STANDARD CATALOG OF

WINCHESTER

THE MOST COMPREHENSIVE PRICE GUIDE EVER PUBLISHED

EDITED BY DAVID D. KOWALSKI

CONTRIBUTORS: TOM WEBSTER · NED SCHWING · RAY GILES · DAN SHUEY · PHIL WHITE

© 2000 by
Krause Publications

All rights reserved.
No part of this publication may be reproduced or transmitted in any form or by any means,
electronic or mechanical, including photocopy, recording or any information storage and retrieval system,
without permission in writing from the author, except by a reviewer who may quote brief passages in a
critical article or review to be printed in a magazine or newspaper or electronically transmitted on radio or
television. The author and publisher assume no liability or responsibility for any loss incurred by users of
this book because of errors, typographical, clerical, or otherwise.

Published by

700 E. State Street • Iola, WI 54990-0001
Telephone: 715/445-2214

Please, call or write us for our free catalog of antiques and collectibles publications. To place an
order or receive our free catalog, call 800-258-0929. For editorial comment and further information,
use our regular business telephone at (715) 445-2214

Library of Congress Catalog Number: 99-68103
ISBN: 0-87341-860-3

Printed in the United States of America

Table of Contents

"As Good As the Gun" - Introduction 4

A Short History of The Winchester Repeating Arms Company 6

Pricing Winchester Products 12

Winchester Firearms 15

Winchester Engraving 106

Cartridge Boxes 126

Cartridges 158

Shotshells (Repeater, Rival) 182

More Shotshells and Shotshell Boxes (Other Brands) 208

Firearms Supplies and Accessories -
    Reloading Tools and Supplies
    Junior Rifle Corps 264

Pocket Knives 283

Winchester - Bright and Beautiful (Color Gallery) 337

Fishing Equipment 369

Baseball and Football Equipment 443

Basketball, Volleyball, Soccer, Boxing, Handball
    Tennis and Golf Equipment 483

Miscellaneous Sports Equipment -
    Skis, Snowshoes, Hockey and Ice Skates,
    Roller Skates, Athletic Supplies, Scooters,
    Wagons and Bicycles 504

Farm, Yard and Garden Tools 522

Axes, Hatchets and Hammers 541

Carpentry Tools -
    Saws, Planes, Levels, Rules,
    Squares, Braces and Bits 563

Mechanic Tools -
    Tool Cabinets, Tool Kits, Chisels, Nail Sets
    Punches, Screwdrivers, Files, Pliers and Wrenches 602

Kitchen and Household Appliances 620

Paints, Brushes and Padlocks 638

Flashlights, Batteries, Household, Cutlery, Scissors and Barber Supplies 662

Winchester Store Products 693

Calendars, Posters and Advertising 713

Trench Art 747

"As Good As The Gun"

by David D. Kowalski

When the typical man or woman on the street hears the name "Winchester" they think of firearms and ammunition. My apologies to Shakespeare, but to paraphrase a famous line from *Hamlet*, there are far more products in the world of Winchester than are dreamt of by the average person.

Within the world of Winchester collectibles, there are many collecting paths to choose from. Some collectors begin with an interest in firearms, then discover cartridge boxes or shotshell boxes or related advertising and are soon collecting in those areas. Or they start with carpentry tools and then pursue a collection of all the tools Winchester made. Did we mention household appliances, cutlery, pocketknives, flashlights, sports equipment, fishing tackle, garden and farm tools, paints or Winchester Store products?

That's part of the excitement of Winchester collecting. There are so many avenues and side streets to go down and you can't predict where they will lead. When my father bought my first gun for me in the early 1960s, a Winchester .22 Model 77, I never dreamed I would be editing the first-ever Winchester price guide some 35 years later.

Historians refer to the 1920s, with American enthusiasm fueled by the end of World War I, as the Roaring 20s. Winchester roared onto the general economic scene in that decade with a vengeance. They bought hardware-related companies with enthusiasm, trying to grow the company as rapidly as possible.

The grandest dreams of management in 1919 and 1920, when many of the acquisitions took shape, probably fell short of imagining just how many products Winchester would distribute by the middle of the decade. The 1927 Catalog for Winchester retailers describes more than 5,000 line items.

If Company management couldn't imagine how vast their enterprise would get during this decade, they surely didn't see those dreams turning to the disaster of bankruptcy by 1929.

Winchester's heroic run for manufacturing and retailing glory in the 1920s produced a veritable smorgasbord of products with the red "Winchester" logo on them. Today's challenge of finding these gems, especially in excellent condition, is motivating collectors across the country and the world. And contrary to the current situation in some other collecting fields, we are still digging Winchester collectibles out of attics and basements. Certainly not with the frequency of 10 or 15 years ago, but often enough to keep the "fever for the hunt" alive.

Winchester's marketing strategy traded heavily on its slogan "As Good As The Gun." Their 1927 Catalog contained this self-assessment of their firearms:

"Exceptional quality of materials and workmanship, dependability and long faithful service have made Winchester guns and ammunition recognized as world standard for more than half a century. Today, as for more than 60 years past, Winchester firearms are the choice of multitudes of sportsmen everywhere."

The editor's gift of a Winchester Model 77, chambered for .22 long rifle and using a tube feed, made him a Winchester fan since the early 1960s. Photo by D. Kowalski.

With their reputation in firearms and ammunition leading the way, they also hammered home the concept to thousands of their authorized retailers that "One Winchester Item Sells Another." That marketing strategy put millions of Winchester products into circulation in the 1920s.

You're holding the most complete collection of surviving Winchester products and advertising from that "Golden Age" ever collected in one volume. It also contains hundreds of new photographs of products contained in premier collections today.

The major inspiration for this book really came from Tom Webster of Missouri. We salute his determined collecting efforts over the past 45 years, beginning well before "Winchester" aroused general collector interest for non-firearms items. He has not only saved a lot of rare pieces from destruction (and allowed us to photograph them) but he has been involved in countless transactions of Winchester collectibles through the years, taking careful note of prices asked and paid. His historical knowledge of "values" helped convince the publishers they could produce this book containing realistic pricing.

We also owe a huge debt of gratitude to our other esteemed contributors. Ned Schwing has again shared his knowledge of Winchester firearms and values. Daniel L. Shuey has taken valuable time from his own collecting and publishing efforts to make sure we had solid, thoroughly researched information on cartridges and shotshells. Ray T. Giles spared no effort in presenting accurate information on cartridge boxes, as well as sharing his valuable collection for photographic purposes. And the combined effort of several contributors has resulted in a major presentation of shotshell boxes, many never seen before in print. We thank Ron Stadt for his photographic contributions. Phil White also added to his previously published material on fishing tackle for our readers.

Another group of dedicated Winchester collectors and experts also helped us immeasurably. A big "thank you" to Thomas I. "Tim" Melcher, who responded promptly and thoroughly with significant photography, as well as serving on our pricing panels. We're indebted to Curt Bowman, Richard Hecht and Ron Willoughby for pricing input and photographs of rare pieces. Finally, we thank Ted Bacyk, Doug Culver and Richard Klinect for their expert pricing help on shotshell boxes.

There are many factors to consider when developing a price guide. That's why we turned to the acknowledged experts mentioned above for this first effort. Some collectibles are, quite frankly, so rare that we can only speculate on their "worth" if one were discovered in a certain condition. With the more common collectibles, multiple transactions in the last few years left little doubt about price ranges.

We had two general pricing goals with this volume. First, to establish clear, published definitions for various grades of condition in several product categories. Second, to help establish a level playing field for both buyers and sellers of Winchester collectibles. In future editions, we will continue to update prices and to clarify both condition and rarity factors in the minor areas.

As a final note on pricing, we will welcome offers from other collectors for their input on future pricing panels.

We have conveyed historical information and product descriptions supplied in Winchester's own catalogs, even preserving some of the unique language and spelling they used in the 1920s. These quotes and paraphrases from Winchester are generally found in *italic type* throughout the book.

As you immerse yourself in this volume, you will find instances where we have used line drawings of products instead of photographs. If you have photographs of some of these items, we would also welcome them for future editions. Use color print film, shoot with natural light on an overcast day, set the product against a neutral background, and make sure your focus is very sharp.

We would also ask that you take a close-up shot of the product's model number. In has been our policy in this first edition to only provide model numbers of photographed products in the caption if we actually saw the model number on the product. If we didn't see it, we made that note. For example, the small pocket level does not have the model number stamped on it but the "Winchester" stamp is clearly visible.

In this first edition, we were also somewhat constrained by page requirements. We have dealt, in a somewhat abbreviated fashion, with cutaway shotshells, salesmen's samples, cartridge boards, wooden cartridge boxes, reloading tools, and the thousands of advertising-related items Winchester produced. We will keep adding to these areas in future editions.

This volume also contains a center section in color. Many of these products are rare or one-of-a-kind. We hope they convey both the beauty of some Winchester packaging and advertising, but also show you more detail of some real rarities. Our upcoming *Winchester Rarities* will be filled with significant pieces, all presented in color, with special focus on Winchester's advertising materials.

Now sit back and enjoy what we hope will be an exciting journey through the vast world of Winchester collectibles.

Iola, Wisconsin (USA)
May, 2000

A Short History of The Winchester Repeating Arms Company

by Ned Schwing

Winchester is a name that is identified with the Old West and the frontier days of America. Winchester rifles and shotguns are prized for their historical significance as well as their collectibility. Not only are the company's firearms of interest to collectors, but its ammunition, both metallic cartridges and shotshells, loading tools, advertising and promotional material, hardware products, fishing tackle, sporting goods, hand tools, appliances, cutlery and any other Winchester-related items as well.

The Winchester Repeating Arms Company was formally established by Oliver F. Winchester on February 20, 1866, and the first model to bear the name of the company was the Model 1866 lever-action rifle chambered for the .44 caliber rimfire cartridge. As with any enterprise it is helpful to study the background and beginnings of the Winchester company so as to better understand the chronological sequence of various rifles and pistols that preceded the Winchester Model 1866.

The story begins with Walter Hunt of New York City who, in 1848, developed the Rocket Ball and Volition Repeater, a unique lever-action, breech-loading, under-barrel magazine tube repeater. This rifle was the origin for future concepts. Hunt's business partner, George Arrowsmith, had as his machinist a man named Lewis Jennings, who improved and simplified Walter Hunt's original concept. Jennings' improvements were granted a U.S. patent in 1849. This 25-shot repeating rifle was promoted by Arrowsmith who found a willing investor in Courtland Palmer, a Connecticut merchant. Palmer bought both the Hunt and Jennings patents and had 5,000 Jennings rifles built by Robbins and Lawrence in Vermont in 1850.

The foreman at Robbins and Lawrence was Benjamin Tyler Henry, a man who would play an important role in future repeating-rifle developments. By 1851 two additional individuals would enter the Hunt-Jennings story: Daniel Wesson and Horace Smith. These two men improved on Lewis Jennings' design, and Smith was granted a patent in 1851, which he assigned to Palmer. Despite the initial achievements with the Jennings rifle, the action proved too complex and the cartridges too light for successful marketability.

In 1854 Horace Smith and Daniel Wesson were granted a U.S. patent for a repeating firearm similar to the earlier Horace Smith design. Courtland Palmer funded the experimental work on the new pistol, which featured a 4" barrel and a full-length under-barrel magazine. Palmer, Smith, and Wesson formed a partnership incorporating the Hunt, Jennings, Smith, and new Smith & Wesson patents. The pistols were made in Norwich, Connecticut, under the name of Smith & Wesson. B. Tyler Henry was an employee of the new firm. Only about 1,000 of these pistols were produced before the company name was changed to Volcanic Repeating Arms Company, an incorporated firm, in 1855.

The new company was formed by Palmer, Smith, and Wesson with the additional financial assistance of Oliver F. Winchester. Winchester was at the time a successful manufacturer of men's clothing in New Haven, Connecticut. The new company bought out Palmer and Smith, while Daniel Wesson stayed on as shop foreman to work on his metallic rimfire cartridge. Volcanic pistols and rifles were first built at the original Smith & Wesson factory in Norwich until 1856 when a new plant was located at New Haven. In 1857 the majority of stock in the Volcanic Repeating Arms Company was owned by Oliver Winchester.

The New Haven Arms Company was structured in April 1857 to assume the business of Volcanic Repeating Arms Company. This new company continued the production of Volcanic pistols and rifles, but these were now marked as "NEW HAVEN CONN. PATENT FEB. 14, 1854". These Volcanics received favorable reports as to their rapidity of fire and ease of operation, but they suffered from low velocity, low energy, and small calibers. These difficulties affected sales, which remained slow.

Perhaps this would be the end of the story had it not been for B. Henry Tyler, who was the shop foreman at New Haven Arms Company after the departure of Daniel Wesson. Tyler had been involved with the predecessors for the past 10 years and he received a patent in 1860 for the improvement in magazine firearms. The success of Henry's new design was twofold: First, the development of a new, more powerful .44 caliber metallic rimfire cartridge was sufficiently potent enough to compete with the single-shot rifles of the day, and second, the advancement in the firing pin design, the addition of an extractor, and improvements in the bolt and feeding mechanisms all helped to make the Henry rifle a success. The first production Henry rfles were delivered in 1862. A number of Henry rfles were used during the latter part of the Civil War.

In 1866 the New Haven Arms Company name was changed to Winchester Repeating Arms Company.

The Model 1866, an improved version of the Henry rifle, was the first firearm to bear the Winchester name. The rifle had a magazine capacity of 17 rounds while the carbine held 12. The Henry rifle was dropped from production and the company embarked on a serious effort to interest governments in adopting the Model 66. In the meantime Winchester purchased the Spencer Repeating Rifle Company. This purchase helped to position the company as the dominant force in the repeating rifle markets. However, in the early 1870s the U.S. Army adopted the Springfield Model 73 carbine instead of the Winchester Model 66, but the company did have success overseas and in Mexico.

With the commercial success of the Henry rifle and Model 66, Winchester needed to supply cartridges for its rifles in use around the world. During this period large quantities of .44 flat rim-fire cartridges were produced for these rifles using the letter "H" headstamp as its trademark on rim-fire ammunition. By 1877 Winchester manufactured 25 different calibers of rim-fire and 24 calibers of centerfire cartridges as well as empty brass shot shells in 8, 10, 11, 12, 14, 15, and 16 gauges. Empty paper shells were also produced during this time.

With the arrival of centerfire cartridges the Model 66 was in danger of becoming outmoded. The company developed the .44-40 centerfire cartridge. It used a .44 caliber bullet and a 40-grain powder charge. The new rifle, designated the New Model of 1873 or more often referred to as the Model 73, was a stronger version of the Model 66 Winchester. This Winchester rifle was really the model that helped to win the west, and its popularity was worldwide.

This successful model was followed by the Model 76, or "Centennial Model". This rifle was chambered for the more powerful .45-70 cartridge. But the success of this rifle was limited even though it was adopted by the Royal Canadian Northwest Mounted Police. Only about 63,000 Model 76s were sold compared to 720,000 Model 73s.

With the advent of Winchester rifles chambered for centerfire cartridges the company manufactured its .44WCF, the .38WCF and, in 1882, the .32WCF cartridges. The Model 76 was the result of Winchester's development of the .45-70 cartridge. In time the Model 76 was chambered for the .50-95 Winchester Express, the .45-60 WCF, and in 1884 the .40-60 cartridge. By 1878 the company manufactured 38 different types and styles of rimfire cartridges and 63 different centerfire cartridges. It was also in the late 1870s that the company, for the first time, featured reloading tools for its centerfire cartridges in its catalogues.

On December 10, 1880 Oliver Winchester died at his home in New Haven at the age of seventy. He must receive credit for establishing a business environment in which the repeating rifle design could reach fruition and flourish as a commercial success. He left the company in the capable hands of his family and in-laws. The new president was William Converse, William Winchester's brother-in-law.

The mid-1880s marked a turning point for Winchester. Up to 1885 the company had almost exclusively manufactured repeating rifles. In that year Winchester began production of the single-shot Model 1885 rifle designed by John Moses Browning. Not only did Winchester enjoy the fruits of Browning's genius with a series of successful rifle designs but the company had in its employ another firearms genius by the name of William Mason. Between the two men Winchester was able to expand and improve its firearms product line well into the 20th century. Both Mason and Browning worked on the new Model 1886, a very strong and rugged lever-action rifle capable of handling the most powerful centerfire cartridges of the day.

The Model 86 was considered by many to be the ultimate big game rifle in the United States, and many felt it suitable for all but the largest African game. In 1886 the company developed for its Model 86 the .45-90 WCF, and the .40-82 WCF. In 1887 the .40-65 WCF, .38-56 WCF, and the .50-110 were added to the Model 86 product line. By 1894 the .40-70 WCF, and the .38-70 WCF were available for the Model 86. In 1895 the .50-100-450 WCF was added, and in 1903 the .33 WCF.

But Winchester was also busy developing other firearms lines outside its traditional lever-action rifles and carbines. In 1880 the company began importing British-made double shotguns. Winchester did not mark its name on all of these guns; instead they were referred to as Match, and Grades A, B, C, and D. These imported shotguns were dropped from the Winchester line in 1884.

The company introduced a lever-action shotgun in 1887, designed by none other than John Browning, named the Model 87. Introduced in the Winchester 1888 catalog it was offered in 10 gauge and 12 gauge.

Beginning in 1885 machine loaded shotshells became more widely available and Winchester began loading paper shells under various brand names. In 1886 the company marketed, for the first time, its brand of black powder shotshells called "Rival". In 1887 the "Star" brand appeared, and in 1888 the "1st Quality" brand. These Winchester shotshells were loaded in a wide variety of loads for 10, 12, 14, 16, and 20 gauge. All paper used in these Rival shells was brown in color. This new era of machine made shotshells was the beginning of one of the company's more profitable product lines. Winchester shotshells are still today one of the most respected brands in the world.

The 1880s was also a period of consolidation for the American firearms industry. In the 1880s Winchester experimented with several different revolver models. Company executives took the prototypes to Colt's for that company's opinion with the result that Colt's discontinued the manufacture and sale of its lever-action rifle, the Colt-Burgess, and Winchester discontinued its development of its improved revolver. In 1887 Winchester purchased Whitney Firearms Company and withdrew the Whitney line of firearms from the market.

In 1888 Winchester, in conjunction with Union Metallic Cartridge Company, purchased the assets of Remington Arms Company. This purchase gave Winchester an increased share of the firearms and ammunition market in the United States. It is interesting to note that during the period of Winchester ownership of Remington that company did not produce a lever-action gun. Winchester owned shares in Remington until it withdrew in 1896.

The decade prior to the 20th century was an important one for Winchester. In 1890 William G. Bennett was elected president of Winchester. He was a son-in-law of Oliver Winchester and the first trained scientific mind to head the company. For the next twenty-five years Bennett would provide the kind of sound leadership that the company needed to compete in the coming century. The decade of the 1890s also marked the introduction of Winchester's first slide-action .22 caliber rifle and the .22 WRF cartridge , made expressly for this model: the Model 1890. This decade futhermore marked the beginning of the introduction of smokeless powder. It was during this ten-year period that the company began to expand its product line in a more aggressive fashion. The introduction of the Model 1890 .22 caliber rifle was followed by the Model 92 lever-action rifle. Another slide-action firearm was added to the product line but this time it was a shotgun; the Model 93. The well known and highly popular Model 94 was also developed and manufactured during this period.

All of these firearms were based on John M. Browning patents and improvements by William Mason.

The famous Winchester Model 94, introduced near the end of 1894, was chambered for two black powder cartridges; the .32-20 and the .38-55. In August of 1895 two new smokeless cartridges were introduced; the Winchester .25-35 and the Winchster .30 caliber or .30-30. The .30-30 and the Model 94 soon became the most popular hunting combination in the U.S. Its introductory price in 1894 was $18.00.

In the middle of the decade Winchester introduced its Model 95. Similar to the Model 94 but with a stronger breech and detachable box magazine, this rifle was chambered for a variety of military cartridges such as the .303 British, .30 M1902 Government, the .30 M1906 Government, and the .30-40 Krag. In addition to these military cartridges the company developed the .35 WCF, the .38-72 WCF, the .40-72 WCF, and the .405 WCF especially for the Model 95. The introductory price for the Model 95 was $25.00.

The decade of the 1890s was a positive one for Winchester and paved the way for continued prosperity into the new century. Only one unfortunate episode was to blemish the company's position as a leader in the development and sale of sporting arms. In 1901 and 1902 Winchester's business relationship with John Browning came to an end. The cause was the failure of the company to meet Browning's request for a royalty payment arrangement for Browning's new semi automatic shotgun design. The inability to reach an agreement with Browning resulted in a loss to Winchester of the services of the preeminent firearms inventor of our time. Browning eventually took his new shotgun design to Fabrique Nationale in Belgium for manufacture. The result was the famous Browning Auto-5 shotgun.

The loss of John Browning's designs was to have long-range consequences for Winchester. But in the meantime the company was fortunate to have a talented designer in T.C. Johnson. At the time of his retirement Johnson had transferred 124 patents to Winchester. Among some of his designs were the series of semi automatic rifles; the Models 03, 05, 07, and 10. But perhaps his greatest design was the famous Model 12 shotgun. First introduced in 1913 at a price of $20.00, Winchester sold 100,000 of these shotguns in two years.

Despite the success in the early part of the 20th century the company was beginning to feel the effects of domestic competition. Companies like Remington, Marlin, Stevens, Parker, L.C. Smith, and Savage began to corrode Winchester's market share. These effects forced the company to aggressively push sales both domestically and foreign. Despite an increase in overall sales Winchester's market share was the same in 1914 as it was in 1890. However, the company was on sound financial footing.

With the breakout of the First World War in Europe in 1914 Winchester was called upon to supply the Allied forces with Enfield rifles, Model 95 rifles in 7.62mm caliber for Russian forces, .303 British cartridges, 18-pound cannon cases and primers. Throughout the war years Winchester continued to expand its facilities to accommodate the wartime orders along with its continued strong peacetime domestic sales. The U.S. declared war on Germany on April 6, 1917 and with this event Winchester was again forced to expand its production to meet this wartime demand. The Winchester plant was used to build 47,123 Browning Automatic Rifles, 545,511 Model 1917 Enfield rifles, Model 12 and Model 96 Riot guns, and literally hundreds of millions of service cartridges.

With the coming of peace in November of 1918 the Winchester plant was left with huge production capacity and substantial debt. In 1919 Winchester Repeating Arms Company was forced to reorganize in order to service its debts and make way for peacetime production.

The new company was called the Winchester Company, but for all practical purposes it was the same company albeit under new management. This new management, under the leadership of John Otterson, was committed to the manufacture of new products in addition to guns and ammunation.These new products would require extensive expansion of existing marketing facilities. The concept was to expand into new products in order to absorb the factory production capacity left over from the war. This expansion would take the company into uncharted waters and in the end provide collectors with a colorful field of collectibles beyond firearms and ammunition.

Winchesters approach was two-fold. First, a group of products had to be selected that would complement its firearms and ammunition business, and secondly, a totally new marketing organization was required in order to sell these new products. The company decided that sporting goods and hardware were among the best possible new lines to pursue. These new products would be sold directly to hardware stores and newly created Winchester retail stores.

In 1919 Winchester began its new expansion in ernest with the acquisition of eight companies. Eagle Pocket Knife Co.; Napanoch Knife Co.; Andrew B. Hendryx Co., a fishing reel and artificial bait concern; Morril Target Co., a clay target manufacturer; E.W. Edwards, a fishing rod company; Barney & Berry, an ice and roller skate manufacturer; Lebonon Machine Co., a manufacturer of auger bits; and Page-Storm Drop Forge Co., a producer of flat wrenches; were all purchased in 1919 by Winchester. In 1920 Mack Axe Co. of Beaver Falls, PA was acquired. Thus, by 1920 Winchester had acquired a broad range of hardware items with which to expand its new product lines. In addition to these acquisitions the company developed, on its own, a line of batteries and flashlights. Winchester also began manufacturing steel fishing rods in order to supplement the split bamboo rods of the recently purchased E.W. Edwards Co.

By the end of 1920 Winchester had a total of 3,400 dealers signed up to become part of the new Winchester dealer network. Not only did Winchester sell them the company's new line of sporting goods and hardware but guns and ammunition as well. In the spring of 1920 Winchester opened its first retail store in Providence, Rhode Island. Before the end of the year nine additional retail stores were opened from Boston to New York City. In spite of these advances into new product lines and sales outlets the cost of doing business on this level was enormous. An even greater volume of sales was needed to reduce the cost of manufacturing and distribution.

By the middle of 1922 a solution for additional sales volume was found in the merger of Winchester with the Associated Simmons Hardware Companies of St. Louis. The merger enabled Simmons to assume responsibility for sales and distribution of Winchester's hardware line and Simmons own hardware line marketed under the Keen Kutter brand. Winchester in turn concentrated on manufacturing not only its hardware lines but its guns and ammunition lines. The new company was called The Winchester-Simmons company.

When the merger took effect the Simmons Company had controlling interest in the Walden Knife Co., the Roanoke Spoke and Handle Co., and the Mound City Paint and Color Co. The products of the first and third companies are self explanatory but the Roanoke Spoke and Handle Co. manufactured handles for tools and the famous Louisville Slugger brand baseball bat. Winchester had already been producing baseball bats under its own brand name and now, with the new line, was involved in the baseball bat business on an extensive scale.

The Walden Knife Co. was a relatively small company and its operations were moved to Winchester's plant in New Haven. The Mound City Paint operation required some expensive upgrading in terms of quality with the result that both Simmons and Winchester marketed high quality paint under both company's brand names. Winchester also undertook the manufacture of cutlery under the Keen Kutter brand. This was in response to the continued need to utilize the additional plant capacity left over from World War I. Despite the merger the additional sales realized by Winchester amounted to only about ten percent of its total sales in 1923.

In the meantime the company continued to manufacture and sell its world-renowned line of guns and ammunition. In 1920 Winchester introduced its Model 52, a high quality .22 caliber bolt-action rifle. It was an expensive rifle to build and carried a retail price of $70.00. However, it had a reputation as the premier bolt-action .22 caliber rifle built in America. Three low-priced shotguns were added to Winchester's product line; the Model 20, a .410 bore single shot, the Model 41 a .410 bolt action, and the Model 36, a 9mm single shot for ball and shot cartridges.

Under the guidance of T.C. Johnson Winchester continued to introduce new models. From 1924 to 1931 the company initiated nine new models. In 1924 the Model 53, a simplified Model 92, and Model 55, a modified version of the Model 94, were first shown to the trade. In 1925 the bolt action centerfire rifle, the Model 54, was introduced. This was the company's first attempt to build a heavy caliber, bolt-action sporting rifle. In 1926 Winchester announced the Model 56 and Model 57, two bolt-action .22 caliber rifles. The Model 58, a single-shot .22 caliber rifle, was also announced in 1926. The Models 59 and 60 were introduced in 1930. But perhaps the greatest offering in the Winchester line was the Model 21, the company's preeminent shotgun. Initially offered in 12, 16, and 20 gauge with a choice of various barrel lengths, the Model 21 would become Winchester's symbol of quality and dependability; the flagship of the company line.

Despite the aggressive move into new product expansion and retail outlets, sales volume did not increase enough to show a profit. Strong efforts were undertaken to increase sales and lower cost but to no avail. The situation became more serious as debt began to increase, and more avenues were explored to increase sales and production capacity. In 1925 Winchester acquired National Refrigerator Company of Boston. By 1926 the company was producing gas-operated refrigerators. But these appliances did not fit well into the Winchester-Simmons product line and the project was abandoned in 1928.

The year 1926 also saw the introduction of Winchester into the washing machine business. Winchester purchased the Whirldry Corporation and moved the production facilities to New Haven. This attempt, like the refrigerator line, was not successful. In 1931 the Whirldry venture had cost Winchester about $1,750,000.

In 1929 the Winchester Repeating Arms Company was reorganized. This reorganization was an attempt to stem the flow of losses and consolidate profitable lines. The result was the dissolution of the Winchester-Simmons Company and eventually, in 1931, Winchester went into receivership. This marked the end of an era for the company. But in many ways the period following the First World War is fertile ground for the Winchester collector. From 1919 to 1931 the company was involved in an incredible array of products that bore the Winchester name. From the traditional guns and ammunition to hardware, flashlights, and even skates, the collector will find a calliope of collectibles. This was also the period that Winchester retail stores were established with the subsequent plethora of advertising and promotional materials from calendars, signs, banners, and counter-display pieces of all shapes and sizes.

In 1931, Winchester was purchased by the Western Cartridge Company owned by the Olin family. Because of the changing times, the new company's focus was now on sporting arms, and the drive for new models and manufacturing techniques came from the vision and foresight of John M. Olin. Olin was responsible for the continued production, despite skimpy profits, of the Model 21 side-by-side shotgun. He was also responsible for adding, in 1934, the Model 42 .410 slide-action shotgun to the Winchester line. Like Oliver Winchester, John Olin had the foresight, expertise, and passion to see his company succeed. He was a hands-on manager, interested in developing new products that would advance the company's reputation for quality and innovation.

If the Model 21 was Winchester's premier shotgun, then the Model 70 was the company's premier bolt action centerfire rifle. Known as the "Rifleman's Rifle" the Model 70 was an improved version of its Model 54. Introduced in 1937 the Model 70 was the epitome of Winchester quality and dependability. Offered in a wide variety of calibers and configurations the Model 70 is not only highly sought after by collectors, but many shooters believe the pre-1963 Winchester Model 70 action is the finest centerfire action ever produced. With various changes-the Model 70 still carries the Winchester name after sixty-three years in production.

When The United States entered World War II Winchester did its part to help facilitate the war effort just as the company had done during the First World War. Winchester built the M1 Garand rifle (Winchester model designation M39) for the U.S. military beginning in 1940 . This model was discontinued in 1945 after 513,582 were built. Winchester also made the .30 caliber M1 carbine for the military. This model, known as the M/31, was designed by Winchester. By the time this model was discontinued in 1945, 818,059 had been manufactured by Winchester in its New Haven plant. Winchester also produced the fully automatic M2 carbine during the same time period.

From 1931 until 1963, Winchester Repeating Arms regained its reputation for quality firearms, and the rifles and shotguns produced during this period in the company's history are as collectible as those guns that preceded them. Other than the Model 42 and Model 21 designed and built prior to the war, Winchester also introduced the popular Model 62 slide action .22 caliber rifle, a modernized version of its Model 1890 and Model 1906. Along with the Model 61, a more contemporary hammerless .22 caliber rimfire version, Winchester built and sold more than two million of its slide-action .22 caliber rifles from 1890 to 1963.

Between 1946 and 1963 Winchester continued to develop new models but on a much smaller scale. After World War II ended the company introduced the bolt action Model 43 and the Model 47 in 1949. The Model 43 was chambered for small-bore centerfire cartridges such as the .218 Bee and .25-20 WCF. The Model 47 was chambered for .22 caliber rimfire cartridges. In 1947 the company introduced the Model 50 recoil operated semiautomatic shotgun in 12 and 20 gauge. The Model 77 semiautomatic .22 caliber was brought out in 1955, as well as the lever-action Model 88. In 1958 the curious Model 55 single-shot semiautomatic .22 caliber rifle was introduced and in 1959 the Model 59 semiautomatic shotgun in 12 gauge was introduced. But by 1960 the handwriting was on the wall. Winchester could no longer continue to offer its high quality, hand-built firearms in an age where the competition offered lower prices and a wider range of choices.

In 1964 the company could no longer afford to mass produce firearms that in reality were hand-fitted and hand-machined. Manufacturing changes were implemented that reflected the mass production psychology that was becoming so commonplace in American industry. With the exception of the Model 21 and a few other select models of Winchester rifles and shotguns, many Winchester guns produced after 1963 are not viewed by collectors necessarily as collectibles, although this attitude is slowly changing. Nevertheless, they were excellent guns for the hunting fields and duck blinds.

One new development that showed a fundamental shift in production philosophy for Winchester was the introduction of the Model 101 shotgun in 1963. Designed by Winchester but built in Japan by Miroku Limited, this partnership between the Olin Corporation and Miroku was in an attempt by the company to reduce manufacturing costs. The answer was the Model 101 in several gauges and configurations followed by other Japanese-built shotguns, such as the Model 23 that lasted until 1987 when the production of Winchester shotguns in Japan ceased.

But the search for lower production costs was unsuccessful, and in 1981 Winchester Repeating Arms Company sold its firearms division to U.S. Repeating Arms Company. This new company continues to the present day to build Winchester rifles and shotguns under license from the Olin Corporation. U.S. Repeating Arms Company has itself been the object of several buyouts and is now owned by the Belgian government. Nevertheless, the Winchester legend lives on; collected and respected by many.

A brief guide to the Winchester Repeating Arms Company corporate and divisional name changes will be of help to the collector to establish the proper company name on various firearms and advertising materials.

WINCHESTER CORPORATE AND DIVISIONAL NAME CHANGES 1931- 1991

WINCHESTER REPEATING ARMS COMPANY
Dec. 22, 1931 - Dec. 31, 1938

WINCHESTER REPEATING ARMS COMPANY
A Division of Western Cartridge Company
Dec. 31, 1938 - Dec. 30, 1944

WINCHESTER REPEATING ARMS COMPANY
A Division of Olin Industries, Inc.
Dec. 30, 1944 - January 1952

WINCHESTER-WESTERN DIVISION
Olin Industries, Inc.
January 1952 - Aug. 31, 1954

WINCHESTER-WESTERN DIVISION
Olin Mathieson Chemical Corporation
Aug. 31, 1954 - Sept. 1, 1969

WINCHESTER-WESTERN DIVISION
OLIN CORPORATION
Sept. 1, 1969- July 21, 1981

U.S REPEATING ARMS COMPANY
July 21, 1981 -Present

Pricing Winchester Products

by Tom Webster

"What's it worth?" In my more than 45 years collecting Winchester products, that's the question I hear most often.

Of course, the classic reply is, "Whatever someone will pay for it." But that's not too helpful if you're the person buying and you want to know whether something is a "good deal" or not.

Actually, this entire book is devoted to answering the question, "What's it worth?" But Winchester produced such a vast array of products, particularly before 1931, that there is no simple answer to the question. And there is no simple formula that applies to all products.

To answer this question, there are really a lot of other questions that need to be asked and answered first.

- What condition is it in?
- Has it been altered from factory-original condition?
- Is it in the original box?
- What condition is the box in?
- Who's selling it?
- Where did it come from?
- Is there documentation of the origin of the piece, particularly if it's claimed to be rare or one-of-a-kind?
- Are you buying it to complete a personal collection? If so, what are the chances you will ever find another one?
- Are you buying it to re-sell? If so, do you have a buyer in mind? Or will you have to hold it for five or ten years for a buyer to come along?

There are also different standards applied to valuations in several Winchester collectible areas. Firearms, cartridges, cartridge boxes, shotshells, shotshell boxes and pocket knives have become very specialized areas. What is considered "Very Good" condition in one area may only be "Good" in another area.

That's why we've taken some pains to describe the standards for valuation in each of these areas. We're doing something here that's never been done before on this scale. We're trying to answer the question "What's it worth?" for all kinds of Winchester products spanning nearly 100 years of production.

As our contributors introduce their area of expertise, they will describe the factors that affect values and prices in that specialty. You've already found that grades of condition changed from one specialty area to another in firearms, ammo boxes and pocket knives. Trench art is also a unique product category.

Now let's look at the considerations affecting values for the rest of the Winchester products in this book.

Rarity and Regional Demand Affect Price

Pricing collectibles involves evaluating both rarity and condition, then adding a dose of experience. New collectors simply have not seen enough of Winchester's broad range of products to accurately price them. They haven't been to enough auctions. They haven't put on enough miles going to shows and visiting antique stores. In this book, our goal is to help you get educated faster.

The other factor that affects pricing is regional demand. Let me give you an example. One of my other interests is oyster cans. Many of the original producers of canned oysters were located on the East Coast. And there was a great deal of demand for their branded products, shipped in colorful, covered "tins" to the West Coast and elsewhere. Over the years oyster cans became fairly plentiful on the West Coast so prices were relatively low. In the meantime, eastern collectors who got interested in this area were having more difficulty finding cans locally. So they were willing to pay more. If you asked a western collector and an eastern collector what a particular oyster can was worth, you might get vastly different prices.

Some of that occurs with Winchester products. With firearms, particularly, some models were very popular in certain parts of the country and scarce in others. Prices reflected those regional differences.

With the growth of national classified advertising publications and now internet auction sites, we don't see the big regional differences we once did.

With Winchester collectibles, we will provide prices that reflect national averages.

Winchester Logos and Model Numbers

First of all, look for the Winchester name on the product. Over the years the wording might have changed but Winchester products typically have the "Winchester" name on it in some form. With items such as tools that may have been heavily used in their day, that logo may now be very faint. A good reading glass will help you inspect the piece in detail.

Speaking of worn logos, they're sometimes a good sign. If the entire product is worn, expect the logo to be worn, as well. If a tool has been heavily used and shows some rust, you wouldn't expect it's Winchester logo to look clean and newly stamped.

Winchester was also very meticulous about stamping product numbers on most of its products, labels or boxes. With the thousands of products they eventually provided in the late 1920s, they had to do this to avoid disaster in their shipping departments.

Some very small items might not have had room for a stamp on the actual product. Winchester's round wooden plinking targets, for example, have no identification on the individual pieces. That's when it's critical to obtain them with their original box.

Another item that comes to mind is the small metal line level. I have never seen one with the model number stamped on it.

Condition Factors Affect Price

Now let's talk about general condition factors in the non-firearms and non-pocket-knives areas of Winchester collectibles.

Moisture, light and handling affect all products to some degree. Metal products can rust and oxidize. Tools, garden equipment and fishing tackle get dinged and dented from use. Labels, boxes and advertising materials can get ruined from water stains, faded by direct sunlight and start to deteriorate from various kinds of acids in older paper and paper matte boards. All these things reduce the value of the collectible.

In fact, there are certain kinds of products I won't even buy if they have severe damage. I have turned down otherwise rare advertising materials because of severe tears and water stains. If they were in perfect condition, they would be worth large sums of money. But most collectors don't want severely damaged goods.

Other products have been severely harmed by dirt and mud, by handwritten stickers put on them at some yard sale, by welds on metal cracks, or by crude taping of seams or tears.

Having said all that, we will provide standards and pricing in three grades of condition: Excellent (Exc.), Very Good (VG) and Good (Good). This will apply from fishing tackle and sporting goods to calendars and advertising items, from tools to household goods, from yard and garden equipment to Winchester Store collectibles.

Excellent

Condition is original and perfect. No fingerprints, scratches, dents, welds, rust, water stains, tears, non-factory stickers, tape, or signs of tape removal. Also no repainting or staining, refinishing, or obvious replacement parts. Colors original and bright.

Very Good

Shows one or two very slight signs of wear or use from the above list. Perhaps a few minor rust spots on metal items. Perhaps a light fading of color on paper items or a few wrinkles along an edge. Slight smudges.

Good

Three or more signs of wear or use to a greater degree than a "very good" item. More rust, minor tears, more fading of color, light water spots.

Products that have been taped, welded, repaired, reinforced, sanded, repainted or water damaged move down into the Fair category or worse.

The Value of Original Boxes

If the product comes in an original box or sleeve, the value doubles, at least. And if both the box and the product it contains are in excellent condition, that factor is even bigger.

If the box or container is factory sealed, it is sometimes impossible to estimate the value "multiplier." Later in this book we will show you the only can of Winchester tennis balls that has ever been found. Even more amazing, the can has never been opened. What does that add to its value? A lot! I'm afraid I can't give you a better answer. Some collectibles are so unique we simply can't plug them into a standard "formula."

Before we begin any major product area, we will attempt to define unique condition factors. We will then describe individual products, provide a picture or line art (if available), then price each product. If there are special pricing considerations you should be aware of, we will try to provide those directly below the value guide for that product.

If you have photos of unique, original Winchester products and would like to see them (instead of the line art we may have used) in future editions, please contact the publisher.

Other Factors Affecting Demand and Price

Besides rarity and condition, there are other factors that enter into pricing Winchester products. For example, some Winchester advertising or calendars or posters are so well done that they are considered art. The "Cock of the Woods" poster from 1905 is a perfect example. Even if you're not a Winchester collector, this painting of a wild turkey is so colorful and lifelike that you can't help but admire it.

Winchester also commissioned various artists to paint the scene for their wall calendar each year. Some of these artists were so good they developed a following among those who simply appreciated outstanding wildlife art, regardless of who it was painted for. The work of Philip R. Goodwin comes quickly to mind.

In this price guide, we have gotten input from a variety of active Winchester collectors. We present prices we believe are accurate and fair today. But something may happen in the marketplace in the next six months that we didn't anticipate. That's part of the excitement and challenge of this area.

If a highly publicized auction generates a high price for an item, that may not represent what would happen the next time a similar item comes into the market.

If you are an experienced Winchester collector, the publisher would welcome your offer to contribute to future price guides.

Product Descriptions

One of the most complete descriptions of the range of Winchester products is the 1927 general product Catalog Winchester produced for its retail customers. In fact, Winchester actually put out two different versions that year. They had not put out a catalog in two years. And some of their line art used actually goes back to 1923 or earlier.

The cover of the catalog gives the retailer a preview of all the categories inside:

- Steel Goods
- Lawn Mowers
- Wheel Barrows
- Food Choppers
- Electric Irons
- Vacuum Bottles
- Radio Batteries
- Flashlights
- Coaster Wagons
- Tools
- Cutlery
- Hair Clippers
- Guns & Ammunition
- Fishing Tackle
- Sporting Goods
- Ice Skates
- Roller Skates
- Paints
- Sales Promotion Equipment

Since Winchester had not put out a general Catalog in two years, they also wanted to alert their retailers to new product categories that had been added in that time. These included:

- Lacquer
- Padlocks
- Golf Clubs
- Rubber Hose
- Family Scales
- Refrigerators
- Ice Cream Freezers
- Tennis Balls and Rackets
- Paint and Varnish Brushes

In reading this list of products, you may see spellings that now seem unusual. For example, we now typically spell "lawnmowers" as one word. But we have preserved the original Winchester spelling of its own products.

We have also used original Winchester Catalog descriptions (where available) for those products. (They are in Italic type directly under the product photo or line art.) Those descriptions may often seem more like the "exaggerations" of advertising copy but Winchester was, after all, trying to sell products. That aside, the descriptions are typically quite accurate in terms of metals used or sizes or colors.

If we have additional information or notes about a particular product, we will provide that in the "Comment" section below the value guide.

Tom Webster has been collecting Winchester products from firearms to washing machines to sporting goods and tools to advertising material since 1954. In addition to his contributions to this volume, he is the co-author of the upcoming Winchester Rarities.

Winchester Firearms: From the Beginning to the Present

by Ned Schwing

The prices given here are for the most part standard guns without optional features that were so often furnished by the factory. These optional or extra-cost features are too numerous to list and can affect the price of a shotgun or rifle to an enormous degree. In some cases these options are one-of-a-kind. Collectors and those interested in Winchester firearms have the benefit of some of the original factory records. These records are now stored in the Cody Firearms Museum, Buffalo Bill Historical Center, P.O. Box 1000, Cody, Wyoming 82414 (307) 587-4771. For a $25 fee for patrons of the museum (non-members charged $40) factory letters containing the original specifications of certain Winchester models using the original factory records of the following models and serial numbers will be provided.

CAUTION: Buyers should confirm by Cody letter any special order feature on any Winchester within the Cody record range before paying a premium for a scarce feature.

Model	Serial Number
1866	124995 to 170101
1873	1 to 720496 (N/A 497-610 and 199551-199598)
1876	1 to 63871
Hotchkiss	1 to 84555
1885*	1 to 109999 (N/A 74459-75556)
1886	1 to 156599 (N/A 146000-150799)
1887 & 1901	1 to 72999
1890	1 to 329999 (N/A 20000-29999)
1906	1 to 79999
1892	1 to 379999
1893	1 to 34050
1897	1 to 377999
1894	1 to 353999
1895	1 to 59999
Lee	1 to 19999
1903	1 to 39999
1905	1 to 29078
1906	1 to 79999
1907	1 to 9999
21	1 to 35000
* Single-Shot	

Pricing Guidelines

In the opinion of the writer all grading systems are subjective. It is our task to offer the collector and dealer a measurement that most closely reflects a general consensus on condition. The system we present seems to come closest to describing a firearm in universal terms. We strongly recommend that the reader acquaint himself with this grading system before attempting to determine the correct price for a particular firearm's condition. Remember, in most cases condition determines price.

NIB-New in Box

This category can sometimes be misleading. It means that the firearm is in its original factory carton with all of the appropriate papers. It also means the firearm is new; that it has not been fired and has no wear. It should be noted that Winchester shotguns and rifles that are described as NIB bring a substantial premium. Beware that unscrupulous individuals are reproducing Winchester boxes and labels with the intention to defraud the collector. Consult with an expert prior to a sale of this desirable and highly collectible category of Winchester.

Excellent

Collector quality firearms in this condition are highly desirable. The firearm must be in at least 98 percent condition with respect to blue wear, stock or grip finish, and bore. The firearm must also be 100 percent factory original without refinishing, repair, alterations or additions of any kind. Sights must be factory original as well. This grading classification includes both modern and antique (manufactured prior to 1898) firearms.

Firearms in this category are also sought after both by the collector and shooter. Firearms must be in working order and retain approximately 92 percent metal and wood finish. It must be 100 percent factory original, but may have some small repairs, alterations, or non-factory additions. No refinishing is permitted in this category. Both modern and antique firearms are included in this classification.

Good

Modern firearms in this category are not considered to be as collectable as the previous grades, but antique firearms are considered desirable. Modern firearms must retain at least 80 percent metal and wood finish, but may display evidence of old refinishing. Small repairs, alterations, or non-factory additions are sometimes encountered in this class. Factory replacement parts are permitted. The overall working condition of the firearm must be good as well as safe. The bore may exhibit wear or some corrosion, especially in antique arms. Antique firearms may be included in this category if their metal and wood finish is at least 50 percent original factory finish.

Fair

Firearms in this category should be in satisfactory working order and safe to shoot. The overall metal and wood finish on the modern firearm must be at least 30 percent and antique firearms must have at least some original finish or old re-finish remaining. Repairs, alterations, non-factory additions, and recent refinishing would all place a firearm in this classification. However, the modern firearm must be in working condition, while the antique firearm may not function. In either case the firearm must be considered safe to fire if in a working state.

Poor

Neither collectors nor shooters are likely to exhibit much interest in firearms in this condition. Modern firearms are likely to retain little metal or wood finish. Pitting and rust will be seen in firearms in this category. Modern firearms may not be in working order and may not be safe to shoot. Repairs and refinishing would be necessary to restore the firearm to safe working order. Antique firearms will have no finish and will not function. In the case of modern firearms their principal value lies in spare parts. On the other hand, antique firearms in this condition may be used as "wall hangers" or as an example of an extremely rare variation or have some kind of historical significance.

Pricing Considerations

Unfortunately for shooters and collectors, there is no central clearinghouse for firearms prices. The prices given in this Winchester firearms section are designed as a guide, not as a quote. This is an important distinction because prices for firearms vary with the time of the year and geographical location. For example, interest in firearms is at its lowest point in the summer. People are not as interested in shooting and collecting at this time of the year as they are in playing golf or taking a vacation. Therefore, prices are depressed slightly and guns that may sell quickly during the hunting season or the winter months may not sell well at all during this time of year.

Geographical location also plays an important part in pricing. For instance, a Winchester Model 70 in a .264 caliber will bring a higher price in the Western states than along the Eastern seaboard. Smaller gauges and calibers seem to be more popular along both coasts and mid-sections of the United States than in the more open western sections of the country.

What is given is a reasonable price based on sales at gun shows, auction houses, *Gun List* prices, and information obtained from knowledgeable collectors and dealers. The firearms prices listed in this section are **RETAIL PRICES** and the gun may bring more or less depending on the variables discussed above. If you choose to sell your gun to a dealer you will not receive the retail price but a wholesale price based on the markup that particular dealer needs to operate.

Also, in certain cases there will be no price indicated under a particular condition but rather the notation "N/A" or the symbol "—". This indicates that there is no known average price for that gun in that condition or the sales for that particular model are so few that a reliable price cannot be given. This will usually be encountered only with very rare guns, with newly introduced firearms, or more likely with antique firearms in those conditions most likely to be encountered. Most antique firearms will be seen in the good, fair and poor categories.

One final note. Due to the nature of business one will usually pay higher prices at a retail store than at a gun show. In some cases auctions will produce excellent buys or extravagant prices, depending on any given situation. Collectors will sometimes pay higher prices for a firearm that they need to fill out their collection when in other circumstances they will not be willing to pay market price if they don't have to have the gun. The point here is that prices paid for firearms is an ever changing affair based on a large number of variables. The prices in this book are a **GENERAL GUIDE** as to what a willing buyer and willing seller might agree on. You may find the item for less, and then you may have to pay more depending on the variables of your particular situation.

Special Features:

Winchester would add just about any option to its guns if the customers were willing to pay for it. The company offered a wide variety of options for most of its models. Some of these options are quite rare and others fairly common. The prices listed in this guide are for standard guns with standard features. We are often asked to add premiums to these prices for factory options. This, in the opinion of the writer, is not possible. Some options were offered for some models for different periods of time and then discontinued. Certain combinations of options may be found that will add substantially to the price in combination but not alone. Sights are an example of this.

To illustrate the complexity of how options might affect price and what Winchester offered in the way of options, the example of the Model 1886 is given.

The Model 1886 was offered with engraving patterns in various styles and coverages; shorter or longer barrels than standard; round, 1/2 octagon, and octagon barrels, heavier barrels than standard; extra length magazine tubes; full and half magazine; set triggers (both single and double); wood carvings; checkering; rifle and shotgun butts; special dimension stocks; straight or pistol grips; silver, nickel, and gold plating; and special sights. Special carrying cases may also be seen. These options are for just one model. Other options for other models were offered at different times. It is therefore strongly suggested that an expert appraisal be obtained prior to a sale if a Winchester is encountered with a number of special-order features.

Acknowledgements

The author would like to acknowledge the assistance in pricing of Don Criswell, Model 21s; David Bichrest, Winchester lever actions; Joe McBride, modern Winchesters; Larry Orr, Winchester .22s; Dean Rinehart, Model 70s; Allan Wilson, Model 70s and Model 52s.

Auction houses that gave freely of their time and photos are Butterfield & Butterfield, Faintich Auction Services, Rock Island Auction Company, Old Town Station, and Amoskeag Auction Company.

Lieutenant Cook's Model 1866 Carbine

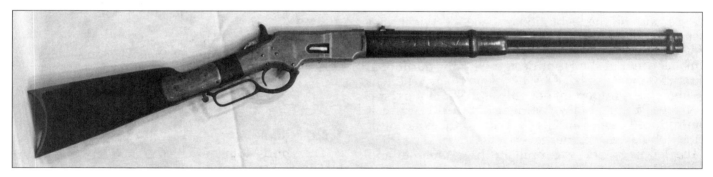

Winchester Model 1866 Carbine that first belonged to General Custer's Adjutant, who died at his side at the Battle of Little Big Horn. It is not known whether this gun was carried by the Adjutant, William W. Cook, during the Battle. This gun was reportedly first sold by Cook's niece, apparently after the family inherited this gun after his death. Barrel is round; overall length is 39 1/2". From the Tom Webster Collection. Photo by D. Kowalski.

A brass plate on the above gun bore the inscription: "1st Lieut. Wm. W. Cook 1869 7th US Cav". Photo by D. Kowalski.

WINCHESTER FIREARMS AND ITS PREDECESSORS

Hunt Repeating Rifle

Walter Hunt described his repeating rifle as the Volition Repeater. Hunt was granted U.S. patent number 6663 in August 1849 for his repeating rifle that was to pave the way for future generations of Winchester repeating rifles. Hunt's rifle design was unique and innovative as was his patent number 5701 for a conical lead bullet that was to be fired in his rifle. This ingenious bullet had a hole in its base filled with powder and closed by a disc with an opening in the middle to expel the ignition from an independent priming source that used priming pellets made of fulminate of mercury. The rifle actually worked but only the patent model was built; it is now in the Cody Firearms Museum.

Jennings

Second in the evolutionary line of Winchester rifles is the Jennings. Made by Robbins & Lawrence of Windsor, Vermont, this rifle incorporated the original concept of the Hunt design with the additional improvements utilized by Lewis Jennings. The Jennings rifle is important not only as a link in the chain of repeating rifle development but also because it introduced Benjamin Henry Tyler to the concept of the tubular magazine, lever-action repeating rifle. The Jennings rifle was built in three separate and distinct models. While total production of the three types was contracted for 5,000 guns, it is probable that only about 1,000 were actually produced.

First Model

The First Model Jennings was built in a .54 caliber, breech-loading, single shot configuration with a ring trigger, oval trigger guard, and 26" barrel. A ramrod was fixed to the underside of the barrel as well. This variation was made from 1850 to 1851.

Courtesy Milwaukee Public Museum. Milwaukee, Wisconsin

Exc.	V.G.	Good	Fair	Poor
—	—	6250	3250	1000

Second Model

The Second Model Jennings was produced adopting the improvements made by Horace Smith. This Second Model is a breech-loading repeating rifle with an under-barrel magazine tube and a 26" barrel. The frame is sculptured, unlike the First Model. The ring trigger is still present, but the trigger guard was removed as part of the design change. The caliber remained a .54, and the rifle was fitted with a 25" barrel. The Second Model was produced in 1851 and 1852.

Courtesy Milwaukee Public Museum. Milwaukee, Wisconsin

Exc.	V.G.	Good	Fair	Poor
—	—	7000	4000	1500

Third Model

The Third Model represents an attempt by investors to use the remaining parts and close out production. The .54 caliber Third Model was a muzzleloading rifle with a ramrod mounted under the barrel and a 26-1/2" barrel. The frame was the same as that used on the First Model, but the trigger was more of the conventional type. The trigger guard had a bow in the middle giving this model a distinctive appearance. This variation was produced in 1852 and marks the end of the early conceptual period in repeating rifle development.

Exc.	V.G.	Good	Fair	Poor
—	—	8500	5000	2500

Smith & Wesson Volcanic Firearms

An interesting connection in the evolution of the lever action repeating firearm is found in the production of a small group of pistols and rifles built in Norwich, Connecticut, by Horace Smith and Daniel Wesson under the firm name of Smith &

Wesson. The company built two types of Volcanic pistols. One was a large-frame model with an 8" barrel and chambered in .41 caliber. About 500 of these large frames were produced. The other pistol was a small-frame version with a 4" barrel chambered in .31 caliber. Slightly more of these small-frame pistols were built, about 700, than the large-frame version. In both variations the barrel, magazine, and frame were blued. Smith & Wesson also produced a lever-action repeating rifle. These rifles are exceedingly rare with less than 10 having been built. They were chambered for the .528 caliber and were fitted with 23" barrels. Because of the small number of rifles built, no value is offered.

Courtesy Buffalo Bill Historical Center, Cody, Wyoming

Courtesy Buffalo Bill Historical Center, Cody, Wyoming

8" Pistol

Exc.	V.G.	Good	Fair	Poor
—	—	12500	5500	1000

Courtesy Buffalo Bill Historical Center, Cody, Wyoming

4" Pistol

Exc.	V.G.	Good	Fair	Poor
—	—	10000	4000	1000

Volcanic Firearms
(Volcanic Repeating Arms Company)

With the incorporation of the Volcanic Repeating Arms Company, a new and important individual became a key figure in the company. Oliver F. Winchester would have an impact on the American arms industry for the next 100 years. This new company introduced the Volcanic pistol using the improvements made by Horace Smith and Daniel Wesson. Volcanic firearms are marked on the barrel, "THE VOLCANIC REPEATING ARMS CO. PATENT NEW HAVEN, CONN. FEB. 14, 1854". The Volcanic was offered as a .38 caliber breechloading tubular magazine repeater with blued barrel and bronze frame. These pistols were available in three barrel lengths.

6" Barrel

Exc.	V.G.	Good	Fair	Poor
—	—	6500	3500	1500

8" Barrel

Exc.	V.G.	Good	Fair	Poor
—	—	6500	3500	1500

16" Barrel

Exc.	V.G.	Good	Fair	Poor
—	—	12500	5500	2500

Courtesy Milwaukee Public Museum, Milwaukee, Wisconsin

Courtesy Buffalo Bill Historical Center, Cody, Wyoming

NOTE: A few Volcanic pistols were produced with detachable shoulder stocks. These are considered quite rare. For original guns with this option, the above prices should be increased by 25%.

Volcanic Firearms (New Haven Arms Company)

In 1857 the New Haven Arms Company was formed to continue the production of the former Volcanic Repeating Arms Company. Volcanic firearms continued to be built but were now marked on the barrel, "NEW HAVEN, CONN. PATENT FEB. 14, 1854". The Volcanic pistols produced by the New Haven Arms Company were built in .30 caliber and used the same basic frame as the original Volcanic. These pistols were produced in 3-1/2" and 6" barrel lengths.

3-1/2" Barrel

Exc.	V.G.	Good	Fair	Poor
—	—	5000	2500	1500

6" Barrel

Exc.	V.G.	Good	Fair	Poor
—	—	5500	3000	1750

Lever Action Carbine

New Haven Arms introduced, for the first time, a Volcanic rifle that featured a full-length slotted magazine tube with a spring-activated, thumbpiece follower that moved along the entire length of the magazine tube. These rifles were chambered for .38 caliber cartridges and were offered in three barrel lengths: 16", 20", and 24".

Courtesy Buffalo Bill Historical Center, Cody, Wyoming

16" Barrel

Exc.	V.G.	Good	Fair	Poor
—	--	12500	6000	2000

20" Barrel

Exc.	V.G.	Good	Fair	Poor
—	—	16000	8000	3000

24" Barrel

Exc.	V.G.	Good	Fair	Poor
—	—	20000	10000	3000

Henry Rifle

With B. Tyler Henry's improvements in the metallic rimfire cartridge and his additional improvements in the Volcanic frame, the direct predecessor to the Winchester lever-action repeater was born. The new cartridge was the .44 caliber rimfire, and the Henry rifle featured a 24" octagon barrel with a tubular magazine holding 15 shells. The rifle had no forearm, but was furnished with a walnut buttstock with two styles of buttplates: an early rounded-heel, crescent shape seen on guns produced from 1860 to 1862 and the later sharper-heel, crescent butt found on guns built from 1863 to 1866. The early models, produced from 1860 to 1861, were fitted with an iron frame, and the later models, built from 1861 to 1866, were fitted with brass frames. About 14,000 Henry rifles were made during the entire production period; only about 300 were iron-frame rifles.

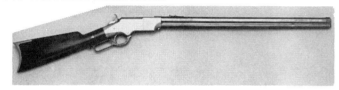

Courtesy Butterfield & Butterfield, San Francisco, California

Iron Frame Rifle

Courtesy Butterfield & Butterfield, San Francisco, California

Exc.	V.G.	Good	Fair	Poor
—	—	75000	25000	—

A Volcanic lever action carbine with 16-1/2" octagon barrel and chambered for .41 caliber was sold at auction for $23,730. The condition was good with 50% finish. Faintich Auction Service, June 1997. Photo by Paul Goodwin

A first model Henry rifle with brass frame and 24" barrel was sold at auction for $41,400. It was used throughout the Civil War and inscribed "A.J. Rolf/Co. D 23rd/Ill." Condition was good to very good. Rock Island Auction Company, April, 1999.

A factory engraved, silver-plated Henry sold at auction for $30,250. Condition was good to very good with 85% silver plating remaining.
Faintich Auction Services, November 1997

Brass Frame Rifle

Exc.	V.G.	Good	Fair	Poor
—	—	25000	8000	—

Exc.	V.G.	Good	Fair	Poor
—	—	50000	15000	7000

Martially Inspected Henry Rifles

Beginning in 1863 the Federal Government ordered 1730 Henry Rifles for use in the Civil War. These Government-inspected rifles fall into serial number range 3000 to 3900. They are marked "C.G.C." for Charles G. Chapman, the Government inspector. These Henry rifles were used under actual combat conditions and for that reason it is doubtful that there are any rifles that would fall into the excellent or very good condition category. Therefore no price is given.

NOTE: There are many counterfeit examples of these rifles. It is strongly advised that an expert in this field be consulted prior to a purchase.

Winchester's Improvement Carbine

Overall length 43-1/2"; barrel length 24"; caliber .44 r.f. Walnut stock with a brass buttplate; the receiver and magazine cover/forend of brass; the barrel and magazine tube blued. The magazine loading port is exposed by sliding the forend forward. This design was protected by O.F. Winchester's British Patent Number 3285 issued December 19, 1865. Unmarked except for internally located serial numbers. Approximately 700 manufactured in December of 1865 and early 1866, the majority of which were sold to Maximilian of Mexico. Prospective purchasers are strongly advised to secure an expert appraisal prior to acquisition.

Martially Inspected Henry Rifle. Courtesy Buffalo Bill Historical Center, Cody, Wyoming

A Winchester Model 1860 Henry rifle with standard finish. Condition was excellent. Very rare to find this model with that kind of condition. Auction price was $63,000. Butterfield & Butterfield, January 1997

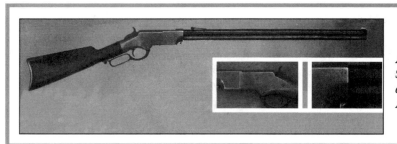

A martially marked Henry sold at auction for $63,250. Condition was very good. These rifles are extremely difficult to find in this condition. Faintich Auction Service, November, 1997

Exc.	V.G.	Good	Fair	Poor
—	—	17500	10000	7500

Model 1866

In 1866 the New Haven Arms Company changed its name to the Winchester Repeating Arms Company. The first firearm to be built under the Winchester name was the Model 1866. This first Winchester was a much-improved version of the Henry. A new magazine tube developed by Nelson King, Winchester's plant superintendent, was a vast improvement over the slotted magazine tube used on the Henry and its predecessor. The old tube allowed dirt to enter through the slots and was weakened because of it. King's patent, assigned to Winchester, featured a solid tube that was much stronger and reliable. His patent also dealt with an improved loading system for the rifle. The rifle now featured a loading port on the right side of the receiver with a spring-loaded cover. The frame continued to be made from brass. The Model 1866 was chambered for the .44 caliber Flat Rimfire or the .44 caliber Pointed Rimfire. Both cartridges could be used interchangeably.

The barrel on the Model 1866 was marked with two different markings. The first, which is seen on early guns up to serial number 23000, reads "HENRY'S PATENT-OCT. 16, 1860 KING'S PATENT-MARCH 29, 1866". The second marking reads, "WINCHESTER'S-REPEATING-ARMS.NEW HAVEN, CT. KING'S-IMPROVEMENT-PATENTED MARCH 29, 1866 OCTOBER 16, 1860". There are three basic variations of the Model 1866:

Courtesy Milwaukee Public Museum, Milwaukee, Wisconsin

1. Sporting Rifle round or octagon barrel. Approximately 28,000 were produced.
2. Carbine round barrel. Approximately 127,000 were produced.
3. Musket round barrel. Approximately 14,000 were produced.

The rifle and musket held 17 cartridges, and the carbine had a capacity of 13 cartridges. Unlike the Henry, Model 1866s were fitted with a walnut forearm. The Model 1866 was discontinued in 1898 with approximately 170,000 guns produced. The Model 1866 was sold in various special-order configurations, such as barrels longer or shorter than standard, including engraved guns. The prices listed below represent only standard Model 1866s. For guns with special-order features, an independent appraisal from an expert is highly recommended.

A First Model carbine with saddle ring and 20" barrel sold at auction for $15,820. Condition was good with traces of original finish. Caliber was .44 rimfire. Faintich Auction Service, June 1997. Photo by Paul Goodwin

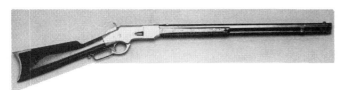

Courtesy Butterfield & Butterfield, San Francisco, California

First Model

This first style has both the Henry and King patent dates stamped on the barrel, a flat loading port cover, and a two-screw upper tang. Perhaps the most distinctive feature of the First Model is the rapid drop at the top rear of the receiver near the hammer. This is often referred to as the "Henry Drop," a reference to the same receiver drop found on the Henry rifle. First Models will be seen up through the 15000 serial-number range.

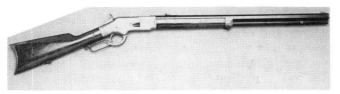

Courtesy Butterfield & Butterfield, San Francisco, California

Rifle

Exc.	V.G.	Good	Fair	Poor
—	20000	12000	5000	2000

Carbine

Exc.	V.G.	Good	Fair	Poor
—	15000	10000	500	2000

Second Model

The second style differs from the first most noticeably in its single-screw upper tang and a flare at the front of the receiver to meet the forearm. The Second Model also has a more gradual drop at the rear of the receiver than the First Model. The second style Model 1866 appears through serial number 25000.

Courtesy Butterfield & Butterfield, San Francisco, California

Rifle

Exc.	V.G.	Good	Fair	Poor
—	15000	7500	4000	3000

Courtesy Butterfield & Butterfield, San Francisco, California

Carbine

Exc.	V.G.	Good	Fair	Poor
—	12000	7500	5000	2000

Third Model

The third style's most noticeable characteristic is the more moderately curved receiver shape at the rear of the frame. The serial number is now stamped in block numerals behind the trigger thus allowing the numbers to be seen for the first time without removing the stock. The barrel marking is stamped with the Winchester address. The Third Model is found between serial numbers 25000 and 149000. For the first time a musket version was produced in this serial number range.

Rifle

Courtesy Butterfield & Butterfield, San Francisco, California

Exc.	V.G.	Good	Fair	Poor
—	12000	7000	4000	2000

Carbine

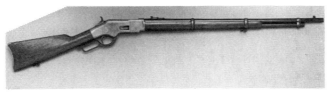

Courtesy Butterfield & Butterfield, San Francisco, California

Exc.	V.G.	Good	Fair	Poor
—	10000	7500	3500	2000

Musket

Exc.	V.G.	Good	Fair	Poor
—	8000	5000	2000	1000

Fourth Model

The fourth style has an even less pronounced drop at the top rear of the frame, and the serial number is stamped in script on the lower tang under the lever. The Fourth Model is seen between serial number 149000 and 170100 with the late guns having an iron buttplate instead of brass.

Iron

Exc.	V.G.	Good	Fair	Poor
—	12000	7500	3500	2000

Carbine

Exc.	V.G.	Good	Fair	Poor
—	10000	5000	2000	1000

Musket

Exc.	V.G.	Good	Fair	Poor
—	9500	5000	1800	1000

Model 1866 Iron Frame Rifle Musket

Overall length 54-1/2"; barrel length 33-1/4"; caliber .45 c.f. Walnut stock with case-hardened furniture, barrel burnished bright, the receiver case-hardened. The finger-lever catch mounted within a large bolster at the rear of the lever. Unmarked except for serial numbers that appear externally on the receiver and often on the buttplate tang. Approximately 25 made during the early autumn of 1866. Prospective purchasers are strongly advised to secure an expert appraisal prior to acquisition. Due to the rarity of this model reliable prices cannot be established.

Model 1866 Iron Frame Swiss Sharpshooters Rifle

As above, but in .41 Swiss caliber and fitted with a Schuetzen-style stock supplied by the firm of Weber Ruesch in Zurich. Marked Weber Ruesch, Zurich, on the barrel and serial numbered externally. Approximately 400 to 450 manufactured in 1866 and 1867. Prospective purchasers are strongly advised to secure an expert appraisal prior to acquisition. Due to the rarity of this model reliable prices cannot be established.

Model 1867 Iron Frame Carbine

Overall length 39-1/4"; barrel length 20"; caliber .44 r.f. Walnut stock with case-hardened furniture; the barrel and magazine tube blued; the receiver case-hardened. The finger-lever catch mounted within the rear curl of the lever. Unmarked except for serial numbers that appear externally on the receiver and often on the buttplate tang. Approximately 20 manufactured. Prospective purchasers are strongly advised to secure an expert appraisal prior to acquisition. Due to the rarity of this model reliable prices cannot be established.

Model 1868 Iron Frame Rifle Musket

Overall length 49-1/2" (.455 cal.), 50-1/2" or 53" (.45 and .47 cal.); barrel length 29-1/2" (.455 cal.) and 30-1/4" or 33" (.45 and .47 cal.); calibers .45 c.f., .455 c.f., and .47 c.f. Walnut stock with case-hardened or burnished bright (.45 and .47 cal.) furniture; the barrel burnished bright; the receiver case-hardened or burnished bright (.45 and .47 cal.). The finger-lever catch mounted on the lower receiver tang. The rear of the finger lever machined with a long flat extension on its upper surface. Unmarked except for serial number. Approximately 30 examples made in .45 and .455 caliber and 250 in .47 caliber. Prospective purchasers are strongly advised to secure an expert appraisal prior to acquisition. Due to the rarity of this model reliable prices for this model cannot be established.

Model 1868 Iron Frame Carbine

Overall length 40"; barrel length 20"; caliber .44 c.f. Walnut stock with case-hardened furniture; barrel and magazine tube blued; the receiver case-hardened. The finger-lever catch as above. Unmarked except for serial numbers (receiver and buttplate tang). Approximately 25 manufactured. Prospective purchasers are strongly advised to secure an expert appraisal prior to acquisition. Due to the rarity of this model reliable prices cannot be established.

Model 1873

This Winchester rifle was one of the most popular lever actions the company ever produced. This is the "gun that won the West" and with good reason. It was chambered for the more powerful centerfire cartridge, the .44-40. Compared to the .44 Henry, this cartridge was twice as good. With the introduction of the single-action Colt pistol in 1878, chambered for the same cartridge, the individual had the convenience of a pistol for protection and the accuracy of the Winchester for food and protection. The .44-40 was the standard cartridge for the Model 1873. Three additional cartridges were offered but were not as popular as the .44. The .38-40 was first offered in 1879 and the .32-20 was introduced in 1882. In 1884 the Model 1873 was offered in .22 caliber rimfire, with a few special-order guns built in .22 extra long rimfire. Approximately 19,552 .22 caliber Model 1873s were produced.

Early Model 1873s were fitted with an iron receiver until 1884, when a steel receiver was introduced. The Model 1873 was offered in three styles:

1. Sporting Rifle, 24" round, octagon, or half-octagon barrel. Equipped standard with a crescent iron buttplate, straight-grip stock and capped forearm.

2. Carbine, 20" round barrel. Furnished standard with a rounded iron buttplate, straight-grip stock, and carbine-style forend fastened to the barrel with a single barrel band.

3. Musket, 30" round barrel. Standard musket is furnished with a nearly full-length forearm fastened to the barrel with three barrel-bands. The buttstock has a rounded buttplate.

The upper tang was marked with the model designation and the serial number was stamped on the lower tang. Caliber stampings on the Model 1873 are found on the bottom of the frame and on the breech end of the barrel. Winchester discontinued the Model 1873 in 1919 after producing about 720,000 guns.

The Winchester Model 1873 was offered with a large number of extra-cost options that greatly affect the value of the gun. For example, Winchester built two sets of special Model 1873s; the 1-of-100 and the 1-of-1000. Winchester sold only 8; 1-of-100 Model 1873s, and 136 of the 1-of-1000 guns that were built. In 1991 a few of these special guns were sold at auction and brought prices exceeding $75,000. The prices listed here are for standard guns only. For Model 1873 with special features, it is best to secure an expert appraisal. Model 1873s with case-colored receivers will bring a premium.

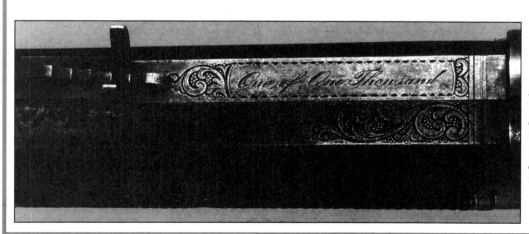

A Model 1873 "One of One Thousand" was sold at auction for $112,500. Condition was good. Only 136 of these rifles were produced. Butterfield & Butterfield, May 1998

Courtesy Butterfield & Butterfield, San Francisco, California

First Model

The primary difference between the various styles of the Model 1873 is found in the appearance and construction of the dust cover. The First Model has a dust cover held in place with grooved guides on either side. A checkered oval finger grip is found on top of the dust cover. The latch that holds the lever firmly in place is anchored into the lower tang with visible threads. On later First Models, these threads are not visible. First Models appear from serial number 1 to about 31000.

Courtesy Milwaukee Public Museum, Milwaukee, Wisconsin

Rifle

Exc.	V.G.	Good	Fair	Poor
—	7500	4000	2000	750

Carbine

Exc.	V.G.	Good	Fair	Poor
—	10000	5000	3000	1000

Musket

Exc.	V.G.	Good	Fair	Poor
—	3500	1500	1000	500

Second Model

The dust cover on the Second Model operates on one central guide secured to the receiver with two screws. The checkered oval finger grip is still used, but on later Second Models this is changed to a serrated finger grip on the rear of the dust cover. Second Models are found in the 31000 to 90000 serial-number range.

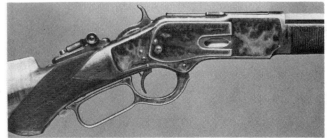

Courtesy Butterfield & Butterfield, San Francisco, California

Rifle

Exc.	V.G.	Good	Fair	Poor
9500	6000	2500	1000	500

Carbine

Exc.	V.G.	Good	Fair	Poor
12000	7500	4000	1500	800

Musket

Exc.	V.G.	Good	Fair	Poor
3500	1500	1000	750	500

Third Model

The central guide rail is still present on the Third Model, but it is now integrally machined as part of the receiver. The serrated rear edges of the dust cover are still present on the Third Model.

Courtesy Butterfield & Butterfield, San Francisco, California

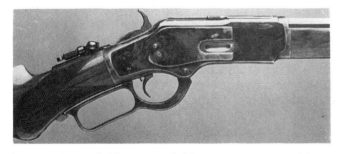

Courtesy Butterfield & Butterfield, San Francisco, California

Rifle

Exc.	V.G.	Good	Fair	Poor
9500	5000	2000	800	400

Carbine

Exc.	V.G.	Good	Fair	Poor
12000	6500	3500	1200	800

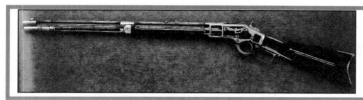

A Model 1873 factory cutaway rifle was sold at auction for $16,100. Entire left side of barrel, magazine tube, frame, forend, and butt stock are cutaway. Condition was excellent. Butterfield & Butterfield, May 1998

Musket

Exc.	V.G.	Good	Fair	Poor
3500	1500	1000	750	300

Model 1873 .22 Rimfire Rifle

Winchester's first .22 caliber rifle and the first .22 caliber repeating rifle made in America was introduced in 1884 and discontinued in 1904. Its drawback was the small caliber. The general preference during this period of time was for the larger-caliber rifles. Winchester sold a little more than 19,000 .22 caliber Model 1873s.

Exc.	V.G.	Good	Fair	Poor
10000	5500	2500	1500	750

Model 1876

Winchester's Model 1876, sometimes referred to as the Centennial Model, was the company's response to the public's demand for a repeater rifle capable of handling larger and more potent calibers. Many single shot rifles were available at this time to shoot more powerful cartridges, and Winchester redesigned the earlier Model 1873 to answer this need. The principal changes made to the Model 1873 were a larger and stronger receiver to handle more powerful cartridges. Both the carbine and the musket had their forearms extended Model 1876to cover the full length of the magazine tube. The carbine barrel was increased in length from 20" to 22", and the musket barrel length was increased from 30 to 32". The Model 1876 was the first Winchester to be offered with a pistol grip stock on its special Sporting Rifle. The Model 1876 was available in the following calibers: .45-77 W.C.F., .50-95 Express, .45-60 W.C.F., .40-60 W.C.F. The Model 1876 was offered in four different styles:

1. Sporting Rifle, 28" round, octagon, or half-octagon barrel. This rifle was fitted with a straight grip stock with crescent iron buttplate. A special sporting rifle was offered with a pistol grip stock.

2. Express Rifle, 26" round, octagon, or half-octagon barrel. The same sporting rifle stock was used.

3. Carbine, 22" round barrel with full-length forearm secured by one barrel band and straight-grip stock.

4. Musket, 32" round barrel with full-length forearm secured by one barrel band and straight-grip stock. Stamped on the barrel is the Winchester address with King's patent date. The caliber marking is stamped on the bottom of the receiver near the magazine tube and the breech end of the barrel. Winchester also furnished the Model 1876 in 1-of-100 and 1-of-1000 special guns. Only 8; 1-of-100 Model 1876s were built and 54; 1-of-1000 76s were built. As with their Model 1873 counterparts, these rare guns often sell in the $75,000 range or more. Approximately 64,000 Model 1876s were built by Winchester between 1876 and 1897. As with other Winchesters, the prices given below are for standard guns.

First Model

As with the Model 1873, the primary difference in model types lies in the dust cover. The First Model has no dust cover and is seen between serial number 1 and 3000.

Courtesy Butterfield & Butterfield, San Francisco, California

Rifle

Exc.	V.G.	Good	Fair	Poor
—	6500	3000	1500	1000

Model 1876

A First Model 1876 "1 of 1000" was sold at auction for $96,000. Chambered for .45 caliber and fitted with a 28" octagon barrel. Scroll engraved and inlaid silver bands at muzzle and breech. Condition was very good. Shipped 1877. Butterfield & Butterfield, February, 1999.

Courtesy Butterfield & Butterfield, San Francisco, California

Carbine

Exc.	V.G.	Good	Fair	Poor
—	5000	3000	1500	1000

Musket

Exc.	V.G.	Good	Fair	Poor
—	7000	4000	2000	1000

Second Model

The Second Model has a dust cover with guide rail attached to the receiver with two screws. On the early Second Model an oval finger guide is stamped on top of the dust cover while later models have a serrated finger guide along the rear edge of the dust cover. Second Models range from serial numbers 3000 to 30000.

Rifle

Exc.	V.G.	Good	Fair	Poor
—	3500	2500	1000	500

Carbine

Exc.	V.G.	Good	Fair	Poor
—	4500	2500	1500	700

Northwest Mounted Police Carbine

The folding rear sight is graduated in meters instead of yards.

Exc.	V.G.	Good	Fair	Poor
—	8000	4000	2000	1100

Musket

Exc.	V.G.	Good	Fair	Poor
—	8000	5000	2000	1000

Third Model

The dust cover guide rail on Third Model 76s is integrally machined as part of the receiver with a serrated rear edge on the dust cover. Third Model will be seen from serial numbers 30000 to 64000.

Rifle

Exc.	V.G.	Good	Fair	Poor
6000	3500	2000	800	500

Carbine

Exc.	V.G.	Good	Fair	Poor
7000	4000	2500	1500	700

Northwest Mounted Police Carbine

The folding rear sight is graduated in meters instead of yards.

Exc.	V.G.	Good	Fair	Poor
—	7500	3750	1750	1000

Musket

Exc.	V.G.	Good	Fair	Poor
12000	8000	4500	2000	1000

Winchester Hotchkiss Bolt Action Rifle

This model is also known as the Hotchkiss Magazine Gun or the Model 1883. This rifle was designed by Benjamin Hotchkiss in 1876, and Winchester acquired the manufacturing rights to the rifle in 1877. In 1879 the first guns were delivered for sale. The Hotchkiss rifle was a bolt-action firearm designed for military and sporting use. It was the first bolt-action rifle made by Winchester. The rifle was furnished in .45-70 Government, and although the 1884 Winchester catalog lists a .40-65 Hotchkiss as being available, no evidence exists that such a chamber was ever actually furnished. The Model 1883 was available in three different styles:

1. Sporting Rifle, 26" round, octagon, or half-octagon barrel fitted with a rifle-type stock that included a modified pistol grip or straight-grip stock.
2. Carbine, 24" round or 22-1/2" round barrel with military style straight-grip stock.
3. Musket, 32" or 28" round barrel with almost-full-length military style straight-grip stock. Winchester produced the Model 1883 until 1899, having built about 85000 guns.

First Model

This model has the safety and a turn-button magazine cutoff located above the trigger guard on the right side. The Sporting Rifle is furnished with a 26" round or octagon barrel while the carbine has a 24" round barrel with a saddle ring on the left side of the stock. The musket has a 32" round barrel with two barrel bands, a steel forearm tip, and bayonet attachment under the barrel. The serial number range for the First Model is between 1 and about 6419.

Sporting Rifle

Courtesy Butterfield & Butterfield, San Francisco, California

Exc.	V.G.	Good	Fair	Poor
5500	2500	1500	900	500

Carbine

Exc.	V.G.	Good	Fair	Poor
5500	2500	1500	900	500

Musket

Exc.	V.G.	Good	Fair	Poor
5500	2500	1500	900	500

Second Model

On this model the safety is located on the top left side of the receiver, and the magazine cutoff is located on the top right side of the receiver to the rear of the bolt handle. The sporting rifle remains unchanged from the First Model with the above exceptions. The carbine has a 22-1/2" round barrel with a nickeled forearm cap. The musket now has a 28" barrel. Serial number range for the Second Model runs from 6420 to 22521.

Sporting Rifle

Courtesy Milwaukee Public Museum, Milwaukee, Wisconsin

Exc.	V.G.	Good	Fair	Poor
4500	2500	1000	750	500

Carbine

Exc.	V.G.	Good	Fair	Poor
4500	2250	1000	750	500

Musket

Exc.	V.G.	Good	Fair	Poor
4500	2250	1000	750	500

Third Model

The Third Model is easily identified by the two-piece stock separated by the receiver. The specifications for the sporting rifle remain the same as before, while the carbine is now fitted with a 20" barrel with saddle ring and bar on the left side of the frame. The musket remains unchanged from the Second Model with the exception of the two-piece stock. Serial numbers of the Third Model range from 22552 to 84555.

Sporting Rifle

Exc.	V.G.	Good	Fair	Poor
4250	2500	1000	750	500

Carbine

Exc.	V.G.	Good	Fair	Poor
4250	2500	1000	700	400

Courtesy Butterfield & Butterfield, San Francisco, California

Musket

Exc.	V.G.	Good	Fair	Poor
4250	2500	750	500	300

Model 1885 (Single Shot)

The Model 1885 marks an important development between Winchester and John M. Browning. The Single Shot rifle was the first of many Browning patents that Winchester would purchase and provided the company with the opportunity to diversify its firearms line. The Model 1885 was the first single-shot rifle built by Winchester. The company offered more calibers in this model than any other. A total of 45 centerfire calibers were offered from the .22 extra long to the .50-100 Express, as well as 14 rimfire caliber from .22 B.B. cap to the .44 Flat Henry. Numerous barrel lengths, shapes, and weights were available as were stock configurations, sights, and finishes. These rifles were also available in solid frame and takedown styles. One could almost argue that each of the 139,725 Model 1885s built are unique. Many collectors of the Winchester Single Shot specialize in nothing else. For this reason it is difficult to provide pricing that will cover most of the Model 1885s that the collector will encounter. However the prices given here are for standard guns in standard configurations.

The Model 1885 was offered in two basic frame types:

A. The High Wall was the first frame type produced and is so called because the frame covers the breech and hammer except for the hammer spur.

B. The breech and hammer are visible on the Low Wall frame with its low sides. This frame type was first introduced around the 5000-serial number range.

Both the High Wall and the Low Wall were available in two frame profiles; the Thickside and the Thinside. The Thickside frame has flat sides that do not widen out to meet the stock. The Thickside is more common on the low wall rifle and rare on the High Walls.

The Thinside frame has shallow-milled sides that widen out to meet the stock. Thinside frames are common on High Wall guns and rare on Low Wall rifles.

1. The standard High Wall rifle was available with octagon or round barrel with length determined by caliber. The butt stock and forearm were plain walnut with crescent buttplate and blued frame.

2. The standard Low Wall featured a round or octagon barrel with length determined by caliber and a plain walnut stock and forearm with crescent buttplate.

3. The High Wall musket most often had a 26" round barrel chambered for the .22 caliber cartridge. Larger calibers were available as were different barrel lengths. The High Wall musket featured an almost-full-length forearm fastened to the barrel with a single barrel band and rounded buttplate.

4. The Low Wall musket is most often referred to as the Winder musket named after the distinguished marksman, Colonel C.B. Winder. This model features a Lyman receiver sight and was made in .22 caliber.

5. The High Wall Schuetzen rifle was designed for serious target shooting and was available with numerous extras including a 30" octagon barrel medium weight without rear sight seat; fancy walnut checkered pistol grip Schuetzen-style cheekpiece; Schuetzen-style buttplate; checkered forearm; double set triggers; spur finger lever, and adjustable palm rest.

6. The Low Wall carbine was available in 15", 16", 18", and 20" round barrels. The carbine featured a saddle ring on the left side of the frame and a rounded buttplate.

7. The Model 1885 was also available in a High Wall shotgun in 20 gauge with 26" round barrel and straight grip stock with shotgun-style rubber buttplate. The Model 1885 was manufactured between 1885 and 1920 with a total production of about 140,000 guns.

Courtesy Butterfield & Butterfield, San Francisco, California

Standard High Wall Rifle

Courtesy Butterfield & Butterfield, San Francisco, California

Exc.	V.G.	Good	Fair	Poor
3750	3000	2250	1300	850

Standard Low Wall Rifle

Courtesy Butterfield & Butterfield, San Francisco, California

Exc.	V.G.	Good	Fair	Poor
3500	2500	1750	1100	750

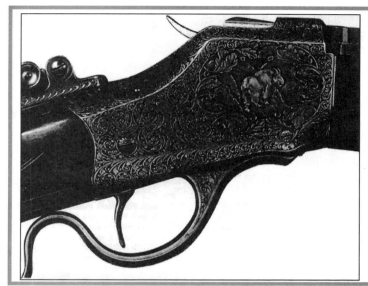

In April of 1997 Rock Island Auction Company sold a custom built Model 1885 High Wall rifle chambered for the .22 caliber rimfire cartridge and fitted with a 28-1/2" octagon barrel. The rifle was engraved by Rudolph Kornbrath in the 1930s. Auction price was $25,300. Condition is near mint.

High Wall Musket

Exc.	V.G.	Good	Fair	Poor
2750	2000	1200	900	700

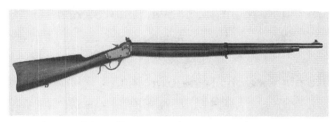

Courtesy Buffalo Bill Historical Center, Cody, Wyoming

Low Wall Musket (Winder Musket)

Exc.	V.G.	Good	Fair	Poor
2250	1500	700	400	250

High Wall Schuetzen Rifle

Exc.	V.G.	Good	Fair	Poor
10500	6000	4000	2000	1200

Low Wall Carbine

Courtesy Buffalo Bill Historical Center, Cody, Wyoming

Exc.	V.G.	Good	Fair	Poor
17500	10000	7000	3000	1500

High Wall Shotgun

Exc.	V.G.	Good	Fair	Poor
3500	2500	1750	1250	850

NOTE: Model 1885s with case-colored frames bring a premium of 25% over guns with blued frames.

NOTE: Model 1885s in calibers .50-110 and .50-100 will bring a premium depending on style and configuration.

Model 1886

Based on a John Browning patent, the Model 1886 had one of the finest and strongest lever-actions ever utilized in a Winchester rifle. Winchester introduced the Model 1886 in order to take advantage of the more powerful centerfire cartridges of the time. The rifle was available in 10 different chambers:

.45-70 U.S. Gov't.	.50-110 Express
.45-90 W.C.F.	.40-70 W.C.F.
.40-82 W.C.F.	.38-70 W.C F.
.40-65 W.C.F.	.50-100-450
.38-56 W.C.F.	.33 W.C. F.

This Deluxe Model 1886 rifle is chambered for the .45-90 cartridge. It is fitted with a 26" octagon barrel. Checkered stock with crescent butt and fancy wood. Condition is excellent. Auction price was $19,775. Photo by Paul Goodwin

The most popular caliber was the .45-70 Government. Prices of the Model 1886 are influenced by caliber, with the larger calibers bringing a premium. The 1886 was available in several different configurations.

1. Sporting Rifle, 26" round, octagon, or half-octagon barrel, full or half magazine and straight-grip stock with plain forearm.
2. Fancy Sporting Rifle, 26" round or octagon barrel, full or half magazine and fancy checkered walnut pistol-grip stock with checkered forearm.
3. Takedown Rifle, 24" round barrel, full or half magazine with straight-grip stock fitted with shotgun rubber buttplate and plain forearm.
4. Extra Lightweight Takedown Rifle, 22" round barrel, full or half magazine with straight-grip stock fitted with shotgun rubber buttplate and plain forearm.
5. Extra Lightweight Rifle, 22" round barrel, full or half magazine with straight-grip stock fitted with a shotgun rubber butt-plate and plain forearm.
6. Carbine, 22" round barrel, full or half magazine, with straight-grip stock and plain forearm.
7. Musket, 30" round barrel, musket-style forearm with one barrel band. Military style sights. About 350 Model 1886 Muskets were produced. Model 1886 rifles and carbines were furnished with walnut stocks, case-hardened frames, and blued barrels and magazine tubes. In 1901 Winchester discontinued the use of case-hardened frames on all its rifles and used blued frames instead. For this reason, case-hardened Model 1886 rifles will bring a premium. Winchester provided a large selection of extra-cost options on the Model 1886, and for rifles with these options, a separate valuation should be made by a reliable source. The Model 1886 was produced from 1886 to 1935 with about 160,000 in production.

Sporting Rifle

Courtesy Butterfield & Butterfield, San Francisco, California

Exc.	V.G.	Good	Fair	Poor
—	6000	3500	1500	650

Fancy Sporting Rifle

Exc.	V.G.	Good	Fair	Poor
—	9500	5000	3500	2000

Takedown Rifle-Standard

Exc.	V.G.	Good	Fair	Poor
—	7000	3500	1750	700

Extra Lightweight Takedown Rifle-.33 caliber

Exc.	V.G.	Good	Fair	Poor
—	2500	1250	600	400

Extra Lightweight Takedown Rifle

Exc.	V.G.	Good	Fair	Poor
—	4500	1500	1000	500

Extra Lightweight Rifle-.33 caliber

Exc.	V.G.	Good	Fair	Poor
—	2500	1100	550	400

Extra Lightweight Rifle

Courtesy Butterfield & Butterfield, San Francisco, California

Exc.	V.G.	Good	Fair	Poor
—	4500	1750	850	500

Courtesy Milwaukee Public Museum, Milwaukee, Wisconsin

Carbine

Exc.	V.G.	Good	Fair	Poor
—	10000	5000	2000	1000

Musket

Exc.	V.G.	Good	Fair	Poor
—	15000	7500	3000	1500

NOTE: For .50 Express add a premium of 20%. Blued frame Model 1886 will bring 20% less than case-colored Model 1886s.

Model 71

When Winchester dropped the Model 1886 from its line in 1935 the company replaced its large-bore, lever-action rifle with the Model 71 chambered for the .348 caliber. The Model 71 is similar in appearance to the Model 1886 with some internal parts strengthened to handle the powerful .348 cartridge. The rifle was available in three basic configurations:

1. Standard Rifle, 24" round barrel, 3/4 magazine, plain walnut pistol-grip stock and semi-beavertail forearm.
2. Standard Rifle, 20" round barrel, 3/4 magazine, plain walnut pistol grip stock and semi-beavertail forearm.
3. Deluxe Rifle, 24" round barrel, 3/4 magazine, checkered walnut pistol-grip stock and checkered semi-beavertail forearm. The frames and barrels were blued on all models of this rifle.

The Model 71 was produced from 1935 to 1957 with about 47,000 built.

Standard Rifle-24" Barrel

Exc.	V.G.	Good	Fair	Poor
1000	800	600	400	300

Standard Carbine-20" Barrel

Courtesy Butterfield & Butterfield, San Francisco, California

Exc.	V.G.	Good	Fair	Poor
3250	2000	1600	1200	650

Deluxe Rifle-24" Barrel

Exc.	V.G.	Good	Fair	Poor
1600	950	700	525	425

Deluxe Carbine-20" Barrel

Exc.	V.G.	Good	Fair	Poor
3750	3000	2000	1250	700

NOTE: For prewar Model 71s add a premium of 20%.

Model 1892

The Model 1892 was an updated successor to the Model 1873 using a scaled-down version of the Model 1886 action. The rifle was chambered for the popular smaller cartridges of the day, namely the .25-20, .32-20, .38-40, .44-40, and the rare .218 Bee. The rifle was available in several different configurations:

1. Sporting Rifle, solid frame or takedown (worth an extra premium of about 20%), 24" round, octagon, or half-octagon barrel with 1/2, 2/3, or full magazines. Plain straight-grip walnut stock with capped forearm.

Model 71, Deluxe Rifle-24" Barrel

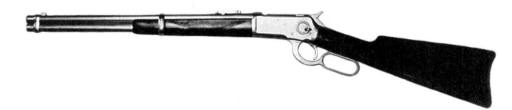

Model 71, Deluxe Carbine-20" Barrel

2. Fancy Sporting Rifle, solid frame or takedown (worth 20% premium), 24" round, octagon, or half-octagon barrel with 1/2, 2/3, or full magazine. Checkered walnut pistol-grip stock with checkered capped forearm.
3. Carbine, 20" round barrel, full or half magazine, plain walnut straight-grip stock with one barrel-band forearm. Carbines were offered only with solid frames.
4. Trapper's Carbine, 18", 16", 15", or 14" round barrel with the same dimensions of standard carbine. (Federal law prohibits the possession of rifles with barrel lengths shorter than 16". The Model 1892 Trapper's Carbine can be exempted from this law as a curio and relic with a federal permit.)
5. Musket, 30" round barrel with full magazine. Almost-full-length forearm held by two barrel bands. Buttstock is plain walnut with straight-grip.

The Model 1892 was built between 1892 and 1932 with slightly more than 1 million sold. The Model 1892 carbine continued to be offered for sale until 1941.

Courtesy Butterfield & Butterfield, San Francisco, California

Fancy Sporting Rifle

Courtesy Butterfield & Butterfield, San Francisco, California

Exc.	V.G.	Good	Fair	Poor
5500	3750	1500	700	300

Carbine

Courtesy Butterfield & Butterfield, San Francisco, California

Courtesy Butterfield & Butterfield, San Francisco, California

Sporting Rifle

Exc.	V.G.	Good	Fair	Poor
3500	2500	700	450	200

Exc.	V.G.	Good	Fair	Poor
4000	3000	1250	700	300

A Winchester Model 1892 chambered for the .25-20 cartridge and fitted with a 20" barrel was sold at auction for $27,600. It was the property of Clyde Barrow, the outlaw. Condition was fair, refinished. Butterfield & Butterfield, April 1997

Trapper's Carbine

Exc.	V.G.	Good	Fair	Poor
7500	4800	2000	850	400

NOTE: Add 20% for 15" barrel. Add 50% for carbines chambered for .25-20 cartridge.

Musket

Exc.	V.G.	Good	Fair	Poor
—	7500	2500	1000	500

Model 53

This model was in fact a slightly more modern version of the Model 1892 offered in the following calibers: .25-20, .32-20, and the .44-40. It was available in only one style: the Sporting Rifle, 22" round barrel, half magazine, straight- or pistol-grip plain walnut stock with shotgun butt. It was available in solid frame or takedown with blued frame and barrel. The Model 53 was produced from 1924 to 1932 with about 25,000 built.

Sporting Rifle

Exc.	V.G.	Good	Fair	Poor
3500	2500	1000	500	300

NOTE: Add 10% for takedown model. Add 40% for rifles chambered for .44-40 cartridge. A few of these rifles were fitted with stainless steel barrel in the early 1930s. If the black paint on these barrels is in good condition they will bring a substantial premium period.

Model 65

This model was a continuation of the Model 53 and was offered in three calibers: .25-20, .32-20, and .218 Bee. It had several improvements over the Model 53, namely the magazine capacity was increased to seven cartridges, forged ramp for front sight, and a lighter trigger pull. The Model 65 was available only in solid blued frame with blued barrel and pistol-grip with plain walnut stock. Only about 5,700 of these rifles were built between 1933 and 1947.

Courtesy Butterfield & Butterfield, San Francisco, California

Standard Rifle

Exc.	V.G.	Good	Fair	Poor
3500	2500	1000	550	250

Model 1894

Based on a John M. Browning patent, the Model 1894 was the most successful centerfire rifle Winchester ever produced. This model is still in production, and the values given here apply to those rifles produced before 1964, or around serial number 2550000. The Model 1894 was the first Winchester developed especially for smokeless powder and was chambered for the following cartridges: .32-40, .38-55, .25-35 Winchester, .30-30 Winchester, and the .32 Winchester Special. The rifle was available in several different configurations:

1. Sporting Rifle, 26" round, octagon, or half-octagon barrel, in solid frame or takedown. Full, 2/3 or 1/2 magazines were available. Plain walnut straight- or pistol-grip stock with crescent buttplate and plain capped forearm.

2. Fancy Sporting Rifle, 26" round, octagon, or half-octagon barrel, in solid frame or takedown. Full, 2/3, or 1/2 magazines were available. Fancy walnut checkered straight- or pistol-grip stock with crescent buttplate and checkered fancy capped forearm.

3. Extra Lightweight Rifle, 22" or 26" round barrel with half magazine. Plain walnut straight-grip stock with shotgun buttplate and plain capped forearm.

4. Carbine, 20" round barrel, plain walnut straight-grip stock with carbine style buttplate. Forearm was plain walnut uncapped with one barrel band. Carbines were available with solid frame only. Carbines made prior to 1925 were fitted with a saddle

Model 1894. Courtesy Butterfield & Butterfield, San Francisco, California.

ring on the left side of receiver and worth a premium over carbines without saddle ring.

5. Trapper's Carbine, 18", 16", 15", or 14". Buttstock, forearm, and saddle ring specifications same as standard carbine. All Model 1894s were furnished with blued frames and barrels, although case-hardened frames were available as an extra-cost option. Case-colored Model 1894s are rare and worth a considerable premium, perhaps as much as 1000 percent. Guns with extra-cost options should be evaluated by an expert to determine proper value. Between 1894 and 1963, approximately 2,550,000 Model 1894s were sold.

Courtesy Butterfield & Butterfield, San Francisco, California

Sporting Rifle

Exc.	V.G.	Good	Fair	Poor
2500	1600	750	500	200

NOTE: Takedown versions are worth approximately 20% more.

Fancy Sporting Rifle

Exc.	V.G.	Good	Fair	Poor
6500	2500	1400	750	400

NOTE: Takedown versions are worth approximately 20% more. Fancy Sporting Rifles were also engraved at the customer's request. Check factory records where possible and proceed with caution. Factory engraved Model 1894s are extremely valuable.

Extra Lightweight Rifle

Exc.	V.G.	Good	Fair	Poor
3500	2500	1100	600	300

Courtesy Butterfield & Butterfield, San Francisco, California

Carbine

Exc.	V.G.	Good	Fair	Poor
2500	1500	600	400	200

NOTE: Above values are for guns with saddle rings. For carbines without saddle rings deduct 35%. Add 25% for carbines chambered for .25-20 cartridge.

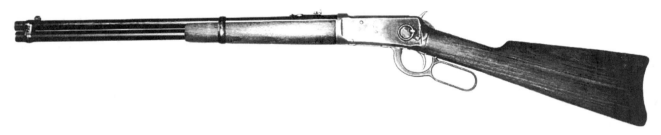

Model 1894 Carbine with saddle ring

A Model 94 takedown deluxe short rifle was sold at auction for $49,500. Chambered for .25-35 caliber and fitted with an 18 1/2" octagon barrel. Engraved in style No. 4 with D carved wood. Steel shotgun butt engraved and inlaid with gold line work. Special Lyman sights. Fancy walnut stock. Condition was excellent. Faintich Auction Service, Aril 1999. Photo Paul Goodwin

Courtesy Butterfield & Butterfield, San Francisco, California

Trappers Carbine

Exc.	V.G.	Good	Fair	Poor
5500	3500	1500	750	400

NOTE: Add 30% for carbines chambered for .25-35 or .38-55 calibers.

Model 55

This model was a continuation of the Model 1894 except in a simplified version. Available in the same calibers as the Model 1894, this rifle could be ordered only with a 24" round barrel, plain walnut straight-grip stock with plain forend and shotgun butt. Frame and barrel were blued with solid or takedown features. This model was produced between 1924 and 1932 with about 21,000 sold. Serial numbers for the Model 55 were numbered separately until about serial number 4500; then the guns were numbered in the Model 1894 sequence.

Standard Rifle

Exc.	V.G.	Good	Fair	Poor
1500	1000	650	450	200

NOTE: .25-35 caliber will bring about a 60% premium. Add 10% for models with solid frame.

Model 64

An improved version of the Model 55, this gun featured a larger magazine, pistol-grip stock, and forged front sight ramp. The trigger pull was also improved. Frame and barrel were blued. Chambered for the .25-35 Win., .30-30 Win., .32 Win. Special, and the .219 Zipper (added in 1938 and discontinued in the Model 64 in 1941). Serial number of the Model 64 was concurrent with the Model 1894. Built between 1933 and 1957, approximately 67,000 were sold. This model was reintroduced in 1972 and discontinued in 1973. The values listed below are for the early version only.

Courtesy Butterfield & Butterfield, San Francisco, California

Standard Rifle

Exc.	V.G.	Good	Fair	Poor
1200	900	500	300	200

Carbine-20" Barrel

Exc.	V.G.	Good	Fair	Poor
1550	1000	650	500	250

NOTE: For Deluxe model add 50% to above prices. For Carbine model add 50% to above prices. For rifles chambered for the .219 Zipper and .25-35 cartridges add 50%.

Model 1895

The Model 1895 was the first non-detachable box magazine rifle offered by Winchester. Built on a John M. Browning patent, this rifle was introduced by Winchester to meet the demand for a rifle that could handle the new high power, smokeless hunting cartridges of the period. The Model 1895 was available in the following calibers: .30-40 Krag, .38-72 Winchester, .40-72 Winchester, .303 British, .35 Winchester, .405 Government, 7.62 Russian, .30-03, and .30-06. The rifle gained fame as a favorite hunting rifle of Theodore Roosevelt. Because of its box magazine, the Model 1895 has a distinctive look like no other Winchester lever-action rifle. The rifle was available in several different configurations:

1. Sporting Rifle, 28" or 24" (depending on caliber) round barrel, plain walnut straight-grip stock with plain forend. The first 5,000 rifles were manufactured with flat-sided receivers, and the balance of production were built with the receiver sides contoured. After serial number 60000 a takedown version was available.

Model 55

2. Fancy Sporting Rifle, 28" round barrel, fancy walnut checkered straight-grip stock and fancy walnut-checkered forearm. Rifles with serial numbers below 5000 had flat-sided frames.

3. Carbine, 22" round barrel, plain walnut straight-grip stock with military style hand-guard forend. Some carbines are furnished with saddle rings on left side of receiver.

4. Musket:
   A. Standard Musket, 28" round barrel, plain walnut straight-grip stock with musket-style forend with two barrel-bands.
   B. U.S. Army N.R.A. Musket, 30" round barrel, Model 1901 Krag-Jorgensen rear sight. Stock similar to the standard musket. This musket could be used for "Any Military Arm" matches under the rules of the National Rifle Association.
   C. N.R.A. Musket, Models 1903 and 1906, 24" round barrel with special buttplate. Also eligible for all matches under "Any Military Arm" sponsored by the N.R.A. This musket was fitted with the same stock as listed above.
   D. U.S. Army Musket, 28" round barrel chambered for the .30-40 Krag. Came equipped with or without knife bayonet. These muskets were furnished to the U.S. Army for use during the Spanish-American War and are "US" marked on the receiver.
   E. Russian Musket, similar to standard musket but fitted with clip guides in the top of the receiver and with bayonet. Approximately 294,000 Model 1895 Muskets were sold to the Imperial Russian Government between 1915 and 1916. The first 15,000 Russian Muskets had 8" knife bayonets, and the rest were fitted with 16" bayonets.

The Model 1895 was produced from 1895 to 1931 with about 426,000 sold.

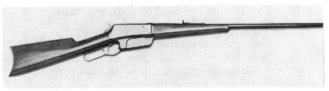

Sporting Rifle

Courtesy Butterfield & Butterfield, San Francisco, California

Exc.	V.G.	Good	Fair	Poor
5000	3000	1200	700	300

NOTE: Flat-side rifles will bring a premium of 100%. Takedown rifles will add an additional 15%.

Fancy Sporting Rifles

Exc.	V.G.	Good	Fair	Poor
6500	4500	1500	1100	500

NOTE: Flat-side rifles will bring a premium of 100%. Takedown rifles will add an additional 15%.

Courtesy Butterfield & Butterfield, San Francisco, California

Carbine

Exc.	V.G.	Good	Fair	Poor
3000	1750	1050	600	300

Standard Musket

Exc.	V.G.	Good	Fair	Poor
3000	1750	1050	600	300

U.S. Army N.R.A. Musket

Exc.	V.G.	Good	Fair	Poor
4500	2000	1200	800	400

N.R.A. Musket, Model 1903 and 1906

Exc.	V.G.	Good	Fair	Poor
5500	2500	1200	800	400

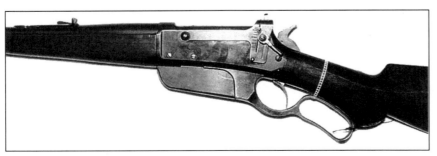

Model 1895 .30-40 Krag. Courtesy Butterfield & Butterfield, San Francisco, California

Imported English Double Shotguns

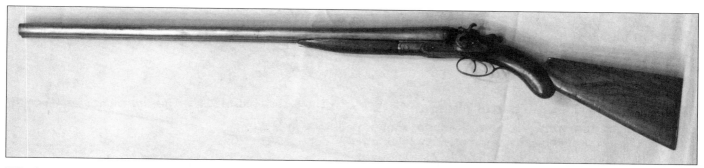

Winchester imported double-barreled shotguns from England from 1880-1884. This 12 Gauge made by C.G. Bonehill of London. "C.G. Bonehill" is inscribed on receiver. Barrel length is 30"; overall length 46 3/4". From the Tom Webster Collection. Photo by D. Kowalski.

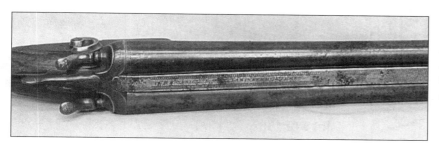

Rib bears the inscription: "The Bonehill Special BB London Street Damascus" Also "Winchester Repeating Arms Co. (Class D) New Haven, Conn. USA" Photo by D. Kowalski.

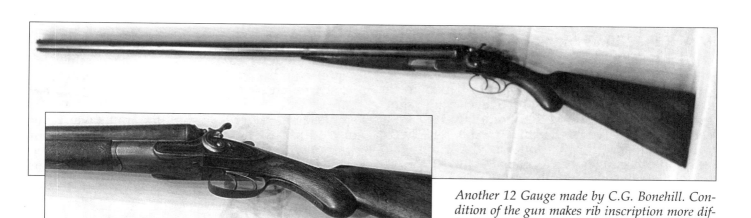

Another 12 Gauge made by C.G. Bonehill. Condition of the gun makes rib inscription more difficult to read. It says "New Model C.G. Bonehill London Laminated Steel" Then it has the same Winchester identification but stacked in two lines reading "Winchester Repeating Arms Co. (Class D) New Haven, Conn. USA" Barrel length is 30"; overall length 46 3/4". From the Tom Webster Collection. Photo by D. Kowalski.

Receiver of "New Model" above. Photo by D. Kowalski.

Closeup of receiver. Photo by D. Kowalski.

U.S. Army Musket

Exc.	V.G.	Good	Fair	Poor
—	3000	1500	850	450

Russian Musket

Exc.	V.G.	Good	Fair	Poor
4000	2500	1000	500	250

Breechloading Double Barrel Shotgun

Winchester imported an English-made shotgun sold under the Winchester name between 1879 and 1884. The gun was available in 10 and 12 gauge with 30" or 32" Damascus barrels. It was sold in five separate grades referred to as "classes." The lowest grade was the "D" and the best grade was called the "Match Grade." These were marked on the sidelocks. The center rib was stamped "Winchester Repeating Arms Co., New Haven, Connecticut, U.S.A." About 10,000 of these guns were imported by Winchester.

Class A, B, C, and D

Exc.	V.G.	Good	Fair	Poor
2500	2250	1250	850	500

Match Gun

Exc.	V.G.	Good	Fair	Poor
2500	2250	1250	850	500

Model 1887 Shotgun

Winchester enjoyed a great deal of success with its imported English shotgun, and the company decided to manufacture a shotgun of its own. In 1885 it purchased the patent for a lever-action shotgun designed by John M. Browning. By 1887 Winchester had delivered the first model 1887 in 12 gauge and shortly after offered the gun in 10 gauge. Both gauges were offered with 30" or 32" full-choked barrels, with the 30" standard on the 12 gauge and 32" standard on the 10 gauge. A Riot Gun was offered in 1898 both in 10, and 12 gauge with 20" barrels choked cylinder. Both variations of the Model 1887 were offered with plain walnut pistol-grip stocks with plain forend. The frame was case-hardened and the barrel blued. Between 1887 and 1901 Winchester sold approximately 65,000 Model 1887 shotguns.

Courtesy Milwaukee Public Museum, Milwaukee, Wisconsin

Courtesy Butterfield & Butterfield, San Francisco, California

Standard Shotgun

Exc.	V.G.	Good	Fair	Poor
1700	1200	850	500	300

Riot Shotgun

Exc.	V.G.	Good	Fair	Poor
2000	1500	950	600	400

Model 1901 Shotgun

This model is a redesign of the Model 1887 shotgun and was offered in 10 gauge only with a 32" barrel choked full, modified, or cylinder. The barrel was reinforced to withstand the new smokeless powder loads and the frame was blued instead of case-hardened. The stock was of plain walnut with a modified pistol-grip and plain forearm. The Model 1901 was built between 1901 and 1920 with about 65,000 guns sold.

Standard Shotgun

Exc.	V.G.	Good	Fair	Poor
1200	800	600	400	250

Model 1901, Standard Shotgun

Model 1893

This was the first slide-action repeating shotgun built by Winchester. It featured an exposed hammer and side ejection. Based on a John M. Browning patent this model was not altogether satisfactory. The action proved to be too weak to handle smokeless loads even though the gun was designed for black powder. The gun was offered in 12 gauge with 30" or 32" barrels choked full. Other chokes were available on special order and will command a premium. The stock was plain walnut with a modified pistol grip, grooved slide handle, and hard-rubber buttplate. The receiver and barrel were blued. Winchester produced the Model 1893 between 1893 and 1897, selling about 31,000 guns.

Courtesy Butterfield & Butterfield, San Francisco, California

Standard Shotgun

Exc.	V.G.	Good	Fair	Poor
1000	700	500	325	150

Model 1897

The Model 1897 replaced the Model 1893, and while similar to the Model 1893, the new model had several improvements such as a stronger frame, chamber made longer to handle 2-3/4" shells, frame top was covered to force complete side ejection, the stock was made longer and with less drop. The Model 1897 was available in 12 or 16 gauge with the 12 gauge offered either in solid or takedown styles and the 16 gauge available in takedown only. The Model 1897 was available with barrel lengths of 20", 26", 28", 30", and 32" and in practically all choke options from full to cylinder. The shotgun could be ordered in several different configurations:

1. Standard Gun, 12 or 16 gauge, 30" barrel in 12 gauge and 28" barrel in 16 gauge, with plain walnut modified pistol-grip stock and grooved slide handle. Steel buttplate standard.
2. Trap Gun 12 or 16 gauge, 30" barrel in 12 gauge and 28" barrel in 16 gauge, fancy walnut stock with oil finish checkered pistol-grip or straight-grip stock with checkered slide handle. Marked "TRAP" on bottom of frame.
3. Pigeon Gun, 12 or 16 gauge, 28" barrel on both 12 and 16 gauge, straight- or pistol-grip stock same as Trap gun, receiver hand engraved.
4. Tournament Gun, 12 gauge only with 30" barrel, select walnut checkered straight-grip stock and checkered slide handle, top of receiver is matted to reduce glare.
5. Brush Gun, 12 or 16 gauge, 26" barrel, cylinder choke, has a slightly shorter magazine tube than standard gun, plain walnut modified pistol-grip stock with grooved slide handle.
6. Brush Gun, Takedown, same as above with takedown feature and standard length magazine tube.
7. Riot Gun, 12 gauge, 20" barrel bored to shoot buckshot, plain walnut modified pistol-grip stock with grooved slide handle. Solid frame or takedown.
8. Trench Gun, same as Riot Gun but fitted with barrel hand guard and bayonet.

The Winchester Model 1897 was a great seller for Winchester. During its 60-year production span 1,025,000 guns were sold.

Standard Gun

Exc.	V.G.	Good	Fair	Poor
700	600	450	250	150

Trap Gun

Exc.	V.G.	Good	Fair	Poor
850	550	400	325	250

Pigeon Gun

Exc.	V.G.	Good	Fair	Poor
2700	2200	1600	1250	1000

Tournament Gun

Exc.	V.G.	Good	Fair	Poor
900	600	450	350	250

Brush Gun

Exc.	V.G	Good	Fair	Poor
850	550	400	325	250

Courtesy Butterfield & Butterfield, San Francisco, California

Riot Gun

Courtesy Butterfield & Butterfield, San Francisco, California

Exc.	V.G.	Good	Fair	Poor
700	600	500	350	200

Trench Gun

Exc.	V.G.	Good	Fair	Poor
2000	1500	1000	500	300

NOTE: Add 25% for 16 gauge guns in excellent, very good, and good condition.

Winchester-Lee Straight Pull Rifle

This rifle was a military firearm that Winchester built for the U.S. Navy in 1895. The Navy version was a musket type with 28" round barrel and musket-style forearm and plain walnut pistol-grip stock. In 1897 Winchester offered a commercial musket version for public sale as well as a Sporting Rifle. All of these guns were chambered for the 6mm Lee (236 caliber) cartridge. The Sporting Rifle featured a 24" round barrel with plain walnut pistol-grip stock and finger grooves in the forearm. Built from 1895 to 1905, Winchester sold about 20,000 Lee rifles; 15,000 were sold to the U.S. Navy; 3,000 were sold in the commercial version; and 1,700 were Sporting Rifles.

U.S. Navy Musket

Exc.	V.G.	Good	Fair	Poor
2500	2000	1500	700	500

Commercial Musket

Exc.	V.G.	Good	Fair	Poor
2500	2000	1500	700	500

Sporting Rifle

Exc.	V.G.	Good	Fair	Poor
2500	2000	1500	700	500

Model 1890

The Model 1890 was the first slide-action rifle ever produced by Winchester. Designed by John and Matthew Browning, this rifle was chambered for the .22 Short, Long, and Winchester Rimfire cartridges (the WRF cartridge was developed by Winchester specifically for the Model 1890), but not on an interchangeable basis. In 1919 the .22 Long Rifle cartridge was offered as well. The rifle was a slide-action top-ejecting rifle with an 18" under-barrel magazine tube. All Model 1890s were furnished standard with plain walnut straight stocks with crescent buttplate and 12" grooved slide handle. This rifle was one of the company's best-selling small-caliber firearms and was in worldwide use. The Model 1890 came in three separate and distinct variations that greatly affect its value:

1. First Model, solid frame, 24" octagon barrel, case-hardened frame and fixed rear sight. Approximately 15,552 of these First Model guns were produced, and their distinctive features are concealed locking lugs and solid frame. Serial numbered on the lower tang only. Built from 1890 to 1892.

2. Second Model, takedown, 24" octagon barrel, case-hardened frame, and adjustable rear sight. Serial numbered from 15,553 to 112,970 (on lower tang only) these Second Model guns feature the same concealed locking lugs but with the added takedown feature. A Deluxe version was offered with fancy walnut checkered straight- or pistol-grip stock and grooved slide handle.

2A. Second Model (Blued Frame Variation), same as above but with blued frame. Serial numbered from 112,971 to 325,250 (on lower tang until 232,328, then also on bottom front end of receiver) these blued-frame Second Models are much more numerous than the case-hardened variety. A Deluxe version was offered with fancy walnut checkered straight- or pistol-grip stock and grooved slide handle.

3. Third Model, takedown, 24" octagon barrel, blued frame, adjustable rear sight. Serial numbered from 325,251 to as high as 853,000 (numbered on both the lower tang and bottom front of receiver) the distinctive feature of the Third Model is the locking cut made on the front top of the receiver to allow the breech bolt to lock externally. A Deluxe version was offered with fancy walnut checkered stock, straight or pistol grip with grooved slide handle. Winchester offered many extra-cost options for this rifle that will greatly affect the value. Secure an expert appraisal before proceeding. The Model 1890 was produced from 1890 to 1932 with approximately 775,000 guns sold.

U.S. Navy Musket

First Model-Standard Grade

Exc.	V. G.	Good	Fair	Poor
9000	5000	2500	1250	750

Second Model-Case-hardened Frame

Standard

Exc.	V. G.	Good	Fair	Poor
5500	3500	2000	1000	500

Deluxe

Exc.	V. G.	Good	Fair	Poor
10000	7000	3500	2000	1000

Courtesy Butterfield & Butterfield, San Francisco, California

Courtesy Butterfield & Butterfield, San Francisco, California

Second Model-Blued Frame

Standard

Exc.	V. G.	Good	Fair	Poor
4000	2250	1500	750	500

Deluxe

Exc.	V. G.	Good	Fair	Poor
7500	5500	3000	1500	1000

Courtesy Butterfield & Butterfield, San Francisco, California

Third Model

Standard

Exc.	V.G.	Good	Fair	Poor
2750	1750	1200	750	500

Deluxe

Exc.	V.G.	Good	Fair	Poor
5000	3500	2000	1000	750

NOTE: For Third Models chambered for .22 Long Rifle add 25% premium.

Model 1906

In 1906 Winchester decided to offer a lower-cost version of the Model 1890. The Model 1906 used the same receiver but was fitted with a 20" round barrel and plain gumwood straight-grip stock. When the Model 1906 was first introduced, it sold for 2/3 of the price of the Model 1890. For the first two years the gun was chambered for the .22 Short cartridge only. In 1908 the rifle was modified to shoot .22 Short, Long, and Long Rifle cartridges interchangeably. This modification ensured the Model 1906's success, and between 1906 and 1932 about 800,000 were sold. All Model 1906s were of the takedown variety. The Model 1906 is available in three important variations:

1. 22 Short only, 20"-round barrel, straight-grip gumwood stock and smooth slide handle. These were built from serial number 1 to around 113000.

2. Standard Model 1906, 20" round barrel, straight-grip gumwood stock with 12" grooved slide handle. Serial numbered from 113000 to 852000.

3. Model 1906 Expert, 20" round barrel, pistol-grip gumwood stock with fluted smooth slide handle. Expert was available from 1918 to 1924 and was offered in three different finishes; regular blued finish; half nickel (receiver, guard, and bolt); and full nickel (receiver, guard, bolt, and barrel nickeled).

Courtesy Butterfield & Butterfield, San Francisco, California

Model 1906 .22 Short Only

Courtesy Butterfield & Butterfield, San Francisco, California

Exc.	V.G.	Good	Fair	Poor
3000	1750	750	500	200

Standard Model 1906

Courtesy Butterfield & Butterfield, San Francisco, California

NIB	Exc.	V.G.	Good	Fair	Poor
4000	2000	1000	650	400	200

Model 1906 Expert

Exc.	V.G.	Good	Fair	Poor
3250	1700	850	500	300

NOTE: Prices are for all blued Experts. Add 25% for half nickel and 100% for full nickel.

Model 62 and 62A

When the Model 1890 and Model 1906 were dropped from the Winchester product line in 1932, the company introduced the Model 62 to take their place. An updated version of the earlier slide-action .22 rifles, the Model 62 was fitted with a 23" round barrel and was capable of shooting .22 Short, Long, and Long Rifle cartridges interchangeably. Winchester offered a Gallery version of the Model 62 that was chambered for .22 Short only. Some of these Gallery guns have "Winchester" stamped on the left side of the receiver. Winchester Model 62 Gallery rifles have a triangular loading port on the loading tube that the standard models did not have. A change in the breech-bolt mechanism brought about a change in the name designation from Model 62 to Model 62A. This occurred around serial number 98000. The letter "A" now appears behind the serial number. This model stayed in production until 1958, and collectors will concede a premium for guns built prior to WWII with small slide handles. The stock was of plain walnut with straight grip and grooved slide handle. Both the receiver and barrel were blued. All Model 62 and 62As were takedown. Approximately 409,000 guns were sold.

Prewar Model 62

NIB	Exc.	V.G.	Good	Fair	Poor
2250	1500	700	400	250	150

NOTE: Barrels marked with Model 62 are worth more than barrels marked with Model 62A by approximately 15%. Gallery models will bring a premium of 400%.

Postwar Model 62

NIB	Exc.	V.G.	Good	Fair	Poor
1700	750	450	325	225	125

Model 62 Gallery-.22 Short Only w/triangular loading port

NIB	Exc.	V.G.	Good	Fair	Poor
4250	1750	1000	650	400	200

Model 61

Winchester developed the Model 61 in an attempt to keep pace with its competitors' hammerless .22 rifles. The Model 61 featured a 24" round or octagonal barrel and could be ordered by the customer in a variety of configurations. Collector interest in this rifle is high because of the fairly large number of variations. The Model 61 is often considered a companion to the Winchester Model 12 and Model 42 shotguns. The following is a list of chamber and barrel variations found in this model:

1. 24" round barrel, .22 Short, Long, Long Rifle.
2. 24" octagonal barrel, .22 Short only.
3. 24" octagonal barrel, .22 Long Rifle only.
4. 24" octagonal barrel, .22 W.R.F. only.
5. 24" round barrel, .22 Long Rifle Shot only.
6. 24" round barrel, .22 W.R.F. only.
7. 24" round barrel, .22 Long Rifle only.
8. 24" round barrel, .22 Winchester Magnum.
9. 24" round barrel, .22 Short only.

The Model 61 was fitted with a plain walnut pistol-grip stock with grooved slide handle. All Model 61s were of the takedown variety. Prewar models

Model 62. Courtesy Butterfield & Butterfield, San Francisco, California

will have a short slide handle. Manufactured between 1932 and 1963, approximately 342,000 guns were sold.

Courtesy Butterfield & Butterfield, San Francisco, California

Prewar Model 61

NIB	Exc.	V.G.	Good	Fair	Poor
2500	1500	700	575	325	200

NOTE: Single-caliber models will command a premium of 50% depending on caliber. Octagon-barrel models will command a premium of 75%. .22 Long Rifle Shot-only models will bring a premium of 250%.

Postwar Model 61

NIB	Exc.	V.G.	Good	Fair	Poor
1750	850	500	450	250	150

Model 61 Magnum

NIB	Exc.	V.G.	Good	Fair	Poor
1850	950	775	600	400	250

NOTE: This variation was produced from 1960 to 1963.

Model 1903

The first semiautomatic rifle produced by Winchester was designed by T.C. Johnson. This rifle was offered in a takedown version only and was available in a 20" round barrel chambered for the .22 Winchester Automatic Rimfire. This ammunition is no longer produced and when found is very expensive. The tubular magazine is located in the butt stock and holds 10 cartridges. The rifle was available in two different configurations:

1. Standard Rifle, 20" round barrel, plain walnut straight-grip stock with plain forend. Steel crescent butt was standard.
2. Deluxe Rifle, 20" round barrel, fancy checkered walnut pistol-grip stock with checkered forearm. Manufactured from 1903 to 1932, about 126,000 were sold.

Standard Rifle

Exc.	V.G.	Good	Fair	Poor
850	550	325	200	100

Deluxe Rifle

Exc.	V.G.	Good	Fair	Poor
2250	1000	700	500	250

NOTE: The first 5,000 guns were built without safeties, and the first 15,000 guns were furnished with bronze firing pins instead of steel. These early Model 1903s will bring a premium of 30%.

Model 63

The Model 63 took the place of the Model 1903 in 1933 in an attempt by Winchester to solve the problem of having to use a special .22 caliber cartridge in the gun to operate the blow back system. It is a very high quality semiautomatic rifle. Many collectors and shooters considered it the best rimfire semiautomatic rifle ever produced. The Model 63

Model 1903. Courtesy Butterfield & Butterfield, San Francisco, California

Model 63. Courtesy Butterfield & Butterfield, San Francisco, California

was chambered for the .22 Long Rifle cartridge and was available in a 20" barrel for the first four years or until about serial number 9800. Thereafter, the model was offered with a 23" round barrel. The gun was fitted with a plain walnut pistol-grip stock and forearm. The tubular magazine was located in the butt stock that came with a steel buttplate. The last 10,000 Model 63s were sold with a grooved receiver top to make the addition of a scope easier. Manufactured between 1933 and 1958, about 175,000 guns were sold.

20" Barrel Model 63

Courtesy Butterfield & Butterfield, San Francisco, California

NIB	Exc.	V.G.	Good	Fair	Poor
2750	1400	800	500	400	250

23" Barrel Model 63

NIB	Exc.	V.G.	Good	Fair	Poor
1750	800	550	400	300	200

NOTE: Grooved top receivers command a premium of 20%.

EDITOR'S COMMENT: There have been reports of Deluxe Model 63s offered for sale. These rifles are often seen with Model 1903 buttstocks with checkering and deluxe wood. Prices are in the $3,000 to $4,000 range. Winchester did not catalog a Deluxe Model 63. However, that does not mean the company did not make them. It is strongly suggested that an expert opinion be obtained prior to a purchase. Proceed with caution.

Model 1905

The Model 1905 was a larger version of the Model 1903, developed by T.C. Johnson to handle the more powerful centerfire cartridges. It was chambered for the .32 Winchester Self-Loading and .35 Self-Loading cartridges, loading by means of a detachable box magazine. Available in takedown only, this model was offered in two different styles:

1. Sporting Rifle, 22" round barrel, plain walnut straight-grip (changed to pistol grip in 1908) stock with plain forend.
2. Fancy Sporting Rifle, 22" round barrel, fancy walnut checkered pistol-grip stock with checkered forend. This model was the first Winchester semiautomatic rifle to fire centerfire cartridges. Produced from 1905 to 1920 with about 30,000 rifles sold.

Sporting Rifle

Exc.	V.G.	Good	Fair	Poor
500	350	250	175	125

Fancy Sporting Rifle

Exc.	V.G.	Good	Fair	Poor
600	400	300	200	150

Model 1907

The Model 1907 was an improved version of the Model 1905 and chambered for the new .351 Winchester Self-Loading cartridge. Outward appearance was the same as Model 1905 except for 20" round barrel. This rifle was available in three different styles:

1. Sporting Rifle, 20" round barrel, plain walnut pistol-grip stock with plain forend. Discontinued in 1937.
2. Fancy Sporting Rifle, 20" round barrel, fancy walnut checkered pistol-grip stock and checkered forend.
3. Police Rifle, 20" round barrel, plain walnut pistol-grip stock and beavertail forend. This version was fitted with a leather sling and with or without knife bayonet. First introduced in 1937. Winchester discontinued this model in 1957 after having sold about 59,000 guns.

Sporting Rifle

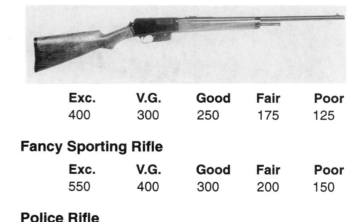

Exc.	V.G.	Good	Fair	Poor
400	300	250	175	125

Fancy Sporting Rifle

Exc.	V.G.	Good	Fair	Poor
550	400	300	200	150

Police Rifle

Exc.	V.G.	Good	Fair	Poor
450	350	275	200	150

Model 1910

This model was similar to the Model 1907 but the action was made stronger to handle the new

Winchester .401 Self-Loading cartridge. The specifications for this model are the same as the Model 1907. Built between 1907 and 1936, only about 21,000 of these guns were sold.

Courtesy Butterfield & Butterfield, San Francisco, California

Sporting Rifle

Exc.	V.G.	Good	Fair	Poor
400	300	250	175	125

Fancy Sporting Rifle

Exc.	V.G.	Good	Fair	Poor
550	400	300	200	150

Model 55 (Rimfire Rifle)

Not to be confused with the lever-action model, this .22 caliber rifle was a semiautomatic single shot with a 22" round barrel. Fitted with a plain walnut pistol-grip, one-piece stock and forend. The safety goes on when each cartridge is inserted into the chamber. This model was not serial numbered and was produced from 1957 to 1961 with about 45,000 guns sold.

Standard Rifle

Exc.	V.G.	Good	Fair	Poor
200	125	100	90	60

Model 74

This was a semiautomatic chambered for either the .22 Short or the .22 Long Rifle. The rifle has a tubular magazine in the buttstock and a 24" round barrel. The bolt on this rifle was designed to be easily removed for cleaning or repair. The stock was plain walnut pistol grip with semi-beavertail forend. A Gallery Special was offered that was chambered for the .22 Short and fitted with a steel shell deflector. This gallery model was also available with chrome trimmings at extra cost.

Courtesy C.H. Wolfersberger

Sporting Rifle

Exc.	V.G.	Good	Fair	Poor
400	300	225	150	100

Gallery Special-.22 Short Only

Exc	V.G.	Good	Fair	Poor
600	450	325	225	150

NOTE: For Gallery models with chrome trimmings, add a premium of 50%.

Model 77

This rifle was built on the blow-back design for semiautomatic rifles and is chambered for the .22 Long Rifle. It features a 22" round barrel and either a detachable box magazine or under-barrel tubular magazine. The rifle has a trigger guard made of nylon. It has a plain walnut pistol-grip stock with semi-beavertail forend and composition buttplate. Built between 1955 and 1963, Winchester sold about 217,000 of these rifles.

Standard Rifle

Exc.	V.G.	Good	Fair	Poor
250	175	150	100	50

NOTE: Models with tubular magazines will bring a premium of 10% to 20%.

Model 100

This rifle is gas operated, semiautomatic and chambered for the .243, .308, and .284 caliber centerfire cartridges. It was available in a rifle version with a 22" round barrel and a carbine version with a 19" barrel. Both were furnished with a detachable box magazine. The stock was a one-piece design with pistol grip and was offered in either hand-cut checkering or pressed-basket-weave checkering. Rifles were introduced in 1961 and the carbine in 1967. The Model 100 was last produced in 1973 with about 263,000 guns sold.

WARNING: The Model 100 has been recalled. Do not purchase this model without first determining if the problem has been repaired.

Model 100 Rifle

Exc.	V.G.	Good	Fair	Poor
475	400	300	250	200

NOTE: Pre-1964 models will bring a 15% premium. Cut checkered add 10%. Prices given are for .308 caliber; for .243 add 15%, for .284 add 20%.

Model 100 Carbine

Exc.	V.G.	Good	Fair	Poor
575	475	375	325	225

NOTE: Add 25% premium for .243, and 100% for .284.

Model 88

The Model 88 was a modern short-stroke lever-action chambered for the .243, .308, .284, and .358 calibers. It was available in a rifle version with 22" round barrel and a carbine version with 19" round barrel. The carbine model was not chambered for the .358 cartridge. Both were furnished with a detachable box magazine. The stock was a one-piece design with pistol grip and was offered with hand-cut checkering or pressed-basket-weave checkering after 1964. The rifle was introduced in 1955 and the carbine was first offered in 1968. Both versions were discontinued in 1973 with about 283,000 sold.

Model 88 Rifle

Exc.	V.G.	Good	Fair	Poor
500	400	300	250	150

NOTE: Pre-1964 models add 25% premium. Prices above are for .308 caliber; for .243 add 15%, .284 add 50%, and for .358 add 100%.

Model 88 Carbine

Exc.	V.G.	Good	Fair	Poor
950	800	650	400	300

NOTE: Add 25% for .243, add 100% for .284 calibers.

Model 1900

This single-shot bolt-action .22 caliber rifle was based on a John M. Browning design. The rifle was furnished with an 18" round barrel and chambered for the .22 Short and Long interchangeably. The stock was a one-piece plain gumwood straight grip without a buttplate. The rifle was not serial numbered. It was produced from 1899 to 1902 with about 105,000 sold.

Courtesy Buffalo Bill Historical Center, Cody, Wyoming

Exc.	V.G.	Good	Fair	Poor
2500	1250	750	500	300

Model 1902

Also a single shot, this model was of the same general design as the Model 1900 with several improvements: a special shaped metal trigger guard was added, a shorter trigger pull, a steel buttplate, a rear peep sight, and the barrel was made heavier at the muzzle. The rifle was chambered for the .22 Short and Long cartridges until 1914 when the .22 Extra Long was added. In 1927 the .22 Extra Long was dropped in favor of the more popular .22 Long Rifle. All of these cartridges were interchangeable. The stock was a one-piece plain gumwood with straight grip (the metal trigger guard added a pistol grip feel) and steel buttplate, which was changed to composition in 1907. This model was not serial numbered. About 640,000 Model 1902s were sold between 1902 and 1931 when it was discontinued.

Exc.	V.G.	Good	Fair	Poor
1000	750	400	225	125

Model 99 or Thumb Trigger

This rifle was a modification of the Model 1902 without a traditional trigger. The rifle was fired by depressing the trigger with the thumb, which was part of the sear and extractor located behind the bolt. The

Model 88 Rifle

rifle was chambered for the .22 Short and Long until 1914 when it was also chambered for the .22 Extra Long. All cartridges could be shot interchangeably. The stock was the same as the Model 1902, Gumwood stained walnut, without the trigger or trigger guard. This model was not serial numbered. Built between 1904 and 1923. Winchester sold about 76,000 rifles.

Courtesy Butterfield & Butterfield, San Francisco, California

Exc.	V.G.	Good	Fair	Poor
2250	1250	600	300	100

Model 1904

This model was a slightly more expensive version of the Model 1902. It featured a 21" round barrel, a one-piece plain gumwood straight-grip stock (the metal trigger guard gave the rifle a pistol grip feel) with a small lip on the forend. Rifle was chambered for the .22 Short and Long until 1914 when the .22 Extra Long was added. The .22 Long Rifle cartridge was added in place of the Extra Long in 1927. This model was not serial numbered. Produced between 1904 and 1931, about 303,000 rifles were sold.

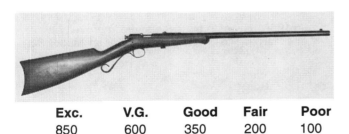

Exc.	V.G.	Good	Fair	Poor
850	600	350	200	100

Model D Military Rifle

Overall length 46-3/8"; barrel length 26"; caliber 7.62 mm. Walnut stock with blued barrel, receiver, magazine housing and furniture. Receiver ring over barrel breech stamped with serial number and Winchester proofmark. A total of 500 Model D Rifles were shipped to Russia for trial in March of 1917.

Prospective purchasers are strongly advised to secure an expert appraisal prior to acquisition. Due to the recent identification of this model pricing schedules have yet to be established.

Imperial Bolt Action Magazine Rifle (Model 51)

Designed by T.C. Johnson, approximately 25 of these rifles were made during 1919 and 1920 in two different styles and three calibers. The takedown variation has an overall length of 42-1/4", barrel length of 22" and was made in .27, .30-06 and .35 Newton calibers. The solid frame version is identical in form, dimensions and calibers. Sight configurations and markings vary.

Winchester Imperial Takedown

Winchester Imperial Solid Frame

A Winchester prototype single shot pistol similar to the Model 1904 breech barrel was sold at auction for $4,025. Fitted with an 11" round barrel and chambered for .22 caliber. Walnut grips. Condition was excellent. Rock Island Auction Company, March 1998

Model 43

Introduced in 1949, this rifle was chambered for the .218 Bee, .22 Hornet, .25-20 Winchester, and the .32-20 Winchester. The rifle was a bolt-action with detachable box magazine, fitted with a 24" round barrel and front sight ramp forged integrally with barrel. This model was not drilled and tapped for scope blocks except for a few late rifles. This model was available in two styles:

1. Standard Rifle, 24" round barrel, plain walnut pistol-grip stock and forend. One-inch sling swivels are standard.
2. Special Rifle, 24" round barrel, select walnut checkered pistol-grip stock and checkered forend. Furnished with either open sporting rear sight or Lyman 57A micrometer receiver sight.

The Model 43 was produced from 1949 to 1957 with about 63,000 sold.

Standard Rifle

Exc.	V.G.	Good	Fair	Poor
600	500	300	250	175

Special Rifle or Deluxe

Exc.	V.G.	Good	Fair	Poor
750	650	550	250	175

NOTE: For rifles chambered for .25-20 and .32-20 add a 25% premium.

Model 47

This model was a single shot bolt-action rifle chambered for the .22 Short, Long, and Long Rifle interchangeably. The rifle was furnished with a 25" round barrel, plain walnut pistol-grip stock and forend. The bolt, bolt handle, and trigger are chrome plated. This model has a special bolt with a post on the underside. This moves into the safety position when the bolt is closed. This model was not serial numbered. Produced between 1948 and 1954, Winchester sold about 43,000 guns.

Courtesy Buffalo Bill Historical Center, Cody, Wyoming

Model 47 Target Rifle

Fitted with a 28" round standard weight or heavyweight barrel, plain walnut modified pistol-grip stock with correct bolt.

Exc.	V.G.	Good	Fair	Poor
350	300	200	150	100

Model 52

One of the finest small caliber bolt-action rifles ever built, the Model 52 was Winchester's answer to the increased demand for a military style target rifle following WWI. The Model 52 was a well-made quality-built bolt-action rifle. The rifle was chambered for the .22 Long Rifle cartridge. Designed by T.C. Johnson, this rifle was built in several different configurations over its production life:

1. Model 52 with finger groove in forend and one barrel band. Produced from 1920 to 1929.
2. Model 52 Target Rifle, same as above but without finger groove in forend and has first speed lock. Made from 1929 to 1932.
3. Model 52A Target Rifle, same as above with addition of reinforced receiver and locking lug. Made from 1932 to 1935.
4. Model 52B Target Rifle, same as above with addition of adjustable sling swivel and single-shot adaptor. Made from 1935 to 1947.
5. Model 52C Target Rifle, same as above with addition of an easily adjustable vibration-free trigger mechanism. Made from 1947 to 1961.
6. Model 52D Target Rifle, this is a single-shot rifle with free-floating barrel and new-design stock with adjustable hand-stop channel.
7. Model 52 Bull Gun, same as target rifle but fitted with extra heavyweight barrel. Made from 1939 to 1960.
8. Model 52 International Match, a free-style stock with thumb hole and adjustable buttstock and forend introduced in 1969. An International Prone model with no thumb hole or adjustable buttplate and forend was introduced in 1975. Both discontinued in 1980.
9. Model 52 Sporter, 24" round barrel, select walnut checkered pistol-grip stock with cheekpiece and forend with black plastic tip. Pistol grip was furnished with hard rubber grip cap. The Model 52 Sporter was introduced in 1934 and discontinued in 1958. It went through the same improvements as the Target Rifle, thus the designation Model 52A Sporter; etc.

Model 52 Target

Exc.	V.G.	Good	Fair	Poor
500	400	300	275	225

Model 52 Target-Speed Lock

Exc.	V.G.	Good	Fair	Poor
550	450	350	300	250

Model 52A Target-Rare

Exc.	V.G.	Good	Fair	Poor
700	600	500	400	300

Model 52 Target-Speed Lock

Model 52 Sporter

Model 52B Target

Exc.	V.G.	Good	Fair	Poor
600	500	375	325	250

Model 52C Target

Exc.	V.G.	Good	Fair	Poor
650	600	450	375	300

Model 52D Target

Exc.	V.G.	Good	Fair	Poor
600	500	375	325	250

Model 52B Bull Gun

Exc.	V.G.	Good	Fair	Poor
800	600	500	300	250

Model 52C Bull Gun

Exc.	V.G.	Good	Fair	Poor
850	650	550	350	300

Model 52 International Match

Approximately 300 manufactured.

Free Style

Exc.	V.G.	Good	Fair	Poor
1500	1250	950	600	350

Model 52 International Prone

Exc.	V.G.	Good	Fair	Poor
600	500	375	325	250

Model 52 Sporter

Exc.	V.G.	Good	Fair	Poor
2750	1750	1250	900	700

EDITOR'S COMMENT: According to Winchester factory records, Model 52 barrels were, "originally drilled and tapped for Winchester telescope bases designed for use with the Winchester 3A, 5A, and Lyman telescopes. These bases had a 6.2" center to center spacing ... a change in the bases and the spacing to be used was authorized on January 11, 1933. These new bases had a specially shaped Fecker type notch added on the right hand side of both bases. They are known as Winchester Combination Telescope Sight Bases and are satisfactory for use with Winchester, Lyman, Fecker, and Unertl telescopes. Bases are spaced 7.2" center to center ... All Model 52 targets were factory drilled for scope mounting but only the "C" series Sporters were factory drilled for scopes."

Model 54

The Model 54 was to centerfire cartridges what the Model 52 was to rimfire cartridges. The Model 54 was also a quality made bolt-action rifle with a non-detachable box magazine and was chambered for a variety of calibers: .270, .30-06, .30-30, 7mm, 7.65mm, 9mm, .250-3000, .22 Hornet, .220 Swift, and .257 Roberts. This was Winchester's first bolt-action rifle built for heavy, high-velocity ammunition. The rifle was available in several different styles:

1. Standard Rifle, 24" or 20" round barrel (except .220 Swift which was 26"), plain walnut checkered pistol-grip stock and forend.

2. Carbine, 20" round barrel, plain walnut pistol-grip stock with finger groove on each side of forend.
3. Sniper's Rifle, 26" round heavyweight barrel, plain walnut pistol-grip stock and forend.
4. N.R.A. Rifle, 24" round barrel, select walnut checkered pistol-grip stock and forend.
5. Super Grade Rifle, 24" round barrel, select walnut checkered pistol-grip stock with cheekpiece and checkered forend with black plastic tip. Pistol grip was capped with hard rubber cap. Super Grade was equipped with 1" detachable sling swivels.
6. Target Rifle, 24" round heavyweight barrel, plain walnut checkered pistol-grip stock and forend.
7. National Match Rifle, 24" round barrel, plain walnut special target stock and forend.

The Model 54 was introduced in 1925 and was discontinued in 1936 with about 50,000 guns sold.

Standard Rifle

Exc.	V.G.	Good	Fair	Poor
650	550	400	300	225

Carbine

Exc.	V.G.	Good	Fair	Poor
700	600	450	350	275

Sniper's Rifle

Exc.	V.G.	Good	Fair	Poor
900	750	600	500	350

N.R.A. Rifle

Exc.	V.G.	Good	Fair	Poor
900	750	600	500	350

Super Grade Rifle

Exc.	V.G.	Good	Fair	Poor
900	750	600	450	375

Target Rifle

Exc.	V.G.	Good	Fair	Poor
900	750	600	450	375

National Match Rifle

Exc.	V.G.	Good	Fair	Poor
900	750	600	450	375

NOTE: The rare calibers are the 7.65 and the .30-30, which bring considerable premiums (in some cases as much as 250%) over standard calibers. Popular calibers such as .22 Hornet, .220 Swift, and .257 Roberts will also bring a premium. Proceed with caution on Model 54s with rare caliber markings.

Model 56

This model was designed to be a medium-priced bolt-action rimfire rifle. It featured a detachable box magazine and was chambered for the .22 Short or .22 Long Rifle cartridges. The rifle was offered in two styles;

1. Sporting Rifle, 22" round barrel, plain walnut pistol-grip stock and forend.
2. Fancy Sporting Rifle, 22" round barrel, fancy walnut checkered pistol-grip stock and forend.

Both styles had a forend with a distinctive lip on the forend tip. The rifle was introduced in 1926 and was discontinued in 1929 with about 8,500 rifles sold.

Sporting Rifle

Exc.	V.G.	Good	Fair	Poor
1500	1000	750	525	400

Fancy Sporting Rifle (Very Rare, Use Caution)

Exc.	V.G.	Good	Fair	Poor
3000	2000	1500	900	750

NOTE: Add a 25% premium for rifles chambered for .22 Short only.

Model 57

The Model 57 was close in appearance to the Model 56 with the addition of a heavier stock, target sights, and swivel bows attached to the stock. The rifle was chambered for the .22 Short or .22 Long Rifle and featured a 22" round barrel with

Model 54

detachable box magazine. The stock was plain walnut with pistol grip and plain forend. The rifle was introduced in 1927 and dropped from the Winchester line in 1936 having sold only about 19,000 guns.

Exc.	V.G.	Good	Fair	Poor
750	600	450	325	250

Model 58

This model was an attempt by the company to market a low-priced .22 caliber rimfire rifle in place of its Models 1902 and 1904. This was a single-shot bolt-action, cocked by pulling the firing pin head to the rear. It had an 18" round barrel and was chambered for the .22 Short, Long, and Long Rifle interchangeably. The stock was a one-piece plain wood with straight grip. This model was not serial-numbered. The Model 58 was introduced in 1928 and discontinued in 1931. About 39,000 were sold.

Exc.	V.G.	Good	Fair	Poor
850	600	425	250	125

Model 59

The Model 59 was essentially a Model 58 with the addition of a pistol-grip stock and a 23" round barrel. Introduced in 1930, it was dropped from the product line in the same year with a total sales of about 9,000 guns.

Courtesy Olin Corporation

Exc.	V.G.	Good	Fair	Poor
600	475	350	200	125

Model 60 and 60A

This rifle used the same action as that of the Model 59. When the rifle was first introduced in 1931, it was furnished with a 23" round barrel which was changed to 27" in 1933. Several other mechanical improvements were included with this model; perhaps the most noticeable were the chrome-plated bolt, bolt handle, and trigger. The stock was plain wood with pistol grip. In 1933 the Model 60A was added, which was the same rifle but in a target configuration. The front sight was a square-top military blade with a Lyman 55W receiver sight. The Model 60 was discontinued in 1934 with about 166,000 rifles sold. The Model 60A was dropped in 1939 with only about 6,100 rifles sold.

Courtesy Buffalo Bill Historical Center, Cody, Wyoming

Model 60

Exc.	V.G.	Good	Fair	Poor
300	250	150	125	100

Model 60A

Exc.	V.G.	Good	Fair	Poor
400	300	225	150	100

Model 67

Winchester again upgraded and improved the Model 60 with an expansion of the styles offered to the shooting public. The standard chamber for the rifle was .22 Short, Long, and Long Rifle interchangeably. The W.R.F. was only added in 1935:

1. Sporting Rifle, 27" round barrel, stock similar to the Model 60.
2. Smoothbore Rifle, 27" barrel, chambered for the .22 Long Shot or .22 Long Rifle Shot.
3. Junior Rifle, 20" round barrel and shorter stock.
4. Rifle with miniature target boring, 24" round barrel, chambered for .22 Long Rifle Shot.

Model 67s were not serial numbered for domestic sales but were numbered for foreign sales. Introduced in 1934, the gun was dropped from the line

Model 58

in 1963, having sold about 384,000. Many of these models were fitted at the factory with telescopes, and the bases were mounted on the rifle and the scope was packed separately.

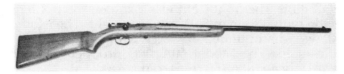

Courtesy C.H. Wolfersberger

Courtesy Buffalo Bill Historical Center, Cody, Wyoming

Sporting Rifle

Exc.	V.G.	Good	Fair	Poor
200	150	125	100	75

Smoothbore Rifle

Courtesy Buffalo Bill Historical Center, Cody, Wyoming

Exc.	V.G.	Good	Fair	Poor
450	350	300	250	200

Junior Rifle

Exc.	V.G.	Good	Fair	Poor
250	200	175	150	125

Model 677

This model looked the same as the Model 67 but was manufactured without iron sights and therefore will have no sight cuts in the barrel. The rifle was furnished with either 2-3/4 power scopes or 5 power scopes. This model was not serial numbered. Introduced in 1937 and discontinued in 1939.

Exc.	V.G.	Good	Fair	Poor
2250	1350	900	600	300

NOTE: Add a 50% premium for rifles chambered for .22WRF.

Model 68

Another takeoff on the Model 67, this model differed only in the sight equipment offered. Winchester fitted this rifle with its own 5 power telescopes. First sold in 1934 the Model 68 was dropped in 1946 with sales of about 101,000.

Courtesy C.H. Wolfersberger

With Scope

Exc.	V.G.	Good	Fair	Poor
750	500	300	200	150

Without Scope

Exc.	V.G.	Good	Fair	Poor
200	175	150	100	75

NOTE: Rifles with factory scopes and no sights add 40%. For rifles with factory scopes and no sights chambered for .22 WRF add 100%.

Model 69 and 69A

This model was designed by Winchester to answer the demand for a medium-priced hunting and target .22 rimfire bolt-action rifle. The rifle had a detachable box magazine, and many were offered with factory-installed telescopes in 2-3/4 and 5 power. The stock was plain walnut with pistol grip and plain forend. This model was not serial num-

Model 69

bered. The 69A version was introduced in 1937 and featured an improved cocking mechanism. Introduced in 1935 as the Model 69, this gun was dropped in 1963 with sales of about 355,000 guns.

Exc.	V.G.	Good	Fair	Poor
450	350	300	175	100

NOTE: Add 25% for Target Model. Add 20% for grooved receiver.

Model 69A

The Model 69A was similar in appearance to the Model 69 except A was equipped exclusively for a telescope. Winchester offered either a 2-3/4 or 5 power scope with the bases attached at the factory and the scope packed separately. Built between 1937 and 1941 with small sales, this model was not serial numbered.

Exc.	V.G.	Good	Fair	Poor
1500	900	600	400	200

NOTE: For factory scopes with no sights add 50%.

Model 70

Considered by many as the finest bolt-action rifle ever built in the United States, the pre-1964 Model 70 is highly sought after by shooters and collectors alike. Its smooth, strong action has no peer. It is often referred to as "The Riflemen's Rifle." The Model 70 is an updated and improved version of the Model 54 and features a hinged floorplate, new speed locks, new safety design that does not interfere with telescope, manually releasable bolt stop, more attractive buttstock and forend, and forged steel trigger guard. Like many Winchesters, the Model 70 was available with several extra-cost options that should be evaluated by an expert. The values listed below are given for pre-1964 Model 70s with serial numbers from 1 to 581471. This rifle was available in several different styles:

1. Standard Grade, 24" round barrel (except 26" round barrel for .220 Swift and .300 H&H Magnum—25-inch round barrel for .375 H&H Magnum after 1937), plain walnut checkered pistol-grip stock and forend. Built from 1936 to 1963.
2. Standard Grade Carbine, 20" round barrel, chambered for .22 Hornet, .250-3000, .257 Roberts, .270, 7mm, and 30-06, same stock as Standard Grade. Built from 1936 to 1946.
3. Super Grade Rifle, same barrel and calibers as Standard Grade, select walnut checkered and capped pistol-grip stock with cheekpiece and checkered forend with plastic tip. Built from 1936 to 1960.
4. Featherweight, 22" round barrel chambered for .243, .264, .270, .308, .30-06, and .358. Fitted with aluminum trigger guard, aluminum buttplate, and aluminum floor plate. Later versions with plastic buttplate. Built from 1952 to 1963.
5. Featherweight Super Grade, same as above except not chambered for the .358 cartridge, but fitted with Super Grade stock. Built from 1952 to 1963.
6. National Match, same as Standard Grade but fitted with target-type stock and telescope bases. Chambered for .30-06 only. Discontinued in 1960.
7. Target, 24" round medium-weight barrel with same stock as National Match in .243 and 30-06 calibers. Discontinued in 1963.
8. Varmint, 26" round heavy barrel, with heavier stock, chambered for .243 and .220 Swift. Built from 1956 to 1963.
9. Westerner, 26" round barrel with Standard Grade stock, chambered for .264 Winchester Magnum. Built from 1960 to 1963.
10. Alaskan, 25" round barrel, with Standard Grade stock, chambered for .338 Winchester Magnum and .375 H&H Magnum. Built from 1960 to 1963.
11. Bull Gun, 28" round barrel, same stock as National Match, chambered for .30-06 and .300 H&H Magnum. Built from 1936 to 1963.

The standard calibers offered for the Model 70 are as follows in order of rarity: .300 Savage, .35 Rem., .458 Win. Magnum, 7mm, .358 Win., .250-3000 Savage, .300 Win. Magnum, .338 Win. Magnum, .375 H&H Magnum, .257 Roberts, .220 Swift, .22 Hornet, .264 Win. Magnum, .300 H&H Magnum, .308 Win., .243 Win., .270 W.C.F., .30-06.

NOTE: Prices for the Model 70 are, in many cases, based on the caliber of the rifle; the more rare the caliber, the more premium the gun will command. Many pre-1964 Model 70s are still available in new condition in the original box with all papers. Add 100% if the box is serial numbered to the gun. Use caution prior to purchase of NIB guns due to fake boxes and papers.

PRICING NOTE: The asterisk (*) signifies the value of the rifle with respect to a usable action. Model 70 receivers bring $500 regardless of the condition of the barrel and stock. If the receiver is unusable then the rifle is worth the value of its usable parts, i.e. less than $500.

For Model 70s with "X" or "D" prefix add a premium of 10%. These letters indicate that there were two rifles stamped with the same serial number.

Standard Rifle

.30-06 Springfield (1937-1963)

Pre-War

Exc.	V.G.	Good	Fair	Poor
850	700	450*	365*	300*

Post-War

Exc.	V.G.	Good	Fair	Poor
650	550	450*	365*	300*

.270 Win. (1937-1963)
Pre-War

Exc.	V.G.	Good	Fair	Poor
950	750	450*	365*	300*

Post-War

Exc.	V.G.	Good	Fair	Poor
800	650	450*	365*	300*

.243. Win. (1955-1963)

Exc.	V.G.	Good	Fair	Poor
1000	850	600	420*	315*

.300 H&H Magnum (1937-1963)
Pre-War

Exc.	V.G.	Good	Fair	Poor
1200	950	750	600	370*

Post-War

Exc.	V.G.	Good	Fair	Poor
1000	800	625	580	370*

.264 Win. Magnum (1959-1963)

Exc.	V.G.	Good	Fair	Poor
995	815	630	580	370*

.22 Hornet (1937-1958)
Pre-War

Exc.	V.G.	Good	Fair	Poor
1850	1200	850	580	370*

Post-War

Exc.	V.G.	Good	Fair	Poor
1400	995	650	580	370*

.220 Swift (1937-1963)
Pre-War

Exc.	V.G.	Good	Fair	Poor
1200	995	650	580	370*

Post-War

Exc.	V.G.	Good	Fair	Poor
1000	800	650	580	370*

.257 Roberts (1937-1959)
Pre-War

Exc.	V.G.	Good	Fair	Poor
1900	1500	850	680	370*

Post-War

Exc.	V.G.	Good	Fair	Poor
1250	995	650	580	370*

.375 H&H Magnum (1937-1963)
Pre-War

Exc.	V.G.	Good	Fair	Poor
1900	1500	900	630	420*

Post-War

Exc.	V.G.	Good	Fair	Poor
1250	995	650	580	370*

.338 Win. Magnum (1959-1963)

Exc.	V.G.	Good	Fair	Poor
1475	1150	750	565	390*

.300 Win. Magnum (1962-1963)

Exc.	V.G.	Good	Fair	Poor
1475	1100	700	530	390*

.250-3000 Savage (1937-1949)

Exc.	V.G.	Good	Fair	Poor
2100	1525	840	680	420*

7mm (1937-1949)

Exc.	V.G.	Good	Fair	Poor
2990	2050	1300	995	630

.35 Rem. (1944-1947)

Exc.	V.G.	Good	Fair	Poor
4095	2890	1950	1260	950

.300 Savage (1944-1950s?)

Exc.	V.G.	Good	Fair	Poor
3500	2890	1825	1260	950

.300 Savage (1944-1950s?)

Model 70 Bull Gun

.458 African (Built in Supergrade only, 1956-1963)

Exc.	V.G.	Good	Fair	Poor
4500	3500	2750	1750	1000

Featherweight

Exc.	V.G.	Good	Fair	Poor
800	650	550	450	370*

NOTE: Add 100% for .358 Win. For .264 and .270 calibers add 25%.

Featherweight Super Grade

Exc.	V.G.	Good	Fair	Poor
3500	2750	1900	1250	1000

Standard Grade Carbine

Exc.	V.G.	Good	Fair	Poor
2500	1750	1000	700	650

NOTE: For calibers other than standard add a premium of 100% to Standard Grade prices. For Super Grade rifles add 100%.

National Match

Exc.	V.G.	Good	Fair	Poor
1325	1100	825	650	550

Target

Exc.	V.G.	Good	Fair	Poor
1325	1100	825	650	550

Varmint

Exc.	V.G.	Good	Fair	Poor
900	775	600	500	375*

Bull Gun

Exc.	V.G.	Good	Fair	Poor
2750	1650	1100	825	650

Model 72

This model is a bolt-action rifle with tubular magazine. It is chambered for the .22 Short, Long, and Long Rifle cartridges interchangeably. Early rifles were available with 2-3/4 or 5 power telescopes, but the majority were furnished with either open sights or peep sights. This rifle was available in two different configurations:

1. Sporting Rifle, 25" round barrel, chambered for the .22 Short, Long, and Long Rifle cartridges, one-piece plain walnut pistol-grip stock and forend.

2. Gallery Special, 25" round barrel, chambered for .22 Short only, stock same as Sporting Rifle.

This model was not serial numbered. It was built between 1938 and 1959 with about 161,000 rifles sold.

A Winchester Model 70 chambered for .35 Whelen sold at auction for $6,325. It was a first-year production gun. Barrel length was 24". Condition excellent. Rock Island Auction, March 1998

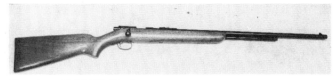

Courtesy C.H. Wolfersberger

Exc.	V.G.	Good	Fair	Poor
375	300	250	200	125

NOTE: Gallery Special will command a premium of 100%. For rifles with factory scopes and no sights add 200% depending on condition. Add 25% premium for peep sights.

Model 75

Styles:

1. Sporting Rifle, 24" round barrel, chambered for .22 Long Rifle, select walnut checkered pistol-grip stock and forend. This rifle was furnished with either open rear sights or a Lyman 57 E receiver sight.
2. Target Rifle, 28" round barrel, chambered for .22 Long Rifle, plain walnut pistol-grip stock and forend. The Target Rifle was furnished with either a Winchester 8 power telescope or a variety of target sights.

This model was discontinued in 1958 with about 89,000 sold.

Model 75 Sporter

NIB	Exc.	V.G.	Good	Fair	Poor
1500	750	600	450	350	200

Model 75 Target

Exc.	V.G.	Good	Fair	Poor
650	525	400	250	200

Model 12

This model was designed by T.C. Johnson and was the first slide-action hammerless shotgun built by Winchester. The Model 12 has enjoyed great success in its 51-year history, and over 1,900,000 were sold. This was a high quality, well-made shotgun that is still in use in the hunting and shooting fields across the country. All Model 12s were of the takedown variety. The Model 12 was dropped from regular product line in 1963, but a special model was produced in the Custom Shop until 1979. In 1972 Winchester resurrected the Model 12 in its regular production line in 12 gauge only and ventilated rib. This reintroduced Model 12 was dropped in 1980. The prices listed below are for guns made prior to 1964 or for guns with serial numbers below 1968307. This shotgun was offered in several different styles:

1. Standard Grade, 12, 16, 20, and 28 gauge, with plain, solid rib, or vent rib round barrels of standard lengths (26", 28", 30", 32"), plain walnut pistol-grip stock with grooved slide handle. Built from 1912 to 1963.
2. Featherweight, same as above with lightweight alloy trigger guard. Built between 1959 and 1962.
3. Riot Gun, in 12 gauge only with 20" round choked cylinder, stock same as Standard Grade. Built between 1918 and 1963.
4. Trench Gun, chambered for 12 gauge only with 20" round barrel with ventilated hand guard over barrel, fitted with bayonet lug. All metal surfaces are "Parkerized," and these shotguns should be U.S. marked as a military firearm. Introduced in 1918 and built for U.S. Armed Forces on special order.
5. Skeet Grade, chambered for 12, 16, 20, and 28 gauge with 26" round barrel with solid or ventilated rib, select walnut checkered pistol stock and special checkered extension slide handle (longer than standard). Built from 1933 to 1963.
6. Trap Grade, chambered for 12 gauge only with 30" round barrel with solid rib or ventilated rib, select walnut pistol- or straight-grip stock, checkered extension slide handle. Built from 1914 to 1963.
7. Heavy Duck Gun, chambered in 12 gauge only with 30" or 32" round barrel with plain, solid, or ventilated rib, plain walnut pistol-grip stock fitted with Winchester solid red rubber recoil pad, plain grooved slide handle. Built from 1935 to 1963.
8. Pigeon Grade, chambered for 12, 16, 20, and 28 gauges with standard barrel lengths and choice of ribs. This was a special-order shotgun and will be seen in many different variations, most of these guns were factory engraved. Built 1914 to 1963.

The Model 12 shotgun will be seen in many different combinations of gauges, barrel lengths, ribs,

Model 75 Sporter

and stocks, all of which determine value. The more rare a particular combination, the higher the price. The buyer is urged to be extremely cautious before purchasing the more rare combinations, such as a 28 gauge. The best advice is to seek assistance from an expert and get as many opinions as possible. The prices listed below are for guns in standard configurations.

Courtesy Butterfield & Butterfield, San Francisco, California

Standard Grade-12 Gauge

Exc.	V.G.	Good	Fair	Poor
600	400	300	300	125

Featherweight

Exc.	V.G.	Good	Fair	Poor
500	400	325	275	250

Riot Gun

Exc.	V.G.	Good	Fair	Poor
750	650	550	400	250

Trench Gun

Exc.	V.G.	Good	Fair	Poor
1750	1200	950	550	400

Skeet Grade

Exc.	V.G.	Good	Fair	Poor
1250	750	550	400	350

Trap Grade

Exc.	V.G.	Good	Fair	Poor
800	700	600	450	400

Heavy Duck Gun

Exc.	V.G.	Good	Fair	Poor
750	600	500	325	300

NOTE: For Heavy Duck Guns with solid ribs add 25% premium.

Pigeon Grade

Exc.	V.G.	Good	Fair	Poor
1950	1400	1200	650	500

NOTE: For 16 Gauge deduct 20%. For 20 gauge add 20%. For 28 gauge add 600%. For guns with solid rib add 20%. For guns with Winchester Special Ventilated Rib add 30%. For guns with Milled Rib add 40%. Add 10% for 32" barrels on any Model 12 model. Add 30% premium for original box and papers.

Model 25

This model is similar in appearance to the Model 12 but does not have the takedown feature. All guns were solid frame. The Model 25 was furnished in 12 gauge with 26" or 28" plain round barrel, plain walnut pistol-grip stock with grooved slide handle. This was an attempt by Winchester to introduce a less-expensive version of the Model 12. Introduced in 1949 it was dropped from the product line in 1954 having sold about 88,000 guns.

Exc.	V.G.	Good	Fair	Poor
300	200	175	125	75

Model 20

In order to utilize the expanded production facilities left over from WWI, Winchester introduced a series of three different models of single-shot shotguns; the Model 20 was the first of the three. This model has a visible hammer and a top lever frame. It was the first Winchester to have this type of breakdown action. It was chambered for the .410, 2-1/2" shell. The barrel is 26" round choked full, plain walnut pistol-grip stock with hard rubber buttplate. The forend has a small lip on the front end. The Model 20 was dropped from the product line in 1924 having sold about 24,000 guns.

Courtesy C.H. Wolfersberger

Exc.	V.G.	Good	Fair	Poor
600	500	350	200	150

Model 25

Model 36

The Model 36 was the second of the single-shot shotguns to be introduced in 1920. This model features a bolt action that is cocked by pulling the firing pin head to the rear. It is fitted with an 18" round barrel, chambered for the 9mm Long Shot, 9mm Short Shot, and 9mm Ball interchangeably, plain gumwood straight-grip stock with special metal pistol-grip trigger guard. Winchester referred to this model as the "Garden Gun" for use against birds and pests around the house and barn. This model was not serial numbered. It was dropped from the product line in 1927 having sold about 20,000 guns.

Exc.	V.G.	Good	Fair	Poor
750	475	375	300	225

Model 41

This was the third of the low-priced single-shot shotguns to be announced in 1920. Like the Model 36, the Model 41 was a bolt-action arrangement but of much stronger construction and design. It features a 24" round barrel, chambered for the .410 2-1/2" shell, plain walnut pistol-grip stock and forend. Straight-grip stocks were furnished at no extra charge. This model was not serial numbered. It was discontinued in 1934 having sold about 22,000 guns.

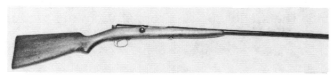

Courtesy C.H. Wolfersberger

Exc.	V.G.	Good	Fair	Poor
600	500	350	300	200

Model 21

The Model 21 was Winchester's finest effort with regard to quality, reliability, and strength. Developed in the late 1920s the introduction of this fine side-by-side shotgun was delayed by the company's financial troubles. When Winchester was purchased by the Olin family, the Model 21 was assured the attention it richly deserved due to John M. Olin's love for the gun. Despite the Model 21 being offered as a production gun it was, in fact, a hand-built, custom-made shotgun. Almost each Model 21 built has a personality of its own because each shotgun is slightly different with regard to chokes, barrel lengths, stock dimensions, and embellishments. The gun was introduced in 1931. From 1931 to 1959 the Model 21 was considered a production line gun and about 30,000 were sold. In 1960, when the Custom Shop was opened, the Model 21 was built there using the same procedures. Sales during the Custom Shop era were about 1,000 guns. Winchester changed the name of some of the Model 21 styles but the production methods stayed the same. In 1981 Winchester sold its firearms division to U.S. Repeating Arms Company including the right to build the Model 21. Again the production procedures stayed the same as did many of the former employees. U.S. Repeating Arms expanded and changed some of the style designations for the Model 21. Production was discontinued in about 1991. No sales figures are available for this time period. Collectors and shooters will be given the price breakdown for all three eras of production separately.

Model 21-1931 to 1959

The Model 21 was available in several different styles and configurations:

1. Standard Grade, chambered in 12, 16, and 20 gauge with barrel length from 26", 28", 30", and 32" with matted rib or ventilated rib, select walnut checkered pistol- or straight-grip stock with checkered beavertail forend. Built from 1931 to 1959.

2. Tournament Grade, same as above with special dimension stock. Marked "TOURNAMENT" on bottom of trigger plate. Built from 1933 to 1934.

Model 21

Rare 12 Gauge Cutaway of Model 21

Winchester produced ten cutaways of the Model 21, all bearing serial numbers. This one, serial number 5161, is the only one owned by a private party. From the Tom Webster Collection. Photo by D. Kowalski.

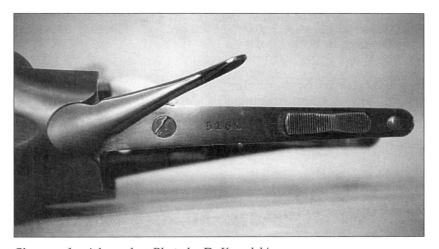

Closeup of serial number. Photo by D. Kowalski.

Where Do All The Old Guns Go?

Winchester produced millions of firearms. Why have we found only a fraction of them? They get dropped in lakes and ponds, lost in the debris of the forest floor, burned in fires, perhaps hidden by owners who never live to recover them. If only some of these guns could talk, what a story they would tell. This old Winchester was recovered from a swamp. From the Tom Webster Collection. Photo by D. Kowalski.

3. Trap Grade, same as above with slightly better grade wood and stock made to customers' dimensions. Marked "TRAP" on trigger plate. Built from 1940 to 1959.

4. Skeet Grade, same as above with the addition of the 28 gauge, stock furnished with checkered butt. Marked "SKEET" on trigger plate. Built from 1936 to 1959.

5. Duck Gun, chambered for 12 gauge 3" magnum shells, 30" or 32" barrels, Standard Grade stock except for shorter length of pull. Marked "DUCK" on trigger plate. Built from 1940 to 1952.

6. Magnum Gun, chambered for 3" 12 or 20 gauge, same stock as Duck Gun. Not marked on trigger plate. Built from 1953 to 1959.

7. Custom Built/Deluxe Grade, chambered for 12, 16, 20, 28, and .410, barrel lengths from 26" to 32", stock built to customer's specifications using fancy walnut. Marked "CUSTOM BUILT" on top of rib or "DELUXE" on trigger plate. These grades are frequently but not always engraved. Built from 1933 to 1959.

NOTE: Some early Model 21s were furnished with double triggers, extractors, and splinter forends. This combination reduces the price of the gun regardless of grade. Deduct about 25%.

Standard Grade

	Exc	V.G.	Good	Fair	Poor
12 gauge	3800	3300	2800	2600	2300
16 gauge	4600	4000	3500	3200	2700
20 gauge	5500	5000	4600	4300	3700

Tournament Grade

	Exc.	V.G.	Good	Fair	Poor
12 gauge	4000	3500	3000	2700	2300
16 gauge	5000	4500	4000	3200	2600
20 gauge	5900	5500	4900	4500	3800

Trap Grade

	Exc.	V.G.	Good	Fair	Poor
12 gauge	4000	3600	3100	2800	2300
16 gauge	5000	4500	4000	3300	2900
20 gauge	6000	5600	5000	4500	4100

Skeet Grade

	Exc.	V.G.	Good	Fair	Poor
12 gauge	3900	3400	2800	2400	2100
16 gauge	5000	4500	4000	3300	2900
20 gauge	5700	5300	4700	4300	3700

A Winchester Model 21 special order engraved with three sets of barrels sold at auction for $37,375. Barrels have vent ribs and are chambered for 20, 28, and .410 bore. Pistol grip with leather cover pad. Engraved by John Kusmit and shipped in 1977. Rock Island Auction, March 1998

Duck/Magnum Gun

Exc	V.G.	Good	Fair	Poor
4200	3800	3200	2900	2500

NOTE: Add 20% for 20 gauge Magnum.

NOTE: Factory ventilated ribs command a premium of about $400 on 12 gauge guns and $1,500 on 20 and 16 gauge guns. Models 21s with factory furnished extra barrels will bring an additional premium of about $1,500.

NOTE: Refinished and restored Model 21s are in a somewhat unique category of American made collectible shotguns. A gun that has been professionally refinished by a master craftsman will approximate 90% of the value of factory original guns.

Custom Built/Deluxe Grade

The prices paid for guns of this grade are determined by gauge, barrel and choke combinations, rib type, stock specifications, and engraving.

	Exc.	V.G.	Good	Fair	Poor
12 gauge	6000	5500	4400	3500	3000
16 gauge	7000	6500	5400	4500	3500
20 gauge	7500	7000	6000	5000	4000

It is best to secure a factory letter from the Cody Firearms Museum. With respect to such letter it is important to note that these records are incomplete and may be inaccurate in a few cases. Records for Model 21s built during the 1930s may be missing. Special order guns may have incomplete records. In such cases a written appraisal from an authoritative collector or dealer may be helpful.

Custom Built .410 Bore

Exc.	V.G.	Good	Fair	Poor
35000	30000	26000	22000	20000

NOTE: Less than 50 .410 Model 21s were built between 1931 and 1959 in all grades. The number of 28 gauge Model 21s built is unknown but the number is probably no greater than the .410 bore.

Custom Shop Model 21s - 1960 to 1981

When Winchester moved the production of the Model 21 into the Custom Shop the number of styles was greatly reduced. There were now three distinct styles:

1. Custom Grade, chambered in 12, 16, 20, 28 gauge, and .410 bore in barrel lengths from 26" to 32". Matted rib, fancy walnut checkered pistol- or straight-grip stock with checkered forend. Guns with pistol grips furnished with steel grip cap. A small amount of scroll engraving was provided on the frame of this grade.

2. Pigeon Grade, same chambers and barrel lengths as above with the addition of choice of matted or ventilated-rib, leather-covered recoil pad, style "A" carving on stock and forend, and gold engraved pistol-grip cap. The frame was engraved with the 21-6 engraving pattern.

3. Grand American Grade, same chambers and barrel lengths as Pigeon Grade with the addition of "B" carving on the stock and forend, 21-6 engraving with gold inlays, extra set of interchangeable barrels with extra forend. All of this was enclosed in a leather trunk case.

Custom Grade - 12 Gauge

Exc.	V.G.	Good	Fair	Poor
7500	6000	5500	4700	4200

NOTE: Add $4,000 for 16 gauge. Add $3,000 for 20 gauge.

Pigeon Grade - 12 Gauge

Exc.	V.G.	Good	Fair	Poor
12000	10000	8000	6500	6000

NOTE: Add $5,000 for 16 gauge. Add $4,000 for 20 gauge.

Grand American - 12 Gauge

Exc.	V.G.	Good	Fair	Poor
18000	14500	12000	10500	9500

NOTE: Add $10,000 for 16 gauge. Add $4,000 for 20 gauge.

A Model 21 Grand American with special order engraving for the Premier of Alberta, Canada, sold at auction for $28,750. Condition was near mint. Rock Island Auction Company, August 1998

EDITOR'S COMMENT: There were eight 28 gauge Model 21s built during this period and five .410 bores built. These guns obviously command a large premium. Factory letters are available on these guns.

ENGRAVED MODEL 21s

Winchester catalogued a number of special order engraving patterns which ranged from a small amount of scroll (#1) to full coverage game scene and scroll (#6). In addition, there were a few guns engraved on special order to the customer's request. Engraved guns are extremely rare, and the value added will vary with the rarity of the gauge and the date of manufacture. The following table represents the value added for various standard engraving patterns on 12 gauge guns for the "Custom Shop" (1960-1982) and "Pre-Custom Shop" (1932-1959) periods. However, it is advisable to seek the opinion of an authoritative collector or dealer prior to a purchase.

Engraving Pattern	Pre-Custom Shop	Custom Shop
#1	25%	10%
#2	35%	15%
#3	50%	30%
#4	55%	35%
#5	65%	45%
#6	75%	50%

Custom Shop Model 21s-1982 to Present

When U.S. Repeating Arms Company took over the production of the Model 21 the Pigeon Grade was dropped from the line. The Grand American Grade was retained with all the features of its predecessor but with the addition of a small bore set featuring a 28 gauge and .410 bore set of barrels. Two new grades were introduced in 1983; the Standard Custom Grade and the Special Custom Built. In addition to these grades the factory would undertake to build for its customers whatever was desired. Due to the unique nature of these guns it is advised that an expert appraisal be sought to establish a value. While the changeover from Winchester to U.S. Repeating Arms was a transfer of business assets and the craftsmen and personnel remained the same, collectors are reluctant to assign the same values to U.S. Repeating Arms Model 21s as those produced by Winchester. No official production figures are available for U.S.R.A. Model 21s but the number is most likely small; perhaps around 200 guns.

Standard Custom Built

NIB	Exc.	V.G	Good	Fair	Poor
6500	4700	3700	3400	2900	2500

Grand American

NIB	Exc.	V.G.	Good	Fair	Poor
16000	10000	8500	7500	5500	4500

Grand American - Small Gauge Set - 28 or .410 bore

NIB	Exc.	V.G.	Good	Fair	Poor
47000	35000	30000	23000	20000	17000

Model 24

The Model 24 was Winchester's attempt to develop a medium-priced double-barrel shotgun. Like the Model 21, it was a top-lever breakdown model that was available in 12, 16, and 20 gauge in various barrel lengths from 26" to 30". Offered in a Standard model only with double triggers, raised matted rib, plain walnut pistol- or straight-grip stock with semi-beavertail forend, the Model 24 was introduced in 1939 and was discontinued in 1957 with about 116,000 guns sold.

Exc.	V.G.	Good	Fair	Poor
500	400	350	250	200

Model 37

This model was developed to keep pace with Winchester's competitors in the low-price, single-barrel, exposed-hammer shotgun market. The shotgun was available in 12, 16, 20, 28 gauge, and .410 bore with barrel lengths from 26" to 30". The stock was plain walnut with pistol grip and semi-beavertail forend. This model was not serial numbered.

Model 24

Introduced in 1936 it stayed in the company line until 1963 having sold slightly over 1,000,000 guns.

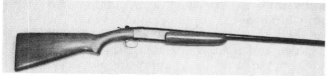

Courtesy C.H. Wolfersberger

	Exc.	V.G.	Good	Fair	Poor
12 gauge	350	300	250	150	50
16 gauge	200	175	150	100	60
20 gauge	300	275	225	135	90
20 gauge	400	350	275	175	100

Youth Model-26" modified barrel, Win. factory pad.

	Exc.	V.G.	Good	Fair	Poor
28 gauge	1500	1000	800	600	450
.410 bore	350	300	275	200	100

NOTE: For 12 and 16 gauge guns add a 50% premium for 32" barrels. Use caution for 28 gauge guns. Many fakes are seen for sale.

Model 42

This was the first slide-action shotgun ever developed exclusively for the .410 bore. Invented by William Roemer, the Model 42 was in effect, at least in outward appearance, a miniature Model 12. This shotgun was a quality built, fast handling, racy looking shotgun that many refer to as "Everybody's Sweetheart." The Model 42 was offered in several different configurations throughout its production. These configurations will greatly influence value:

1. Standard Grade, 26" or 28" plain or solid-rib barrel, plain walnut pistol-grip stock with grooved slide handle, fitted with composition buttplate. Built from 1933 to 1963.
2. Skeet Grade, 26" or 28" plain, solid-rib, or ventilated-rib barrel, select walnut checkered pistol- or straight-grip stock with checkered extension slide handle. The Skeet Grade was offered in chokes other than skeet. Skeet Grade Model 42s are seen in full, modified cylinder, improved cylinder, and skeet chokes. Built from 1933 to 1963.
3. Trap Grade, 26" or 28" plain or solid-rib barrel, fancy walnut special checkered pistol- or straight-grip stock with special checkered extension slide handle. The Trap Grade checkering pattern has one closed diamond on each side of the pistol grip or, in the case of the straight grip, the diamond is located on the underside of the grip. The extension slide handle has two diamonds on each side. Stamped "TRAP" on the bottom of the receiver. Built from 1934 to 1939.
4. Deluxe Grade, same as above, available with ventilated rib in 1954. Some early models stamped "DELUXE" on bottom of receiver. Built from 1940 to 1963.
5. Pigeon Grade, same as above Deluxe Grade but engraved with a pigeon on the lower magazine tube. Very few of this grade were built by Winchester, and the majority were done in the late 1940s.

Engraved Model 42s will occasionally be seen. Collectors are urged to seek expert advice on these rare and expensive guns. The Model 42 was produced from 1933 to 1963. About 160,000 were sold.

Standard Grade

NIB	Exc.	V.G.	Good	Fair	Poor
1750	950	650	450	350	250

NOTE: For guns with solid ribs add 50%.

Skeet Grade-Solid Rib

Exc.	V.G.	Good	Fair	Poor
2500	1750	900	500	350

An example of a prewar Standard Grade Model 42. Notice the distinctive grip on the butt stock and the round slide handle.

A postwar Standard Grade Model 42. The pistol grip has a new shape as does the flat-bottom slide handle.

A Skeet Grade Model 42 with solid rib. Notice the extension slide handle which was used on all Model 42 Skeet Grades. The pistol grip is fitted with a gripcap.

A Skeet Grade with factory ventilated rib. Winchester began to install ventilated ribs on the Model 42 in 1954 and continued until the end of production in 1963.

An example of a Deluxe Grade Model 42. Notice the single diamond in the pistol grip and the two diamonds on the extension slide handle. This particular gun has a solid rib, but Winchester built Deluxe Grades with ventilated ribs as well.

NOTE: Add 25% to guns chambered for 2-1/2" shells.

Skeet Grade-Ventilated Rib

NIB	Exc.	V.G.	Good	Fair	Poor
5000	3500	2500	1250	850	600

NOTE: Add 25% to guns chambered for 2-1/2" shells.

EDITOR'S COMMENT: Contrary to traditional views, Winchester did install factory ventilated ribs on its Model 42. Former employees and factory drawings substantiate this fact. However, the subject of what is a factory rib and what is not has been covered in great detail in an excellent book on the Model 42. Seek expert advice before selling or purchasing any Model 42 with a ventilated rib.

Trap Grade

Exc.	V.G.	Good	Fair	Poor
8500	5500	3500	1750	700

Deluxe Grade-Solid Rib

Exc.	V.G.	Good	Fair	Poor
5500	2750	1500	750	400

Deluxe Grade-Ventilated Rib

Exc.	V.G.	Good	Fair	Poor
7500	4000	2250	900	500

NOTE: For Pigeon Grade Model 42s add 50%.

Model 1911

This was Winchester's first self-loading shotgun and was developed by T.C. Johnson in order to keep pace with the Remington Auto-Loading Shotgun Model 11, which was developed by John M. Browning with help from T.C. Johnson. Because of the delays involved in developing a brand new design, the Model 1911 was introduced on October 7, 1911. The shotgun was a recoil operated mechanism, had a tubular magazine and had the takedown feature. The shotgun was available in two styles:

1. Plain Model 1911, 26" or 28" barrel, 12 gauge, choked full, modified, or cylinder, plain birch laminated pistol-grip stock and forend with hard rubber buttplate.
2. Fancy Model 1911, same as above with fancy birch laminated stock.

Because of the hurry in getting the model ready for production, the shotgun demonstrated design weakness and never proved satisfactory. It was discontinued in 1925 with about 83,000 guns sold.

Model 1911-Plain

Exc.	V.G.	Good	Fair	Poor
550	375	300	250	200

Model 1911-Fancy

Exc.	V.G.	Good	Fair	Poor
800	500	400	300	250

Model 40

This model represents Winchester's second attempt to build a self-loading-long-recoil-operated repeating shotgun. This shotgun was a hammerless tubular magazine gun without the hump at the rear of the receiver. Available in 12 gauge only with barrel lengths from 28" to 30". The Standard Grade had plain walnut pistol-grip stock and forend. The Skeet Grade was fitted with select walnut checkered pistol-grip stock and checkered forend. The Model 40 suffered from the same design problems as the Model 11, and sales were small. Introduced in 1940 and discontinued in 1941, Winchester sold about 12,000 guns.

Standard Grade

Exc.	V.G.	Good	Fair	Poor
600	500	400	275	200

Skeet Grade

Exc.	V.G.	Good	Fair	Poor
800	600	500	300	250

Model 50

The Model 50 was the company's third attempt to produce a satisfactory self-loading repeating shotgun. Winchester went to the short recoil system, utilizing a floating chamber design. This model was available in several different styles:

1. Standard Grade, 12 or 20 gauge with plain or ventilated rib in lengths from 26" to 30", plain walnut checkered pistol-grip stock and forend.
2. Skeet Grade, 12 or 20 gauge with 26" ventilated rib barrel. Walnut checkered pistol-grip stock and forend.
3. Trap Grade, 12 gauge with 30" ventilated rib barrel, walnut checkered Monte Carlo stock and forend.
4. Pigeon Grade, 12 or 20 gauge with barrel lengths to customers' specifications. Fancy walnut checkered stock and forend. Made on special orders only.
5. Featherweight, a lighter version of all the above except Trap Grade.

This model begins with serial number 1000. This model was successful and was built between 1954 and 1961. Winchester sold about 200,000 guns.

Standard Grade

Exc.	V.G.	Good	Fair	Poor
450	350	300	200	150

Model 50

Skeet Grade

Exc.	V.G.	Good	Fair	Poor
600	500	350	250	200

Trap Grade

Exc.	V.G.	Good	Fair	Poor
600	500	350	250	200

Pigeon Grade

Exc.	V.G.	Good	Fair	Poor
1250	900	750	450	250

Featherweight

Exc.	V.G.	Good	Fair	Poor
500	400	325	225	150

NOTE: Add 10% for 20 gauge.

Model 59

The fourth and final pre-1964 Winchester self-loading shotgun featured a steel and fiberglass barrel with aluminum alloy receiver. The gun was available in 12 gauge only with barrel lengths from 26" to 30" with a variety of chokes. In 1961 Winchester introduced the "Versalite" choke tube, which gave the shooter a choice of full, modified, or improved cylinder chokes in the same barrel. This model was available in two different styles:

1. Standard Grade, plain walnut checkered pistol-grip stock and forend.
2. Pigeon Grade, select walnut checkered pistol-grip and forend.

Winchester sold about 82,000 of these guns between 1960 and 1965.

Courtesy Butterfield & Butterfield, San Francisco, California

Standard Grade

Exc.	V.G.	Good	Fair	Poor
500	375	325	225	150

Pigeon Grade

Exc.	V.G.	Good	Fair	Poor
1500	1100	850	600	300

NOTE: Add 30% premium for barrels with 3 Versalite chokes and wrench. Add 20% premium for orginal box and papers.

This shotgun was also made in 10 gauge (very rare), 20 gauge, and 14 gauge. If any of these very low production or prototype guns are encountered use extreme caution and seek an expert appraisal.

POST-1963 RIFLES AND SHOTGUNS

Rifles

Model 121
This is a single-shot, bolt-action rifle chambered for the .22 rimfire cartridge. It has a 20.75" barrel with open sights. The finish is blued, with a plain walnut stock. It was manufactured between 1967 and 1973. A youth model with a shorter stock was designated the 121Y and is valued the same.

Courtesy Buffalo Bill Historical Center, Cody, Wyoming

Exc.	V.G.	Good	Fair	Poor
125	100	80	60	40

Model 131
This is a bolt-action repeater chambered for the .22 rimfire cartridge. It has a 20.75" barrel with open sights and a 7-round, detachable magazine. The finish is blued, with a plain walnut stock. It was manufactured between 1967 and 1973. A tubular magazine version was designated the Model 141 and is valued the same.

Exc.	V.G.	Good	Fair	Poor
140	110	90	75	50

Model 310
This is a single-shot, bolt-action rifle chambered for the .22 rimfire cartridge. It features a 22" barrel with open sights. The finish is blued, with a checkered walnut stock. It was manufactured between 1972 and 1975.

Courtesy Buffalo Bill Historical Center, Cody, Wyoming

Exc.	V.G.	Good	Fair	Poor
200	150	125	100	75

Model 320
This is a bolt-action repeating rifle that is similar in configuration to the Model 310 single shot. It has a 5-round, detachable box magazine. It was manufactured between 1972 and 1974.

Exc.	V.G.	Good	Fair	Poor
350	300	250	175	125

Model 250
This is a lever-action repeating rifle with a hammerless action. It is chambered for the .22 rimfire cartridge and has a 20.5" barrel with open sights and a tubular magazine. The finish is blued, with a checkered pistol-grip stock. It was manufactured between 1963 and 1973.

Exc.	V.G.	Good	Fair	Poor
125	100	80	60	40

Model 250 Deluxe
This version is similar to the Model 250 and is furnished with select walnut and sling swivels. It was manufactured between 1965 and 1971.

Exc.	V.G.	Good	Fair	Poor
150	125	100	75	50

Model 255
This version is simply the Model 250 chambered for the .22 WMR cartridge. It was manufactured between 1964 and 1970.

Exc.	V.G.	Good	Fair	Poor
145	120	90	70	50

Model 255 Deluxe

This version was offered with select walnut and sling swivels. It was manufactured between 1965 and 1973.

Exc.	V.G.	Good	Fair	Poor
175	150	125	100	75

Model 270

This is a slide action rifle chambered for the .22 rimfire cartridge. It has a 20.5" barrel and a tubular magazine. The finish is blued, with a checkered walnut stock. It was manufactured between 1963 and 1973.

Exc.	V.G.	Good	Fair	Poor
125	100	75	50	35

Model 490

This is a blowback-operated, semiautomatic rifle chambered for the .22 Long Rifle cartridge. It has a 22" barrel with open sights and a 5-round, detachable magazine. The finish is blued, with a checkered stock. It was manufactured between 1975 and 1980.

Exc.	V.G.	Good	Fair	Poor
250	200	150	100	75

Model 63

Introduced in 1997 this is a recreation of the famous Model 63 .22 caliber auto. Fitted with a 23" barrel and 10-round tubular magazine. The receiver top is grooved for scope mounting.

Grade I

NIB	Exc.	V.G.	Good	Fair	Poor
675	525	—	—	—	—

High Grade-engraved receiver with gold accents and select walnut stock.

NIB	Exc.	V.G.	Good	Fair	Poor
1075	850	—	—	—	—

Model 94

This is the post-1964 lever-action carbine chambered for the .30-30, .7-30 Waters, and the .44 Magnum cartridges. It is offered with a 20" or 24" barrel and has a 6- or 7-round, tubular magazine depending on barrel length. The round barrel is offered with open sights. The forearm is held on by a single barrel band. The finish is blued, with a straight-grip walnut stock. In 1982 it was modified to angle ejection to simplify scope mounting. It was introduced as a continuation of the Model 94 line in 1964.

NIB	Exc.	V.G.	Good	Fair	Poor
275	225	175	125	100	75

Model 94 Ranger-Base Model

NIB	Exc.	V.G.	Good	Fair	Poor
240	200	175	150	100	75

Model 63

Model 94 Ranger Compact

Introduced in 1998 this model features a 16" barrel with 12.5" lop. Chambered for .30-30 or .357 Magnum. Furnished with black recoil pad. Post-style front sight with adjustable rear sight. Hardwood stock. Weight is approximately 5.87 lbs.

NIB	Exc.	V.G.	Good	Fair	Poor
325	250	—	—	—	—

Model 94 Black Shadow

This model features a black synthetic stock with non-glare finish and black recoil pad. Offered in .30-30, .44 Magnum, or .444 Marlin. Fitted with a 20" barrel. Weight is about 6.5 lbs. Introduced in 1998.

NIB	Exc.	V.G.	Good	Fair	Poor
350	275	—	—	—	—

Model 94 Deluxe-Checkered Stock

NIB	Exc.	V.G.	Good	Fair	Poor
300	250	200	150	125	100

Model 94 Win-Tuff-Laminated Stock

NIB	Exc.	V.G.	Good	Fair	Poor
300	250	200	150	125	100

Model 94 XTR-Select, Checkered Walnut Stock-Discontinued 1988

Exc.	V.G.	Good	Fair	Poor
275	225	150	100	85

Model 94 XTR Deluxe-Fancy Checkering

Exc.	V.G.	Good	Fair	Poor
350	300	200	150	110

Model 94 Trapper-16" Barrel

NIB	Exc.	V.G.	Good	Fair	Poor
300	225	175	125	100	75

Model 94 Antique Carbine-Gold-plated Saddle Ring

Exc.	V.G.	Good	Fair	Poor
250	200	175	125	90

Model 94 Wrangler-.32 Win. Special

Exc.	V.G.	Good	Fair	Poor
325	275	175	125	100

Model 94 Wrangler II-Loop Lever

NIB	Exc.	V.G.	Good	Fair	Poor
375	300	250	200	150	100

Model 94 Trapper-16" Barrel

Model 94 Trapper Walnut Saddle Ring Carbine

Model 94 XTR Big Bore

Model 94 Legacy

This Model 94 is fitted with a 20" barrel and chambered for the .30-30 Win. but it is fitted with a half-pistol-grip stock. Both walnut buttstock and forearm are cut checkered. Weight is 6.5 lbs.

NIB	Exc.	V.G.	Good	Fair	Poor
350	300	250	200	150	100

Model 94 XTR Big Bore

This version is chambered for the .307, .356, or the .375 Win. cartridges. It features the angle-ejection and is blued with a walnut, Monte Carlo-type stock and recoil pad. The round barrel is 20" in length. It has a 6-round, tubular magazine. It was introduced in 1978.

NIB	Exc.	V.G.	Good	Fair	Poor
300	250	200	150	125	100

Model 94 Centennial Limited Editions

Introduced in 1994 these models celebrate the 100-year anniversary of the Winchester Model 1894. Offered in three grades these models are of limited production. The Grade I is limited to 12,000 rifles while the High Grade is limited to 3,000 rifles. Only 94 of the Custom Limited model will be produced. Each Limited model has different grades of select walnut and engraving coverage. All are chambered for the .30-30 Winchester cartridge.

Grade I

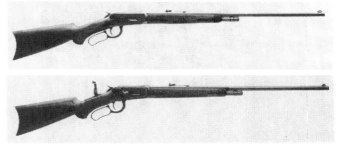

NIB	Exc.	V.G.	Good	Fair	Poor
750	700	600	450	300	200

High Grade

NIB	Exc.	V.G.	Good	Fair	Poor
1200	950	700	500	300	200

Custom High Grade

NIB	Exc.	V.G.	Good	Fair	Poor
4500	3900	2500	1000	750	450

Model 94 Trails End

This model is chambered for the .357 Mag., .44 Mag., and .45 Colt. Offered with standard-size loop lever or Wrangler-style loop. Introduced in 1997.

Model 94 Trails End

NIB	Exc.	V.G.	Good	Fair	Poor
400	325	250	—	—	—

Model 94 Timber Carbine

Introduced in 1999 this model is chambered for the .444 Marlin cartridge. Barrel is 17.75" long and ported. Hooded front sight. Magazine capacity is 5 rounds. Weight is about 6 lbs. Finish is blue. Walnut stock.

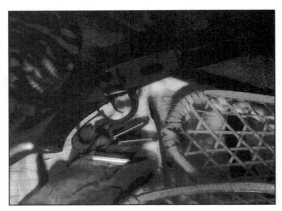

NIB	Exc.	V.G.	Good	Fair	Poor
520	400	—	—	—	—

Model 9422

Introduced in 1972 this model is chambered for the .22 rimfire and .22 Magnum rimfire cartridges. It was fitted with a 20.5" barrel, front ramp sight with hood, and adjustable semi-buckhorn rear sight. Tubular magazine holds 21 Shorts, 17 Longs, and 15 Long Rifle cartridges. The Magnum version holds 11 cartridges. Weight is about 6.25 lbs. Two-piece American walnut stock with no checkering. Between 1972 and 1992 approximately 750,000 Model 9422s were produced.

NIB	Exc.	V.G.	Good	Fair	Poor
275	225	200	175	150	100

Model 9422 XTR

This is a deluxe lever-action rifle chambered for the .22 rimfire cartridge. It is a takedown rifle with a 20.5" round barrel and a tubular magazine. The finish is blued with a checkered, high-gloss, straight-grip walnut stock. It was introduced in 1978. A .22 Magnum version is also available and would be worth approximately $10 additional.

NIB	Exc.	V.G.	Good	Fair	Poor
325	275	225	175	125	100

Model 9422 XTR Classic

This version is similar to the standard Model 9422 XTR except that it features a 22.5" barrel and a satin-finished, plain, pistol-grip walnut stock. It was manufactured between 1985 and 1987.

NIB	Exc.	V.G.	Good	Fair	Poor
650	550	350	250	200	125

Model 9422 WinTuff

This model features an uncheckered laminated wood stock that is brown in color. Chambered for both the .22 Rimfire and the .22 Winchester Magnum Rimfire. Weighs 6.25 lbs. Other features are the same as the standard Model 9422.

NIB	Exc.	V.G.	Good	Fair	Poor
300	250	200	150	100	75

Model 9422 WinTuff

Model 9422 WinCam

This model is chambered only for the .22 Winchester Magnum Rimfire. The laminated stock is a green color. Weighs 6.25 lbs.

NIB	Exc.	V.G.	Good	Fair	Poor
315	260	200	150	100	75

Model 9422 Trapper

Introduced in 1996 this model features a 16.5" barrel. It has an overall length of 33". Weight is 5.5 lbs.

NIB	Exc.	V.G.	Good	Fair	Poor
350	300	250	200	150	100

Model 9422 High Grade

This variation of the Model 9422 series features a specially engraved receiver and fancy wood stock. Barrel length is 20.5". Weight is about 6 lbs.

NIB	Exc.	V.G.	Good	Fair	Poor
450	400	300	250	175	125

Model 9422 25th Anniversary Rifle

Introduced in 1997 this model features 20.5" barrel. Limited quantities.

Grade I-Engraved Receiver

NIB	Exc.	V.G.	Good	Fair	Poor
600	475	—	—	—	—

Model 9422 25th Anniversary, Grade I

Model 9422 25th Anniversary, High Grade

High Grade-Engraved Receiver With Silver Border

NIB	Exc.	V.G.	Good	Fair	Poor
1350	1100	—	—	—	—

Model 9422 Legacy

This model has a semi-pistol-grip stock of checkered walnut, will shoot .22 caliber LR, L, or S cartridges. Fitted with a 16" barrel. Weight is about 6 lbs. Introduced in 1998.

NIB	Exc.	V.G.	Good	Fair	Poor
400	325	—	—	—	—

Model 9422 Large Loop & Walnut

Introduced in 1998 this model features a walnut stock with large loop lever. Large loop offered on .22 LR, L, or S model. Standard lever on .22 WMR version. Fitted with 16" barrel. Weight is about 6 lbs.

NIB	Exc.	V.G.	Good	Fair	Poor
350	275	—	—	—	—

Model 9422 High Grade Series II

This model features a high grade walnut stock with cut checkering. Receiver engraved with dogs and squirrels. Fitted with 16" barrel. Weight is about 6 lbs. Introduced in 1998.

NIB	Exc.	V.G.	Good	Fair	Poor
500	400	—	—	—	—

Model 64

This is a post-1964 version of the lever-action Model 64. It is chambered for the .30-30 cartridge and has a 24" round barrel with open sights and a 5-round, 2/3-length tubular magazine. The finish is blued with a plain walnut pistol-grip stock. It was manufactured between 1972 and 1974.

Exc.	V.G.	Good	Fair	Poor
250	200	150	100	85

Model 1885 Low Wall

Introduced in the fall of 1999 this single shot model is chambered for the .22 Long Rifle cartridge. It is fitted with a 24.5" half-octagon barrel with leaf rear sight. Drilled and tapped for a tang sight. Crescent steel buttplate. Walnut stock. Weight is about 8 lbs. Limited to 2,400 rifles.

Grade I

NIB	Exc.	V.G.	Good	Fair	Poor
750	600	—	—	—	—

High Grade

NIB	Exc.	V.G.	Good	Fair	Poor
1175	950	—	—	—	—

Model 1892

Introduced in mid-1997 this model is chambered for the .45 Colt cartridge. It features a straight grip, full magazine, and crescent butt plate.

Grade I-2,500 Rifles With Engraved Receiver

NIB	Exc.	V.G.	Good	Fair	Poor
725	575	—	—	—	—

High Grade-1,000 Rifle With Gold Accents.

NIB	Exc.	V.G.	Good	Fair	Poor
1275	1050	—	—	—	—

Model 1892 Short Rifle

This model is fitted with a 20" barrel and chambered for the .45 Colt, .357 Magnum, .44 Magnum, and .44-40 cartridges. Walnut stock and blued barrel and receiver. Weight is about 6.25 lbs. Introduced in 1999.

NIB	Exc.	V.G.	Good	Fair	Poor
740	575	—	—	—	—

Model 1886

Introduced to the Winchester line in 1997 this was a non-catalogued item. This model features a 26" octagon barrel, semi-pistol grip, and crescent buttplate.

Grade I-2,500 Rifles Blued Receiver

NIB	Exc.	V.G.	Good	Fair	Poor
1000	800	—	—	—	—

High Grade-1,000 rifles with gold accents on receiver.

High Grade-1,000 rifles with gold accents on receiver.

NIB	Exc.	V.G.	Good	Fair	Poor
1575	1300	—	—	—	—

Model 1886 Take Down Classic

Introduced in 1999 this model is chambered for the .45-70 cartridge and features a 26" barrel with takedown feature. Walnut stock with pistol grip and crescent butt. Magazine capacity is 8 rounds. Weight is about 9.25 lbs.

NIB	Exc.	V.G.	Good	Fair	Poor
1140	900	—	—	—	—

Model 1895 Limited Edition

Introduced in 1995 this reproduction of the famous Model 1895 is offered in .30-06 caliber with 24" barrel. Magazine capacity is 4 rounds. Weight is approximately 8 lbs. Available in two grades each limited to 4,000 rifles.

Grade I

NIB	Exc.	V.G.	Good	Fair	Poor
800	700	—	—	—	—

High Grade

NIB	Exc.	V.G.	Good	Fair	Poor
1300	1000	—	—	—	—

Model 52B Sporting Rifle

A 1993 limited edition rifle (6,000 guns) that is a faithful reproduction of the famous Winchester Model 52 Sporter. Equipped with a 24" barrel, adjustable trigger, and "B" style cheekpiece. This model was reissued in 1997 and limited to 3,000 rifles.

NIB	Exc.	V.G.	Good	Fair	Poor
500	400	350	300	200	100

Post-1964 Model 70S

These post-Model 70 rifles were fitted with redesigned actions and bolt with free-floating barrels, and new style stock with impressed checkering.

Model 1895 Limited Edition, Grade I

Model 52B Sporting Rifle

Model 70-Standard Grade

This is a bolt-action sporting rifle chambered for various popular calibers such as the .22-250, .222 Rem., .243 Win., .270 Win., .30-06, and .308 Win. It features a 22" barrel with open sights and a 5-round, integral box magazine. The finish is blued with a Monte Carlo-type stock furnished with sling swivels. It was manufactured between 1964 and 1971.

Exc.	V.G.	Good	Fair	Poor
350	250	200	150	100

Model 70 Varmint

Chambered for the .22-25, .222 Rem., and .243 Win. cartridges this rifle is fitted with a 24" heavyweight barrel with no sights. Magazine capacity is 5 rounds. Weight is about 9.75 lbs. Built from 1964 to 1971.

Exc.	V.G.	Good	Fair	Poor
—	—	—	—	—

Model 70 Westerner

This model is chambered for the .264 Win. Magnum and .3" Win. Magnum cartridges. Open sights, 24" barrel. Ventilated recoil pad. Weight is about 7.25 lbs. Built from 1964 to 1971.

Exc.	V.G.	Good	Fair	Poor
—	—	—	—	—

Model 70 African

Chambered for the .458 Win. Magnum cartridge this rifle is fitted with a 22" barrel with open sights. Magazine capacity is 3 rounds. Weight is about 8.5 lbs. Built from 1964 to 1971.

Exc.	V.G.	Good	Fair	Poor
—	—	—	—	—

Model 70 Magnum

Chambered for the 7mm Rem. Mag., .300 Win. Mag., and .375 H&H cartridges. Barrel length is 24". Weight is about 7.75 lbs. Built from 1964 to 1971.

Exc.	V.G.	Good	Fair	Poor
—	—	—	—	—

Model 70 Deluxe

Built from 1964 to 1971 this rifle features a Monte Carlo stock with hand checkering and ebony forend tip. Offered in .243, .270, .30-06, and .300 Win. Mag. Fitted with 22" barrel except magnums with 24" barrel. Weight is about 7.5 lbs.

Exc.	V.G.	Good	Fair	Poor
—	—	—	—	—

Model 70 Mannlicher

This is a full-length, Mannlicher-type stocked version of the Model 70 bolt-action rifle that is chambered for the .243, .270, .308, and the .30-06 cartridges. It was introduced in 1969. It features a 19" barrel with open sights. The finish is blued. It was discontinued in 1972. Only 2,401 were produced. Excellent quality.

Exc.	V.G.	Good	Fair	Poor
750	600	500	400	300

Model 70 Target Rifle

This version is chambered for the .308 or the .30-06 cartridges. It was offered with a 24" heavy barrel without sights. It is furnished with bases for a target scope. The finish is blued with a heavy walnut target stock with a palm rest. Weight is approximately 10.25 lbs.

Exc.	V.G.	Good	Fair	Poor
650	550	450	350	250

Model 70 International Match Army

This version is chambered for the .308 cartridge and has a 24" heavy barrel furnished without sights. It has an adjustable trigger and is blued, with a target-type heavy stock that had an accessory rail and an adjustable butt.

Exc.	V.G.	Good	Fair	Poor
750	650	500	400	300

Model 70A

This is a utility version of the bolt-action post-1964 Model 70. It was furnished without a hinged floorplate. The finish is blued, with a walnut stock. It was manufactured between 1972 and 1978.

Exc.	V.G.	Good	Fair	Poor
300	275	225	175	100

Model 70 XTR Featherweight

This gun was built after the takeover by the U.S.R.A. Company. It is a bolt-action sporting rifle chambered for various calibers from .22-250 up to the .30-06 cartridges. It has a 22" barrel that is furnished without sights and features either a short- or medium-length action. It has a 5-round, integral magazine. The finish is blued, with a checkered walnut stock. It was introduced in 1981.

NIB	Exc.	V.G.	Good	Fair	Poor
450	400	325	300	250	200

Model 70 Fiftieth Anniversary Model

This is a commemorative version of the post-1964 Model 70 bolt-action rifle. It is chambered for the .300 Win. Mag. and is offered with a 24" barrel. It is engraved and high-gloss blued with a deluxe, checkered walnut stock. There were 500 manufactured in 1987. In order to realize collector potential, it must be NIB with all supplied materials.

NIB	Exc.	V.G.	Good	Fair	Poor
1000	800	400	300	250	200

Model 70 XTR Super Express

This is a heavy-duty version of the Post-1964 Model 70 chambered for the .375 H&H and the .458 Win. Mag. cartridges. It is offered with a 22" or 24" heavy barrel and a 3-round, integral box magazine. This version has extra recoil lugs mounted in the stock and is blued with a select, straight-grain walnut stock and a recoil pad standard.

NIB	Exc.	V.G.	Good	Fair	Poor
650	500	400	300	200	100

Model 70 XTR Varmint

This version is chambered for the .22-250, .223, and the .243 cartridges. It has a 24" heavy barrel and is furnished without sights. It has a 5-round magazine and is blued with a heavy walnut stock. It was introduced in 1972.

NIB	Exc.	V.G.	Good	Fair	Poor
400	350	300	250	200	100

Model 70 Winlight

This version is offered in various calibers between .270 and the .338 Win. Mag. It features a matte-blue finish and a fiberglass stock. It is offered with a 22" or a 24" barrel and a 3- or 4-round magazine. It was introduced in 1986.

NIB	Exc.	V.G.	Good	Fair	Poor
400	350	300	250	200	100

Ranger

This is a utility-grade, bolt-action rifle chambered for the .270 Win., .30-06, and the 7mm Rem. Mag. cartridges. It is offered with a 22" or a 24" barrel with open sights and has a 3- or 4-round box magazine. The finish is blued with a plain hardwood stock.

NIB	Exc.	V.G.	Good	Fair	Poor
350	300	275	225	150	100

Model 70 Featherweight Classic

A U.S.R.A. model with 22" barrel, walnut stock, and claw-controlled round feeding. The bolt is jeweled and the bolt handle knurled. Comb is straight. Available in .270, .280, and .30-06 calibers. In 1997 this model was offered in the 6.5x55mm Swedish caliber. Rifle weighs about 7.25 lbs.

NIB	Exc.	V.G.	Good	Fair	Poor
600	450	350	250	200	100

Model 70 Winlight

Model 70 Featherweight Classic

Model 70 Classic Laredo

Model 70 Featherweight Ultra Grade

Limited to 1,000 rifles this model is profusely engraved with game scene and gold line inlaid. Serial number inlaid in gold. Offered in .270 caliber with very-fine-figured walnut stock with fine-line checkering. Mahogany fitted case. The retail price was $5,000. Due to lack of active sales no price is given. Strongly suggest a qualified appraisal before sale.

Model 70 Featherweight Classic All-Terrain

Introduced in 1996 this model features a weather-resistant stainless steel barrel and action with fiberglass/graphite black synthetic stock. Offered in .270 Win., .30-06, 7mm Rem. Mag., and .330 Win. Mag. Weight is about 7.25 lbs. Also offered with the BOSS system.

NIB	Exc.	V.G.	Good	Fair	Poor
600	550	450	300	200	150

NOTE: Add $100 for BOSS.

Model 70 Classic Laredo

First offered in 1996 this model features a heavy 26" barrel with pre-1964 action on a gray synthetic stock. Chambered for the 7mm Rem. Mag and the .300 Win. Mag. The forearm is a beavertail. Finish is matte blue. In 1997 this model was offered chambered for the 7mm STW cartridge. In 1998 this model was offered with fluted barrel.

NIB	Exc.	V.G.	Good	Fair	Poor
750	650	550	500	400	300

NOTE: Add $100 for BOSS. Add $125 for fluted barrel.

Model 70 Classic Compact

Introduced in 1998 this model is a scaled-down version of the Featherweight. It has a lop of 12.5" and a 20" barrel. Chambered for .243, .308, and 7mm-08 calibers. Checkered walnut stock. Weight is about 6.5 lbs.

NIB	Exc.	V.G.	Good	Fair	Poor
525	425	—	—	—	—

Model 70 Classic Sporter LT

Introduced in 1999 this model is chambered for a wide variety of calibers from .25-06 to .338 Win. Mag. Fitted with a 24" or 26" barrel depending on caliber and no sights. Walnut stock with butt pad. Blued finish. Also offered in left-hand models from .270 to .338 Win. Mag. Weight is about 8 lbs.

NIB	Exc.	V.G.	Good	Fair	Poor
630	500	—	—	—	—

NOTE: Add $30 for left-hand models.

Model 70 Classic Safari Express

This model is chambered for the .375 H&H Mag, .416 Rem. Mag, and .458 Win. Mag. Fitted with 24" barrel Magazine capacity is 4 rounds. Walnut stock with open sights. Left-hand model offered in .375 H&H. Weight is about 8.5 lbs. Introduced in 1999.

NIB	Exc.	V.G.	Good	Fair	Poor
925	750	—	—	—	—

NOTE: Add $30 for .375 H&H left hand model.

Model 70 Super Grade

Another U.S.R.A. rifle that features a select walnut stock, claw-controlled round feed, a single reinforced cross bolt, 24" barrel shipped with bases and rings. The buttstock has a straight comb with classic cheekpiece and deep-cut checkering. Available in .270, .30-06, 7mm Rem. Mag., .300 Win. Mag., and .338 Win. Mag. Rifle weighs approximately 7.75 lbs. Currently in production.

NIB	Exc.	V.G.	Good	Fair	Poor
800	650	550	450	300	150

Model 70 Super Express

A U.S.R.A. version of the post-1964 XTR Super Express. Specifications are the same as the earlier model. Rifle weighs 8.5 lbs. Introduced in 1993.

NIB	Exc.	V.G.	Good	Fair	Poor
650	500	400	300	200	100

Model 70 Custom Sharpshooter

A U.S.R.A. Custom Shop gun. This model is fitted with a stainless steel Schneider barrel with hand-honed action and hand fitted. The stock is a custom McMillan A-2 glass-bedded stock. Offered in .223 Rem., .22-250 Rem., .308 Win. and .300 Win. Mag. Comes from the factory with a hard case. Currently in production.

NIB	Exc.	V.G.	Good	Fair	Poor
1300	950	750	500	300	150

Model 70 Custom Classic Sharpshooter II

Same as above but introduced in 1996 with an H-S heavy target stock, a pre-1964 action stainless steel H-S barrel. Weight is about 11 lbs. Offered in .22-250, .308, .30-06, and .300 Win. Mag.

NIB	Exc.	V.G.	Good	Fair	Poor
1800	1400	—	—	—	—

Model 70 Custom Sporting Sharpshooter

Essentially a take-off on the Custom Sharpshooter but configured for hunting. Fitted with a McMillan sporter-style gray stock and Schneider stainless steel barrel. Offered in .270 Win., .300 Win., and 7mm STW. Introduced in 1993.

Model 70 Super Express

Winchester Model 70 Grey Sporting Sharpshooter

NIB	Exc.	V.G.	Good	Fair	Poor
1250	900	750	500	300	150

Model 70 Custom Classic Sporting Sharpshooter II

Introduced in 1996 this is an updated version of the model above. It features a pre-1964 action with H-S special fiberglass stock and stainless steel barrel. Available in .7mm S.T.W., and .300 Win. Mag. Weight is about 8.5 lbs.

NIB	Exc.	V.G.	Good	Fair	Poor
1700	1400	—	—	—	—

Model 70 Custom Grade

This custom-built Model 70 is hand-finished, polished, and fitted in the Custom Shop. Internal parts are hand-honed while the barrel is lead-lapped. The customer can order individual items to his or her own taste, including engraving, special stock dimensions and carvings, etc. Each Custom Grade Model 70 should be priced on an individual basis.

Model 70 Custom Express

Also built in the Custom Shop this model features figured walnut, hand-honed internal parts, bolt and follower are engine turned. A special 3-leaf rear sight is furnished also. Offered in .375 H&H Mag., .375 JRS, .416 Rem. Mag., .458 Win. Mag., and .470 Capstick.

NIB	Exc.	V.G.	Good	Fair	Poor
1700	1400	900	500	300	150

Model 70 African Express

Introduced in 1999 this model is chambered for the .340 Wby, .358 STA, .375 H&H, .416 Rem. Mag., and the .458 Win. Mag. Fitted with a 24" barrel and a magazine capacity of 4 rounds. Express sights. Weight is about 9.75 lbs. Ebony pistol-grip cap, and select walnut stock.

NIB	Exc.	V.G.	Good	Fair	Poor
3850	3000	—	—	—	—

Model 70 Custom Safari Express

This model has a figured walnut stock with the bolt and follower engine turned. Express sights. Chambered in .340 Wby., .358 STA, .375 H&H, .416 Rem. Mag., and .458 Win. Mag. Barrel length is 24". Weight is about 9.5 lbs. Introduced in 1999.

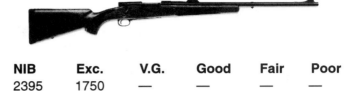

NIB	Exc.	V.G.	Good	Fair	Poor
2395	1750	—	—	—	—

Model 70 Custom Mannlicher

This model features a full-length stock of figured walnut with smooth-tapered barrel and blued action. Chambered for .260 Rem., .308 Win., and 7mm-08. Fitted with a 19" barrel with optional open sights. Weight is about 6.75 lbs. Introduced in 1999.

NIB	Exc.	V.G.	Good	Fair	Poor
2700	2000	—	—	—	—

Model 70 Ultimate Classic

This model features a number of special options as standard. Included is a pre-1964 action, choice of round, round-fluted, 1/2-octagon 1/2-round barrel, full-tapered-octagon barrel, blued or stainless steel barrel actions, Fancy American walnut stock, special Custom Shop serial numbers and proof stamp, inletted swivel bases, red recoil pad, fine-cut checkering, and a hard case. Offered in a wide variety of calibers from .25-06 to .338 Win. Mag. Weight is about 7.5 to 7.75 lbs. depending on caliber. Also available in stainless steel.

NIB	Exc.	V.G.	Good	Fair	Poor
2450	1950	1500	—	—	—

Model 70 Custom Express

NOTE: In 1997 this model was introduced in a left hand version.

Model 70 Custom Take Down

Introduced in 1998 this composite stock rifle has a special take-down feature. Chambered for .375 H&H, .416 Rem. Mag., .300 Win Mag., and 7mm STW. Magazine capacity is 3 rounds. Barrel length is 26". Weight is between 8.5 and 9 lbs. Offered in fluted barrel in .300 Win. Mag. and 7mm STW.

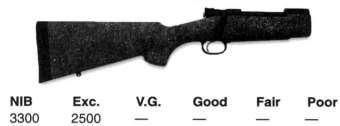

NIB	Exc.	V.G.	Good	Fair	Poor
3300	2500	—	—	—	—

Model 70 Heavy Varmint

Introduced by U.S.R.A. in 1993 this rifle features a fiberglass/graphite stock with heavy 26" stainless steel barrel. Offered in .223, .22-250, .243, and .308. In 1997 this model was offered chambered for the .222 Rem. cartridge. Rifle weighs about 10.75 lbs.

NIB	Exc.	V.G.	Good	Fair	Poor
550	475	400	300	200	100

Model 70 Heavy Varmint-Fluted Barrel

Introduced in 1997 this model is similar to the above Varmint with the addition of a fluted barrel. Calibers are also the same as the above model.

NIB	Exc.	V.G.	Good	Fair	Poor
550	475	400	—	—	—

Model 70 Stainless

All metal parts are stainless steel, including the barrel, with synthetic stock. Available with 24" barrel and chambered for .270, .30-06, 7mm Rem. Mag., .300 Win. Mag., and .338 Win. Mag. Weighs about 7.5 lbs. Currently in production.

NIB	Exc.	V.G.	Good	Fair	Poor
485	425	375	300	200	100

Model 70 Classic Laminated Stainless

Introduced in 1998 this model features a laminated stock and stainless steel barrel and action. Offered in .270, .30-06, 7mm Rem. Mag., .300 Win. Mag., and .338 Win. Mag. Pre-1964 action. Bolt is jeweled and bolt handle is knurled. Barrel lengths are 24" and 26" depending on caliber. Weight is about 8 lbs.

NIB	Exc.	V.G.	Good	Fair	Poor
700	475	—	—	—	—

Classic Camo Stainless

This model features a Sporter-style stock with 24" or 26" barrel and Mossy Oak Treestand camo on the stock. Chambered for .270 Win., .30-06, 7mm Rem. Mag., and .300 Win Mag. Magazine capacity is 5 rounds. Weight is about 7.5 lbs. Introduced in 1998.

NIB	Exc.	V.G.	Good	Fair	Poor
725	550	—	—	—	—

Model 70 SM

This rifle features a synthetic stock with black matte finish. Barrel length is 24". Available in 10 calibers from .223 Rem. to .375 H&H Mag. Depending on caliber rifle weighs between 7 and 8 lbs. Currently in production.

NIB	Exc.	V.G.	Good	Fair	Poor
475	400	300	200	150	100

Model 70 DBM-S

Similar to the Model 70 SM but fitted with a detachable box magazine. The metal parts are blued and the stock is synthetic. Offered in 8 calibers from .223 Rem. to .338 Win. Mag. Furnished with scope bases and rings are open sights. Rifle weighs about 7.25 lbs. depending on caliber. Introduced in 1993.

Winchester Model 70 Synthetic Stock w/Detachable Box Magazine

NIB	Exc.	V.G.	Good	Fair	Poor
500	425	325	225	150	100

Model 70 Varmint

Similar to the Model 70 Heavy Varmint but furnished with a traditional walnut stock and 26" medium-heavy barrel. Offered in .223 Rem., .22-250, .243, and .308. Weighs 9 lbs.

NIB	Exc.	V.G.	Good	Fair	Poor
465	400	300	200	150	100

Model 70 DBM

DBM stands for detachable box magazine. Fitted with a straight comb walnut stock. Jeweled bolt with blued receiver. Shipped with scope bases and rings or open sights. Rifle offered in 8 calibers from .223 Rem. to .300 Win. Mag. Rifle weighs about 7.35 lbs. depending on caliber. Introduced in 1993.

NIB	Exc.	V.G.	Good	Fair	Poor
480	425	325	225	150	100

Model 70 Sporter

U.S.R.A.'s basic Model 70 offering. Straight-comb walnut stock with checkering, jeweled bolt and blued receiver and barrel are standard. Available in 12 calibers from .223 Rem. to .338 Win. Mag. including .270 Weatherby Mag. and .300 Weatherby Mag. Barrel length is 24" and is available with either scope bases and rings or open sights. Rifle weighs about 7.5 lbs.

NIB	Exc.	V.G.	Good	Fair	Poor
450	400	300	200	150	100

Model 70 WinTuff

Similar to the Sporter except fitted with a laminated hardwood straight-comb stock with cheekpiece. Offered in 24" barrel lengths with a choice of 6 calibers from .270 Win. to .338 Win. Mag. Furnished with scope bases and rings. Rifle weighs about 7.65 lbs. depending on caliber.

NIB	Exc.	V.G.	Good	Fair	Poor
450	400	300	200	150	100

Model 70 Lightweight

Similar to the Model 70 Winlight. Offered with straight-comb checkered walnut stock with knurled bolt and blued receiver and barrel. The barrel is 22" without sights. Offered in 5 calibers: .223, .243, .270, .308, and .30-06. Rifle weighs about 7 lbs. depending on caliber.

NIB	Exc.	V.G.	Good	Fair	Poor
400	350	300	200	150	100

Model 70 Black Shadow

Chambered for the .270, .30-06, 7mm Rem. Mag., and .300 Win. Mag. and fitted with a 22" or 24" barrel depending on caliber. Finish is matte black with composite stock. Push-feed action. Weight is 7.25 lbs. Introduced in 1998.

NIB	Exc.	V.G.	Good	Fair	Poor
425	350	—	—	—	—

Model 70 Ladies/Youth Ranger

A scaled-down version of the Ranger. Length of pull is 1" shorter than standard. Rifle weighs 6.5 lbs. Chambered in .243 and .308. In 1997 this model was offered chambered for the .223 Rem. and the 7mm-08 Rem. cartridges.

NIB	Exc.	V.G.	Good	Fair	Poor
375	350	300	200	150	100

NOTE: In 1994 U.S. Repeating Arms reintroduced the pre-1964 Model 70 action on many of its Model 70 rifles. At the present time this new action does not affect values but may do so in the future depending on shooter reaction.

POST-1964 SHOTGUNS
Model 12 "Y" Series

Model 12 Field Grade
This is a later version of the slide-action Model 12, chambered for 12 gauge only. It was offered with a 26", 28", or 30" vent rib barrel with various chokes. The finish is blued with a jeweled bolt and a hand-checkered, select walnut stock. This version is easily recognizable as it has the letter Y serial number prefix. It was manufactured between 1972 and 1976.

Exc.	V.G.	Good	Fair	Poor
650	550	400	350	275

Model 12 Super Pigeon Grade
This is a deluxe version that features extensive engraving and fancy checkering. It was offered with a turned action and select, fancy-grade walnut. It was a limited-production item produced between 1964 and 1972. It was briefly reintroduced in 1984 and discontinued again in 1985.

Exc.	V.G.	Good	Fair	Poor
3000	2500	1850	1400	950

Model 12 Skeet
This version is similar to the Field Grade but is offered with a 26", vent rib, skeet-bored barrel. The finish is blued, with a skeet-type stock and recoil pad. It was manufactured between 1972 and 1975.

Exc.	V.G.	Good	Fair	Poor
700	650	550	350	300

Model 12 Trap Grade
This version features a 30" vent rib barrel with a full choke. It is blued with a trap-type, standard, or Monte Carlo stock with a recoil pad. It was manufactured between 1972 and 1980.

Exc.	V.G.	Good	Fair	Poor
650	600	500	300	200

Model 12 (Limited Edition)
Available in 20 gauge only. Furnished with a 26" vent rib barrel choked improved cylinder. The walnut stock is checkered with pistol grip. Introduced in 1993 and available in three different grades.

Grade 1 (4,000 guns)

NIB	Exc.	V.G.	Good	Fair	Poor
700	600	450	350	200	100

Grade IV (1,000 guns) Gold Highlights

NIB	Exc.	V.G.	Good	Fair	Poor
1150	900	650	400	200	100

Model 12 (Limited Edition)

Ducks Unlimited Model

Available through Ducks Unlimited chapters. An independent appraisal is suggested.

Model 42 (Limited Edition)

A reproduction of the famous Winchester Model 42 .410 bore slide-action shotgun. Furnished with a 26" ventilated rib barrel choked full. The receiver is engraved with gold border. Introduced in 1993 and limited to 850 guns.

NIB	Exc.	V.G.	Good	Fair	Poor
1250	900	600	400	300	150

Model 1200

This is a slide-action shotgun chambered for 12, 16, or 20 gauge. It was offered with a 26", 28", or 30", vent rib barrel with various chokes. It has an alloy receiver and is blued, with a checkered walnut stock and recoil pad. It was manufactured between 1964 and 1981. This model was offered with the plastic Hydrocoil stock, and this would add approximately 35% to the values given.

Exc.	V.G.	Good	Fair	Poor
225	175	150	100	75

Model 1300 Series

Model 1300 XTR

This is the current slide-action shotgun offered by Winchester. It is chambered for 12 and 20 gauge with 3" chambers. It is a takedown gun that is offered with various-length vent-rib barrels with screw-in choke tubes. It has an alloy frame and is blued with a walnut stock. It was introduced in 1978.

Exc.	V.G.	Good	Fair	Poor
300	250	200	150	100

Model 1300 Waterfowl

This version is chambered for 12 gauge, 3" only. It has a 30" vent-rib barrel with screw-in choke tubes. It is matte-blued, with a satin-finished walnut stock and a recoil pad. It was introduced in 1984. A laminated WinTuff stock was made available in 1988 and would add $10 to the value.

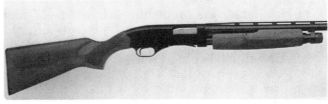

NIB	Exc.	V.G.	Good	Fair	Poor
350	300	250	200	150	100

Model 1300 WinCam Turkey Gun

This version is similar to the Model 1300 Turkey Gun, with a green, laminated hardwood stock. It was introduced in 1987. A WinTuff version is also available and would add $20 to the values given.

NIB	Exc.	V.G.	Good	Fair	Poor
375	325	250	200	150	125

Model 1300 Stainless Security

This version is chambered for 12 or 20 gauge and is constructed of stainless steel. It has an 18" cylinder-bore barrel and a 7- or 8-shot tubular magazine. It is available with a pistol-grip stock, which would add approximately 50% to the values given.

NIB	Exc.	V.G.	Good	Fair	Poor
250	225	200	150	125	100

Model 1300 Turkey

This slide-action model features a 22" vent rib barrel chambered for 3" 12 gauge shells. Supplied with choke tubes. Gun weighs 7.25 lbs.

NIB	Exc.	V.G.	Good	Fair	Poor
350	300	250	200	150	100

Model 1300 Realtree® Turkey

Model 1300 Black Shadow Turkey

Model 1300 National Wild Turkey Federation Series III

Model 1300 Realtree® Turkey

Introduced in 1994 this model features a synthetic stock camouflaged with Realtree® pattern. The receiver and 22" barrel are matte finish.

NIB	Exc.	V.G.	Good	Fair	Poor
375	275	225	200	150	100

Model 1300 Black Shadow Turkey

This model was also introduced in 1994 and features a black composite stock with a non-glare finish on the barrel, receiver, bolt, and magazine. Barrel has vent rib and is 22" in length.

NIB	Exc.	V.G.	Good	Fair	Poor
250	200	175	150	125	100

Model 1300 National Wild Turkey Federation Series III

Engraved receiver, camo stock, open sights on a 22" plain barrel, and all metal and wood parts are non-glare. Comes with a quick detachable sling. Offered in 12 gauge only. Gun weighs 7.25 lbs.

NIB	Exc.	V.G.	Good	Fair	Poor
370	320	250	200	150	100

Model 1300 National Wild Turkey Federation Series IV

Introduced in 1993 this model is similar to the Series II with the addition of a 22" vent rib barrel. Stock is black laminated. Comes with quick detachable sling. Gun weights 7 lbs.

Winchester Model 1300 National Wild Turkey Federation Series IV Shotgun

NIB	Exc.	V.G.	Good	Fair	Poor
370	320	250	200	150	100

Model 1300 Whitetails Unlimited Slug Hunter

This slide-action model features a full-length rifle barrel chambered for 3" 12 gauge shells. Barrel is choked cylinder. Fitted with a checkered walnut stock with engraved receiver. Receiver is drilled and tapped for bases and rings, which are included. Comes equipped with camo sling. Weighs 7.25 lbs.

NIB	Exc.	V.G.	Good	Fair	Poor
350	300	250	200	150	100

Model 1300 Slug Hunter

Similar to the Whitetails Unlimited model, but without the engraved receiver.

NIB	Exc.	V.G.	Good	Fair	Poor
350	300	250	200	150	100

Model 1300 Black Shadow Deer

Introduced in 1994 this Model 1300 features a black composite stock with non-glare finish on the bolt, barrel, receiver, and magazine. Barrel is 22" with ramp front sight and adjustable rear sight.

NIB	Exc.	V.G.	Good	Fair	Poor
250	200	175	150	125	100

Model 1300 Black Shadow Deer

Model 1300 Black Shadow Field

Same as above but fitted with a 26" or 28" vent rib barrel chambered for 3" Mag. shells. Weight is about 7 lbs.

NIB	Exc.	V.G.	Good	Fair	Poor
275	225	200	150	100	80

Model 1300 Slug Hunter Sabot (Smoothbore)

Similar to the Slug Hunter but furnished with a smoothbore barrel with a special extended screw-in choke tube that is rifled.

NIB	Exc.	V.G.	Good	Fair	Poor
275	250	200	175	150	100

Model 1300 Upland Special

This 12 gauge slide-action shotgun is fitted with a 24" vent rib barrel and straight-grip walnut stock. Weight is about 7 lbs. Introduced in 1999.

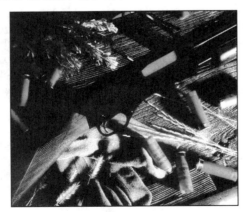

NIB	Exc.	V.G.	Good	Fair	Poor
360	275	—	—	—	—

Model 1300 Ranger

This slide-action shotgun is a lower-cost version of the Model 1300. Furnished with a hardwood stock and available in 12 or 20 gauge with 26" or 28" vent rib barrel. WinChokes are included.

NIB	Exc.	V.G.	Good	Fair	Poor
235	200	175	150	125	100

Model 1300 Ranger Ladies/Youth

Available in 20 gauge only this model has a 1" shorter-than-standard length of pull and a 22" vent rib barrel. Choke tubes are included. Gun weighs 6.75 lbs.

NIB	Exc.	V.G.	Good	Fair	Poor
250	200	175	150	125	100

Model 1300 Ranger Deer Slug

Comes in two principal configurations: a 12 gauge 22" smooth barrel with cylinder choke; and a 12 gauge 22" rifled barrel. Both are chambered for 3" shells and weigh 6.75 lbs.

NIB	Exc.	V.G.	Good	Fair	Poor
250	200	175	150	125	100

Model 1300 Ranger Deer Combo

The Model 1300 Ranger Deer Combos are available in three different configurations. One: 12 gauge 22" smooth barrel and 28" vent rib barrel with WinChokes. Two: 12 gauge 22" rifled barrel with 28" vent-rib barrel with WinChokes. Three: 20 gauge 22" smooth barrel with 28" vent-rib barrel with WinChokes.

12 Gauge Combo

NIB	Exc.	V.G.	Good	Fair	Poor
300	250	200	175	150	100

Model 1300 Ranger Deer Combo

20 Gauge Combo

NIB	Exc.	V.G.	Good	Fair	Poor
300	250	200	175	150	100

Model 1300 Defender Combo

This personal-defense slide-action shotgun features an 18" cylinder-choked barrel and a 28" vent rib barrel with modified WinChoke and an accessory pistol grip. A hardwood stock comes fitted to the gun.

NIB	Exc.	V.G.	Good	Fair	Poor
300	250	200	175	150	100

Model 1300 Defender 5-Shot

Same as above but furnished with a hardwood stock only and 18" barrel.

NIB	Exc.	V.G.	Good	Fair	Poor
250	200	175	150	125	100

Model 1300 Camp Defender

Introduced in 1999 this 12 gauge model features a 22" barrel and walnut stock. Magazine capacity is 5 rounds. Barrel fitted with rifle sights. Weight is about 7 lbs. Comes with cylinder choke tube.

NIB	Exc.	V.G.	Good	Fair	Poor
	345	275	—	—	—

Model 1300 Defender 8-Shot

Same as above but furnished with an 18" barrel with extended magazine tube.

NIB	Exc.	V.G.	Good	Fair	Poor
250	200	175	150	125	100

Model 1300 Defender Synthetic Stock

Same as above but fitted with a black synthetic full stock. Available in either 12 or 20 gauge.

NIB	Exc.	V.G.	Good	Fair	Poor
250	200	175	150	125	100

Model 1300 Defender Pistol Grip

Same as above but fitted with a black synthetic pistol grip and extended magazine tube.

NIB	Exc.	V.G.	Good	Fair	Poor
250	200	175	150	125	100

Model 1300 Lady Defender

Chambered for the 20 gauge shell this model features a 18" barrel with 8-round capacity. Pistol-grip stock. Introduced in 1997.

NIB	Exc.	V.G.	Good	Fair	Poor
	275	225	—	—	—

Model 1300 Stainless Marine

Model 1300 Stainless Marine

This 12 gauge slide-action shotgun comes with a black synthetic full stock with all metal parts chrome-plated. Barrel is 18" and magazine tube holds 7 rounds. Gun weighs 6.75 lbs.

NIB	Exc.	V.G.	Good	Fair	Poor
350	300	250	200	150	100

Model 1300 Stainless Marine with Pistol Grip

Same as above with black synthetic pistol-grip in place of full butt-stock. Gun weighs 5.75 lbs.

NIB	Exc.	V.G.	Good	Fair	Poor
350	300	250	200	150	100

Model 1500 XTR

This is a gas-operated, semiautomatic shotgun chambered for 12 or 20 gauge, with a 28" vent-rib barrel with screw-in chokes. The finish is blued, with a walnut stock. It was manufactured between 1978 and 1982.

Exc.	V.G.	Good	Fair	Poor
300	250	225	175	125

Super X Model I

This is a self-compensating, gas-operated, semi-automatic shotgun chambered for 12 gauge. It was offered with a 26", 28", or 30" vent rib barrel with various chokes. It features all-steel construction and is blued, with a checkered walnut stock. It was manufactured between 1974 and 1981.

Exc.	V.G.	Good	Fair	Poor
400	325	250	200	150

Super X Model 1 Custom Competition

This is a custom-order trap or skeet gun that features the self compensating, gas-operated action. It is available in 12 gauge only from the Custom Shop. It is offered with a heavy degree of engraving on the receiver and a fancy, checkered walnut stock. Gold inlays are available and would add approximately 50% to the values given. This model was introduced in 1987.

NIB	Exc.	V.G.	Good	Fair	Poor
1300	1000	850	700	600	450

Super X2 Magnum

Introduced in 1999 this model is a gas-operated design chambered for 3.5" 12 gauge shells. Fitted with a black synthetic stock and choice of 24", 26", or 28" vent-rib barrels. Invector chokes. Magazine capacity is 5 rounds. Weight is about 7.5 lbs depending on barrel length. Matte black finish.

NIB	Exc.	V.G.	Good	Fair	Poor
850	675	—	—	—	—

Super X2 Turkey

Similar to the X2 Magnum but with 24" vent-rib barrel with Truglo sights. Extra Full choke. Weight is about 7.25 lbs. Black synthetic stock. Introduced in 1999.

NIB	Exc.	V.G.	Good	Fair	Poor
860	675	—	—	—	—

Super X2 Camo Waterfowl

Chambered for 12 gauge 3.5" shells and fitted with a 28" vent rib barrel this model features a Mossy Oak camo finish. Introduced in 1999.

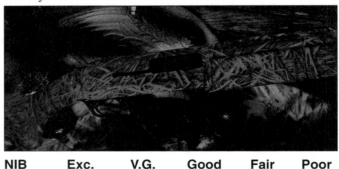

NIB	Exc.	V.G.	Good	Fair	Poor
930	725	—	—	—	—

Super X2 Magnum Field

This model is chambered for the 12 gauge 3" shell and is offered with either a walnut stock or black synthetic stock. Choice of 26" or 28" vent rib barrel with Invector chokes. Weight is about 7.25 lbs. Introduced in 1999.

NIB	Exc.	V.G.	Good	Fair	Poor
725	575	—	—	—	—

Model 1400

This is a gas-operated, semiautomatic shotgun chambered for 12, 16, or 20 gauge. It was offered with a 26", 28", or 30" vent rib barrel with various chokes. The finish is blued, with a checkered walnut stock. It was manufactured between 1964 and 1981. The Hydrocoil plastic stock was available on this model and would add approximately 35% to the values given.

Exc.	V.G.	Good	Fair	Poor
250	225	200	150	100

New Model 1400

This is a gas-operated, semiautomatic shotgun chambered for 12 or 20 gauge. It is offered with a 22" or 28" vent rib barrel with screw-in chokes. The finish is blued, with a checkered walnut stock. It was introduced in 1989.

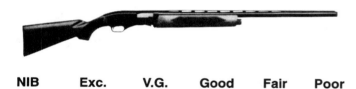

NIB	Exc.	V.G.	Good	Fair	Poor
400	350	300	250	200	125

Model 1400 Ranger

This is a utility-grade, gas-operated, semiautomatic shotgun chambered for 12 or 20 gauge. It is offered with a 28" vent rib barrel with screw-in chokes, as well as a 24" slug barrel with rifle sights. The finish is blued, with a checkered stock. A combination two-barrel set that includes the deer barrel would be worth approximately 20% additional. This model was introduced in 1983 and is currently produced.

NIB	Exc.	V.G.	Good	Fair	Poor
340	300	250	200	150	100

Model 1400 Quail Unlimited

This 12 gauge semiautomatic shotgun model was introduced in 1993. It features compact engraved receiver with 26" vent-rib barrel supplied with WinChoke tubes. Stock is checkered walnut. Gun weighs 7.25 lbs.

NIB	Exc.	V.G.	Good	Fair	Poor
340	300	250	200	150	100

Model 1400 Ranger Deer Combo

This model features a 12 gauge 22" smooth barrel and a 28" vent rib barrel with three WinChokes.

NIB	Exc.	V.G.	Good	Fair	Poor
340	300	250	200	150	100

Model 22

Introduced in 1975 this side-by-side shotgun was manufactured by Laurona in Spain to Winchester's specifications for the European market. It had an oil-finished stock with checked pistol-grip semi-beavertail forearm and hand-engraved receiver. The finish was black chrome. The gun was fitted with double triggers, matted rib and offered in 12 gauge only with 28" barrels. It weighed 6-3/4 lbs.

NIB	Exc.	V.G.	Good	Fair	Poor
1250	950	700	550	400	200

Model 91

This over and under shotgun was built for Winchester by Laurona for its European markets. Offered in 12 gauge only with 28" barrels the barrels were fit-

Model 1400 Quail Unlimited

ted with a ventilated rib. The gun was offered with single or double triggers with hand checkered walnut stock with oil finish and hand engraved receiver. The finish was black chrome. Gun weighs 7-1/2 lbs.

NIB	Exc.	V.G.	Good	Fair	Poor
1000	800	600	500	400	200

Model 23 Series

Model 23 XTR

This is a side-by-side, double-barrel shotgun chambered for 12 or 20 gauge. It is offered with 25.5", 26", 28", or 30" vent rib barrels with 3" chambers and various choke combinations. It is a boxlock gun that features a single trigger and automatic ejectors. It is scroll-engraved with a coin-finished receiver, blued barrels, and a checkered, select walnut stock. It was introduced in 1978. This model is available in a number of configurations that differ in the amount of ornamentation and the quality of materials and workmanship utilized in their construction. These models and their values are as follows:

Grade I-Discontinued

Exc.	V.G.	Good	Fair	Poor
900	750	650	500	400

Pigeon Grade-With WinChokes

Exc.	V.G.	Good	Fair	Poor
1000	850	750	600	500

Pigeon Grade Lightweight-Straight Stock

Exc.	V.G.	Good	Fair	Poor
1300	1000	900	750	600

Golden Quail

This series was available in 28 gauge and .410, as well as 12 or 20 gauge. It features 25.5" barrels that are choked improved cylinder/modified. It features a straight-grip, English-style stock with a recoil pad. The .410 version would be worth approximately 10% more than the values given. This series was discontinued in 1987.

Exc.	V.G.	Good	Fair	Poor
1500	1250	1100	850	750

Model 23 Light Duck

This version is chambered for 20 gauge and was offered with a 28" full and full-choked barrel. There were 500 manufactured in 1985.

Exc.	V.G.	Good	Fair	Poor
1500	1250	1100	850	750

Model 23 Heavy Duck

This version is chambered for 12 gauge with 30" full and full-choked barrels. There were 500 manufactured in 1984.

Exc.	V.G.	Good	Fair	Poor
1500	1250	1100	850	750

Model 21

This is a high-quality, side-by-side, double-barrel shotgun that features a boxlock action and is chambered for 12, 16, 20, and 28 gauges, as well as .410. It is featured with various barrel lengths and choke combinations. Since 1960 the Model 21 has been available on a custom-order basis only. It is available in five basic configurations that differ in the options offered, the amount of ornamentation, and the quality of materials and workmanship utilized in their construction. See previous Model 21 entry.

MODEL 101 SERIES

Model 101 Field Grade

This is an over/under, double-barrel shotgun chambered for 12, 20, and 28 gauge, as well as .410. It was offered with 26", 28", or 30" vent rib barrels with various choke combinations. As of 1983 screw-in chokes have been standard, and models so furnished would be worth approximately $50 additional. This is a boxlock gun with a single selective trigger and automatic ejectors. The receiver is engraved; the finish blued with a checkered walnut stock. It was manufactured between 1963 and 1987.
28 Gauge-Add 40%. .410-Add 50%.

Exc.	V.G.	Good	Fair	Poor
750	650	500	375	300

Waterfowl Model

This version of the Model 101 is chambered for 12 gauge with 3" chambers. It has 30" or 32" vent rib barrels and a matte finish.

Exc.	V.G.	Good	Fair	Poor
1250	1000	850	650	500

Model 101 Magnum

This version is similar to the Field Grade, chambered for 12 or 20 gauge with 3" Magnum chambers. It was offered with 30" barrels with various chokes. The stock is furnished with a recoil pad. It was manufactured between 1966 and 1981.

Exc.	V.G.	Good	Fair	Poor
775	675	525	400	325

Model 101 Skeet Grade

This version was offered with 26" skeet-bored barrels with a competition rib and a skeet-type walnut stock. It was manufactured between 1966 and 1984.

Exc.	V.G.	Good	Fair	Poor
950	850	750	500	400

Model 101 Three-Gauge Skeet Set

This combination set was offered with three barrels, chambered for 20 and 28 gauge, as well as .410. It was furnished with a fitted case and manufactured between 1974 and 1984.

Exc.	V.G.	Good	Fair	Poor
1850	1450	1000	750	650

Model 101 Trap Grade

This version is chambered for 12 gauge only and was offered with 30" or 32" competition-ribbed barrels, choked for trap shooting. It is furnished with a competition-type stock. It was manufactured between 1966 and 1984.

Exc.	V.G.	Good	Fair	Poor
1250	1000	850	650	500

Model 101 Pigeon Grade

This is a more deluxe engraved version of the Model 101, chambered for 12, 20, or 28 gauge, as well as .410. It features a coin-finished receiver with a fancy checkered walnut stock. It was introduced in 1974.

Exc.	V.G.	Good	Fair	Poor
1500	1250	1000	800	700

Super Pigeon Grade

This is a deluxe version of the Model 101, chambered for 12 gauge. It is heavily engraved with several gold inlays. The receiver is blued, and it features a high-grade walnut stock with fleur-de-lis checkering. It was imported between 1985 and 1987.

Exc.	V.G.	Good	Fair	Poor
4000	3500	2750	2000	1650

Model 101 Diamond Grade

This is a competition model, chambered for all four gauges. It was offered in either a trap or skeet configuration with screw-in chokes, an engraved matte-finished receiver, and a select checkered walnut stock. The skeet model features recoil-reducing muzzle vents.

Exc.	V.G.	Good	Fair	Poor
1600	1250	1000	750	600

Model 501 Grand European

This is an over/under, double-barreled shotgun chambered for 12 or 20 gauge. It was available in trap or skeet configurations and was offered with a 27", 30", or 32" vent rib barrel. It is heavily engraved and matte-finished, with a select checkered walnut stock. It was manufactured between 1981 and 1986.

Exc.	V.G.	Good	Fair	Poor
1500	1150	950	700	550

Model 501 Presentation Grade

This is a deluxe version chambered in 12 gauge only. It is ornately engraved and gold-inlaid. The stock is made out of presentation-grade walnut. It was furnished with a fitted case. It was manufactured between 1984 and 1987.

Exc.	V.G.	Good	Fair	Poor
3000	2500	2000	1500	1250

Combination Gun

This is an over/under rifle/shotgun combination chambered for 12 gauge over .222, .223, .30-06, and the 9.3x74R cartridges. It features 25" barrels. The shotgun tube has a screw-in choke. It is engraved in the fashion of the Model 501 Grand European and features a select checkered walnut stock. It was manufactured between 1983 and 1985.

Exc.	V.G.	Good	Fair	Poor
2250	2000	1750	1250	1000

Express Rifle

This is an over/under, double-barreled rifle chambered for the .257 Roberts, .270, 7.7x65R, .30-06, and the 9.3x74R cartridges. It features 23.5" barrels with a solid rib and express sights. It is engraved with game scenes and has a satin-finished receiver. The stock is checkered select walnut. It was manufactured in 1984 and 1985.

Exc.	V.G.	Good	Fair	Poor
1750	1500	1250	1000	750

Model 96 Xpert

This is a utility-grade, over/under, double-barreled shotgun that is mechanically similar to the Model 101. It is chambered for 12 or 20 gauge and was offered with various barrel lengths and choke combinations. It has a boxlock action with single selective trigger and automatic ejectors. The plain receiver is blued, with a checkered walnut stock. It was manufactured between 1976 and 1982. A competition-grade model for trap or skeet was also available and would be worth approximately the same amount.

Exc.	V.G.	Good	Fair	Poor
650	550	450	350	275

Model 1001 Field

A new addition to the U.S.R.A. product line for 1993. This over/under shotgun is available in 12 gauge only, with a 28" ventilated rib barrel furnished with WinPlus choke tubes. A walnut checkered pistol stock is standard. The finish is blued with scroll engraving on the receiver. The receiver top has a matte finish. The gun weighs 7 lbs.

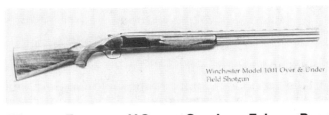

Winchester Model 1001 Over & Under Field Shotgun

NIB	Exc.	V.G.	Good	Fair	Poor
875	750	650	500	300	150

Model 1001 Sporting Clays I & II

This model features different stock dimensions, a fuller pistol grip, a radiused recoil pad, and a wider vent rib fitted on a 28" barrel (Sporting Clays I model, the Sporting Clays II features a 30" barrel). Comes complete with choke tubes. The frame has a silver-nitrate finish and special engraving featuring a flying clay target. Introduced in 1993. Gun weighs 7.75 lbs.

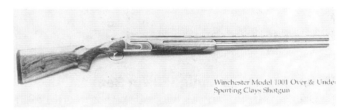

Winchester Model 1001 Over & Under Sporting Clays Shotgun

NIB	Exc.	V.G.	Good	Fair	Poor
1000	800	700	550	300	150

WINCHESTER COMMEMORATIVE RIFLES

Since the early 1960s, Winchester has produced a number of special Model 1894 rifles and carbines that commemorated certain historic events, places, or individuals. In some cases they are slightly embellished and in others are quite ornate. The general liquidity of these commemoratives has not been as good as would be expected. In some cases they were produced in excessive amounts and could not, in all honesty, be considered limited-production items. In any case, in our opinion one should purchase weapons of this nature for their enjoyment factor as the investment potential is not sufficient reason for their purchase. As with all commemoratives, in order to realize the collector potential they must be NIB with all supplied materials including, in the case of Winchester, the colorful outer sleeve that encased the factory carton. If a Winchester commemorative rifle has been cocked leaving a line on the hammer or the lever, many collectors will show little or no interest in its acquisition. If they have been fired, they will realize little premium over a standard, Post-1964 Model 94. A number of commemoratives have been ordered by outside concerns and are technically not factory issues. Most have less collectibility than the factory-issued models. There are a number of concerns that specialize in marketing the total range of Winchester commemorative rifles. We list the factory-issue commemoratives with their current value, their issue price, and the number manufactured.

1964 Wyoming Diamond Jubilee-Carbine

NIB	Issue	Amt. Mfg.
1295	100	1,500

1966 Centennial-Rifle

NIB	Issue	Amt. Mfg.
450	125	102,309

1966 Centennial-Carbine

NIB	Issue	Amt. Mfg.
425	125	102,309

1966 Nebraska Centennial-Rifle

NIB	Issue	Amt. Mfg.
1195	100	2,500

1967 Canadian Centennial-Rifle

NIB	Issue	Amt. Mfg.
450	125	

1967 Canadian Centennial-Carbine

NIB	Issue	Amt. Mfg.
425	125	90,301

1967 Alaskan Purchase Centennial-Carbine

NIB	Issue	Amt. Mfg.
1495	125	1,500

1968 Illinois Sesquicentennial-Carbine

NIB	Issue	Amt. Mfg.
395	110	37,648

1968 Buffalo Bill-Carbine

NIB	Issue	Amt. Mfg.
425	130	112,923

1968 Buffalo Bill-Rifle

NIB	Issue	Amt. Mfg.
450	130	

1968 Buffalo Bill "1 or 300"-Rifle

NIB	Issue	Amt. Mfg.
2650	1000	300

1969 Theodore Roosevelt-Rifle

NIB	Issue	Amt. Mfg.
450	135	—

1969 Theodore Roosevelt-Carbine

NIB	Issue	Amt. Mfg.
425	135	52,386

1969 Golden Spike Carbine

NIB	Issue	Amt. Mfg.
395	120	69,996

1970 Cowboy Commemorative Carbine

NIB	Issue	Amt. Mfg.
450	125	27,549

1970 Cowboy Carbine "1 of 300"

NIB	Issue	Amt. Mfg.
2650	1000	300

1970 Northwest Territories (Canadian)

NIB	Issue	Amt. Mfg.
850	150	2,500

1970 Northwest Territories Deluxe (Canadian)

NIB	Issue	Amt. Mfg.
1100	250	500

1970 Lone Star-Rifle

NIB	Issue	Amt. Mfg.
450	140	

1970 Lone Star-Carbine

NIB	Issue	Amt. Mfg.
425	140	38,385

1971 NRA Centennial-Rifle

NIB	Issue	Amt. Mfg.
425	150	21,000

1971 NRA Centennial-Musket

NIB	Issue	Amt. Mfg.
425	150	23,400

1971 Yellow Boy (European)

NIB	Issue	Amt. Mfg.
1150	250	500

1971 Royal Canadian Mounted Police (Canadian)

NIB	Issue	Amt. Mfg.
795	190	9,500

1971 Mounted Police (Canadian)

NIB	Issue	Amt. Mfg.
795	190	5,100

1971 Mounted Police, Presentation

NIB	Issue	Amt. Mfg.
9995	—	10

1973 Texas Ranger-Carbine

NIB	Issue	Amt. Mfg.
695	135	4,850

1973 Texas Ranger Presentation Model

NIB	Issue	Amt. Mfg.
2650	1000	150

1974 Apache (Canadian)

NIB	Issue	Amt. Mfg.
795	150	8,600

1974 Commanche (Canadian)

NIB	Issue	Amt. Mfg.
795	230	11,500

1974 Klondike Gold Rush (Canadian)

NIB	Issue	Amt. Mfg.
795	240	10,500

1975 Klondike Gold Rush-Dawson City Issue (Canadian)

NIB	Issue	Amt. Mfg.
8500	—	25

1976 Sioux (Canadian)

NIB	Issue	Amt. Mfg.
795	280	10,000

1976 Little Bighorn (Canadian)

NIB	Issue	Amt. Mfg.
795	300	11,000

1976 U.S. Bicentennial Carbine

NIB	Issue	Amt. Mfg.
595	325	19,999

1973 Texas Ranger-Carbine

1977 Wells Fargo

1977 Legendary Lawmen

1977 Wells Fargo

NIB	Issue	Amt. Mfg.
495	350	19,999

1977 Legendary Lawmen

NIB	Issue	Amt. Mfg.
495	375	19,999

1977 Limited Edition I

NIB	Issue	Amt. Mfg.
1395	1500	1,500

1977 Cheyenne-.22 Cal. (Canadian)

NIB	Issue	Amt. Mfg.
695	320	5,000

1977 Cheyenne-.44-40 Cal. (Canadian)

NIB	Issue	Amt. Mfg.
795	300	11,225

1977 Cherokee-.22 Cal. (Canadian)

NIB	Issue	Amt. Mfg.
695	385	3,950

1977 Cherokee-.30-30 Cal. (Canadian)

NIB	Issue	Amt. Mfg.
795	385	9,000

1978 "One of One Thousand" (European)

NIB	Issue	Amt. Mfg.
7500	5000	250

1978 Antler Game Carbine

NIB	Issue	Amt. Mfg.
495	375	19,999

1979 Limited Edition II

NIB	Issue	Amt. Mfg.
1395	1500	1,500

1981 John Wayne

1979 Legendary Frontiersman Rifle
NIB	Issue	Amt. Mfg.
495	425	19,999

1979 Matched Set of 1,000
NIB	Issue	Amt. Mfg.
2250	3000	1,000

1979 Bat Masterson (Canadian)
NIB	Issue	Amt. Mfg.
795	650	8,000

1980 Alberta Diamond Jubilee (Canadian)
NIB	Issue	Amt. Mfg.
795	650	2,700

1980 Alberta Diamond Jubilee Deluxe (Canadian)
NIB	Issue	Amt. Mfg.
1495	1900	300

1980 Saskatchewan Diamond Jubilee (Canadian)
NIB	Issue	Amt. Mfg.
795	695	2,700

1980 Saskatchewan Diamond Jubilee Deluxe (Canadian)
NIB	Issue	Amt. Mfg.
1495	1995	300

1980 Oliver Winchester
NIB	Issue	Amt. Mfg.
695	375	19,999

1981 U.S. Border Patrol
NIB	Issue	Amt. Mfg.
595	1195	1,000

1981 U.S. Border Patrol-Member's Model
NIB	Issue	Amt. Mfg.
595	695	800

1981 Calgary Stampede (Canadian)
NIB	Issue	Amt. Mfg.
1250	2200	1,000

1981 Canadian Pacific Centennial (Canadian)
NIB	Issue	Amt. Mfg.
550	800	2,000

1981 Canadian Pacific Centennial Presentation (Canadian)
NIB	Issue	Amt. Mfg.
1100	2200	300

1981 Canadian Pacific Employee's Model (Canadian)
NIB	Issue	Amt. Mfg.
550	800	2,000

1981 John Wayne (Canadian)
NIB	Issue	Amt. Mfg.
1095	995	1,000

1981 John Wayne
NIB	Issue	Amt. Mfg.
895	600	49,000

1981 Duke
NIB	Issue	Amt. Mfg.
2950	2250	1,000

1981 John Wayne "1 of 300" Set
NIB	Issue	Amt. Mfg.
6500	10000	300

1982 Annie Oakley

1983 Chief Crazy Horse

1982 Great Western Artist I

NIB	Issue	Amt. Mfg.
1195	2200	999

1982 Great Western Artist II

NIB	Issue	Amt. Mfg.
1195	2200	999

1982 Annie Oakley

NIB	Issue	Amt. Mfg.
695	699	6,000

1983 Chief Crazy Horse

NIB	Issue	Amt. Mfg.
595	600	19,999

1983 American Bald Eagle

NIB	Issue	Amt. Mfg.
595	895	2,800

1983 American Bald Eagle-Deluxe

NIB	Issue	Amt. Mfg.
3000	2995	200

1985 Boy Scout 75th Anniversary-.22 Cal.

1985 Boy Scout 75th Anniversary-Eagle Scout

1986 120th Anniversary Model-Carbine-.44-40 Cal.

1983 Oklahoma Diamond Jubilee

NIB	Issue	Amt. Mfg.
1395	2250	1,001

1984 Winchester-Colt Commemorative Set

NIB	Issue	Amt. Mfg.
2250	3995	2,300

1985 Boy Scout 75th Anniversary-.22 Cal.

NIB	Issue	Amt. Mfg.
595	615	15,000

1985 Boy Scout 75th Anniversary-Eagle Scout

NIB	Issue	Amt. Mfg.
3000	2140	1,000

Texas Sesquicentennial Model-Rifle-.38-55 Cal.

NIB	Issue	Amt. Mfg.
2400	2995	1,500

Texas Sesquicentennial Model-Carbine-.38-55 Cal.

NIB	Issue	Amt. Mfg.
695	695	15,000

Texas Sesquicentennial Model Set with Bowie Knife

NIB	Issue	Amt. Mfg.
6250	7995	150

1986 Model 94 Ducks Unlimited

NIB	Issue	Amt. Mfg.
650	—	2,800

1986 Statue of Liberty

NIB	Issue	Amt. Mfg.
7000	6500	100

1986 120th Anniversary Model-Carbine-.44-40 Cal.

NIB	Issue	Amt. Mfg.
895	995	1,000

1986 European 1 of 1,000 Second Series (European)

NIB	Issue	Amt. Mfg.
7000	6000	150

1987 U.S. Constitution 200th Anniversary-.44-40

NIB	Issue	Amt. Mfg.
13000	12000	17

1990 Wyoming Centennial-.30-30

NIB	Issue	Amt. Mfg.
1095	895	500

1991 Winchester 125th Anniversary

NIB	Issue	Amt. Mfg.
5500	4995	61

1992 Arapaho-.30-30

NIB	Issue	Amt. Mfg.
1095	895	500

1992 Ontario Conservation-.30-30

NIB	Issue	Amt. Mfg.
1195	1195	400

1992 Kentucky Bicentennial-.30-30

NIB	Issue	Amt. Mfg.
1095	995	500

1993 Nez Perce-.30-30

NIB	Issue	Amt. Mfg.
1095	995	600

1995 Florida Sesquicentennial Carbine

NIB	Issue	Amt. Mfg.
1195	1195	360

1996 Wild Bill Hickok Carbine

NIB	Issue	Amt. Mfg.
1195	1195	350

WINCHESTER SERIAL NUMBERS

MODEL 100

Records at the factory indicate the following serial numbers were assigned to guns at the end of the calendar year.

Year	Serial	Year	Serial
1961 —	1 to 32189	1968 —	210053
62 —	60760	69 —	A210999
63 —	78863	70 —	229995
64 —	92016	71 —	242999
65 —	135388	72 —	A258001
66 —	145239	73 —	A262833
67 —	209498		

MODEL 74

Records at the factory indicate the following serial numbers were assigned to guns at the end of the calendar year.

Year	Serial	Year	Serial
1939 —	1 to 30890	1948 —	223788
40 —	67085	49 —	249900
41 —	114355	50 —	276012
42 —	128293	51 —	302124
43 —	None	52 —	328236
44 —	128295	53 —	354348
45 —	128878	54 —	380460
46 —	145168	55 —	406574
47 —	173524		

MODEL 88

Records at the factory indicate the following serial numbers were assigned to guns at the end of the calendar year.

Year	Serial	Year	Serial
1955 —	1 to 18378	1965 —	162699
56 —	36756	66 —	192595
57 —	55134	67 —	212416
58 —	73512	68 —	230199
59 —	91890	69 —	H239899
60 —	110268	70 —	H258229
61 —	128651	71 —	H266784
62 —	139838	72 —	H279014
63 —	148858	73 —	H283718
64 —	160307		

MODEL 71

Records at the factory indicate the following serial numbers were assigned to guns at the end of the calendar year.

Year	Serial	Year	Serial
1935 —	1 to 4	1947 —	25758
36 —	7821	48 —	27900
37 —	12988	49 —	29675
38 —	14690	50 —	31450
39 —	16155	51 —	33225
40 —	18267	52 —	35000
41 —	20810	53 —	37500
42 —	21959	54 —	40770
43 —	22048	55 —	43306
44 —	22051	56 —	45843
45 —	22224	57 —	47254
46 —	23534		

MODEL 70

Records at the factory indicate the following serial numbers were assigned to guns at the end of the calendar year.

Year	Serial	Year	Serial
1935 —	1 to 19	1950 —	173150
36 —	2238	51 —	206625
37 —	11573	52 —	238820
38 —	17844	53 —	282735
39 —	23991	54 —	323530
40 —	31675	55 —	361025
41 —	41753	56 —	393595
42 —	49206	57 —	425283
43 —	49983	58 —	440792
44 —	49997	59 —	465040
45 —	5 0921	60 —	504257
46 —	58382	61 —	545446
47 —	75675	62 —	565592
48 —	101680	63 —	581471
49 —	131580		

All post-64 Model 70s began with the serial number 700000

Year	Serial	Year	Serial
1964 —	740599	1973 —	G1128731
65 —	809177	74 —	G1175000
66 —	833795	75 —	G1218700
67 —	869000	76 —	G1266000
68 —	925908	77 —	G1350000
69 —	G941900	78 —	G1410000
70 —	G957995	79 —	G1447000
71 —	G1018991	80 —	G1490709
72 —	G1099257	81 —	G1537134

MODEL 63

Records at the factory indicate the following serial numbers were assigned to guns at the end of the calendar year.

Year	Serial	Year	Serial
1933 —	1 to 2667	1946 —	61607
34 —	5361	47 —	71714
35 —	9830	48 —	80519
36 —	16781	49 —	88889
37 —	25435	50 —	97259
38 —	30934	51 —	105629
39 —	36055	52 —	114000
40 —	41456	53 —	120500
41 —	47708	54 —	127000
42 —	51258	55 —	138000
43 —	51631	56 —	150000
44 —	51656	57 —	162345
45 —	53853	58 —	174692

MODEL 62

Factory records indicate the following serial numbers were assigned to guns at the end of the calendar year.

Year	Serial	Year	Serial
1932 —	1 to 7643	1946 —	183756
33 —	10695	47 —	219085
34 —	14090	48 —	252298
35 —	23924	49 —	262473
36 —	42759	50 —	272648
37 —	66059	51 —	282823
38 —	80205	52 —	293000
39 —	96534	53 —	310500
40 —	116393	54 —	328000
41 —	137379	55 —	342776
42 —	155152	56 —	357551
43 —	155422	57 —	383513
44 —	155425	58 —	409475
45 —	156073		

MODEL 61

Records at the factory indicate the following serial numbers were assigned to guns at the end of the calendar year.

Year	Serial	Year	Serial
1932 —	1 to 3532	1948 —	115281
33 —	6008	49 —	125461
34 —	8554	50 —	135641
35 —	12379	51 —	145821
36 —	20615	52 —	156000
37 —	30334	53 —	171000
38 —	36326	54 —	186000
39 —	42610	55 —	200962
40 —	49270	56 —	215923
41 —	57493	57 —	229457
42 —	59871	58 —	242992
43 —	59872	59 —	262793
44 —	59879	60 —	282594
45 —	60512	61 —	302395
46 —	71629	62 —	322196
47 —	92297	63 —	342001

This model was discontinued in 1963. For some unknown reason there are no actual records available from 1949 through 1963. The serial number figures for these years are arrived at by taking the total production figure of 342,001, subtracting the last known number of 115281, and dividing the difference equally by the number of remaining years available, (15).

MODEL 55 CENTERFIRE

Records at the factory indicate the following serial numbers were assigned to guns at the end of the calendar year.

Year	Serial	Year	Serial
1924 —	1 to 836	1929 —	12258
25 —	2783	30 —	17393
26 —	4957	31 —	18198
27 —	8021	32 —	19204
28 —	10467	33 —	Clean-up 20580

MODEL 54

Records at the factory indicate the following serial numbers were assigned to guns at the end of the calendar year.

Year	Serial	Year	Serial
1925 —	1 to 3140	1931 —	36731
26—	8051	32 —	38543
27 —	14176	33 —	40722
28 —	19587	34 —	43466
29 —	29104	35 —	47125
30 —	32499	36 —	50145

MODEL 53

In the case of the Model 53 the following list pertains to the number of guns produced each year rather than a serial number list.

The Model 53 was serially numbered concurrently with the Model 92.

MODEL 53s PRODUCED

1924 —	1488	1929 —	1733
25 —	2861	30 —	920
26 —	2531	31 —	621
27 —	2297	32 —	206
28 —	1958		

This model was discontinued in 1932, however, a clean-up of production continued for nine more years with an additional 486 guns.

TOTAL PRODUCTION APPROXIMATELY - 15,100

MODEL 52

Records at the factory indicate the following serial numbers were assigned to guns at the end of the calendar year.

1920 —	None indicated	1950 —	70766
21 —	397	51 —	73385
22 —	745	52 —	76000
23 —	1394	53 —	79500
24 —	2361	54 —	80693
25 —	3513	55 —	81831
26 —	6383	56 —	96869
27 —	9436	57 —	97869
28 —	12082	58 —	98599
29 —	14594	59 —	98899
30 —	17253	60 —	102200
31 —	21954	61 —	106986
32 —	24951	62 —	108718
33 —	26725	63 —	113583
34 —	29030	64 —	118447
35 —	32448	65 —	120992
36 —	36632	66 —	123537
37 —	40419	67 —	123727
38 —	43632	68 —	123917
39 —	45460	69 —	E124107
40 —	47519	70 —	E124297
41 —	50317	71 —	E124489
42 —	52129	72 —	E124574
43 —	52553	73 —	E124659
44 —	52560	74 —	E124744
45 —	52718	75 —	E124828
46 —	56080	76 —	E125019
47 —	60158	77 —	E125211
48 —	64265	78 —	E125315
49 —	68149		

This model was discontinued in 1978. A small clean-up of production was completed in 1979 with a total of 125,419.

MODEL 50

Records at the factory indicate the following serial numbers were assigned to guns at the end of the calendar year.

1954 —	1 to 24550	1958 —	122750
55 —	49100	59 —	147300
56 —	73650	60 —	171850
57 —	98200	61 —	196400

MODEL 42

Records at the factory indicate the following serial numbers were assigned to guns at the end of the calendar year.

1933 —	1 to 9398	1949 —	81107
34 —	13963	50 —	87071
35 —	17728	51 —	93038
36 —	24849	52 —	99000
37 —	30900	53 —	108201
38 —	34659	54 —	117200
39 —	38967	55 —	121883
40 —	43348	56 —	126566
41 —	48203	57 —	131249
42 —	50818	58 —	135932
43 —	50822	59 —	140615
44 —	50828	60 —	145298
45 —	51168	61 —	149981
46 —	54256	62 —	154664
47 —	64853	63 —	159353
48 —	75142		

MODEL 24

Records at the factory indicate the following serial numbers were assigned to guns at the end of the calendar year.

1939 —	1 to 8118	1944 —	33683
40 —	21382	45 —	34965
41 —	27045	46 —	45250
42 —	33670	47 —	58940
43 —	None recorded	48 —	64417

There were no records kept on this model from 1949 until its discontinuance in 1958. The total production was approximately 116,280.

MODEL 12

Records at the factory indicate the following serial numbers were assigned to guns at the end of the calendar year.

1912 —	5308	1938 —	779455
13 —	32418	39 —	814121
14 —	79765	40 —	856499
15 —	109515	41 —	907431
16 —	136412	42 —	958303
17 —	159391	43 —	975640
18 —	183461	44 —	975727
19 —	219457	45 —	990004
20 —	247458	46 —	1029152
21 —	267253	47 —	1102371
22 —	304314	48 —	1176055
23 —	346319	49 —	1214041
24 —	385196	50 —	1252028
25 —	423056	51 —	1290015
26 —	464564	52 —	1328002
27 —	510693	53 —	1399996
28 —	557850	54 —	1471990
29 —	600834	55 —	1541929
30 —	626996	56 —	1611868
31 —	651255	57 —	1651435
32 —	660110	58 —	1690999
33 —	664544	59 —	1795500
34 —	673994	60 —	1800000
35 —	686978	61 —	1930029

36 —	720316	62 —	1956990
37 —	754250	63 —	1962001

A clean-up of production took place from 1964 through 1972 with the ending serial number 1970899.

New Style M/12

1972 —	Y2000100-Y2006396
73 —	Y2015662
74 —	Y2022061
75 —	Y2024478
76 —	Y2025482
77 —	Y2025874
78 —	Y2026156
79 —	Y2026399

MODEL 1911 S.L.

Records at the factory indicate the following serial numbers were assigned to guns at the end of the calendar year.

1911 —	1 to 3819	1919 —	57337
12 —	27659	20 —	60719
13 —	36677	21 —	64109
14 —	40105	22 —	69132
15 —	43284	23 —	73186
16 —	45391	24 —	76199
17 —	49893	25 —	78611
18 —	52895		

The model 1911 was discontinued in 1925. However, guns were produced for three years after that date to clean up production and excess parts. When this practice ceased there were approximately 82,774 guns produced.

MODEL 1910

Records at the factory indicate the following serial numbers were assigned to guns at the end of the calendar year.

1910 —	1 to 4766	1924 —	17030
11 —	7695	25 —	17281
12 —	9712	26 —	17696
13 —	11487	27 —	18182
14 —	12311	28 —	18469
15 —	13233	29 —	18893
16 —	13788	30 —	19065
17 —	14255	31 —	19172
18 —	14625	32 —	19232
19 —	15665	33 —	19281
20 —	Not Available	34 —	19338
21 —	15845	35 —	19388
22 —	16347	36 —	19445
23 —	16637		

A clean-up of production continued into 1937 when the total of the guns were completed at approximately 20786.

MODEL 1907

Records at the factory indicate the following serial numbers were assigned to guns at the end of the calendar year.

1907 —	1 to 8657	1933 —	44806
08 —	14486	34 —	44990
09 —	19707	35 —	45203
10 —	23230	36 —	45482
11 —	25523	37 —	45920
12 —	27724	38 —	46419
13 —	29607	39 —	46758
14 —	30872	40 —	47296
15 —	32272	41 —	47957
16 —	36215	42 —	48275
17 —	38235	43 —	None
18 —	39172	44 —	None
19 —	40448	45 —	48281
20 —	Not Available	46 —	48395
21 —	40784	47 —	48996
22 —	41289	48 —	49684
23 —	41658	**49 —	50662
24 —	42029	**50 —	51640
25 —	42360	**51 —	52618
26 —	42688	**52 —	53596
27 —	43226	**53 —	54574
28 —	43685	**54 —	55552
29 —	44046	**55 —	56530
30 —	44357	**56 —	57508
31 —	44572	**57 —	58486
32 —	44683		

Actual records on serial numbers stops in 1948. The serial numbers ending each year from 1948 to 1957 were derived at by taking the last serial number recorded (58486) and the last number from 1948, (49684) and dividing the years of production, (9), which relates to 978 guns each year for the nine year period.

MODEL 1906

Records at the factory indicate the following serial numbers were assigned to guns at the end of the calendar year.

1906 —	1 to 52278	1920 —	None
07 —	89147	21 —	598691
08 —	114138	22 —	608011
09 —	165068	23 —	622601
10 —	221189	24 —	636163
11 —	273355	25 —	649952
12 —	327955	26 —	665484
13 —	381922	27 —	679692
14 —	422734	28 —	695915
15 —	453880	29 —	711202
16 —	483805	30 —	720116
17 —	517743	31 —	725978
18 —	535540	32 —	727353
19 —	593917		

A clean-up of production took place for the next few years with a record of production reaching approximately 729,305.

MODEL 1905

Records at the factory indicate the following serial numbers were assigned to guns at the end of the calendar year.

Year	Serial	Year	Serial
1905	1 to 5659	1913	25559
06	15288	14	26110
07	19194	15	26561
08	20385	16	26910
09	21280	17	27297
10	22423	18	27585
11	23503	19	28287
12	24602	20	29113

MODEL 1903

Records at the factory indicate the following serial numbers were assigned to guns at the end of the calendar year.

Year	Serial	Year	Serial
1903	Not Available	1918	92617
04	6944	19	96565
05	14865	20	Not Available
06	23097	21	97650
07	31852	22	99011
08	39105	23	100452
09	46496	24	101688
10	54298	25	103075
11	61679	26	104230
12	69586	27	105537
13	76732	28	107157
14	81776	29	109414
15	84563	30	111276
16	87148	31	112533
17	89501	32	112992

This model was discontinued in 1932, however, a clean up of parts was used for further production of approximately 2,000 guns. Total production was stopped at serial number 114962 in 1936.

MODEL 1901 SHOTGUN

Records at the factory indicate the following serial numbers were assigned to guns at the end of the calendar year.

Year	Serial	Year	Serial
1904	64856 to 64860	1913	72764
05	66483	14	73202
06	67486	15	73509
07	68424	16	73770
08	69197	17	74027
09	70009	18	74311
10	70753	19	74872
11	71441	20	77000
12	72167		

MODEL 1897

Records at the factory indicate the following serial numbers were assigned to guns at the end of the calendar year.

Year	Serial	Year	Serial
1897	to 32335	1928	796806
98	64668	29	807321
99	96999	30	812729
1900	129332	31	830721
01	161665	32	833926
02	193998	33	835637
03	226331	34	837364
04	258664	35	839728
05	296037	36	848684
06	334059	37	856729
07	377999	38	860725
08	413618	39	866938
09	446888	40	875945
10	481062	41	891190
11	512632	42	910072
12	544313	43	912265
13	575213	44	912327
14	592732	45	916472
15	607673	46	926409
16	624537	47	936682
17	646124	48	944085
18	668383	49	953042
19	691943	50	961999
20	696183	51	970956
21	700428	52	979913
22	715902	53	988860
23	732060	54	997827
24	744942	55	1006784
25	757629	56	1015741
26	770527	57	1024700
27	783574		

Records on this model are incomplete. The above serial numbers are estimated from 1897 through 1903 and again from 1949 through 1957. The actual records are in existence from 1904 through 1949.

MODEL 1895

Records at the factory indicate the following serial numbers were assigned to guns at the end of the calendar year.

Year	Serial	Year	Serial
1895	1 to 287	1914	72082
96	5715	15	174233
97	7814	16	377411
98	19871	17	389106
99	26434	18	392731
1900	29817	19	397250
01	31584	20	400463
02	35601	21	404075
03	42514	22	407200
04	47805	23	410289
05	54783	24	413276
06	55011	25	417402
07	57351	26	419533
08	60002	27	421584
09	60951	28	422676
10	63771	29	423680
11	65017	30	424181
12	67331	31	425132
13	70823	32	425825

MODEL 94

Records at the factory indicate the following serial numbers were assigned to guns at the end of the calendar year.

Year	Serial	Year	Serial
1894	1 to 14579	1939	1101051
95	44359	40	1142423
96	76464	41	1191307
97	111453	42	1221289
98	147684	43	No Record Avail.
99	183371	44	No Record Avail.

Year	Serial	Year	Serial
1900 —	204427	45 —	No Record Avail.
01 —	233975	46 —	No Record Avail.
02 —	273854	47 —	No Record Avail.
03 —	291506	48 —	1500000
04 —	311363	49 —	1626100
05 —	337557	50 —	1724295
06 —	378878	51 —	1819800
07 —	430985	52 —	1910000
08 —	474241	53 —	2000000
09 —	505831	54 —	2071100
10 —	553062	55 —	2145296
11 —	599263	56 —	2225000
12 —	646114	57 —	2290296
13 —	703701	58 —	2365887
14 —	756066	59 —	2410555
15 —	784052	60 —	2469821
16 —	807741	61 —	2500000
17 —	821972	62 —	2551921
18 —	838175	63 —	2586000
19 —	870762	*1964 —	2700000
20 —	880627		2797428
21 —	908318	65 —	2894428
22 —	919583	66 —	2991927
23 —	938539	67 —	3088458
24 —	953198	68 —	3185691
25 —	978523	69 —	3284570
26 —	997603	70 —	3381299
27 —	1027571	71 —	3557385
28 —	1054465	72 —	3806499
29 —	1077097	73 —	3929364
30 —	1081755	74 —	4111426
31 —	1084156	75 —	4277926
32 —	1087836	76 —	4463553
33 —	1089270	77 —	4565925
34 —	1091190	78 —	4662210
35 —	1099605	79 —	4826596
36 —	1100065	80 —	4892951
37 —	1100679	81 —	5024957
38 —	1100915	62 —	5103248

The post-64 Model 94 began with serial number 2700000.

Serial number 1000000 was presented to President Calvin Coolidge in 1927.

Serial number 1500000 was presented to President Harry S. Truman in 1948.

Serial number 2000000 was presented to President Dwight D. Eisenhower in 1953.

Serial numbers 2500000 and 3000000 were presented to the Winchester Gun Museum, now located in Cody, Wyoming.

Serial number 3500000 was not constructed until 1979 and was sold at auction in Las Vegas, Nevada. Serial number 4000000—whereabouts unknown at this time.

Serial number 4500000—shipped to Italy by Olin in 1978. Whereabouts unknown.

Serial number 5000000—in New Haven, not constructed as of March 1983.

MODEL 1892

Records at the factory indicate the following serial numbers were assigned to guns at the end of the calendar year.

Year	Serial	Year	Serial
1892 —	1 to 23701	1913 —	742675
93 —	35987	14 —	771444
94 —	73508	15 —	804622
95 —	106721	16 —	830031
96 —	144935	17 —	853819
97 —	159312	18 —	870942
98 —	165431	19 —	903649
99 —	171820	20 —	906754
1900 —	183411	21 —	910476
01 —	191787	22 —	917300
02 —	208871	23 —	926329
03 —	253935	24 —	938641
04 —	278546	25 —	954997
05 —	315425	26 —	973896
06 —	376496	27 —	990883
07 —	437919	28 —	996517
08 —	476540	29 —	999238
09 —	522162	30 —	999730
10 —	586996	31 —	1000727
11 —	643483	32 —	1001324
12 —	694752		

MODEL 1890

Records on the Model 1890 are somewhat incomplete. Our records indicate the following serial numbers were assigned to guns at the end of the calendar year beginning with 1908. Actual records on the firearms that were manufactured between 1890 and 1907 will be available from the "Winchester Museum," located at The "Buffalo Bill Historical Center", P.O. Box 1020, Cody, WY 82414

Year	Serial	Year	Serial
1908 —	330000 to 363850	1920 —	None
09 —	393427	21 —	634783
10 —	423567	22 —	643304
11 —	451264	23 —	654837
12 —	478595	24 —	664613
13 —	506936	25 —	675774
14 —	531019	26 —	687049
15 —	551290	27 —	698987
16 —	570497	28 —	711354
17 —	589204	29 —	722125
18 —	603438	30 —	729015
19 —	630801	31 —	733178
		32 —	734454

The Model 1890 was discontinued in 1932, however, a clean-up of the production run lasted another 8+ years and included another 14,000 to 15,000 guns. Our figures indicate approximately 749,000 guns were made.

MODEL 1887

Records at the factory indicate the following serial numbers were assigned to guns at the end of the calendar year.

Year	Serial	Year	Serial
1887 —	1 to 7431	1893 —	54367
88 —	22408	94 —	56849
89 —	25673	95 —	58289
90 —	29105	96 —	60175
91 —	38541	97 —	63952
92 —	49763	98 —	64855

According to these records no guns were produced during the last few years of this model and it was therefore discontinued in 1901.

MODEL 1886

Records at the factory indicate the following serial numbers were assigned to guns at the end of the calendar year.

Year	Serial	Year	Serial
1886 —	1 to 3211	1905 —	138838
87 —	14728	06 —	142249
88 —	28577	07 —	145119
89 —	38401	08 —	147322
90 —	49723	09 —	148237
91 —	63601	10 —	150129
92 —	73816	11 —	151622
93 —	83261	12 —	152943
94 —	94543	13 —	152947
95 —	103708	14 —	153859
96 —	109670	15 —	154452
97 —	113997	16 —	154979
98 —	119192	17 —	155387
99 —	120571	18 —	156219
1900 —	122834	19 —	156930
01 —	125630	20 —	158716
02 —	128942	21 —	159108
03 —	132213	22 —	159337
04 —	135524		

No further serial numbers were recorded until the discontinuance of the model, which was in 1935 at 159994.

MODEL 1885 SINGLE SHOT

Records at the factory indicate the following serial numbers were assigned to guns at the end of the calendar year.

Year	Serial	Year	Serial
1885 —	1 to 375	1900 —	88501
86 —	6841	01 —	90424
87 —	18328	02 —	92031
88 —	30571	03 —	92359
89 —	45019	04 —	92785
90 —	None	05 —	93611
91 —	53700	06 —	94208
92 —	60371	07 —	95743
93 —	69534	08 —	96819
94 —	None	09 —	98097
95 —	73771	10 —	98506
96 —	78253	11 —	99012
97 —	78815	12 —	None
98 —	84700	13 —	100352
99 —	85086		

No further serial numbers were recorded until the end of 1923. The last number recorded was 139700.

MODEL 1876

Records at the factory indicate the following serial numbers were assigned to guns at the end of the calendar year.

Year	Serial	Year	Serial
1876 —	1 to 1429	1988 —	63539
77 —	3579	89 —	None
78 —	7967	90 —	None
79 —	8971	91 —	None
80 —	14700	92 —	63561
81 —	21759	93 —	63670
82 —	32407	94 —	63678
83 —	42410	95 —	None
84 —	54666	96 —	63702
85 —	58714	97 —	63869
86 —	60397	98 —	63871
87 —	62420		

MODEL 1873

Records at the factory indicate the following serial numbers were assigned to guns at the end of the calendar year.

Year	Serial	Year	Serial
1873 —	1 to 126	1897 —	513421
74 —	2726	98 —	525922
75 —	11325	99 —	541328
76 —	23151	1900 —	554128
77 —	23628	01 —	557236
78 —	27501	02 —	564557
79 —	41525	03 —	573957
80 —	63537	04 —	588953
81 —	81620	05 —	602557
82 —	109507	06 —	613780
83 —	145503	07 —	None
84 —	175126	08 —	None
85 —	196221	09 —	630385
86 —	222937	10 —	656101
87 —	225922	11 —	669324
88 —	284529	12 —	678527
89 —	323956	13 —	684419
90 —	363220	14 —	686510
91 —	405026	15 —	688431
92 —	441625	16 —	694020
93 —	466641	17 —	698617
94 —	481826	18 —	700734
95 —	499308	19 —	702042
96 —	507545		

No last number available: 1920, 21, 22, 23—720609.

MODEL 1866

Records at the factory indicate the following serial numbers were assigned to guns at the end of the calendar year.

Year	Serial	Year	Serial
1866 —	12476 to 14813	1883 —	162376
67 —	15578	84 —	163649
68 —	19768	85 --	163664
69 —	29516	86 —	165071
70 —	52527	87 —	165912
71 —	88184	88 —	167155
72 —	109784	89 —	167401
73 —	118401	90 —	167702
74 —	125038	91 —	169003
75 —	125965	92 —	None
76 —	131907	93 —	169007
77 —	148207	94 —	169011
78 —	150493	95 —	None
79 —	152201	96 —	None
80 —	154379	97 —	169015
81 —	156107	98 —	170100
82 —	159513	99 —	Discontinued

Winchester Engraving: A Synthesis

Winchester factory engraving on its guns is very rare and highly sought after by collectors. It is a subject that has been discussed and studied in detail over the last sixty years.

Many Winchester engraved rifles and shotguns built during the 19th century can be verified by factory records. A few models built prior to World War I can also be verified as well. The Winchester Model 21 has most of the factory records relating to style, gauge, special features, and engraving patterns. But a number of popular Winchester rifles and shotguns, the Models 12, 42, and 70, to name a few, have no such records, leaving the collector to rely on his own judgement. It is therefore imperative that if an engraved Winchester has available records to substantiate its genuineness the buyer must use that opportunity.

Winchester often used outside contractors to provide various firearm components such as barrels, sights, stocks, etc. Engraving was often given to outside contractors, particularly when the factory was understaffed or backlogged with too many orders. The incomparable master L. D. Nimschke worked from about 1850 to 1900 and engraved many outstanding Winchesters as an outside contractor. He often signed his work. Some Winchester engravings are signed by the engraver and others are not. A few Winchester factory engravers are considered by many collectors to be exceptional artisans and thus more collectible, with a resulting higher premium for the gun.

Beginning in 1871 Winchester began to employ factory engravers. The first of these was Herman L. Ulrich (1870 to 1880 & 1897 to 1923) in 1870, followed a year later by Conrad F. Ulrich (1871 to 1894) in 1871. Another family member, John Ulrich (1875 to 1918) joined Winchester in 1875. In 1905 John A. Gough (1905 to 1918) and Angelo J. Stokes (1905 to 1917) joined Winchester. Both of these engravers, Gough and Stokes, had distinctive styles that many collectors regard as exceptional craftsmanship. More Ulrichs became employed at Winchester with Leslie B. Ulrich in 1908 (1908 to 1925) and Alden George Ulrich (1919 to 1949) in 1919.

A knowledge of these dates will assist the collector in establishing whether or not a particular engraver could have engraved certain models. For example, Alden George Ulrich almost never signed his work, but he was responsible for some outstanding engraving on the Model 21 shotgun, introduced in 1930. Between 1930 and his death in 1949 Alden George was the only factory engraver at Winchester. Outside contractors, such as the master Rudolph Kornbrath, engraved Model 21s, as well, but not in the factory.

Modern factory engravers such as the Kusmit brothers, John and Nick, began engraving in 1949 and 1952, respectively, and were still active when the company was sold in 1981. Jasper Salerno, Joe Crowley and Pauline Muerrle, the company's first female engraver, worked at Winchester in the 1970s and 1980s. Some of these engravers did contract work for Winchester after 1981. Because factory records are almost non-existent for models, other than the Model 21, after World War II, it is important to secure the services of an expert prior to the purchase of an engraved Winchester.

There is an additional sub-category to collecting engraved Winchesters, and that is engraved guns presented to historically important individuals or to commemorate an important historical event. These Winchesters, if verifiable, are in a class by themselves. Many of these guns are priced in the hundreds of thousands of dollars. Since only a small number of individuals can have the pleasure of owning such a Winchester, some of these more outstanding examples will appear throughout the firearms section.

Whatever the collector's preferences regarding engraved Winchesters, I have yet to meet one who did not, at the very least, appreciate the beauty and historical significance of these rare and scarce firearms.

WINCHESTER ENGRAVING ARTISTRY

Krause Publications wishes to acknowledge and thank Wallace Bienfeld for the use of his outstanding photos of engraved Winchesters.

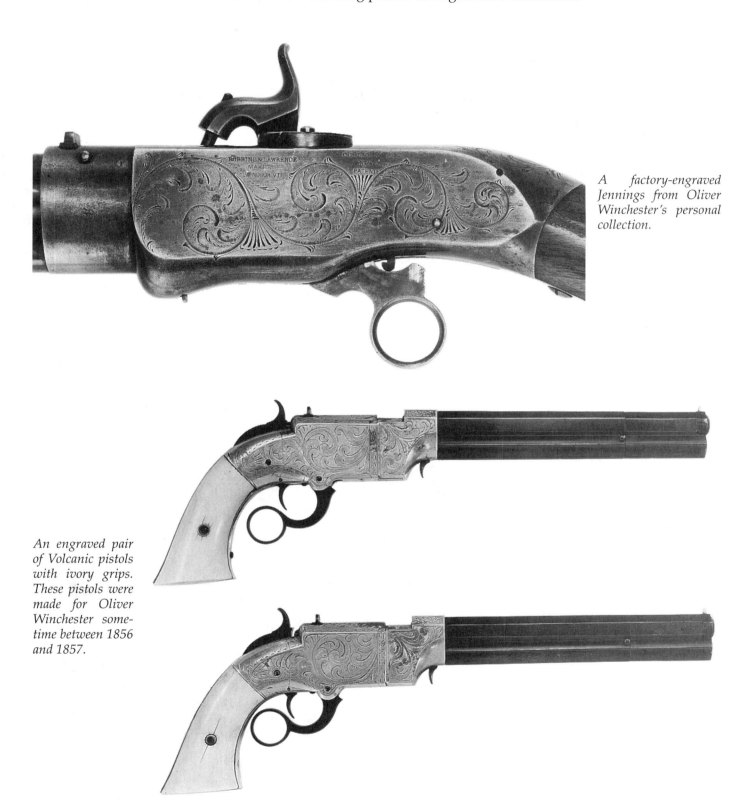

A factory-engraved Jennings from Oliver Winchester's personal collection.

An engraved pair of Volcanic pistols with ivory grips. These pistols were made for Oliver Winchester sometime between 1856 and 1857.

108 • *Winchester Engraving*

This Nimschke-engraved Henry rifle has a silver-plated brass frame. This a classic pattern employed by the engraver. Such Winchesters are highly sought after and very expensive.

The frame on this Winchester Model 1866 is solid silver. It is engraved by the master L.D. Nimschke. It was made for the President of Bolivia.

This Winchester Model 1866 was engraved by Conrad Ulrich. Ulrich's game scenes are legendary, and are a legacy that is part of the Winchester mystique.

This outstanding example of a John Ulrich-engraved Winchester is this Model 1876. The frame is gold-plated. The caliber is .50-95. It was presented to General Philip Sheridan in June of 1881.

This Model 1866 by Conrad Ulrich shows the strong influence of Gustave Young, under whom Ulrich studied.

This Model 1873 was engraved by John Ulrich, brother of Conrad Ulrich. The engraving patterns on this rifle are quite unusual in their themes. The rifle was shipped in February of 1883.

This Model 1873 was engraved by John Ulrich. The rifle has a silver-plated frame and is done in semi-relief.

This Model 1876 is chambered for the .45-75 cartridge and engraved by John Ulrich. It was built for Theodore Roosevelt. Stock is inlaid with a gold oval with engraved bear. A very historic Winchester.

This Winchester High Wall rifle is chambered for the .38-55 cartridge. It features a typical John Ulrich-type scroll-engraving pattern with game scene.

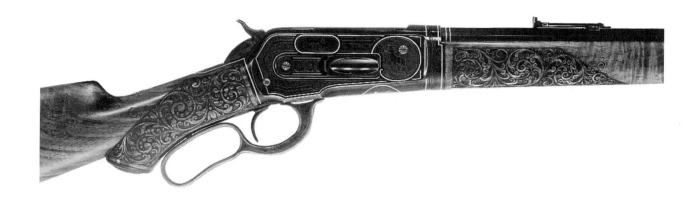

A Winchester Model 1886 engraved by John Ulrich. Chambered for .45-70 cartridge and engraved and inlaid in the Number 3 style. The fancy walnut stock is carved in the B style. This rifle was produced in September of 1899 as a factory sample.

116 • Winchester Engraving

This Winchester Model 1886 takedown rifle is engraved in the Number 1 style with Style A carved stocks. Caliber is .45-70. Engraved and inlaid by John Ulrich.

This Winchester Model 1892 is engraved in the Number 4 style with E carved stocks. A gold band borders the frame and takedown mount. Instead of a gold inlay on the barrel, platinum is used instead.

This Winchester Model 1892 may be the most elaborate gold-inlaid Winchester ever executed by John Ulrich. The stock carving is A style, the most expensive and intricate offered by the factory. This rifle is a **masterpiece** *of the engraver's art.*

This Winchester Model 1894 was shipped from the factory in November of 1902. It is engraved in the Number 2 style by John Ulrich. The stock carving is Style B. This Model 94 might have been a factory sample and display rifle.

This Winchester Model 1895 is chambered for the .405 cartridge. It is engraved in the Number 1 style with gold and platinum inlays. The stocks are carved in the B style.

This Winchester Model 1910 rifle was engraved in the Number 1 style, but with many custom touches. The rifle may have been executed by Winchester engraver George Ulrich, son of Conrad Ulrich.

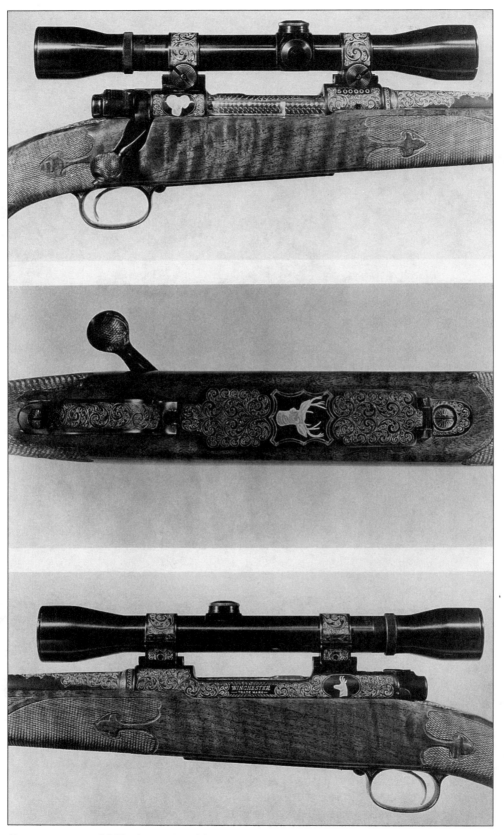

Factory-engraved Winchester Model 70s are quite rare. This Model 70 is the 500,000th and is done with gold inlays. The work was done by John or Nick Kusmit.

This Winchester Model 50 was engraved by John Kusmit and presented to General Curtis LeMay. A historic and rare Winchester.

This Winchester Model 12 was engraved by John Kusmit early in his career, sometime in the late 1940s. It is done in the 12-5 pattern. A close examination will give the reader an idea of the style of engraving used by John Kusmit during his career with Winchester.

This Winchester Model 94 rifle is an example of today's factory engraving. Winchester no longer has in-house engravers but the work is contracted out, much like it was in the 19th century, to master engravers.

Winchester Cartridge Boxes For Winchester Calibers

by Ray T. Giles

While Winchester guns have long been considered prime articles of collectible Americana, original boxes of antique ammunition have only recently begun to find broadened interest. Old boxed ammo was once the near-exclusive bailiwick of cartridge collectors. Now, however, it has become a highly sought-after collectible due mainly to the "cross-over" demand from gun collectors wishing to match up their guns with boxes of contemporary ammo. Winchester collectors are often heard to say something like, "I don't collect ammo; I just want an old, full box of .44-40's to go with my Model 73." Perhaps you've said similar words yourself. If you have, guess what? You're an ammo collector!

Unfortunately, most collectors would be hard pressed to date a pre-WWII ammo box to within five years of its date of manufacture. If it were pre-1906, they'd be lucky to come within ten years. There are a couple of good reasons for this.

First, early Winchester catalogs didn't picture contemporary ammo boxes. There were pictures of nearly every cartridge, but no boxes. Between WWI and WWII *some* catalogs as well as advertising flyers and posters pictured *some* boxes, but not regularly. Second, there are no books on the subject (yet)! The main reason for this is simply that there are virtually no original resources from which to research ammo box data. Cartridges, yes; boxes, no. Hence, a large amount of the "data" in such an undertaking must be somewhat speculative, relying largely on empirical knowledge and observation as well as anecdotal evidence, only a step away from hearsay and rumor. In other words a researcher's nightmare, a place where only fools would dare to tread, especially in print. Like me.

But over the years I've seen a lot of boxed ammo and picked the brains of many people who have seen still more. And, of course, I've read what there is to read. This chapter will be limited to boxes of ammunition in calibers made *by* Winchester *for* Winchester rifles (comparable to Dan Shuey's treatment of cartridges in this book in a Level 3 collection). I will attempt to bring together some of this accumulated knowledge in a way that will enable the reader to better date a box as well as have some idea of its value.

While a much broader work is still needed to cover *all* the calibers Winchester produced over the years, the scope of that undertaking far exceeds that contemplated here. Importantly, however, much of what the reader will find in this chapter will relate quite directly to Winchester boxes in the other, non-Winchester calibers.

Factors Affecting Collectibility

As with any collectible, several factors contribute to the desirability and value of ammo boxes. Condition and rarity rank at the top, as they do with most collectibles, so these will be dealt with first. All references to ammo box collectibility and pricing assumes boxes full of their original cartridges, not empty, partial or varying in any other particular from the way they were shipped from the factory.

The Condition Factor

Since the labels are the focal point of any ammo box, label condition is paramount. Starting with a perfect label with all its original color, detractions can be seen as scratches, tears and other missing paper; blotches, stains, fading or discoloration; price stickers or other non-factory labels or handwritten notations; tape residue; and of course, dirt and grime.

The box itself should be solid, retaining its original integrity without internal or external reinforcement or other obvious "help." The worst "help" (unfortunately, the most often seen) is tape, *any* kind of tape. I've seen 'em all ... transparent, cellophane, masking, white, surgical, black, paper, even duct tape ... and they *all* detract significantly. Sometimes tape can be removed with heat or solvents but the risk of losing label and/or ink in the process is high and some residue or staining is a virtual certainty. If I do nothing more in this chapter than underscore the fact that one should never put tape or price labels on a box, I'll feel I've added something important to the literature on the care and feeding of cartridge boxes.

Split seams or edge separations are not serious detractions and most often should be left as they are. However, if a box is obviously deteriorating under the load of its contents, I do not find it objectionable to effect a skillful repair with a clear, flexible paste but without reinforcements. If you're not skilled enough to do a first-rate job, forget this remedy. A second-rate job ends up being about as attractive as tape.

While most gun collectors tend to disdain refinished guns, thin cardboard ammo boxes that have been carrying around a load of lead, brass, copper and corrosive chemicals for 50 to 140 years may need some help just to preserve them for future generations. In many cases, it's either fix 'em or lose 'em and I hate to see a piece of history self-destruct. Just be careful not to destroy something in the process of attempting to fix it.

The Rarity Factor

Antique ammo boxes in "Excellent" condition (see below for grading definitions) are not common, with few exceptions, in any of the Winchester calibers except .22's. Relative to the number of loose rounds in existence, the boxes are quite scarce. Over time, as the boxes deteriorated, they were thrown away while their contents survived in coffee cans or other containers. If the rounds got shot up the boxes were generally discarded and disappeared along with the cartridges.

What we don't know is how many boxes were made in any given caliber or style. About all we have to go on are beginning and ending appearances in catalog listings coupled with what experience tells us may have survived. Some collectors assume that the quantity of guns produced in a given caliber is an indication of the rarity of the attendant ammo. I don't find this to be true. For instance, in the Winchester Model 86, .38-70 is a rare gun (under 1000 having been manufactured) but the ammo is not much scarcer than .40-82 or .40-65, calibers in which many more guns were manufactured. On the other hand, a full box of .50-100-450 is even less likely to be encountered than the Model 1886 that is chambered for it, rare though it is. Or try finding a nice two-piece box of 7.62 Russian (of which 100s of thousands were made) or .303 British for the Model 1895!

Other Value Factors

Demand for common calibers will always be high simply because of the number of guns out there for which people will want to have an original box of display ammo. Some people, like myself, avidly collect ammo boxes as collectibles in their own right. Shotshell boxes have become extremely popular, as have .22 rimfire boxes. The other metallics, from .22s on up, have also caught on in recent years, adding to the demand from those gun collectors who didn't know (or wouldn't admit) they were also ammo box collectors.

Graphics and color are very important in determining cartridge box popularity, just as they are for shotshell boxes. The Grizzly Bear design of the early 1940s is a very popular collectible, bringing higher prices than most other one-piece boxes, before or since. The yellow, blue and red box from the late 1930s lacks a bear but is still very colorful and out-sells the still older blue and white box even though the latter is Winchester's first one-piece box and is much scarcer in nice condition. The "Rainbow" Precision and Indoor Precision .22 boxes from the 1930s combine great graphics with rarity and both readily sell for more than $1000.

Grading and Grading Definitions

Grading, like beauty, lies in the eyes of the beholder. For instance, an "80%" condition gun may suggest a very different image in the minds of different people. So it is here. Overall box condition is the sum total of many variables, each of which will be weighted differently in accordance with the personal preferences of the individual collector or dealer. As a result, it is important to understand that assigning condition, even according to the objective criteria set forth below, remains, in the end, a very subjective exercise.

Also, please bear in mind that these are *guidelines* and by no means will every box fit readily into one or the other of these categories.

Note: Sealed boxes, while worth a premium within their grade, must be judged by the same standards as other boxes. In other words, just because a box is sealed doesn't mean it is "Excellent." In *all* grades it is assumed that the box is full and correct in all respects.

Excellent

While not necessarily "as new", the box is solid and labels are clean with only negligible flaws or light scuffing. Colors will be bright and original. If it's a two-piece 50-round box, the side seal will be virtually all there. There will be no tape or signs of tape removal.

Very Good-Fine

Box may be a little weak or separated at the edges but is otherwise sound (exception: .22 boxes are not permitted any edge or seam separations in this grade). The labels may have *minor* staining, scratches or scuffs but will be completely readable. Colors may show slight fading. There will be no tape, though tape removal marks may be present on boxes other than .22s. If it's a 50-round two-piece box, the side seal will be more than half present. If it's a one-piece box, end flaps will be sound.

Good

Box may have some repairs, reinforcements, splits or loose edges but no missing cardboard. Labels will have scuff marks, chips, stains and other detractions but no major pieces will be missing. On two-piece, 50-round boxes, side label may be partial or roughly opened. End flaps will be present on one-piece boxes, but may have folds.

Note: Later one-piece boxes are not generally collectible in condition below V.G.-Fine. Pricing is included for completeness only and is based largely on the value of the contents.

Pricing and Value Charts

In pricing these boxes many generalizations obviously had to be made. There are simply too many variations to be included here. It is very important to keep in mind that, in many cases, the prices listed in this chapter represent the best judgment of a group of active collectors, in various areas of specialty, who regularly collect, buy and sell these boxes. Through experience they have developed a fairly good idea of their relative scarcity and corresponding demand levels.

These prices do not purport to be representative of actual trades like the prices-realized sheet of a past auction or tomorrow's *Wall Street Journal*. Auction prices for ammo boxes have been considered here but, in the majority of instances, are too incomplete and reflect a market too imperfect to be relied upon.

Some prices will undoubtedly appear too high or too low, and if the rapid price changes of recent years are any indication, the future course of trading will simply exacerbate these appearances. Of all this I have no doubt.

Yet, intrepid souls that we are, we present here our "first cut" effort at a complete pricing guide for Winchester cartridge boxes for Winchester rifles, the first ever in print. Your comments will be welcome; in fact, you may be offered a place on a future pricing panel.

Premium Factors That Affect Pricing

While many varieties of cartridge boxes are discussed in the following pages, the number of sub-varieties expands exponentially with each minor label change within each basic format. Many of these sub-varieties are quite rare and will bring significant premiums among knowledgeable collectors, especially in the .22 box categories. Unfortunately, an attempt to list all these sub-varieties lies well beyond the scope of this chapter.

That having been said, here are further considerations that significantly affect the value charts:

Add 25-50% for factory-sealed boxes.
Add 20% for "Full Patch" (full metal jacket) except the Self-Loading calibers (.32, .35, .351, .401) and two-piece .30-30 (.30 W.C.F.) boxes.
Add 100-200% for "Full Patch, High Velocity" loadings in .25-20, .32-20, .32-40 and .38-55.
Add 50-100% for "Full Patch, High Velocity" loadings in .45-90 and .50-110.
Add 50% for "High Velocity" loadings in .25-20, .32-20, .32-40, .38-40, .38-55, .44-40, .45-70, .45-90 and .50-110.
Add 50% for Hollow Point loadings in .38-40 & .44-40.
Add 25-50% for Lesmok loadings in .44 Henry (25%) and Center Fire calibers (50%).
Add 50-100% for .45-70 or .45-90 marked "Gould Hollow Ball."
Add 50-100% for Short Range or Miniature loadings.
Add 30% for one-piece yellow/blue/red box with "Winchester Repeating Arms Co." line on front (pre-Western Cartridge Co.).
Add 50-100% for blue labels on any Winchester caliber *except* .45-60, .50-110, and .50-100-450.

Dating By Box Types

One thing that must be kept firmly in mind when dating Winchester items is that transitions in *anything* this company produced were likely to have been gradual, with old stocks of boxes, labels or parts being used up before, during or after introduction of the new stocks. As a result, and as records are also incomplete, *all dates and time periods, especially in a generalized work such as this, must be considered approximate.*

Photograph note: Unless otherwise noted, boxes used for illustration are from the Ray T. Giles collection. If you would like your photographs of other boxes included in future editions, please contact the publisher.

Where to Find Your Cartridge Boxes and Their Prices

One of our challenges in presenting this material was organizational. We have put each caliber's value chart in the text according to its date of introduction and listed them in descending order by caliber. You may be interested in pricing a box of Blue/White Staynless .32-40 ammo in 20-round boxes for your Model '94. You know that box era was 1928-1937. But the .32-40 cartridge was first loaded in 1885. So we've placed the value chart for that caliber in the section with dates 1876-1886.

Section I - Small Rifle Caliber Boxes (Including M1885 Express Calibers and .44 Henry R.F.)

Box Styles

The boxes discussed in this section held between 10 and 100 cartridges, with the 50-box being by far the most common. Three basic box styles will be observed.

The earliest is the "half-split" box. The top and bottom halves meet in the middle and, beginning in the 1870s, were sealed by a label that wrapped all the way around the four sides of the box. This style predominated until around 1920 when the two-piece, full-cover box took over. These boxes had a full-cover top that covered the bottom portion on all sides and had semi-circular thumb-cuts at the bottom edge to facilitate opening. Labels extended over the top and both ends and lapped over onto the bottom, sealing it. The third box style is a one-piece outer box containing a cartridge tray. It came into being in 1928 and it's the one common today.

Circa 1860 - late-1870s

As the only Winchester (& Henry, its predecessor) guns produced in this period were the Henry, the M1866 and the M1873, there are only two calibers to be dealt with here, the .44 Henry rimfire and the .44 W.C.F. (Winchester Center Fire) or .44-40, as it came to be called.

The first Henry box is generally believed to be the black (actually dark purple) 100-box with gold print made by New Haven Arms Co. in the 1861-62 period. With fewer than 10 known and an auction record of $19,800 (Butterfield and Butterfield, July, 1994), this is the reigning "king" of cartridge boxes.

Another "black" Henry box, a loose-pack box of 50 produced without a manufacturer's name (and generally referred to as the "generic" black box), has been assumed by some to be New Haven Arms in origin. That's because one was found with an early, authenticated Henry in its original casing. Indeed it was a common occurrence in the early years to sub-contract the manufacture of cartridges and cartridge boxes to another maker and this could well have been just such an instance. In the absence of other corroborating evidence, however, I am reluctant to ascribe this box to Hew Haven. Whatever its origins it remains a very rare and desirable box.

There are also two main styles of the green New Haven 50-round boxes from the 1862-66 period. One has a relatively plain black border, while the other has a much fancier scroll border. Which is older remains the subject of debate. It's likely they were produced simultaneously since both types have been observed with pointed bullet rounds, both headstamped and unheadstamped. Only the plain border box, however, has been observed with an end label identifying "flat" bullets, which followed the earlier pointed ones and resemble those found in the first Winchester box. The scroll-border-label format, by contrast, bears a very close resemblance to the first Winchester box, while the plain-border version clearly does not. Hence, both New Haven boxes have strong antecedent claims to the first Winchester box of 1866. At least three minor variations of the scroll-border box exist as well as an interesting "small label" variety of the plain border box. The .44 Henry boxes would remain 50-round boxes until the end of production.

The "king" of cartridges boxes is the New Haven Arms 100-round Henry box made in 1861 or 1862. Photo by M. Allyson.

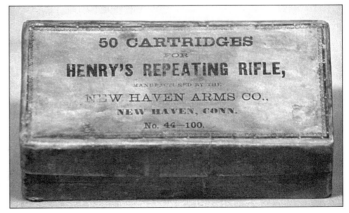

New Haven Arms Co. box with .44 Rim-Fire Henry shells showing the plain border. Photo by D. Kowalski.

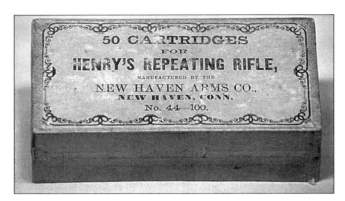

This New Haven Arms Co. box of .44 Rim-Fire Henry shells has a scroll border. Photo by D. Kowalski.

The first Winchester box, as stated above, has all the look of the green scroll-border New Haven box. What is apparently the second Winchester box, however, bears almost no resemblance to the first. This particular box, except for its relatively plain green Winchester label, closely resembles the various Union Metallic Cartridge Co. boxes of the period. It had purple/white plaid paper covering the cardboard and was probably a UMC sub-contract. Both of these first and second Winchester boxes are much rarer than either of the green New Haven boxes.

Winchester's first box design looks very much like the green scroll-border New Haven box. Photo by M. Allyson.

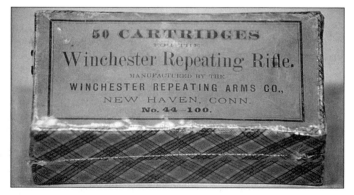

Winchester's second box (late 1860s), with its purple/plaid paper, appears to have more of a U.M.C. heritage than New Haven or Winchester. Photo by D. Kowalski.

The next box is one of the more common ones, having a picture of the cartridge in the lower left corner. The earliest of these, circa 1870-71, had no reference to the Stetson's Patent date.

Cartridge drawing in lower left corner helps date this box as circa 1870-1890. Photo by D. Kowalski.

Somewhere in the early 1870s the label (one of the scarcer blue labels) also covers one end of the top. Later in the 1870s, as mentioned above, side-seal labels began to appear, the earlier boxes having been plain and unsealed. A scarce variation of this era is the "Pointed Bullet" box that had a red label. As far as I can determine, it was the only *Winchester* .44 Henry label that wasn't green. Considering the length of time this box was in use, surprisingly few variations are to be found. Fortunately, its longevity, reaching well into the next period, has provided collectors with a relatively large number of these boxes. However, their pricing varies greatly as auction records attest.

The earliest .44-40 box, illustrating a Milbank-primed round on a yellow label, is also the rarest of .44-40 boxes. I am aware of only one. The second box of this early period had fairly plain green labels without scroll borders and featured a picture of the cartridge in the center. This box is seldom seen and almost never in Excellent condition.

Box of .44 Henry Flats dates from 1890-WWI period. Photo by M. Allyson.

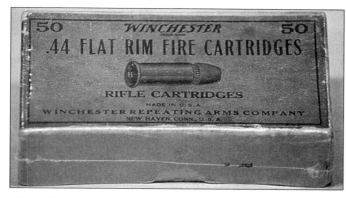

This full-cover box of .44 Henry Flats is from the period 1920s. Photo by D. Kowalski.

Second .44-40 box, circa 1870s. Photo by M. Allyson.

Values: .44 Henry R.F. (50-Round Box)
Winchester Gun Models: Henry, 1866

	Exc.	VG/F	Good
Pre-1875:			
100-rd "Black" New Haven	20,000	15,000	10,000
50-rd Green New Haven	7500	5000	3500
1st Win Bx (New Haven style)	8500	6000	4000
2nd Win Bx (UMC style)	8000	5500	3750
"Pointed Bullet" - Red Label	5000	3000	2000
Late 1870s - 1892:			
Green Label	3000	1500	850
"Pointed Bullet" - Red Label	4000	2500	1500
1892 - 1906	2000	1400	1000
1906 - 1920	1850	1300	900
1920 - 1930	1550	1200	850
Blue/white Staynless	(Not loaded in these)		
1937 - 1946 Yellow/blue/red	(Not loaded in these)		
1946 - 1958 Red/yellow	(Not loaded in these)		

Values: .44-40 (50-Round Box)
Winchester Gun Models: 1873, 1892, 53, 43

	Exc.	VG/F	Good
Pre-1875	1000	500	250
Late 1870s - 1892	400	275	150
1892 - 1906	300	200	125
1906 - 1920	250	175	125
1920 - 1930	175	125	75
Blue/white Staynless	125	90	50
1937 - 1946 Yellow/blue/red	125	85	50
1946 - 1958 Red/yellow	60	45	35

Circa Late 1870s - 1892

Though incorrect, the October 24, 1871, Stetson's Patent date remained on Henry boxes throughout the period. (The correct date, October 31, 1871, was not used on Henry labels until sometime near, or possibly after, the turn of the century. There was no specific year when the Company made this correction on its rimfire labels. I have seen 1880s boxes with the correct date and some after 1907 with the old date.)

Again, labels are usually green, though blue and blue-green also will be found occasionally and are worth a premium, the bluer the better. I must comment here on the belief by some that these labels all left the factory as green and faded toward blue. I've seen .44 Henrys and .44-40s in too many blue and near-blue boxes that appear, to me at least, to be original color. And if these faded to blue, why didn't all the other calibers in 1870s-1880s green boxes fade also? Anyone who has seen a lot of .45-60 labels knows they are more common in blue than the other M1876 calibers, which are virtually never, in my experience, blue.

This favorite of collectors has bright green top label and M1873 carbine on the side. Photo by D. Kowalski.

Henry boxes from this period continue to picture the cartridge in the lower left part of the top label. Also remaining in this period will be the seldom-encountered Pointed Bullet red label box.

The .44-40, .38-40 and .32-20 boxes mention the M1873 on both top and side labels, although the formats among the various calibers differ somewhat. The most coveted of these boxes (and actually the most common) is the .44-40 box that pictures the M1873 carbine on the side label.

In order to avoid possible confusion in nomenclature, the calibers .44 W.C.F., .38 W.C.F., and .32 W.C.F. will continue to be referred to in this chapter by their more "generic" caliber callouts of .44-40, .38-40, and .32-20, respectively.

Values: .38-40 (50-Round Box)
Winchester Gun Models: 1873, 1892

	Exc.	VG/F	Good
Pre-1875	(First loaded 1879)		
Late 1870s - 1892	375	225	125
1892 - 1906	300	200	100
1906 - 1920	250	175	80
1920 - 1930	200	135	75
Blue/white Staynless	100	75	45
1937 - 1946 Yellow/blue/red	100	65	45
1946 - 1958 Red/yellow	55	45	35

Values: .32-20 (50-Round Box)
Winchester Gun Models: 1873, 1892, 53, 65, 43

	Exc.	VG/F	Good
Pre-1875	(First loaded 1882)		
Late 1870s - 1892	225	150	75
1892 - 1906	150	90	60
1906 - 1920	125	80	55
1920 - 1930	90	65	50
Blue/white Staynless	80	50	40
1937 - 1946 Yellow/blue/red	75	50	35
1946 - 1958 Red/yellow	40	30	25

The M1885 single shot (the "High Wall") caused Winchester to develop four new "Express" cartridges in .38-90, .40-110, .45-125 and .50-140. First appearing in 1886, these came in 10-round, full-cover, two-piece green label boxes with a picture of the cartridge featured diagonally across the top. That the .50-140 Express came in this box is strictly conjecture on my part, as I have not personally seen one.

These calibers, supposedly brought out by Winchester to fill the gap left by the bankrupt Sharps Rifle Co., unfortunately came too late to be of any value on the buffalo circuit. That era in American history had already come to an end.

All center fire boxes discussed above have the "Central Fire" wording during this period. According to George Watrous, however, 50-round pistol calibers began to be called Center Fire rather than Central Fire in Company nomenclature beginning in 1885. This change very probably found its way onto the box labels around the same time.

Values: .45-125 Express (10-Round Box)
Winchester Gun Models: 1885

	Exc.	VG/F	Good
1876 - 1886	(First loaded 1886)		
1886 - 1898	750	650	500
1898 - 1906	700	600	500
1906 - 1914	650	550	475

Values: .40-110 Express (10-Round Box)
Winchester Gun Models: 1885

	Exc.	VG/F	Good
1876 - 1886	(First loaded 1886)		
1886 - 1898	600	500	325
1898 - 1906	550	450	300
1906 - 1914	500	400	275

Values: .38-90 Express (10-Round Box)
Winchester Gun Models: 1885

	Exc.	VG/F	Good
1876 - 1886	(First loaded 1886)		
1886 - 1898	400	350	250
1898 - 1906	375	330	275
1906 - 1914	375	320	250

Values: .25-20 Single Shot (50-Round Box)
Winchester Gun Model: 1885

	Exc.	VG/F	Good
Pre-1875	(First loaded 1890)		
Late 1870s - 1892	175	130	100
1892 - 1906	150	115	90
1906 - 1920	125	100	85
1920 - 1930	110	95	80

Values: .22 WCF (50-Round Box)
Winchester Gun Models: 1885

	Exc.	VG/F	Good
Pre-1875	(First loaded 1890)		
Late 1870s - 1892	150	115	50
1892 - 1906	125	100	50
1906 - 1920	115	80	45
1920 - 1930	100	65	45
Blue/white Staynless	90	65	40

Circa 1892 - 1906

Many changes in Winchester box labels began to occur as the M1892s, M1894s and M1895s debuted and, in 1894, smokeless powder loadings appeared along with a variety of bullet types. Label color for black powder remained green. However, labels for smokeless loadings progressed from a specially designed green label (pre-1900) to a dark orange (on a few circa-1902 boxes), to light orange (soft point), and a red (full patch) label sometime after 1902. Smokeless labels were always denoted as such while black powder continued with no powder call-out.

Henry labels were all green, the red "pointed" box having been discontinued. The picture of the cartridge, however, moved to the center of the box. In both center fire and rimfire labels, several minor varieties are in evidence. The words "Trade Mark" appear under the Winchester name and reference is made to U.S. Patent Office Registration. Also a new fancy WRACO (Winchester Repeating Arms Co.) logo appears on the ends of many of the boxes in this period.

The new Winchester Repeating Arms (WRACO) logo, circa late 1890s-1906, was predecessor to the commonly found "Red W" of 1907. Photo by D. Kowalski.

The .38-40 black powder box, circa 1898-1906, has "Center Fire" callout. Photo by M. Allyson.

As mentioned earlier, "Central Fire" became "Center Fire" in most pistol calibers in 1885. This change in wording occurred in the *rifle* calibers in 1898. (Exceptions will be found, however, in both cases.) According to my own observations, the M1873 and M1892 calibers, i.e. .44-40, .38-40, .32-20 and .25-20, were included in this later change.

Values: .25-20 WCF (50-Round Box)
Winchester Gun Models: 1892, 53, 65, 43

	Exc.	VG/F	Good
Pre-1875	-	-	-
Late 1870s - 1892	(First loaded 1895)		
1892 - 1906	150	90	45
1906 - 1920	125	80	40
1920 - 1930	90	65	40
Blue/white Staynless	75	50	35
1937 - 1946 Yellow/blue/red	70	50	30
1946 - 1958 Red/yellow	40	30	20

Circa 1906 - 1920

This period, like the previous one, exhibited numerous changes in boxes and labels. Unlike earlier periods, however, this one allows us to date boxes quite readily, usually to within a year or two of their manufacture. In 1906, the label design date (month-year) began to be included on the labels. Also during this time-frame, changes in the treatment of the Winchester name went from block letters (pre-1906); to block letters in quotation marks (circa 1906); to italics with quotation marks (circa 1911); to italics without quotation marks (circa 1913). And, as always, exceptions are to be found; for instance, I have a January 1908 label .38-40 box with italicized "Winchester."

Orange smokeless box of .38-40 shells, circa 1906-1910, has "Trade Mark" line under company name. Photo by M. Allyson.

Box of .32 Winchester (.32-20) High Velocity, yellow label, circa 1906-1910. Photo by D. Kowalski.

Red label, Full Patch, .351 self-loaders date from 1906-20. Photo by M. Allyson.

Label colors became more standardized. Green denoted black powder or Lesmok powder (introduced in 1911) and red, purple or orange denoted smokeless. The Lesmok labels became more of a light green or gray-green in the later years.

The self-loading caliber labels (.32 SL, .35 SL, and .351 SL) exhibit the color consistency that will be described later in the chapter among the 20-round boxes: red representing smokeless full patch and orange being smokeless soft point.

Scarcer, more unusual loadings include hollow points, Lesmok in center fire calibers, and the yellow WHV (Winchester High Velocity), as well as lavender WHV Full Patch boxes, all of which command premium prices.

Values: .32 & .35 Self-Loading (50-Round Box)
Winchester Gun Models: 1905

	Exc.	VG/F	Good
Pre-1875	-	-	-
Late 1870s - 1892	(First loaded 1905)		
1892 - 1906	125	90	65
1906 - 1920	100	80	60
1920 - 1930	90	75	60
Blue/white Staynless	85	65	60
1937 - 1946 Yellow/blue/red	90	70	60
1946 - 1958 Red/yellow	775	65	60

Values: .351 Self-Loading (50-Round Box)
Winchester Gun Models: 1907

	Exc.	VG/F	Good
Late 1870s - 1892	-	-	-
1892 - 1906	(First loaded 1907)		
1906 - 1920	100	75	60
1920 - 1930	85	65	55
Blue/white Staynless	70	60	50
1937 - 1946 Yellow/blue/red	75	65	50
1946 - 1958 Red/yellow	70	65	60

Circa 1920 - Mid-1930s

By the end of 1920 (earlier in some rimfire calibers) the old half-split two-piece box had given way to the full-cover lift-top box. The following color code was still in effect: orange labels indicated smokeless soft point; red was smokeless full patch; and yellow was WHV soft point.

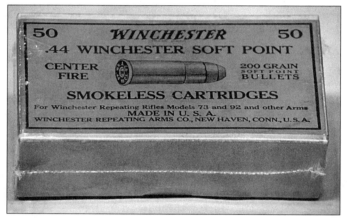

Red, full-cover, two-piece, Smokeless .44-40 box from early 1920s. Photo by D. Kowalski.

Inexplicably, green, in addition to its continued use for black powder loadings, was chosen to introduce the Company's newest offering, the high-velocity Super Speed full-jacketed hollow points in .25-20 and .32-20 that debuted in 1925. Continuing the oddity, this green two-piece Super Speed box appears to have carried on into the early 1930s where it was shown in Winchester catalogs.

The .44 Winchester (.44-40) High Velocity, Soft Point, yellow label, circa late 1920s. Photo by M. Allyson.

Lavender continued to represent "WHV Full Patch" in the 20-round boxes, although I do not recall seeing that label on a 1920- or 1930s-style full-cover box.

Also in this period, circa 1921-22, we find the advent of Winchester's K-code, a "K" followed by four digits (relating to the caliber which it signified) and a letter (R= rimfire, C= center fire rifle, T= center fire pistol, S= shot, etc.). For example, "K-3302 C" represented .33 WCF.

Blue/White Staynless Boxes, Circa 1928 - 1937

With the advent of Staynless priming in 1927, Winchester created new packaging consisting of a blue and white pre-printed one-piece box with red "Winchester" lettering across the top. These boxes were made from 1928 until the mid- to late-1930s with a 1932 label addition of the words "Non-Mercuric" above Staynless.

During this period several calibers remained in the full-cover, two-piece box of the early 1920s, such as the WHV and Super Speed loadings as well as many of the slower-selling calibers with black powder origins.

A couple of interesting anomalies occur during this period as well. There exists a blue/yellow/red Super-W-Speed box in .22 Hornet that apparently pre-dates the 1936-38 change from the blue/white box to the yellow/blue/red box. My best guess dates this between 1933 and 1936.

Another unique box from this period I have yet to explain is a .44-40 two-piece, half-split box without powder or primer callouts and stating "Division of Western Cartridge Co." This box type is a throwback to the pre-1920 style with a label that dates from the 1938-44 period! Such discoveries keep collectors interested, researchers thoughtful and writers modest.

Winchester's first .22 Hornet box, 1932. Photo by M. Allyson.

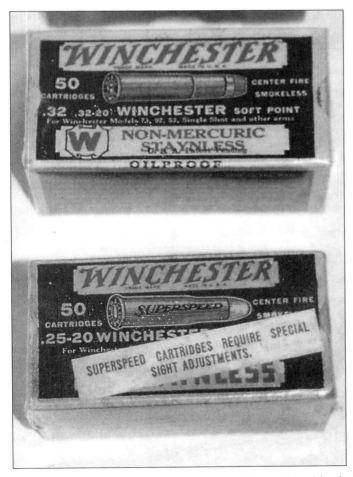

Blue/white Staynless boxes in standard and Super Speed loadings. Bottom box of .25-20 is earlier and lacks "Non-Mercuric" callout of post-1931 top box of .32-20 cartridges. Photo by M. Allyson.

This striking .22 Hornet box from the 1933-1936 period differs from other box styles of the 1930s, making it a very desirable collector's item. Photo by M. Allyson.

Yellow/blue/red late-1930's version of Winchester High Velocity box, this one in .25-20 caliber. Photo by M. Allyson.

Example of the first box of .218 Bee, circa 1938-39. Photo by D. Kowalski.

Designs resurrected from earlier times such as this "Division of Western Cartridge Co." label on a two-piece .44-40 box can sometimes baffle collectors. Photo by D. Kowalski.

In late 1937, Western Cartridge Co. converted Winchester Repeating Arms Co., which had been a subsidiary since its 1931 acquisition, into a division. As a result, by 1939, the boxes had moved the "Winchester" line from the front to the side and added "Division of Western Cartridge Company". This lasted until late 1944 or 1945 when "Division of Olin Industries" replaced the Western reference. This last version of the yellow/blue/red box would make it seem fairly scarce as it was only around for perhaps two years.

On the other hand, non-military ammunition for the public was scarce in all calibers after 1941. So the "Division of Western Cartridge" box may be equally as scarce, especially considering much of it would have been shot up during the war when everyone had to rely on their old stocks of ammo for the duration.

Values: .22 Hornet (50-Round Box)
Winchester Gun Models: 54, 70, 43

	Exc.	VG/F	Good
1906 - 1920	-	-	-
1920 - 1930	(First loaded 1932)		
Blue/white Staynless	100	65	40
Super-W-Speed	100	80	60
Super-W-Speed, Full Patch	125	100	80
1937 - 1946 Yellow/blue/red	65	50	30
1946 - 1958 Red/yellow	45	35	25

Yellow/Blue/Red Boxes, Circa 1937 - 1946

One of the most colorful boxes Winchester ever produced, these one-piece boxes began to replace the Blue/White Staynless box around 1937. There are three main varieties corresponding to specific time periods. The first, circa 1937-38, shows a "Winchester Repeating Arms Co., New Haven, Conn." line near the bottom of the box.

Scarce, early post-war red/yellow, "Full Patch" box of .218 Bee uses the K-code and still references the Winchester Model 65 (discontinued in 1947). Photo by M. Allyson.

Values: .218 Bee (50-Round Box)
Winchester Gun Models: 65, 43

	Exc.	VG/F	Good
Pre-1875	-	-	-
Late 1870s - 1892	-	-	-
1892 - 1906	-	-	-
1906 - 1920	-	-	-
1920 - 1930	-	-	-
Blue/white Staynless	(First loaded 1939)		
1937 - 1946 Yellow/blue/red	75	50	35
1946 - 1958 Red/yellow	50	40	30

Red /Yellow Boxes, Circa 1947 - 1958

After WWII, virtually the entire Winchester ammo line, from .22s on up, was packaged in their new red and yellow box. The .22s actually debuted in 1946, while the other calibers phased in through 1948. The earlier boxes retained the K-codes but, sometime in the late 1940s, they began to shift toward a slightly revised system. In .218 Bee (and probably .25-20 and .32-20), these early boxes made reference on a side panel to the M65, which was discontinued in 1947, while the later ones referenced the M43, introduced in 1949.

The Olin Industries labeling gave way to "Winchester-Western Division, Olin-Mathieson Chemical Corp." This was in late 1954 or early 1955 and continued to the end of the box style in approximately 1958. While most of the red/yellow series are not very collectible in less than Excellent condition, there were a few relatively scarce items produced. For instance, try to find a red/yellow box of .218 Bee Full Patch.

Later red/yellow box of .218 Bee; note "W" code has replaced K-code; callout is now for Winchester Model 43 (introduced in 1949). Photo by M. Allyson.

Two Rare Cartridge Boxes

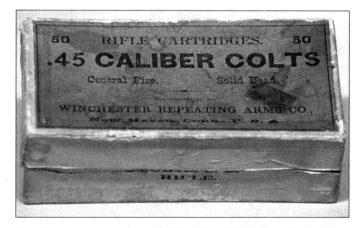

Here's a rarely seen box of .45 caliber "Colts" made by Winchester in the early 1880's that would be highly sought after in a "Level 3" collection. Photo by D. Kowalski.

A rare diagonal label, 10-round box of .44-90/105 probably dating from the late 1870s. Photo by D. Kowalski.

Section II - Large Rifle Calibers, Lever-Action and Bolt-Action Rifles (20-Round Boxes)

Circa 1876 - 1886

The "Centennial Model" of 1876, the first of Winchester's *big* lever-action rifles, was chambered only in .45-75 until 1879. The earliest of these boxes had a green label with a picture of the cartridge showing no headstamp and a bullet with a deep grease groove. The lower part of the box had a wide green label listing three (later, six) recommended powder manufacturers. It is doubtful these powder labels lasted more than a year or two, although the box picturing the unheadstamped round probably continued until the early 1880s.

The second M1876 "Centennial" .45-75 box, circa 1877-78. Photo by M. Allyson.

The second version of the first .50-95 Express box, circa early 1880s. Photo by M. Allyson.

In 1879, both the .45-60 and .50-95 Express were introduced and, like the .45-75s, had green labels picturing unheadstamped cartridges. The .50-95 label had the word "Express" in tall letters on the front, the second version much bolder than the first.

An interesting variation is the earliest .50-95 box with the word "Keene" stamped under the word "Express", signifying a loading with Keene bullets, a supposedly expansive lead bullet partitioned into quadrants with tissue paper (barely discernible without magnification). These are quite scarce, even rare, and command a substantial premium.

The later boxes in this period, including the .40-60 introduced in 1884, show pictures of headstamped rounds and use bold block lettering, rather than italics, in the caliber and powder weight callouts on the right side of the cartridge picture. This is the box style that carried the M1876 calibers into and through the next period.

A black powder box of .45-90 from the 1886-1898 period with early red "Metal Patched" label. Photo by D. Kowalski.

A scarce .50-100-450 black powder box from the 1886-1898 period. Photo by D. Kowalski.

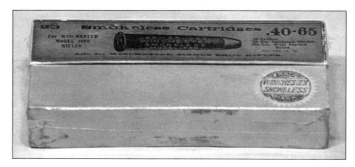

Another box from the 1886-1898 period; this one is .40-65 with early green Smokeless label with powder grains callout and yellow "Winchester Smokeless" sunburst sticker. Photo by D. Kowalski.

Values: .50-95 (20-Round Box)
Winchester Gun Models: 1876, 1885 (First loaded 1879)

	Exc.	VG/F	Good
1876 - 1886	1500	1000	600
1886 - 1898	1350	1000	550
1898 - 1906	1250	950	500
1906 - 1914	1250	950	500
1914 - 1941 (two-piece)	-	-	-

Values: .45-75 (20-Round Box)
Winchester Gun Models: 1876, 1885 (First Loaded 1876)

	Exc.	VG/F	Good
1876 - 1886	650	450	200
1886 - 1898	475	350	185
1898 - 1906	375	300	175
1906 - 1914	350	285	165
1914 - 1941 (two piece)	325	250	150

Values: .45-60 (20-Round Box)
Winchester Gun Models: 1876, 1885 (First loaded 1879)

	Exc.	VG/F	Good
1876 - 1886	500	350	185
1886 - 1898	450	325	165
1898 - 1906	425	315	150
1906 - 1914	400	290	150
1914 - 1941 (two-piece)	375	275	135

Values: .40-60 (20-Round Box)
Winchester Gun Models: 1876, 1885 (First loaded 1884)

	Exc.	VG/F	Good
1876 - 1886	425	325	165
1886 - 1898	400	300	135
1898 - 1906	375	310	125
1906 - 1914	350	285	125
1914 - 1941 (two-piece)	325	275	125

Values: .32-40 (20-Round Box)
Winchester Gun Models: 1885, 1894

	Exc.	VG/F	Good
1876 - 1886	(First loaded 1885)		
1886 - 1898	135	100	45
1898 - 1906	110	80	40
1906 - 1914	95	75	40
1914 - 1941 (two-piece)	90	75	40
Blue/white Staynless	75	60	40
1937 - 1946 Yellow/blue/red	75	60	45
1946 - 1958 Red/yellow	60	50	40

Circa 1886 - 1898

When Winchester rolled out the Model 1886, they entered a ten-year period in which no fewer than 19 proprietary calibers would be introduced in their models 1885, 1886, 1892, 1894 and 1895, along with other cartridges either developed earlier and/or elsewhere.

The varieties within these calibers were endless given the various bullet styles and powder loadings in both black and smokeless. Labels remained green, however, with the notable exceptions of .45-60, .50-110 and .50-100-450 that were commonly blue.

Even the new smokeless loads were introduced in a newly designed green-labeled box with a smokeless call-out, the "Green Smokeless" box. The earlier of these, circa 1895-96, listed the actual number of grains of smokeless powder. Before they introduced the Green Smokeless box, Winchester's black powder boxes sported yellow, sunburst-shaped "Winchester Smokeless" stickers. A second sunburst label also was used, where appropriate, to label the box as containing "Soft Point Metal Patched Bullets."

One very scarce box produced late in this period (1896-97) is the smokeless .50-95 loading; the only smokeless offering of a Model 1876 caliber ever listed in the Winchester catalogs. The only box I have ever seen was a Green Smokeless box in ratty condition holding six jacketed hollow point cartridges with "w" primers, all of which would appear to be correct.

Other intriguing new products in this era were Gould Hollow Ball loadings in .45-70 and .45-90; low-powered Short Range and "Miniature" loadings; and calibers like .45-82, .45-85 and .40-75, all designed by Winchester for calibers for which they had no firearms specifically chambered. The .45-82-405, .45-85-300 Express and .45-85-350 were just different loadings for the .45-90.

Early green Smokeless box is first .30 W.C.F. (.30-30) box with callout for 30 grains smokeless powder, circa 1895. Photo by D. Kowalski.

The .40-75 was, in effect, a copper-tubed express bullet loading of the .40-82. The .40-75 never had its own headstamp, always appearing as a .40-82 in spite of its distinct .40-75 box labeling. All of these boxes are scarce and, when full and correct, will command $250-$750 prices, with the .40-75s bringing even more.

For those seeking a real collecting challenge, Winchester's 1890 "Single W" cartridge board holds a dummy round with a .50-105 headstamp. I still hope to find a box of those.

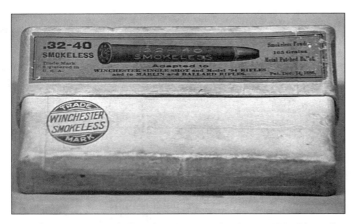

Another green Smokeless box in .32-40, circa 1900. Photo by D. Kowalski.

Values: .50-110 (20-Round Box)
Winchester Gun Models: 1886, 1885

	Exc.	VG/F	Good
1876 - 1886	(First loaded 1887)		
1886 - 1898	650	500	350
1898 - 1906	500	425	325
1906 - 1914	450	375	325
1914 - 1941 (two-piece)	425	375	325

Values: .50-100-450 (20-Round Box)
Winchester Gun Models: 1886

	Exc.	VG/F	Good
1876 - 1886	-	-	-
1886 - 1898	(First loaded 1895)		
1898 - 1906	1500	1000	800
1906 - 1914	1400	1000	800
1914 - 1941 (two-piece)	-	-	-

Values: .45-90 (20-Round Box)
Winchester Gun Models: 1886, 1885

	Exc.	VG/F	Good
1876 - 1886	(First loaded 1886)		
1886 - 1898	350	250	150
1898 - 1906	300	225	130
1906 - 1914	275	200	125
1914 - 1941	250	200	125

Values: .45-70-405, Marked for M86 (20-Round Box)
Winchester Gun Models: 1886, 1885

	Exc.	VG/F	Good
1886 - 1898	200	140	75
1898 - 1906	185	135	65
1906 - 1914	175	125	60
1914 - 1941 (two-piece)	150	100	50
Blue/white Staynless	100	75	40
1937 - 1946 Yellow/blue/red	115	85	45
1946 - 1958 Red/yellow	65	45	30

Values: .40-82 (20-Round Box)
Winchester Gun Models: 1886, 1885

	Exc.	VG/F	Good
1876 - 1886	(First loaded 1886)		
1886 - 1898	300	225	125
1898 - 1906	275	200	125
1906 - 1914	250	185	125
1914 - 1941 (two-piece)	225	175	120

Values: .40-72 (20-Round Box)
Winchester Gun Models: 1895

	Exc.	VG/F	Good
1876 - 1886	(First loaded 1896)		
1886 - 1898	150	125	80
1898 - 1906	135	120	75
1906 - 1914	130	115	75
1914 - 1941 (two-piece)	125	110	65

Values: .40-70 (20-Round Box)
Winchester Gun Models: 1886, 1885

	Exc.	VG/F	Good
1876 - 1886	(First loaded 1894)		
1886 - 1898	325	250	135
1898 - 1906	275	225	125
1906 - 1914	250	200	125
1914 - 1941 (two-piece)	225	195	120

Values: .40-65 (20-Round Box)
Winchester Gun Models: 1886, 1885

	Exc.	VG/F	Good
1876 - 1886	(First loaded 1887)		
1886 - 1898	375	275	150
1898 - 1906	300	225	125
1906 - 1914	250	200	125
1914 - 1941 (two-piece)	225	195	120

Values: .38-72 (20-Round Box)
Winchester Gun Models: 1895

	Exc.	VG/F	Good
1876 - 1886	(First loaded 1896)		
1886 - 1898	165	135	85
1898 - 1906	150	125	80
1906 - 1914	150	115	70
1914 - 1941 (two-piece)	135	100	60

Values: .38-70 (20-Round Box)
Winchester Gun Models: 1886, 1885

	Exc.	VG/F	Good
1876 - 1886	(First loaded 1894)		
1886 - 1898	325	225	135
1898 - 1906	275	210	130
1906 - 1914	250	200	125

Values: .38-56 (20-Round Box)
Winchester Gun Models: 1886, 1885

	Exc.	VG/F	Good
1876 - 1886	(First loaded 1887)		
1886 - 1898	300	200	125
1898 - 1906	265	215	120
1906 - 1914	250	190	110
1914 - 1941 (two-piece)	220	175	100

Values: .38-55 (20-Round Box)
Winchester Gun Models: 1885, 1894

	Exc.	VG/F	Good
1876 - 1886	(First loaded 1886)		
1886 - 1898	140	95	45
1898 - 1906	115	85	40
1906 - 1914	100	75	40
1914 - 1941 (two-piece)	100	65	40
Blue/white Staynless	85	60	35
1937 - 1946 Yellow/blue/red	90	65	45
1946 - 1958 Red/yellow	50	35	25

Values: .30-30 (20-Round Box)
Winchester Gun Models: 1894, 55, 64

	Exc.	VG/F	Good
1876 - 1886	(First loaded 1895)		
1886 - 1898	165	135	85
1898 - 1906	100	80	50
1906 - 1914	80	60	30
1914 - 1941 (two-piece)	70	50	25
Blue/white Staynless	50	30	20
1937 - 1946 Yellow/blue/red	60	40	25
1946 - 1958 Red/yellow	25	15	10

Values: .25-35 (20-Round Box)
Winchester Gun Models: 1894, 55, 64

	Exc.	VG/F	Good
1876 - 1886	(First loaded 1895)		
1886 - 1898	140	115	85
1898 - 1906	95	70	50
1906 - 1914	85	60	40
1914 - 1941 (two-piece)	75	55	35
Blue/white Staynless	65	40	25
1937 - 1946 Yellow/blue/red	60	40	25
1946 - 1958 Red/yellow	30	20	15

Circa 1898 - 1906

As mentioned earlier, the long-used "Central Fire" term was changed to "Center Fire" in 1898 for rifle calibers. Also around 1900, many boxes changed from a square-edged construction to rounded ends. Unlike smokeless offerings, black powder boxes had no powder call-out on labels until around 1920 and then not on all such labels. Sunburst labels show up, however, on virtually any style box of the period, whether black powder or smokeless.

Later .45-75 "Centennial" square-corner box, circa 1898-1900. Photo by D. Kowalski.

The Dark Orange, first .32 Special box of unique design is thought to be the precursor of what became the standard line of orange label Smokeless boxes. (This photo also shows top of box.) Photo by D. Kowalski.

The orange Smokeless box seems to have hit the market around 1902-1903, and perhaps a little earlier. The existence of a dark orange .32 Special box of unique design, probably the first .32 Special box from 1902, leads me to believe it was the precursor to the lighter orange-label series.

Earliest .50-110 WHV, yellow box without label dates, circa 1905. Photo by M. Allyson.

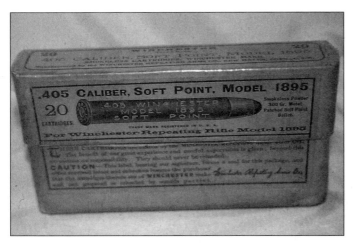

Typical early orange-label box, this one for .405 Soft Point cartridges for Model 1895. Photo by M. Allyson.

These new orange-label designs, as well as the ones described below, covered the full front of the box, forming a seal rather than just covering the top and front of the box lid. These were the first of the "factory-sealed" large-caliber boxes. It is this light-orange-labeled box that dominates the two-piece format until its demise in 1941-42.

Besides the ubiquitous green labeling of black powder boxes, the other commonly seen box in this period is the red (or purple) Smokeless Full Patch (FMJ) loading. Winchester created smokeless versions of the old black powder loads in the 1890s. They, and others (especially the world's militaries), introduced numerous new calibers specifically designed for smokeless powder. While many of the old cartridges would be loaded with both types of powder for another 15-40 years, the new smokeless offerings were destined to dominate the future.

Shortly after the turn of the century the Company introduced several new smokeless calibers such as the .32 Special, .33 WCF, .35 WCF and .405 WCF. Winchester found that, with the new powders, they had the ability to attain higher velocities with acceptable pressures for use in the older, black powder guns.

This led to the introduction of their new "Winchester High Velocity, Low Pressure Smokeless" (WHV) loadings beginning with .38-40, .44-40, .45-90 and .50-110 in 1903. They filled out the line with the addition of .25-20, .32-20, .32-40, .38-55 and .45-70 in 1905.

Top box of .38-55, Full Patch WHV has lavender label; bottom box of .32-40 WHV has yellow label. Photo by M. Allyson.

The new WHV line was marketed with yellow labels for soft points and lavender labels for full patch bullets. Neither featured a picture of the cartridge. These boxes will also frequently be found with sunburst "Smokeless" and "Metal Patched Bullets" labels, a redundancy in the sense that *all* WHV loadings contained smokeless powder and jacketed bullets.

Though little more than a footnote to these years, the colorful red or dark orange Smokeless Short Range boxes make for very interesting collecting. In my own research I have identified five minor label variations of the .30-30 Short Range box between 1897 and 1906, a slightly different label roughly every other year for a cartridge that was never popular.

Values: .405 WCF (20-Round Box)
Winchester Gun Models: 1895

	Exc.	VG/F	Good
1876 - 1886	-	-	-
1886 - 1898	(First loaded 1904)		
1898 - 1906	160	125	100
1906 - 1914	140	110	95
1914 - 1941 (two-piece)	125	100	90
Blue/white Staynless	100	90	80
1937 - 1946 Yellow/blue/red	95	85	75
1946 - 1958 Red/yellow	90	80	70

Values: .32 Special (20-Round Box)
Winchester Gun Models: 1894, 64

	Exc.	VG/F	Good
1876 - 1886	-	-	-
1886 - 1898	(First loaded 1902)		
1898 - 1906*	100	80	55
1906 - 1914	80	60	30
1914 - 1941 (two-piece)	70	50	25
Blue/white Staynless	50	30	20
1937 - 1946 Yellow/blue/red	60	40	25
1946 - 1958 Red/yellow	25	15	10

Add 100% for Dark Orange first box.

Values: .35 WCF (20-Round Box)
Winchester Gun Models: 1895

	Exc.	VG/F	Good
1876 - 1886	-	-	-
1886 - 1898	(First loaded 1903)		
1898 - 1906	135	100	65
1906 - 1914	125	90	60
1914 - 1941 (two-piece)	110	80	60
Blue/white Staynless	85	75	50
1937 - 1946 Yellow/blue/red	90	75	50
1946 - 1958 Red/yellow	-	-	-

Values: .33 WCF (20-Round Box)
Winchester Gun Models: 1886

	Exc.	VG/F	Good
1876 - 1886	-	-	-
1886 - 1898	(First loaded 1903)		
1898 - 1906	180	140	100
1906 - 1914	165	135	90
1914 - 1941 (two-piece)	135	120	80
Blue/white Staynless	100	80	70
1937 - 1946 Yellow/blue/red	100	80	70
1946 - 1958 Red/yellow	90	75	70

Circa 1906 - 1914

Beginning in 1906, as noted in the Small Rifle Caliber section, Winchester began to make our research a little easier by adding label design dates. The practice continued until around 1931 on most two-piece boxes (although, for some reason, there exists a 1941-dated .45-90 box label). Winchester's practice of using up old boxes and labels, however, meant that some older, undated boxes and labels were present along with later, dated ones.

Frequently in such cases, the only dated (and easily overlooked) labels are the "Red W" end labels which were designed in 1906 for the 1907 introduction of that new logo. In dating boxes of this period it is important to find the latest date on the box. As many as seven dated labels appear on some boxes. In addition, a "fair trade" label, voided on later boxes, is found on the bottoms of many boxes from the period 1910-13. For those calibers picturing the cartridge, such illustrations remained on the lid (top) part of the front label through 1914.

Label-dated, round-corner box of .45-60 picturing cartridge on top, circa 1906-1914. Note label now covers front of box forming seal. Photo by M. Allyson.

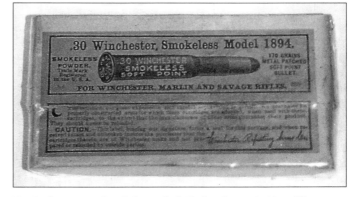

Typical orange Smokeless, Soft-Point box of .30 caliber cartridges, circa 1906-1914. Photo by M. Allyson.

For a brief time in the early Teens Winchester produced .32-40 and .38-55 black powder rounds in both soft point and full patch with a bright blue label. As usual, though, black powder boxes were green, but with a difference. Like the new smokeless boxes of the prior period, the new black powder labels formed a front seal over both top and bottom as opposed to the old style which covered just the top and front of the lid. Most label-dated boxes from 1914 represented the end of the old-style box construction (this was a paper covering on the cardboard that wrapped over the bottom and was pasted in place in a pattern of folds). The new box style is described in the next section. This change affected the smaller-sized boxes of the Model 1894 calibers as well as the Model 1895 calibers, which tended to be tall but narrow.

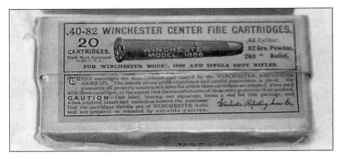

"Center Fire" labeling on Black Powder box (.40-82), circa 1906-14. Photo by M. Allyson.

Values: .401 Self-Loading (20-Round Box)
Winchester Gun Models: 1910

	Exc.	VG/F	Good
1886 - 1898	-	-	-
1898 - 1906	(First loaded 1910)		
1906 - 1914*	125	90	75
1914 - 1941 (two-piece)*	100	85	65
Blue/white Staynless	100	75	60
1937 - 1946 Yellow/blue/red	100	85	65
1946 - 1958 Red/yellow	75	65	60

Add 25% for 250 grain.

Circa 1915 - 1941, Two-Piece Boxes

This period opened with a change in box construction for some calibers (see prior section) to a folded cardboard design with visible seams glued only on the ends of both lid and bottom. The "Red W" end labels were discontinued and replaced by a simple red "W" printed or stamped directly on the end of the lower part of the box. The picture of the cartridge on the front sealing label was also moved to the lower (bottom) part of the box. Except for minor changes in wording, the boxes and their labels and colors would stay much the same until their discontinuance early in WWII.

From 1928 on, the Winchester calibers went to the new Staynless priming and those calibers that remained in two-piece boxes, mainly with black powder origins, had the word "Staynless" stamped or printed on the labels. In dating such boxes, many with label design dates in the Teens and early 1920s, it is important to subordinate label dates to this 1928 (and later) Staynless call-out. In the late 1930s, several years after Western acquired Winchester, the words "Division of Western Cartridge Company," show up on some two-piece orange label boxes, mostly Model 1886 calibers.

Example of 1915-1941 box label with cartridge (.45-60) pictured on bottom of front label. Photo by M. Allyson.

Green K-coded, two-piece box (.45-70-405) with Black Powder callout, circa 1920s. Photo by M. Allyson.

The final addition to the run of two-piece boxes occurred in 1925. The Company introduced the Super Speed line of lightweight, full-jacketed, hollow point bullets in calibers .32 Special, .30-30 and .25-35 (as well as three Remington calibers and the 50-round boxes covered in the Small Rifle Calibers section). These boxes were green and carried the Super Speed logo but are most often seen in the Remington calibers.

For a discussion of the K-codes on boxes from 1921-1950s, refer to the section on Small Rifle Calibers, Circa 1920 - Mid-1930s.

Very few collectors have seen the first green label, two-piece Winchester Super Speed box. Photo by D. Kowalski.

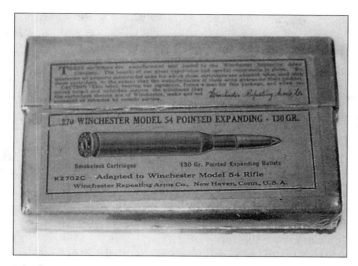

The first .270 box, orange, circa 1925. Photo by M. Allyson.

The scarce Super Speed blue/white, one-piece box from the late 1920s, this one in .32 Winchester Special caliber. Photo by M. Allyson.

Values: .270 Winchester (20-Round Box)
Winchester Gun Models: 54, 70

	Exc.	VG/F	Good
1898 - 1906	-	-	-
1906 - 1914	(First loaded 1925)		
1914 - 1941 (two-piece)	130	100	70
Blue/white Staynless	100	65	45
1937 - 1946 Yellow/blue/red	70	45	25
1946 - 1958 Red/yellow	25	15	10

Blue/White Staynless Boxes, Circa 1928 - 1937

As mentioned in the Small Rifle Caliber section, the Company brought out its new Staynless non-corrosive priming mixture in one-piece blue and white boxes. They continued the design into the late 1930s. Some rare and interesting boxes are found in this series, however.

Winchester High Velocity offerings (with WHV headstamps) are generally believed to have been issued only in two-piece boxes. I have seen but one exception: a .32-40 WHV loading in the blue/white Staynless box. I suspect there may be a .38-55 WHV in this style box as well, but I have yet to see it.

Another scarce blue/white box, though not as rare as the WHV, is the box that succeeded the green two-piece Super Speed. This one typically exhibits a paste-on over-label stating: "Super Speed Cartridges Require Special Adjustments."

It is assumed .25-35, .30-30 and .32 Special Super Speeds are all found in the blue/white box. However, I have seen only the .30-30 and .32 Special. Other blue/white boxes to watch for are the .219 Zipper and .348; both are reported to exist but have eluded *my* grasp.

Values: .220 Swift (20-Round Box)
Winchester Gun Models: 54, 70

	Exc.	VG/F	Good
1906 - 1914	-	-	-
1914 - 1941 (two-piece)	(First loaded 1936)		
Blue/white Staynless	90	65	30
1937 - 1946 Yellow/blue/red	40	30	20
1946 - 1958 Red/yellow	25	15	10

Yellow/Blue/Red Boxes, Circa 1937 - 1946

The big news in this box type started in 1940 when the Grizzly Bear box was designed to hold the Company's new Silvertip bullet. At the same time it launched one of the most collectible series of all Winchester ammo boxes. Fortunately for the collector, these boxes are not rare, but some are getting hard to find in nice condition. The scarcest ones in Winchester calibers appear to be the .32 Special and .30-30, in that order; but the 220 grain .30-40 and .30-06 are also tough to find.

For comments on yellow/blue/red boxes *without* the Bear, I refer you again to the Small Rifle Caliber section.

Beautiful example of the highly collectible Grizzly Bear box in the scarce .32 Special caliber. Photo by M. Allyson.

Examples of the first two .219 Zipper boxes. Lower part of the top box has "Winchester Repeating Arms Co." line. Photo by M. Allyson.

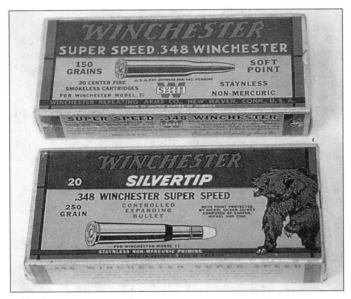

Top is early .348 box with "WRACO" line, bottom is .348 Grizzly box of early 1940s. Photo by M. Allyson.

Values: .348 WCF (20-Round Box)
Winchester Gun Models: 71

	Exc.	VG/F	Good
1914 - 1941 (two-piece)	-	-	-
Blue/white Staynless	(First loaded 1936)		
1937 - 1946 Yellow/blue/red	70	60	45
1946 - 1958 Red/yellow	50	45	45

*Add 50% for 250 grain bullet.

Red/Yellow Boxes, Circa 1947-1958

For a general discussion of this box type, please see the Small Rifle Caliber section.

Surprisingly, there are a few interesting and collectible boxes even this late. The scarcest red/yellow box I've run into is the .30-30 Full Patch. Although not yet expensive, the first .243 box (with a 6 M/M call-out), the first .358 box (with an 8.8 M/M call-out) and the first .458 box are all quite desirable in Excellent condition.

An attractive and colorful box style, I believe it will become more collectible as years go by, especially as many of its calibers are becoming, or have already become, obsolete. Remember, this was the last box type to offer such great Winchester calibers as the .33 WCF and the .405!

Red and yellow box of 1946-58. While this one is a .458 magnum "experimental" loading the standard commercial box is valued at $60 in excellent condition. Photo by M. Allyson.

First .358 Winchester box, marked "8.8 m/m" is for Winchester gun models 70 and 88 and, like the first .243 Winchester red/yellow box, is valued at $45 in excellent condition. Photo by M. Allyson.

Section III - .22 Rimfire Cartridge Boxes

Interest in the larger calibers has historically resided predominantly with gun collectors. But .22 boxes have, especially during the 1990s, spawned a legion of avid collectors specializing in this relatively new area of collectibility. The oldest and by far the most popular of all cartridges for the past 140 years, the colorful .22 box provides an interesting and challenging pursuit for today's cartridge collector.

One of the biggest challenges, unfortunately, has been, as with the larger calibers, a lack of published material. The late Tony Dunn created *A Catalog of the .22 Boxes of the U.S.A.*, with updates and revisions still being added by collectors today. (For more information contact: *The .22 Box*, 4321 Bluff Rd., Spokane, WA 99224 or e-mail: rlr22box@aol.com.) It remains a three-inch stack of unpublished work, without prices, in a 3-ring binder. As research progresses, I hope a descendant of this *magnum opus* will find its way onto the market. Meanwhile, information in this chapter will provide at least a framework for the beginning collector of Winchester .22 boxes as well as an acquaintance with some of its more arcane corners of collectibility.

Types of .22 Cartridges

As with the larger calibers, not all .22 cartridges produced by Winchester will be covered here. The .22 BB caps and CB caps, developed for "saloon pistols," "parlor rifles" and such were not of Winchester origin, nor were they originally intended for Winchester guns; likewise, the .22 extra long rimfire.

On the other hand, Winchester chamberings for the .22 Short, Long and Long Rifle are common. And Winchester developed the .22 W.R.F. (M1890) and Winchester Automatic (M1903) specifically for Winchester rifles.

Labeling tended to be distinctive for the two-piece boxes in each powder, as explained earlier. So we'll cover two-piece boxes for the five cartridges listed above by loadings: black powder, Lesmok and smokeless. By the time black powder faded from the scene, one-piece boxes in smokeless and Lesmok had become fairly standardized and those boxes will therefore be discussed simultaneously.

We've also included a separate section on target and gallery loadings and highlighted a few other interesting and highly collectible box varieties.

Two-Piece Boxes for .22 Cartridges

Black Powder, Two-Piece Boxes

Introduced in 1873, the earliest Winchester boxes, both .22 Long and Short, held 100 cartridges in bulk or "loose" pack and had yellow, blue or green labels in half-split boxes. Since they all appear to be from the early- to mid-1870s, it is unknown what the differences in color meant or even whether they were produced concurrently or consecutively.

An early 100-round .22 box style with a yellow label. Photo by D. Kowalski.

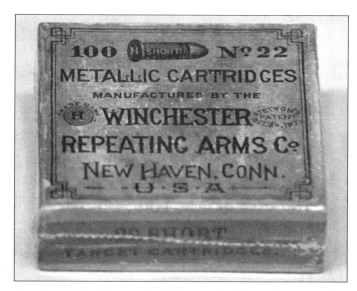

Another early 100-round .22 box style, this with green label. Photo by D. Kowalski.

While most of the early 50-round boxes had cartridges arranged "heads and tails," ten rows of five cartridges alternating bullet down, bullet up, some remained bulk-packed. These 50-rounders frequently had "1/2" printed on the end, signifying that what is today a standard box of fifty was then a half-box, 100 having been the norm. These early boxes prominently featured the word "Metallic Cartridges" on their labels and the (incorrect) October 24, 1871 Stetson's Patent date.

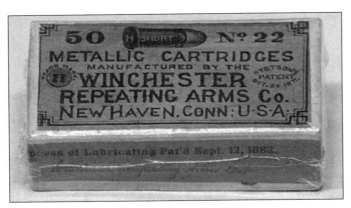

"Metallic Cartridges" in .22 Short, green box, circa 1880. Photo by D. Kowalski.

The next significant label variety, probably dating from the mid-1880s, features the words "Rifle Cartridges" rather than "Metallic Cartridges" on its top line. This half-split box with its old-style, green label contained either Short or Long cartridges and remained in the line, with modest changes, through about 1910. While the earlier labels still exhibited the October 24 Stetson's date, later ones, probably in the mid-1890s, had the correct October 31, 1871 date.

Another box, less Victorian-looking, with straight borders and more modern typefaces (but lacking a Stetson's date), made its appearance around the turn of the century. Hollow point bullets were offered in Short in the January, 1896 catalog and in Long in June 1902. Hollow points are always scarcer and more highly desired in any of the two-piece boxes. From 1906 on, as was seen earlier in the discussion of the larger calibers, label design dates appear on the boxes.

In 1890, the Company introduced their M1890 rifle that was chambered for the newly developed .22 Winchester Rimfire (WRF) cartridge. Although their new rifle wasn't yet chambered for it, 1890 also saw Winchester's first loading of the .22 Long Rifle. These two new Winchester offerings were packaged with labels different from the Short and Long versions described above. Both featured a new green-label box with the more modern type fonts and straight-edged borders referred to previously. The WRF box also prominently displayed a picture of the cartridge and could be found with either green or, occasionally, blue labels. Hollow points were first offered in WRF in 1911.

The Stetson's Patent references were omitted on most labels early in this period but returned after the turn of the century, lasting, on an irregular basis, into the 1920s. These labels continued with a number of variations until Lesmok and smokeless powders made the black powder loadings obsolete. When they disappeared from the marketplace is not a certainty. While Winchester lists black powder .22s in their 1918 catalog, Dunn makes no reference to black powder loads (except one .22 Long Shot box) in his section on Winchester's "1920" box style. And, as with the center-fire calibers, smokeless and Lesmok had label call-outs while black powder did not.

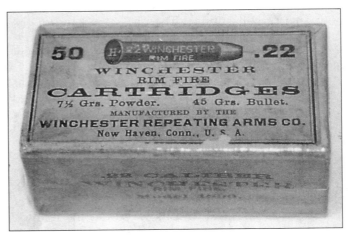

Example of what is thought to be first .22 W.R.F. box for Model 1890 rifle. Photo by M. Allyson.

Values: Black Powder, Two-Piece Boxes (.22)

	Exc.	VG/F	Good
Early 100-Box	350	250	150
Early 50-Box (Metallic)	125	95	60
Rifle Cartridges, old style	85	65	40
Rifle Cartridges, 1900s style	75	60	40
1900s style (above), Hol.Pt.	250	185	125
WRF, undated label, pre-'06	75	60	40
WRF, dated label	60	50	35
WRF, Hollow Point	125	90	60

Lesmok Powder, Two-Piece Boxes

Lesmok, a blend of black and smokeless powders, was offered as an alternative to the pure black or smokeless powders in the October, 1911 Winchester Catalog. All rimfire (and some center fire) calibers were listed at black-powder prices and it quickly supplanted black powder as the loading of choice among many shooters. It was somewhat less likely to foul the barrel and (dare I say it?) produced less smoke. It was also preferred to smokeless at the time because the early smokeless loadings in .22s were not as consistent or accurate as Lesmok, partly a fault of the priming compounds of the period and partly the powders themselves.

The light green (or gray-green) labels in solid bullet and hollow point offerings varied little from their inception in 1911 until Winchester introduced the one-piece box in 1926-27. The earlier boxes are found in both half-split and full-cover types, neither being decidedly more valuable than the other. By 1920, however, the full-cover box clearly predominates. One interesting difference between the black powder boxes of the period and Lesmok boxes was the fact that the latter carried a picture of the cartridge on the label whereas black-powder labels did not.

Lesmok loads retained substantial popularity with target shooters through WWII, and many of Winchester's premium target loads featured it. The difference on the labels during their fifteen-year existence in the two-piece box was mostly confined to changes in the "Winchester" line and their treatment of the trademark registration.

As mentioned earlier, the Winchester name went from block letters (pre-1906); to block letters in quotation marks (circa 1906); to italics with quotation marks (circa 1911); to italics without quotation marks (circa 1913).

The words "Trade Mark" were, before 1913, found under the Winchester logo and the words "Trade Mark Registered in U.S. Patent Office," or contractions thereof, surrounded a circled "H" logo. The 1913 design, however, placed the entire patent registration line directly below the Winchester logo and removed it from the circled "H" logo. In 1920, "Trade Mark" returned to its former spot underneath "Winchester" and the patent registration wording was omitted in favor of a return to the Stetson's Patent reference. (The temptation to dub this the "Neo-classical" box is great).

Taken together, the variations in the Company's treatment of the Winchester name and trademark registration line are widely used as reference points in categorizing .22 boxes. They are certainly more important here than they are in the Center Fire calibers.

Values: Lesmok Powder, Two-Piece Boxes (.22)

	Exc.	VG/F	Good
1910-19, dated label	50	35	25
1910-19, Hollow Point	175	135	80
1910-19, WRF	75	45	30
1910-19, WRF Hollow Point	125	100	60
1920-25 issue	60	40	25
1920-25, Hollow Point	175	135	80
1920-25, WRF	65	45	30
1920-25, WRF Hollow Point	125	100	60

Smokeless Powder, Two-Piece Boxes

Winchester began loading .22 Short and Long in smokeless powder in 1896. Other introductions in smokeless were the W.R.F. and .22 Winchester Automatic in 1903 and, finally, .22 Long Rifle in 1905. The early Short and Long were packaged in green-label, half-split boxes with pictures of the cartridges, a circled "H" logo and "Smokeless" in bold, bright letters across the labels, horizontally on Long, diagonally on Short.

These boxes, with variations in the Winchester logo and patent registration treatment, as mentioned above with regard to Lesmok boxes, continued through the Teens, including some "Target" marked. Smokeless Short, Long and Long Rifle in hollow points, and W.R.F.s were business-like red labels on which the fanciest feature was the circled "H" logo. Except on the W.R.F.s, the picture of the cartridge disappeared and "Smokeless" now appeared as a subdued afterthought.

The .22 Winchester Auto introduced in 1903 was given a label of unique design that lasted, with vari-

Lesmok offerings in .22 Short. Top box is circa 1911; bottom one circa 1913. Photo by M. Allyson.

.22 Short, early smokeless label with a 10-8 label-design date. Photo by D. Kowalski.

ations, throughout its life as a two-piece box. The bright yellow label featured a red band within which ".22 Automatic" stretched nearly from the left margin to the right margin under a picture of the cartridge. One of the more eye-catching boxes the company ever produced, it also had one of the most interesting variations. This was a label on which the ".22 Automatic" line was further stretched to ".22 Automatic Rifle" and pictured a pair of double-bodied lion heads, one on either side of the cartridge. To my knowledge, no one has yet divined the meaning of this label with any certainty.

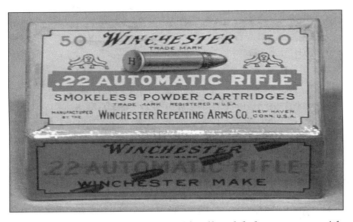

These unique lion heads on a vivid yellow label present us with an enigma yet to be solved. Was the box produced for export to the Middle East? The author doubts it, but no proof has been found to explain its existence. Photo by D. Kowalski.

This two-piece box of .22 Winchester Automatic cartridges is dated 6-15. Photo by M. Allyson.

The solid red "hollow point" label, a 1911 introduction, may be considered an exception to all the above except formatting.

Beginning in 1920, most .22 shells could be found in full-cover, two-piece boxes with red or purple smokeless labels, light green (or gray-green) Lesmok and, possibly, green black powder labels, and a circle "H" logo. One exception to this orderly array was a "greased" smokeless loading, in both Short and Long, that came in a green label box. Another exception was the .22 Automatic, solid bullet, which remained in its yellow box.

Winchester had come perilously close to label standardization by 1920. It lasted about five years. Then *everything* changed.

Values: Smokeless Powder, Two-Piece Boxes (.22)

	Exc.	VG/F	Good
1890s style, undated, pre-'06	85	60	40
1890s style, dated label	75	55	35
1900s style, Hollow Points	200	160	100
1920-25; S, L, LR	65	40	25
1920-25, WRF	100	65	40
1920-25, Hollow Points	200	160	100
.22 Win Auto, 1903-25	90	50	25

One-Piece Boxes for .22 Cartridges

One-Piece Box, Two-Piece Graphics, 1926-27

The printed one-piece box (outer box with end flaps, cardboard cartridge tray inside) was, in .22s only, introduced sometime before the 1927 announcement of Staynless. How much before is another question. Tony Dunn called it the "1925 Issue." My guess is that this box, displaying the graphics of the earlier 1920s boxes, was only a stopgap box in 1926-27. The Company had probably been caught short in trying to run out stocks of two-piece boxes before the planned introduction of the new Staynless one-piece box sometime in 1927. In any event they are quite scarce and missing from most collections.

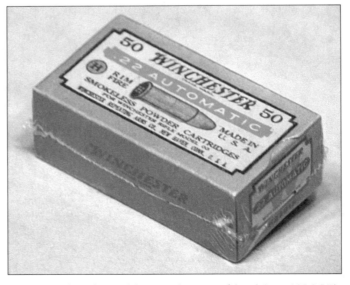

Rare one-piece box with two-piece graphics (circa 1926-27); this one in .22 Winchester Automatic. (Note "thumb cut" on box end to help pull down the end flap.) Photo by D. Kowalski.

Blue/White Boxes
(Staynless, Kopper Klad)

This box, in .22s as with the larger calibers, launched the Company's new Staynless-primed loadings in 1927 and stayed in the line until 1937-38. Unlike the larger calibers, the .22 line provided us with a myriad of variations, some significant, most minor, but possessed of wide collector interest.

The first of the blue/white Staynless, one-piece boxes (circa 1928). This one contains Long Rifle cartridges. Photo by M. Allyson.

On the first of these boxes the word "Staynless" appeared in a broad white banner with a red "W" in a plain or shaded shield that dominated the lower part of the box. Above this banner was a picture of the cartridge. The red "Staynless" was replaced with "Kopper Klad Bullet" in 1929. It described the Company's new non-fouling, copper coating of lead bullets.

Red/White Boxes
(Super-W-Speed, Lestayn)

Winchester continued their Lesmok loadings in a new Staynless-primed offering in 1927-28 called "Lestayn." (Dunn called the Lestayn issue a 1932

Scarce .22 Long Hollow Point box in Kopper Klad (circa 1929). Photo by M. Allyson.

introduction, but Winchester mentioned it in a 1928 ad.) Box graphics were very similar to the above Staynless and Kopper Klad boxes with a major exception: red replaced blue as the dominant box color. The banner now held only the word "Lestayn" separated by the Company's red "W" logo. Never a popular cartridge, it was discontinued in 1934. These boxes have become very collectible, especially in their hollow point loadings.

Red and white Lestayn box, this one containing Long Rifle cartridges, was introduced circa 1932. Photo by M. Allyson.

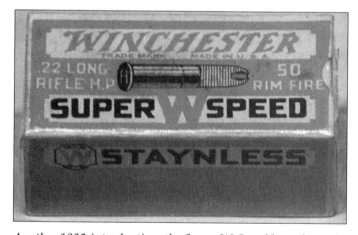

Another 1932 introduction, the Super-W-Speed box, shown in a Long Rifle, Hollow Point version. Photo by D. Kowalski.

The Company's famous Super-W-Speed high-velocity loadings first appeared in 1932. Like Lestayn, the box was red and white but the banner now contained the words "Super-W-Speed." This loading would eventually span four decades.

Yellow/Blue/Red Boxes (Super Speed, Leader)

This new box probably came to market in late 1936 or 1937. Dunn called it a 1938 issue. If correct, that would mean the center-fire calibers in this style box preceded the .22s in the marketplace by at least a year, when, in fact, .22s usually led the way in Winchester product and packaging changes. In any event these colorful boxes in "Super Speed" and "Leader" (standard velocity) formats, now lacking a cartridge picture, brought the era of the Winchester stand-alone name to an end.

The first of these boxes appeared with only "Winchester Repeating Arms Company, New Haven, Conn., USA" on the front side of the box. The second variety, beginning in 1939, added the line "Division of Western Cartridge Company." The 1944 change to "Division of Olin Industries" was the last for this box, which concluded its run in 1946.

A post-WWII red/yellow Leader box in Long Rifle. Photo by D. Kowalski.

Popular yellow/blue/red Super Speed box of late-1930s, this one in .22 Long Rifle Hollow Point. Photo by M. Allyson.

Red/Yellow Boxes (Super Speed, Leader)

The first of this series, with K-codes (explained earlier in Small Rifle Caliber Boxes, Circa 1920 - Mid-1930s), retained the Olin Industries line on the side of the box from its introduction in 1946 until the 1954-55 change to "Winchester-Western Division, Olin Mathieson Chemical Corporation."

There are few notable varieties in this box. Differing hollow-point call-outs on the end flaps of the 1940's boxes, however, have received little attention and do provide some interest in this series. Otherwise, only boxes in "Excellent" to "New" condition are generally deemed collectible.

Super Speed .22 Long Rifle Hollow Point in red/yellow box, circa 1946-58. Photo by D. Kowalski.

Values: One-Piece Boxes (.22)

	Exc.	VG/F	Good
1920-25 format; S, L, LR	275	200	150
1920-25 format, WRF or Auto	200	165	125
1927 Staynless, blue/white	75	50	30
1927 Staynless, bl/wh, Hol.Pt.	200	150	100
1929 Kopper Klad, bl/wh, all	100	75	50
1929 Kop.Kl., bl/wh, Hol.Pt.	200	150	100
1932 Super-W-Speed, red/wh	100	65	30
1932 Super-W-Sp., red/wh, HP	200	150	100
1932 Lestayn, red/wh, all	200	150	100
1932 Lestayn, red/wh, Hol.Pt.	250	175	125
1936-46, yellow/blue/red, all	20	15	10
1936-46, yel/bl/red, Hol.Pt.	30	20	15
1946-58, red/yellow, all	15	10	5
1946-58, red/yellow, Hol.Pt.	25	15	10

A pre-WWII Leader box in Long Rifle. Photo by M. Allyson.

These prices are for Short boxes. Long boxes will be higher; Long Rifle somewhat lower.

Target and Gallery Boxes

While many of the two-piece "target" or "gallery" boxes were only marked on the side-labels, the later ones were very prominently marked. By the time the one-piece boxes came out the target versions were specially designed. These are premium boxes that are among today's most highly collectible .22 boxes.

It is not necessary to fully describe these boxes in order to identify them as the box graphics fully describe themselves. They will be listed here simply to provide a checklist and show the chronology of their production.

Pre-1923 ... Two-piece, light green Lesmok box with "Precision 75" or "Precision 200" overlabels.

1923 ... Two-piece, light green Lesmok box, pre-printed label featuring a diagonal red "Precision 75" or "Precision 200" band over the top.

1931 ... Precision Five Star, red/blue oversized box with ammo all placed "bullets down" in a special cartridge holder insert.

1933 ... One-piece blue/red box in "Precision 75" or "Precision 200."

1933 ... Indoor Precision Staynless, black/red/yellow box with "Indoor Precision" in "rainbow" logo.

1935 ... Precision Staynless in box similar to above except logo just says "Precision."

1936 ... Long Range EZXS, Lesmok yellow/blue box with "EZXS" in diagonal blue band.

1936 ... Staynless EZXS, yellow/red box, with "Staynless EZXS" in a diagonal red band.

1938 ... EZXS, Lesmok, blue/yellow box, graphics similar to above Long Range EZXS.

1940 ... All-X Match, smokeless, yellow/blue/red with "x" ring target in center.

1946 ... Staynless EZXS, new red/yellow box.

1947 ... Smokeless EZXS, red/yellow box similar to above.

1954 ... Improved L.V. EZXS blue/yellow/red box showing Olin Industries until late 1954 or early 1955, after which "Olin Mathieson" appears.

Winchester's gallery and indoor target offerings were also a very interesting lot. The unsuccessful and extremely rare 1906 U.S. Armory issue is one of the premier Winchester .22 boxes. Although cataloged in all three powder offerings, Dunn contends only the red smokeless and green black powder boxes have been found.

The Company introduced one of its most fascinating offerings in 1913 -- the Spotlight cartridge. This was a gallery cartridge containing a special bullet that produced a small flash of light upon striking a metal target or backstop. In this way a gallery shooter could see where his shots were hitting. While all Spotlight boxes displayed "Spotlight" boldly across the top of the box, the earlier ones featured a distinctive "light burst" in the center of the label.

"Precision 75" overlabel highlights this early two-piece box of Lesmok .22 Long Rifle. Photo by D. Kowalski.

Bright red diagonal band is printed directly on the label of this "Precision 75" .22 Long Rifle box from the 1920's. Photo by D. Kowalski.

The "Precision 200" version of the two-piece box with a bright red printed diagonal band. Photo by D. Kowalski.

More bold graphics characterize this oversized Precision Five Star .22 Long Rifle box. Photo by D. Kowalski.

Bold graphics accent this "Precision 200" box of .22 Long Rifle, a 1933 introduction. Photo by D. Kowalski.

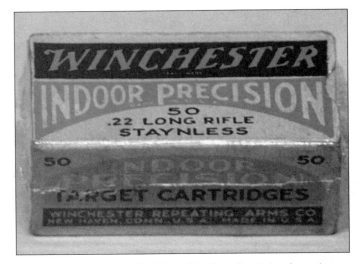

Rare .22 box showing "rainbow" Indoor Precision logo, introduced in 1935. Photo by D. Kowalski.

Another rare "rainbow" logo on this Precision .22 box, circa 1935. Photo by D. Kowalski.

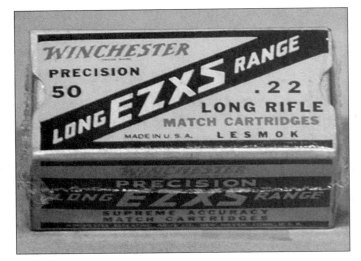

Blue band Lesmok .22 caliber Long Range EZXS box (1936). Photo by D. Kowalski.

Red band Staynless smokeless .22 caliber EZXS box (1936). Photo by D. Kowalski.

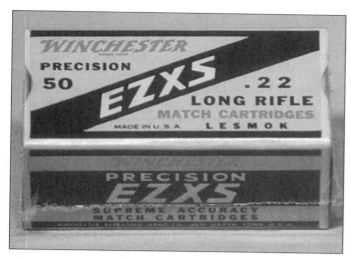

Blue/yellow Lesmok .22 caliber EZXS box (1938) has dropped "Long Range" from banner. Photo by D. Kowalski.

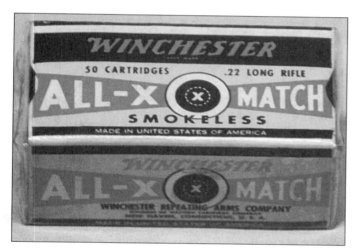

This .22 box of "All-X Match" from the early 1940s differs markedly from the EZXS target loads that dominated the period 1936-1958. Photo by D. Kowalski.

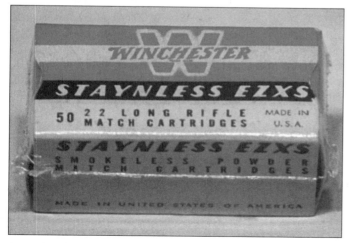

Staynless red/yellow .22 caliber EZXS box introduced in 1946. Photo by D. Kowalski.

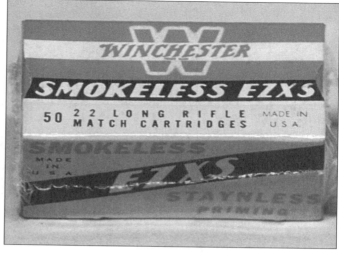

Staynless smokeless red/yellow .22 EZXS box also has EZXS on diagonal dark band on side (1947). Photo by D. Kowalski.

Blue/yellow/red EZXS box - Improved L.V. (1954). Photo by M. Allyson.

Lesmok and Lestayn loadings appeared in light green boxes, smokeless in red. Many varieties of these exist, all in two-piece boxes except the final one which is a Spatterproof box (see below) with a "Spotlight Bullet" overlabel. The .22 Winchester Automatic was also produced in this series, but is very rarely encountered.

The Spotlight series was replaced by the Spatterproof loading after an overlap of about five years in the mid-1930s. Spatterproof packaging contained a new composition bullet that would break up without danger of lead fragments or ricochets when it hit metal targets or backstops. A very colorful special loading with its red, white and blue diamond-pattern boxes in either 50 or 1000 rounds, these earliest boxes have become highly desirable collectors' items.

Three .22 Spotlight boxes: top one is rare 1000-round loose-pack; lower left is light green Lesmok half-split, two-piece box, circa 1913; and lower right is red full-cover, two-piece box. Photo by M. Allyson.

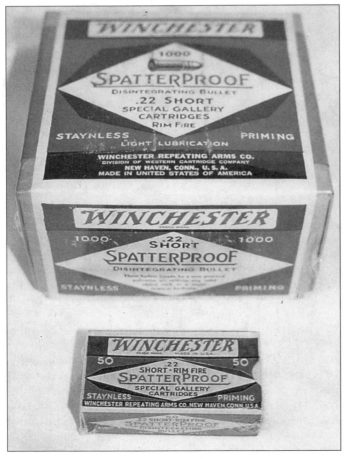

Two colorful red, white and blue, pre-war Spatterproof boxes, including the scarce 1000-rounder. Photo by M. Allyson.

Only one known example of the "Indoor Spatterproof" variety exists. With readers' help, perhaps one or two more will surface.

Unlike the rest of Winchester's 1946 box styles, the "Spatterpruf" (note the new spelling) box remained in its original colors until the more typical post-war red and yellow box appeared after 1950, this box containing 500 rounds. A new 15-grain composition bullet was first marketed in 1955 in a newly designed red, yellow, and white 500-round box with the Olin-Mathieson markings.

Values: Target Boxes (.22)

	Exc.	VG/F	Good
Pre-1923, Precision 75, 2-pc	250	200	125
Pre-1923, Precision 200, 2-pc	225	175	115
1923 Precision 75, 2-pc	175	135	95
1923 Precision 200, 2-pc	125	100	75
1931 Precision 5-Star	175	130	85
1933 Precision 75, 1-pc	550	400	250
1933 Precision 200, 1-pc	110	85	60
1933 Indoor Prec. Staynless	1500	1250	800
1935 Precision Staynless	1350	1100	700
1936 Long Range EZXS	150	110	75
1936 Staynless EZXS	200	150	100
1938 EZXS	50	35	25
1940s All-X Match	200	150	100
1946 Staynless EZXS	100	75	50
1947 Smokeless EZXS	45	35	25
1954 Improved L.V. EZXS	40	30	20

Values: Gallery and Other Boxes (.22)

	Exc.	VG/F	Good
1906 U.S. Armory, 2-pc	1750	1300	800
1920s Jr. Rifle Corps, 2-pc	2500	1800	1250
Spotlight, red, smokeless	175	135	90
Spotlight, green, Lesmok	325	200	135
Spotlight, green, Lestayn	375	250	150
Spotlight, 1000-round	1650	1300	1000
Spatterproof, 50-rd, red/wh/blue	500	375	200
Spatterproof, 1000-rd, r/wh/blue	1000	750	500
Spatterpruf, later 250-round	125	90	75
Shot, Super-W-Speed, 1938	200	165	100
Shot, Super-W-Speed, 1939	175	140	90
Shot, "Clay Pigeon"	80	55	35

A Couple of Parting "Shots" ...

Most box and label formats of .22 Shot boxes fit in with their lead-bullet counterparts and have therefore not been separately covered. This does not reflect a lack of interest, however, as these boxes have caught the attention of a good many collectors.

While all the two-piece Shot boxes, in both Long and Long Rifle are quite collectible, two one-piece box styles from the 1930s are also desirable. The first of these, and the more unusual, is the

"Long Range Super Speed" Long Rifle Shot box which, except for the Winchester logo at the top, is unlike any other .22 offering of this period. This was a black and yellow box with a large "W" in the center and superimposed upon it, "Super Speed," the two words stacked and sharing a common capital "S". The earlier, a "pure" Winchester box is considered a 1938 issue while the succeeding box, stating "Division of Western Cartridge Company," is 1939.

The other interesting .22 Long Rifle Shot box is the "Clay Pigeon" box of 1939-40. This was a marketing appeal to the then-popular sport of short-range (sometimes-indoor) .22 clay-target shooting. Although the box closely resembles the standard blue, yellow and red boxes of the period, the words "Clay Pigeon" were centered across the middle of the box.

Highly collectible box of Long Range Super-W-Speed Shot from the 1930s. Photo by M. Allyson.

Winchester promoted indoor "clay pigeon" shooting by offering special loads such as this late-1930s box. Photo by M. Allyson.

... And a Final Challenge

Winchester produced a boxed target shooting set for their Junior Rifle Corps in the early 1920s. This was a marketing effort designed to introduce youngsters to the shooting sports and create future Winchester customers. This set included specially designed blue-green boxes of .22 Short ammunition, stating under the italicized red Winchester logo, "Junior Rifle Corps," and under that, "Official Cartridges." Like the U.S. Armory boxes of 1906, this is one of the rarest and most highly sought Winchester .22 boxes. Maybe you can find one.

Good luck with your collecting efforts!

Acknowledgments

Many thanks to Robert Buttweiler, Richard Rains, Keith Shepard, and Dan Shuey for their time, help and expertise. Valuable input from these generous friends and experts is greatly appreciated.

Bibliography

Buttweiler, Robert. *American .22 Rimfire Cartridge Boxes.* Houston, TX. Robert T. Buttweiler, Ltd. 1990.

Dunn, A.G. "Tony." *A Catalog of the .22 Boxes of the U.S.A.* Sturgis, MI. Association for the Study of .22 Caliber Rimfire Cartridges. (Privatelyprinted). 1983.

Watrous, G.R. *Winchester Metallic Ammunition, Brass and Paper Shotshells.* (An internal monograph, Winchester Repeating Arms Co., New Haven, CT). 1943.

Winchester Repeating Arms Co. Catalogs of New Haven Arms Co. and Winchester Repeating Arms Co. 1865-1918. 12 volumes. Reprinted by Armory Publications. 1991.

Ray T. Giles began dealing in antique boxed ammunition in 1989, following a 30-year career on Wall Street. A veteran of the national gun show circuit, he is a graduate of Lake Forest College; attended the Graduate School of Business, University of Illinois; and is a Chartered Financial Analyst. Now living in Dallas, Ray can be reached at RTG Sporting Collectibles, LLC; Box 670894, Dallas, TX 75367; or through his website: www.rtgammo.com

Winchester Cartridges

by Daniel L. Shuey

The subject of Winchester cartridges and their production is really too deep to do in passing, in my view. That's because most calibers of ammunition were made over a period of several years. And each of those time periods for each cartridge had a unique headstamp used on it.

However, having pointed out the existence of multiple variations for most cartridges, the purpose of this volume is to give both new and more advanced collectors an organized view of each of the Winchester collectible areas as well as real-world prices. We have applied this challenge to cartridges, as well. This has not been done before.

As my contribution, I wanted to share my special knowledge on center fire cartridges and also give you a good grasp of rimfire cartridges, a much smaller subject area. The history of these cartridges is fascinating. But collectors and would-be collectors want to know ... "What are they worth?"

That's a tough task but we tackled it here. It is virtually impossible to price cartridges with as many grades of condition as we give to guns. Guns have so many critical parts where finish and condition can vary, even on the same gun.

Cartridge values are really more a function of rarity, rather than just condition. For years I've felt that single cartridge prices have not reflected rarity as far as loading or headstamp variations. And it is a challenge to price cartridges where there are so few in existence that no "commercial" price has been established. Quite frankly, when these rare cartridges are found or become available, they're only available to a private collector who knows the owner or they go to an auction where a bidding frenzy may escalate the price beyond the expected level.

The other thing you will notice about this section is that there are not a lot of photographs of actual cartridges. First of all, it's a challenge to take photographs that capture minute cartridge detail. Secondly, it is difficult to get access to very rare cartridges. If you're reading this and have actual photographs of rare cartridges or would like to have your rare cartridges seen in future editions, please contact the publishers of this volume.

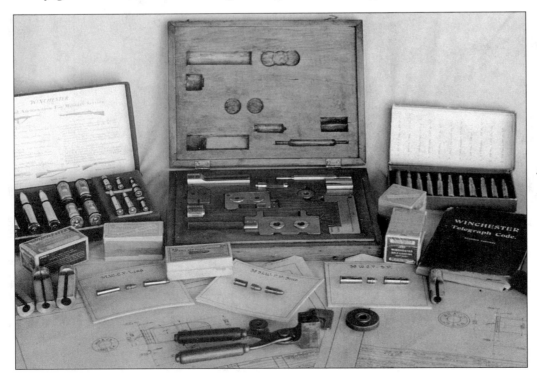

Collectors of cartridges usually don't stop there. They often collect a variety of related items ... from factory cartridge blueprints to reloading tools, from salesman's samples to calibration gauges, from company order code books to full boxes of shells. From the Daniel L. Shuey collection. Photo by D. Kowalski.

Winchester Rimfire and Center Fire Cartridges

Cartridges played a larger role in the business operations of the Winchester Repeating Arms Company (W.R.A. Co.) than most collectors realize. Because ammunition is a high-volume, high-profit product, it literally carried the W.R.A. Co. for most of its existence.

Winchester bragged that they sold their firearms at or near cost. Adding their many give-away guns, the only real moneymakers of the line were the large contract sales. During the 1920s, as a result of cancelled WWI contracts and excess parts and material left over from contracts actually filled, firearms sales brought additional revenue into the company. At that point, the firearms line approached the ammunition line for profits.

During the early years of center fire cartridge production, the 1870s to the mid-1880s, it shared equal footing with the rimfire line for breadth of product and profit. By the late-1880s shotgun target sports had become extremely popular, enough so to allow shot shells to become the company's top-selling ammunition line. In the early 1900s the rimfire line, mainly .22 caliber, became the premier seller and remained so.

Because ammunition was such a high-profit business, it led to Winchester's active participation in the Ammunition Manufacturer's Association (A.M.A.). Winchester either bought many small ammunition companies or forced them out of business. Increased ammunition sales and profits were also a major reason for the W.R.A. Co. to acquire the U.S.C. Co. in 1926.

Another little-known fact is that after Western's takeover of Winchester in late 1931, part of New Haven's ammunition production was transferred to East Alton, Illinois. East Alton's production mix also changed. Certain calibers and types of loadings were moved to New Haven, Connecticut. The changeover was in place by 1933 and not only Winchester but also U.S.C. Co. and Western cartridges were being made on the same lines in New Haven.

The W.R.A. Co. employed many trick or sharpshooters over the years. The most notable of these were the Topperweins, a husband-and-wife team. They, along with the others, helped boost ammunition sales.

Ammunition was handed out gratis at large shooting meets such as various large- and small-bore national matches and the Grand American trap shoot. Any shooter winning or finishing well in those competitions who used Winchester ammunition was highly touted in magazine advertising. All of which led to increased sales.

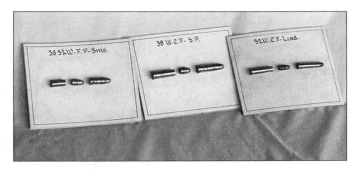

For trade shows Winchester would create sample display cards for all the calibers they produced. From the Daniel L. Shuey Collection. Photo by D. Kowalski.

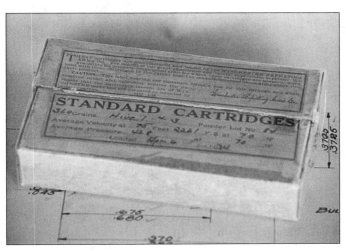

Production runs of ammunition included samples put in boxes and hand-labeled for testing and storage. From the Daniel L. Shuey Collection. Photo by D. Kowalski.

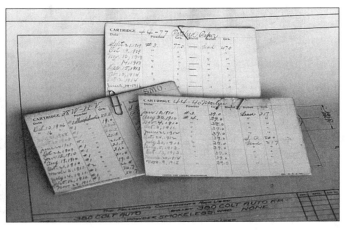

Here are samples of factory production record cards with entries ranging from 1906 to 1916 for .38 WHV, .44-77 and .44-40 Marlin cartridges. From the Daniel L. Shuey Collection. Photo by D. Kowalski.

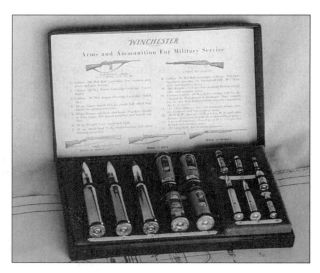

Military Ammunition clearly played a huge role in Company fortunes. This salesman's sample box starts with sample #1, the .50 M-2 Ball Cartridge, and goes through #14, .22 Long Rifle, "for training purposes." From the Daniel L. Shuey Collection. Photo by D. Kowalski.

Government contract orders also played a major role in overall sales at the W.R.A. Co. Many lots were filled for the U.S. Army and Navy along with various state militias during the late 1800s. Work for the U.S. Government began again for the .30-03 caliber and continued on through the years.

Though commercial ammunition production at New Haven ceased in 1956, the Winchester brand continues on at East Alton.

Rimfire (RMF) Cartridges

When the W.R.A. Co. was formed in 1866, the existing ammunition production was continued from the earlier New Haven Arms Co. A raised "H" headstamp, in honor of plant superintendent B.T. Henry, was already in use and continued on.

This raised H will be found in varying sizes on the cartridge's head and gradually gave way to the more common impressed H during the 1880s. A Winchester letter of 1936, which details headstamp histories, states that the form of the H on the headstamp was modified slightly from time to time to

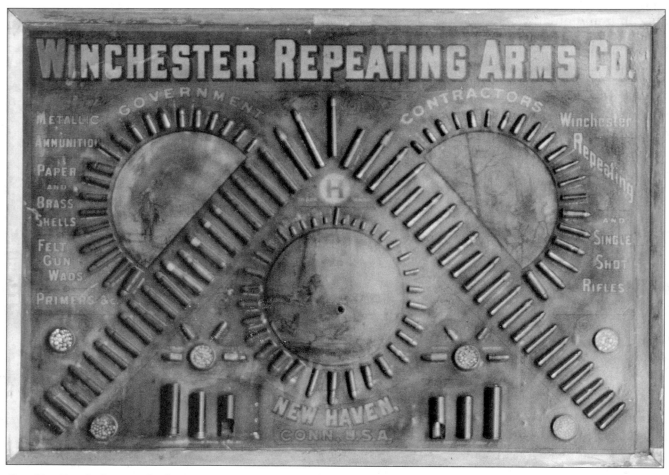

Cartridge Boards, because they're large and dramatic, are often sought by collectors who may not have a companion collection of cartridges. This 1890 "Single W" board is from the Tom Webster Collection and it depicts a variety of Winchester military ammunition. Photo by D. Kowalski.

denote special lots and/or their destinations. An impressed "W" headstamp was begun in 1971 on rimfire calibers and it replaced the well-known H.

Winchester also used a very rare raised "W" headstamp in the early 1880s. Though no records exist to confirm this, it is speculated that this headstamp was used to commemorate the death of Oliver Winchester.

For many years the rimfire line lead a rather mundane life compared to the achievements of the center fire line. The George Stetson patent of 1871 for fastening the bullet to the case mouth is probably the most notable landmark. Rimfire blank cartridges were first offered in the Catalog of 1880 and shot cartridges in 1893.

The addition of the .22 W.R.F. to the Winchester line was another milestone. Brought out for the Model 1890 rifle, it was a great improvement over other .22 calibers. Soon after smokeless loadings became a popular item. The Catalog of 1895 is the first to offer them, but in the .22 Short caliber only. This same year hollow point bullets also became available.

In the early 1900s when the rimfire line became the primary moneymaker of the Winchester ammunition line, its mundane life soon changed. This transition began with the introduction of the Model 1903 rifle and its special, smokeless-powder-only, .22 caliber cartridge. In 1911 Lesmok cartridges were offered. Lesmok is a blend of black and smokeless powders and gave much cleaner shooting than the old black powder cartridges.

Gallery shooting had become increasingly popular, although it would be several years before its own specialized loading would be marketed. The first and most notable appeared in 1914. Those were the Spotlight cartridges. Made using a hollow point bullet coated with aluminum and magnesium powder, they gave a flash when they hit the backstop.

Target shooting and club-oriented matches had become popular and grew very rapidly after WWI. Winchester's own Junior Marksman program along with D.C.M. and N.R.A. programs led to a variety of specialized target loadings. The Precision series, both the 75 and the later 200, came out in 1920. Soon a Precision 5 Star was added. Those along with the Junior Marksman cartridges are identical in outward appearances to other standard loadings. Proper identification is feasible only by removing rounds from an original box.

Staynless priming was announced for the rimfire line in 1927. This priming composition contained no free mercury in its formula thus eliminating pitting of barrels. Smokeless powder cartridges were then known as Staynless, while the Lesmok loadings were called Lestayn. Because of its smooth pressure curve, Lestayn became very popular for small bore competition shooting. Some of the Precision series and the later EZXS series featured this though it was not always noted on box labels or in Catalogs.

Kopperklad bullets were first featured in 1928 and Super Speed rimfires made their appearance in 1932. Between 1936 and 1937 brass began to replace copper for casing material on some grades of .22 caliber ammunition. Copper continued in use for many target grades and those using Lestayn. Steel was considered for case material after WWII, but tried on an experimental basis only.

Many large rimfire sizes, those above .32 caliber, had been discontinued prior to WWI. The remaining few - Spencers, .44 Henry, .41 Swiss - were gradually phased out of the line prior to WWII.

The .22 Winchester Magnum, announced in 1959, was a huge leap in .22 caliber performance. With it began a series of high performance and specialty loadings, particularly in .22 Long Rifle throughout the 1960s and 1970s.

It must be stated that many early large caliber rimfire cartridges listing in Catalogs, i.e. .52-70, Joslyn, .58 Gatling, .50 pistol, etc., were not headstamped. These have not been proven to be made by the W.R.A. Co. and may have been U.M.C. Co. products sold by Winchester.

Center Fire (CF) Ammunition

Indications are that experimental work on center fire cartridges was begun in 1871. Because of the limited and sometimes dysfunctional priming systems and cartridge case manufacturing methods of the era, progress was slow. Patent rights with priming and case making also had to be overcome.

The first mass-produced center fire ammunition made by the W.R.A. Co. used the Milbank primer and folded head case construction. Milbank primers are small diameter, made of copper, and show an indent which makes them look like they've been fired. After having trouble with this primer and folded head case, royalties were paid to use the Berdan primer and its associated solid head case for certain calibers. By 1874 Milbank primers were still in use but with Winchester's own designed solid head case. Later this same year a newly patented boxer-type primer was put into production. Designed by W.R.A. Co. employee John Gardner, it was improved in 1879 and its basic design remains with us to this day.

For many years solid lead bullets in various forms were the only choice in Winchester ammunition. The Express bullet, a hollow point lead bullet with a copper tube in its nose, was offered in 1879. A plain hollow point lead bullet first appeared in the Catalog in 1891.

Another solid lead bullet introduced for the Model 86, 94 and 95, is the Short Range series.

Designed for the shooter who desired lower-priced, low-velocity cartridges for plinking and small game hunting, the Short Range cartridge filled this need. They were first introduced in 1894 and are easily identified by their case cannelure and plain lead bullet.

Full patch or full metal jacket bullets were the next offering. Patented in 1892 by the W.R.A. Co., the few calibers made early on used a copper alloy for their jackets. In approximately 1896 tin plating was added to the jacket to reduce bore fouling. This was continued until 1928. A small number of military-oriented calibers used cupronickel, which was discontinued in 1898 on most commercial calibers. Cupronickel continued in use for metric and some military patch loadings until the late 1930s. Then many of these calibers and loadings were discontinued. Of interest is that cupronickel, also called "German silver," was also tried as a case material.

Soft point bullets, first offered in 1896, follow the same characteristics and time frames as the full patch. Another feature of both of these bullets is a "W" that was stamped on the sides of the jackets. First started in 1903, this "W" was used to denote factory-loaded ammunition. The use of this "W" was discontinued in 1932.

To make a rifle dual purpose, shot cartridges were made popular and were loaded by Winchester. Only a small number of calibers were available when they were first offered in the Catalog of 1886 but more calibers were added over the years. Almost all shot cartridges had been eliminated from the line by WWII. Of interest is that many trick shooters employed shot loadings and some were noted as being made to the shooter's specifications. The normal identification for shot cartridges is a blue over-shot wad.

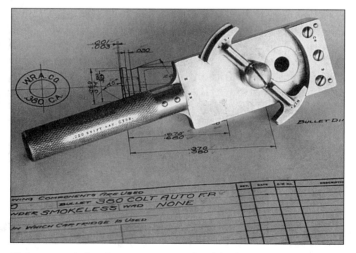

Primer seat depth was measured with factory instruments such as this one for the .220 Swift. (Original factory schematic for the .380 cartridge used as a backdrop.) From the Daniel L. Shuey Collection. Photo by D. Kowalski.

The W.R.A. Co. would make blanks in any caliber and advertised them in their early Catalogs. By 1915 the movie industry was fast becoming a large concern and Winchester began to offer a line of picture blanks. Available in only popular calibers, they were discontinued in the early 1920s. By this time specialty companies were cranking out blanks for the movie studios. Many of those will be found with Winchester headstamps and a variety of colored wads. While Winchester factory-loaded blanks normally used a white wad, the other companies used lavender, pink, red and yellow. Those were made using fired or new-primed cases and are not a W.R.A. Co. product. The exception to this is the later 5-in-1 blank.

Center Fire Head Markings

Many early Winchester solid head rifle cartridges will show a small raised ring. Those would be larger calibers such as Sharps, Remington and many Winchester center fires. During the same time, pistol sizes and small rifle calibers will show a smooth flat head. Those could be either folded or solid heads. The above types will not be headstamped. Identification is easier if the collector remembers that the W.R.A. Co. used only two sizes of boxer primers - large .210" diameter and small .175" diameter. The U.M.C. Co. primers are mostly Berdan and their size is considerably larger than the Winchesters. Raised ring heads on U.M.C. cartridges are also larger and more rounded.

The first headstamp noted on center fire rifle and pistol ammunition is on U.S. Government contract .45-70 cartridges. The format used was "R W month year" - R meaning rifle; W meaning Winchester. "R W 10 78" is the earliest of these known. The .50-70 government rifle contract ammunition also used this same type of markings.

The next format used the "W.R.A. Co." followed by the caliber. No records exist to determine the first usage of this headstamp for either time or caliber. However, 1886 is the first Catalog to show cartridges with headstamps. Some collectors indicate 1884 is the first year Winchester actually used headstamps. The W.R.A. Co. headstamp continued until the 1930s when it was gradually phased out. After WWII, two calibers continued to use this headstamp with the last of them being discontinued in 1954.

The "W.R.A." format was first shown in the 1928 Catalog on the .45 Autorim cartridge. The .30 Krag contract ammunition dated 1930 also used the W.R.A. format. A company memo from 1930 indicated that this headstamp was to be adapted "... as bunters wear out ..." and as " ... new products are added to the line." The 1933 Catalog is the next to show a W.R.A. headstamp. This is on a .22 Hornet.

Headstamps ... W.R.A. Co. and W.R.A.

Headstamps ... Super Speed, W-W, and W-W Super

Winchester also modified the W.R.A. headstamp by using it without periods after each letter. The difference between using the "W.R.A." and the "WRA" headstamps is unknown. It is thought (and actually mentioned in factory notes) that the W.R.A. was for ammunition loaded in New Haven and WRA for loadings from East Alton. This seems to hold true except in a few instances. The WRA headstamp was used on standard velocity and some soft point, full patch target loadings. Its use continued until the late 1960s when the W-W format was instituted.

Next in lineage is the "Super Speed" headstamp. First shown in the catalog of 1933 on the .38 Special caliber, this headstamp would see increased use during the 1930s. It was used only on the higher velocity calibers and hollow point loadings. The company used it until the late 1960s when the "W-W Super" headstamp was adopted.

The plain "Winchester" headstamp was first used around 1890 on .43 Mauser ammunition made for the Chinese Government. This was a raised headstamp. The Winchester headstamp appears again on .458 Winchester Magnum cartridges made in the late 1950s. Though discontinued on the .458 in the late 1960s, the Winchester headstamp is still in use on a few select calibers.

Several calibers do not use a Winchester marking, but just their caliber. Two examples would be the .450 Wesley Richards No. 1 Musket and the 7.65 M/M Belg. (7.65 x 53 Belgian contract ammunition). Others, mainly contract loadings for foreign governments, use various forms of W and a date.

This set of factory sizing or calibration gauges for the 7.65 M/M Mauser Marina Argentina cartridge measured such parameters as shell length, head diameter, head thickness and loading lengths. From the Daniel L. Shuey Collection. Photo by D. Kowalski.

U.S. Government contract ammunition made for use during the Spanish-American War used commercial headstamps. Those would include the 6 M/M U.S.N., .30 U.S.G., and .45-70. No special dates were used until the .30-03 caliber was adapted. As with earlier dated rounds, these cartridges also used the month and year of manufacture in their headstamps. This system continued until mid-1917 when the Ordnance Department specifications called for just year of manufacture. Winchester continued to use this format on most of its U.S. Government ammunition. The last use of this appears on 5.56 M/M NATO experimental cartridges made in 1970.

As with previously mentioned Spanish-American War contract ammunition, many contracts for other governments were filled with commercial headstamped cartridges. This was done either to expedite wartime production or because the contract had no specifications for markings. This is quite evident with large amounts of 7 M/M Mauser ammunition made during WWI, as well as 9 M/M Parabellum and .45 A.C. during WWII. With these commercially marked cartridges, it helps the collector to have taken the round from the original box to aid in identification.

Cartridge Condition

Finding a cartridge specimen in perfect, like-new condition may be difficult. They're more typically quite old and well handled. Several factors can affect the condition of a cartridge or bullet.

Oxidation is the most prevalent factor affecting condition. Storage in some types of wood cabinets, acid from certain types of cardboard, and various chemicals will cause lead and other cartridge metals to oxidize. Some oxidation, in its early stages, will be a very light dust and easily cleaned off. More severe oxidation will involve large pits or flaking of the lead. This severe damage on a bullet should be avoided.

Cracked necks or split cases are evident problems with many of the early smokeless cartridges. This problem, caused by manufacturing techniques, also should be avoided when purchasing a cartridge. However, in some calibers, cases without cracked necks are very difficult to find. Therefore the pricing should reflect this.

Fingerprint and lubricant stains on the cartridge case are also commonly found. Handling cartridges with bare hands leaves oils on them. If not thoroughly wiped off, these acids and oils produced by the human body will cause stains on casings. Also oils and grease from gun lubricants sometimes cause the same effect. While those stains usually can be removed with chemical cleaners, their use should be avoided if possible. Many collectors will not buy a cartridge that has been cleaned. These same chemicals will also remove tin plating on bullet jackets, which will then make proper identification difficult.

Small scratches, dents, dings and nicks on older cartridge cases are often found and cannot be remedied. Again pricing should reflect this condition.

Sealing the cartridge with clear lacquer is another detraction to many collectors. While the polishing and the lacquer make for a bright, classy piece, it does detract from its original condition and natural patina. Serious collectors will not buy a cartridge finished like this.

Loaded cartridges with blackish-green spots or apparent leaking are on the verge of destruction. Some types of early smokeless powders cause these problems. It is not only difficult or sometimes impossible to clean these cases but their corrosion may spread to other specimens stored with them in the collection.

A cartridge with a snapped primer would detract approximately 50 percent from its value. The only place such a round would be beneficial is to fill in a void in a collection until a better specimen can be found.

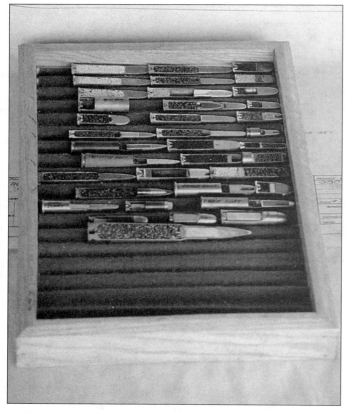

Winchester regularly produced cutaway display shells for their salesman's sample kits. Dan Shuey has also cut many cartridges in half as part of his education (pictured here). From the Daniel L. Shuey Collection. Photo by D. Kowalski.

Pricing and Grades of Condition

We have provided pricing on cartridges in four grades of condition. These are New In Box (NIB.), Excellent (Exc.), Very Good (V.G.) and Good.

New In Box (NIB) - Mint condition that is only possible because the cartridge has not been handled, harmed or oxidized.

Excellent (Exc.) - Perfect condition with no detectable dent, blemish, fingerprint or oxidation.

Very Good (V.G.) - Has only one of the following conditions to a very minor degree: slight oxidation, a small nick or scratch or a light fingerprint.

Good - Has two of the following three conditions: oxidation, nicking or scratching, fingerprints.

If a cartridge has all three problems - oxidation; nicking, scratches or dents; and fingerprint damage - it moves into the Fair category. The more severe these problems, the more it moves down the ladder of condition and value to the typical collector.

A Fair category was not included in our pricing structure, as many of the cartridges have virtually no value in Fair condition. It should also be noted that some NIB prices are considerably higher than one would normally expect. This is because the particular round cannot be properly identified unless it's actually removed from its original box. Or else the original box for the cartridge is very rare or even unknown. In the latter case, a photo or Xerox of the box label adds a valuable premium for the collector.

Cartridge Rarity

Rarity adds the other important dimension to pricing cartridges. There are six levels of rarity as applied to headstamps only. These do not apply to various loadings available with that headstamp. For example, we would consider a "W.R.A. Co." headstamp "Rare" if there were only 25 rounds or less known to exist. But a .22 High Power Pointed shell with a soft point bullet might be "Very Rare" if only five rounds were known to exist. Here are the six levels of rarity.

1. **Very Common** - Found in all collections and easily found at gun shows.
2. **Common** - Found in all collections and found at most gun shows.
3. **Uncommon** - Found in most collections and at some gun or cartridge shows.
4. **Scarce** - Found in some collections and at some cartridge auctions.
5. **Rare** - 25 rounds or less known to exist.
6. **Very Rare** - 5 rounds or less known to exist.

These multiple factors of condition combined with rarity are what make definitive pricing a difficult challenge. We wanted to help you define the parameters of pricing and the important considerations. But it is impossible to create an exact formula. And the situation is complicated further by the determined collector for whom price is no object. If he or she decides that they must have a rare piece to complete their collection, the price they pay may not be equaled again for a long time.

How to Start a Cartridge Collection

The least productive way to start cartridge collecting is to buy a box full of odds and ends, hoping to discover some rare piece that someone has overlooked. Kind of like the kid who starts a penny collection by buying rolls of pennies from his local bank. He'll have lots of pennies but if he finds an old one, it will very likely be severely damaged from years of bouncing around in peoples' pockets.

I recommend that you make a decision to collect certain cartridges based on a pre-determined plan. Let's call these the "levels" of collecting. Here are some of your options.

Level 1 - One or more cartridges and boxes for a particular rifle, i.e. a .270 caliber Model 54 or 70 rifle with assorted cartridge variations and boxes. This could be accomplished easily and displayed nicely.

Level 2 - All cartridges for a favorite model rifle, i.e. the Model 92 rifle available in .25-20 W.C.F., .32-20 W.C.F., .38 W.C.F. and .44 W.C.F. You'd look for standard cartridge variations, their W.H.V. equivalents and associated boxes. This level could be readily achieved and would make a nice grouping.

Level 3 - Collect all Winchester-designed, commercially available cartridges, i.e. all W.C.F., W.H.V., Super Speed, and Winchester Magnum variations. With a few exceptions, this also could be readily achieved. However, display and storage may become a problem.

Level 4 - Collect all commercial calibers chambered in Winchester rifles. This would include many metric calibers. While there are a significant number of headstamp and loading variations, it is an obtainable goal.

Level 5 - Collect all commercial calibers Winchester loaded including pistol calibers. With the many headstamp and loadings available, this would be a lofty goal but could be achieved. Storage and display would become a problem.

Level 6 - Collect everything Winchester ever made in their ammunition line. This would include not only the previously mentioned ammunition but also cannon shells, military contract shells, special purpose and experimental cartridges. To date no single collector has attained this level and, in fact, it may be impossible to achieve.

Among the many challenges of collecting are the twin challenges of storage and display. The collection needs to be housed in custom or specially made units. Or the owner gets lucky and finds old or odd furnishings that can be converted to displays. Here are "recycled" storage trays for a portion of the Daniel L. Shuey cartridge collection. Photo by D. Kowalski.

Similarities in Center Fire Ammunition

Several calibers in the Winchester Center Fire line use the same cartridge case. But they have entirely different names and, in some instances, loadings. This leads to some confusion in identification if the cartridge is not headstamped. If it is headstamped, some confusion may still exist among novice collectors.

The .44 W.C.F. is a classic example as it is used for a number of different loadings and firearms, all having different names. However, those in the W.R.A. Co. line are headstamped to aid in identification. Examples of these would be .44 W.C.F., .44 W.H.V. M-92, .44-40 (Marlin), .44 G.G. (Game Getter), .44 X.L. (Extra Long Shot).

The .40-60 Marlin Casing

One casing, for the .40-60 Marlin, is used for several different calibers. The difficulty in identification is that some, in their early loadings, are not headstamped. Below are the calibers that use the .40-60 Marlin casing. Note the distinctive shapes of each bullet and their primer sizes. Those features will help identify cartridges without headstamps.

.40-60 Marlin

Introduced in the Catalog of 1882 for the Marlin Model 1881 rifle, it was also produced without a headstamp. Its main identification feature is its use of a small No. 1 size primer and its bullet profile.

Primer: No. 1 Win.
Powder: 60 Gr.
Bullet: 260 Gr.

.40-70 Bullard

First listed in the Catalog of 1884, it was made for the Bullard Heavy Frame Repeater. While it also uses the No. 1 size primer, it has a distinct bullet profile. It is also found without headstamp.

Primer: No. 1 Win.
Powder: 72 Gr.
Bullet: 232 Gr.

.40-60 Colt

Introduced for the large frame Colt Lightning rifle, it was not listed in W.R.A. Co. Catalogs. It was made in quantity and appears on cartridge boards. This cartridge is headstamped.

Primer: No. 1 Win.
Powder: 60 Gr.
Bullet: 260 Gr.

.40-65 Hotchkiss

Listed only in the Catalog of 1884, it was an experimental cartridge of its day. The Hotchkiss also appears on the 1884 cartridge board. It is not headstamped.

Primer: No. 1 Win.
Powder: 65 Gr.
Bullet: 260 Gr.

.40-65 Winchester Center Fire (W.C.F.)

This cartridge was first listed in the 1887 Catalog for the M-86 rifle. It is a .40-60 Marlin casing with an increased powder charge and a larger No. 2 1/2 size primer.

Primer: No. 2 1/2 Win.
Powder: 65 Gr.
Bullet: 260 Gr.

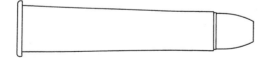

The .32 Winchester Center Fire Cartridge

Here is another example of the variations possible in one shell casing. The .32 W.C.F. was made for the Model 92 rifle. As you will see in the following chart, it was produced with seven different headstamps combined with seven different bullet configurations.

We will show each of the seven headstamps, followed by the bullet configurations available in each.

Headstamp A

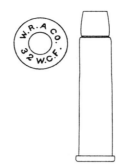

Configuration (one factory load) ... Lead

Headstamp B

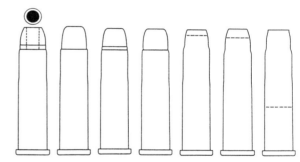

Configurations (from left) ... Hollow Point; Lead; Lead; Full Patch; Shot; Shot; Blank; Blank

Headstamp C

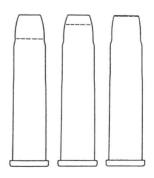

Configurations (from left) ... Shot; Shot; Shot

Headstamp D

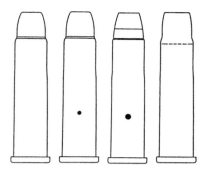

Configurations (from left) ... Lead; Dummy; Dummy; Smokeless Shot

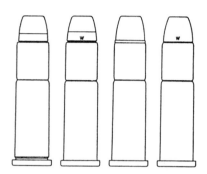

Configurations (from left) ... Soft Point; Soft Point; Lead; Full Patch

Headstamp E

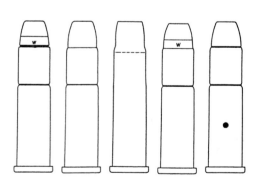

Configurations (from left) ... Soft Point; Lead; Shot; Soft Point; Dummy

Headstamp F

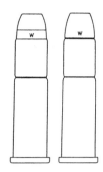

Configurations (from left) ... Soft Point; Full Patch

Headstamp G

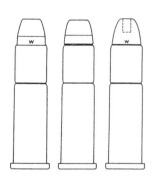

Configurations (from left) ... Soft Point; Soft Point; Hollow Point

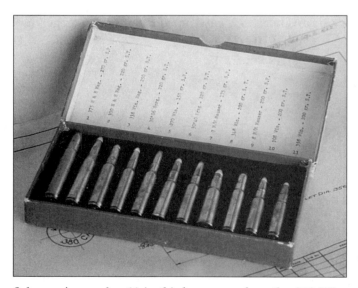

Salesman's samples, 11 in this box, range from the .270 Winchester to the .375 Holland & Holland Magnum to the 7 M/M and 8 M/M Mauser cartridges. From the Daniel L. Shuey Collection. Photo by D. Kowalski.

Winchester Cartridge Pricing

This price guide is set up for two groups of collectors. First we have both Rimfire and Center Fire cartridges for a collection through Level 3. These are the commercial cartridges Winchester designed and made at their New Haven, Connecticut production facility for Winchester Model rifles. We will list the cartridge caliber, followed by any headstamp and configuration notes in parenthesis. Next we'll indicate the Winchester Model rifle the cartridge was made for. Production dates will follow; these will begin with first year of production. If the production date is followed by - ?, that indicates the cartridge was still being made at New Haven when Winchester ceased commercial cartridge production there in 1956.

We'll then follow that list with additional cartridges to take the would-be collector through Level 4. These include all cartridges that could be chambered in Winchester rifles.

Pricing grades are, in order, New In Box (NIB), Excellent (Exc.), Very Good (V.G.) and Good. Finally, we will provide notes on valuation for special versions of the cartridge.

Prices are stated in U.S. Dollars for standard loaded single rounds. Prices are for single specimen collector cartridges (not the prices for shooting purposes). It is especially important to note that single round prices do not reflect nor should they be used to determine full box prices. In most cases, a full box is worth far more than the sum of the single cartridges.

If you are an experienced collector, the publisher would welcome your offer to be a member of future pricing panels.

Note: Line drawings of headstamps were made by E.L. Scranton and are the copyrighted property of Daniel L. Shuey.

All cartridge loading data for primers, grains of powder, and bullet weights were taken directly from original Winchester Catalogs, memos and drawings. They are used here strictly for historical reference. This data is not meant or intended to be used as a guideline for the loading of ammunition. No responsibility is assumed, meant or implied by the author, editor or publisher for its use in the loading of ammunition.

Cartridge Values -
General Rules on Price Premiums

Add 25 percent for shot loading (W.C.F.)
Add 25 percent for blank cartridge (W.C.F.)
Add 75 percent for cartridge board dummy

Values: Rimfire (RMF) Cartridges (Level 3)

.22 W.R.F.
Model 1890, 61, 67, 68, 85   1890 ---

NIB	Exc.	V.G.	Good
0.60	0.50	0.30	

Add 50 percent for hollow point.

.22 WINCHESTER AUTOMATIC
Model 1903   1903 ---

NIB	Exc.	V.G.	Good
0.60	0.50	0.30	

Add 50 percent for hollow point.

.22 WINCHESTER MAGNUM RIMFIRE (WMRF)
                                                            1959 ---

NIB	Exc.	V.G.	Good
0.30	0.20		

The .22WMRF design began in 1952; production began in 1958 and it was announced to the trade in 1959. Shown in Catalog in 1960. Small lots made at New Haven prior to move to East Alton.

.44 HENRY (RAISED H, ROUND NOSE, NEW HAVEN)
Model 1866   1862 - ?

NIB	Exc.	V.G.	Good
50.00	45.00	30.00	20.00

.44 Henry Round Nose thought to be first style made. A New Haven Arms product but later shipped in Winchester Repeating Arms Co. boxes so listed here.

.44 HENRY (RAISED H, POINTED NOSE)
Model 1866   1864 - ?

NIB	Exc.	V.G.	Good
40.00	30.00	20.00	15.00

The early .44 Henry and Colt had a shorter case for a time, then both went to a longer case.

170 • Winchester Cartridge Pricing

.44 HENRY (RAISED H, FLAT NOSE)
Model 1866   1866 - ?

NIB	Exc.	V.G.	Good
20.00	15.00	12.00	10.00

.44 HENRY (IMPRESSED H, FLAT NOSE)
Model 1866   ? - 1937

NIB	Exc.	V.G.	Good
15.00	12.00	10.00	8.00

Values: Center Fire (CF) Cartridges (Level 3)

.218 BEE
Model 43, 65   1939 ---

NIB	Exc.	V.G.	Good
2.00	1.50	1.00	0.75

.219 ZIPPER
Model 64   1938 ---

NIB	Exc.	V.G.	Good
2.25	1.75	1.00	0.75

.22 HORNET
Model 43, 54, 70   1931 ---

NIB	Exc.	V.G.	Good
0.75	0.50	0.30	

Add 100 percent for "WRA" headstamp. The .22 Hornet was a wildcat cartridge of the 1920s and earlier. The Winchester Repeating Arms Co. did the ballistics and chamber standards for the industry and named it the .22 Winchester Hornet.

.22 W.C.F.
Model 1885   1885-1937

NIB	Exc.	V.G.	Good
1.50	1.00	0.75	0.50

.220 SWIFT
Model 54, 70   1936 ---

NIB	Exc.	V.G.	Good
2.00	1.50	1.00	0.75

.236 U.S.N. (SO HEADSTAMPED)
Win - Lee (Rimless)   1895-1897

NIB	Exc.	V.G.	Good
25.00	20.00	15.00	12.00

The U.S. Navy designed a rimmed cartridge. Winchester did the design work for a rimless version, later called "6 M/M U.S.N."

6 M/M U.S.N. (S0 HEADSTAMPED)
Win-Lee   1897-1938

NIB	Exc.	V.G.	Good
4.00	3.50	2.00	1.00

.243 WINCHESTER (PREVIOUSLY CALLED 6 M/M WINCHESTER X: HAS SUPER-X HEADSTAMP)
Model 70   1955 ---

NIB	Exc.	V.G.	Good
0.75	0.50	0.30	

.25-20 W.C.F.
Model 1892, 43, 53, 65   1895 ---

NIB	Exc.	V.G.	Good
1.00	0.75	0.50	0.25

Add 25 percent for full patch.

.25-20 W.H.V.
Model 1892, 43, 53, 65   1903 ---

NIB	Exc.	V.G.	Good
1.25	1.00	0.75	0.50

Add 50 percent for "Super Speed" headstamp.

.25-35 W.C.F.
Model 1894, 55, 64, 85   1895 ---

NIB	Exc.	V.G.	Good
2.00	1.50	1.00	0.75

Add 50 percent for Short Range.

.270 W.C.F. (.27 W.C.F.)
Model 54, 70   1925 ---

NIB	Exc.	V.G.	Good
1.00	0.75	0.50	

Add 100 percent for "W.R.A." headstamp.

.30 W.C.F. (.30-30)
Model 1894, 54, 55, 64, 85   1895 ---

NIB	Exc.	V.G.	Good
0.50	0.40		

Add 200 percent for Short Range; add 50 percent for "WRA" headstamp.

.308 WINCHESTER (7.62 M/M NATO)
Model 70, 88   1953 ---

NIB	Exc.	V.G.	Good
0.75	0.50	0.25	

.32 W.C.F. (.32-20)
Model 1873, 43, 53, 65, 92, 85   1882 ---

NIB	Exc.	V.G.	Good
0.75	0.50	0.25	

Add 400 percent for hollow point.

.32 W.H.V. M-92 (.32-20 W.H.V.)
Model 1892, 43, 53, 65   1903 ---

NIB	Exc.	V.G.	Good
1.50	1.00	0.75	0.50

Add 25 percent for full patch; add 50 percent for "Super Speed" headstamp.

.32 S.L. (SELF-LOADING)
Model 1905   1909-1956

NIB	Exc.	V.G.	Good
1.25	1.00	0.75	0.50

.32 S.L.C.F. (SO HEADSTAMPED)
Model 1905   1905-1908

NIB	Exc.	V.G.	Good
10.00	8.00	5.00	3.00

.32 WINCHESTER SPECIAL
Model 1894, 55, 64, 85   1902 ---

NIB	Exc.	V.G.	Good
1.00	0.75	0.50	0.25

Add 75 percent for "W.R.A. Co." headstamp with hollow point.

.32-40 W.C.F. (SO HEADSTAMPED)
Model 1894   1894 - ?

NIB	Exc.	V.G.	Good
125.00	100.00	75.00	50.00

The only reference found for this cartridge is on the cover illustration of "Shooting And Fishing Times" of October 10, 1895. And only one box, to date, has been found. It's a scarce cartridge with a brief and confusing history that I discuss in my book, <u>W.R.A. Co. - Headstamped Cartridges And Their Variations, Vol. I</u>, pages 234-5.

.33 W.C.F
Model 1886, 85   1903-1954

NIB	Exc.	V.G.	Good
3.50	3.00	2.00	1.50

.348 WINCHESTER (.34 W.C.F.)
Model 71   1936 ---

NIB	Exc.	V.G.	Good
2.00	1.50	1.00	0.75

Add 50 percent for 250 grain bullet.

.35 S.L. (SELF-LOADING)
Model 1905   1909-1956

NIB	Exc.	V.G.	Good
1.25	1.00	0.75	0.50

.35 S.L.C.F. (SO HEADSTAMPED)
Model 1905   1905-1908

NIB	Exc.	V.G.	Good
10.00	8.00	6.00	4.00

.35 W.C.F.
Model 1895, 85   1903-1948

NIB	Exc.	V.G.	Good
3.50	2.50	1.50	1.00

Add 25 percent for "WRA" headstamp.

.351 S.L. (SELF-LOADING)
Model 1907   1907 ---

NIB	Exc.	V.G.	Good
0.75	0.50	0.25	

Winchester Cartridge Pricing • 173

.358 WINCHESTER

Model 70, 88   1955 ---

NIB	Exc.	V.G.	Good
1.25	1.00	0.75	0.50

.38 EXPRESS

Model 1885   1886-1918

NIB	Exc.	V.G.	Good
20.00	15.00	10.00	8.00

.38 W.C.F.

Model 1873, 92, 85   1879 ---

NIB	Exc.	V.G.	Good
1.00	0.75	0.50	0.25

Add 400 percent for hollow point; add 100 percent for full patch.

.38-40 W.H.V. (SO HEADSTAMPED)

Model 1892   1903 ---

NIB	Exc.	V.G.	Good
500.00	400.00	350.00	200.00

.38 W.H.V. M-92

Model 1892, 53   1903-1942

NIB	Exc.	V.G.	Good
2.00	1.50	0.75	0.50

Add 25 percent for full patch.

.38-55 W.H.V.

Model 1894   1904-1940

NIB	Exc.	V.G.	Good
4.00	3.00	2.00	1.00

Add 25 percent for full patch.

.38-56 W.C.F.

Model 1886, 85   1887-1946

NIB	Exc.	V.G.	Good
3.50	2.50	1.50	1.00

Add 25 percent for full patch.

.38-70 (NO W.C.F. - SO HEADSTAMPED)

Model 1886   1894 - ?

NIB	Exc.	V.G.	Good
12.00	10.00	8.00	6.00

.38-70 W.C.F. (SO HEADSTAMPED)

Model 1886   1894-1918

NIB	Exc.	V.G.	Good
4.50	4.00	3.00	2.00

Add 25 percent for soft point or full patch.

.38-72 W.C.F.

Model 1895   1896-1946

NIB	Exc.	V.G.	Good
3.50	3.00	2.50	1.50

.40 EXPRESS
Model 1885   1886-1916

NIB	Exc.	V.G.	Good
25.00	20.00	15.00	12.00

.40-60 W.C.F.
Model 1876, 85   1884-1938

NIB	Exc.	V.G.	Good
4.50	4.00	2.00	1.50

.40-65 HOTCHKISS
Model 1883 Sporting Rifle   1884 - ?

NIB	Exc.	V.G.	Good
500.00	400.00	350.00	250.00

Note: Shown only in Catalog of 1884. No weapons chambered for this cartridge known to exist. Also appears on 1884 cartridge board.

.40-65 W.C.F.
Model 1886, 85   1887-1946

NIB	Exc.	V.G.	Good
5.00	4.00	3.00	2.00

Add 25 percent for full patch.

.40-70 (NO W.C.F. - SO HEADSTAMPED)
Model 1886   1894 - ?

NIB	Exc.	V.G.	Good
12.00	10.00	8.00	6.00

.40-70 W.C.F. (SO HEADSTAMPED)
Model 1886   1894-1918

NIB	Exc.	V.G.	Good
6.00	5.00	4.00	3.00

Add 25 percent for soft point or full patch.

.40-72 W.C.F.
Model 1895   1896-1940

NIB	Exc.	V.G.	Good
4.50	4.00	3.00	2.00

Add 30 percent for lead.

.40-75 W.C.F. (.40-82 W.C.F. WITH EXPRESS BULLET)
Model 1886, 85   1887-1916

NIB	Exc.	V.G.	Good
20.00	15.00	12.00	10.00

Note: The .40-75 has a .40-82 W.C.F. headstamp. It has a lighter-weight, copper-tubed Express bullet.

.40-82 W.C.F.
Model 1886, 85   1886-1947

NIB	Exc.	V.G.	Good
5.00	4.00	3.00	2.00

Add 25 percent for full patch.

.401 S.L. (SELF-LOADING)
Model 1910   1910-1955

NIB	Exc.	V.G.	Good
3.00	1.50	1.00	0.75

Add 50 percent for full patch, 250 grain bullet or "WRA" headstamp.

.405 W.C.F.
Model 1895, 85   1904-1955

NIB	Exc.	V.G.	Good
4.00	3.50	2.50	2.00

.44 W.C.F.
Model 1873, 53, 92, 85   1873 ---

NIB	Exc.	V.G.	Good
0.75	0.50	0.25	

Add 400 percent for hollow point; add 25 percent for full patch.

.44 W.C.F. (RAISED HEADSTAMP)
Model 1873   ?

NIB	Exc.	V.G.	Good
60.00	40.00	30.00	20.00

.44 W.H.V. M-92
Model 1892, 53   1903-1940

NIB	Exc.	V.G.	Good
2.50	2.00	1.75	1.50

Add 50 percent for full patch.

.45 EXPRESS
Model 1885   1886-1916

NIB	Exc.	V.G.	Good
45.00	40.00	35.00	20.00

.45-60 W.C.F.
Model 1876, 85   1879-1938

NIB	Exc.	V.G.	Good
6.00	5.00	4.00	2.00

.45-70 W.C.F. (MODEL 86 WITH FLAT NOSE BULLET)
Model 1886, 85   1886-1920

NIB	Exc.	V.G.	Good
3.00	2.00	1.50	1.00

Add 25 percent for full patch; add 25 percent for 350 grain bullet.

.45-70 W.H.V.
Model 1886   1903-1940

NIB	Exc.	V.G.	Good
5.00	4.50	3.00	1.50

Add 10 percent for full patch.

.45-75 W.C.F.
Model 1876, 85   1876-1940

NIB	Exc.	V.G.	Good
6.00	5.00	3.00	1.50

Add 300 percent for Express bullet.

.45-82 W.C.F. (SO HEADSTAMPED)
Model 1886   1886-1916

NIB	Exc.	V.G.	Good
25.00	20.00	15.00	10.00

Add 20 percent for soft point or full patch.

.45-85 W.C.F. (SO HEADSTAMPED)
Model 1886   1886-1916

NIB	Exc.	V.G.	Good
10.00	8.00	6.00	3.50

Add 50 percent for hollow point or full patch.

.45-90 W.C.F.
Model 1886, 85   1886-1946

NIB	Exc.	V.G.	Good
6.00	5.00	4.00	2.00

Add 50 percent for Express bullet or hollow point; add 25 percent for full patch.

.45-90 WINCHESTER SPECIAL (LONG RANGE PAPER PATCH BULLET - .45-75 WCF WITH 450 GRAIN BULLET)
Model 1876   1878 Only

NIB	Exc.	V.G.	Good
500.00	400.00	350.00	250.00

Note: Shown only in Catalog of 1878. Even though it is listed above for Model 1876, memos indicate this cartridge will not chamber in existing Model 1876 weapons.

.45-90 W.H.V.
Model 1886   1903-1920

NIB	Exc.	V.G.	Good
8.00	6.50	4.50	2.50

.458 WINCHESTER MAGNUM
Model 70   1957 ---

NIB	Exc.	V.G.	Good
7.00	6.00	4.00	3.00

Design work began in 1955 and first lots made at New Haven.

.50-95 EXPRESS (SO HEADSTAMPED)
Model 1876, 85   1879-1918

NIB	Exc.	V.G.	Good
25.00	20.00	15.00	12.00

Add 20 percent for hollow point, full patch or lead.

.50-95 W.C.F. (SO HEADSTAMPED)
Model 1876, 85   1886 - ?

NIB	Exc.	V.G.	Good
30.00	25.00	20.00	15.00

Add 20 percent for hollow point or lead; add 200 percent for smokeless powder.

.50-100-450 (SO HEADSTAMPED)
Model 1886   1895-1920

NIB	Exc.	V.G.	Good
35.00	30.00	25.00	20.00

Add 25 percent for full patch.

.50-105 EXPRESS
Model 1886, 85   1886 - ?

NIB	Exc.	V.G.	Good
600.00	500.00	400.00	350.00

This cartridge not listed in Catalogs. Appears on 1890 cartridge boards. No loaded rounds known to exist at this time (February 2000).

.50-110 EXPRESS
Model 1886, 85   1887-1940

NIB	Exc.	V.G.	Good
12.00	10.00	8.00	5.00

Add 25 percent for hollow point, lead or full patch.

.50-110 W.H.V.
Model 1886   1903-1920

NIB	Exc.	V.G.	Good
18.00	15.00	12.00	8.00

Add 50 percent for full patch.

.50-140 EXPRESS
Model 1885   1886 - ?

NIB	Exc.	V.G.	Good
800.00	700.00	500.00	400.00

This cartridge not listed in Catalogs. Appears on 1890 cartridge boards.

Values: Rimfire (RMF) Cartridges (Level 4)

.22 SHORT (RAISED H)
Model 1885, 73   1873 - ?

NIB	Exc.	V.G.	Good
12.00	10.00	7.00	3.00

.22 SHORT (IMPRESSED H)
Model 1885, 73, 90, 06, 56, 57,
62, 61, 72, 74, 00, 02, 04, 99   ? ---

NIB	Exc.	V.G.	Good
	0.25		

Add 100 percent for hollow point; add 300 percent for Spotlight cartridge.

.22 LONG (RAISED H)
Model 1885, 93   1873 - ?

NIB	Exc.	V.G.	Good
8.00	6.00	3.00	2.00

.22 LONG (IMPRESSED H)
Model 1885, 73, 90, 00, 02,
04, 99, 58, 53, 60, 62, 61,
67, 68, 63, 637, 677, 72, 47   ? ---

NIB	Exc.	V.G.	Good
0.30	0.25		

.22 LONG RIFLE
Model 1885, 90, 52, 56, 57,
61, 63, 75, 74, 02, 04, 06,
58, 59, 60, 62, 60A, 67, 68,
69, 697, 677, 72, 47   1890 ---

NIB	Exc.	V.G.	Good
0.25			

Add 50 percent for copper case.

.25 STEVENS (LONG)
Model 1885   1890-1942

NIB	Exc.	V.G.	Good
1.00	0.75	0.50	0.25

.25 STEVENS (SHORT)
Model 1885   1902-1946

NIB	Exc.	V.G.	Good
0.75	0.50	0.25	

.32 SHORT (RAISED H)
Model 1885   1873 - ?

NIB	Exc.	V.G.	Good
3.00	2.00	1.00	0.50

.32 SHORT (IMPRESSED H)
Model 1885   ? - 1942

NIB	Exc.	V.G.	Good
0.75	0.50	0.25	

.32 LONG (RAISED H)
Model 1885   1873 - ?

NIB	Exc.	V.G.	Good
3.50	2.50	1.50	0.50

.32 LONG (IMPRESSED H)
Model 1885   ? ---

NIB	Exc.	V.G.	Good
0.75	0.50	0.25	

9 M/M BALL
Model 36   1920-1928

NIB	Exc.	V.G.	Good
2.50	2.00	1.50	1.00

9 M/M SHOT - LONG (RED, PINK, ORANGE CASE)
Model 36   1920-1958

NIB	Exc.	V.G.	Good
2.00	1.50	1.25	1.00

Add 100 percent for green case; add 200 percent for blue case.

9 M/M SHOT - SHORT (BLUE CASE)
Model 36   ?

NIB	Exc.	V.G.	Good
8.00	6.00	4.00	3.00

Values: Center Fire (CF) Cartridges (Level 4)

.25-20 STEVENS
Model 1885   1890-1946

NIB	Exc.	V.G.	Good
2.00	1.75	1.00	0.75

Add 25 percent for soft point; add 50 percent for full patch.

.250-3000 SAVAGE
Model 54, 70   1923 ---

NIB	Exc.	V.G.	Good
1.00	0.75	0.50	0.25

Add 100 percent for "WRA Co." headstamp; add 50 percent for full patch.

.257 ROBERTS
Model 54, 70   1935 ---

NIB	Exc.	V.G.	Good
1.75	1.50	1.00	0.75

.30 G. 1903 (.30-03)
Model 1895   1905-1940

NIB	Exc.	V.G.	Good
3.00	2.50	1.50	1.00

.30 G. 1906 (.30-06)
Model 1895, 54, 70   1908 ---

NIB	Exc.	V.G.	Good
0.50	0.25		

Add 100 percent for "WRA" headstamp; add 200 percent for Wimbledon Cup; add 800 percent for tracer.

.30 U.S.G. (.30 ARMY, .30-40 KRAG)
Model 1895, 85   1894 ---

NIB	Exc.	V.G.	Good
1.00	0.75	0.50	0.25

Add 200 percent for Short Range; add 50 percent for "WRA" headstamp or for pointed full patch bullet.

.300 SAVAGE
Model 70   1928 ---

NIB	Exc.	V.G.	Good
1.00	0.75	0.50	0.25

Add 100 percent for "WRA Co." headstamp; add 50 percent for full patch.

.303 BRITISH
Model 1895, 85   1897 ---

NIB	Exc.	V.G.	Good
1.00	0.75	0.50	0.25

Add 50 percent for "WRA Co." headstamp; add 50 percent for full patch; add 100 percent for "WRA" headstamp.

.32-40 (MARLIN & BALLARD, LEAD BULLET)
Model 1885, 94   1885-1937

NIB	Exc.	V.G.	Good
2.00	1.75	1.00	0.75

Add 150 percent for paper patch.

.32-40 (WINCHESTER, SOFT POINT & FULL PATCH)
Model 1894, 85   1895 ---

NIB	Exc.	V.G.	Good
2.50	2.00	1.00	0.75

Add 50 percent for Short Range.

.32 IDEAL
Model 1885   1894-1918

NIB	Exc.	V.G.	Good
6.00	5.00	3.50	2.00

.35 REMINGTON
Model 70   1907 ---

NIB	Exc.	V.G.	Good
0.75	0.50	0.25	

Add 100 percent for "WRA Co." or "WRA" headstamps.

.300 H&H (HOLLAND & HOLLAND)
Model 70   1937 ---

NIB	Exc.	V.G.	Good
1.50	1.25	0.75	0.50

Add 50 percent for "WRA" headstamp.

.375 H&H (HOLLAND & HOLLAND)
Model 70   1936 ---

NIB	Exc.	V.G.	Good
2.00	1.75	1.50	1.00

Add 50 percent for "WRA" headstamp.

.40-50 SHARPS STRAIGHT
Model 1885   1879-1916

NIB	Exc.	V.G.	Good
15.00	12.00	8.00	5.00

.40-70 SHARPS STRAIGHT
Model 1885   1879-1914

NIB	Exc.	V.G.	Good
15.00	12.00	8.00	5.00

Deduct 30 percent for plain lead.

.40-70 BALLARD
Model 1885   1882-1916

NIB	Exc.	V.G.	Good
25.00	20.00	12.00	8.00

.40-85 BALLARD
Model 1885   1885-1913

NIB	Exc.	V.G.	Good
40.00	35.00	25.00	15.00

Note: *Factory records indicate barrels made for this caliber and to substitute this ammunition when .40-90 Ballard not in stock.*

.40-90 BALLARD
Model 1885   1884-1916

NIB	Exc.	V.G.	Good
35.00	30.00	25.00	15.00

.40-90 SHARPS STRAIGHT
Model 1885   1884-1916

NIB	Exc.	V.G.	Good
25.00	20.00	15.00	10.00

.45-70 (U.S. GOVERNMENT, LEAD BULLET)
Model 1885, 86   1878-1935

NIB	Exc.	V.G.	Good
1.25	1.00	0.75	0.50

Add 50 percent for 500 grain lead bullet; add 100 percent for tin case.

.45-70 (WINCHESTER, SOFT POINT & FULL PATCH)
Model 1885, 86   1895 ---

NIB	Exc.	V.G.	Good
1.50	1.00	0.75	0.50

Add 200 percent for Short Range; add 1000 percent for 500 grain full patch.

.45-70 & .45-75 SHARPS
Model 1885   1886-1916

NIB	Exc.	V.G.	Good
30.00	25.00	15.00	10.00

.50 ELEY (3" EXPRESS)
Model 1885   See Note

NIB	Exc.	V.G.	Good
300.00	250.00	200.00	150.00

Note: *No known headstamped rounds, factory drawings and test data 1902-1912. Appears in 1910-1916 Catalogs under Single Shot Rifles.*

7 M/M MAUSER (7X57)
Model 54, 70   1899 ---

NIB	Exc.	V.G.	Good
0.75	0.50	0.25	

Add 200 percent for "WRA" headstamp. Add 1000 percent for tracer.

7.65 M/M (BELGIAN)
Model 54   1900-1938

NIB	Exc.	V.G.	Good
2.00	1.50	0.75	0.50

Add 100 percent for pointed full patch.

8 M/M MAUSER (7.9 M/M)
Model 70   1918 ---

NIB	Exc.	V.G.	Good
0.75	0.50	0.25	

Add 100 percent for pointed full patch or "W.R.A. Co." headstamp. **Note:** *The 8 M/M cartridge previously listed in Catalogs was for Mauser & Mannlicher rifles 1904-1914. The 7.9 M/M appears in 1918 Catalog.*

9 M/M MAUSER
Model 54, 70   1905-1938

NIB	Exc.	V.G.	Good
2.50	2.00	1.00	0.75

Add 50 percent for full patch.

Bibliography

Houze, Herbert G. *Winchester Repeating Arms Company. Its History & Development from 1865 to 1981.* Iola, Wisconsin: Krause Publications, Inc., 1994.

Shuey, Daniel L. *W.R.A. Co. - Headstamped Cartridges And Their Variations, Volume I.* Rockford, Illinois: WCF Publications, Inc. 1999.

Various notes and ledgers from former Winchester employees.

Watrous, George. *Metallic Ammunition - Brass and Paper Shotshells.* Unpublished Winchester In-house Booklet.

Watrous, George. *Winchester Rifles & Shotguns.* Unpublished Winchester In-house Booklet.

Winchester Repeating Arms Company. *Catalogs;* 1920 - 1961. *Price Lists;* 1873-1956.

Winchester Repeating Arms Company. *Catalogs* of New Haven Arms Co. and Winchester Repeating Arms Co. 1865-1918. 12 volumes. Reprinted by Armory Publications, Tacoma, Washington. 1991.

Daniel L. Shuey has been collecting cartridges since 1970. He is the author of W.R.A. Co. - Headstamped Cartridges And Their Variations, Vol. 1, published in 1999.

Winchester Shotshells

by Daniel L. Shuey

To visualize the scope at which Winchester shotshells could be collected, W.R.A. Co. employee George Watrous once calculated that 14,383 single loading combinations were possible. This list was compiled of available gauges, grades, shot sizes, shot types (soft or chilled), shot charges, powder brands, powder charges and shell lengths offered in Winchester Catalogs prior to World War I.

The goal of this book, generally, is to give collectors both accurate historical information and insights to help them date Winchester products they find; and then to provide a guide to pricing these collectibles. An exhaustive, chronological listing of the estimated 14,383 shotshell variations (and their values) is beyond the scope of this book. But we intend to give you enough history and enough pricing data to get you started in this vast and complex arena of Winchester shotshells.

A Brief History of Winchester Paper Shotshells

The growth in the ammunition and explosives industry during WWI made all involved aware that industry standards must be developed and applied to their related fields. Those standards involved cartridge and chamber sizes, proof testing methods, ballistic and accuracy testing, powder grading and measurements. The standards would eventually include shipping methods and enclosures for ammunition, primers and powder along with cartridge names and markings.

During the later stages of the War a loose-knit group of the concerned manufacturers was formed under the title, "Society of American Manufacturers of Small Arms and Ammunition." The Society was disbanded after a few years. Through their early efforts the simplification and standardization of shotshells began. In the mid-1920s the group reorganized under the title "Sporting Arms and Ammunition Manufacturer's Institute (SAMMI)."

SAMMI is still in existence and with collateral input from the U.S. Commerce Department began to pare down the vast amount of shotshell loading combinations. By 1939 the total number of combined loadings was 262. By 1954 the Winchester line had been reduced to 105 line items including blanks and rifled slugs.

As indicated in the rimfire and center fire text, Winchester commercial ammunition production at New Haven, Connecticut was discontinued in the latter half of 1956. We will make that cut-off date part of our timeline in this section. The coverage of shotshells in this text will be limited to pre-1956 grades and loadings.

Of interest is that after Winchester acquired the United States Cartridge Company in 1926, the U.S. brand of shotshells was made on some of the same production lines as Winchester shells. The same would hold true for the Western line of shotshells. After Western took over the W.R.A. Co. in 1931, plans were formulated to move some of the New Haven production to Western's plant in East Alton, Illinois and vice versa.

By 1933 this plan was in effect and certain grades of each company's shells were being made at the other's facility. By 1956 both brands were being made in all grades; in fact they were being made simultaneously at each plant. The only exceptions were that blanks and rifled slugs were made solely at New Haven. In 1954, alone, total production of both facilities approached 300 million shells.

To begin a history of Winchester shotshell grades and loadings, several dates need to be clarified and set in place. Because much of the W.R.A. Company's early records and memos concerning the subject no longer exist (when Western took over Winchester, a lot of early files were destroyed or lost), or are sketchy or, at best, incomplete, several sources must be pieced together to form time frames.

The earliest Catalog offering shotshells (empty) is the 1875 issue. The list shown mimics that of the Union Metallic Cartridge Company's offering of the same period. It is known Winchester did not have the capability to make paper shells at this time and specimens are not known to exist. So we can only speculate that if these shells were, in fact, sold by Winchester, they were bought from the U.M.C. Co. It is also thought that this 1875 Catalog listing was presented to customers as a "trial balloon." Orders received would help Winchester assess the viability of producing their own line of shotshells.

So when did Winchester actually first offer their own in-house shotshell production for sale? Information exists to confirm that the company laid out plans to begin shotshell production, both paper and metallic, in 1877. George Watrous indicates these shells were being produced in 1877. However, the earliest-known offering for sale of the in-house-produced shotshells is a price list of 1878. The list shows the "W.R.A. Co." headstamp on both brass and paper shells. A notation made by a factory employee indicates August 1, 1878, as the date shipments were ready. It is the author's opinion that 1878 is the proper production date for these earliest shotshells.

Pinpointing the exact date the W.R.A. Co. offered loaded shells is also difficult. The earliest reference to them is 1886 when Rival shells, loaded with black powder, were sold. This, however, was not to the public, but to a business concern for retail sales. The Star grade of shells was likewise sold loaded in 1887. Factory memos indicated that no loaded shells were offered in Catalogs but were offered in supplements to Catalogs.

The Catalog of 1891 is the first found to actually offer loaded shells, black powder in Star and Rival grades.

Winchester experimented with smokeless powder loadings as early as 1889. The first Catalog found to offer loaded shells, smokeless powder, is the 1893 for the Rival grade only.

During the mid-1890s the Winchester shotshell line began a rapid evolution. Many production techniques were tried and a wide range of shell grades were offered. By the early 1900s Winchester stabilized both the basic product line and their production methods.

The early 1920s saw a consolidation of some grades and by the 1930s the line grades had been scaled down considerably. After World War II the Winchester shotshell line featured only two grades, the Super Speed and the Ranger. These two corresponded to Western's Super-X and Xpert, respectively. Gone were the days of endless variety in the Winchester shotshell line; only three types of powder and six sizes of shot were offered.

Five Levels of Shotshell Collecting

As mentioned earlier Winchester, at one time, offered or could have loaded some 14,383 different shotshell combinations. This would be an enormous collecting task; and it would be complicated by the reality that some of these possible variations may never have been loaded.

To give collectors a better grasp of the collecting possibilities, I have also broken down the category into five levels. The same basic collecting levels used for rimfire and center fire cartridges are also used here for shotshells. Some of the levels have been modified as follows:

Level 1 - One or more shells and boxes for a particular shotgun. For example, a Model 42 shotgun produced in 1936 and the grades of .410 shells produced during the same time period.

Level 2 - All shells and boxes for a certain model shotgun. For example, the Model 12. You could collect all gauges and grades of the gun and all shells and boxes in corresponding field and target loadings of the periods.

Level 3 - All commercially loaded shells and gauges applicable to Winchester-produced shotguns. This would form a sizeable collection and storage would become a problem. The period from 1887 on in 10, 12, 16, 20, 28 and .410 gauges would be covered.

Level 4 - Collect all commercially offered Winchester shotshells (those offered in Catalogs). This would cover the period from 1887 on and would add the 4, 8, 14, 24 and 32 gauges to those previously mentioned. Metallic shotshells would also be included.

Level 5 - Collect all shells and gauges made by Winchester. This would include contract loadings, loadings for outside sources, and the many experimentals. Case construction and color variants, as well as many odd loadings (blanks, proofs and dummies) would be included.

In this volume, we will give you an example of a "Level 1" collection in both paper and brass shotshells. Then we will also detail a general "Level 3" collection in both types of shells. Finally, we will narrow our paper shotshell focus to the "Repeater" line; on the metallic shotshell side, we will provide details on the "Winchester" and "Rival" brands.

Individual shotshells can be displayed in a variety of ways. Here is how Daniel L. Shuey displays part of his paper and metallic shotshell collection (including various primer boxes on the top rows) in this wall rack with a drop cover to keep out dust. Photo by D. Kowalski.

Value Guide for Repeater Shotshells

The format followed here is very similar to what we used for cartridge pricing. We will list the shotshell gauge, followed by any headstamp and configuration notes. Production dates will follow; these will begin with first year of production. After we price shotshells in one of four grades, we will provide notes on valuation for special versions of the shotshell.

Prices are stated in U.S. Dollars for factory-loaded single shells unless noted. Top wads have common powders: Dupont, E.C., New E.C., Hazard, Infallible and Ballistite. Prices are for single specimen collector shotshells (not the prices for shooting purposes).

All shotshell loading data for primers, wads, washers, grains of powder, and shot sizes were taken directly from original Winchester Catalogs, memos and drawings. They are used here strictly for historical reference. This data is not meant or intended to be used as a guideline for the loading of ammunition. No responsibility is assumed, meant or implied by the author, editor or publisher for its use in the loading of ammunition.

Shotshell Pricing and Grades of Condition

We have provided pricing on shotshells in four grades of condition. (These grades are generally adapted from the cartridge area. And readers would be well served to go back and read all the general comments made there about condition and valuation.) These conditions are New In Box (NIB.), Excellent (Exc.), Very Good (V.G.) and Good.

New In Box (NIB) - Mint condition that is only possible because the shotshell has not been handled or harmed.

Excellent (Exc.) - Perfect condition with no detectable dent, blemish, fingerprint or oxidation.

Very Good (V.G.) - Has only one of the following conditions to a very minor degree: slight oxidation, a small nick or scratch or a light fingerprint. In the case of empty paper shotshells, may have only slight blemishes along the leading edge of the shell. May have slight smudges on case wall. Top wad is totally readable. Bright hull color.

Good - Has at least two of the following conditions: nicking or slight blemishes, scratching, fingerprints. Top wad only partially readable. Hull color fading.

If a shotshell has at least three imperfections - oxidation (causes the hull to swell); nicking, scratches or dents; fingerprint damage, unreadable hull, poor color - it moves into the Fair category. The more severe these problems, the more it moves down the ladder of condition and value to the typical collector. A Fair category was not included in our pricing structure, as many shotshells have virtually no value in Fair condition.

It should also be noted that some NIB prices for individual shells are considerably higher than one would normally expect based on the price for a full box. That's because most collectors would not normally pay 25 times the price of a single shell in a box of 25. Such pricing would really put full-box prices into the stratosphere.

As a collector, it's also important to know that a particular shotshell actually came from a specific box. Some shotshells cannot be properly identified unless they're actually matched up with or removed from their original box. It's important to know your seller, especially when it comes to buying a collectible that could be controversial.

Shotshell Rarity

Rarity adds the other important dimension to pricing shotshells. There are six levels of rarity as applied to headstamps only. These do not apply to various gauges available with that headstamp. Here are the six levels of rarity.

1. **Very Common** - Found in all collections and easily found at gun shows.
2. **Common** - Found in all collections and found at most gun shows.
3. **Uncommon** - Found in most collections and at some gun or cartridge and shotshell shows.
4. **Scarce** - Found in some collections and at some shotshell auctions.
5. **Rare** - 25 rounds or less known to exist.
6. **Very Rare** - 5 rounds or less known to exist.

These multiple factors of condition combined with rarity are what make definitive pricing a difficult challenge. We wanted to help you define the parameters of pricing and the important considerations. But it is impossible to create an exact formula.

Presenting Shotshells and Boxes Together

We're going to change our presentation in this section from what we did with cartridges. As you recall, in the cartridge section, we dealt with the cartridges themselves in a separate section after we covered cartridge boxes.

With shotshells, we're going to present examples of boxes and their values right along with the shotshells. As we've indicated, the shotshell arena is vastly more complex than cartridges. And it's perhaps even more important (than it is with cartridges) to understand that some "unexpected" shotshells were packed in certain boxes.

For example, when we cover the Repeater brand, we will deal with the shotshells, then illustrate as many Repeater boxes as possible. We'll do the same thing for the metallic shells we've decided to cover in detail in this first volume.

In the next chapter, we will provide several other shotshell brands and box examples with very little text. We will, however, provide some basic information on them in captions and then offer valuations.

Many shotshell boxes are visually striking and there is growing interest in them. So we will attempt to give the reader an introduction to them, as well as a framework for a fuller presentation in future editions.

Shotshell Box Grading and Grading Definitions

The grading definitions we present here, as well as the following comments regarding the pricing and value charts, are adapted from an earlier chapter by Ray T. Giles on cartridge box condition and grading. Once again, the reader is encouraged to go back and read those comments in their entirety. *Ed.*

Overall box condition is the sum total of many variables, each of which will be weighted differently in accordance with the personal preferences of the individual collector or dealer. As a result, it is important to understand that assigning condition, even according to the objective criteria set forth below, remains, in the end, a very subjective exercise.

Also, please bear in mind that these are *guidelines* and by no means will every box fit readily into one or the other of these categories.

Note: Sealed boxes, while worth a premium within their grade, must be judged by the same standards as other boxes. In other words, just because a box is sealed doesn't mean it is "Excellent." In *all* grades it is assumed that the box is full and correct in all respects.

Excellent - While not necessarily "as new", the box is solid and labels are clean with only negligible flaws or light scuffing. Colors will be bright and original. If it's a two-piece box, the seal will be virtually all there. There will be no tape or signs of tape removal.

Very Good-Fine - Box may be a little weak or separated at the edges but is otherwise sound. The labels may have *minor* staining, scratches or scuffs but will be completely readable. Colors may show slight fading. There will be no tape, though tape removal marks may be present on boxes. If it's a two-piece box, the seal will be more than half present. If it's a one-piece box, end flaps will be sound.

Good - Box may have some repairs, reinforcements, splits or loose edges but no missing cardboard. Labels will have scuff marks, chips, stains and other detractions but no major pieces will be missing. On two-piece boxes, label may be partial or roughly opened. End flaps will be present on one-piece boxes, but may have folds.

Shotshell Box Pricing and Value Charts

In pricing these boxes many generalizations obviously had to be made. There are simply too many variations to be included here. The prices listed in this chapter represent the best judgment of a group of active collectors, in various areas of specialty, who regularly collect, buy and sell these boxes. Through experience they have developed a fairly good idea of their relative scarcity and corresponding demand levels.

Some prices will undoubtedly appear too high or too low, and if the rapid price changes of recent years are any indication, the future course of trading will simply exacerbate these appearances.

We present here the beginnings of a pricing guide for Winchester shotshell boxes for Winchester shotguns. Your comments will be welcome.

And if you are an experienced collector, your offer to be a member of future pricing panels will also be welcome.

Premium Factors That Affect Box Pricing

Here are additional considerations that significantly affect the shotshell box value charts:
Add 25-50% for factory-sealed boxes.

A "Level 1" Paper Shotshell Collection Built Around the Model 42

With dates of use for certain Winchester brand shells given, the collector can match those with the known dates of production for a certain gun(s). Using the Model 42 as our focus for this example, here is a Level 1 collection for that famous gun.

The Model 42 was made from 1933 to 1963 in .410 gauge only. For illustration purposes, let's suppose you have a Model 42 with a serial number in the 12000 range, being made in 1934. Now for the shotshells.

Repeater Super Speed in .410 had the 3-inch shell length added to the line in 1934 to correspond with the introduction of the Model 42. These shells would come in a two-piece box. The shells would have a red hull with black print "Super Speed" placed horizontally. These early 3-inch .410 shells would use a Staynless-type primer and have a 1/2" base with three corrugations and a "W.R.A. .410 Made in U.S.A." headstamp. The top wad was marked with a shot size. A roll crimp was used.

Values: Repeater Super Speed, .410, 3 inch (1/2" base) "W.R.A. .410 Made in U.S.A." head-stamp

NIB	Exc.	V.G.	Good
2.00	1.50	1.00	0.75

Values apply to any shot size. Add 50 percent for no case wall print.

This early variant was followed closely by the use of the newly adapted No. 209 battery cup primer, and a longer 3/4" high base with four corrugations. The same headstamp was used. Shot sizes began to be printed on the hull.

Values: Repeater Super Speed, .410, 3 inch (3/4" base) "W.R.A. .410 Made in U.S.A." headstamp

NIB	Exc.	V.G.	Good
1.50	1.00	0.75	0.50

Values apply to any shot size. Deduct 25 percent for shot size on case wall.

Next would be a shotshell with a new headstamp. It would be "Super Speed WRA .410 Made in USA." The case-wall print was turned vertical on later versions. Pie-style crimp replaced the roll crimp on later production.

Values: Repeater Super Speed, .410, 3 inch (3/4" base) "Super Speed WRA .410 Made in USA" headstamp

NIB	Exc.	V.G.	Good
1.00	0.75	0.50	

Values apply to any shot size. Add 50 percent for horizontal case wall print or roll crimp.

The above three shells show the evolution of a new product using one or more features from a previous product. What happened was that old stocks of materials were used up before material with the intended change got into the production stream. Changes on a production line often amount to several items being changed over a period of time.

Often a minor change like the orientation of case wall print might happen in the middle of a several-hundred-thousand-round run. Or hull paper, pre-printed from a previous run would be incorporated into a current run, thus resulting in these differences. Even though the third shell in the above series was intended to have vertical case wall print, for example, there was undoubtedly a large supply of horizontal print stock from the previous shell that company management decided would be used first on the new shell.

Anyone familiar with manufacturing processes knows how costly it is to throw out old inventory, especially if you're a young company or one being reorganized or absorbed into another company. The economies of production typically demand long runs of such things as shell casings or boxes. If sales projections don't materialize, you've got components left over. And especially in a company or market already accustomed to several product variations, you can understand how a production manager would be very reluctant to throw anything useable away.

The result was that "old parts" often appeared on "new products." It saved the company a lot of money. But it created a giant jigsaw puzzle for collectors trying to sort it out 75 or 100 years later.

A "Level 3" Paper Shotshell Collection

Because so many variations are available, this will be a general listing of grades and gauges.

10 Gauge	*Grades Applicable*
Model 1887 (Black Powder only)	Winchester (First Quality), S.Q., Star, Rival, Blue Rival, Yellow Rival New Rival, Nublack
Model 1901	Leader, Metal Lined, Repeater, Pigeon, Speed Load, Ranger, Super Speed
12 Gauge	
Model 1887 (Black Powder only)	Winchester (First Quality), S.Q., Star, Rival, Blue Rival, New Rival, Nublack
Model 1893, 1897, 1911, 1912, 21, 24, 25, 37, 40	Rival, Leader, Metal Lined, Repeater, Pigeon, Speed Load, Ranger, Super Speed
16 Gauge	
Model 1897, 1912, 21, 24, 37	Leader, Repeater, Speed Load, Ranger, Super Speed
20 Gauge	
Model 1885, 1912, 21, 24, 37	Leader, Repeater, Speed Load, Ranger, Super Speed
28 Gauge	
Model 1912, 21, 37	Repeater, Ranger, Super Speed
.410 Gauge	
Model 20, 37, 41, 42	Repeater, Speed Load, Super Speed

Our intention with this first issue is to provide the reader with an introduction to shotshells and their pricing. To cover every variation in this level would not be possible. However, we will lay out the Repeater grade in detail. This was a popular, middle line of paper shotshell using smokeless powder.

Repeater Grade Shotshells

From their introduction in 1896 the Repeater used a yellow hull. They were first offered as an empty shell (not loaded) only. Gauges listed are 10, 12, 16 and 20. One year later (1897) the 14 gauge was added.

In 1900 the Repeater was offered loaded with smokeless powder only and only in 10, 12, 16 and 20 gauges. The Company added 24 and 28 gauge in 1904. These two could be ordered with black or smokeless powder and they used a red hull rather than the standard yellow. In 1919 the 24 and 28 gauge reverted to the yellow hull color.

The .410, 2-inch length only, and the 32 gauge were first offered in 1916 but were not headstamped Repeater; simply "Winchester" and the gauge and metric equivalent. They did, however, use the yellow hull and were only offered as smokeless loadings.

In 1921 the 24 gauge loaded shell was discontinued; it was now available as an empty shell only. A .410 in 2 1/2-inch length was added in 1923.

Repeater Speed Loads were introduced in 1927 for 10, 16, and 20 gauges. Speed Loads covered single ball and buckshot loads and used the standard Repeater headstamp but with a red hull. Repeater Speed Loads were discontinued in 1932 when a separate "Speed Load" line, and so titled, was added. During this same time frame the standard Repeaters switched to a red tube. By 1938 the Repeater grade was dropped from the line.

During their life Repeaters used three corrugations on their head, except for the earliest issues in the 1890s which had two corrugations.

Several loadings, besides the usual shot sizes, became quite popular. The most popular of these were the Brush Loads. They were first offered in 1905 in 10, 12, 16 and 20 gauges and had cardboard shot "separators." Winchester also used shot "concentrators" in some shells to hold the discharged shot in a tighter group.

Brush Loads were so marked on their hulls. The layout of the marking changed several times over the years. The "lightning strike" typeface for the Winchester logo was adopted for most boxes and brands in 1910 which helps date some of these changes. The red "W" was added in 1907.

The first Brush Load markings were stamped with red ink. This quickly changed to black ink which continued for the life of the loads. Brush Loads used green top wads.

Single ball and buckshot options were added in 1907 and became very popular. They were likewise offered in 10, 12, 16 and 20 gauges.

Using Primers for Dating Repeater Shotshells

A key in identifying time periods during which any shotshell or cartridge was made is the primer. With the Repeater, the first issues used the small (.175" diameter) No. 6 copper primer. This plain, rounded primer, even with improved priming mixtures, would not always give sure ignition. Its small size coupled with loose-fitting firing pins and weak sear springs of many period guns would also cause misfires.

In 1902 the No. 4 primer was substituted. This primer, of flat, copper construction, was marked with a "W" and was of much larger size to accommodate larger priming charges. During 1903 the No. 4 primer had a protective ring added to it and was renamed the No. 4 1/2. Shells with this primer are very scarce and were not manufactured for very long.

Then in 1904 the No. 4 1/2 primer changed its name to the "New No. 4." This well-known primer had its protective ring marked "W.R.A. Co. New No. 4" and it continued in use in this form until the advent of the Staynless No. 4 in 1927.

Staynless No. 4 primers featured a larger vent opening and copper construction with a brass, unmarked ring. In approximately 1930 a standard Staynless primer using a nickel-plated center was adopted. This version was used until 1933 when the No. 209 Battery Cup primer was made standard for all Winchester shells.

Using Top Wads for Dating Repeater Shotshells

Top wads are also another feature to help date a shell. The wad was printed with the powder brand, powder charge, shot size and shot charge. "W.R.A. Co." was added to the wad to show it was a factory load.

With the many combinations possible the information sometimes gets confusing. And the number of combinations listed in Catalogs could be increased if the customer special-ordered a favorite brand of powder or amount of charge.

Two types of smokeless powders were used in the early years: bulk powder measured in drams and dense powder measured in grains. Popular bulk powders were Dupont, E.C., New E.C., and Hazard. Schultze, New Schultze and Deadshot were also offered but are not encountered as often as the first three brands. Empire and Mullerite bulk powders are also listed but seldom encountered.

Dense powder brands used included the more popular Laflin & Rand "Infallible" and Ballistite; Walsrode and Rifleite were more scarce.

In 1925 Dupont "Oval" smokeless became a standard, well-accepted powder. Standard top wads were an off-white or buff color. A factory memo indicates top wad print was red before 1919 and black after that date.

Repeater Shot Sizes

Shot sizes available ranged from 1 to 10. BB and Dust were also available. Buckshot sizes were listed in two ranges, eastern and western. Eastern sizes were 000, 00, 0, 2, 3, 4. Corresponding western sizes were 2, 3, 4, 5-6, 7, 8-9. There was no western size to correspond to the eastern "4" shot.

Shot was offered as either soft or chilled. Round or single-ball sizes ranged from 1 1/8 ounce for 10 gauge to 1/2 ounce for 28 gauge. Brush Loads were only listed in shot sizes from 6 to 10.

Repeater Headstamps, Bases and Washers

Throughout its life the headstamp used was "Winchester Repeater." The first series through 1919 used "No. (gauge)." In 1920 "No." was replaced by "GA." The change must have been short-lived as this variation is quite scarce. The use of "No." was begun again and continued until the grade was discontinued.

Approximately 1924 "Made in U.S.A." was added to the headstamp and remained so as required by a new U.S. tariff law.

Repeater shotshells were advertised with a 3/4" reinforced base. The reinforcement was usually a brass washer. The washer was changed to steel at an unknown date, thought to be sometime in the 1906-1908 period. For several years the steel washer was used virtually exclusively. During the late 1920s the brass washer was used again, now almost interchangeably with the steel washer.

The "1901" Repeater Shells

Because smokeless powder, in its infancy, was produced in numerous types, grades and brands, this variability resulted in several manufacturing problems. Not only did the major companies have problems developing proper loads and primers to ignite them, shotshell construction had to be improved to handle the increased pressures of more potent powders.

All these dilemmas at the commercial level were compounded by consumers who handloaded their own shells. Improper smokeless handloads, along with the sometimes-inferior condition and quality of some guns of the day, led to frequent firing failures and shooting injuries.

To circumvent these problems, Winchester offered its 1901 Brand in most grades of shotshells. Named for their date of introduction, the 1901 Brands were first retailed only as new-primed empties for the handloader. The headstamp would also indicate the shell was not a factory load. However, in time, the 1901 Brand was factory loaded in most grades.

The 1901 Repeaters used the same yellow hull as regular Repeaters. All other information, except the headstamp, would also be the same for both shells. The 1901 headstamp reads "1901 Repeater No. (gauge)." All grades of the 1901 were discontinued in 1919.

Premium Factors That Affect Repeater Shotshell Values - General Rules on Prices and Deductions

Add 50 percent for blank or dummy
Add 50 percent for "Speed Load" on hull
Deduct 50 percent for red hull or "Made in USA" on headstamp
Deduct 50 percent for NPE (New Primed Empty)
Deduct 25 percent for "1901" headstamp
"Window Shell" (salesmen's sample shells) worth minimum of $25.00

Values: Repeater Paper Shotshells

10 GAUGE YELLOW HULL

2 5/8", 2 7/8" length   1896-1938

NIB	Exc.	V.G.	Good
2.00	1.50	1.00	0.75

Add 50 percent for two corrugations on base; or for Walsrode, Rifleite, Empire, or Mullerite top wads. Add 25 percent for steel reinforced base, Dead Shot top wad, No. 6 or No. 4 primer, odd length, round ball load.

12 GAUGE YELLOW HULL

2 5/8", 2 3/4" length   1896-1938

NIB	Exc.	V.G.	Good
	1.50	1.00	0.75

Add 50 percent for two corrugations on base; or for Walsrode, Rifleite, Empire, or Mullerite top wads. Add 25 percent for steel reinforced base, Dead Shot top wad, No. 6 or No. 4 primer, odd length, round ball load. Add 100 percent for Brush Load.

14 GAUGE YELLOW HULL

2 9/16" length   1897

NIB	Exc.	V.G.	Good
	3.00	2.50	1.50	1.00

Not sold as loaded shell.

16 GAUGE YELLOW HULL

2 9/16" length   1896-1938

NIB	Exc.	V.G.	Good
2.50	2.00	1.00	0.75

Add 50 percent for two corrugations on base; or for Walsrode, Rifleite, Empire, or Mullerite top wads. Add 25 percent for steel reinforced base, Dead Shot top wad, No. 6 or No. 4 primer, odd length, round ball load. Add 100 percent for Brush Load.

20 GAUGE YELLOW HULL

2 1/2", 2 3/4" length   1896-1938

NIB	Exc.	V.G.	Good
3.00	2.50	2.00	1.00

Add 50 percent for two corrugations on base; or for Walsrode, Rifleite, Empire, or Mullerite top wads. Add 25 percent for steel reinforced base, Dead Shot top wad, odd length, round ball load. Add 100 percent for Brush Load, GA. headstamp.

24 GAUGE YELLOW HULL

                                                    1904-1921

NIB	Exc.	V.G.	Good
4.50	4.00	3.00	1.50

Add 50 percent for red hull. Add 25 percent for No. 4 1/2 primer.

28 GAUGE YELLOW HULL

                                                    1904-1938

NIB	Exc.	V.G.	Good
3.50	3.00	2.00	1.00

Add 50 percent for red hull. Add 25 percent for No. 4 1/2 primer. Add 100 percent for GA. headstamp.

32 GAUGE YELLOW HULL

                                                    1916-1925

NIB	Exc.	V.G.	Good
6.00	5.00	3.00	2.00

Deduct 25 percent for "Made in USA" headstamp.

.410 GAUGE YELLOW HULL

2", 2 1/2" length   1916-1927

NIB	Exc.	V.G.	Good
5.00	4.00	3.00	1.00

Add 100 percent for "W.R.A. Co." headstamp.

Now that you have value guides for the Repeater shells, both empty and loaded, we want to take you on a photographic tour through Repeater shotshells and companion or related shotshell boxes. Our organization of the material is intended to be roughly chronological. Once again, please keep in mind that there is often considerable overlap of headstamps, brands and box styles, adding to the immense variations possible in this area.

We also provide the following tour as a sneak preview of the next chapter. There we will take you through several Winchester brands, weaving shotshell photos and shotshell box photos together. The values for each shell and box will directly follow each photograph and caption.

Repeater Empty Shotshells

Repeater empty shells were popular for four decades. They typically had yellow hulls. Gauges, year introduced, and year discontinued were: 10 and 12, 1896-1937; 14, 1897-1921; 16 and 20, 1896-1937; 24, 1904-1927; 28, 1904-1937; 32, .410 2 inch and .410 2 1/2 inch, 1920-1937; .410 3 inch, 1936-1937.

Photo not available of pre-"1901" Repeater headstamp.

Shell Values: Repeater Empty Shotshells - See page 189

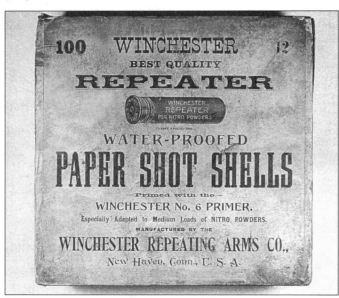

Very early Repeater Empty, box of 100, 12 gauge. Believed to be the earliest Repeater empty box of 100. Label is cream color with brown print. No red "W" on side panels. From TIM collection. Photo from R. Stadt.

Box Values:	Exc.	VG/F	Good
	450.00	300.00	200.00

Comment: *Very rare box with less than five known to exist.*

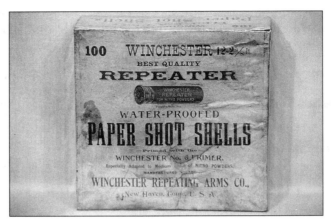

Early Repeater Empties, box of 100, 12 gauge. The second-earliest Repeater empties. No red "W" on side panels. This box was included to show the Winchester tendency to make sometimes "minute" changes on various label runs. This box differs from the previous one by having added "12-2 5/8 In." to the upper right corner instead of just "12." Winchester first offered shells in 2 5/8-inch and 2 3/4-inch lengths in about 1899 and other lengths to order. Early boxes printed with 2 5/8 or 2 3/4. Later boxes had this area left open to use a paste-on label or rubber stamp to denote shell length. This was common on all 100-round boxes. From T. Webster collection. Photo by D. Kowalski.

Box Values:	Exc.	VG/F	Good
	450.00	300.00	200.00

Comment: *Another very rare box with less than five known to exist.*

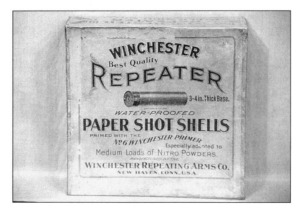

Box of Repeater Empty paper shells, box of 100, 10 gauge ("Winchester Repeater No. 10" shown on headstamp on shell illustration.) Side label indicates it's a box of 100. This version shows "Winchester" set in a blockier typeface on a "crescent" pattern. "Repeater" is also set with a "roller coaster" pattern. These empty shells were primed with the #6 primer, so this box pre-dates upcoming one with similar typeface for "1901" empties that touts the #4 primer and the newer smokeless powder. From T. Webster collection. Photo by D. Kowalski.

Box Values:	Exc.	VG/F	Good
	225.00	150.00	100.00

Comment: *More common than first two boxes.*

Late Repeater Empties, box of 100, 12 gauge. A 1920-era box with the rare and short-lived "12 GA" headstamp; also has "Winchester" on headstamp of shell drawing. Label is buff color with black type. The date stamp in lower right corner is 9-19 (indicating box was made in September 1919) and further corroborates the other dating clues on this label. Also note that this is the first box we've seen with the so-called "lightning strike" typeface used for the logo; Winchester first used this typeface in 1910. Photo from R. Stadt.

Box Values: Exc.   VG/F   Good
                              325.00   225.00   150.00

Comment: *Even though it's newer than the previous boxes, it's actually a scarce box.*

Repeater empty shell, "1901" headstamp. This 28 gauge shell has the typical yellow hull. Photos from R. Stadt.

Shell Values: Repeater Empty "1901" Shotshells - See page 189

Repeater "1901" Empty paper shells, box of 100, 12 gauge. Side label indicates it's a box of 12 gauge. This version very similar to the third box shown with "Winchester" on a "crescent" pattern and "Repeater" set with the "roller coaster" pattern. This box has the newer smokeless powder that replaced Nitro powder. It also has the No. 4 primer that replaced the No. 6 primer; this would indicate box was made in 1902 or later, per the primer dating guidelines given earlier. Also, if it were made after 1906-07 it would have a date code in lower right corner similar to previous box. Of course, we always have to keep in mind that the company would use up old boxes before ordering new ones. From T. Webster collection. Photo by D. Kowalski.

Box Values: Exc.   VG/F   Good
                              250.00   200.00   125.00

Comment: *Considered a common box.*

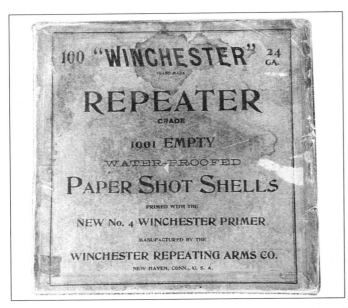

Early and unusual box of Repeater "1901" Empties, box of 100, 24 gauge. Note backward slant of "Winchester" and use of quote marks around logo name. Ron Stadt speculates that this was an export box and it's very rare; perhaps the only one like it to survive. Label is cream color with brown print. While the prior box used the No. 4 primer, this box and the three 1901 Empties that follow all use the later "New No. 4" primer. Photo from R. Stadt.

Box Values: Exc.   VG/F   Good
                       425.00   300.00   200.00

Comment: *Any 24 gauge box is rare. Deduct 20 percent for other gauges.*

Another box of Repeater "1901 Empty paper shells, box of 100, 24 gauge. Compared to previous box, this version shows "Winchester" *logo slanted to right, the "lightning strike" logo (first used in 1910). Note also that the "Trade Mark" line is longer and more detailed. From T. Webster collection. Photo by D. Kowalski*

Box Values: Exc.   VG/F   Good
                       325.00   250.00   175.00

Comment: *Considered a scarce box. Deduct 20 percent for gauges other than 20 gauge.*

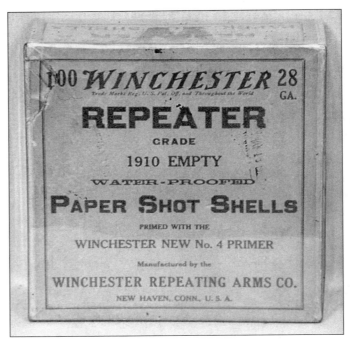

Repeater "1901" Empties, box of 100, 28 gauge. Here's a misprinted box from Winchester that reads "1910" instead of "1901." They put stickers on some of the incorrect boxes. Label is cream color with brown print. Large red "W" on side panel. This box should have a label date on the side or on the sealing label if it was made for the U.S. commercial market after 1907. Any "lightning strike" box (dating from 1910 or later) that does not have a label date was likely for the export market. From T. Webster collection. Photo by D. Kowalski.

Box Values: Exc.   VG/F   Good
                       300.00   225.00   150.00

Comment: *There are at least two variations of this label-error box. It probably dates from 1913 - 1916.*

Repeater "1901" Empties, box of 100, 16 gauge. Another post-1910 box with "lightning strike" logo. Label is cream color with brown print. The "primer" line is much more detailed than previous box. Photo from R. Stadt.

Box Values: Exc.   VG/F   Good
                     275.00   225.00   175.00

Comment: *We would look for a label date on this box (and it would probably be in the later part of the 1913 - 1919 date range).*

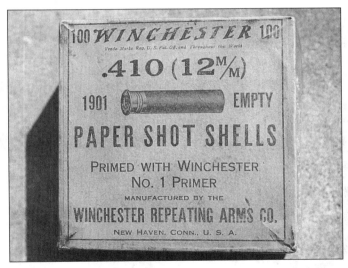

Repeater Empties, box of 100, .410 gauge. Has "lightning strike" logo and red "W" on two sides. Also has hand stamp in red ink on side panel that reads: "Nov. 15, 1919 Rec'd." Box is also full of new primed empties with brown packing ticket having an inspector's mark that reads: "No. 93, 290M 5-19" referring, of course, to May, 1919. From TIM collection. Photo by T. Melcher.

Box Values: Exc.   VG/F   Good
                     700.00   600.00   450.00

Comment: *A highly desirable box in the popular .410 gauge.*

Repeater Loaded Shotshells

Loaded Repeater shells in the four most popular gauges were sold for nearly forty years. Hulls were yellow. Gauges, year introduced, and year discontinued were: 10, 12, 16 and 20, 1900-1938; 24, 1904-1921; 28, 1904-1938; 32, 1916-1925; .410 2 inch, 1916-1927; .410 2 1/2 inch, 1923-1927. The 24 and 28 gauge were loaded in red hulls until 1919, when they switched to yellow.

Photo not available.

Shell Values: Repeater Loaded Shotshells - See page 189

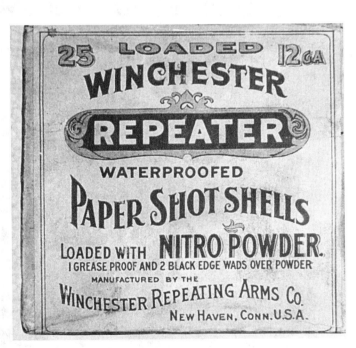

Very early Repeater loaded shells, box of 25, 12 gauge. Believed to be earliest loaded box. Refers to Nitro powder that was used before smokeless powder. Label is cream color with brown type. From TIM collection. Photo from R. Stadt.

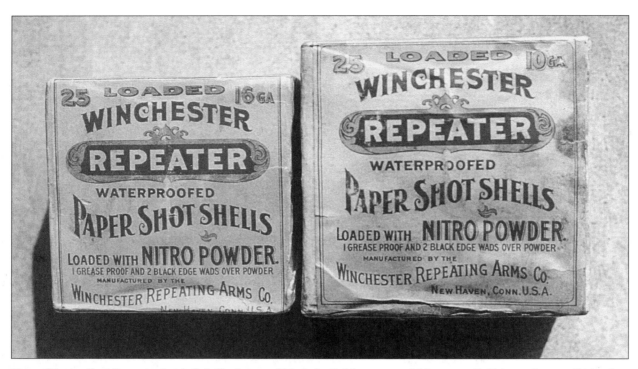

Two of the earliest Repeater loaded shells, boxes of 25, in both 16 gauge and 10 gauge. Both boxes have split-top box construction, which stopped about 1902. The 10 gauge box is a very rare, full sealed box. From TIM collection. Photo by T. Melcher.

End labels for the above boxes. The 10 gauge box promotes the use of "Dupont Powder" as part of Winchester's early efforts to focus on the benefits of shooters buying loaded shells, rather than continuing to load their own. From TIM collection. Photo by T. Melcher.

Box Values:	Exc.	VG/F	Good
	425.00	325.00	250.00

Comment: *Values are for 12 gauge and 16 gauge. Add 20 percent premium for 10 gauge and 20 gauge. In general, the largest and smallest gauges in any series are the rarest.*

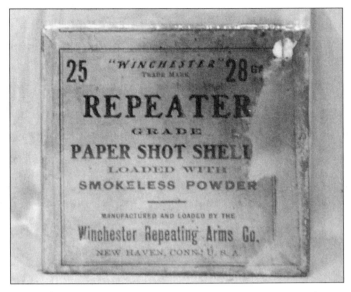

Repeater loaded shells, box of 25, 28 gauge. Very similar to previous box; Label is cream color with black type (and has no red type). However, we now see the "lightning strike" Winchester logo, dating this box after 1910 (probably 1911-13). From T. Webster collection. Photo by D. Kowalski.

Box Values: Exc.   VG/F   Good
                              275.00   200.00   125.00

Early Repeater loaded shells, box of 25, 24 gauge. These 25-round boxes, known as "quarters," had not become popular with empty shells. "Smokeless Powder" has replaced "Nitro Powder" seen on previous earliest boxes. Label is cream color with black type and since it has no red type on box, we would date it between 1900 and 1908, perhaps even before 1907. From T. Webster collection. Photo by D. Kowalski.

Box Values: Exc.   VG/F   Good
                              325.00   225.00   175.00

Loaded Repeater shell, headstamped "24 GA." A rare loaded shell. This "(gauge) GA" headstamp was used briefly starting in 1920, then Winchester switched back to the "No. (gauge)" format. Photos from R. Stadt.

Shell Values: "(Gauge) GA" Shotshell - See page 189

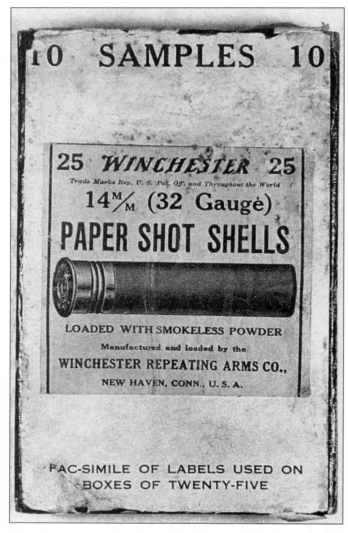

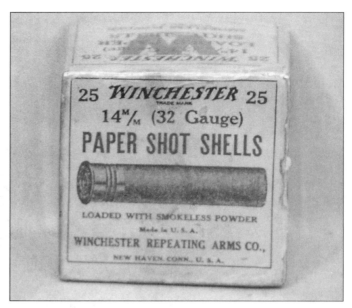

Repeater paper shells, box of 25, 32 gauge. "Made in U.S.A." line puts box at 1924 or later. Side label is cream color with brown type; top label has red "W." From T. Webster collection. Photo by D. Kowalski.

Box Values: Exc.   VG/F   Good
                         225.00   150.00   125.00

Comment: *There are several variations of this box.*

Repeater Rojo, box of 25, 20 gauge. Bright red label is Spanish version with "lightning strike" logo dating this box after 1910. Does not have "Made in U.S.A." line so it was made prior to 1924. This box is actually a sealed, empty box that may only have been made up as a salesman's sample. There is currently no proof that it was ever put into production. From TIM collection. Photo by T. Melcher.

Box Values: Exc.   VG/F   Good
                         700.00   600.00   450.00

Comment: *Only two examples are known to exist.*

Rare Repeater samples, box of 10, 32 gauge. This box of loaded samples is among the rarest of Repeater boxes. The extended "Trade Mark" line was used from 1912-1916 or perhaps a little later. Label is cream color with brown type. Photo from R. Stadt.

Box Values: Exc.   VG/F   Good
                         400.00   300.00   200.00

Comment: *A rare box with at least 10 known examples.*

Repeater box, 25 loaded shells, 28 gauge. A colorful "lightning strike" box with "starburst" visual. It was made after 1912 (see extended "Trade Mark" line) and before 1924 (no "Made in U.S.A."). Label is white with yellow/gold highlights and blue and red type. Would have production date on sealing label. From TIM collection. Photo from R. Stadt.

Box Values: Exc.   VG/F   Good
                  250.00   200.00   175.00

Comment: *Values are for this scarcer box in 28 gauge. Deduct 25 percent for other gauges.*

Early Repeater box, 25 loaded shells, 12 gauge. Another colorful "lightning strike" and "starburst" box with the "Made in U.S.A." line dating it after 1924. Label is white with yellow/gold highlights and blue and red type. "Smokeless Powder" line is printed in red. Would have production date on sealing label. From T. Webster collection. Photo by D. Kowalski.

Box Values: Exc.   VG/F   Good
                  125.00   100.00   75.00

Comment: *Fairly common box.*

Repeater Oval box, 25 loaded shells, 10 gauge. The "Oval" smokeless powder introduced in 1925. Would have production date on sealing label. From TIM collection. Photo from R. Stadt.

Box Values: Exc.   VG/F   Good
                  275.00   175.00   125.00

Comment: *Very colorful but not uncommon.*

Repeater Brush Loads, 12 gauge, two versions of the many variations. Available in four gauges, these were popular loads. Gauges, year introduced, and year discontinued were: 10, 12, 16, and 20, 1905-1938. (Some collectors have even questioned whether any 10 gauge brush loads were ever made.) These had red hulls after 1928-29. Photos from R. Stadt.

Shell Values: Brush Loads - See page 189

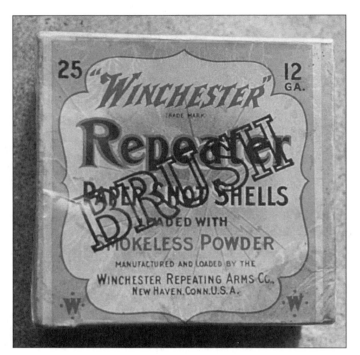

Repeater Brush Load, box of 25, 12 gauge. Here's a variation of the previous box notable for three reasons. First of all, it does not have the "Made in U.S.A." line; so the basic box was made prior to 1924. Since Winchester simply overprinted the word "Brush" on a basic box, here was an obvious situation where old boxes were being used up when the "Brush" loads were first developed. The "W" in each bottom corner has four red dots placed around it. Finally, the "lightning strike" Winchester logo has both quote marks around it and a more exaggerated "Devil's tail" typeface (see the "W" particularly) than the previous box. From TIM collection. Photo by T. Melcher.

Box Values:	Exc.	VG/F	Good
	200.00	150.00	100.00

Comment: *These "four-dot" variations are valued about 10 percent higher than a similar box without them.*

Repeater Brush Loads, box of 25, 12 gauge. "Brush" was overprinted on "lightning strike" box with "starburst" visual. Has "Made in U.S.A." line dating this box as produced after 1924. Label is white with yellow/gold highlights and blue and red type. From TIM collection. Photo from R. Stadt.

Box Values:	Exc.	VG/F	Good
	175.00	125.00	75.00

Comment: *Relatively common.*

Repeater Speed Loads, 12 gauge. They typically had red hulls. They were introduced in 1927 in 10, 12, 16, and 20 gauges, .410 2 inch, and .410 2 1/2 inch. The .410 2-inch shells were discontinued in 1930; the remainder were dropped in 1932. Some early "Speed Load" boxes contained shells that had "Repeater" headstamps. Photos from R. Stadt.

Shell Values: Repeater Speed Loads - See page 189

Repeater Speed Loads, .410 gauge. These shells came out of the following box. Photos from R. Stadt.

Shell Values: Repeater Speed Loads - See page 189

Repeater Speed Loads, box of 25 shells, 12 gauge. These boxes date from 1927 to 1932, when Speed Loads were discontinued. Label is white with blue and red print. From TIM collection. Photo from R. Stadt.

Box Values:	Exc.	VG/F	Good
	150.00	125.00	100.00

Comment: *Values are for 12 gauge. Add 20 percent premium for 10 gauge, 16 gauge or 20 gauge.*

Repeater Speed Loads box, 25 shells, .410 gauge. This box held the previous shell. There are several variations of this box. This variation has 12 M/M in upper right corner that was dropped from some later versions. From TIM collection. Photo from R. Stadt.

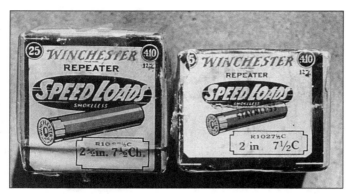

Repeater Speed Loads, two boxes of 25, .410 gauge. These side labels show more variations of this box. This .410 shell was made in both 2-inch and the scarcer 2 1/2-inch lengths. Both of these boxes still have the 12 M/M in the upper right corner on both the top and side labels. However, the 2-inch box has now added the word "Staynless" in blue type on the red hull of the shell. This box, in its last days before 1932, was used for "Staynless" shells in both lengths before Winchester switched to the following boxes for Speed Loads and Staynless Speed Loads. From TIM collection. Photo by T. Melcher.

Box Values: Exc.   VG/F   Good
                       300.00   225.00   175.00

Comment: *Values are for this box in .410 gauge, regardless of variation. Collectors actively seek out the several variations of this box.*

Repeater loaded shells, box of 25, 24 gauge. "Made in U.S.A." line puts box at 1924 or later. The label is cream color and the fact it also has blue and red type brings it into the Staynless era that was post-1928. According to Daniel L. Shuey, most boxes with these plain tan or cream-colored labels produced after WWI were for export. Photo from R. Stadt.

Box Values: Exc.   VG/F   Good
                       325.00   225.00   175.00

Comment: *A scarce box.*

Repeater Staynless shells, such as this 12 gauge example, featured a new primer that was stainless. The Staynless primer came out in 1928. Winchester also would change placements of the corrugations around shell head. Photos from R. Stadt.

**Shell Values: Repeater Staynless -
See page 189**

Repeater Speed Loads, Staynless, box of 25 shells, 12 gauge. These boxes also date from the late 1920s and early 1930s and are available in 10, 12, 16 and 20 gauge. Label is dark blue with white trim and panels; oval behind "Speed Loads" is red, so are words "Winchester" and "W Staynless." Photo from R. Stadt.

Box Values: Exc.   VG/F   Good
                       150.00   125.00   100.00

Comment: *Values are for 12 gauge. Add 10 percent premium for 10 gauge, 16 gauge or 20 gauge.*

Repeater Speed Loads, box of 10 shells, 16 gauge. Only produced in 1932-1933. Photo from R. Stadt.

Box Values:	Exc.	VG/F	Good
	175.00	125.00	75.00

Comment: *Values are for these 10-shell boxes in any gauge (come in 12 and 20 gauge, as well); they are very scarce.*

Repeater Staynless box, 25 shells, 12 gauge. This Staynless box dates from the late 1920s and early 1930s. From TIM collection. Photo from R. Stadt.

Box Values:	Exc.	VG/F	Good
	150.00	100.00	75.00

Repeater Speed Load shell, 12 gauge. Shows "Speed Load" with "Winchester" headstamp and red hull; these were introduced in 1932 in 10, 12, 16, 20, and .410 in 2 1/2-inch length, but they remained in production only until the following year. They were also packed in boxes of 10. These kinds of short runs and odd packaging add to the immense variations in Winchester shotshells. Photos from R. Stadt.

Shell Values: Speed Loads - See page 189

Repeater Staynless "Pheasant" box. Box is pre-1937, unless it says "Div. Of Western Cartridge Co.," which would make it post-1937. Examples exist in 10, 12, 16, 20 and 28 gauge, as well as "Brush" loads. Label is yellow on lower portion and red on upper portion with red and blue type. Photo from R. Stadt.

Box Values:	Exc.	VG/F	Good
10 Ga.	1,200.00	900.00	700.00
12 Ga.	700.00	500.00	400.00
16 Ga.	700.00	500.00	400.00
20 Ga.	900.00	750.00	500.00
28 Ga.	1,500.00	1,100.00	800.00

Comment: *After the "Christmas Boxes," these colorful boxes are highly collectible and still relatively available. The order of rarity for these boxes is 28 gauge (most rare), then 10 gauge, 20 gauge, 16 gauge and 12 gauge (most common). Add 20 percent premium for "Brush" loads, which have only been found in 12 gauge and 16 gauge to date.*

Repeater "Pheasant" Boxes, all five gauges. This is one of only two full sets known in any collection. From TIM collection. Photo by T. Melcher.

Repeater Super Speed shell, 12 gauge. The "Speed Load" was reintroduced in 1933 as the "Super Speed," then discontinued in 1937. Note the battery cup primer and the print on the case wall. Photos from R. Stadt.

Shell Values: Super Speed - See page 189

Super Speed, box of 25, 12 gauge, Steel Heads. During early years of WWII, Winchester used steel or zinc heads on these shells due to metal shortages. (The shell shown has an orange hull and a bright silver head.) The box is an early Super Speed box in two-piece version. Box is white, border is red, panels are yellow; type is blue and red. From TIM collection. Photo by T. Melcher.

Box Values:	Exc.	VG/F	Good
	150.00	140.00	125.00

Comment: *Values are for this first Super Speed box. Add 25 percent for steel heads.*

Repeater Super Speed, one-piece box was not used until 1935, then not on all gauges. It also continued to be used during and after WWII for some gauges. This version has "Repeater" stamped on side; some versions do not. Label is cream with blue and red print. Photo from R. Stadt.

Box Values:	Exc.	VG/F	Good
	150.00	140.00	125.00

Comment: *Values are for one-piece boxes with "Repeater" stamped on side. Without "Repeater" on side, boxes are 1/3 these values.*

Winchester Metallic (Brass) Shotshells

The beginnings of the metallic shotshell, better known as brass shells, follows the same dates and details as laid out in the paper shell section. There is one exception; Winchester did have the capabilities to manufacture brass shells in 1875. However, as with paper shells, existing patents on design and manufacturing techniques had to be overcome.

As detailed in the paper shell section, the price list of 1878 is the first to show shells (empty). These were headstamped "W.R.A. Co. No. (gauge)." Only the 10 and 12 gauges were listed. An employee's note indicates the 8 gauge was also made in 1878 and examples are known. Specimens in 14, 16 and 20 gauges are also known. However, these gauges were not listed until 1879 under the "First Quality" title.

The "First Quality" line was first offered in 1879 and bore the headstamp "Winchester No. (gauge)." Gauges available were 8, 10, 12, 14, 16 and 20. The 4 gauge was offered later. Also in 1879 a "Second Quality" shell was added using a "W.R.A. Co. No. (gauge) XX" headstamp. Even though 14, 16 and 20 gauges were listed, only examples of 10 and 12 gauge are known to exist.

It is reported the Second Quality shell was discontinued in 1881. In 1884 the Rival shell took its place as the "second quality" line. The Rival shell was made with thinner material and could be sold for less. Headstamped "W.R.A. Co. No. (gauge) Rival," it was only offered in 10 and 12 gauge and remained listed in Winchester Catalogs and price lists until 1929. A 28 gauge was listed in 1914 and remained in production until 1949.

The .58 caliber shell was first listed in 1881. Headstamped "Winchester 58," it was made for converted military smooth bore muskets. The .58 was discontinued in 1919.

Brass shells were offered in varying lengths and eventually tin or nickel plating could be added for a nominal charge. Throughout their life, brass shells used a No. 2 size primer (.210 diameter). Later shells, for smokeless powder, used a No. 3 primer but it was the same diameter as the No. 2.

Metallic shotshells were always offered empty. However, in the 1930s the Company noted it would load brass shells on special order. As collectors have discovered (to add yet another layer of mystery to the already complicated arena of shotshell collecting), factory-loaded brass shells do exist that can be dated back to 1898-99 for loaded brass shells with sawtooth and other various types of mouth crimps. These shells are clearly "commercial" items but it's typical to find them in U.S. military contract loadings using 0 and 00 buck.

Several special brass shells and gauges were made over the years, mostly for export, and are extremely scarce.

"Level 1" Brass Shell Collection for Model 1901

Both the first quality "Winchester" and the second quality "Rival" shells in 10 gauge would be applicable to this gun.

The readers should note that values given here for brass shells are NPE - New Primed Empty. Winchester offered brass shells as empties. If you find factory loaded brass shells, you will have to have them evaluated by an expert appraiser.

For values, please refer to the following section. Grading definitions used are the same ones used for metallic cartridges in a previous chapter.

"Level 3" Brass Shotshell Values

10 GAUGE   FIRST QUALITY "WINCHESTER"
Model 1887, 1901

NIB	Exc.	V.G.	Good
8.00	6.00	4.00	3.00

10 GAUGE   SECOND QUALITY "RIVAL"
Model 1887, 1901

NIB	Exc.	V.G.	Good
10.00	8.00	6.00	4.00

12 GAUGE   FIRST QUALITY "WINCHESTER"
Model 1887, 1893, 1897, 1911, 1912, 21, 24, 37, 40

NIB	Exc.	V.G.	Good
8.00	6.00	4.00	3.00

12 GAUGE   SECOND QUALITY "RIVAL"
Model 1887, 1893, 1897, 1911, 1912, 21, 24, 37, 40

NIB	Exc.	V.G.	Good
10.00	8.00	6.00	4.00

16 GAUGE   FIRST QUALITY "WINCHESTER"
Model 1897, 1912, 21, 24, 37

NIB	Exc.	V.G.	Good
20.00	18.00	15.00	10.00

20 GAUGE   FIRST QUALITY "WINCHESTER"
Model 1885, 1912, 21, 24, 37

NIB	Exc.	V.G.	Good
30.00	25.00	20.00	15.00

28 GAUGE   SECOND QUALITY "RIVAL"
Model 1912, 21, 37

NIB	Exc.	V.G.	Good
15.00	12.00	8.00	5.00

Empty Brass Shotshells

W.R.A. Co. "XX" brass empty shell, "No. 12." Gauges, year introduced, and year discontinued were: 10, 1879-1881; 12, 1879-1881. Photos from R. Stadt.

Shell Values: Same as First Quality "Winchester" - See page 203

First Quality "Winchester" Empty Brass Shells

Winchester's "first quality" brass shells were headstamped "Winchester" along with "No (gauge)." Note the two sizes of headstamps on these 12 gauge shells. Gauges, year introduced, and year discontinued were: 4, 1886-1909; 8, 1879-1923; 10, 1879-1949; 12, 1879-1949; 14, 1879-1919; 16, 1879-1949; .410 gauge, 1927-1933; .58 caliber, 1881-1919. Winchester also sold No. 3 Yacht Cannon empty brass shells but did not list them in price lists. Photos from R. Stadt.

Shell Values: First Quality "Winchester" - See page 203

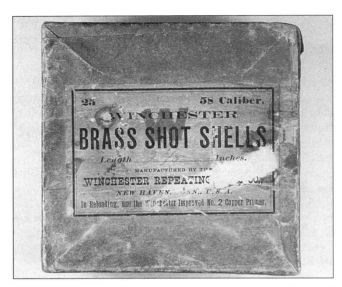

Brass shells, box of 25, in .58 caliber. Advised reloading with "Improved No. 2 Copper Primer." (Note that removing a piece of tape on right side of label also pulled off some type. Most collectors would agree that the tape, if it was clear, should have been left on the box.) Photo from R. Stadt.

Box Values:	Exc.	VG/F	Good
	400.00	325.00	200.00

Comment: *The only box type for .58 caliber ever seen to date. One of the brass shotshell labels, although the presence of the red "W" on this version would place it after 1906.*

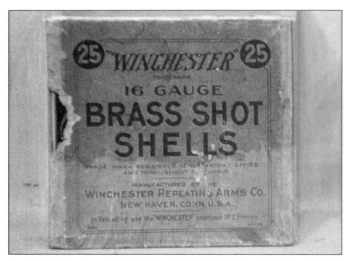

Winchester brass shells, box of 25, 16 gauge. Has "lightning strike" logo with quote marks and also a 1910 date mark in bottom right corner, indicating this is the earliest of the "lightning strike" labels. Bright green label, black type; red "W" on side label. Advised reloading with "Improved No. 2 Primer." From T. Webster collection. Photo by D. Kowalski.

Box Values:	Exc.	VG/F	Good
	200.00	175.00	150.00

Comment: *Values for 16 gauge box.*

adopted until 1913-14 but not advertised until 1920-21. "Made in U.S.A." line was mandated by 1924 U.S. tariff law; however, label date in bottom right corner shows 1922 production. Did Winchester anticipate coming tariff law? Did they help spearhead it with their own voluntary use of this line prior to the law? Or did they simply overprint the "Made in U.S.A." line in a convenient place on the label. Gold label, black type; red "W" on side label. From T. Webster collection. Photo by D. Kowalski.

Box Values: | Exc. | VG/F | Good
| --- | --- | --- |
| 250.00 | 200.00 | 150.00 |

Comment: *Values for this 20 gauge box.*

Winchester brass shells, box of 25, 20 gauge. Also has "lightning strike" logo with quote marks and a "10-10" date mark in bottom right corner. Note that this box and prior one also have "25" inside black circles. Bright green label, black type; red "W" on side label. Advised reloading with "Improved No. 2 Primer." From TIM collection. Photo from R. Stadt.

Box Values: | Exc. | VG/F | Good
| --- | --- | --- |
| 175.00 | 150.00 | 125.00 |

Comment: *Values for 20 gauge box. Also note that for this and the prior box, the simple "Trade Mark" line used in 1910 with this particular logo. Some collectors also speculate that these box labels may have been used for as long as five years until supplies were exhausted.*

Winchester brass shells, box of 25, 10 gauge. Yellow label, black type. As for dating, the comments made about the last box apply here, except that we now have advice to reload with "No. 3 Primer." Label date is "1,1-22." Photo from R. Stadt.

Box Values: | Exc. | VG/F | Good
| --- | --- | --- |
| 200.00 | 175.00 | 125.00 |

Comment: *Values for this 10 gauge box.*

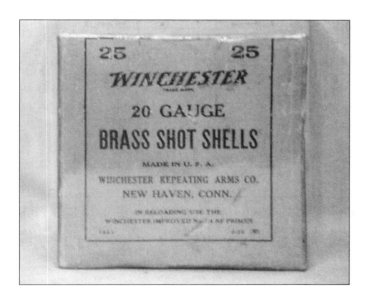

Winchester brass shells, box of 25, 20 gauge. Here's a box that typifies the often-contradictory dating clues available. Advised reloading with "Improved No. 4 NF Primer;" the "NF" not

Winchester brass shells, box of 25, 12 gauge. "Made in U.S.A." line dates this as post-1924. No longer a date code in bottom right corner; it has now been moved to bottom sealing label. Yellow label, black type. Advised reloading with "No. 3 Primer." Photo from R. Stadt.

Box Values:

	Exc.	VG/F	Good
	200.00	175.00	125.00

Comment: *Values for this 12 gauge box.*

Rival Brass Shotshells

Rival replaced the "XX" brass shells. They were "second quality" shells (with thinner walls), and more economically priced than the headstamped "Winchester" shells. Gauges, year introduced, and year discontinued were: 10, 1884-1929; 12, 1884-1929; 28, 1914-1949. Photos from R. Stadt.

Shell Values: Rival Brass - See page 203

Winchester brass shells, box of 25, 28 gauge. "Made in U.S.A." line dates this as post-1924. No longer a date code in bottom right corner; it has now been moved to bottom sealing label. Bright green label, black type; red "W" on side label. Advised reloading with "Improved No. 2 Primer." From TIM collection. Photo from R. Stadt.

Box Values:

	Exc.	VG/F	Good
	200.00	150.00	100.00

Comment: *Values for this 28 gauge box.*

Early Rival brass shells, box of 25 shells, 12 gauge. Some early Rival boxes, such as this one, had only side or end labels. One of earliest and most common types of Rival label. Promotes use of "Improved No. 2 Primer." From TIM collection. Photo from R. Stadt.

Box Values:

	Exc.	VG/F	Good
	300.00	250.00	200.00

Comment: *Values for this side-label type box.*

Rival brass shells, box of 25, 12 gauge. Promotes use of "Improved No. 2 Primer." A "lightning strike" logo with quote marks and a very tall typeface (compared to later box that follows); also has "10-10" date stamp in lower right corner. Lower trademark line reads: "Trade Mark Registered in U.S. Patent Office and Throughout the World." The "25" also inside black circles. Photo from R. Stadt.

Box Values:	Exc.	VG/F	Good
	300.00	250.00	200.00

Comment: *Values for any gauge.*

Rival brass shells, box of 25, 28 gauge. Another post-1910 "lightning strike" logo with quote marks but now in a short typeface (compared to previous box). No date stamp in lower right corner. Has "Patented June 28, 1910" line. The "25" no longer inside black circles. These box labels varied from light red to dark red in color. Print was typically black. Promotes use of "Improved No. 2 Primer." Photo from R. Stadt.

Box Values:	Exc.	VG/F	Good
	300.00	250.00	175.00

Comment: *Values for any gauge. The patent-date line is not often seen and must have denoted a unique primer composition.*

Bibliography

Houze, Herbert G. *Winchester Repeating Arms Company - Its History & Development from 1865 to 1981.* Iola, Wisconsin: Krause Publications, Inc., 1994.

Shuey, Daniel L. *W.R.A. Co. - Headstamped Cartridges And Their Variations, Volume I.* Rockford, Illinois: WCF Publications, Inc. 1999.

Stadt, Ronald W. *Winchester Shotguns and Shotshells - From the Hammer Double to the Model 59.* 2nd edition. Iola, Wisconsin: Krause Publications, Inc., 1995.

Various notes, ledgers, memos and personal correspondence from former Winchester employees.

Watrous, George. *Metallic Ammunition - Brass and Paper Shotshells.* Unpublished Winchester In-house Publication.

Watrous, George. *Winchester Rifles & Shotguns.* Unpublished Winchester In-house Publication.

Winchester Repeating Arms Company. *Catalogs.* 1920 - 1961.

Winchester Repeating Arms Company. *Catalogs* of New Haven Arms Co. and Winchester Repeating Arms Co. 1865-1918. 12 volumes. Reprinted by Armory Publications, Tacoma, Washington. 1991.

Winchester Repeating Arms Company. *Price Lists.* 1877 - 1956.

More Shotshells and Shotshell Boxes

by David D. Kowalski

While the previous chapter has provided a great deal of information about Repeater paper shotshells and boxes, as well as the Winchester and Rival brass shotshells and related boxes, there's a bigger world out there. In this chapter we will start painting the much bigger picture of the entire collectible arena of Winchester shotshells and shotshell boxes. As Dan Shuey intimated in the last chapter, that potential picture stretches all the way to the horizon.

We are indebted to Ronald W. Stadt, whose <u>Winchester Shotguns and Shotshells, 2nd edition</u>, served as a source for a great deal of information, insight and photography contained in this shotshell section. Daniel L. Shuey has added several layers of clarifying research to this complex area, then came back to do it again. His effort was particularly important because many of the dates that shotshell and shotshell box collectors have been working with have not always been accurate. Quite frankly, this chapter would not have been possible without his attention to detail and his pricing input. Thank you, Dan!

We are also indebted to Tom Webster for access to his shotshell box collection. To Ray T. Giles for his corroborating oversight and comment on shotshell box dating. To Thomas I. "Tim" Melcher for his pricing help, as well as generously adding photographs of about 15 rare boxes to fill in some of the "era" and "variation" gaps he saw. Finally, another big "Thank You" to Ted Bacyk, Doug Culver, Ron Willoughby and Richard Klinect for taking time from their busy schedules to serve on our pricing panel.

A totally exhaustive examination of Winchester shotshells and shotshell boxes would have taken us far beyond anything we anticipated with this first volume. However, with the dedicated help of our contributors, this chapter and the previous one give you a very substantial, detailed view of this area. It should clearly help any collector add to his or her ability to pinpoint style changes and production eras when presented with shotshell-related collectibles.

In the following pages, you will find shotshells and shotshell boxes organized by brand in rough chronological order. But even this is a challenge because Winchester produced several brands simultaneously and their introductions and phase-outs overlapped each other.

You will also find shotshells and boxes from the same general era in rough chronological order within

Shotshell boxes, especially in quantity, present a storage and display challenge common to many collectibles. And sunlight and certain kinds of artificial light can damage the vivid colors of some products. Tom Webster solves the display challenge with a series of low shelves in a larger room where he's made his Rival "Christmas Box" the centerpiece of the collection. He also limits the amount of time lights are on in display rooms, as well as putting special light-filtering sleeves on his fluorescent lighting. Photo by D. Kowalski.

each brand. We kept shells and boxes together because there are some instances where unexpected headstamps, for example, came out of certain boxes.

Consistent with Dan Shuey's coverage of Repeater shotshells in the previous chapter, we have generally not included shotshell or box examples newer than 1956. (However, we couldn't resist making a few exceptions in an "oddities" section at the end of the chapter.)

We have tried to provide information and relevant observations in caption form. To deal coherently with this whole area is like watching a movie with a major plot and several minor subplots. Actors come on the screen, tell a part of their story, then exit, only to return five scenes later. That's analogous to how Winchester created headstamp and box design changes. Headstamps were typically the "major plot" but Winchester box designers were constantly creating minor "subplots" in the form of additions and deletions to box labels. And to really confuse the collector, sometimes the box would be the major plot and the headstamps would provide the variations.

After we cover each shotshell and box variation, we give a range of values after each one. We will continue to use categories and grading definitions provided by Daniel L. Shuey for cartridges and shotshells in earlier chapters. And we will use the standards Ray T. Giles articulated for cartridge boxes and that we adapted for shotshell boxes.

In future editions of this volume, we will add more examples and continue to "fill in the gaps" in the shotshell and shotshell box area. If you have rare or striking examples of boxes, for example, that you believe should be seen by the wider world, we would welcome your submissions.

Before you launch off into this chapter, we have created the following "Shotshell Timeline" to help your orientation process. Beginning and end dates for each brand include all gauges. You will find exact dates for each brand and gauge in their appropriate sections later in the chapter.

Winchester Shotshell Timeline

METALLIC (BRASS) EMPTY

Brand	Introduced	Discontinued
W.R.A. Co.	1878	1881
Winchester (1st Quality)	1879	1949
W.R.A. Co. "XX"	1879	1881
Rival	1884	1949

PAPER (EMPTY) OR (LOADED)

Brand	Introduced	Discontinued
WRA Co. (Empty)	1878	1879
Winchester (Empty - 1st Quality)		
Brown Hull	1879	1883
Gray Hull	1883	1885
Black Hull	1884	1897
Winchester (Loaded)	1888	1898
W.R.A. Co. "XX" (Empty)	1884	1884
Star (Empty)	1884	1894
Star (Loaded)	1887	1894
S.Q. (Empty)	1884	1889
Rival (Empty)	1884	1897
Rival (Loaded)	1886	1897
Blue Rival (Empty)	1894	1904
Blue Rival (Loaded)	1894	1903
Metal Lined (Empty)	1897	1907
Metal Lined (Loaded)	1894	1907
Pigeon (Empty)	1898	1907
Pigeon (Loaded)	1898	1907
New Rival Green (Empty)	1897	1920
New Rival Green (Loaded)	1897	1920
New Rival Blue (Loaded)	1901	1929
New Rival Blue (Empty)	1920	1927

Brand	Introduced	Discontinued
Yellow Rival (Empty)	1899	1904
Nublack (Loaded)	1905	1938
Nublack (Empty)	1927	1937
Leader (Empty)	1894	1943
Leader (Loaded)	1894	1928
Leader Brush	1905	1921
Leader Oval	1925	1927
Leader Staynless	1928	1943
Leader Lacquered	1929	1937
Leader Super Speed	1933	1947
Leader Trap	1935	1939
Repeater (Empty)	1896	1937
Repeater (Loaded)	1900	1928
Repeater Brush	1905	1938
Repeater Staynless	1928	1941
Repeater Speed Load	1927	1932
Repeater Trap	1935	1939
Winchester Speed Load	1932	1933
Repeater Super Speed	1933	1937
Ranger (Loaded)	1925	1928
Ranger Staynless	1928	Current
Ranger Brush	1925	1938
Ranger Skeet	1933	1939
Ranger Super Skeet	1939	1954
Ranger Trap	1935	1939
Ranger Super Trap	1939	1954
Ranger (Empty)	1937	Current
Winchester Super Speed	1937	Current
Wonder	1919	1930

Winchester Empty Paper Shotshells

The first Winchester paper shotshells were empty, brown in color, and headstamped "W.R.A. Co." They were offered (with brown hulls) from 1879-1883. This one is an example of the so-called "Chamberlin crimp." Photos from R. Stadt.

Shell Values: NIB 150.00   Exc. 100.00   V.G. 75.00   Good 50.00

Comment: "W.R.A. Co." headstamp. Brown hull.

"Winchester No. 10" headstamp. The second Winchester empty shells were also brown in color, headstamped "Winchester" along with the "No. (gauge)." These were considered their "first quality" shells. They were made from 1879-1883 in 4, 8, 10, 12, 14, 16 and 20 gauge. Photos from R. Stadt.

Shell Values: NIB 100.00   Exc. 80.00   V.G. 65.00   Good 50.00

Comment: "Winchester" headstamp. Brown hull.

"Winchester No. 10." The next empty paper shotshells were dark gray in color, and headstamped "Winchester" along with the "No. (gauge)." These were also considered "first quality" shells. They were made from 1883-1885 in 4, 8, 10, 12, 14, 16, and 20 gauge. (Note the very visible seam line.) Photos from R. Stadt.

Shell Values: NIB 10.00   Exc. 8.00   V.G. 6.00   Good 4.00

Comment: "Winchester" headstamp. Dark gray hull.

Winchester changed its entire line of "first quality" empty paper shotshells in 1884. They had black hulls. Headstamp was "Winchester" along with the "No. (gauge)." (The .58 caliber did not have "No." on the headstamp.) These were available in 4 and 8 gauge from 1884-1897; and in 10, 12, 14, 16 and 20 gauge from 1884-1894; .58 caliber unknown. Photos from R. Stadt.

Shell Values: NIB 7.00   Exc. 5.00   V.G. 3.00   Good 2.00

Comment: "Winchester" headstamp. Black hull.

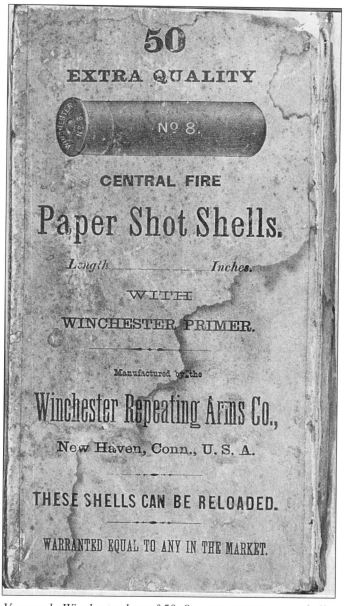

Very early Winchester box of 50, 8 gauge empty paper shells, showing heavy water marks. From TIM collection. Photo from R. Stadt.

Box Values:	Exc.	VG/F	Good
	1,400.00	1,200.00	900.00

Comment: *Shells could be ordered in several lengths; so box shows blank space here.*

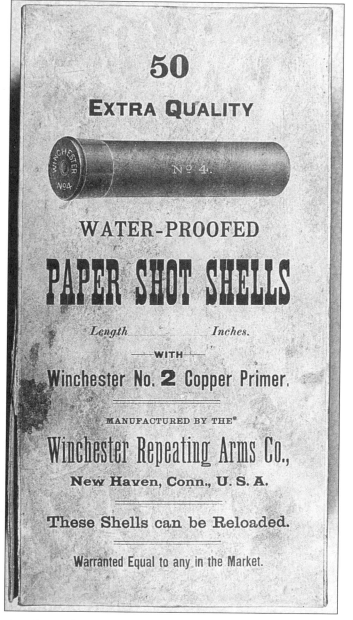

Another early, very rare Winchester box of 50, 4 gauge empty paper shells. Promotes "No. 2 Copper Primer." Box shows split along box seam. From TIM collection. Photo from R. Stadt.

Box Values:	Exc.	VG/F	Good
	3,000.00	2,500.00	2,000.00

Comment: *May be only one or two in existence.*

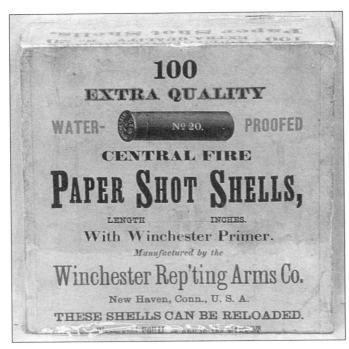

Another early Winchester box of 100, 20 gauge empty paper shells, with one of the few instances where "Rep'ting" has not been completely spelled out on the label. Label is buff with black type. "Water-proofed" is printed in red on both the top and side of box. Water-proofed not offered until 1886. Daniel Shuey has a factory note indicating that these shells had gray hulls but the waterproofing turned them black. Box also has reference to "Central Fire" that was used prior to 1890; later boxes use the term "Centerfire." From T. Webster collection. Photo by D. Kowalski.

Box Values:	Exc.	VG/F	Good
	550.00	500.00	400.00

Comment: *Only two of these boxes are currently known to exist.*

Very rare, early Winchester box of 100, 10 gauge empty paper shells, with simple, readable typeface. Also has the "Central Fire" designation. Note also that unlike three earlier boxes, this one makes reference to a shell length. From TIM collection. Photo from R. Stadt.

Box Values:	Exc.	VG/F	Good
	550.00	500.00	400.00

Comment: *Less than five examples known.*

Winchester Second Quality "S.Q." Paper Shells

"W.R.A. Co. No. 12 SQ." Winchester's "S.Q." empty paper shotshells were "Second Quality." They were offered from 1884-1889 in 10 gauge (black) and 12 gauge (gray). Photos from R. Stadt.

Shell Values:	NIB	Exc.	V.G.	Good
	85.00	70.00	50.00	25.00

Comment: *Fairly rare.*

More Shotshells and Shotshell Boxes • 213

Rare, early "SQ" box of 100, 10 gauge empty paper shells. Note that "Good For One Shot" meant not suitable for reloading. Also note "Central Fire" designation. From TIM collection. Photo from R. Stadt.

Box Values: Exc.   VG/F   Good
                        1,800.00   1,600.00   1,300.00

Comment: *Only two "SQ" boxes are currently known to exist.*

Star Paper Shotshells (Empty)

Star shell, empty, 10 gauge. Star shells were offered empty in 10 and 12 gauge from 1884-1894. Hull paper color was black. Photos from R. Stadt.

Shell Values: NIB   Exc.   V.G.   Good
                    25.00   20.00   15.00   10.00

Comment: *Fairly rare.*

Star Paper Shotshells (Loaded)

Loaded Star shells were offered in 10 and 12 gauge from 1887-1894. Paper color was black.

Photo not available.

Shell Values: NIB   Exc.   V.G.   Good
                    25.00   20.00   15.00   10.00

Comment: *Also fairly rare.*

Very rare Star box, 25 shells, 12 gauge, with duck on front. A highly collectible item. From TIM collection. Photo from R. Stadt.

Box Values: Exc.   VG/F   Good
                        4,000.00   3,000.00   2,500.00

Comment: *Less than five of these 12 gauge boxes currently known to exist.*

Star box, 25 loaded shells, 10 gauge, with duck on front is rare and sought after by collectors. Compared to previous box, Winchester now makes it clear these are loaded shells. Photo from R. Stadt.

Box Values:

	Exc.	VG/F	Good
	4,000.00	3,000.00	2,500.00

Comment: *Less than five of these 10 gauge boxes currently known to exist.*

Star shells, box of 25, 10 gauge loaded paper shells. Winchester took the concept of the two earlier boxes with duck images on them and created a "Duck Cartridges" box. They have also changed the duck image and background somewhat. Also note addition to top line; "Load No. 144 1/2." This is a very rare box and is considered highly collectible. Photo from R. Stadt.

Box Values:

	Exc.	VG/F	Good
	3,800.00	3,000.00	2,500.00

Comment: *Less than five of this variation of "Duck Cartridges" are currently known to exist.*

Star "Goose Cartridges" box, 25 loaded, 10 gauge paper shells. All the Star boxes have split-top box construction and this seam clearly shows though label. Water stains and chunks of label missing (none major) would push this particular very rare box into the "Good" category. From TIM collection. Photo from R. Stadt.

Box Values:

	Exc.	VG/F	Good
	5,000.00	4,500.00	3,500.00

Comment: *The only "Goose Cartridges" box known to exist.*

Star shells, box of 25 loaded shells, 12 gauge. A very rare "Prairie Chicken" box. This label also shows evidence of the split-top seam underneath. Photo from R. Stadt.

Box Values: Exc.   VG/F   Good
                        4,000.00   3,000.00   2,500.00

Comment: *The only example of the "Prairie Chicken" box currently known to exist.*

W.R.A. Co. "XX" Paper Shotshells (Empty)

"W.R.A. Co. No. 12 XX." The "XX" paper shotshells with "W.R.A. Co." headstamp were only sold for about nine months in 1884. Paper color was black. Photos from R. Stadt.

Shell Values: NIB   Exc.   V.G.   Good
                     120.00   100.00   80.00   60.00

Comment: *Very rare.*

Rival Paper Shotshells (Empty)

"W.R.A. Co. Rival No. 12." Rival empty paper shotshells were brown. Gauges, year introduced, and year discontinued were: 10, 1894-1897; 12, 1884-1897; 14, 1890-1897; 16, 1890-1897; 20, 1890-1897. Photos from R. Stadt.

Shell Values: NIB   Exc.   V.G.   Good
                     5.00   4.00   3.00   1.00

Comment: *Old but fairly common.*

Very early Rival paper shells, box of 100, 12 gauge. Perhaps the earliest Rival label version. Top has 1/4-inch overlap on lip. Label is cream color with black type. A "Water-Proofed" post-1886 box. Uses "No. 2 Copper Primer." From TIM collection. Photo from R. Stadt.

Box Values: Exc.   VG/F   Good
                         2,000.00   1,500.00   1,000.00

Comment: *Very rare.*

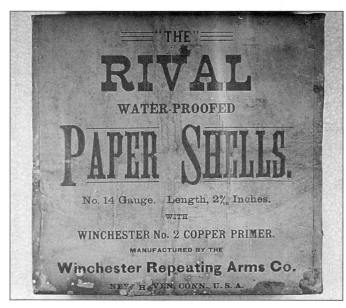

Another very early box of "The" Rival paper shells, 14 gauge. Label is cream color with blue type. A "Water-Proofed" post-1886 box. Uses "No. 2 Copper Primer." Photo from R. Stadt.

Box Values: Exc.   VG/F   Good
                         1,500.00   1,300.00   1,000.00

Comment: *Also very rare.*

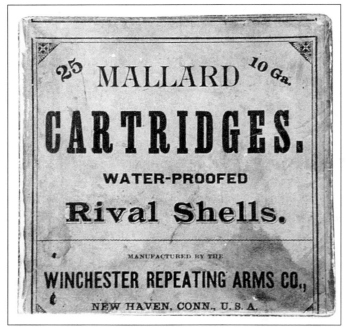

Rival shells, box of 25, 10 gauge. These "Mallard Cartridges" reportedly have a stamp on the bottom that reads "11/13/80." (However, this date would be too early for the generally recognized launch of Rival paper empties in 1884. Perhaps the year was either "88" or "90?") Note ornate triangle corner decorations. Label color is buff with black type. Photo from R. Stadt.

Box Values: Exc.   VG/F   Good
                         2,500.00   2,000.00   1,500.00

Comment: *Yet another very rare box.*

More Shotshells and Shotshell Boxes • 217

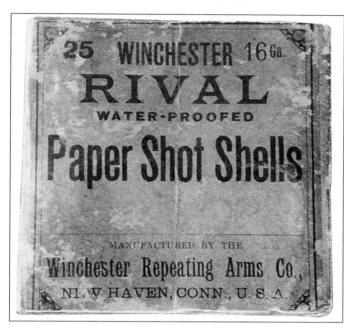

Rival paper shells, box of 25, 16 gauge. Label is gray/green with black type. Probably from early 1890s; note ornate triangle corner decorations similar to previous box. From TIM collection. Photo from R. Stadt.

Rival "Turkey Cartridges" in box of 25, 10 gauge. The first box of Rival loaded shells. Also the only early Rival box displaying a game bird on label. Label is tan with greenish-blue type. From TIM collection. Photo by T. Melcher.

Box Values:

	Exc.	VG/F	Good
	1,100.00	900.00	750.00

Comment: *Note also that this box and previous one are 25-round boxes, an option for empties that never became very popular.*

Rival Paper Shotshells (Loaded)

Winchester also offered the Rival brand as loaded shells from 1887-1897 in 10, 12, 14, and 16 gauge.

Photos not available.

Shell Values:	NIB	Exc.	V.G.	Good
	15.00	10.00	8.00	5.00

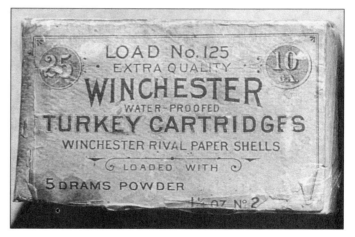

Rival "Turkey Cartridges," side of box. Dating this box as 1886 or 1887 would make sense since "Water-proofed" was introduced in 1886, as were Rival loaded shells. From TIM collection. Photo by T. Melcher.

Box Values:

	Exc.	VG/F	Good
	10,000.00	9,000.00	8,000.00

Comment: *The only box of its kind known.*

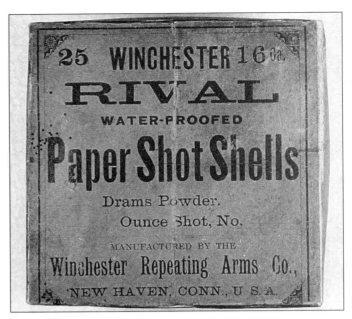

Loaded Rival paper shells, box of 25, 16 gauge. Perhaps slightly later than previous box but from the same era. From TIM collection. Photo from R. Stadt.

Box Values: Exc.   VG/F   Good
                    1,000.00   850.00   600.00

Comment: *Values for any gauge.*

Early loaded Rival paper shells, box of 25, 12 gauge. Note "Drams Powder" and "Ounce Shot No." lines, also ornate triangular corner decorations, very similar to following box. This box probably from early 1890s since Winchester reportedly stopped the private labeling in the mid-1890s. Label is buff with black type. From T. Webster collection. Photo by D. Kowalski.

Box Values: Exc.   VG/F   Good
                    1,100.00   900.00   750.00

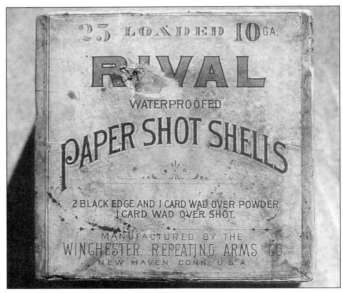

Rival loaded shells, box of 25, 10 gauge. A box from mid- to late-1890s that appears to be a transition between previous box and next one. "Rival" name is very dominant. Box is tan; label is egg-white with "rival" in gold; other copy is black. From TIM collection. Photo by T. Melcher.

Box Values: Exc.   VG/F   Good
                     750.00   600.00   500.00

Comment: *Values for any gauge.*

More Shotshells and Shotshell Boxes • 219

Loaded Rival paper shells, box of 25, 12 gauge. Now "Winchester" has taken over the position of prominence at top of label. From TIM collection. Photo from R. Stadt.

Box Values: | Exc. | VG/F | Good
| 400.00 | 350.00 | 275.00

Comment: *A fairly common Rival label.*

The Rival "Christmas Box." A very coveted box; containing 100 shells, came in either 10 or 12 gauge, very ornate with beautiful four-color scenes on all sides. (See color section in center of this book for another excellent example, a box of 12 gauge empty shells showing the top and three sides.) From TIM collection. Photo from R. Stadt.

Box Values: | Exc. | VG/F | Good
| 5,000.00 | 4,500.00 | 3,500.00

Comment: *This is perhaps the most generally sought-after Winchester shotshell box. A much rarer version holding "Star" shells (one of only two known) sold at auction in January 2000 for more than $39,000.*

Blue Rival Paper Shotshells (Empty)

"Winchester Blue Rival No. 12." Blue Rival empty paper shotshells were also offered. Gauges, year introduced, and year discontinued were: 10, 1894-1904; 12, 1894-1904; 14, 1896-1904; 16, 1894-1904; 20, 1896-1904. Photos from R. Stadt.

Shell Values:	NIB	Exc.	V.G.	Good
	3.50	2.50	2.00	1.00

Early Blue Rival empty paper shells, box of 100, 14 gauge. Likely the first Blue Rival label. Note reference to "Nitro Powder" and "No. 3W Primer." Photo from R. Stadt.

Box Values:	Exc.	VG/F	Good
	450.00	400.00	300.00

Comment: *As we've indicated elsewhere, 14 gauge boxes of any kind are rare.*

Blue Rival empty box, 100 shells, 10 gauge. Label is buff color with dark blue print. Note that Winchester has started to use a shell illustration on the box. Also note continuing reference to "Nitro Powder" and "No. 3W Primer." From T. Webster collection. Photo by D. Kowalski.

Box Values:	Exc.	VG/F	Good
	400.00	325.00	200.00

Comment: *Most common of the Blue Rival boxes.*

More Shotshells and Shotshell Boxes • 221

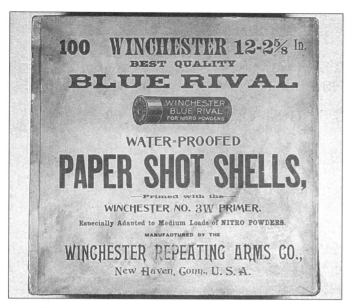

Blue Rival empty paper shells, box of 100, 12 gauge. The same as previous box, but in 12 gauge. This box is less ornate than the following one. Here Winchester has specifics about shell gauge, length and number of shells on the front of the box. From TIM collection. Photo from R. Stadt.

Box Values: Exc.   VG/F   Good
                         450.00   400.00   325.00

Comment: *Values similar for all gauges of this box.*

Blue Rival empty paper shells, box of 100, 12 gauge. Probably slightly newer than previous two boxes. "Blue Rival" logo has gotten more ornate and it and "Paper Shot Shells" are now in what we might call a "double crescent" pattern. Also note continuing reference to "Nitro Powder" on shell illustration and on box; however, box reference has been stricken and another overprint added above it: "Primed for Black Powder." Still references "No. 3W Primer." A classic example of using up old boxes for new product. Label is cream color with black type. From TIM collection. Photo from R. Stadt.

Box Values: Exc.   VG/F   Good
                         325.00   250.00   175.00

Comment: *Values similar for all gauges of this box.*

Blue Rival Paper Shotshells (Loaded)

Blue Rival loaded paper shells were sold for slightly shorter period of time than empty shells, from 1894-1903.

Photos not available.

Shell Values: NIB   Exc.   V.G.   Good
                    5.00   4.00   3.00   2.00

Blue Rival loaded paper shells, box of 25, 10 gauge. Has split-top construction. Note use of dark-colored banners behind both "Winchester" references; uncommon for any Winchester brand from that era. From TIM collection. Photo from R. Stadt.

Box Values: Exc.   VG/F   Good
                   750.00   650.00   500.00

Comment: *Blue Rival boxes of 25 are very rare; less than 10 are known to exist.*

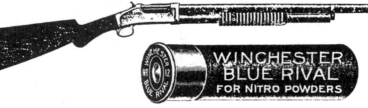

Winchester advertising frequently used the names of celebrity shooters who won competitions with their ammunition. The illustration of the early Blue Rival shell shows a smooth base with no corrugations. From R. Stadt.

Metal Lined Paper Shotshells (Empty)

"Winchester Metal Lined No. 12." Metal Lined empty paper shotshells were much higher quality than their predecessors. The base of the shell was lined with metal on the inside. They were made in various shades of green as empty shells. Gauges, year introduced, and year discontinued were: 4, 1897-1907; 8, 1897-1907; 10, 1894-1907; 12, 1897-1907. Photos from R. Stadt.

Shell Values:	NIB	Exc.	V.G.	Good
	90.00	75.00	50.00	40.00

Comment: *Significantly rarer than "1901" version.*

Metal Lined empty paper shells box, box of 100, 12 gauge. Has "Winchester" headstamp on shell illustration. And the last patent date under the shell illustration is "Dec. 8, 1896." According to Daniel Shuey, this is a "second generation" box. The first "Metal Lined" shells had smooth base with no corrugations (as seen on previous shell) and used the No. 3W primer. The shell on this box has corrugations and shells in box primed with "No. 4 Primer." From TIM collection. Photo from R. Stadt.

Box Values:	Exc.	VG/F	Good
	2,000.00	1,600.00	1,000.00

Comment: *One of only two Metal Lined boxes known.*

Metal Lined "1901" Empty Paper Shotshells

"1901 Metal Lined No. 8." Beginning in 1901, Winchester started to produce Metal Lined empty shells with "1901" headstamp that replaced "Winchester." Photos from R. Stadt.

Shell Values:	NIB	Exc.	V.G.	Good
	35.00	30.00	25.00	20.00

Comment: *Values are for 8 gauge shells.*

Metal Lined Paper Shotshells (Loaded)

Winchester sold Metal Lined loaded shells in only 10 and 12 gauge from 1894-1907.

Photos not available.

Shell Values:	NIB	Exc.	V.G.	Good
	100.00	90.00	75.00	65.00

Comment: *The rarest of the Metal Lined shells.*

Yellow Rival Empty Shotshells

"Winchester Yellow Rival No. 12." Yellow Rival shells were offered empty only in 10, 12, 14, 16, and 20 gauges from 1899-1904. The 14 and 16 gauge shells are rare. Photos from R. Stadt.

Shell Values:	NIB	Exc.	V.G.	Good
	8.50	6.50	4.00	3.00

Comment: *Values are for 10 and 12 gauge shells. For rarer 14, 16 and 20 gauge, add 100 percent premium.*

Yellow Rival box, 100 round, 20 gauge. Since Yellow Rival was only made from 1899-1904, it is also valuable (other than as an obvious collectible in its own right) for helping to date other boxes. Boxes from all brands tended to have similar design changes at the same time (keeping in mind that old stock had to be used up before new stock was rolled out). It is possible there was only one version of the Yellow Rival box in its five-year history; Tim Melcher reports his 10 gauge and 20 gauge boxes have identical top labels. From TIM collection. Photo from R. Stadt.

Box Values:	Exc.	VG/F	Good
	2,200.00	1,800.00	1,200.00

Comment: *Only four Yellow Rival boxes (all 100-round boxes) are known to exist.*

Pigeon Shotshells (Empty)

"Winchester Pigeon No. 10 and No. 12." Pigeon shells (empty) were similar to the Metal Lined shells but had paper base wads. They were light green and were offered in 10 and 12 gauge from 1898-1907. Photos from R. Stadt.

Shell Values:	NIB	Exc.	V.G.	Good
	65.00	50.00	35.00	20.00

Comment: *Values for 12 gauge; 10 gauge would be 1/3 these prices.*

Pigeon Shotshells (Loaded)

Loaded Pigeon shells were also offered in 10 and 12 gauge from 1898-1907.

Shell Values:	NIB	Exc.	V.G.	Good
	75.00	65.00	45.00	35.00

Comment: *Extremely rare.*

New Rival Shotshells (Empty - Green)

A rare empty New Rival shell with sunburst around the primer; 12 gauge. This was a trademark registration sample shell that shows the "Winchester" headstamp that pre-dates the "1901." New Rival empty shells were olive green. They were offered both empty and loaded in 10, 12, 14, 16, and 20 gauges from 1897-1920. The one exception was that the 14 gauge shell was not loaded after 1917.

Shell Values:	NIB	Exc.	V.G.	Good
	3.00	2.00	1.00	

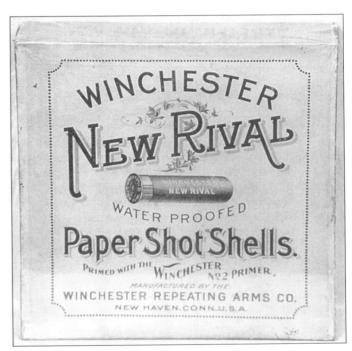

Early New Rival box, 100 empty shells, 10 gauge. Mimics the previous Yellow Rival label. But now this New Rival box touts the "No. 2 Primer." No trademark line. This box probably produced between 1900-1909. Shows headstamp of early "Winchester New Rival" (No. 10) shell that pre-dated the "1901" headstamped shell. Label is buff color with black type. From T. Webster collection. Photo by D. Kowalski.

Box Values:	Exc.	VG/F	Good
	300.00	250.00	150.00

Comment: *Values for all gauges.*

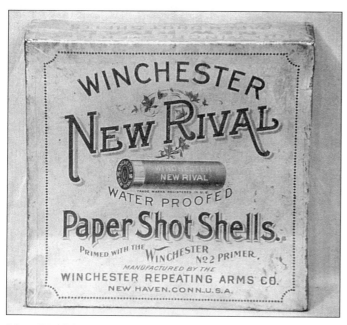

New Rival box, 100 empty shells, 16 gauge. Very similar to previous box with shotshell illustration showing headstamp of early "Winchester New Rival" (No. 16) shell that pre-dated the "1901" headstamped shell. This box has added "Trade Marks Registered in U.S." line under shell illustration, used from 1910-1913+. Box label is cream color with green type. From T. Webster collection. Photo by D. Kowalski.

Box Values: Exc.   VG/F   Good
                    300.00   250.00   150.00

Comment: *Values for all gauges.*

Later New Rival box, 100 empty shells, 12 gauge. Shell illustration has "Winchester New Rival" headstamp. Has "lightning strike" logo typeface used in 1910 and later. Winchester continued to use the "Winchester" headstamp even though they were also making the "1901" version. Box has blue type and the "dotted" border no longer has "indents" in each corner. Photo from R. Stadt.

Box Values: Exc.   VG/F   Good
                    350.00   300.00   250.00

Comment: *Values are for all gauges. A very desirable box.*

New Rival "1901" Shotshells (Empty)

New Rival empty shell, "1901" headstamp, 12 gauge. The "1901" headstamp was launched after the "Winchester" headstamp but both were produced concurrently for many years. Photos from R. Stadt.

Shell Values: NIB   Exc.   V.G.   Good
                     3.00   2.00   1.00

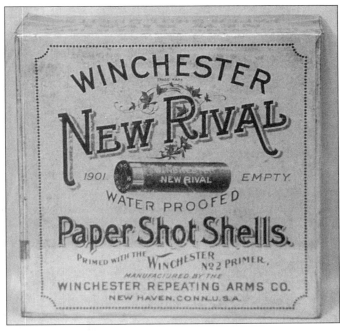

New Rival "1901" box of 100 empty shells, 16 gauge. This box does not have "Trade Marks Registered in U.S.A." line under shell illustration. Has "1901" headstamp on shell illustration. "Dotted" border has corner "indents." Box is pre-1910. Label is cream color with green type. From T. Webster collection. Photo by D. Kowalski.

Box Values: Exc.   VG/F   Good
                        300.00   250.00   175.00

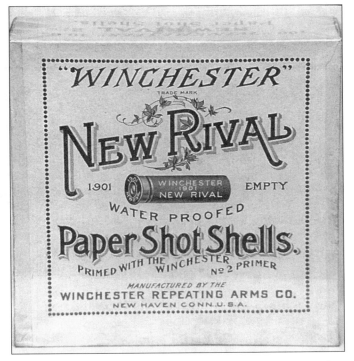

New Rival "1901" box of 100 empties, 10 gauge. A rather unique box in this series of New Rival 100 empty boxes. This box does not show shell gauge on headstamp (the gauge is on the side label). The shell illustration on this box also has an added "1901" not seen on any of the other 100-round boxes we show here. Does not have "Trade Marks Registered in U.S.A." line under shell illustration as did the prior pre-"1901" box. Finally, the "dotted" border around label has square corners. Label color is buff with black type; there is also red "W" on side label, which was used after 1907. Also has earliest of "lightning strike" logos with quotes marks. There are several overlapping design features between this box and the ones before and after; it's possible it was something of an experimental design that was a short-lived transition between the two. From T. Webster collection. Photo by D. Kowalski.

Box Values: Exc.   VG/F   Good
                        300.00   250.00   175.00

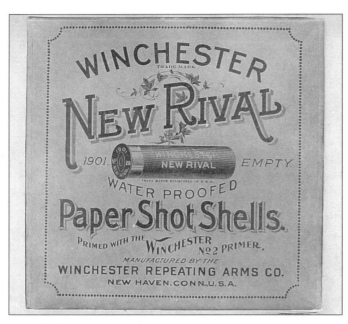

New Rival "1901" box of 100 empty shells, 20 gauge. This box does have the "Trade Marks Registered in U.S.A." line under shell illustration, which Winchester used from 1910-1913+. "Dotted" border still has corner "indents." Box label is cream color with green type. From TIM collection. Photo from R. Stadt.

Box Values: Exc. 300.00   VG/F 250.00   Good 175.00

New Rival Green Shotshells (Loaded)

"Winchester New Rival No. 12 and No. 20." These early loaded New Rival shells were first produced in 1897 and have the "Winchester" headstamp. Hull color is light green. (Winchester also added blue hulls for loaded New Rival shells in 1901 and produced both hull colors concurrently.) Photos from R. Stadt.

New Rival box, 25 loaded shells, 10 gauge. Box label is cream color with green type and green color inside black outlined type. Refers to "Waterproofed" which was added in 1896. From T. Webster collection. Photo by D. Kowalski.

Box Values: Exc. 450.00   VG/F 375.00   Good 250.00

Comment: *Values for 10 gauge.*

Shell Values: NIB 3.00   Exc. 2.00   V.G. 1.00   Good

Comment: *Add 100 percent premium for 14 gauge.*

More Shotshells and Shotshell Boxes • 229

New Rival, box of 25 loaded shells, 12 gauge. Same style as previous box. Box label is cream color with green type. From TIM collection. Photo from R. Stadt.

Box Values: | Exc. | VG/F | Good
| 400.00 | 325.00 | 200.00

Comment: *Values for 12 gauge.*

New Rival, box of 25 loaded shells, 20 gauge. Same design as previous two boxes. Box label is cream color with green type. From TIM collection. Photo from R. Stadt.

Box Values: | Exc. | VG/F | Good
| 450.00 | 375.00 | 250.00

Comment: *Values for 20 gauge.*

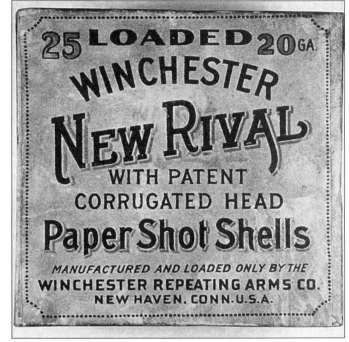

Later New Rival, box of 25 loaded shells, 20 gauge. Doesn't have the ornate vines and leaves but now features the patented "Corrugated Head" that was first used in 1897. Believed to be the last box for loaded green New Rival shells. Photo from R. Stadt.

Box Values: | Exc. | VG/F | Good
| 450.00 | 375.00 | 250.00

Comment: *This label in much better condition than following one.*

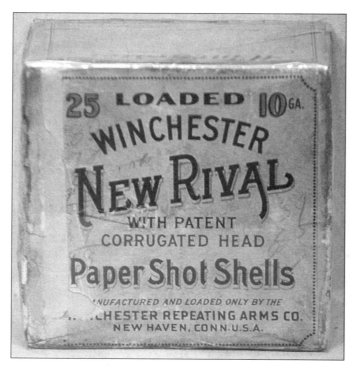

Later New Rival box, 25 loaded shells, 10 gauge. Same label style as previous one. Box label is cream color with black type and green color inside black outlined type on "25" and "10." (See the following two photos of the side labels on this box.) From T. Webster collection. Photo by D. Kowalski.

Other side of same box has black-print sticker promoting "Laflin & Rand Powder." Shells could be ordered with specific brands of powder. From T. Webster collection. Photo by D. Kowalski.

Box Values:	Exc.	VG/F	Good
	450.00	375.00	250.00

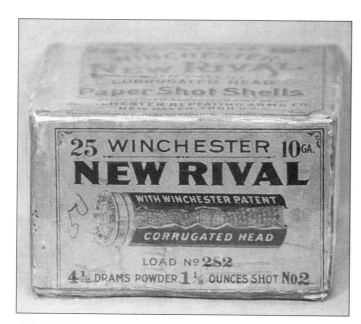

Side label for previous box clearly shows corrugation around shell head. Label is cream color with bright yellow shell head. Shell hull is bright green. From T. Webster collection. Photo by D. Kowalski.

New Rival Blue Shotshells (Loaded)

Blue hulls, "Winchester New Rival No. 12 and No. 20." New Rival paper was changed to blue for a portion of this brand in 1901. These blue loaded shells had one corrugation around the base as did some of the earlier olive green ones. New Rival loaded shells were offered in 14 gauge until 1917; in 10, 16, and 20 gauges until 1927; and in 12 gauge until 1929. Photos from R. Stadt.

Shell Values:	NIB	Exc.	V.G.	Good
	3.00	2.00	1.00	

Comment: *Add 100 percent premium for 14 gauge.*

New Rival, box of 25 loaded shells, 16 gauge. Probably a pre-1924 box. Does not yet have the expected "Made in U.S.A." line that began to be used after the tariff law of 1924; it still retains the "Manufactured and Loaded only by the Winchester Repeating Arms Co." phrasing. New trademark line reads: "Trade Marks Reg. U.S. Pat. Off. And throughout the World." Shell on box still has "Winchester New Rival" headstamp. Box label is white with blue type and trim; "Winchester" and "New Rival" are in red. From TIM collection. Photo from R. Stadt.

Box Values:	Exc.	VG/F	Good
	225.00	190.00	100.00

Comment: *Values for this design, all gauges.*

New Rival, box of 25 loaded shells, 12 gauge. "Devil's tail" logo in quote marks from early 1920s. Note stylized "W" in bottom corners each has four dots around them. Has simple "Trade Mark" line under logo. Shell on box has "Winchester New Rival" headstamp. Box label is white with yellow copy within blue border trim and then a yellow shadow within the blue border. "Winchester" and "New Rival" are in red, as are the bottom two lines of copy. The two lines immediately below "New Rival" are black type. From T. Webster collection. Photo by D. Kowalski.

Box Values:	Exc.	VG/F	Good
	250.00	200.00	125.00

Comment: *Values for this style, all gauges.*

232 • More Shotshells and Shotshell Boxes

New Rival, box of 25 loaded shells, 20 gauge. The 20 gauge shell was produced between 1920-1927; this box would be post-1924. Unlike last two boxes, this one has line "Made in U.S.A. Otherwise box shows many design features of the last one. Has less-stylized "lightning strike" logo without quotes. "W" in each bottom corner has block typeface without serifs. But now Winchester has gone back to the simple "Trade Mark" line. Shell on box has "Winchester New Rival" headstamp. From TIM collection. Photo from R. Stadt.

Box Values:

Exc.	VG/F	Good
225.00	190.00	100.00

Comment: *Values for this design, all gauges.*

Nublack Shotshells (Loaded)

"WinchesterNublack No. 10, No. 12 and No. 24." Nublack loaded shells were listed from 1905-1938 in 10, 12, 16, and 20 gauges. They were also offered in 24 and 28 gauge from 1911-1921. Most Nublack shells are yellow but there are some red and orange ones in small gauges, both empty and loaded. Photos from R. Stadt.

Shell Values:

NIB	Exc.	V.G.	Good
5.00	3.50	2.50	1.50

Nublack Shotshells (Empty)

Nublack empty shells were available from 1927-1937 in 10, 12, 16, and 20 gauges. Most empty Nublack shells are yellow but there are some red ones in small gauges. Most late Nublack shells were natural or Manila color.

Photos not available.

Shell Values:

NIB	Exc.	V.G.	Good
5.00	3.50	2.50	1.50

More Shotshells and Shotshell Boxes • 233

Nublack box, loaded shells, box of 25, 12 gauge. Probably pre-1924. Does not yet have the expected "Made in U.S.A." line that began to be used after the tariff law of 1924; it still retains the "Manufactured and Loaded only by the Winchester Repeating Arms Co." phrasing. The trademark line reads: "Trade Marks Reg. U.S. Pat. Off. And throughout the World." Label is white, border is green, ring around ducks is yellow. Type on "Loaded Black Powder Shells" is black; rest of type is red. Flying trio of mallards are in four color, right down to the orange feet and legs. (See following side label.) From T. Webster collection. Photo by D. Kowalski.

Side label of previous Nublack box is almost more brilliantly colored than top (probably due to fading by the sun or artificial lights). Border is green and both "W" and black-outlined "Nublack" are bright red. Photograph also shows this is clearly a two-piece box, where top slides over bottom, commonly used for this shell (note "Cut Seal Here" phrase). From T. Webster collection. Photo by D. Kowalski.

Box Values: Exc. VG/F Good
300.00 250.00 175.00

Comment: *Values for 12 gauge box, this variation. These boxes have variations seen with the previously shown New Rival boxes from the 1920s: i.e. different trademark lines; with and without dots around the bottom 'W"; and with and without the "Made in U.S.A." line. Note that label on this box was placed in slightly off-center position, a common production problem. This has always been a popular collectible due, no doubt, to the flying ducks. This picture actually adapted from a poster from the early 1900s.*

Nublack box, 25 shells, 16 gauge. An "oddities" box shows a typical two-piece label on a one-piece box. Winchester started to see a drastic decrease in demand for black powder shells in the late 1920s and early 1930s. However, at the time they switched to one-piece box production, they had these labels left from earlier days so they went ahead and used them. Although the photograph doesn't make it obvious, this is actually a one-piece box (with top-opening lid) but Winchester used a post-1924 ("Made in U.S.A.") label on it. From TIM collection. Photo by T. Melcher.

Box Values: Exc. VG/F Good
400.00 300.00 250.00

Comment: *Values for this "oddity" box. Tim Melcher's comment was, "this variation even escapes the eyes of all but the truly dedicated (fanatical?) collector."*

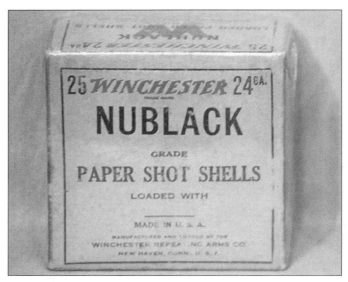

Later Nublack box of 25 loaded shells, 24 gauge. This label is buff color with "Winchester" and "Trade Mark" colored red on top label; other type is black. Side label has red "W" and "Winchester." The "Made in U.S.A." line indicates this was produced after 1924; bottom label would have the actual date. If it didn't have a date, this would be an export box, which is likely since 24 gauge was a much more common gauge overseas than in the U.S. From T. Webster collection. Photo by D. Kowalski.

Box Values: Exc. VG/F Good
300.00 250.00 175.00

Comment: *Values for 24 gauge.*

Leader Paper Shotshells (Empty)

Early Leader, empty shell, 12 gauge. Leader empty shells were introduced in 1894 (some nine years before the first loaded ones) and became the industry standard for nearly 50 years. Empty shells were packed in 100-round boxes. Gauges, year introduced, and year discontinued were: 4 and 8, 1897-1920; 10, 1894-1937; 12 and 16, 1894-1943; 20, 1897-1943. Most Leader shells were red, but pink or peach, tan and medium brown were also common. The first issue had a smooth head (no corrugations) and the No. 3W primer. After June, 1896 they had corrugations. Photos from R. Stadt.

Shell Values: NIB Exc. V.G. Good
4.50 3.50 2.50 1.50

Comment: *Values are for corrugated head. Add 50 percent for smooth heads; smooth heads may only be found today in 10 and 12 gauge.*

More Shotshells and Shotshell Boxes • 235

Leader box, 100 empty shells, 10 gauge. Headstamp on shell illustration is "Winchester Leader No. 10" and the patent line under the shell illustration has the date "June 9-30, 1896." This was the patent date for corrugations around the head. Shells have "No. 4W Primer" that came out in 1902; also refers to early "Nitro Powders." Would probably date this box between 1902-1904. Label is buff color with red type. From T. Webster collection. Photo by D. Kowalski.

Box Values:	Exc.	VG/F	Good
	250.00	200.00	125.00

Comment: *Values for any gauge.*

Leader box, 100 empty shells, 12 gauge. Headstamp on shell illustration is "Winchester Leader 12 GA" that dates this box from 1920 when that "GA" headstamp variation was used for a brief time. Lower right corner of box references 1918. Label is buff color with red type. From T. Webster collection. Photo by D. Kowalski.

Box Values:	Exc.	VG/F	Good
	300.00	250.00	200.00

Comment: *Values for any gauge. A scarce box.*

Leader "1901" Paper Shotshells (Empty)

From 1901 to 1920 Leader empty shells had "1901" at the top of the headstamp instead of "Winchester." They were available in several lengths, including this 12 gauge empty, 4-inch version. Photos from R. Stadt.

Shell Values:	NIB	Exc.	V.G.	Good
4-inch	12.00	10.00	8.00	6.00
Other	5.00	4.00	3.00	1.00

Comment: *Values are for corrugated head.*

Very early Leader "1901" box, 100 empty shells, 12 gauge. This unique transitional box appears to have been printed for shells made prior to the introduction of the "1901." The headstamp on the shell illustration is "Winchester Leader No. 12" and the two lines under the shell illustration read "Trade Mark Registered in the U.S. Pat. June 9-30 and Dec. 8, 1896, July 17, 1900." Label is buff color with red type. But the words "1901." and "Empty." have been overprinted in black which would have been consistent with the production department trying to use old labels before new ones were put in service. The "No. 4 Primer" came out in 1902; also refers to "Nitro Powders" so this box would be dated about 1902-1904. From T. Webster collection. Photo by D. Kowalski.

Box Values:	Exc.	VG/F	Good
	250.00	200.00	125.00

Comment: *A fairly common box.*

Early Leader "1901" box, 100 empty shells, 16 gauge. Compared to prior box, headstamp is now the expected "1901" headstamp. It reads "1901 Leader No. 16." There is no patent date line under shell illustration. Label is buff color with red type. The words "1901." and "Empty." are also printed in red, now apparently done at the same time as the rest of the label. References the "New No. 4 Primer" that came out in 1904; also refers to "Smokeless Powders" so this box would be dated post-1904. From T. Webster collection. Photo by D. Kowalski.

Box Values: Exc.   VG/F   Good
                                   275.00   225.00   150.00

Comment: *Values for any gauge.*

Leader "1901" box, 100 empties, 10 gauge. A slightly newer version of the last box. Headstamp on shell illustration is the expected "1901 Leader No. 10." While the previous box had no trademark line or dates, this one has a line above the shell illustration that reads "Trade Mark Registered in the U.S." Below the shell illustration it reads "Pat. June 9-30, Dec. 8, 1896; July 17, 1900" and then "July 14, 1903." by itself on the next line. Continues to reference the "New No. 4 Primer" that came out in 1904; also refers to "Smokeless Powders" so this box probably came out in late 1904 or 1905. Label color is buff with all copy in red. From T. Webster collection. Photo by D. Kowalski.

Box Values: Exc.   VG/F   Good
                                   250.00   200.00   125.00

Comment: *This box was used for several years and is quite common.*

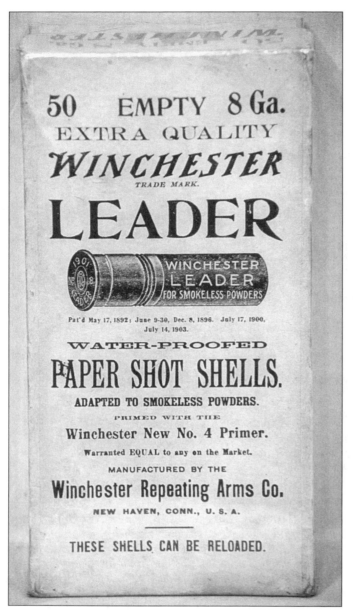

Early "1901" Leader box, 50 empty shells, 8 gauge. Shell illustration shows "1901" headstamp. A rare "shoebox" of Leader empties produced about 1910. Like previous two boxes, this one continues the references to the "New No. 4 Primer" that came out in 1904; and also to "Smokeless Powders." The last of four patent dates shown below shell illustration is July 14, 1903. The new feature here is the "lightning strike" logo that was commonly adopted in 1910. Label on top of this box is buff color with black type. (See following end label.) From T. Webster collection. Photo by D. Kowalski.

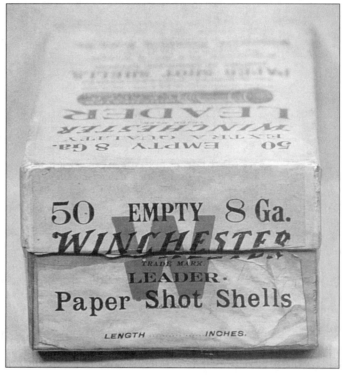

"1901" Leader box, 50 empty shells, 8 gauge; this end label of previous box clearly shows how top of box slides down over bottom. "W" printed in red, which was not done until after 1907. The wraparound label would have had an actual date code on it. From T. Webster collection. Photo by D. Kowalski.

Box Values:

	Exc.	VG/F	Good
	1,200.00	1,000.00	700.00

Comment: *Values for any gauge.*

Leader Shotshell Specialty Items

Here's a "1901" Leader empty shell in 8 gauge produced as a banquet favor for the Bristol (New Hampshire) Gun Club held January 20, 1916. Photos from R. Stadt.

Shell Values:	NIB	Exc.	V.G.	Good
	85.00	65.00	50.00	40.00

Comment: *Menu would have been rolled up in shell at each place setting. Would Winchester corporate have done this? Not necessarily. Would they have to approve it? Again, not necessarily. An aggressive local Winchester representative could have come up with this creative way to promote Winchester locally. Even the president or program director of the gun club, who might have been a Winchester fan, could have done the same thing.*

Leader box, Gilbert label. During the early 1900s, Winchester enlisted the services of five famous trapshooters of the day who won championships using Leader loaded shotshells. These personalities each appeared on a series of very rare die-cut store displays. They also had their images used on labels that were simply pasted on standard production-run Leader shotshell boxes of the period. This particular box seems to support the theory that the labels were provided by Winchester to various retailers, who would then simply paste them on boxes they had in stock. The pictures would serve as a form of "testimonial" advertising for the box of Leader shells. This box from the Tim Melcher collection has the label on a pre-1907 Leader box that does not have a red "W" on the side. (It is generally believed that these rare boxes date from 1902-1907, but before we totally accept this theory, let's look at the next box.) Photo by T. Melcher.

Box Values:	Exc.	VG/F	Good
	2,000.00	1,800.00	1,500.00

Comment: *Values for any box labeled with this or similar over-label (less than 10 known to exist in series). This version shows photo of Fred Gilbert. Copy on right reads: "Live Bird."*

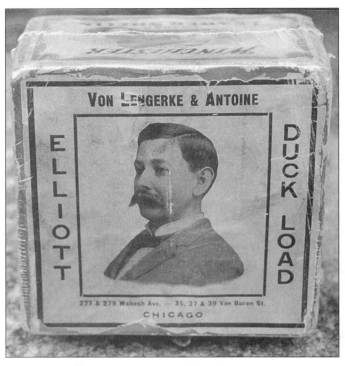

Leader box, Elliott label. While Fred Gilbert was on the previous box, this one pictures J.A.R. Elliott, another of the famous trapshooters of the day who won championships using Winchester Leader loaded shotshells. This box from the Ron Willoughby collection has the label on a Leader box that may date as late as the early 1920s. It also clearly shows the address of the Chicago retailer, Von Lengerke and Antoine. The fact that Von Lengerke and Antoine put this Elliott label on a box perhaps 15 years older than the previous one raises a host of new questions. Did Winchester produce these labels? Or did Von Lengerke and Antoine, being aggressive and progressive retailers, simply take the Winchester images and create their own labels? These were just black and white labels and would have been easy to create and cheap to print. Furthermore, if they were a large Winchester account, the corporate office would have been very hesitant to chastise them or restrain them from using "old" labels on "new" boxes. Perhaps the only stipulation they would have insisted on is that the labels were only glued on Leader boxes. Photo by R. Willoughby.

Box Values:	Exc.	VG/F	Good
	2,000.00	1,800.00	1,500.00

Comment: *Values for any box labeled with this or similar over-label (less than 10 known to exist in series). This version shows photo of J.A.R. Elliott.*

Leader brass shell heads were used to make up powder sample shells. This cutaway shell, made about 1898, is one of four variations known to exist. The Winchester Repeating Arms Co. received patent no. 719,876 for them. Photo from R. Stadt.

Sample Values:	NIB	Exc.	V.G.	Good
	400.00	300.00	200.00	125.00

Leader Shotshells (Loaded)

Leader, early loaded shell with plain base, 12 gauge, with No. 3W primer. Gauges, year introduced, and year discontinued for loaded Leader shells were: 8, 1900-1921; 10, 1894-1938; 12, 1894-1943; 16, 1894-1943; 20, 1900-1943. Leader 8 gauge shells were also loaded with black powder from 1907-1921. Photos from R. Stadt.

Shell Values:	NIB	Exc.	V.G.	Good
	10.00	8.00	6.00	5.00

Comment: *These rarer smooth heads only made for a few years.*

Leader shell, loaded, corrugated base, 12 gauge, with No. 4 primer. After 1896 Leader shells came with three corrugated rings (sometimes four) around the base. That's when John Gardner, superintendent of the Winchester cartridge department, was granted patent no. 25611 for circular grooves or corrugations around the metal base of a shell. A fourth corrugation was added in 1903. Photos from R. Stadt.

Shell Values:	NIB	Exc.	V.G.	Good
	5.00	4.00	3.00	2.00

Comment: *Values for shells with three corrugations. Deduct 10 percent for four corrugations. Add 400 percent premium for 8 gauge.*

Early Leader box, 25 loaded shells, 12 gauge. Nitro powder has now given way to "Loaded with Smokeless Powder." From TIM collection. Label is buff color with red type. Photo from R. Stadt.

Box Values:	Exc.	VG/F	Good
	450.00	400.00	300.00

Comment: *Values for any gauge.*

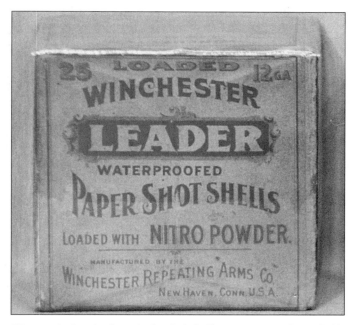

Very early Leader box, 25 loaded shells, 12 gauge. These shells are "Loaded with Nitro Powder." Probably the first loaded Leader box. Label is buff color with red type. From T. Webster collection. Photo by D. Kowalski.

Box Values:	Exc.	VG/F	Good
	450.00	400.00	300.00

Comment: *Values for any gauge.*

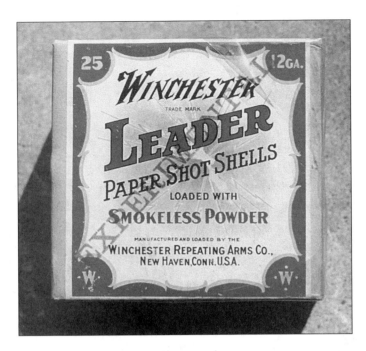

Leader "Experimental" box, 12 gauge (top and side views). Winchester was always looking at new designs and new loadings. And they created actual sample boxes for management review, marking them "Experimental" (this one overprinted in red ink). Box does not have the red "W" on the side, which was generally adopted in 1907. It does have the "Devil's tail" version of the "lightning bolt" logo that appeared on some boxes in late 1907, 1908 and 1909 before being generally adopted on all boxes in 1910. Note also that box claims shells were loaded with "Empire" Smokeless powder. Tim Melcher reports about 20 of these boxes have been found, nearly all in mint condition. This would support the view that this particular loading never made it into the marketplace. From TIM collection. Photos by T. Melcher.

Box Values: Exc.   VG/F   Good
                       400.00   350.00   300.00

Comment: *A very collectible box.*

Leader box, 25 loaded shells, 12 gauge, with "Devil's tail" version of the "lightning strike" logo with "sunburst" image behind brand name. This "Devil's tail" logo does not have quote marks around "Winchester." This box probably from the early 1920s. Also has four dots around each bottom "W" and short "Trade Mark" line. Label has red border (with yellow type) on white background; lightning strike is yellow; other type is black and red. From T. Webster collection. Photo by D. Kowalski.

Box Values: Exc.   VG/F   Good
                       200.00   160.00   100.00

Comment: *Values for 12 gauge. Add 20 percent premium for 10, 16 and 20 gauge. This is another box with multiple versions revolving around trademark lines, dots around the "W", quote marks around logo and logo variations.*

More Shotshells and Shotshell Boxes • 243

Leader Oval box, 25 shells, 12 gauge. Oval smokeless powder was used from 1925-1927. Note "Made in U.S.A." line put on boxes starting in 1924. Label is white with red outside trim with yellow highlights and yellow shadow inside red trim. "Leader" is dark silver with black border. "Winchester" and "Oval" are in red; other copy is black. From T. Webster collection. Photo by D. Kowalski.

Box Values:

	Exc.	VG/F	Good
	300.00	250.00	200.00

Comment: *Values for any gauge.*

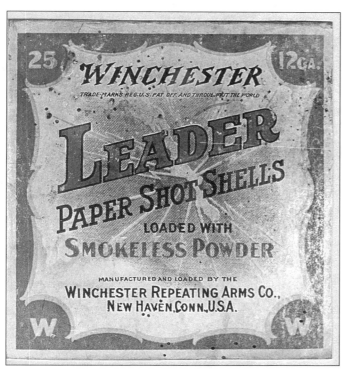

Leader box, 25 loaded shells, 12 gauge, with standard "lightning strike" logo that was widely adopted by Winchester in 1910. This box probably dates from about 1921-1924, prior to Winchester putting "Made in U.S.A." on its boxes. Has longer trademark line that reads: "Trade Marks Reg. U.S. Pat. Off. And throughout the World." Now uses a blockier "W" in each bottom corner. Label has red border (with yellow type) on white background; "sunburst" visual is gold; other type is blue and red. Photo from R. Stadt.

Box Values:

	Exc.	VG/F	Good
	200.00	160.00	100.00

Comment: *Values for 12 gauge. Add 20 percent premium for 10, 16 and 20 gauge.*

Leader "Brush" Shotshells (Loaded)

Winchester Leader "Brush" 12 gauge. Leader Brush shells are rare, especially in 16 and 20 gauge. Gauges, year introduced, and year discontinued were: 12, 1905-1921; 16, 1905-1921; 20, 1913-1921. Photos from R. Stadt.

Shell Values:	NIB	Exc.	V.G.	Good
12 Ga.	65.00	60.00	50.00	40.00
16 Ga.	80.00	75.00	65.00	50.00
20 Ga.	125.00	115.00	100.00	75.00

Comment: *The 20 gauge shell is extremely rare.*

244 • *More Shotshells and Shotshell Boxes*

Leader boxes, "Brush" in 12 and 16 gauge (top and side views). Even though Winchester made "Brush" shells from 1905-1921, very few boxes have survived. The "Brush" stamp was typically an overprint on the standard Leader box of the day. The 12 gauge box is older than the 16 gauge one. And here we see another cause for speculation. The newer 16 gauge box has the "Made in U.S.A." line mandated by the 1924 tariff law. Yet it is generally agreed Winchester stopped making Brush shells in 1921. We raised the questions earlier ... Did Winchester anticipate the coming legislation? Or did their prior use of the "Made in U.S.A." line help shape pending legislation? Or did they just discover a few extra Brush shells in storage after 1924 and dump them back into the retail pipeline by doing what they typically did - stamp a regular box? From TIM collection. Photos by T. Melcher.

Box Values:	Exc.	VG/F	Good
	750.00	600.00	500.00

Comment: *There have only been four or five Brush boxes found. Values for 12 and 16 gauge boxes, any era. For 20 gauge, add 50 percent premium (no 20 gauge Brush box has been found to date that we're aware of).*

Leader Shotshells (Loaded) - "Made in U.S.A."

Leaders, 12 and 16 gauge, loaded. Here are examples of another headstamp variation of loaded Leader shells with an additional "Made in U.S.A." line below "Leader." This additional line was added to headstamps about 1924, as it was with boxes at that time. Photos from R. Stadt.

Shell Values:

NIB	Exc.	V.G.	Good
1.50	1.00	0.75	0.50

Leader Staynless box, 25 shells, 12 gauge. The new primer was stainless. These boxes date from the late 1920s and early 1930s. Box is dark blue with "Winchester," "Leader," "W," and "Staynless" in red; rest of copy is white. Photo from R. Stadt.

Box Values:

Exc.	VG/F	Good
200.00	150.00	100.00

Comment: *Values for any gauge.*

Leader "proof" shells were used for factory testing. These are post-1924. They are distinguishable by a tinned base. Photos from R. Stadt.

Shell Values:

NIB	Exc.	V.G.	Good
15.00	12.00	10.00	8.00

Comment: *Values for any gauge of Leader "proof" shell.*

Leader Lacquered box, 25 shells, 12 gauge. The lacquered shells were produced from 1929-1937. Boxes date from the late 1920s and early 1930s. Box is dark blue with "Winchester," "Leader," "W," and "Lacquered" in red; rest of copy is white. Photo from R. Stadt.

Box Values: Exc.   VG/F   Good
                            200.00   150.00   100.00

Comment: *Values for any gauge.*

Leader, Staynless and Lacquered, 20 gauge. Winchester has combined both the stainless primer and the lacquered finish. Box copy addresses both features. Box would have been from about 1930-1937. Color is dark blue with "Winchester," "Leader," "W," and both "Staynless" and "Lacquered" in red; rest of copy is white. From TIM collection. Photos by T. Melcher.

Box Values: Exc.   VG/F   Good
                            250.00   200.00   150.00

Comment: *The rarest variation of this series of boxes. Values for any gauge.*

More Shotshells and Shotshell Boxes • 247

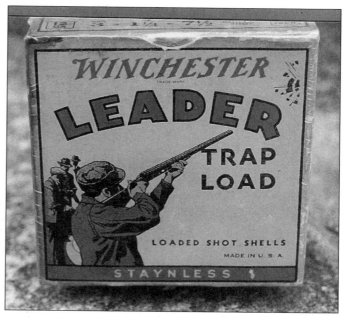

Leader Trap Load, box of 25, 12 gauge. This was probably the second version of the Leader Trap Load boxes; the first (as with the Ranger series) would have had "Leader" at the top of the side label and a small "Winchester" logo at the bottom above the "Staynless" panel. Box is yellow with red "Winchester," "Leader" and panel behind "Staynless." Rest of copy is black. Shooter is wearing a brown coat and tan cap; waiting shooters dressed in gray. From Ron Willoughby collection. Photo by R. Willoughby.

Box Values:

	Exc.	VG/F	Good
	500.00	450.00	350.00

Comment: *A very collectible box.*

Another Leader Staynless box, a rare and colorful "Quail" box from the late 1930s and early 1940s. If it says: "Div. Of Western Cartridge Co." it would be post-1938. Label of this one-piece box is yellow and red with red and blue print. Photo from R. Stadt.

Box Values:

	Exc.	VG/F	Good
	700.00	550.00	400.00

Comment: *Values for any gauge. Condition is extremely important for this box, even though it is generally very sought after.*

Leader Shotshells - "Super Speed"

Leader "Super Speed" shells replaced the progressive powder Leader shells. Gauges, year introduced, and year discontinued were: 10, 1933-1938; 12, 1933-1947; 12 Magnum, 1939-1947; 16 and 20, 1933-1943. Photos from R. Stadt.

Shell Values:

	NIB	Exc.	V.G.	Good
	2.00	1.50	1.00	0.75

Leader Super Speed box, one-piece. The second-to-last Super Speed box. Has cream label with red and blue type. Photo from R. Stadt.

Box Values:	Exc.	VG/F	Good
	225.00	150.00	100.00

Comment: *Values for 12 gauge. The most common box is the 12 gauge, 3-inch shell. Add 10 percent for other gauges. There are also several variations revolving around Staynless and Lacquered.*

The last of the Leader Super Speed boxes from the mid- to late-1940s (after WWII). Red and black type on yellow box. Photo from R. Stadt.

Box Values:	Exc.	VG/F	Good
	175.00	150.00	100.00

Comment: *Values for any gauge. Even though the box is only 50 years old, some collectors consider it highly collectible and relatively scarce.*

Repeater Shotshells (See Prior Chapter - "Winchester, Repeater and Rival Shotshells")

Ranger Shotshells (Loaded)

"Winchester Ranger No. 12." Very early Ranger loaded shells all had red hulls. Patented in 1924, they were introduced commercially in 1925 in 12, 16, and 20 gauges, then in 10 and 28 gauges in 1937. After WWII Winchester also made them for a time in 24 gauge. Photos from R. Stadt.

Shell Values:	NIB	Exc.	V.G.	Good
	2.00	1.00	0.75	0.50

Ranger 12 gauge loaded, "Made in U.S.A." headstamp. Another Ranger shotshell (with a light hull) made after 1924 and prior to 1932. It has the battery cup primer. Photos from R. Stadt.

Shell Values:	NIB	Exc.	V.G.	Good
	1.00	0.75	0.50	0.25

Ranger box, 25 shells, 12 gauge (contained the previous "Made in U.S.A." shell). Note the two separate "Trade Mark" lines, under "Winchester" and under "Ranger." Label was white and cream background with black and red print. From TIM collection. Photo from R. Stadt.

Box Values:	Exc.	VG/F	Good
	275.00	250.00	200.00

Comment: *Values for any gauge.*

Early Ranger box label for loaded shells. Note single "Trade Mark" under "Winchester." Label was white and cream background with black and red print. From TIM collection. Photo from R. Stadt.

Box Values:	Exc.	VG/F	Good
	275.00	250.00	200.00

Comment: *Values for any gauge. Another popular collectible because it depicts wildlife. There are several variations, including side label differences.*

Ranger Shotshells (Loaded) - "Staynless"

Ranger Staynless shells were patented in 1927. They had the stainless primer that was introduced in 1928 and is still in use. This 12 gauge shell shows the tendency of red hulls to fade to light brown. Later shells were made with brown hulls to help distinguish them from the red-hulled Leader shells. Photos from R. Stadt.

Shell Values:	NIB	Exc.	V.G.	Good
	1.50	1.00	0.75	0.50

Ranger Staynless, box of 25 shells, 12 gauge. Box from late 1920s and early 1930s. Label is dark blue with "Winchester," "Ranger," "W," and "Staynless" in red; rest of copy is white. From TIM collection. Photo from R. Stadt.

Box Values:	Exc.	VG/F	Good
	200.00	150.00	100.00

Comment: *Values for any gauge.*

Ranger Staynless, box of 25 shells, 12 gauge. Box from mid-1940s, right after WWII; used through the late 1950s. Box is yellow with blue and red print. Photo from R. Stadt.

Box Values:	Exc.	VG/F	Good
	75.00	50.00	25.00

Comment: *Values for any gauge. Has many variations, including "brush" loads.*

Ranger Shotshells - "Skeet Load"

Ranger Skeet Load 12 gauge. Ranger Skeet Loads were introduced in 1932 in 12, 16, and 20 gauges, and in 1937 in 28 gauge. They were discontinued in 1939. Photos from R. Stadt.

Shell Values:	NIB	Exc.	V.G.	Good
	1.50	1.00	0.75	0.50

Comment: *Add 25 percent for 28 gauge.*

Ranger Skeet Load box (no "Winchester" logo). Some Skeet Load and Trap Load boxes can be found without "Winchester" on them. Some Winchester designer's failure to check his work along with a printer's failure to spot the error rapidly becomes a collectible item. This may also be the first Ranger Skeet Load box. From TIM collection. Photo from R. Stadt.

Box Values: | Exc. | VG/F | Good
| --- | --- | --- |
| 600.00 | 450.00 | 350.00 |

Comment: *Values for any gauge.*

Ranger Skeet Load, 25 shells, 16 gauge; top label of previous box. "Winchester" and "W" are red. From T. Webster collection. Photo by D. Kowalski.

Box Values: | Exc. | VG/F | Good
| --- | --- | --- |
| 250.00 | 200.00 | 150.00 |

Comment: *Values for any gauge.*

Ranger Shotshells - "Super Skeet Load"

Ranger Super Skeet loads were introduced in 1939 in 12, 16, and 20 gauges. They were discontinued in 1954. Photos from R. Stadt.

Shell Values: | NIB | Exc. | V.G. | Good
| --- | --- | --- | --- |
| 1.50 | 1.00 | 0.75 | 0.50 |

Ranger Super Skeet Load, box of 25 shells, 20 gauge. The "Super Seal Crimp" was introduced in late 1939. Box from early 1940s if it says "Div. Of Western Cartridge Co.; after December 1944, it would say "Div. Of Olin Industries." Label color is cream with a blue frame; print is blue and red. From TIM collection. Photo from R. Stadt.

Box Values: | Exc. | VG/F | Good
| --- | --- | --- |
| 150.00 | 100.00 | 75.00 |

Comment: *Values for any gauge.*

Ranger Shotshells - "Trap Load"

Ranger Trap loads were introduced in 1935, then discontinued in 1939. This 12 gauge shell is from the second Trap Load box with the "Winchester" logo at the top. Photos from R. Stadt.

Shell Values:	NIB	Exc.	V.G.	Good
	1.50	1.00	0.75	0.50

Ranger Trap Load, box of 25 shells, 12 gauge. Box from late-1930s. Box is yellow with red "Ranger" and red panel behind "Staynless." Shooter is dressed in red; waiting shooters dressed in black. Print is red, black and yellow. A very colorful box. (Previous shell is from this box.) From TIM collection. Photo from R. Stadt.

Box Values:	Exc.	VG/F	Good
	200.00	175.00	125.00

Comment: *Values for any gauge. Add 25 percent for "U.S. Property" stamp (from government contract sale).*

Ranger Trap Load, box of 25. This first Trap Load box had "Ranger" logo at top; "Winchester" logo at bottom. Box has white rim around edge of side panel; background is yellow. Both "Ranger" and "Winchester" are red, as well as panel behind "Staynless," which is yellow type. "Trap Load" in black type. Shooter is dressed in red with white cap; waiting shooters dressed in black. From TIM collection. Photos by T. Melcher.

Box Values:	Exc.	VG/F	Good
	500.00	450.00	400.00

Comment: *A very collectible version of a very colorful box.*

Ranger Shotshells - "Super Trap Load"

Ranger Super Trap loads were introduced in 1939 in 12, 16, and 20 gauges and remained in production until 1954. Just as there were specially made 16 and 20 gauge trap guns, there were corresponding "trap" shells. Here's a 16 gauge shell from the following box. Photos from R. Stadt.

Shell Values: | NIB | Exc. | V.G. | Good
| --- | --- | --- | --- |
| 1.50 | 1.00 | 0.75 | 0.50 |

Ranger Shotshells - "Blanks"

Ranger Blank, this one a 10 gauge black powder shell. Made through the 1960s for Salute Cannons. Photos from R. Stadt.

Shell Values: | NIB | Exc. | V.G. | Good
| --- | --- | --- | --- |
| 3.00 | 2.00 | 1.50 | 0.75 |

Ranger Super Trap Load, box of 25 shells, 16 gauge. Box from early 1940s. Box is yellow with blue and red print. Note "Made in United States of America" copy line. From TIM collection. Photo from R. Stadt.

Box Values: | Exc. | VG/F | Good
| --- | --- | --- |
| 175.00 | 150.00 | 100.00 |

Comment: *Values for any gauge.*

Ranger Blanks box, 25 shells, 10 gauge. Box probably from early 1940s. This one was overprinted and held the previous blank. Box is yellow with blue and red print. Some examples have stamp "U.S. Property" from WWII contracts. Photo from R. Stadt.

Box Values: | Exc. | VG/F | Good
| --- | --- | --- |
| 150.00 | 125.00 | 100.00 |

Comment: *Add 100 percent premium for the very scarce 28 gauge versions.*

Ranger Blank Load, box of 25 shells, 10 gauge. Last Ranger box logo for paper shells. Box is yellow with red "W" and blue field behind "Ranger." Photo from R. Stadt.

Box Values:	Exc.	VG/F	Good
	75.00	50.00	25.00

Comment: *For this box style, generally, the .410 shells are most collectible.*

Ranger box, 100 empty shells, 12 gauge (see following side label). This box dates from the December 1938 to December 1944 era when Winchester was a "Division of Western Cartridge Company." Note the "Made in United States of America" copy line. Label is buff color with red type. From T. Webster collection. Photo by D. Kowalski.

Ranger Shotshells (Empty)

Ranger empty, 12 gauge. Ranger empties were sold in 10, 12, 16, 20, and 28 gauges beginning in 1937 and are still in the line. The 28 gauge was not listed after WWII. They were offered in boxes of 10, 25 and 100 during various times. Photos from R. Stadt.

Side label of previous Ranger box. But here we see a 10 gauge sticker has been placed over the original 12 gauge spot, presumably at the Winchester factory. From T. Webster collection. Photo by D. Kowalski.

Shell Values:	NIB	Exc.	V.G.	Good
	1.00	0.75	0.50	

Comment: *Values for paper empties.*

Box Values:	Exc.	VG/F	Good
	250.00	200.00	150.00

Comment: *Relatively scarce box.*

Later Ranger box, 100 empty shells, 20 gauge. Also dating from the Winchester - Western era from August 1954 - September 1969 period when Winchester - Western was a division of the Olin Mathieson Chemical Corporation. Label color is buff with black print. From T. Webster collection. Photo by D. Kowalski.

Box Values:	Exc.	VG/F	Good
	150.00	100.00	75.00

Later Ranger box, 25 empty shells, 12 gauge. Winchester - Western box from the August 1954 - September 1969 period when Winchester - Western was a division of the Olin Mathieson Chemical Corporation. Has "3 66" date stamp in the upper left corner referring to March 1966.) A very plain label for export; when exported often sent only with powder. From TIM collection. Photo from R. Stadt.

Box Values:	Exc.	VG/F	Good
	150.00	100.00	75.00

Comment: *Another relatively scarce box.*

Winchester Super Speed Shotshells

Super Speed shell, .410 gauge. Super Speed loads were introduced during 1937 in 10, 12, 16, 20, 28, .410 2 1/2 inch, and .410 3 inch. They provided more knockdown power and range. This .410 shell from the first of the following "Super Speed" boxes has a "WRA" headstamp. Note "Super Speed" not stacked on headstamp, probably for space reasons. Photos from R. Stadt.

Shell Values:	NIB	Exc.	V.G.	Good
	2.00	1.50	1.00	0.75

Comment: *Values for .410 gauge, tan or red hull.*

Winchester Super Speed shell, 12 gauge. This one shows a stacked "Super Speed" headstamp. Tan hull was used from the middle to late 1940s. Photos from R. Stadt.

Shell Values: | NIB | Exc. | V.G. | Good
| 1.75 | 1.25 | 1.00 | 0.75

Comment: *Values for any gauge, tan hull.*

Winchester Super Speed Loads box, 25 shells, .410 gauge. This box contained previous .410 gauge shell. Note dark outline around oval enclosing "Super Speed." Box from late 1930s and early 1940s. Photo from R. Stadt.

Box Values: | Exc. | VG/F | Good
| 125.00 | 90.00 | 75.00

Comment: *Values for .410 boxes of this style and following variation.*

Another Winchester Super Speed shell, also showing a stacked "Super Speed" headstamp, with a star-crimped paper shell. It was produced right after WWII in a red hull and was used through the early 1950s. Shell copy horizontal. Photos from R. Stadt.

Shell Values: | NIB | Exc. | V.G. | Good
| 1.75 | 1.25 | 1.00 | 0.75

Comment: *Values for any gauge, red hull.*

More Shotshells and Shotshell Boxes • 257

Winchester Super Speed box, 25 loaded shells, 28 gauge, side label (see next photo of top label). Box is post-WWII. "Super Speed Shotgun Shells" are in black type; rest of copy is red on yellow background. From T. Webster collection. Photo by D. Kowalski.

Winchester Super Speed box, 12 gauge. This box is a variation of the previous one from the late 1930s and early 1940s. It differs from the previous one because it does not have a dark outline around the oval behind "Super Speed." Box background color is yellow and red with blue and red print. Photo from R. Stadt.

Box Values: Exc. VG/F Good
             100.00 75.00 50.00

Comment: *Values for boxes of this style and previous variation, any gauge except .410.*

Super Speed box, 25 loaded shells, 28 gauge, top label of previous box; load and gauge specifications stamped here. The 28 gauge shell is rare and so is No. 4 shot. From T. Webster collection. Photo by D. Kowalski.

Box Values: Exc. VG/F Good
             75.00 60.00 30.00

Comment: *Values for this scarce version in 28 gauge. Other gauges deduct 25 percent.*

Winchester Super Speed Magnum box, 12 gauge. The "Magnum" shell was introduced in the 1953-1955 era. This box is the "Magnum" version of the previous one and was used through the late 1950s. Box background color is yellow and red with blue and red print. Photo from R. Stadt.

Box Values: Exc.   VG/F   Good
                       75.00   60.00   30.00

Comment: *Values for this "Magnum" version of this box and previous one, any gauge. Add 25 percent for 28 gauge.*

Winchester Super Speed box, 12 gauge. The last box logo for paper Super Speed shells. The "warning label" was added in 1962 or 1963. Box is yellow with red "W" and blue and red print. Photo from R. Stadt.

Box Values: Exc.   VG/F   Good
                       50.00   40.00   25.00

Comment: *Values for this version with "warning label," any gauge.*

Miscellaneous Shotshell and Cartridge Items

In this vast field of Winchester shotshells, shotshell boxes, cartridges and cartridge boxes, there are a lot of items that don't fit neatly into major categories. In this volume, for example, we have elected not to put cartridge boards in a separate section. In fact, the cartridge boards don't fit neatly into either shotshells or cartridges because they contain both. However, we did want to show you a few. In the next volume, we will give you examples of all six versions with then updated prices.

And to give new collectors, particularly, some idea of other unusual boxes and box designs that Winchester created, we present a few "extras." Some of these extras may become parts of new sections in upcoming editions. This will certainly happen as more collectors make photographic records of their collections and make them available to us.

Winchester Wonder box, 12 gauge, with Spanish-version label for South America. Label photo actually taken from a Winchester brochure. Label color is red. Photo from R. Stadt.

Box Values: | Exc. | VG/F | Good
| 2,500.00 | 2,000.00 | 1,800.00

Comment: *A very rare box. Values for any gauge.*

Winchester "Wonder" 12 gauge with "12 GA" headstamp. This was probably the first headstamp used only for a year or two. The Wonder shells were offered from 1919-1930 for export to South America. They were available as green 12 and 16 gauge empties, yellow 12 gauge empties, green 12 gauged loaded and likely 16 gauge loaded shells. Have huge battery cup primer. Photos from R. Stadt.

Shell Values: | NIB | Exc. | V.G. | Good
| 250.00 | 200.00 | 150.00 | 100.00

Comment: *Values for any gauge. Among the rarest of Winchester shells.*

"Winchester Winco No. 12." Winco shells were very similar to Wonder shells, though little is really known about them. Winchester apparently considered four names for them: Winco, Wonder, American and Winner. They finally settled on "Winco." They have smaller battery cup primer than the Wonder shell. This 12 gauge example was factory loaded. Photos from R. Stadt.

Shell Values: | NIB | Exc. | V.G. | Good
| 500.00 | 400.00 | 300.00 | 200.00

Comment: *Values for any gauge. Extremely rare.*

Austin Cartridges, 25 shells, 12 gauge, loaded in Winchester shells. Cleveland's Austin Cartridge Company, as well as Western, Robinhood and others bought Winchester new primed empty (NPE) shells and loaded their own brands if they didn't have primary production facilities. These companies would then produce labeled boxes for distributors ordering large quantities. From T. Webster collection. Photo by D. Kowalski.

Winchester .410 shell, 2 inch. Early loaded shell offered with Junior Trap Outfit in the 1920s. Photos from R. Stadt.

Shell Values:	NIB	Exc.	V.G.	Good
	6.00	5.00	3.50	2.00

Comment: *Values for .410 gauge.*

Austin Cartridges, side label of previous box. Austin loaded these shells for the S. Hamill Company, Keokuk, Iowa. From T. Webster collection. Photo by D. Kowalski.

Box Values:	Exc.	VG/F	Good
	1,800.00	1,500.00	1,000.00

Comment: *Values for any gauge, private label. Such boxes are very rare.*

Winchester .410 box, 25 paper shells, 10 gauge. Shell on box shows early "Winchester" headstamp." These boxes were included in the Junior Trap Outfit sold in the 1920s. This one has "Made in U.S.A." line used after 1924. Photo from R. Stadt.

Box Values:	Exc.	VG/F	Good
	450.00	375.00	300.00

Comment: *A rare box. Values for .410 gauge.*

Super Speed Staynless Rifled Slugs, box of 5, .410 gauge. Rifles Slugs were introduced after 1936. The "Progressive" powder was not used until after 1940. Box is buff color with black type; "Winchester" and "Trade Mark" are in red on front and top labels. From T. Webster collection. Photo by D. Kowalski.

Box Values: Exc.   VG/F   Good
                      125.00   100.00   75.00

Comment: *Values for this box of 2 1/2-inch length in .410. Other gauges deduct 25 percent.*

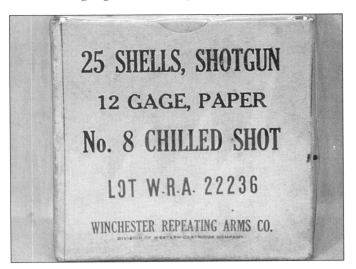

Winchester box, 25 paper shells, 12 gauge, No. 8 Chilled Shot. Many shells packaged for the military had plain labels. Note spelling of "Gage." This box produced between December 1938 and December 1944 when Winchester Repeating Arms Co. was a "Division of Western Cartridge Company." These would have been used for skeet shooting to train aerial gunners. Label was cream with black print. From T. Webster collection. Photo by D. Kowalski.

Box Values: Exc.   VG/F   Good
                      125.00   100.00   75.00

Comment: *Values for any gauge.*

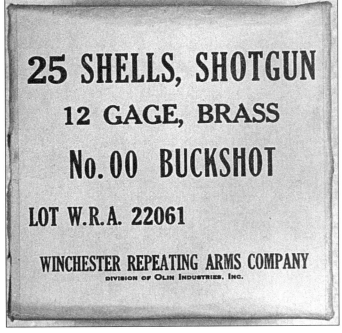

Winchester box, 25 brass shells, 12 gauge, buckshot. Another plain military box. The buckshot loads probably for guard use and even some offensive situations. Again note spelling of "Gage." This box produced between December 1944 and January 1952 when Winchester Repeating Arms Co. was a "Division of Olin Industries, Inc." Curiously, a newer box than last one has a lower lot number; number on this box must have been a subsequent series of lot numbers. Label was cream with black print. Photo from R. Stadt.

Box Values: Exc.   VG/F   Good
                      150.00   125.00   100.00

Comment: *Values for any gauge.*

Winchester "Pest Destruction Load," box of 25 plastic shells, 12 gauge. According to Tim Melcher, this box introduces an entirely new category we haven't dealt with: Winchester's non-domestic production. This was apparently produced by Winchester Australia Pty. For the destruction of wild ducks and other types of declared pests that raided rice crops. Box is probably from late 1970s early 1980s. Box is cream color with red type. From T. Webster collection. Photo by D. Kowalski.

The .70-150 cartridge is best known from being included on the Winchester 1890 "Big W" cartridge display board. It was never loaded commercially. This specimen does not have a headstamp. And it has a wood spacer in the case and two holes drilled on the back side so it could be wired to the board. It also has a thick, flat head. Photo from R. Stadt.

Shell Values:	NIB	Exc.	V.G.	Good
	1,500.00	1,000.00	750.00

Comment: *Some "so-called" .70-150 cartridges have thin rims, probably an indication they've been "forged" from brass shotshells. It can be difficult to assess the authenticity of these shells unless they come from cartridge boards because replicas have been created from 12 gauge brass shotshells. Since they were never loaded commercially, we cannot provide a New In Box (NIB) price.*

Top label for previous "Pest Destruction Load" box. The "5" (or other shot size) was overprinted in "Shot Size" square at time of loading and is the only black copy on the entire box. From T. Webster collection. Photo by D. Kowalski.

Box Values:	Exc.	VG/F	Good
	75.00	50.00	25.00

Comment: *Values for any gauge.*

Winchester 1890 "Big W" or "Single W" cartridge display board. This board holds more than 160 Winchester shotshells and cartridges. These were made available to Winchester retailers to promote company products. "Winchester" in red with yellow highlights. Outdoor scenes and ducks are in four-color. From T. Webster collection. Photo by D. Kowalski.

Board Values:	Exc.	VG/F	Good
	15,000.00	12,000.00	9,000.00

Comment: Values for this board. We will present all the variations in the next edition of this volume.

This stunning 1897/1898 "Double W" Winchester cartridge display board holds more than 215 original Winchester shotshells and cartridges. Central scene was adapted from the top scene of the 1895 Winchester wall calendar painted by A.B. Frost. "Winchester" logo is in red with white outline. Other copy red and white on a deep blue background. Curt Bowman has made this board the centerpiece that dominates one side of a display room. Photo by C. Bowman.

Board Values:	Exc.	VG/F	Good
	16,000.00	13,000.00	10,000.00

Comment: Values are only for this board. There are also variations of this 1897 board since it was made for five or more years.

Firearms Supplies and Accessories
Reloading Tools and Supplies
Winchester Junior Rifle Corps

To cover the broad gamut of Winchester's general firearms area, we come back to the miscellaneous equipment and supplies developed to maintain firearms in good working order, to various firearms and shooting accessories, and to their reloading tools and supplies. Winchester was always on the look-out for ways and products to create add-on sales for retailers.

At the end of this chapter, we will also present products revolving around Winchester's Junior Rifle Corps. This was a bright and intriguing chapter in company history. And it gave us many unique and sought-after collectibles.

Detailed product descriptions (with Winchester's unique spellings and the frequent use of capital letters) have been adapted from their 1927 Catalog. In many cases, Winchester's descriptions of their own products read better than ones we could create some 75 years later.

Breech Loading Cannon. *Model 98, No. 9801, 10 Gauge Only; Weight Each about 14 lbs. One in a Wood Box. 12 in. Tapered Rolled Steel Barrel, Cylinder Bored, Mounted on a Shapely Cast Iron Carriage Substantially Built with two Heavy Wheels at the Forward End 3 1/2 in. in Diameter. The Carriage and Wheels are Nicely Japanned, the Barrel Blued, and Breech Closure Hardened Black. The Length of the Cannon over all is 17 in.; 7 1/4 in. High and 7 in. Wide. In it can be used 10 Gauge Paper or Brass Shells; We recommend Shells Loaded with 9 Drams of Black Powder with Two Black Edge and one Card Wad, to produce the Loudest Report. The Cannon has so Few Parts it cannot readily get out of order or cause any trouble in its operation; It can easily be dismounted.*

Breech-Loading Cannon was first listed in the March 1903 Winchester catalog. Muzzle diameter was increased from 1" to 1 1/4" in 1907. A few other changes were made in 1911. Ron Stadt details these in Chapter 5 of his <u>Winchester Shotguns and Shotshells</u>. *Photo by Curt Bowman.*

A chromium-plated Salute Cannon with rubber wheels was introduced in 1931. There were also other minor variations over the years, including a version introduced in 1955 with larger rubber tires bearing the Firestone trademark. Salute Cannons were discontinued in 1958; none of them had serial numbers. Photo from R. Stadt.

Values:	Exc.	VG	Good
Metal Wheels	900.00	700.00	500.00
Rubber Wheels	3,000.00	2,750.00	2,500.00

Comment: *Also called a "Salute Cannon." Values are for basic models within each group. Here's an interesting situation where the newer, rubber-wheeled models generally have a higher value.*

Telescope Sight.

Values:	Exc.	VG	Good
	1,000.00+		200.00

Comment: *Winchester produced scopes ranging from very low-end models (valued at the minimum price we show) to substantial and expensive high-end models that would currently be valued at the upper end of our scale and beyond. Winchester also sold several pieces of equipment separately for mounting sights including: Rear Mount and Base, Front Mount and Base, Sight Mount Bases, Reticules, and Offset Adapters. They also produced Leather Telescope Sight Cases with Slings, as well as a variety of smaller adjustable and peep sights. They sold other firearms accessories such as recoil pads, extra barrels and magazines. As photos become available, we will add these specific pieces to this volume and price them.*

Two boxes for telescopic sights. Bottom one for an 8 power scope has a white label with black type and red "Winchester" logo and red "Trade Mark" line. Top one held a Style A52 scope; it has yellow label with black type and red "W." From T. Webster collection. Photo by D. Kowalski.

Values:	Exc.	VG	Good
	300.00	225.00	175.00

Comment: *Values are for empty telescope sight boxes.*

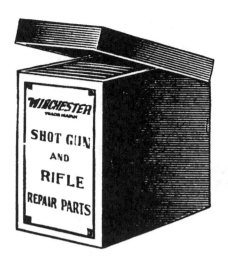

Gun and Rifle Parts Assortment. *No. WGP-Assortment; Weight per Assortment about 2 lbs. Heavy Karatol Covered Cardboard Box, 6 1/4 in. High, 4 in. Wide, 6 1/2 in. Deep, with Lid supported at side with Tape. Each item is put up in an Individual Heavy Metal Top Turned over Envelope, 3 1/2x6 in., on which is typed at the Head the Name and Number of the Item, and parts can be replenished as they run out. The envelopes stand erect and are easily read and removed. Per Assortment consists of the following:*

Model 1897 Shot Gun Repairs

    4 only 5097 Ejector Springs
    3 only 30997 R. H. Extractors
    2 only 36297 Action Slide Hook Screws
    3 only 31097 L. H. Extractors
    2 only 14797 Ext. Plunger R. H.

Model 1912 Shot Gun Repairs

    4 only 37812 Mag. Band Bush Screws
    1 only 50712 Ejector With Spring
    1 only 2512 Firing Pin
    1 only 30912 R. H. Ejector
    1 only 31012 L. H. Extractor

Model 1890-1906 Rifle Repairs

    4 only 2390 Extractors
    1 only 2590 Firing Pin and Spring
    2 only 7090 Main Springs
    8 only 35590 Action Slide Handle Screws
    3 only 13390 Carrier Lever Springs
    2 only 8990 Trigger Springs
    2 only 13290 Carrier Levers
    3 only 25890 Firing Pin Stop Screws

Values:	Exc.	VG	Good
	600.00	500.00	400.00

Comment: *Values are for Assortment Box containing at least several parts packages with pieces inside.*

Sling Straps. *Can be attached to all Winchester Rifles except Models 02, 04, 06 and 90; Also to Shot Guns. Strap fitted with Patent Buckle to permit lengthening and shortening. No. 3260, Selected tan leather strap complete with screw eyes and swivel hooks.*

Values:	Exc.	VG	Good
	150.00	125.00	100.00

Comment: *Values are for leather sling strap. Winchester also made a web strap (No. 3263); valued at $25.00 less than the leather strap in each grade of condition.*

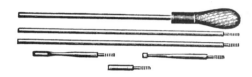

Rifle Cleaning Rods. *High Grade Steel, Accurately Machined and Threaded. Walnut Stained Hardwood Handle, with Dead Black Finish Ferrule. Complete with Three Tip Joints (1 Slotted, 1 with Knob and 1 for Threaded Swabs or Brushes). All Joints Interchangeable. The First Joint is secured to Handle and Swiveled to permit turning of Rod in Rifled Barrel without twisting the Hand or Loosening the Joints. Comes in cloth bag. Four Joint for .30 caliber or larger rifles. No. 3219 - Length 44 in.; Weight per dozen about 6 lbs.*

Values:	Exc.	VG	Good
	150.00	125.00	100.00

Comment: *Values are for either the four-joint rod set in bag or for the three-joint set (No. 3220 - Length 44 in.) made to clean .410 gauge shotguns.*

Rifle Cleaners. *Flexible - for .22 caliber rifles. Galvanized Flexible Wire Cord with Loop on End for Cleaning Cloths; Can be Pushed Through Barrel; Bristle Brush, with Hook. Complete.*

    No. 3212, 24 inches
    No. 3213, 30 inches
    No. 3214, 36 inches

Values:	Exc.	VG	Good
	400.00	350.00	300.00

Comment: *Values are for flexible wire sets in original boxes or bags so authentic origin can be verified. (There is some question whether these pieces were even marked since many veteran collectors have not even seen these flexible wire versions.)*

Winchester also sold individual pieces of the kit, sent to retailers in boxes of one dozen.

Cleaner Cords Only
No. 3215, 24 inches
No. 3216, 30 inches
No. 3217, 36 inches

Cleaner Brushes
No. 3218, one dozen.

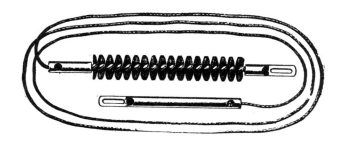

Rifle Cleaners. U.S. Government. *Consists of Bristle Brush with Slot on End and Extra Slotted Wiper; Strong Cord. Cannot be used in Models 73, 92 or 03 Rifles.*

No. 3221, For 6 M/M or .25 Caliber Rifles.
No. 3222, For .30 to .351 Caliber Rifles.
No. 3227, For .38 to .44 Caliber Rifles.
No. 3229, For .45 to .50 Caliber Rifles.

Values:	Exc.	VG	Good
	400.00	350.00	300.00

Comment: *Values are for sets in original boxes or bags so authentic origin can be verified.*

Cleaning Rods. Iron rod, with slot
No. 3201, For .22 Caliber Rifles; Models 02, 04, 06.
No. 3202, For .22 Caliber Rifles; Model 90.
No. 3203, For .22 Caliber Rifles; Model 03.

Wood Rods
No. 3208, For .30 Caliber Rifles; Long.
No. 3209, For .30 Caliber Rifles; Short.
No. 3210, For .38 Caliber Rifles; Long.
No. 3211, For .38 Caliber Rifles; Short.

Brass Rod, with slot
No. 3236, For Model 52 Rifles; 37 1/2 in. Long.
No. 3237, For .22 Caliber Rifles; 27 1/2 in. Long.

Jointed Wood, with wiper swab and brush
No. 3240, For 10 to 20 Gauge Shotguns.

Values:	Exc.	VG	Good
	125.00	100.00	75.00

Comment: *Values for single rod, any model. Sold to retailers in boxes of one dozen pieces, packed loose.*

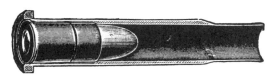

Supplemental chamber for rifle shooting a .30 caliber Winchester cartridge; also cutaway drawing of supplemental chamber with pistol cartridge inserted.

Supplemental Chambers. *To be inserted, same as Cartridge, in High Power Rifles, making it possible to use the Popular Pistol Cartridges with Adjustment of Sights Only; Does not interfere with instant use of regular ammunition and can be extracted same as empty shell. Gives excellent results for Short Range Shooting or Indoor Target Practice and is a great aid in attaining efficiency in the use of Regular Hunting Rifle at a Minimum Cost for Ammunition.*

Nos.	For Use In Rifle/Caliber	Permits Use Of Pistol Cartridges
3280	.30 Army	.32 S. & W.
3281	.30 Govt. Model 1906	.32 S. & W.
3282	.30 Winchester	.32 S. & W.
3283	.303 British	.32 S. & W.
3284	.303 Savage	.32 S. & W.
3285	.32 Winchester Special	.32 Short Colt .32 Long Colt
3286	.32 - .40	.32 Short Colt .32 Long Colt

NOTE - *Smokeless Powder Cartridges Only should be used with Supplemental Chambers, as Black Powder Cartridges soon foul Barrels having Quick Twists as in Rifles listed above.*

Values:	Exc.	VG	Good
	90.00	70.00	50.00

Comment: *Values are for a single supplemental chamber.*

This full box of six individually paper-wrapped supplemental chambers for use of either Short or Long .32 Colt cartridges in .32 Winchester Special rifles. From T. Webster collection. Photo by D. Kowalski.

Values:	Exc.	VG	Good
	550.00	475.00	325.00

Comment: *Values are for full box of supplemental chambers.*

Barrel Reflectors. *For Examining the Inside of Winchester Rifle Barrels. Used by withdrawing Breech Block, placing Reflector on top of Carrier, Mirror toward the Chamber, then by holding Muzzle of Gun toward the light the inside of Barrel will be seen reflected in the mirror. Wrought Brass; Satin Finish.*

No. 3271, Small; For Model '03 Rifle; Length 3/4 in.: Width 5/16 in.; Height 3/4 in.; Weight each about 1/4 oz. No. 3272, Large; For Model 90 Rifles; Length 1 5/8 in. Width 1/2 in.; Height 1/8 in.; Weight each about 3/4 oz.

Values:	Exc.	VG	Good
	145.00	130.00	90.00

Comment: *Values are for any size.*

Extremely rare full tube of Leather Dressing from T. Webster collection. Photo by D. Kowalski.

Leather Dressing. *Specially prepared Oil Paste that Preserves and Softens leather. Particularly recommended for Baseball Gloves and Mitts, but also excellent for Razor Strops, Harness, Leather Gun Slings, etc. No. 2945. One Dozen collapsible 1 oz. Tubes In a Display Carton.*

Values:	Exc.	VG	Good
	250.00	225.00	175.00

Comment: *Values are for single tube. The full tube pictured above is the only one (full or partial) that has ever been found.*

Gun Grease and box (model 1075) - box is light pea green and red; tube is almost blue green with red "Winchester" logo. From T. Webster collection. Photo by D. Kowalski.

Gun Grease. *A Heavy, Non-flow Lubricant to be applied lightly to Metal Parts of Guns, Revolvers and Rifles after cleaning; Prevents Rust and keeps them in good Condition. No. 1075. One Dozen collapsible 2 oz. Tubes in a Cardboard Box.*

Values:	Exc.	VG	Good
	45.00	35.00	25.00

Comment: *Values are for single tube not in a box.*

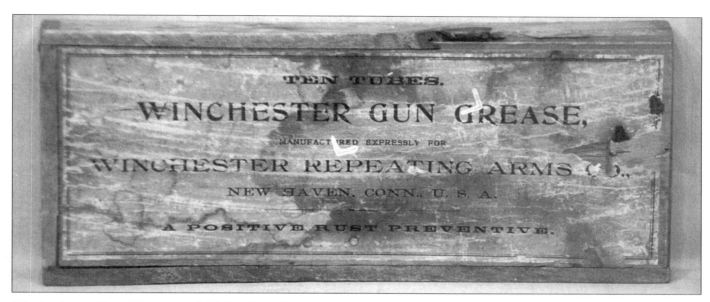

Wooden box with a sliding cover held 10 tubes of Winchester Gun Grease. It measures 11 3/4" x 5" x 1 1/2" and has dovetail joints. From T. Webster collection. Photo by D. Kowalski.

Values:

Exc.	VG	Good
225.00	200.00	175.00

Comment: *Values are for wooden box only.*

Gun Oil. *An excellent preservative that should be applied to Inside of Barrel of Guns, Rifles and Revolvers and to Mechanism after cleaning, preparatory to storing. Also for Lubricating Sewing Machines, Bicycles, Typewriters, etc. Will not Dry, Gum or Cake; Does not become rancid in hot weather nor thicken in extreme cold; Protects the Metal, Lubricates the Parts and keeps them free from rust.*

Gun Oil (Heavy), No. 1050, 1 oz. bottle. Bottle has forest green label with red "Winchester" logo and cork stopper. From T. Webster collection. Photo by D. Kowalski.

Values:

Exc.	VG	Good
250.00	210.00	175.00

Comment: *Values for one bottle, heavy.*

Gun Oil (Heavy), No. 1052, 3 oz. can with spout. Can has olive green label with red "Winchester" logo and thin red edge lines along the green borders. From T. Webster collection. Photo by D. Kowalski.

Values:

Exc.	VG	Good
300.00	250.00	200.00

Comment: *Values for one can, heavy.*

270 • Firearms Supplies and Accessories

Gun Oil, 3 oz. can with spout. Winchester produced cans of gun oil that were not labeled "heavy." This example has brighter green label and different logo style than Heavy Gun Oil. "Winchester" logo is in red; "Gun Oil" in white; rest of copy is green. From T. Webster collection. Photo by D. Kowalski.

Values:	Exc.	VG	Good
	300.00	250.00	200.00

Comment: Values for one 3 oz. can. Also produced in one-gallon cans.

Gun and Machine Oil, No. 2176. Here's a hybrid product that bridges the gap between Gun Oil and General Utility Oil. Early plain label style is brown on both the empty bottle and the box; "W" is red on both. From T. Webster collection. Photo by D. Kowalski.

Values:	Exc.	VG	Good
	325.00	285.00	250.00

Comment: Values for bottle only, gun and Machine Oil.

General Utility Oil. *A High Quality Light Lubricant for High Speed Motors, Drills, etc.; Excellent for Cleaning Tools of Watchmakers, Barbers, Dentists, etc.; Polishes Wood or Metal Ware; Prevents Rust on Nickel Plated Ware, Cutlery, Guns, etc. Will not Gum, become rancid or dry out; Flows freely and is easily applied: Contains neither Grease nor acid and will not collect dirt.*

General Utility Oil, 1 oz. bottle. Early bottle, partially full with corked top, has brown label with black type. From T. Webster collection. Photo by D. Kowalski.

Values:	Exc.	VG	Good
	275.00	250.00	200.00

Comment: Values for one bottle, 1 oz.

General Utility Oil, 1 oz. bottle. Newer version of bottle (and box) both show brighter colors than previous label. Bottle label is cream with red border; "W" is red inside the black "tombstone" and "General Utility Oil" also in red. Box is red with gray top and side panels; both "Winchester" logos are in red. From T. Webster collection. Photo by D. Kowalski.

Values:	Exc.	VG	Good
	250.00	235.00	190.00

Comment: *Values for one newer bottle only. Add 75 percent for box.*

General Utility Oil, 3 oz. can with spout. Can has brown label with red "Winchester" logo and red bars inside the horizontal black bars at top and bottom. From T. Webster collection. Photo by D. Kowalski.

Values:	Exc.	VG	Good
	325.00	280.00	225.00

Comment: *Values for one can. This product was also available in one-gallon cans.*

Crystal Cleaner. *This preparation dissolves the Copper and Nickel Fouling in Rifles without injury to the Barrel.*

Crystal Cleaner, No. 1002, 3 oz. bottle. A later label in excellent condition on bottle; box also in excellent condition with bright colors. Bottom panel of each label is yellow; top is red; top of box also red. From T. Webster collection. Photo by D. Kowalski.

Crystal Cleaner label and box packaging got brighter and more colorful through the years, as did virtually all of Winchester's labels. (The two bottles and boxes on left would be early product labels. Middle bottle shows switch from cork stopper to plastic screw top.) From T. Webster collection. Photo by D. Kowalski.

Values:	Exc.	VG	Good
	75.00	60.00	40.00

Comment: *Values for one bottle only of earlier versions. One of the more common Winchester lubricants, especially later versions. Add 75 percent for box.*

Rust Remover. *Removes Rust Quickly and Completely; Is nonabrasive and will not Cut or Scratch Finely Finished Metals; Easily applied. For use on Guns, Rifles, Revolvers, Skates, Shears, Golf Clubs and other Rusted Metal Surfaces.*

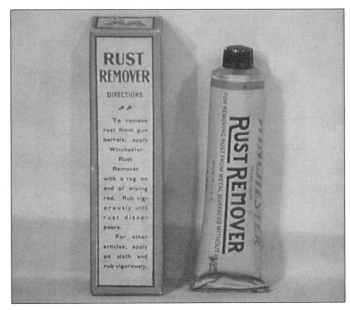

Rust Remover, No. 1020, 2 oz. tube. Box is yellow and red; full tube is bright green with red highlights. Ironically, the tube shows a few rust spots at bottom and along the bottom seam. From T. Webster collection. Photo by D. Kowalski.

Values:	Exc.	VG	Good
	45.00	35.00	25.00

Comment: *Values for one tube only.*

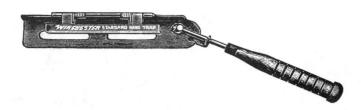

Targets, Paper.

Trapshooting Score Sheets. *Printed in Black (one side only) ON HEAVY PAPER. No. 1975. Sheet 13 1/2 in. x 39 in.; Weight per 1000 about 44 lb.*

Values:	Exc.	VG	Good
	4.00	3.00	2.00

Comment: *Values for single sheet.*

Hand Traps. *For throwing Standard Clay Targets; By inserting Target in Slide and giving a little swing and snap with hand the target will sail along like a live bird. Heavy Blued Steel Frame and Hinged Section; Hinged Section fitted with Coil Springs to hold Target in Place; Oiled Corrugated Wood Handle, with Blued Steel Ferrule. No. 1102. Length, Open, 19 1/4 in.; Folded, 11 3/4 in.; Weight each about 7/8 lb. One in a Cardboard Box.*

Values:	Exc.	VG	Good
	225.00	200.00	175.00

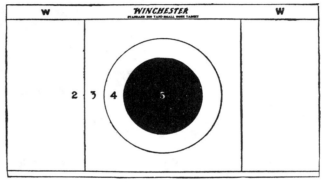

Target, 200 Yard Small Bore, *Printed in Black on HEAVY PAPER. No. 1974. Scoring 5 to 2; Bull - 7 3/16 in.; "4" Ring - 10 3/4 in.; "3" Square - 14 3/8 in.; Sheet - 17 1/2 x 30 in.; Weight per 1000 about 50 lbs.*

Values:	Exc.	VG	Good
	4.00	3.00	2.00

Comment: *Values for single sheet.*

Targets, Cardboard.

Small Clay Target for Junior Trapshooting. These were made to be thrown by the "Midget Hand Trap" that came with the "Junior Trap Shooting Outfit." Winchester reportedly used at least three different logos on these targets through the years. Photo from R. Stadt.

Target, Standard Gallery, *No. 1971. Scoring 5 to 1; Black Bull - 3/4 in.; Outer Ring - 3 3/8 in.; Card - 5 1/4 in. x 6 1/2 in.; Weight per 1000 about 10 lbs.*

Values:	Exc.	VG	Good
	50.00	40.00	30.00

Comment: *Values for single small clay target made prior to 1931.*

Values:	Exc.	VG	Good
	4.00	3.00	2.00

Comment: *Values for single sheet.*

Firearms Supplies and Accessories • 273

Target, 50 Feet Small Bore, *No. 1966. Scoring 10 to 5; Card - 5 1/4 in. x 6 1/2 in. Bull - 5/16 in.; Black, Including 7 Ring - 1 5/16 in.; Outer Ring - 2 in.; Weight per 1000 about 16 lbs.*

Values: Exc.   VG   Good
             4.00   3.00 2.00

Comment: *Values for single sheet.*

Target, 25 Yard Small Bore, *No. 1968. Scoring 10 to 5; Card - 5 1/4 in. x 6 1/2 in. Bull - 1/2 in.; Black, Including 7 Ring - 2 1/16 in.; Outer Ring - 3 in.; Weight per 1000 about 16 lbs.*

Values: Exc.   VG   Good
             4.00   3.00 2.00

Comment: *Values for single sheet. Same design as No. 1966.*

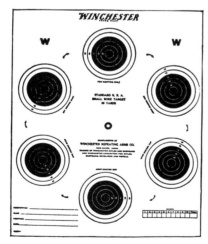

Target, N.R.A. Standard, 50 Feet Small Bore, *No. 1967. Scoring 10 to 5; Card - 11 in. x 14 1/2 in.; SIX TARGETS ON EACH CARD, ALL ALIKE. Bulls - 5/16 in.; Blacks, Including 7 Ring - 1 5/16 in.; Outer Ring - 2 in.; Weight per 1000 about 46 lbs.*

Values: Exc.   VG   Good
             5.00   4.00 3.00

Comment: *Values for single sheet.*

Target, N.R.A. Standard, 25 Yard Small Bore, *No. 1969. Scoring 10 to 5; Card 11 in. x 14 1/2 in.; SIX TARGETS ON EACH CARD, ALL ALIKE. Bulls - 1/2 in.; Blacks, Including 7 Ring - 2 1/16 in.; Outer Ring - 3 in.; Weight per 1000 about 46 lbs.*

Values: Exc.   VG   Good
             5.00   4.00 3.00

Comment: *Values for single sheet. Same design as No. 1967.*

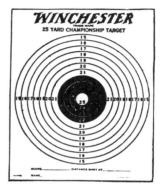

Target, 25 Yard Championship, *No. 1977. Scoring 24 to 15; White Bull - 1/2 in.; Black - 1 15/16 in.; Outer Ring - 5 7/16 in.; Card - 6 in. x 7 1/2 in.; Weight per 1000 about 12 lbs.*

Values: Exc.   VG   Good
             4.00   3.00 2.00

Comment: *Values for single sheet.*

Target, 50 Yard Small Bore, *No. 1972. Scoring 10 to 5; Bull - 1 in.; Black - 2 in.; Outer Ring - 6 in.; Card - 7 in. x 10 in.; Weight per 1000 about 20 lbs.*

Values: Exc.   VG   Good
             4.00   3.00 2.00

Comment: *Values for single sheet.*

274 • Firearms Supplies and Accessories

Target, 100 Yard Small Bore and 25 Yard Revolver, No. 1973. Scoring 10 to 5; Bull - 2 in.; Black - 4 in.; Outer Ring - 12 in.; Card - 14 in. x 16 in.; Weight per 1000 about 64 lbs.

Values:	Exc.	VG	Good
	4.00	3.00	2.00

Comment: *Values for single sheet. Same design as No. 1972.*

Target, 20 Yard Revolver, No. 1970. Scoring 10 to 5; Bull - 1 1/8 in.; Black - 2 3/4 in.; Outer Circle - 6 5/8 in.; Card - 8 1/4 in. x 10 in.; Weight per 1000 about 24 lbs.

Values:	Exc.	VG	Good
	4.00	3.00	2.00

Comment: *Values for single sheet.*

Plinker Targets, box of 50. Each wooden disk measures 1 1/4" in diameter and has a small, tack-size shaft (about 1/4" long) embedded in the back so the target could be fastened to a tree or a post. There is no "Winchester" identification on the individual disks. From T. Webster collection. Photo by D. Kowalski.

Values:	Exc.	VG	Good
	400.00	350.00	300.00

Comment: *Values are for full box. Aside from condition, partial boxes would be priced lower than full boxes.*

Large leather revolver holster is 11" from top of belt loop to barrel end. "Winchester" logo clearly stamped on narrow safety strap. Very few of these "cowboy" style holsters have ever been found. From T. Webster collection. Photo by D. Kowalski.

Values:	Exc.	VG	Good
	1,500.00	1,250.00	1,000.00

Comment: *We're actually aware of only one of these being found to date.*

Leather holster with wide cover flap for small pistol is 5 5/8" long from top of closed flap to tip of muzzle end. From T. Webster collection. Photo by D. Kowalski.

Values:	Exc.	VG	Good
	500.00	450.00	400.00

Comment: *This style of Winchester holster is the one ordinarily seen.*

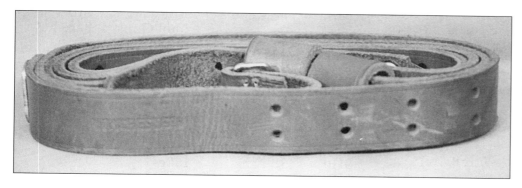

Leather belt is 1" wide. "Winchester" logo is stamped to the left of the buckle holes. From T. Webster collection. Photo by D. Kowalski.

Values:

Exc.	VG	Good
225.00	200.00	175.00

Comment: *Old leather belts are not typically found in the excellent condition displayed here.*

Two woven fiber or canvas cartridge belts, each slightly more than 1" wide. A grizzly bear head has been stamped on each. Bottom buckle is nickel-plated and the insert piece has an inscription that reads, "Pat. Feb. 15, 1981." The top buckle is rarer and has bronze plating on it; the insert piece does not have an inscription. From T. Webster collection. Photo by D. Kowalski.

Values:

Exc.	VG	Good
1,000.00	900.00	800.00

Comment: *Values are for bronze-plated version. For the nickel-plated version, deduct $300.00 from above values. The nickel-plated version also came in a slightly larger size having the same value range as the smaller one.*

Nos.	For Models	Rifles or Shot Guns	In. - With Barrel
3001	03	Rifles	20
3002	06	Rifles	20
3003	07	Rifles	20
3004	10	Rifles	20
3014	90	Rifles	24
3007	92 & 95	Rifles	24
3008	12	Shot Guns	25
3009	86 & 94	Rifles	
	12, 20 & 97	Shot Guns	26
3011	95	Rifles	
	12 & 97	Shot Guns	28
3012	12 & 97	Shot Guns	30
3013	12 & 97	Shot Guns	32

Values:

Exc.	VG	Good
250.00	225.00	175.00

Leather Gun Case, Style 25W. FOR WINCHESTER TAKE-DOWN SHOT GUNS WITH INTERCHANGEABLE BARREL. For Models 12 AND 97.

Nos.	Length Barrel, inches	ExtraBarrel, inches
3019	26	26

Nos.	Length Barrel, inches	ExtraBarrel, inches
3020	28	26
3021	30	28
3022	32	30
3023		32 28

Values:

Exc.	VG	Good
250.00	225.00	175.00

Leather Gun Case, Style 15W. FOR WINCHESTER TAKE-DOWN RIFLES AND SHOT GUNS. Heavy Russet Leather, Maroon Colored Flannel Lined; Patent Hinge Partition; Heavy Brass Trimmings; Lock Buckle; Leather Handle and Sling.

Leather Gun Case, Style 35W. *FOR WINCHESTER TAKE-DOWN SHOT GUNS.*

Nos.	For Models	In. - With Barrel
3030	12	25
3031	97	26
3032	11	26
3035	11	28
3034	12 & 97	28
3036	12	30
3037	12 & 97	32
*3038	12	30

*For Gun with Ventilated Rib and Extension Action Slide Handle.

Values:	Exc.	VG	Good
	250.00	225.00	175.00

Leather Gun Case, Style 45W. *FOR WINCHESTER TAKE-DOWN SHOT GUNS, WITH INTERCHANGEABLE BARREL.*

Nos.	For Models	Length Barrel - In.	Extra Barrel - In.
3040	12	25	25
3041	11	26	26
3042	12 & 97	26	26
3044	11	28	28
3043	12 & 97	28	28
3045	12 & 97	30	30
3046	97	32	32

Values:	Exc.	VG	Good
	275.00	235.00	200.00

Comment: This was Winchester's high-end leather gun case. (Style similar to 35W.) Photo not available.

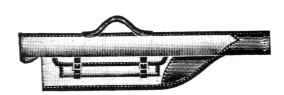

Canvas Gun Cover, Style A. *FOR WINCHESTER TAKE-DOWN RIFLES AND SHOT GUNS.* Heavy Brown Army Duck, Heavy Maroon Colored Flannel Lined; Lock and Muzzle protected with Heavy Orange Leather; Extra Heavy Handle, Orange Leather Bound; Hand Sewed Ends.

Nos.	For Models	Rifles or Shot Guns	In. - With Barrel
3101	02	Rifles	18
3102			20
3104	03	Rifles	20
3108	04	Rifles	
	36	Shot Guns	20
3106	07	Rifles	20
3107	10	Rifles	20
3109			22
3110	86, 92, 95	Rifles	24
3111	90	Rifles	24
3112	12	Shot Guns	25
3113	94	Rifles	
	12, 20, 97	Shot Guns	26
3114	11	Shot Guns	26
3116	11	Shot Guns	28
3119	12 & 97	Shot Guns	28
3117	95	Rifles	
	12 & 97	Shot Guns	28
3118	12 & 97	Shot Guns	32

Values:	Exc.	VG	Good
	200.00	165.00	125.00

Canvas Gun Cover, Style C. *FOR TAKE-DOWN RIFLES AND SHOT GUNS.* Heavy Olive Drab Canvas, Flannel Lined; Leather Reinforced over Muzzle and Action; Leather Handle and Closing Straps; Outside Rod Pockets.

Nos.	For Models	Rifles or Shot Guns	In. - With Barrel
3144	02, 03, 04, 06	Rifles	
	36	Shot Guns	20
3145	07, 10	Shot Guns	20
3146	90	Shot Guns	24
3147	86, 92, 95	Shot Guns	20
3148	94	Shot Guns	26
3150	11	Shot Guns	26
3149	12, 20 & 97	Shot Guns	26
3151	11	Shot Guns	28
3152	12, 95 & 97	Shot Guns	28
3153	12 & 97	Shot Guns	30
3154	12 & 97	Shot Guns	32

Values:	Exc.	VG	Good
	200.00	165.00	125.00

Comment: (Similar to Style A.) Photo not available.

Canvas Gun Cover, Style B. *FOR SOLID FRAME RIFLES AND SHOT GUNS.* Heavy Brown Army Duck, Heavy Maroon Colored Flannel Lined; Lock and Muzzle protected with Heavy Orange Leather; Extra Heavy Combination Sling and Handle, Leather Bound; Hand Sewed Ends.

Firearms Supplies and Accessories • 277

Nos.	For Models	Rifles or Shot Guns	In. - With Barrel
3126			14
3127			15
3128			16
3129	92, 94	Carbine	
	97	Riot Guns	20
3130	95	Carbine	22
3131	92, 95	Rifles	
	41	Shot Guns	24
3132			25
3133	94	Rifles	26
3134	95	Rifles	28
3135			30
3136			32
3141	52	Rifles	28

Values:	Exc.	VG	Good
	200.00	165.00	125.00

Canvas Gun Cover, Style D. *FOR SOLID FRAME RIFLES AND SHOT GUNS. Heavy Olive Drab Canvas, Flannel Lined; Leather Reinforced over Muzzle and Action; Leather Handle and Closing Straps.*

Nos.	For Models	Rifles or Shot Guns	In. - With Barrel
3172			16
3173	92, 94	Carbine	20
	95	Carbine	22
	97	Riot Guns	20
3174	92, 94	Rifle	
	41	Shot Guns	24
3175	94	Rifle	26
3176	95	Rifle	28
3177			30
3178			32

Values:	Exc.	VG	Good
	200.00	165.00	125.00

Comment: *(Similar to Style B.) Photo not available.*

Air Rifle Shot. *Fit practically All Standard Air Rifles; Uniform Size and Hardness; Being of correct Size they fit the Bore properly, increasing the Accuracy, Range and Penetration when used in almost any Air Rifle. No. 1176. 4 oz. Waterproof Cardboard Tube. 100 Tubes in a Case.*

Values:	Exc.	VG	Good
	30.00	25.00	20.00

Comment: *Values for one tube made prior to 1900. Winchester produced these until the 1960s and newer versions would have lesser value.*

Air Rifle Shot, 1 lb. box. No. 1175. Box shows some damage; it's buff colored with black type and red "W." These were originally packed 50 boxes to a case. Boxes are very rare. From T. Webster collection. Photo by D. Kowalski.

Values:	Exc.	VG	Good
	150.00	125.00	100.00

Comment: *Values for one box. Also available in 25 lb. bags (No. 1177).*

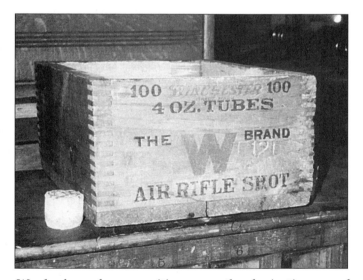

Wooden boxes for ammunition are another fascinating area of Winchester collectibles that are beyond the scope of this first edition ... but we wanted to present an example. This unique box for Winchester 4 oz. Tubes of Air Rifle Shot is in excellent condition with clear graphics. It is also a rare, early box showing heavy dovetailed joints. Photo by Curt Bowman.

Values:	Exc.	VG	Good
	350.00	300.00	250.00

Comment: *Values are for this particular wooden box. In general, newer boxes, particularly the late-model ones with nailed joints would be priced at least 50 percent lower than those with dovetailed joints.*

Winchester Reloading Tools and Supplies

Winchester manufactured a broad selection of these tools in all the calibers of interest to reloaders with patent dates going back to the 1870s. Because of space limitations in this volume, we will provide only a few introductory and unique examples of the tools. For the same reason, even though Winchester made a wide variety of wads, primers and percussion caps, we will only present a few boxes of these related supplies made for the reloading fraternity.

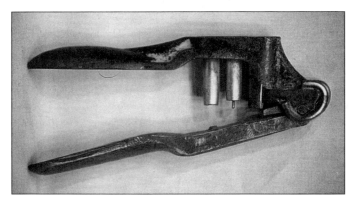

An example of what is believed to be Winchester's first reloading tool. A rare piece with rust, other damage and some apparent repair done to one of the "hinges." Wouldn't it be great if every rare collectible discovered was also in mint condition? From the Tom Webster collection. Photo by D. Kowalski.

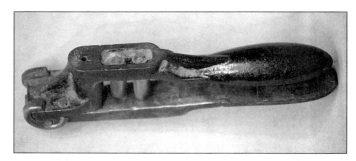

Another view of the same reloading tool. From the Tom Webster collection. Photo by D. Kowalski.

Values: Exc.   VG   Good
                  5,000.00   4,000.00   3,000.00

Comment: *Values are for this first model. Only a very few have ever been found.*

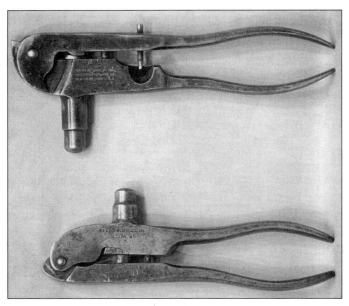

Reloading tools underwent various design changes through the years. Tool on left reads "38 WCF Pat. Oct. 20, 1874 Nov. 7, '82" and measures 8 1/4" in length. Tool on right has inscription "40-60 WCF Pat. Sept. 14, 1880" and it is 9 1/16" long. From T. Webster collection. Photo by D. Kowalski.

Values: Exc.   VG   Good
                   150.00   125.00   90.00

Comment: *Prices are for reloading tools in sizes from .40-50 to .44. For sizes smaller than .40 caliber, deduct 50 percent. For sizes larger than .44 caliber, add a 50 percent premium. The .44 caliber was Winchester's first big game cartridge and their reloading tools are the most common of the large-caliber sizes. The .44-40 and .50 Government were also about three times more common than the other plus-.44-caliber sizes. From T. Webster collection. Photo by D. Kowalski.*

Empty reloading tool box for the Model 1894 rifle measures 8 1/2" x 3 5/8" x 2 1/4". From T. Webster collection. Photo by D. Kowalski.

Values: Exc.   VG   Good
                   225.00   200.00   150.00

Comment: *Prices are for empty reloading tool boxes.*

No. 1 Bullet Breech Caps, box of 100. These were used in gallery rifles. Box is cream color with black print. From Tom Webster collection. Photo by D. Kowalski.

Box of 250 Cardboard Wads to reload 12 gauge shells. Box is cream color with black print. Sample of wad is on top. From T. Webster collection. Photo by D. Kowalski.

Values:	Exc.	VG	Good
	200.00	175.00	150.00

Comment: *Values are for full box. These are extremely rare boxes.*

Values:	Exc.	VG	Good
	75.00	60.00	40.00

Comment: *Prices are for full box.*

The Winchester Junior Rifle Corps (W.J.R.C.)

American youngsters who lived in rural areas grew up with firearms, walking the woods and fields with a .22 or .410 shotgun in search of rabbits, squirrels and crows. Or they might go to the local dump to "plink" rats.

Winchester firearms use and ammunition sales were historically greater in rural areas. However, spurred by the U.S. involvement in World War I, Winchester unveiled its plan to help teach every American youngster, whether they lived in city or country, how to shoot. This was the Winchester Junior Rifle Corps (W.J.R.C.) concept launched in July of 1917. It was first detailed in a Sales Department Bulletin (Number 84, dated July 10, 1917).

In the same month Winchester launched a major sales effort with a related pamphlet they titled,

Junior Rifle Corps belt is made of woven fiber. This rare piece is nearly 1" wide. Metal clamp buckle has "WJRC" stamped on it. From Tom Webster collection. Photo by D. Kowalski.

Values:	Exc.	VG	Good
	2,500.00	2,000.00	1,200.00

Comment: *This was just a small, cheap belt. And today's collectors speculate a lot of them were thrown away for that reason, as well as the fact that "WJRC" was not automatically identified with Winchester.*

"Important Development in Arms and Ammunition Business." There are some who would see the W.J.R.C. promotion as simply an attempt to capture the hearts and minds (and ultimately the dollars) of young shooters and potential shooters. But the "Important Development" pamphlet paints a much broader and more balanced picture of patriotism and national preparedness that takes it beyond just a sales push. In this pamphlet, Winchester management states....

"The development in the international situation that has forced America into war has made every man realize the need of knowing how to handle firearms intelligently."

"American preparedness may avert further international complications that would otherwise arise, and the knowledge by every householder of how to use firearms is the first step in preparedness."

Winchester ran a series of ads in late 1917 on the W.J.R.C. in such magazines as "Arms & The Man" and "Popular Mechanics." These ads promised W.J.R.C. members would learn to be better shooters. And it told them how to set up local chapters.

The company supported the W.J.R.C. program with a variety of products, from boxed range kits to targets, from uniforms to later spin-offs such as "Junior Trap Shooting Outfits" (also in wood cases) in the 1920s. Winchester also organized regional and national shooting competitions under this banner. As you would expect, there are collectors who have made something of a specialty of W.J.R.C. items.

Due to space limitations, we present just a few of these unique pieces to help spotlight a memorable part of Winchester history. We begin with the Winchester Junior Rifle Corps Range Kits still being promoted in the 1927 Catalog.

Winchester Junior Rifle Corps Range Kit. *A Complete Outfit for Target Shooting and Range work all Packed in a Handsome Mission Finish Wood Case with Spring Catches and Handle for Carrying; contains everything for the Young Shooter for Camping and Summer Vacations.*
No. 0204 - COMPLETE WITH RIFLE No. 0201 (Model 02 Single Shot .22); weight each about 11 lbs. (Note: A Winchester five-panel display advertises this rifle as "A Simple Safe Rifle for the Beginner." Ed.)

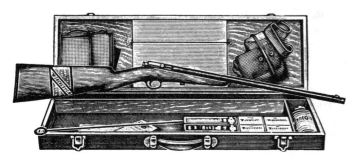

No. 0403 - COMPLETE WITH RIFLE No. 0401 (Model 04 Single Shot .22); weight each about 12 lbs. (Note: The same Winchester five-panel display touts the Model 04 rifle, by comparison, as "A Splendid Accurate Rifle for Older Boys." Ed.)

The following is included in addition to the rifle specified above:

200 .22 Caliber Short Lesmok Cartridges (50 in a box).

1 Cartridge Pouch with Belt.

1 Khaki Covered Canvas Gun Case divided in Two Sections.

50 Official W. J. R. C. Targets in Special Envelope.

1 Tube Winchester Gun Grease.

1 Tube Winchester Rust Remover.

1 Can Winchester Gun Oil.

1 Piece Cheese-cloth.

1 Wire Cleaning Rod.

Values:	Exc.	VG	Good
	7,000.00	6,000.00	5,000.00

Comment: *Above values are for a kit with the Model 02 .22 rifle (illustrated) and at least one original box of cartridges, as well as a WJRC belt. For kit with Model 04, deduct $150.00 if the rifle were in the same condition as a Model 02.*

A complete set with four boxes of .22 shells has never been found. In fact, the special .22 shells that came with this kit are among the rarest of Winchester cartridge boxes and would be valued at $2,000.00 - $3,000.00 each. There are only a few of these cartridge boxes that have ever been found.

In their 1920 Catalog, Winchester offered a shotgun version of this kit that included their Model 20 single shot .410. They called it the "Winchester Junior Trap Shooting Outfit." Instead of .22 shells, this kit contained six boxes of .410 shells, a Midget Hand trap and 100 clay targets. (To the best of our knowledge, a kit has never been found with all 100 targets, a fragile item, intact.) Due to the extra weight of the clay targets, this set tipped the scales at about 40 pounds. It also contained "A Whole New Field of Sport," a brochure describing the outfit with instructions on how to set up a field for trapshooting; a 16-page booklet, "How to Use and Care for the Winchester Junior Trapshooting Outfit;" a 12-page booklet of "General Instructions" on Winchester Repeating Shotguns; a miniature score pad; and instructions on how to use Winchester cleaning materials. For this kit with the basic Model 20, deduct 50 percent from the above values. There are also kits with more ornate Model 20s that would increase the value of the total kit.

Winchester launched the "Junior Trap Shooting Outfit" in 1920 with collateral advertising materials such as this five-panel store display that promised "Your whole family will enjoy the new sport." Photo from R. Stadt.

Throughout its existence, Winchester supported its Junior Rifle Corps with several five-panel displays. This one promotes a "Sharpshooter" Medal that can be won. From the Tom Webster collection. Photo by D. Kowalski.

282 • *Firearms Supplies and Accessories*

Winchester even organized W.J.R.C. shooting matches starting in the late 'teens. This two-sided counter display promoted the first ones held in Camp Perry, Ohio. From T. Webster collection. Photo by D. Kowalski.

The opposite side of the "W.J.R.C. Matches" counter display promoted Winchester rifles to its "target" audience of "keen-eyed boys" with the promise they could become "expert" shots. From Tom Webster collection. Photo by D. Kowalski.

Values:	Exc.	VG	Good
	2,000.00	1,800.00	1,600.00

Comment: *This counter display is fairly rare. Even though we will present other advertising materials later in the book, we wanted to group several W.J.R.C. items here. The companion volume, "Winchester Rarities," will also have several other W.J.R.C. items in four-color.*

Very rare and colorful box in excellent condition for the Model 02 bolt-action, single-shot .22 rifle. This was one of the rifle options offered in the Winchester Junior Rifle Corps Range Kits. From Tom Webster collection. Photo by D. Kowalski.

Values:	Exc.	VG	Good
	750.00	650.00	500.00

Comment: *Values for box only. This version of the Model 02 box was only made for one or two years.*

Winchester Pocket Knives

The end of World War I marked a time of aggressive expansion for Winchester. In fact, 1919 was the year they acquired eight different companies. Among them were the Eagle Pocket Knife Company and the Napanoch Knife Company. And when Winchester merged with the Associated Simmons Hardware Company in 1922, Simmons had a controlling interest in the Walden Knife Company; their designs soon became Winchester designs.

Thus, within a three-year period, Winchester had three knife companies under their corporate umbrella. That meant they went from ground zero to several hundred styles, models and handle materials in a very short time. Winchester finally stopped producing knives from this era in the mid-1940s. In this volume, we will focus on models they produced during the 1920s, 1930s and 1940s.

In the early 1970s a few models appeared in the marketplace, apparently German-made. Then in the late 1980s Blue Brass Cutlery was licensed to make Winchester knives; they subcontracted that production to an American firm. We will not cover these later Winchester-licensed knives here.

We will give you a profile of as many early Winchester knives as possible in this section. In future editions we will expand the list as new models and variations from that era are documented and examples become available. While researching this book, we discovered not all sources agree on the total stock numbers Winchester produced during its days as a knife manufacturer. There are some models that have never been seen. And we also have the challenge of identifying some knife models that may have used spare blades from one knife on another model.

It is also necessary to issue a word of warning. If you begin collecting Winchester knives, know your source. Get a second expert opinion if you have any question about the authenticity of a piece. When you purchase a knife, get a receipt and a money-back guarantee from the seller in the event the knife proves not to be authentic and original.

We are indebted to Mr. Jim Sargent, veteran knife collector and author of the *American Premium Guide to Knives and Razors: Identification and Value Guide*, for his valuable insights and pricing in this chapter.

You will also find many photographs of Winchester pocket knives in his book.

Collecting Winchester pocket knives is also part of a much larger "antique" knife (typically old pocket knives) collecting arena. Several specialty shows host collectors of and dealers in antique knives, including The BLADE Show in Atlanta, held annually in late May or early June.

Analyzing Winchester Knife Model Numbers

Winchester numbered its knife models according to a system. Model numbers were typically composed of four numbers. The first number was the number of blades.

Then the second number generally represented the following handle materials (some exceptions have been discovered):

1. Celluloid
2. Fancy Celluloid
3. Nickel Silver
4. Genuine Pearl
5. Cocobolo or other wood
6. Bone
7. Bone Stag
8. Bone or Stag

Finally, the last two numbers were the factory pattern number. Although, once again, there appears to be some inconsistency in the system, probably due to integrating patterns from three original and separate knife companies.

Detailed Pocket Knife Descriptions

For each of the following selected Winchester pocket knives, we have provided an illustration or a photograph followed by a brief description. The description is paraphrased from material provided by Winchester in catalogs or sales lists. Then we have given the size of the closed knife.

This section will familiarize you with basic Winchester patterns, handle materials, bolster types and blade configurations. It is arranged by pattern.

STABBER PATTERN

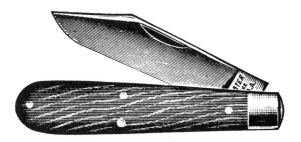

No. 1632. Clip blade, glazed finish. Cocobolo handle. Steel lining and bolster. Size - 3 1/2 in.

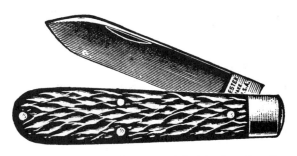

No. 1938. Spear blade, glazed finish. Stag handle. Steel lining and bolsters. Size - 3 1/2 in.

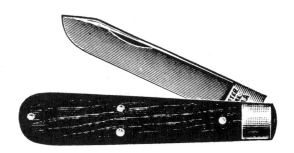

No. 1608. Spey blade, glazed finish. Cocobolo handle. Steel lining and bolster. Size - 3 1/2 in.

No. 2608. Spear and Pen blades, glazed finish. Steel lining and bolster. Comes with Shackle and Chain. Cocobolo handle. Size - 3 1/2 in.

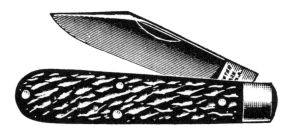

No. 1921. Clip blade, glazed finish. Stag handle. Steel lining and bolster. Size - 3 1/2 in.

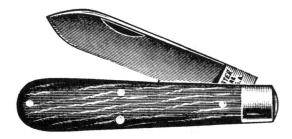

No. 1605. Spear blade, glazed finish. Cocobolo handle. Steel lining and bolster. Size - 3 1/2 in.

No. 2958. Clip and Pen blades, glazed finish. Stag handle. Steel lining and bolster. Size - 3 1/2 in.

No. 2983. Clip and Pen blades, glazed finish. Stag handle. Steel lining and bolster. Comes with Shackle and Chain. Size - 3 1/2 in.

Winchester Pocket Knives • 285

No. 2998. Spear and Pen blades, glazed finish. Stag handle. Steel lining and bolster. Size - 3 1/2 in.

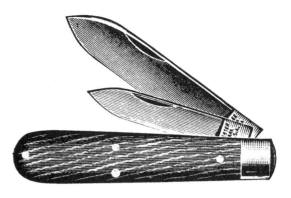

No. 2606. Spear and Pen blades, glazed finish. Cocobolo handle. Steel lining and bolster. Size - 3 1/2 in.

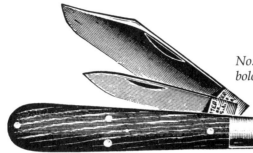

No. 2603. Clip and Pen blades, glazed finish. Cocobolo handle. Steel lining and bolster. Size - 3 1/2 in.

BARLOW PATTERN

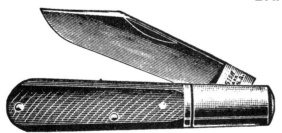

No. 1785. Clip blade, glazed finish. Bone handle. Steel lining and bolster. Size - 3 1/2 in.

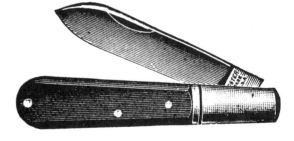

No. 1701. Spear blade, glazed finish. Bone handle. Steel bolster and lining. Size - 3 1/2 in.

No. 2701. Spear and Pen blades, glazed finish. Bone handle. Steel lining and bolster. Size - 3 1/2 in.

No. 2703. Clip and Pen blades, glazed finish. Bone handle. Steel lining and bolster. Size - 3 1/2 in.

PRUNER PATTERN

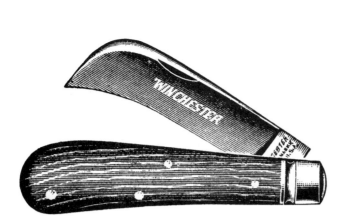

No. 1610. Pruner blade, glazed finish. Cocobolo handle. Steel bolster and lining. Size - 4 in.

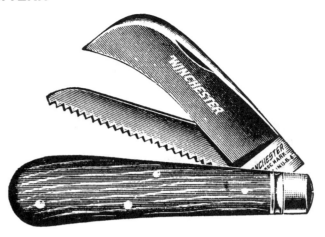

No. 2615. Pruner and Saw blades, glazed finish. Cocobolo handle. Steel bolster and lining. Size - 4 in.

BABY PRUNER PATTERN

No. 1633. Pruner blade, glazed finish. Cocobolo handle. Steel bolster. Brass lining. Crest shield. Common swage and nail mark. Size - 3 1/2 in.

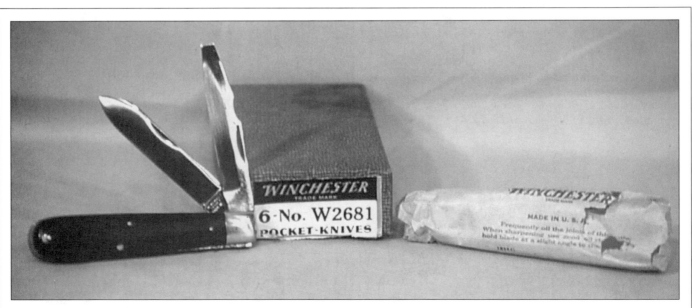

No. 2681. Electrician's knife has Spear blade and long Screwdriver-tipped cutting blade. Ebony handle. We've also shown the paper sleeve that held the knife inside the "6-pak" box. From T. Webster collection. Photo by D. Kowalski.

LONG SLIM JACK PATTERN

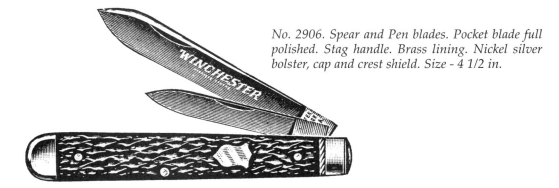

No. 2906. Spear and Pen blades. Pocket blade full polished. Stag handle. Brass lining. Nickel silver bolster, cap and crest shield. Size - 4 1/2 in.

SLEEVEBOARD JACK PATTERN

No. 2905. Spear and Pen blades. Pocket blade full polished. Stag handle. Brass lining. Nickel silver bolster, cap and crest shield. Size - 4 1/4 in.

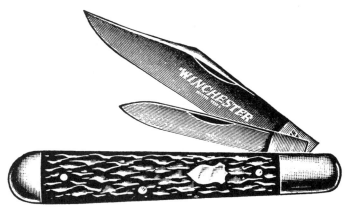

No. 2907. Clip and Pen blades. Pocket blade full polished. Stag handle. Brass lining. Nickel silver bolster, cap and crest shield. Size - 4 1/4 in.

No. 1905. Spear blade, full polished, stag handle. Brass lining. Nickel silver bolster, cap and crest shield. Size - 4 1/4 in.

REGULAR JACK PATTERN

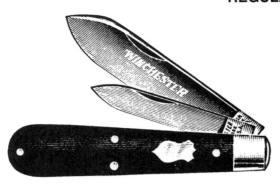

No. 2635. Spear and Pen blades, glazed finish. Cocobolo handle. Brass lining. Steel bolster and nickel silver crest shield. Size - 3 1/2 in.

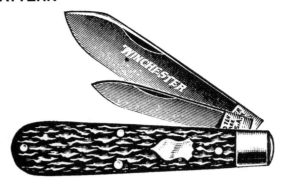

No. 2950. Spear and Pen blades, glazed finish. Stag handle. Steel bolster and brass lining. Nickel silver crest shield. Size - 3 1/2 in.

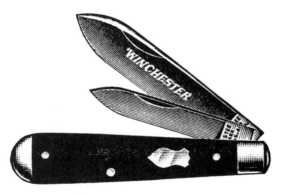

No. 2636. Spear and Pen blades. Pocket blade full polished. Ebony handle. Brass lining. Nickel silver bolster, cap and crest shield. Size - 3 1/2 in.

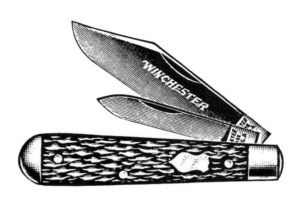

No. 2952. Clip and Pen blades. Pocket blade full polished. Stag handle. Brass lining. Nickel silver bolster, cap and crest shield. Size - 3 1/2 in.

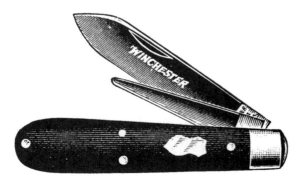

No. 2660. Spear and Punch blades, glazed finish. Ebony handle. Steel bolster. Crest Shield. Brass lining. Size - 3 1/2 in.

No. 2951. Clip and Punch blades, glazed finish. Stag handle. Brass lining. Steel bolster. Nickel silver shield. Size - 3 1/2 in.

No. 2661. Spear and Pen blades, glazed finish. Cocobolo handle. Steel cap and bolster. Crest shield. Brass lining. Size - 3 1/2 in.

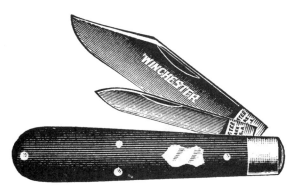

No. 2604. Clip and Pen blades, glazed finish. Cocobolo handle. Steel bolster. Crest Shield. Brass lining. Size - 3 1/2 in.

No. 2662. Clip and Pen blades, glazed finish. Ebony handle. Steel cap and bolster. Crest shield. Brass lining. Size - 3 1/2 in.

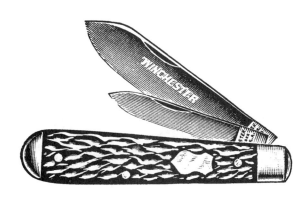

No. 2911. Spear and Pen blades, glazed finish. Stag handle. Steel cap and bolster. Crest shield. Brass lining. Size - 3 1/2 in.

No. 2901. Clip and Pen blades, glazed finish. Stag handle. Steel bolster. Crest shield. Brass lining. Size - 3 1/2 in.

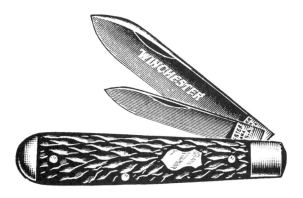

No. 2954. Spear and Pen blades, Pocket blade full polished. Stag handle. Nickel silver cap, bolster and crest shield. Brass lining. Size - 3 1/2 in.

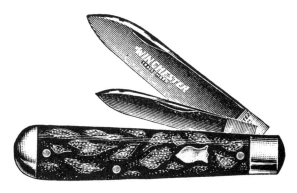

No. 2070. Spear and Pen blades. Large blade full polished. Varicolored brilliant finish celluloid handle. Nickel silver bolster, cap and shield. Brass lining. Size - 3 1/2 in.

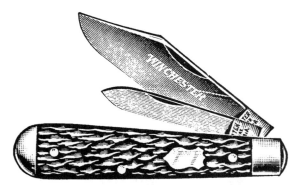

No. 2949. Clip and Pen blades, glazed finish,. Stag handle. Steel cap and bolster. Crest shield. Brass lining. Size - 3 1/2 in.

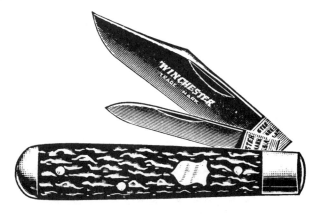

No. 2845. Clip and Pen blades. Pocket blade full polished. Stag handle. Steel bolster and cap. Nickel silver shield. Brass lining. Size - 3 3/4 in.

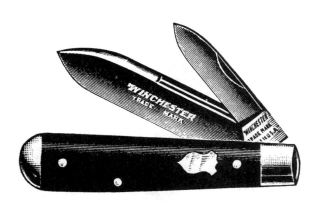

No. 2649. Spear and Pen blade. Pocket blade full polished. Ebony handle. Steel bolster and cap. Nickel silver shield. Brass lining. Size - 3 3/4 in.

HEAVY STRAIGHT JACK PATTERN

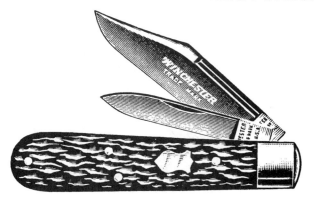

No. 2844. Clip and Pen blades. Pocket blade full polished. Stag handle. Polished steel bolster. Nickel silver shield. Brass lining. Size - 3 3/4 in.

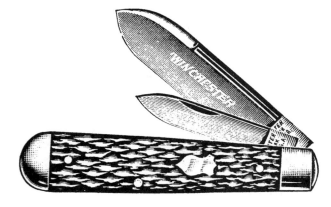

No. 2982. Spear and Pen blades. Pocket blade full polished. Stag handle. Nickel silver crest shield, cap and bolster. Brass lining. Size - 4 in.

Winchester Pocket Knives • 291

No. 2616. Clip and Pen blades. Pocket blade full polished. Cocobolo handle. Nickel silver bolster and crest shield. Brass lining. Size - 4 in.

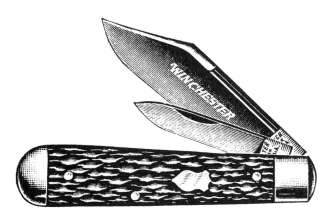

No. 2988. Clip and Pen blades, Pocket blade full polished. Stag handle. Nickel silver bolster and cap. Crest shield. Brass lining. Cut swage and French nail mark. Size - 4 in.

SLIM JACK PATTERN

No. 2627. Spear and Pen blades. Pocket blade full polished. Cocobolo handle. Nickel silver cap, bolsters and crest shield. Brass lining. Size - 3 1/4 in.

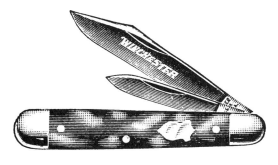

No. 2099. Clip and Pen blades. Pocket blade full polished. Shell celluloid handle. Nickel silver cap, bolster and crest shield. Brass lining. Size - 3 3/4 in.

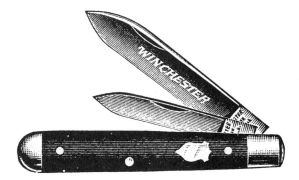

No. 2647. Spear and Pen blades. Pocket blade full polished. Ebony handle. Nickel silver bolster and cap. Brass lining. Nickel silver crest shield. Size - 3 5/8 in.

No. 2931. Clip and Pen blades. Pocket blade full polished. Stag handle. Nickel silver cap, bolsters and crest shield. Brass lining. Size - 3 1/4 in.

No. 2964. Spear and Pen blades. Pocket blade full polished. Stag handle. Nickel silver bolster and cap. Brass lining. Nickel silver crest shield. Size - 3 5/8 in.

No. 2080. Spear and Pen blades. Pocket blade full polished. Shell celluloid handle. Nickel silver cap, bolster and crest shield. Brass lining. Size - 3 5/8 in.

No. 2849. Spear and Pen blades. Pocket blade full polished. Stag handle. Nickel silver bolster, cap and shield. Brass lining. Size - 3 1/4 in.

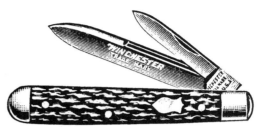

SMALL JACK PATTERN

No. 2083. Spear and Pen blades. Pocket blade full polished. Green celluloid handle. Nickel silver lining. Nickel silver bolster, cap and shield. Size - 3 1/8 in.

No. 2925. Spear and Pen blade. Pocket blade full polished. Stag handle. Nickel silver lining. Nickel silver bolster, cap and crest shield. Size - 3 1/8 in.

No. 2352. Spear and Pen blades. Full polished. Pearl handle. Nickel silver cap, bolster, crest shield and lining. Size - 3 1/8 in.

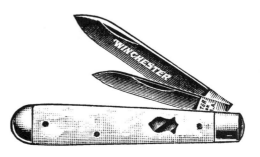

SPEAR JACK PATTERN

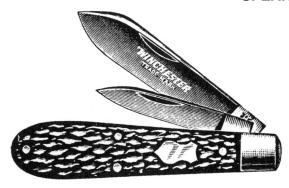

No. 2994. Spear and Pen blades. Pocket blade full polished. Stag handle. Steel bolster. Crest shield. Brass lining. Size - 3 5/8 in.

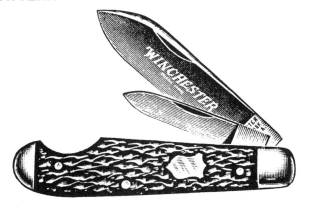

No. 2930. Easy Opener design. Spear and Pen blades. Pocket blade full polished. Stag handle. Brass lining. Steel bolster and cap. Crest shield. Size - 3 5/8 in.

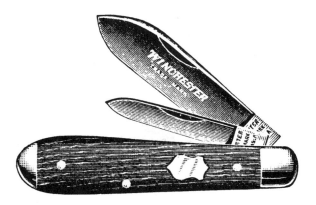

No. 2612. Spear and Pen blades. Pocket blade full polished. Cocobolo handle. Polished steel bolster and cap. Nickel silver shield. Brass lining. Size - 3 5/8 in.

No. 2094. Easy Opener design. Spear and Pen blades, glazed finish. Green and black brilliant finish celluloid handle. Steel bolster, cap and shield. Brass lining. Size - 3 1/2 in.

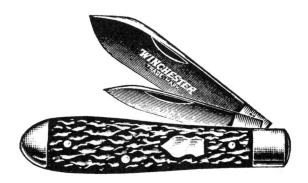

No. 2995. Spear and Pen blades. Pocket blade full polished. Stag handle. Steel bolster and cap. Crest shield. Brass lining. Size - 3 5/8 in.

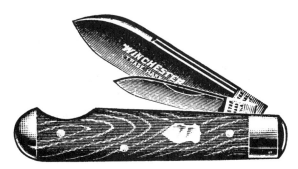

No. 2613. Easy Opener design. Spear and Pen blades. Pocket blade full polished. Cocobolo handle. Polished steel bolster and cap. Nickel silver shield. Brass lining. Size - 3 5/8 in.

SWELL END JACK PATTERN

No. 2340. Spear and Pen blades. Full polished. Pearl handle. Nickel silver bolster, cap, lining and crest shield. Size - 3 3/8 in.

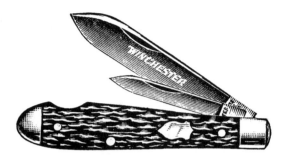

No. 2959. Spear and Pen blades. Glazed finish. Stag handle. Easy opener Steel cap and bolsters. Brass lining. Nickel silver crest shield. Size - 3 3/8 in.

No. 2098. Clip and Pen blades. Pocket blade full polished. Green celluloid handle. Nickel silver cap, bolster, lining and crest shield. Size - 3 3/8 in.

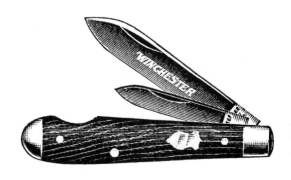

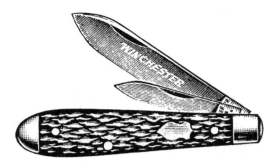

No. 2940. Spear and Pen blades. Pocket blade full polished. Stag handle. Nickel silver cap, bolster and lining. Nickel silver crest shield. Size - 3 3/8 in.

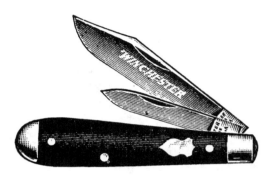

No. 2630. Clip and Pen blades. Pocket blade full polished. Ebony handle. Nickel silver bolster and cap. Nickel silver crest shield and lining. Size - 3 3/8 in.

No. 2987. Spear and Pen blades. Pocket blade full polished. Stag handle. Easy opener. Nickel silver cap, bolster, lining and crest shield. Shackle on end. Size - 3 3/8 in.

No. 2605. Spear and Pen blades. Glazed finish. Cocobolo handle. Easy opener. Steel cap and bolster. Brass lining. Nickel silver crest shield. Size - 3 3/8 in.

BALLOON OR SWELL CENTER JACK PATTERN

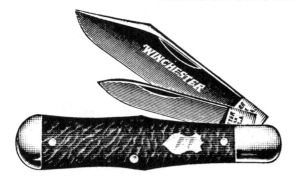

No. 2096. Spear and Pen blades. Pocket blade full polished. Blue celluloid handle. Nickel silver cap, bolster and crest shield. Brass lining. Size - 3 1/2 in.

No. 2984. Clip and Pen blades. Pocket blade full polished. Stag handle. Nickel silver cap, bolster and crest shield. Brass lining. Size - 3 1/2 in.

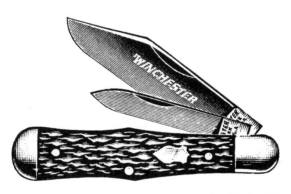

No. 2955. Clip and Pen blades. Pocket blade full polished. Stag handle. Nickel silver cap and bolster. Brass lining. Crest shield. Size - 3 1/2 in.

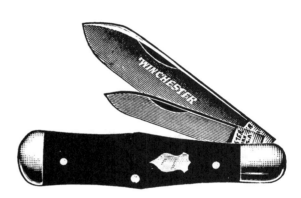

No. 2637. Spear and Pen blades. Pocket blade full polished. Ebony handle. Nickel silver bolster and cap. Brass lining. Crest shield. Size - 3 1/2 in.

EQUAL END JACK PATTERN

No. 2980. Clip and Pen blades. Pocket blade full polished. Stag handle. Nickel silver bolsters. Brass lining. Crest shield. Size - 3 5/8 in.

No. 2991. Spear and Clip blades. Pocket blade full polished. Stag handle. Nickel silver bolsters. Brass lining. Crest shield. Size - 3 5/8 in.

No. 2927. Clip and Punch blades. Pocket blade full polished. Stag handle. Nickel silver bolsters. Brass lining. Crest shield. Size - 3 5/8 in.

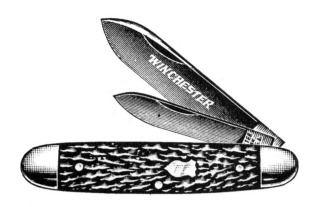

No. 2966. Spear and Pen blades. Pocket blade full polished. Stag handle. Steel bolsters. Nickel silver crest shield. Brass lining. Size - 3 5/8 in.

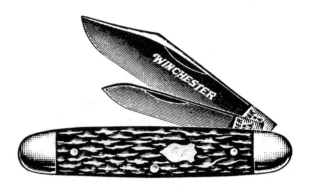

No. 2973. Clip and Pen blades. Pocket blade full polished. Stag handle Nickel silver bolsters. Brass lining. Crest shield. Size - 3 5/8 in.

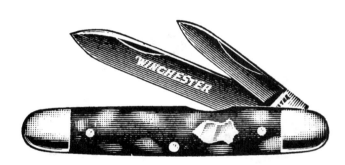

No. 2028. Spear and Pen blades. Pocket blade full polished. Shell celluloid handle. Nickel silver bolsters, lining and crest shield. Size - 3 3/8 in.

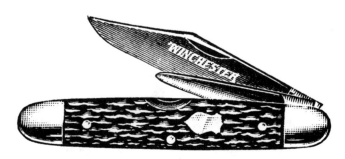

No. 2926. Clip and Punch blades. Pocket blade full polished. Stag handle. Nickel silver bolsters, lining and shield. Size - 3 3/8 in.

No. 2069. Spear and Pen blades. Large blade full polished. Pearl blue celluloid handle. Nickel silver bolsters and shield. Brass lining. Size -3 1/3 in.

Winchester Pocket Knives • 297

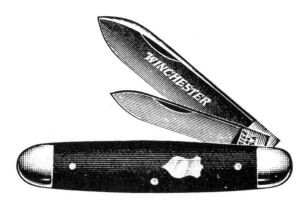

No. 2648. Spear and Pen blades. Pocket blade full polished. Ebony handle. Steel bolsters. Brass lining. Crest shield. Size - 3 5/8 in.

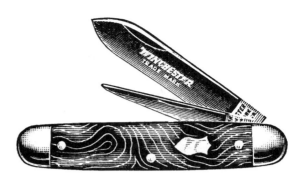

No. 2106. Spear and Patent Leather Punch blades. Pocket blade full polished. Abalone (blue) celluloid handle. Nickel silver bolsters and shield. Brass lining. Size - 3 1/4 in.

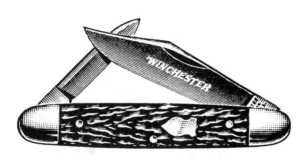

No. 2971. Clip and Pen blades. Pocket blade full polished. Stag handle. Nickel silver bolsters, lining and crest shield. Size - 3 3/8 in.

No. 2665. Spear and Pen blades. Pocket blade full polished. Ebony handle. Nickel Silver bolsters, lining and crest shield. Size - 3 3/8 in.

DOG LEG PATTERN

No. 2611. Spear and Pen blades. Pocket blade full polished. Cocobolo handle. Nickel silver bolsters, cap and shield. Brass lining. Size - 3 in.

No. 2087. Spear and Pen blades. Pocket blade full polished. Shell celluloid handle. Nickel silver bolster and cap. Brass lining. Crest shield. Size - 3 in.

298 • Winchester Pocket Knives

No. 2917. Spear and Pen blades. Pocket blade full polished. Stag handle. Nickel silver bolster and cap. Brass lining. Crest shield. Size - 3 in.

No. 2085. Spear and Pen blades. Large blade full polished. Varicolored brilliant finish celluloid handle. Nickel silver bolster, cap and shield. Brass lining. Size - 3 in.

SERPENTINE PATTERN

No. 2097. Clip and pen blades, pocket blade full polished. Green celluloid handle. Nickel silver cap, bolster and crest shield. Brass lining. Size - 3 1/2 in.

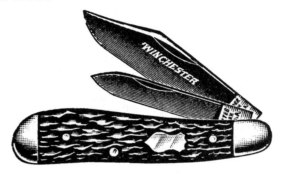

No. 2974. Clip and Pen blades. Pocket blade full polished. Stag handle. Nickel silver bolster, cap and crest shield. Brass lining. Size - 3 1/2 in.

No. 2999. Clip and Pen blades. Pocket blade full polished. Stag handle. Nickel silver bolster, candle end cap and crest shield. Brass lining. Size - 3 1/8 in.

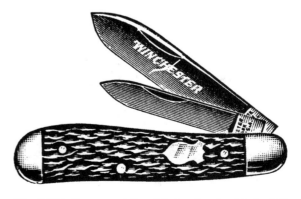

No. 2956. Spear and Pen blades. Pocket blade full polished. Stag handle. Nickel silver bolster, cap and crest shield. Brass lining. Size - 3 1/2 in.

No. 2638. Spear and Pen blades. Pocket blade full polished. Ebony handle. Nickel silver bolster, cap and crest shield. Brass lining. Size - 3 1/2 in.

No. 2990. Sabre Clip and Pen blades. Pocket blade full polished. Stag handle. Nickel silver bolster, cap and crest shield. Brass lining. Size - 2 7/8 in.

CROOKED JACK PATTERN

No. 1937. Sabre Clip Blade, full polished. Stag handle. Nickel silver bolster, lining, cap and crest shield. Size - 3 7/8 in.

No. 2993. Sabre Clip and Pen blades. Pocket blade full polished. Stag handle. Nickel silver bolster, lining, cap and crest shield. Size - 3 7/8 in.

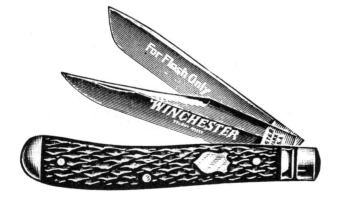

No. 2904. Sabre Clip and Large Spey blades. Pocket blade full polished. Stag handle. Nickel silver bolster, lining, cap and crest shield. Size - 3 7/8 in.

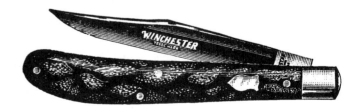

No. 1060. Large Saber Clip blade full polished. Red and black brilliant finish celluloid handle. Nickel silver bolster and shield. Brass lining. Size - 4 1/8 in.

GUNSTOCK JACK PATTERN

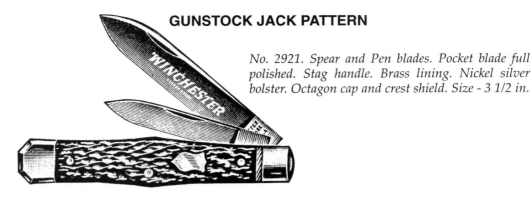

No. 2921. Spear and Pen blades. Pocket blade full polished. Stag handle. Brass lining. Nickel silver bolster. Octagon cap and crest shield. Size - 3 1/2 in.

BALLOON EQUAL END PATTERN

No. 2903. Spear and Pen blades. Pocket blade full polished. Stag handle. Brass lining. Nickel silver bolster and crest shield. Size - 3 1/2 in.

No. 2944. Spear and Pen blades. Pocket blade full polished. Stag handle. Nickel silver bolsters and crest shield. Brass lining. Size - 3 3/8 in.

No. 3902. Clip and two Pen blades. Pocket blade full polished. Stag handle. Brass lining. Nickel silver bolsters and crest shield. Cut swages. Size - 3 1/2 in.

No. 3994. Clip, Pen and Curley file blades. Pocket blade full polished. Stag handle. Nickel silver bolster and crest shield. Brass lining. Size - 3 3/8 in.

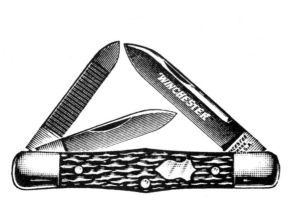

No. 3943. Spear, Pen and Curley file blades. Pocket blade full polished. Stag handle. Nickel silver bolster and crest shield. Brass lining. Size - 3 3/8 in.

SWELL CENTER FLUTED PATTERN

No. 2969. Clip and Spey blades. Clip blade full polished. Stag handle. Nickel silver bolster, lining and crest shield. Size - 3 7/8 in.

No. 2967. Spear and Clip blades. Spear blade full polished. Stag handle. Nickel silver bolster, lining and crest shield. Size - 3 7/8 in.

POWDER HORN OR TOOTHPICK PATTERN

No. 1936. Sabre Clip blade. Glazed finish. Stag handle. Steel cap and bolster. Brass lining. Size - 5 in.

No. 1050. Sabre Clip blade, glazed finish. Abalone celluloid handle. Steel cap and bolster. Brass lining. Size - 5 in.

No. 1051. Large Clip blade, full polished. Red and black brilliant finish celluloid handle. Nickel silver bolster, cap and shield. Brass lining. Size - 4 3/8 in.

SWELL HUNTING PATTERN

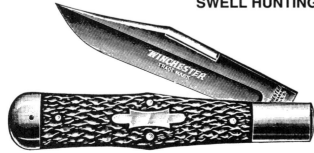

No. 1920. Sabre Clip blade, glazed finish. Stag handle. Nickel silver cap, bolster and shield. Brass lining. Lanyard hole. Size - 5 1/4 in.

SWAY BACK HUNTING PATTERN

No. 1950. Sabre Clip blade. Glazed finish. Genuine stag handle. Nickel silver bolsters and linings. Size - 5 3/8 in.

UTILITY OR MULTIPLE TOOL PATTERN

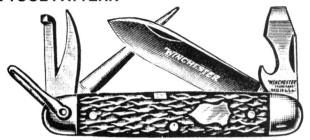

No. 4950. Long Flat Spear, Screwdriver and Cap Lifter combination, Can Opener and Punch blades. Stag handle. Nickel silver bolsters. Brass lining with steel center. Crest shield, Shackle. Size - 3 5/8 in.

No. 4901. Spear, Screwdriver and Cap Lifter combination, Can Opener and Punch blades. Stag handle. Nickel silver bolsters. Brass lining with steel center. Crest shield. Shackle. Size - 3 1/2 in.

YACHTMAN'S UTILITY KNIFE

No. 4951. Long flat Spear, Can Opener, Screwdriver and Cap Lifter combination, and Marlinspike blades. Pocket blade full polished. Stag handle. Nickel silver bolsters and guimpe shield. Brass lining with steel center lining. Shackle. Size - 3 5/8 in.

LIGHT PREMIUM STOCK PATTERN

No. 2919. Clip and Spey blades. Pocket blade full polished. Stag handle. Nickel silver bolsters, lining and crest shield. Size - 3 3/8 in.

No. 3012. Clip, Spey and Punch blades. Pocket blade full polished. Shell celluloid handle. Nickel silver bolster, lining and crest shield. Size - 3 3/8 in.

Winchester Pocket Knives • 303

No. 2972. Clip and Pen blades. Pocket blade full polished. Stag handle. Nickel silver bolsters, lining and crest shield. Size - 3 3/8 in.

No. 2632. Clip and Pen blades. Pocket blade full polished. Ebony handle. Nickel silver bolsters, lining and crest shield. Size - 3 3/8 in.

No. 3340. Full polished Clip, Spey and Sheepfoot blades. Pearl handle. Nickel silver bolsters, lining and crest shield. Size - 3 3/8 in.

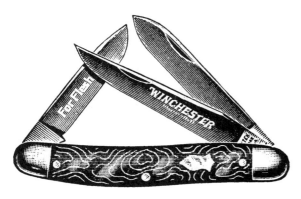

No. 3003. Clip, Spear and Spey blades. Pocket blade full polished. Golden celluloid handle. Nickel silver bolsters and lining. Crest shield. Size - 3 1/2 in.

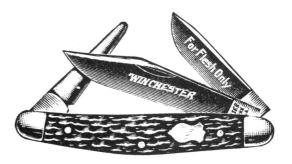

No. 3974. Clip, Spey and Punch blades. Pocket blade full polished. Stag handle. Nickel silver bolsters and lining. Crest shield. Size - 3 3/8 in.

No. 3941. Clip, Spey and Sheepfoot blades. Pocket blade full polished. Stag handle. Nickel silver bolsters, lining and crest shield. Size - 3 3/8 in.

No. 3917. Clip, Spear and Spey Blades. Pocket blade full polished. Stag handle. Nickel silver bolsters and lining. Crest shield. Size - 3 1/2 in.

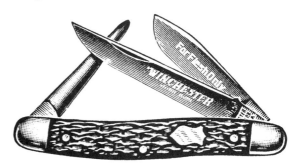

No. 3916. Clip, Spey and Punch blades. Pocket blade full polished. Stag handle. Nickel silver bolsters and lining. Crest shield. Size - 3 1/2 in.

HEAVY PREMIUM STOCKMAN PATTERN

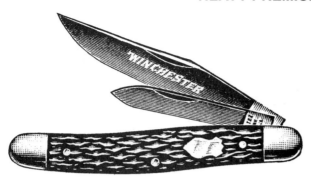

No. 2976. Clip and Pen blades. Pocket blade full polished. Stag handle. Nickel silver bolsters, lining and crest shield. Size - 4 in.

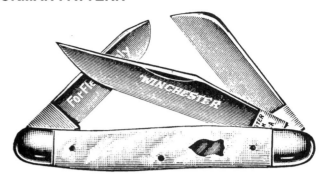

No. 3376. Clip, Sheepfoot and Spey blades. All blades full polished. Pearl handle. Nickel silver bolsters, lining and crest shield. Size - 4 in.

No. 3993. Clip, Spey and Pen blades. Pocket blade full polished. Stag handle. Nickel silver bolsters, lining and crest shield. Size - 4 in.

No. 3961. Clip, Spey and Punch blades. Pocket blade full polished. Stag handle. Nickel silver bolsters, lining and crest shield. Size - 4 in.

No. 3906. Clip, Sheepfoot and Spey blades. Pocket blade full polished. Stag handle. Nickel silver bolsters and lining. Crest shield. Size - 4 in.

No. 2923. Clip and Spey blades. Pocket blade full polished. Stag handle. Nickel silver bolsters, lining and crest shield. Size - 4 in.

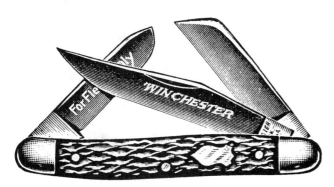

No. 3928. Clip, Sheepfoot and Spey blades. Pocket blade full polished. Stag handle. Nickel silver bolsters, lining and crest shield. Size - 4 in.

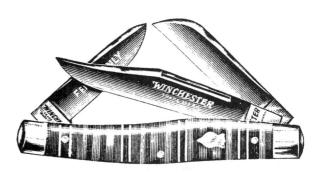

No. 3018. Clip, Sheep Foot and Spey blades. Pocket blade full polished. Red and white celluloid handle. Nickel silver bolsters, shield and lining. Size - 4 in.

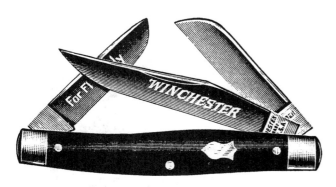

No. 3007. Clip, Sheepfoot and Spey blades. Pocket blade full polished. Black celluloid handle. Nickel silver bolsters, lining and crest shield. Size - 4 in.

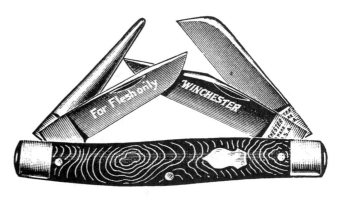

No. 4001. Clip, Sheepfoot, Spey and Punch blades. Pocket blade full polished. Green celluloid handle. Nickel silver bolsters and lining. Crest shield. Size - 4 in.

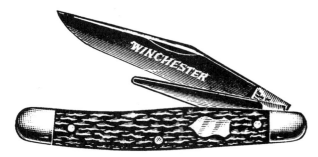

No. 2928. Clip and Punch blades. Pocket blade full polished. Stag handle. Nickel silver bolsters, lining and crest shield. Size - 4 in.

No. 3013. Clip, Spey and Punch blades. Pocket blade full polished. Green celluloid handle. Nickel silver bolsters, shield and lining. Size - 4 in.

No. 3907. Clip, Spey and Punch blades. Pocket blade full polished. Stag handle. Nickel silver bolsters and lining. Crest shield. Size - 4 in.

No. 4961. Clip, Sheepfoot, Spey and Punch blades. Pocket blade full polished. Stag handle. Nickel silver bolsters, lining and crest shield. Size - 4 in.

BALLOON CATTLE PATTERN

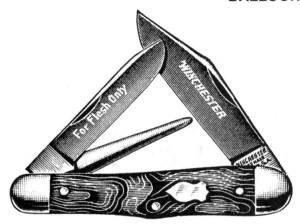

No. 3010. Clip, Spey and Punch blades. Pocket blade full polished. Three springs. Abalone celluloid handle. Nickel silver bolsters, lining and crest shield. Size - 3 3/4 in.

No. 3903. Clip, Spey and Punch blades. Pocket blade full polished. Three springs. Stag handle. Nickel silver lining. Nickel silver bolsters and crest shield. Size - 3 3/4 in.

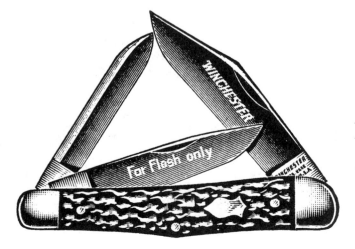

No. 3904. Clip, Spey and Pen blades. Pocket blade full polished. Three springs. Stag handle. Nickel silver bolsters and lining. Crest shield. Size - 3 3/4 in.

LIGHT CATTLE PATTERN

No. 3341. Spear, Sheepfoot and Spey blades. Full polished. Pearl handle. Nickel silver bolsters and lining. Crest shield. Size - 3 3/8 in.

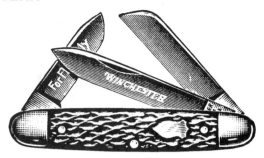

No. 3942. Spear, Sheepfoot and Spey blades. Pocket blade full polished. Stag handle. Nickel silver bolsters, lining and crest shield. Size - 3 3/8 in.

No. 3011. Clip, Spey and Punch blades. Pocket blade full polished. Gray celluloid handle. Nickel silver bolsters and lining. Crest shield. Size - 3 3/8 in.

No. 3975. Clip, Spey and Punch blades. Pocket blade full polished. Stag handle. Nickel silver bolsters and lining. Crest shield. Size - 3 3/8 in.

LIGHT BALLOON CATTLE PATTERN

No. 3001. Spear, Spey and Punch blades. Pocket blade full polished. Gray celluloid handle. Nickel silver bolsters and lining. Crest shield. Size - 3 1/2 in.

No. 3905. Spear, Spey and Punch blades. Pocket blade full polished. Stag handle. Nickel silver bolsters and lining. Crest shield. Size - 3 1/2 in.

CATTLE PATTERN

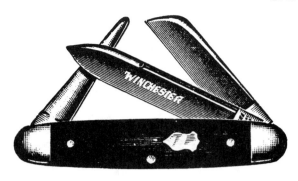

No. 3646. Spear, Sheepfoot and Punch blades. Pocket blade full polished. Ebony handle. Nickel silver bolsters, lining and crest shield. Size - 3 5/8 in.

No. 3937. Spear, Sheepfoot and Pen blades. Pocket Blade full polished. Stag handle. Nickel silver bolsters, lining and crest shield. Size - 3 5/8 in.

No. 3979. Flat Clip, Spey and Punch blades. Pocket blade full polished. Stag handle. Nickel silver bolsters, lining and crest shield. Size - 3 5/8 in.

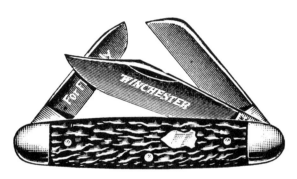

No. 3950. Flat Clip, Sheepfoot and Spey blades. Pocket blade full polished. Stag handle. Nickel silver bolsters, lining and shield. Size - 3 5/8 in.

No. 3008. Spear, Sheepfoot and Spey blades. Pocket blade full polished. White celluloid handle. Has steer's head on reverse side. Nickel silver bolster and lining. Size - 3 5/8 in.

No. 3936. Spear, Clip and Spey blades. Pocket blade full polished. Stag handle. Nickel silver bolsters, lining and crest shield. Size - 3 5/8 in.

Winchester Pocket Knives • 309

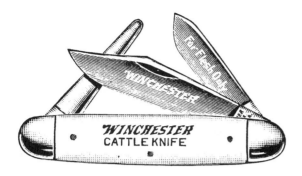

No. 3009. Flat Clip, Spey and Punch blades. Pocket blade full polished. White celluloid handle. Has steer's head on reverse side. Nickel silver bolsters and lining. Size - 3 5/8 in.

No. 3016. Flat Clip, Spey and Punch blades. Pocket blade full polished. Gray celluloid handle. Nickel silver bolsters, lining and crest shield. Size - 3 5/8 in.

No. 3976. Clip, Spey and Punch blades. All blades glazed finish. Stag handle. Nickel silver bolsters and shield. Nickel silver lining. Size - 3 3/8 in.

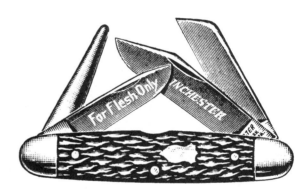

No. 4952. Clip, Spey, Sheepfoot and Punch blades. Pocket blade full polished. Stag handle. Nickel silver bolsters, lining and crest shield. Size - 3 5/8 in.

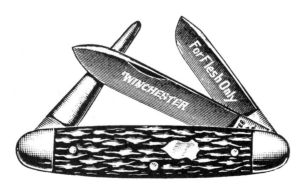

No. 3951. Spear, Spey and Punch blades. Pocket blade full polished. Stag handle. Nickel silver bolsters, lining and crest shield. Size - 3 5/8 in.

BALLOON SLEEVEBOARD PATTERN

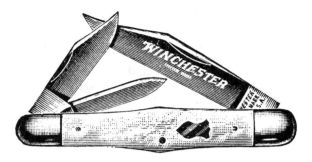

No. 3365. Flat Clip, Small Clip and Pen blades full polished. Pearl handle. Nickel silver bolsters and lining. Crest shield. Size - 3 5/8 in.

No. 3925. Sabre Clip, Small Clip and Pen blades. Pocket blade full polished. Stag handle. Nickel silver bolsters and lining. Crest shield. Size - 3 5/8 in.

No. 3908. Flat Clip, Pen and Punch blades. Pocket blade full polished. Stag handle. Nickel silver bolsters and lining. Crest shield. Size - 3 5/8 in.

No. 2908. Flat Clip and Pen blades. Pocket blade full polished. Stag handle. Nickel silver bolsters and lining. Crest shield. Size - 3 5/8 in.

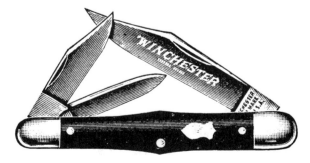

No. 3005. Flat Clip, Small Clip and Pen blades. Pocket blade full polished. Black celluloid handle. Nickel silver bolsters and lining. Crest shield. Size - 3 5/8 in.

No. 3002. Flat Clip, Spey and Punch blades. Pocket blade full polished. Iridescent celluloid handle. Nickel silver bolsters and lining. Crest shield. Size - 3 5/8 in.

Winchester Pocket Knives • 311

WHARNCLIFFE PATTERN

No. 2202. Spear and Pen blades. Pocket blade full polished. Smooth fibre handle. Nickel silver turned edge. Size - 3 in.

No. 2912. Spear and Pen blades. Pocket blade full polished. Stag handle. Nickel silver tips, lining and crest shield. Size - 3 in.

No. 2312. Spear and Pen blades. Full polished. Pearl handle. Nickel silver tips, lining and crest shield. Size - 3 in.

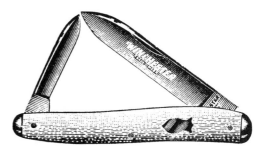

No. 2090. Spear and Pen blades. Large blade full polished. Silvelour finish celluloid handle. Nickel silver tips, shield and lining. Size - 3 in.

No. 2067. Spear and Pen blades, Large blade full polished. Pearl celluloid handle. Nickel silver tips and lining. Size - 3 1/8 in.

No. 2081. Spear and Pen blades. Pocket blade full polished. Shell celluloid handle. Nickel silver tips, lining and crest shield. Size - 3 in.

CARBO PATTERN

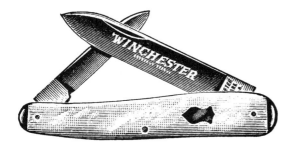

No. 2362. Spear and Pen blades. Full polished. Pearl handle. Nickel silver tips and lining. Crest shield. Size - 3 3/8 in.

No. 2088. Spear and Pen blades. Pocket blade full polished. Gray celluloid handle. Nickel silver tips. Crest shield. Size - 3 3/8 in.

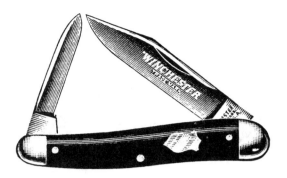

No. 2078. Clip and Pen blades. Pocket blade full polished. Black celluloid handle. Nickel silver bolsters and lining. Crest shield. Size - 3 3/8.

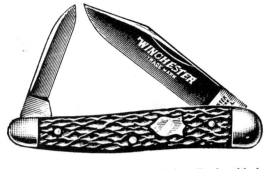

No. 2997. Clip and Pen blades. Pocket blade full polished. Stag handle. Nickel silver bolsters, lining, and crest shield. Size - 3 3/8 in.

No. 3927. Spear, Pen and File blades. Pocket blade full polished. Stag handle. Nickel silver bolsters, lining and crest shield. Size - 3 3/8 in.

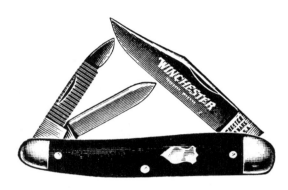

No. 3006. Clip, Pen and File blades. Pocket blade full polished. Black celluloid handle. Nickel silver bolsters and lining. Crest shield. Size - 3 3/8 in.

No. 2918. Spear and Pen blades. Pocket blade full polished. Stag handle. Nickel silver tips and lining. Crest shield. Size - 3 3/8 in.

LARGE SLEEVEBOARD PATTERN

No. 3995. Spear and two Pen blades. Pocket blade full polished. Stag handle. Nickel silver bolsters and crest shield. Brass lining. Size - 4 in.

HEAVY SLEEVEBOARD PATTERN

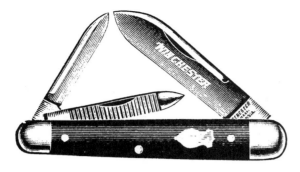

No. 3660. Spear, Pen and Curley File blades. Pocket blade full polished. Ebony handle. Nickel silver bolster and crest shield. Brass lining. Size - 3 1/2 in.

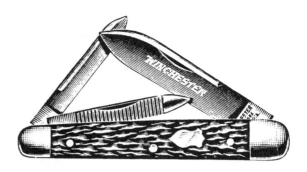

No. 3954. Spear, Pen and Curley File blades. Pocket blade full polished. Stag handle. Nickel silver bolster and crest shield. Brass lining. Size - 3 1/2 in.

LARGE CONGRESS PATTERN

No. 2996. Sheepfoot and Pen blades. Pocket blade full polished. Stag handle. Nickel silver rat-tail bolsters and curved bar shield. Brass lining. Size - 3 3/4 in.

HEAVY CONGRESS PATTERN

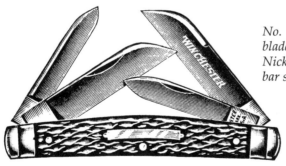

No. 4902. Two Large Sheepfoot and two Pen blades. Sheepfoot blades full polished. Stag handle. Nickel silver rat-tail bolsters. Brass lining. Curved bar shield. Size - 4 1/8 in.

CONGRESS PATTERN

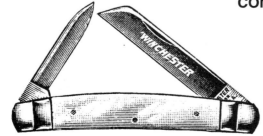

No. 2331. Sheepfoot and Pen blades. Full polished. Pearl handle. Nickel silver rat-tail bolsters. Nickel silver lining. Size - 3 1/4 n.

No. 2095. Sheepfoot and Pen blades. Pocket blade full polished. Shell celluloid handle. Nickel silver smooth bolsters and lining. Size - 3 1/4 in.

No. 3929. Sheepfoot, Pen and File blades. Pocket blade full polished. Stag handle. Nickel silver rat-tail bolsters. Nickel silver lining and curved bar shield. Size - 3 1/4 in.

No. 2932. Sheepfoot and Pen blades. Stag handle. Pocket blade full polished. Nickel silver rat-tail bolsters and lining. Curved bar shield. Size - 3 1/4 in.

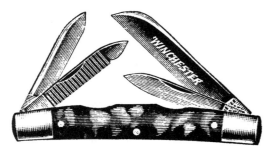

No. 4005. Sheepfoot, File and two Pen blades. Pocket blade full polished. Shell celluloid handle. Nickel silver smooth bolsters and lining. Size - 3 1/4 in.

No. 4930. Sheepfoot, File and two Pen blades. Pocket blade full polished. Stag handle. Nickel silver rat-tail bolsters and lining. Curved bar shield. Size - 3 1/4 in.

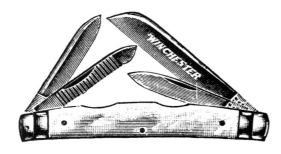

No. 4330. Sheepfoot, File and two Pen blades. Full polished. Pearl handle. Nickel silver rat-tail bolsters. Nickel silver lining. Size - 3 1/4 in.

SLIM SLEEVEBOARD PATTERN

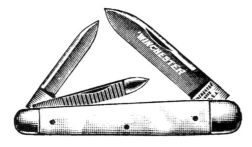

No. 3378. Spear, Pen and File blades. Full polished. Pearl handle. Nickel silver bolsters and lining. Size - 3 in.

No. 2368. Spear and Pen blades. Full polished. Pearl handle. Nickel silver tips and lining. Size - 3 in.

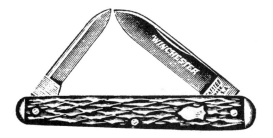

No. 2933. Spear and Pen blades. Pocket blade full polished. Stag handle. Nickel silver tips, lining and crest shield. Size - 3 in.

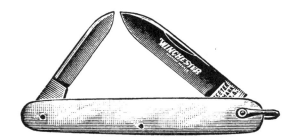

No. 2367. Spear and Pen blades. Full polished. Pearl handle, shadow end. Nickel silver lining. Shackle. Size - 3 in.

SLEEVEBOARD PATTERN

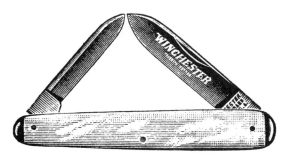

No. 2366. Spear and Pen blades. Full polished. Pearl handle. Nickel silver tips and lining. Size - 3 1/4 in.

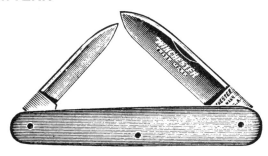

No. 2100. Spear and Pen blades. Pocket blade full polished. Celluloid handle, assorted colors. Nickel lining. Size - 3 3/8 in.

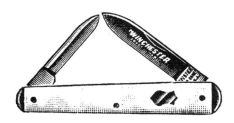

No. 2369. Spear and Pen blades. Full polished. Pearl handle. Nickel silver tips, shield and lining. Size - 2 5/8 in.

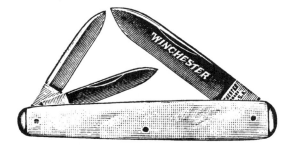

No. 3377. Spear and two Pen blades, all full polished. Pearl handle. Nickel silver tips and lining. Size - 3 1/4 in.

No. 2938. Spear and Pen blades. Pocket blade full polished. Stag handle. Nickel silver tips and lining. Crest shield. Size - 3 1/4 in.

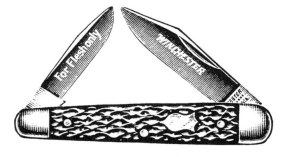

No. 2914. Long Clip and Spey blades. Pocket blade full polished. Stag handle. Nickel silver bolsters. lining and crest shield. Size - 3 1/4 in.

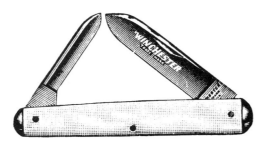

No. 2082. Spear and Pen blades. Large blade full polished. Pearl celluloid handle. Nickel silver tips and lining. Size - 3 1/8 in.

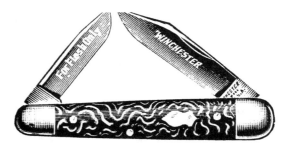

No. 2084. Long Clip and Spey blades. Pocket blade full polished. Blue celluloid handle. Nickel silver bolsters, lining and crest shield. Size - 3 1/4 in.

No. 2068. Clip and Pen blades. Large blade full polished. Fancy red and black brilliant finish celluloid handle. Nickel silver bolsters, shield and lining. Size - 3 3/8 in.

No. 2052. Spear and Pen blades. Pocket blade full polished. Pearl celluloid handle. Nickel silver tip, and lining. Size - 2 5/8 in.

No. 2631. Spear and Pen blades. Pocket blade full polished. Ebony handle. Nickel silver bolsters, lining and shield. Size - 3 1/4 in.

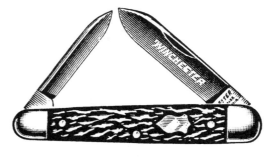

No. 2943. Spear and Pen blades. Pocket blade full polished. Stag handle. Nickel silver bolsters, lining and crest shield. Size - 3 1/4 in.

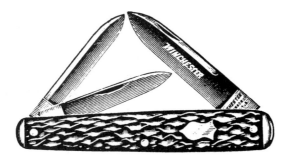

No. 3991. Spear and two Pen blades. Pocket blade full polished. Stag handle, Nickel silver tips and lining. Crest shield. Size - 3 1/4 in.

SMALL SENATOR PATTERN

No. 2902. Spear and Pen blades. Pocket blade full polished. Stag handle. Nickel silver bolsters and lining. Size - 2 5/8 in.

No. 2303. Spear and File blades full polished. Pearl handle. Nickel silver tips and lining. Size - 2 5/8 in.

No. 2306. Spear and File blades. Pocket blade full polished. Short Pearl handle. Long nickel silver bolsters and lining. Size - 2 5/8 in.

No. 2377. Spear and Pen blades. All blades full polished. Pearl handle. Nickel silver bolsters and lining. Size - 2 5/8 in.

No. 3351. Spear, Pen and French File blades, all full polished. Pearl handle. Nickel silver tips and lining. Size - 2 5/8 in.

No. 3914. Spear, Pen and French File blades. Pocket blade full polished. Stag handle. Nickel silver tips and lining. Size - 2 5/8 in.

No. 2375. Spear and File blades, both full polished. Pearl handle. Nickel silver bolsters and lining. Shackle. Size - 2 5/8 in.

No. 2334. Spear and Pen blades, both full polished. Pearl handle, shadow end. Nickel silver lining. Size - 2 5/8 in.

No. 2056. Spear and File blades. Pocket blade full polished. Golden celluloid handle. Nickel silver tips and lining. Size - 2 5/8 in.

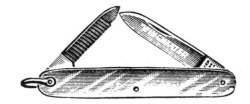

No. 2211. Spear and File blades full polished. Nickel silver skeleton handle. Flush rivets. Shackle. Size - 2 5/8 in.

No. 2206. Spear and Pen blades, both full polished. Nickel silver skeleton handle. Flush rivets. Size - 2 5/8 in.

SLIM SENATOR PATTERN

No. 2965. Spear and Pen blades. Pocket blade full polished. Stag handle. Nickel silver tips, lining and crest shield. Size - 3 1/8 in.

No. 2378. Spear and Pen blades, both full polished. Shadow-end pearl handle. Nickel silver lining and small crest shield. Size - 3 1/8 in.

No. 2204. Spear and Pen blades, both full polished. Nickel silver skeleton handle with flush rivets. Size - 3 1/8 in.

SENATOR PATTERN

No. 2058. Spear and Pen blades. Large blade full polished. Abalone (blue) celluloid handle. Nickel silver bolsters, shield and lining. Size - 3 1/8 in.

Winchester Pocket Knives • 319

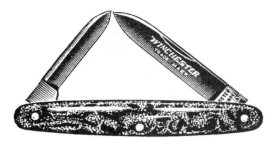

No. 2055. Large Spear Point and Pen blades. Large blade full polished. Red and black brilliant finish celluloid handle. Brass Lining. Size - 3 1/4 in.

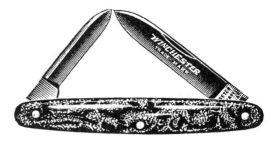

No. 2054. Large Spear Point and Pen blades. Large blade full polished. Green and black brilliant finish celluloid handle. Brass Lining. Size - 3 1/4 in.

No. 2059. Spear and Pen blades. Large blade full polished. Iridescent celluloid handle. Nickel silver bolsters, shield and lining. Size - 3 1/8 in.

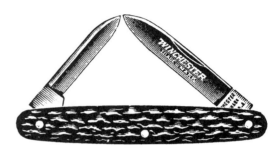

No. 2830. Large Spear Point and Pen blades. Large blade full polished. Stag handle. Brass lining. Size - 3 1/4 in.

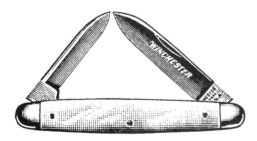

No. 2376. Spear and Pen blades, both full polished. Pearl handle. Nickel silver bolsters and lining. Size - 3 in.

No. 2374. Spear and Pen blades, both full polished. Pearl handle. Nickel silver tips, lining and crest shield. Shackle. Size - 3 in.

No. 2057. Spear and Pen blades. Large blade full polished. Varicolored brilliant finish celluloid handle. Nickel silver bolsters, shield and lining. Size - 3 3/8 in.

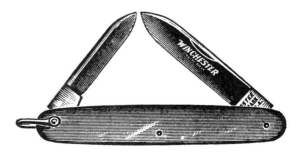

No. 2201. Spear and Pen blades, both full polished. Nickel silver skeleton handle. Flush rivets. Shackle. Size - 3 1/4 in.

No. 2344. Spear and Pen blades, full polished. Pearl handle. Nickel silver lining, crest shield and tips. Size - 3 1/4 in.

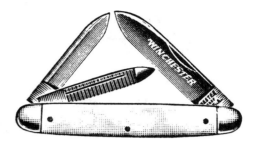

No. 3379. Spear, Pen and Curley File blades, all full polished. Pearl handle. Nickel silver bolsters and lining. Size - 3 in.

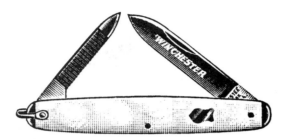

No. 2379. Spear and File blades, full polished. Pearl handle. Nickel silver tips, lining and crest shield. Size - 3 1/4 in.

No. 3345. Spear, Pen and File blades, all full polished. Shadow end pearl handle. Nickel silver lining and crest shield. Size - 3 1/4 in.

No. 3924. Spear, Pen and Curley File blades. Pocket blade full polished. Stag handle. Nickel silver bolsters, lining and crest shield. Size - 3 in.

No. 2963. Spear and Pen blades. Pocket blade full polished. Stag handle. Nickel silver bolsters, lining and crest shield. Size - 3 in.

No. 2945. Spear and Pen blades. Pocket blade full polished. Stag handle. Nickel silver tips, lining and crest shield. Size - 3 1/4 in.

No. 2981. Spear and File blades. Pocket blade full polished. Stag handle. Nickel silver tips, lining and crest shield. Has Shackle on end. Size - 3 1/4 in.

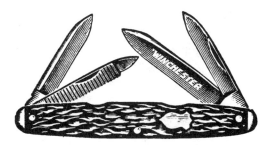

No. 4941. Spear, two Pen and File blades. Pocket blade full polished. Stag handle. Nickel silver lining, tips and crest shield. Size - 3 1/4 in.

No. 3944. Spear, Pen and File blades. Pocket blade full polished. Stag handle. Nickel silver tips, lining and crest shield. Size - 3 1/4 in.

No. 3343. Spear and two Pen blades, all full polished. Pearl handle. Nickel silver bolsters, lining and crest shield. Size - 3 1/4 in.

No. 4340. Spear, two Pen and File blades, all full polished. Pearl handle. Nickel silver bolsters, lining and crest shield. Size - 3 1/4 in.

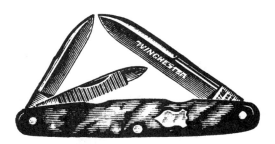

No. 3022. Spear, Pen and File blades. Pocket blade full polished. Shell celluloid handle. Nickel silver lining and crest shield. Shadow end. Size - 3 1/4 in.

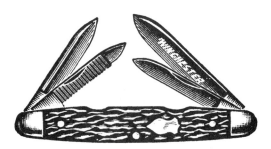

No. 4940. Spear, two Pen and File blades. Pocket blade full polished. Stag handle. Nickel silver bolsters, lining and crest shield. Size - 3 1/4 in.

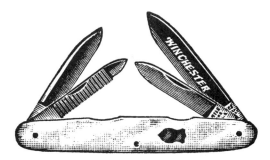

No. 4331. Spear, two Pen and File blades, all full polished. Shadow end pearl handle. Nickel silver lining and crest shield. Size - 3 1/4 in.

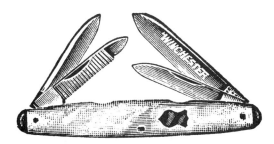

No. 4341. Spear, two Pen and File blades, all full polished. Pearl handle. Nickel silver tips, lining and crest shield. Size - 3 1/4 in.

LARGE SENATOR PATTERN

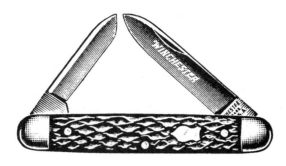

No. 2934. Spear and Pen blades. Pocket blade full polished. Stag handle. Nickel silver bolsters, lining and crest shield. Size - 3 3/8 in.

No. 3909. Clip, Pen and Spey blades. Pocket blade full polished. Stag handle. Nickel silver bolsters and lining. Crest shield. Size - 3 3/8 in.

No. 3366. Spear, Pen and Curley File blades, all are full polished. Pearl handle. Nickel silver lining, bolsters and crest shield. Size - 3 3/8 in.

LARGE SLIM SENATOR PATTERN

No. 2948. Spear and Pen blades. Pocket blade full polished. Stag handle. Nickel silver bolsters, lining and crest shield. Size - 3 3/8 in.

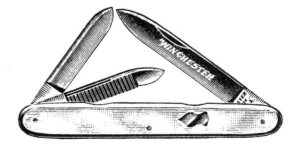

No. 3368. Spear, Pen and File blades, all full polished. Pearl square edge handle with shadow end. Nickel silver lining and crest shield. Size - 3 3/8 in.

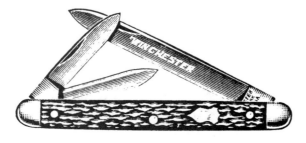

No. 3992. Spear and two Pen blades. Pocket blade full polished. Stag handle. Nickel silver bolsters, lining and crest shield. Size - 3 3/8 in.

PHYSICIAN'S PATTERN

No. 2380. Spear and Pen blades, both full polished. Pearl handle. Nickel silver bolster, cap, and lining. Size - 3 1/2 in.

No. 2978. Spear and Pen blades. Pocket blade full polished. Stag handle. Nickel silver bolster, cap and lining. Crest shield. Size - 3 1/2 in.

OFFICE PATTERN

No. 2079. Spear and Eraser blades. Pocket blade full polished. White celluloid handle marked "Office Knife." Shadow ends. Nickel silver lining. Size - 3 3/8 in.

No. 2089. Spear and Eraser blades. Pocket blade full polished. White celluloid handle marked "Office Knife." Shadow ends. Nickel silver lining. Size - 3 3/4 in.

SLEEVEBOARD LOBSTER PATTERN

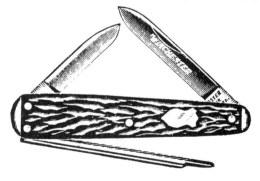

No. 3931. Spear, Pen and Pick File blades, all full polished. Stag handle. Nickel silver tips, lining and crest shield. Size - 3 1/8 in.

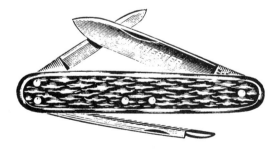

No. 3235. Spear, Pen and Pick File blades. Fibre stag handle with turned edge. Nickel silver lining. Size - 3 1/8 in.

No. 3331. Spear, Pen and Pick File blades, all full polished. Pearl handle. Nickel silver tips, milled lining and crest shield. Sunk joints. Size - 3 1/8 in.

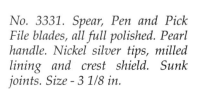

SMALL SLEEVEBOARD LOBSTER PATTERN

No. 3901. Spear, Pen and Pick File blades, all full polished. Stag handle. Nickel silver tips, lining and crest shield. Size - 2 3/4 in.

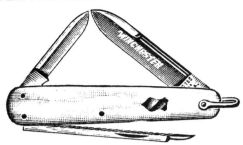

No. 3380. Spear, Pen and Pick File blades, all full polished. Shadow-end Pearl handle. Nickel silver milled lining and crest shield. Shackle. Size - 2 3/4 in.

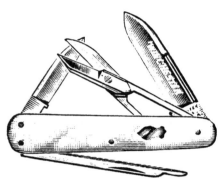

No. 4301. Spear, Pen, Scissors and Pick File blades, all full polished. Shadow-end Pearl handle. Nickel silver milled lining and crest shield. Size - 2 3/4 in.

No. 3301. Spear, Pen and Pick File blades, all full polished. Shadow-end pearl handle. Nickel silver milled lining and crest shield. Size - 2 3/4 in.

ORANGE BLOSSOM LOBSTER PATTERN

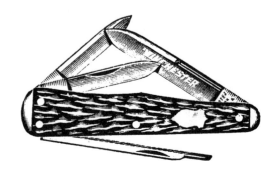

No. 4920. Spear, two Pen and Pick File blades, all full polished. Stag handle. Nickel silver tips, milled lining and crest shield. Size - 3 1/4 in.

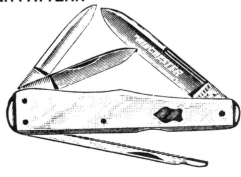

No. 4320. Spear, two Pen and Pick File blades, all full polished. Flat Pearl square-edge handle. Nickel silver tips, small crest shield and milled lining. Size - 3 1/4 in.

FISH CANDLE END LOBSTER PATTERN

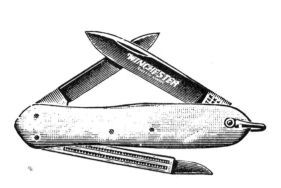

No. 3370. Spear, Pen and French File blades, all full polished. Pearl handle with shadow ends. Nickel silver milled lining. Shackle. Size - 3 in.

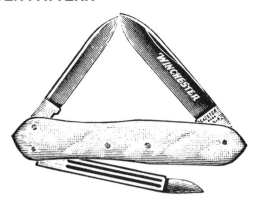

No. 3382. Spear, Pen and French File blades, all full polished. Pearl handle, shadow ends. Nickel silver milled lining. Size - 3 in.

CURVED BALLOON LOBSTER PATTERN

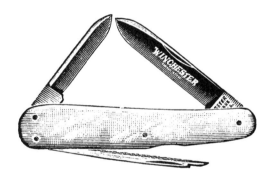

No. 3374. Spear, Pen and Pick File blades, all full polished. Pearl handle with shadow end. Nickel silver milled lining. Size - 3 1/8 in.

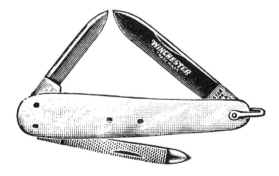

No. 3381. Spear, Pen and Flexible File blades, all full polished. Skeleton Pearl handle. Shackle on end. Size - 3 1/8 in.

SERPENTINE LOBSTER PATTERN

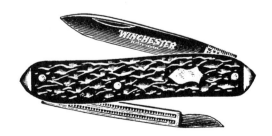

No. 2910. Spear and French File blades, both full polished. Stag handle. Nickel silver tips, lining and crest shield. Size - 3 in.

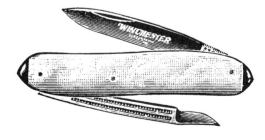

No. 2356. Spear and French File blades, full polished. Pearl handle. Nickel silver tips. Nickel silver milled lining. Size - 3 in.

Stainless Steel Pocket Knives

REGULAR JACK PATTERN

No. 2861. Clip and Pen stainless steel blades. Pocket blade full polished. Stag handle. Nickel silver bolster, cap, shield and lining. Size - 3 1/4 in.

No. 2860. Spear and Pen stainless steel blades. Pocket blade full polished. Stag handle. Nickel silver bolster, cap, shield and lining. Size - 3 1/4 in.

LIGHT PREMIUM STOCK PATTERN

No. 2989. Clip and Spey stainless steel blades, all full polished. Genuine stag handle. Nickel silver bolsters, lining and crest shield. Size - 3 3/8

SLEEVEBOARD PATTERN

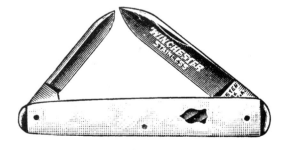

No. 2335. Spear and Pen stainless steel blades, all full polished. Pearl handle. Nickel silver tips, lining and crest shield. Size - 3 1/4 in.

SENATOR PATTERN

No. 3353. Spear, Pen and French File stainless steel blades, all full polished. Pearl handle. Nickel silver tip and lining. Shackle on end. Size - 2 5/8 in.

No. 2205. Spear and Pen stainless steel blades, all full polished. Nickel silver engine turned handle. Shackle. Size - 3 1/2 in.

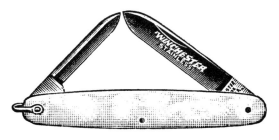

No. 2336. Spear and Pen stainless steel blades, full polished. Pearl handle, shadow ends. Nickel silver lining. Shackle. Size - 3 1/2 in.

No. 2215. Spear and Pen stainless steel blades, all full polished. Nickel silver handle. Size - 3 1/2 in.

No. 3352. Spear, Pen and File stainless steel blades, all full polished. Pearl handle, shadow ends. Nickel silver lining. Size - 3 1/2 in.

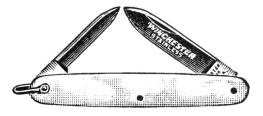

No. 2337. Spear and Pen stainless steel blades, all full polished. Pearl handle, shadow ends. Nickel silver lining. Shackle on end. Size - 2 5/8 in.

Numerical List of Knife Models and Values

Here is the numerical list (from lowest to highest) of Winchester pocket knife model numbers that we're currently aware of. If we have an illustration or photograph and full description of the knife, we will refer you to the prior section with the phrase "See Detailed Description."

If we did not have a Winchester paraphrased description of the model, we will give you a thumbnail sketch here. The size given is closed.

We have also provided a single value for the knife in mint condition, expressed in U.S. dollars. As with other Winchester products, assume that if the knife you have is in its original box (and both the box and the knife are in mint condition), you can conservatively double the values we present here.

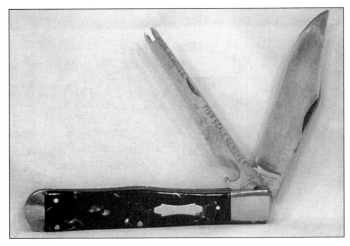

A rare two-bladed version of the basic Model 1920 Folding Hunter. This is sometimes called a "Fisherman's Knife" because the second blade is both a "Hook Remover" and a serrated "Fish Scale Remover" and also has a bottle opener. Both blades have the Winchester stamp. Handle is black smooth celluloid with a few white swirls in it. Value in mint condition is $1,500. From T. Webster collection. Photo by D. Kowalski.

Model	Description	Value
1050	See Detailed Description	350
1051	See Detailed Description	350
1060	See Detailed Description	325
1068	Cocobolo handle. Size - 3 3/8"	125
1201	Jack pattern, easy opener, sheepfoot blade, Nickel silver. Size - 3 3/8"	225
1605	See Detailed Description	115
1608	See Detailed Description	125
1610	See Detailed Description	150
1611	Mariner's Knife, Cocobolo handle. Size - 3 1/4"	120
1613	Maize pattern, Cocobolo handle. Size - 3 3/8"	165
1614	Maize pattern, Cocobolo handle. Size - 4 1/8"	165
1621	Budding pattern, ebony handle. Size - 4 3/4"	175
1624	Maize pattern. Size - 4"	150
1632	See Detailed Description	125
1633	See Detailed Description	150
1701	See Detailed Description	225
1703	Barlow pattern, smooth bone handle. Size - 5"	475
1704	Barlow, bone stag handle, easy opener. Size - 5"	625
1785	See Detailed Description	250
1905	See Detailed Description	325
1920	See Detailed Description	1,275

Model	Description	Value
1921	See Detailed Description	175
1922	Stag handle. Size - 3 3/8"	175
1923	Stag handle. Size - 4 1/8"	275
1924	Powder horn pattern, stag handle. Size - 4 1/4"	375
1925	Jack pattern, stag handle. Size - 3 1/2"	325
1936	See Detailed Description	375
1937	See Detailed Description	225
1938	See Detailed Description	150
1950	See Detailed Description	1,500
2028	See Detailed Description	200
2037	Jack pattern, celluloid handle. Size - 3"	150
2038	Jack pattern, pearl celluloid handle. Size - 3"	195
2039	Jack pattern, celluloid handle. Size - 3 "	125
2047	Equal-end jack pattern, white celluloid handle. Size - 4 1/4"	325
2051	Senator pattern, white celluloid handle. Size - 2 5/8"	175
2052	Senator pattern, pearl celluloid tip bolsters. Size - 2 5/8"	125
2053	Senator pattern, celluloid handle. Size - 2 5/8"	145

Model	Description	Value
2054	See Detailed Description	115
2055	See Detailed Description	115
2056	See Detailed Description	125
2057	See Detailed Description	150
2058	See Detailed Description	150
2059	See Detailed Description	140
2067	See Detailed Description	175
2068	See Detailed Description	225
2069	See Detailed Description	250
2070	See Detailed Description	200
2078	See Detailed Description	200
2079	See Detailed Description	175
2080	See Detailed Description	150
2081	See Detailed Description	200
2082	See Detailed Description	200
2083	See Detailed Description	200
2084	See Detailed Description	225
2085	See Detailed Description	200
2086	See Detailed Description	175
2087	See Detailed Description	200
2088	See Detailed Description	175
2089	See Detailed Description	190
2090	See Detailed Description	175
2094	See Detailed Description	275
2095	See Detailed Description	150
2096	See Detailed Description	200
2097	See Detailed Description	150
2098	See Detailed Description	250
2099	See Detailed Description	210
2106	See Detailed Description	185
2107	Dog leg pattern, gold celluloid handle. Size - 2 3/4"	185
2109	Sleeveboard pattern, gold celluloid handle. Size - 2 7/8"	135
2110	Jack pattern, celluloid tear drop handle. Size - 3 1/2"	175
2111	Jack, celluloid. Size - 3 1/2"	175
2112	Jack, celluloid. Size - 3 1/2"	175
2113	Peanut, celluloid. Size - 2 3/4"	150
2114	Candle end pattern, celluloid handle. Size - 3"	175
2115	Sleeveboard pattern, pearl celluloid handle. Size - 2 7/8"	185
2116	Sleeveboard pattern, celluloid handle. Size - 3 3/8"	175
2117	Serpentine jack pattern, black celluloid handle. Size - 3 1/8"	200
2201	See Detailed Description	125
2202	See Detailed Description	105
2204	See Detailed Description	125
2205	See Detailed Description	150
2206	See Detailed Description	100
2207	Jack pattern, easy opener, nickel silver. Size - 3 3/8"	185
2208	Jack pattern, nickel silver. Size - 3 3/8"	185
2211	See Detailed Description	125
2215	See Detailed Description	105
2301	Senator pattern, pearl without bail. Size - 2 1/4"	150
2302	Senator pattern, pearl with bail. Size - 2 1/4"	175
2303	See Detailed Description	185
2306	See Detailed Description	175
2307	Senator pattern, pearl handle. Size - 2 7/8"	175
2308	Senator pattern, pearl handle. Size - 2 7/8"	175
2309	Senator pattern, pearl handle. Size - 3"	200
2312	See Detailed Description	250
2314	Serpentine jack pattern, pearl handle. Size - 3"	250
2316	Serpentine jack pattern, pearl handle. Size - 3"	250
2317	Serpentine jack pattern, pearl handle. Size - 3"	225
2320	Sleeveboard pattern, pearl handle. Size - 2 7/8"	150
2324	Senator pattern pen knife, pearl handle. Size - 3"	200
2330	Senator pattern pen knife, pearl handle. Size - 3 1/4"	200
2331	See Detailed Description	300
2334	See Detailed Description	125
2335	See Detailed Description	325
2336	See Detailed Description	175
2337	See Detailed Description	250
2338	Senator pattern, pearl handle. Size - 3 1/4"	225
2340	See Detailed Description	200
2344	See Detailed Description	225
2345	Senator pattern, pearl handle. Size - 3 1/4"	225
2346	Lobster pattern, pearl handle. Size - 3"	225
2352	See Detailed Description	200
2356	See Detailed Description	275
2361	See Detailed Description	200
2362	See Detailed Description	200
2363	Congress pattern, pearl handle. Size - 3"	250

Model	Description	Value
2366	See Detailed Description	325
2367	See Detailed Description	225
2368	See Detailed Description	225
2369	Senator pattern, pearl handle. Size - 2 5/8"	225
2374	See Detailed Description	175
2375	See Detailed Description	175
2376	See Detailed Description	175
2377	See Detailed Description	225
2378	See Detailed Description	175
2379	See Detailed Description	200
2380	See Detailed Description	625
2603	See Detailed Description	185
2604	See Detailed Description	200
2605	See Detailed Description	225
2606	See Detailed Description	225
2608	See Detailed Description	200
2610	Jack pattern, Cocobolo handle. Size - 3 3/8"	200
2611	Serpentine jack pattern, Cocobolo handle. Size - 3"	175
2612J	ack pattern, Cocobolo handle. Size - 3 5/8"	250
2613	Jack pattern, Cocobolo handle. Size - 3 5/8"	225
2614	Jack pattern, Cocobolo handle. Size - 3 5/8"	225
2615	See Detailed Description	125
2616	See Detailed Description	125
2627	See Detailed Description	200
2629	Jack pattern, ebony handle. Size - 3 1/2"	225
2630	See Detailed Description	225
2631	See Detailed Description	150
2632	See Detailed Description	200
2633	Premium stockman pattern, ebony handle. Size - 3 1/4"	200
2635	See Detailed Description	175
2636	See Detailed Description	200
2637	See Detailed Description	150
2638	See Detailed Description	225
2640	Balloon jack pattern, ebony handle. Size - 3 3/4"	350
2641	Trapper pattern, Cocobolo handle. Size - 3 7/8"	425
2647	See Detailed Description	175
2648	See Detailed Description	150
2649	See Detailed Description	250
2660	See Detailed Description	225
2661	See Detailed Description	225
2662	See Detailed Description	225
2665	See Detailed Description	200
2666	Jack pattern, ebony handle. Size - 3 3/8"	175
2681	See Detailed Description	200
2690	Texas jack pattern, ebony handle. Size - 4 1/2"	525
2701	See Detailed Description	300
2702	Barlow pattern, bone handle, spey and pen blades. Size - 3 1/2"	350
2703	See Detailed Description	325
2820	Jack pattern, bone handle. Size - 3 3/8"	225
2830	See Detailed Description	175
2840	Stag handle, Size - 2"	200
2841	Stag handle, Size - 3"	200
2842	Senator pattern, stag handle. Size - 3 1/4"	225
2843	Stag handle, Size - 3 3/8"	225
2844	See Detailed Description	300
2845	See Detailed Description	275
2846	Premium stockman pattern, stag handle.	225
2847	Senator pattern, spey and pen blades, brown bone handle. Size - 3 1/4"	200
2848	Jack pattern, stag handle with chain. Size - 3 1/2"	225
2849	Jack pattern, stag handle. Size - 3 3/8"	275
2850	Jack 2-blade coke pattern, stag handle. Size - 3 3/4"	475
2851	Gunstock jack pattern, stag handle. Size - 3"	325
2852	Serpentine cattle pattern, stag handle. Size - 3"	325
2853	Jack pattern, stag handle. Size - 3 3/8"	275
2854	Jack pattern, stag handle. Size - 3 3/8"	225
2855	Jack pattern, stag handle. Size - 3 3/8"	225
2856	Dog leg pattern, stag handle. Size - 2 3/4"	250
2857	Serpentine jack pattern, stag handle. Size - 3 1/8"	275
2858	Serpentine jack pattern, stag handle. Size - 3"	200
2859	Serpentine jack pattern, stag handle. Size - 3 1/8"	
2860	See Detailed Description	275
2861	See Detailed Description	275
2862	Sleeveboard pattern, stag handle. Size - 3 3/8"	250

Model	Description	Value
2863	Congress pattern, stag handle. Size - 3 1/4"	325
2864	Swell center pattern, stag handle. Size - 3 3/8"	325
2865	Swell center pattern, stag handle. Size - 3 1/2"	350
2866	Senator pattern, stag handle. Size - 2 7/8"	200
2867	Senator pattern, stag handle. Size - 3 3/8"	200
2868	Equal-end pen pattern, stag handle. Size - 3 3/8"	200
2869	Gunstock pattern, stag handle. Size - 3 3/4"	425
2870	Gunstock pattern, stag handle. Size - 3 3/4"	425
2871	Gunstock pattern, stag handle. Size - 3 3/4"	425
2872	Gunstock pattern, stag handle. Size - 3 3/4"	425
2874	Jack pattern, stag handle. Size - 3 1/2"	275
2875	Premium stockman pattern, stag handle. Size - 3 1/4"	325
2876	Small muskrat pattern, brown bone handle, clip and spey blades. Size - 3 1/4"	375
2878	Texas jack pattern, stag handle. Size - 4 1/4"	475
2879	Sleeveboard jack pattern, stag handle. Size - 4 1/2"	925
2880	Half whittler pattern, stag handle. Size - 4 1/2"	525
2881	English jack pattern, stag handle. Size - 4 1/2"	525
2901	See Detailed Description	225
2902	See Detailed Description	130
2903	See Detailed Description	300
2904	See Detailed Description	625
2905	See Detailed Description	625
2906	See Detailed Description	350
2907	See Detailed Description	625
2908	See Detailed Description	300
2910	See Detailed Description	175
2911	See Detailed Description	225
2912	See Detailed Description	300
2914	See Detailed Description	225
2917	See Detailed Description	275
2918	See Detailed Description	250
2919	See Detailed Description	250
2921	See Detailed Description	475
2923	See Detailed Description	275
2924	Congress pattern, stag handle. Size - 3"	275
2925	See Detailed Description	225
2926	See Detailed Description	300
2927	See Detailed Description	300
2928	See Detailed Description	325
2930	See Detailed Description	325
2931	See Detailed Description	225
2932	See Detailed Description	275
2933	See Detailed Description	200
2934	See Detailed Description	175
2938	See Detailed Description	225
2940	See Detailed Description	275
2943	See Detailed Description	225
2944	See Detailed Description	250
2945	See Detailed Description	175
2948	See Detailed Description	225
2949	See Detailed Description	275
2950	See Detailed Description	225
2951	See Detailed Description	250
2952	See Detailed Description	250
2954	See Detailed Description	275
2955	See Detailed Description	300
2956	See Detailed Description	275
2958	See Detailed Description	275
2959	See Detailed Description	325
2961	Jack pattern, stag handle. Size - 3 3/8"	225
2962	See Detailed Description	200
2963	See Detailed Description	200
2964	See Detailed Description	275
2965	See Detailed Description	200
2966	See Detailed Description	275
2967	See Detailed Description	525
2969	See Detailed Description	350
2971	See Detailed Description	300
2972	See Detailed Description	300
2973	See Detailed Description	275
2974	See Detailed Description	275
2976	See Detailed Description	175
2978	See Detailed Description	625
2980	See Detailed Description	275
2981	See Detailed Description	200
2982	See Detailed Description	345
2983	See Detailed Description	225
2984	See Detailed Description	250
2987	See Detailed Description	300
2988	See Detailed Description	350
2989	See Detailed Description	300
2990	See Detailed Description	250
2991	Serpentine peanut pattern, brown bone handle. Size - 2 3/8"	250

Model	Description	Value
2992	See Detailed Description	275
2993	See Detailed Description	525
2994	See Detailed Description	275
2995	See Detailed Description	275
2996	See Detailed Description	325
2997	See Detailed Description	250
2998	See Detailed Description	250
2999	See Detailed Description	300
3001	See Detailed Description	425
3002	See Detailed Description	400
3003	See Detailed Description	375
3005	See Detailed Description	425
3006	See Detailed Description	425
3007	See Detailed Description	425
3008	See Detailed Description	475
3009	See Detailed Description	475
3010	See Detailed Description	525
3011	See Detailed Description	450
3012	See Detailed Description	400
3013	See Detailed Description	500
3014	Premium stockman pattern, pearl celluloid handle. Size - 4"	525
3015	Swell center pattern, gold celluloid handle. Size - 3 5/8"	425
3016	See Detailed Description	475
3017	Premium stockman, variegated celluloid handle. Size - 4"	475
3018	See Detailed Description	525
3019	Whittler pattern, red celluloid handle. Size - 4"	475
3020	Whittler pattern, celluloid handle. Size - 3 1/2"	425
3022	See Detailed Description	375
3023	Whittler pattern, red celluloid handle. Size - 3 5/8"	425
3024	Whittler pattern, celluloid handle. Size - 3 5/8"	425
3025	Premium stockman, abalone (blue) celluloid handle. Size - 3 1/2"	375
3026	Premium stockman, variegated celluloid handle. Size - 3 1/4"	375
3027	Premium stockman, red celluloid handle. Size - 3 1/4"	275
3028	Premium stockman pattern, celluloid handle. Size - 3 1/4"	350
3029	Premium stockman pattern, celluloid handle. Size - 3 1/4"	325
3030	Senator pattern, abalone (blue) celluloid handle. Size - 3 3/8"	325
3031	Senator pattern, gray celluloid handle. Size - 3 3/8"	375
3033	Serpentine pattern, gold celluloid handle. Size - 3"	325
3034	Serpentine cattle pattern, abalone (blue) celluloid handle. Size - 3"	325
3035	Gold celluloid handle. Size - 3 3/8"	325
3036	Cattle pattern, celluloid handle. Size - 3 3/8"	325
3040	Whittler pattern, celluloid handle. Size - 3"	325
3041	Senator pattern, celluloid handle. Size - 3"	325
3042	Senator pattern, celluloid handle. Size - 3 3/8"	300
3043	Senator pattern, celluloid handle. Size - 3 3/8"	300
3044	Senator pattern, celluloid handle. Size - 3 3/8"	300
3045	Whittler pattern, celluloid handle. Size - 3 1/4"	325
3046	Whittler pattern, celluloid handle. Size - 3 1/4"	325
3047	Premium stockman, celluloid Handle. Size - 3 1/2"	300
3048	Premium stockman, celluloid Handle. Size - 4"	425
3049	Cattle pattern, imitation white bone handle. Size - 3 5/8"	425
3235	See Detailed Description	150
3301	See Detailed Description	175
3331	See Detailed Description	200
3338	Sleeveboard pattern, pearl handle. Size - 3"	200
3340	See Detailed Description	400
3341	See Detailed Description	525
3343	See Detailed Description	400
3345	See Detailed Description	425
3347	Whittler pattern, pearl handle. Size - 3 1/4"	425
3349	Sleeveboard whittler pattern, pearl handle. Size - 3"	375
3350	Whittler senator pattern, pearl handle. Size - 3 1/4"	325
3351	See Detailed Description	200
3352	See Detailed Description	325
3353	See Detailed Description	250
3357	Senator pattern, pearl handle. Size - 3 1/8"	425
3360	Bartender pattern, pearl handle. Size - 3 1/4"	425
3361	Equal-end cattle pattern, pearl handle. Size - 3 3/4"	525
3365	See Detailed Description	450
3366	See Detailed Description	375
3368	See Detailed Description	400
3370	See Detailed Description	225

Model	Description	Value
3371	Lobster pattern, pearl handle. Size - 3"	250
3373	Whittler senator pattern, pearl handle. Size - 2 7/8"	300
3374	See Detailed Description	200
3376	See Detailed Description	600
3377	See Detailed Description	325
3378	See Detailed Description	325
3379	See Detailed Description	325
3380	See Detailed Description	225
3381	See Detailed Description	225
3382	See Detailed Description	225
3625	Cattle pattern, ebony handle. Size - 3 5/8"	325
3646	See Detailed Description	350
3660	See Detailed Description	350
3901	See Detailed Description	200
3902	See Detailed Description	425
3903	See Detailed Description	1,000
3904	See Detailed Description	1,000
3905	See Detailed Description	425
3906	See Detailed Description	475
3907	See Detailed Description	525
3908	See Detailed Description	425
3909	See Detailed Description	325
3911	Senator whittler pattern, stag handle. Size 3"	325
3914	See Detailed Description	250
3915	Swell center (balloon) cattle pattern, stag handle. Size - 3 1/2"	350
3916	See Detailed Description	350
3917	See Detailed Description	325
3924	See Detailed Description	250
3925	See Detailed Description	425
3927	See Detailed Description	325
3928	See Detailed Description	475
3929	See Detailed Description	425
3931	See Detailed Description	225
3932	Senator whittler pattern, stag handle. Size - 3 3/8"	350
3933	Senator whittler pattern, stag handle. Size - 3 3/8"	325
3936	See Detailed Description	475
3937	See Detailed Description	450
3938	Senator whittler pattern, stag handle. Size - 3 3/8"	325
3939	Senator whittler pattern, stag handle. Size - 3 3/8"	325
3941	See Detailed Description	350
3942	See Detailed Description	350
3943	See Detailed Description	300
3944	See Detailed Description	325
3948	Reverse gunstock pattern, brown bone handle. Size - 3 5/8"	625
3949	Serpentine cattle pattern, stag handle. Size - 3"	275
3950	See Detailed Description	425
3951	See Detailed Description	425
3952	Cattle pattern, brown bone handle. Size - 3 3/4"	425
3953	Bartender pattern, stag handle. Size - 3 1/4"	325
3954	See Detailed Description	400
3959	Stockman pattern, brown bone handle. Size - 4"	475
3960	Premium stockman pattern, stag handle. Size - 4"	475
3961	See Detailed Description	475
3962	Premium stockman pattern, buffalo horn handle. Size - 4"	425
3963	Stockman pattern, stag handle. Size - 4"	475
3964	Premium stockman pattern, stag handle. Size - 4"	475
3965	Premium stockman pattern, stag handle. Size - 3 1/4"	375
3966	Premium stockman pattern, stag handle. Size - 3 1/4"	375
3967	Premium stockman pattern, stag handle. Size - 3 1/4"	375
3968	Whittler pattern, stag handle. Size - 3 1/4"	375
3969	Premium stockman whittler pattern, stag handle. Size - 3 1/4"	375
3971	Swell center whittler pattern, stag handle. Size - 3 5/8"	425
3972	Swell center whittler pattern, stag handle. Size - 3 5/8"	425
3973	Cattle pattern, stag handle. Size - 3 1/2"	375
3974	See Detailed Description	400
3975	See Detailed Description	425
3976	See Detailed Description	450
3977	Cattle pattern, stag handle. Size - 3 3/8"	375
3978	Serpentine stockman pattern, brown bone handle. Size - 3 1/4"	350
3979	See Detailed Description	425
3980	Serpentine cattle pattern, stag handle. Size - 3"	350
3991	See Detailed Description	375
3992	See Detailed Description	375
3993	See Detailed Description	475
3994	See Detailed Description	300

Model	Description	Value
3995	See Detailed Description	500
4001	See Detailed Description	475
4005	See Detailed Description	400
4301	See Detailed Description	250
4313	Senator pattern, pearl handle. Size - 3"	325
4320	See Detailed Description	400
4330	See Detailed Description	450
4331	See Detailed Description	250
4340	See Detailed Description	325
4341	See Detailed Description	325
4901	See Detailed Description	425
4902	See Detailed Description	800
4910	Utility or multiple blade pattern, stag handle. Size - 3 3/4"	625
4918	Congress pattern, stag handle. Size - 3"	325
4920	See Detailed Description	400
4930	See Detailed Description	375
4931	Congress pattern, stag handle. Size - 3 1/2"	425
4940	See Detailed Description	300
4941	See Detailed Description	325
4950	See Detailed Description	525
4951	See Detailed Description	425
4952	See Detailed Description	525
4961	See Detailed Description	525
4962	Premium stockman pattern, stag handle. Size - 4"	525
4963	Premium stockman pattern, stag handle. Size - 4"	525
4975	Bartender pattern, stag handle. Size - 3 1/4"	425
4990	Utility pattern, stag handle. Size - 3 5/8"	425
4991	Utility pattern, stag handle. Size - 3 1/2"	475

Pocket Knife Boxes and Assortments

Winchester typically shipped knives to retail accounts in boxes containing six knives, each individually wrapped in paper. In some cases, collectors have discovered these boxes without the knives; those were already sold. We will show a few examples of such empty boxes and price them. They are sought after by both general Winchester collectors and Winchester knife collectors.

Values:

	Exc	VG	Good
	175.00	125.00	75.00

Comment: *Values are for empty six-knife boxes only.*

Four pocket knife boxes (some brightly colored) that each originally contained six pieces. The individual knives were either wrapped in paper or held in a paper sleeve. From the bottom, these boxes were for models 2681; 3011; 2958; and 2846. From T. Webster collection. Photo by D. Kowalski.

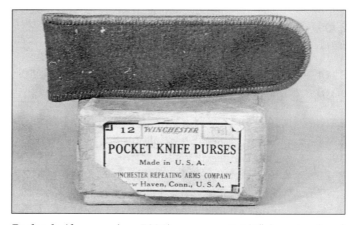

Pocket knife purse (no. 7031) measures 3 3/8" long in closed position and 1" wide. It was made of gray suede. Some had flap without snap; others had flap with snap. Some also had "The Winchester Store" printed on them in black ink. From T. Webster collection. Photo by D. Kowalski.

Values:

	Exc	VG	Good
	200.00	175.00	150.00

Comment: *Values are for the purse only.*

Winchester also created several different knife assortments through the years. These, too, were shipped to retail accounts with a selection of models, grouped in various ways. These were either cardboard or wood boxes that could be converted to counter displays. They were generally available in 12- and 36-knife boxes.

Some of these displays were shipped as self-contained counter displays. Other displays and trays could be purchased. Finally, still other displays were also offered as free or low-cost premiums to retailers who qualified with different levels of purchase.

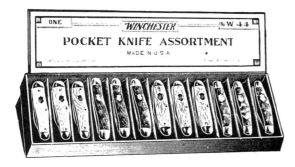

Pocket Knife Assortment (W44) consists of 12 cattle and stock knives, three each of models 3012, 3011, 3003 and 3001. This would have been a likely display for a rural or Western retailer. The cardboard case box is black Karatol covered and constructed to permit converting into a counter display box with the lithographed label on flap facing the customer. This example is 15 in. long x 4 1/4 in. wide x 1 in. high.

Values: | Exc | VG | Good
| 4,500.00 | 4,000.00 | 3,500.00

Comment: *Values are for complete assortment with box and all twelve knives in mint condition. Obviously the box with its complement of original knives would bring the highest price. Some collectors, however, might try to piece together a version with the box and/or some of the knives in less than mint condition or with knives of different model numbers. Then pricing becomes a much more complex exercise that really depends more on the condition and rarity of the individual pieces. Winchester grouped these knife assortments in various ways, quite often by handle material.*

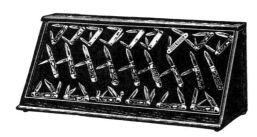

Wood Show Case for Pocket Knife Assortment. Has mahogany finish slanting glass front with removable felt-covered tray. Case is 28 1/2 in. long x 10 1/2 in. wide at base; and 3 3/8 in. wide at the top. Has hinged cover. Height at back is 12 in. Also has compartment for duplicate stock, with hinged door and friction ball catch.

Values: | Exc | VG | Good
| 1,500.00 | 1,400.00 | 1,200.00

Comment: *Values are for the case only.*

Another style of wood display case for Pocket Knife Assortment (No. 2454). Wood display case is 15 1/4 in. square, painted black. Has 11 3/4 in. x 14 1/2 in. heavy glass front. Winchester label in color at top. Equipped with easel back for upright display on counters or in showcase. Three cardboard trays are black Karatol-covered, cloth-lined and racked for 12 knives each; they slide out at the right side.

Values: | Exc | VG | Good
| 1,800.00 | 1,500.00 | 1,200.00

Comment: *Values are for the case only.*

Wooden showcase display tray (No. 3151) with plain bottom covered in green "plush." Wood frame is stained and finished oak. Measures 7 3/4" x 11 3/4".

Values: | Exc | VG | Good
| 500.00 | 400.00 | 300.00

Comment: *Values are for the case only.*

Wooden showcase 20-compartment display tray (No. 3161) is ideally suited to pocket knife display. All trays and dividers covered in green "plush" or felt. Wood frame is stained oak. Measures 7 3/4" x 11 3/4".

Values: | **Exc** | **VG** | **Good**
| 600.00 | 500.00 | 400.00

Comment: *Values are for the case only.*

Larger wooden showcase display tray (No. 3162) for pocket knife display holds 30 pieces, 10 compartments in each of the three rows. All trays and dividers covered in green "plush" or felt. Wood frame is stained and finished oak. Measures 11 3/4" x 11 3/4". From T. Webster collection. Photo by D. Kowalski.

Values: | **Exc** | **VG** | **Good**
| 900.00 | 800.00 | 600.00

Comment: *Values are for the case only.*

Larger wooden showcase display tray (No. 3152) with plain bottom covered in green "plush" or felt. Wood frame is stained and finished oak. Measures 11 3/4" x 11 3/4".

Values: | **Exc** | **VG** | **Good**
| 600.00 | 500.00 | 400.00

Comment: *Values are for the case only.*

Winchester - Bright and Beautiful

Some Winchester collectors will collect anything the company produced during its "Golden Age" prior to 1931. Nevertheless, they all have their favorite pieces. They're often the same pieces sought by collectors who are not especially focused on Winchester products. These collectibles are enthusiastically pursued, in large part, because of their bright colors and realistic, beautifully rendered graphics.

The Winchester advertising people instinctively knew that bright packaging sells. The outdoorsman of 80 years ago also responded to wildlife subjects and outdoor scenes. We present some of these bright and beautiful collectibles here in full color.

We have also included several pieces from virtually every area where Winchester supplied products. Some of these are quite rare. If you've enjoyed seeing these colorful treasures, you'll treasure **Winchester Rarities**, coming in the fall of 2000. It's filled with more rarely seen Winchester collectibles, particularly their broad range of five-panel advertising displays, posters, calendars and other specialties, all in vibrant color.

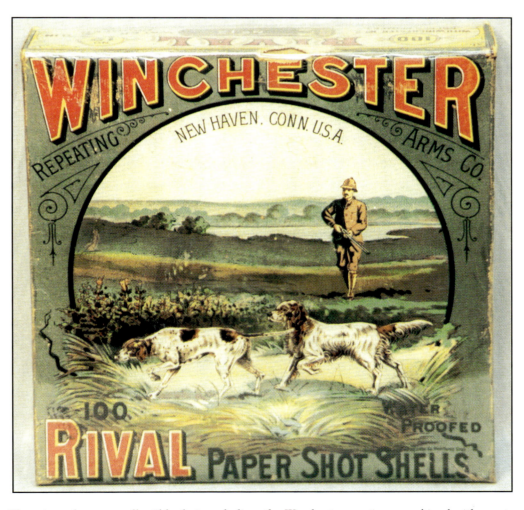

There is perhaps no collectible that symbolizes the Winchester mystique combined with great graphics more than the so-called "Christmas Box" shown here in the Rival brand in 12 gauge (empties). One of the rare variations of this box containing Star brand shells sold at auction in early 2000 for more than $39,000. From T. Webster collection. Photo by D. Kowalski.

Three other side panels of the "Christmas Box" are equally colorful and stunning. From T. Webster collection. Photo by D. Kowalski.

The highly collectible "Pheasant" boxes of Repeater shells from the 1940s. These came in 10, 12, 16, 20 and 28 gauge and Brush loads. Here is one of only two known full sets of the five boxes. From T. Melcher collection. Photo by TIM.

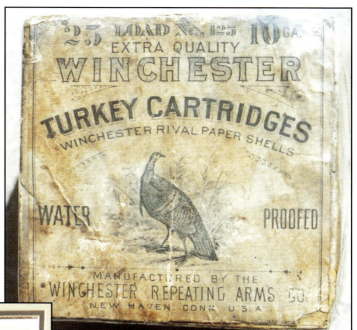

The earliest box of Rival loaded shells in a 25-round box. This is the only example that has ever been found. From T. Melcher collection. Photo by TIM.

Even if you're not a Winchester collector, you've got to be impressed by the world-class quality of the painting on this "Cock of the Woods" poster from the first decade of the 1900s. From T. Webster collection. Photo by D. Kowalski.

A rare treat for shotshell box fans! A box of 12 gauge Leader Brush shells that have never been seen in another book. From TIM collection. Photo by T. Melcher.

Retailers could telegraph their orders to Winchester using codes for each product supplied in this book entitled "Winchester Telegraph Code." Here's the frontispiece from the 1905 second edition. From Daniel Shuey collection. Photo by D. Kowalski.

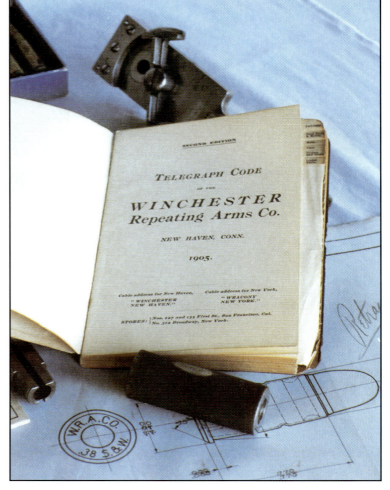

Large leather revolver holster is 11 inches from top of belt loop to barrel end. "Winchester" logo clearly stamped on narrow safety strap. There is currently only one of these known to have been found. From T. Webster collection. Photo by D. Kowalski.

Extremely rare full tube of Leather Dressing; the only one (full or partial) that has ever been found to date. Consumable items have always been more scarce than the non-consumable ones. From T. Webster collection. Photo by D. Kowalski.

Winchester launched one of its most collectible series of cartridge boxes in 1940 when it put its new Silvertip bullets in the colorful Grizzly Bear box. Fortunately for collectors, they are not particularly rare although they are getting hard to find in good condition. From R.T. Giles collection. Photo by M. Allyson.

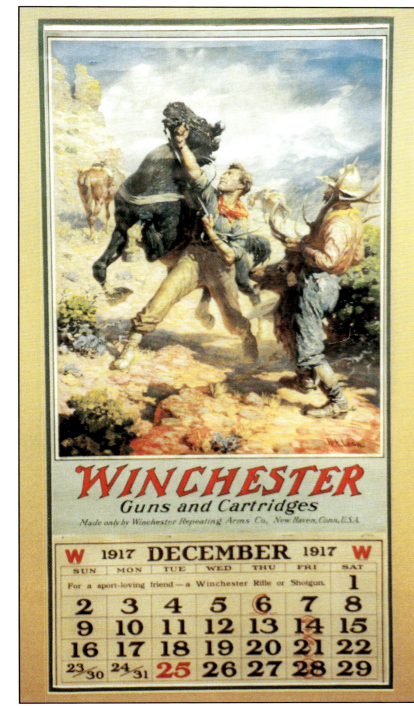

The 1917 Calendar painted by W.K. Leigh, is sought after by Winchester collectors and also by collectors of both Western and cowboy art, making it one of the higher-priced calendars. From T. Webster collection. Photo by D. Kowalski.

Two double-bodied lions are a rare visual on a Winchester box. Collectors speculate this .22 box from the late 'teens or early 1920s was for export. From the Ray T. Giles collection. Photo by D. Kowalski.

Two woven fiber or canvas cartridge belts, each slightly more than 1" wide. A grizzly bear head has been stamped on each. Bottom buckle (the smaller of two sizes available) is nickel-plated and the insert piece has an inscription that reads, "Pat. Feb. 15, 1881." The top buckle is rarer and has bronze plating on it; the insert piece does not have an inscription. Many collectors are not aware Winchester made two versions. From Tom Webster collection. Photo by D. Kowalski.

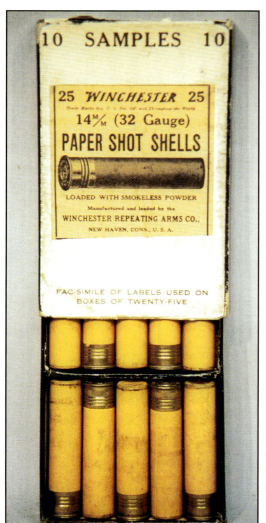

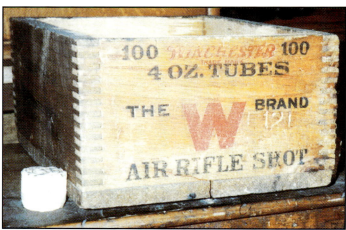

Wooden boxes for ammunition are another fascinating area of Winchester collectibles with many variations. In fact, a wooden box holding 5,000 rounds recently came on the market. Such large boxes apparently were sent to live bird shoots and other competitions. This box (pictured) for Winchester 4 oz. Tubes of Air Rifle Shot is in excellent condition with clear graphics. From Curt Bowman collection. Photo by C. Bowman.

Rare box of early "Repeater" samples, 32 gauge. These boxes of ten 10 loaded shells are among the rarest of the Repeater boxes. Shells were packed head to tail in two compartments. From the Tom Webster collection. Photo by D. Kowalski.

Another rare and colorful box in excellent condition; this one for the Model 58 bolt-action, single-shot .22 rifle. Box is 23 1/4" long. From Tom Webster collection. Photo by D. Kowalski.

Winchester organized shooting matches starting in the late 'teens to promote the Winchester Junior Rifle Corps. This two-sided counter display promoted the first ones held in Camp Perry, OH. From the Tom Webster collection. Photo by D. Kowalski.

Very rare and colorful box in excellent condition for the Model 02 bolt-action, single-shot .22 rifle. This was one of the rifle options offered in the Winchester Junior Rifle Corps Range Kits. Box is 23" long. From Tom Webster collection. Photo by D. Kowalski.

Four pocket knife boxes (some brightly colored) that each originally contained six pieces. The individual knives were either wrapped in paper or held in a paper sleeve. From the bottom, these boxes were for models 2681; 3011; 2958; and 2846. From T. Webster collection. Photo by D. Kowalski.

Counter pad for gun departments in retail stores. Versions with all-red type are the rarest. From T. Webster collection. Photo by D. Kowalski.

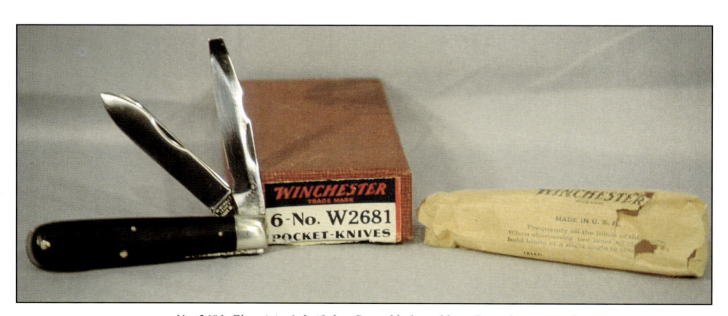

No. 2681. Electrician's knife has Spear blade and long Screwdriver-tipped cutting blade. Ebony handle. We've also shown the paper sleeve that held the knife inside the "6-pak" box. From T. Webster collection. Photo by D. Kowalski.

This stunning 1897/1898 "Double W" Winchester cartridge display board holds more than 215 original Winchester shotshells and cartridges. Central scene was adapted from the top scene of the 1895 Winchester wall calendar painted by A.B. Frost. Curt Bowman has made this board the centerpiece that dominates one side of a display room. Photo by C. Bowman.

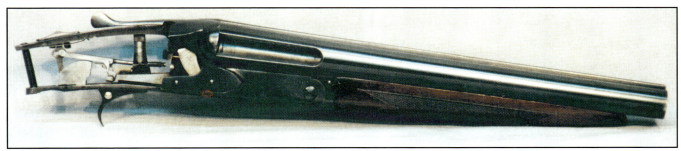

Winchester produced ten cutaways of the Model 21 shotgun, all bearing serial numbers. This one, serial number 5161, is the only one owned by a private party. From the Tom Webster Collection. Photo by D. Kowalski.

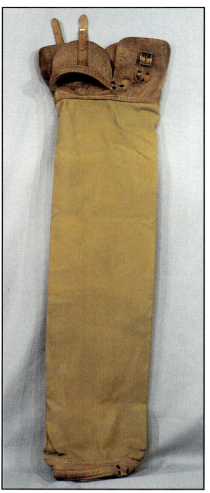

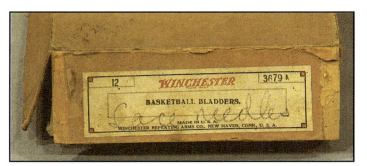

Box for Basketball Bladders is not in good shape but it's rare, like many basketball products. From T. Webster collection. Photo by D. Kowalski.

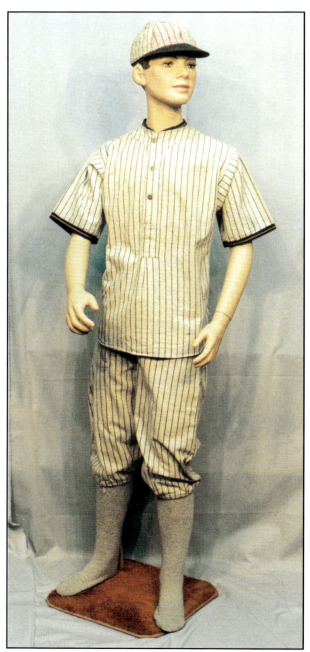

Model 1933 bat bag holds six bats. This bag was never used. Measures about 37 inches when closed. From T. Webster collection. Photo by D. Kowalski.

Boy's Baseball Uniform on manikin with the only known original cap. Gray with blue stripes (No. 7495). From T. Webster collection. Photo by D. Kowalski.

Model 1935 bat bag holds two bats. Another unused bag in excellent condition. Measures 35 1/2 inches closed. From T. Webster collection. Photo by D. Kowalski.

Boy's Footballl Uniform on manikin includes Helmet (model 3243), Shoulder Pads (model 3203), and Pants (model 3282). The jersey and socks are not original Winchester items. From T. Webster collection. Photo by D. Kowalski.

Boys' Football Helmet (model 3236) on a manikin has ¼ inch of felt lining covered by artificial leather. Shoulder Pads are model 3204. From T. Webster collection. Photo by D. Kowalski.

Three footballs stacked - High School (No. 3003) on left; Intercollegiate (No. 3000) on right; American Boy Rugby Football on top. All in excellent condition with clear logo stamps. From T. Webster collection. Photo by D. Kowalski.

Model 3806. Boxing Gloves with box. A set of gloves, two pair, came with this box. The original box more than doubles the value of the gloves. From T. Webster collection. Photo by D. Kowalski.

This No. 3844 Striking Bag probably saw only limited use. The "Winchester" logo and model No. are very clearly stamped in the leather just above the centerline of the bag (although they are not visible in this photograph). From T. Webster collection. Photo by D. Kowalski.

Striking Bag Disk looks like a bicycle wheel with a wooden tire. To the unitiated finder, this item is unique enough to keep, yet the owner or his or her heirs didn't realize there was other hardware that went with the whole kit. That would explain why these disks have sometimes gotten separated from the rest of the hardware. From T. Webster collection. Photo by D. Kowalski.

The only pair of Handball Gloves (of either style) we're aware of that have ever been found. These were never used. From T. Webster collection. Photo by D. Kowalski.

A stabilizer frame for a tennis racket will nearly double the value of the racket it holds. From T. Webster collection. Photo by D. Kowalski.

These three right-hand drivers with wood handles include two older examples with plain "non-corrugated" hitting face on the club. From T. Webster collection. Photo by D. Kowalski.

The tips of this pair of 7-foot cross country skis are typical of the design of all five lengths Winchester sold. Winchester used decals on this product line and they could be worn off by rough use or too much exposure to moisture and sunlight. From T. Webster collection. Photo by D. Kowalski.

Here is the only authentic pair of Winchester snowshoes of which we're aware. Each member of this pair measures 39 3/8" long. From T. Webster collection. Photo by D. Kowalski.

Hockey pucks are difficult to find in excellent condition. From T. Webster collection. Photo by D. Kowalski.

The only tennis ball retail display box that has ever been found. From T. Webster collection. Photo by D. Kowalski.

This is the only can of tennis balls that has ever been found, and it was still factory sealed at the time of this photo in late 1999. From Richard Hecht collection. Photo by R. Hecht.

Now the world knows what a Winchester tennis ball looks like. From the rare can owned by Richard Hecht. Photo by R. Hecht.

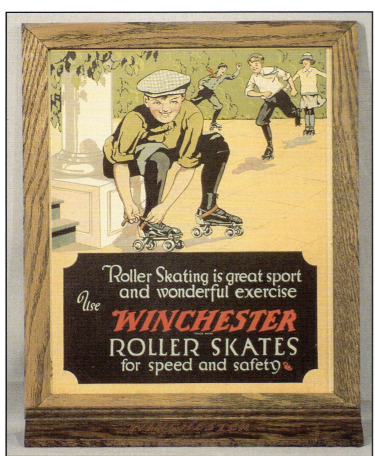

Roller Skates counter sign is from the 1920s. The other side of this reversible display promotes Red W Brand House Paint. Live matter area of sign measures 12 7/8" wide x 16 1/4" high. From T. Webster collection. Photo by D. Kowalski.

Box of Roller Skate Ankle Pads. Winchester designed them (shown front and back) with double slots for the leather skate straps so the skater could use the outer slots first. When they broke, the straps could be inserted through the inside slots. From T. Webster collection. Photo by D. Kowalski.

This box of Roller Skate Rolls (resting on one end) shows the effects of holding its heavy contents. The individual rolls are not marked. From T. Webster collection. Photo by D. Kowalski.

Box for Roller Skates from the 1960s really piles on the advertising claims ... "The Skate with a Backbone, Most Mileage, Utmost Strength, Light Weight, Free Wheeling." From T. Webster collection. Photo by D. Kowalski.

Model WS2. Coaster Wagon has box that can slide backward and off to create a flat-bed-type wagon. Actual measurements of the box of the pictured wagon are 34 7/8" long x 14 3/4" wide x 5" high. From T. Webster collection. Photo by D. Kowalski.

Model WS1. This is the Junior Coaster Wagon with a stationary box. Actual measurements of the box of the pictured wagon are 30 3/4" long x 14 3/4" wide x 4 1/8" high. From T. Webster collection. Photo by D. Kowalski.

Boy's Bicycle is painted light brown (that almost looks "metallic") with white trim. This one has a wire front basket. From T. Webster collection. Photo by D. Kowalski.

Girl's Bicycle is painted dark blue with white trim. This one has a battery-powered light mounted on front fender. From T. Webster collection. Photo by D. Kowalski.

Logo plate on the front neck of Girl's model is clean and clear; it has large red "W" in white circle. "WINCHESTER" is printed in gold letters on a blue banner below the white circle. This photograph also shows original paint job is in better condition than on Boy's Bicycle shown. We speculate that the white-walled tire on the front wheel was a replacement for an original black-walled one. From T. Webster collection. Photo by D. Kowalski.

Common "D" wood handles of early spades were skillfully cut and finished. From T. Webster collection. Photo by D. Kowalski.

Garden Plow (No. W25) is in Excellent to Very Good condition with very little rust. It is the only one discovered to date. The "Winchester" logo is a red-letter decal on the metal frame between the hand grips and the junction of the vertical support with the main frame. From T. Webster collection. Photo by D. Kowalski.

Metal wheelbarrow in Very Good to Good condition showing much of the original color and striping. In Excellent condition, tray would show red stripe around edge. From T. Webster collection. Photo by D. Kowalski.

Winchester-Simmons Co. Wooden Wheelbarrow was produced after 1922 when Winchester merged with the Simmons Hardware Company. The front of the tray bears the following three-line inscription overprinted in black: First line - WINCHESTER - SIMMONS CO.; Second line - OF BOSTON; Third line - NO. 6. From Richard Hecht collection. Photo by R. Hecht.

Model WL13. Low Wheel Lawn Mower. Logos are located several places. The outside hubs of the wheels have indented inscriptions "WINCHESTER DOUBLE GEAR WL13." The inside hubs have "WINCHESTER REPEATING ARMS CO." inscription. Close-up of top of handle shows words "WINCHESTER" and "BALL BEARING" painted in red. From T. Webster collection. Photo by D. Kowalski.

The Whirldry portable electric washing machine fit easily on a table or counter top. This one measures 16 ½ inches high and 14 inches across the top. It also came with a tin lid. From T. Webster collection. Photo by D. Kowalski.

Looking down into the Whirldry machine showing the perforated inner basket and the four-armed agitator. From T. Webster collection. Photo by D. Kowalski.

Model W50 Iron is smaller and rarer than models W100 and W110. From T. Webster collection. Photo by D. Kowalski.

Ironing Board measures 53 ¾ inches from end to end of the wooden top and stands 31 ½ inches high. One of only two ironing boards known. From T. Webster collection. Photo by D. Kowalski.

Label of Ironing Board glued to the underside of top identifies this model as a "Winchester Store" version. From T. Webster collection. Photo by D. Kowalski.

One Quart and Eight Quart Ice Cream Freezers, side by side. These are the largest and smallest of six sizes and are also the rarest. From T. Webster collection. Photo by D. Kowalski.

Wooden Carpet Sweeper measures 14 1/2 inches wide at the base and the case is 4 1/2 inches high. This rare early version is the only one known. Has wooden handle. From T. Webster collection. Photo by D. Kowalski.

This Winchester Electric Sewing Machine came with a full wooden cabinet cover. The wooden base is 20 1/4 inches long. From T. Webster collection. Photo by D. Kowalski.

This Carpet Sweeper has a metal case. It is slightly smaller than the wooden one, measuring 14 inches wide at the base and 4 inches high. This model is also a "Winchester Store" version. Wooden handle. From T. Webster collection. Photo by D. Kowalski.

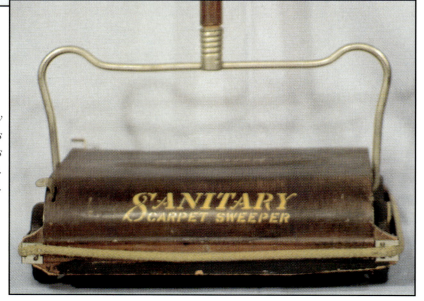

Electric Fans were sold in three sizes. The largest one (on left) is 17 1/2 inches high. The smallest one (right) measures 10 3/4 from the base to the top of the wire blade cage. From T. Webster collection. Photo by D. Kowalski.

The Electric Space Heater (model 600) is old but not that rare. Total height is 16 inches. From T. Webster collection. Photo by D. Kowalski.

Winchester offered both a table model Electric Radio in a wood cabinet (shown here), as well as a console model. Only three of the consoles have been found to date. From T. Webster collection. Photo by D. Kowalski.

Electric Toaster is 7 1/4 inches long at the base and 7 1/8 inches high. Only five or six have been found. This one is in Excellent condition. From T. Webster collection. Photo by D. Kowalski.

Winchester made Electric Coffee Pots in two sizes. Only one nine-cup model (on left) has ever been found. The six-cup model on right is 9 5/8 inches high. From T. Webster collection. Photo by T. Webster.

Vacuum Bottles were also made in one-gallon size and all sizes are very rare. From T. Webster collection. Photo by D. Kowalski.

Brass Vacuum Bottle, quart size, showing bottom detail and cap. From T. Webster collection. Photo by D. Kowalski.

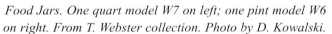

Food Jars. One quart model W7 on left; one pint model W6 on right. From T. Webster collection. Photo by D. Kowalski.

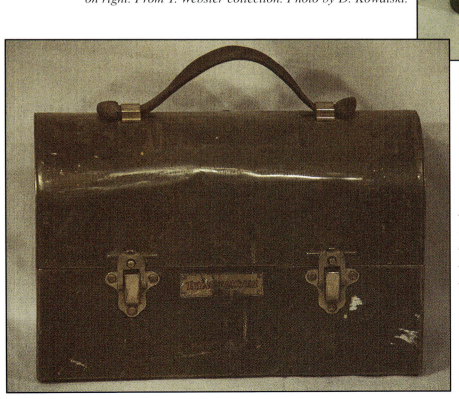

Lunch Boxes are fairly rare. This one shows the effects of having been "on the job." From T. Webster collection. Photo by D. Kowalski.

Wooden flashlight display for retail countertops was designed to hold 18 flashlights in standing position. One of only two ever discovered. From T. Webster collection. Photo by D. Kowalski.

Winchester padlocks in a variety of styles nicely displayed in the Curt Bowman collection. Photo by C. Bowman.

Doctor's Examination Kit is a rare version with a flashlight. From T. Webster collection. Photo by D. Kowalski.

Wooden wall-mounted paint brush display measures 30 1/2 inches long x 15 3/4 inches high. It is the only one found to date. From T. Webster collection. Photo by D. Kowalski.

Two 1/4 pint cans of Varnish Stain - Mahogany. The can on the right is the only one known in the "Winchester Store" version. From T. Webster collection. Photo by D. Kowalski.

The 1-inch "Fitch Flowing" paint brush on the right may be the only Winchester paint brush ever found. The shaving soap brush is in very good condition. From T. Webster collection. Photo by D. Kowalski.

Colorful 3 1/2-ounce can of After Shave Talc has shaker top. From T. Webster collection. Photo by D. Kowalski.

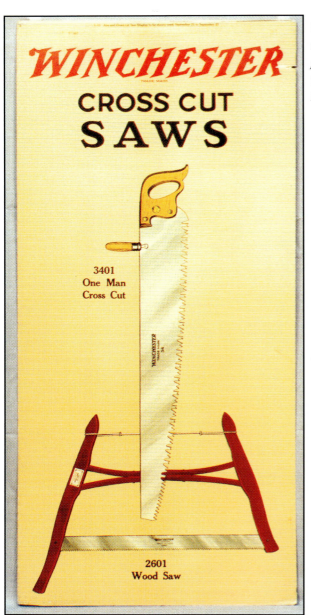

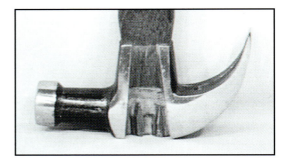

Winchester created more than 100 five-panel floor displays that promoted their various products. This was the far right panel on cross cut and wood saws (#L23, #5) that promoted various tools. A panel for screwdrivers is on the back. From the Tom Webster Collection. Photo by D. Kowalski.

Close-up of the cutaway head of a claw hammer (Model 6008). Another rare piece. From the Tom Webster Collection. Photo by D. Kowalski.

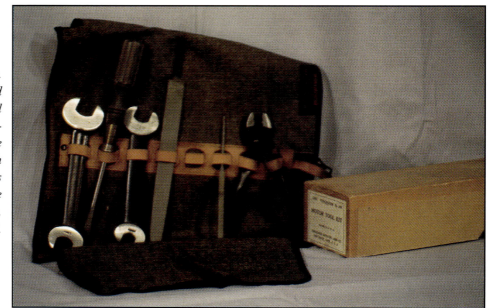

Here's a Motor Tool Kit (No. 1982) that was never used and contained six of the original seven tools. Having the original box probably doubles the value of this collectible, which is one of only a few that has ever been found. From the Tom Webster Collection. Photo by D. Kowalski.

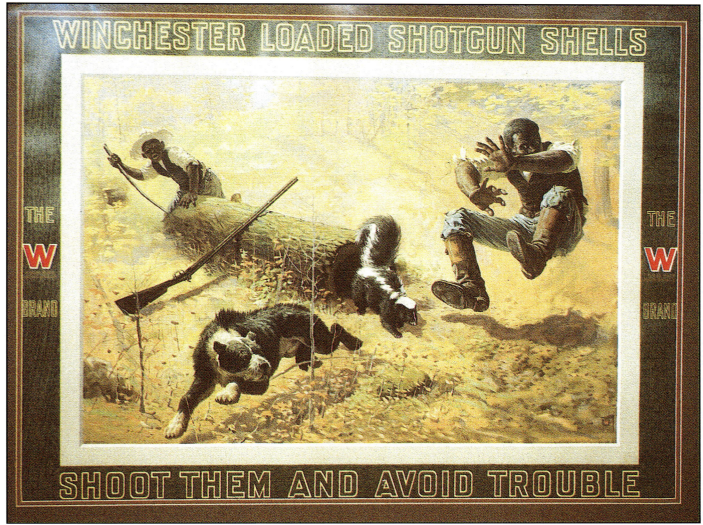

"Shoot Them and Avoid Trouble" poster has always been controversial and highly collectible. The originals had the border shown here. From T. Webster collection. Photo by D. Kowalski.

Wooden Folding Spring Joint Rules were made in both yellow and white models in several lengths. From T. Webster collection. Photo by D. Kowalski.

Plug Baits in the three styles of Crackle Back Pattern are difficult to find in excellent condition because Winchester used decals on them. The Multi-Wobbler (No. 9205) is on left; Minnow with three hooks (No. 9015) is in front; and Minnow with five hooks (No. 9215) is in back. Winchester produced eight distinct colors and patterns in each of the three styles. From T. Webster collection. Photo by D. Kowalski.

Boxes for Plug Baits - Multi-Wobbler (No. 9201) and Minnow with five hooks (No. 9216) used attention-getting graphics. From T. Webster collection. Photo by D. Kowalski.

Winchester Fishing Equipment

by Phil White

Collectors gather up things for many reasons. Some enjoy the beauty, some are reliving their childhood, a few are looking for an investment, and some start collecting just to have something to do.

Winchester fishing tackle collectors are one of the few groups of collectors who are really collecting a name only. Many other companies produced fishing tackle of higher quality, but it does not have the appeal of the trademarked "Winchester Repeating Arms Company" lightning letter logo. The wooden lures had only medium quality paint jobs, spoonbaits are similar to many earlier manufacturers in style and quality, and the reels (with a few exceptions) were not of very high quality. However, Winchester tackle is some of the highest-priced tackle on the collector market. The Winchester lightning letters are the attraction.

Winchester tackle now has a dual following that has produced a great deal of competition for available items as they come on the market. For many years the only collectors interested in fishing tackle stamped with the famous lightning letters were a small group of people who collected miscellaneous Winchester things – the tools, sporting goods, and household products that were manufactured by Winchester in the 1920s. These collectors were usually hunters or gun collectors who learned of the mind-numbing list of products that bore the Winchester name. They felt that some fishing tackle would add a nice touch to their gunroom.

This small group of collectors had a great thing going for many years, but not any longer. In the 1980s it was possible to go to the few fishing tackle shows then held around the country, and purchase Winchester tackle for low prices. If the pieces were not what you wanted for your collection, you could take it to gun shows and sell to Winchester collectors at a good profit. This situation no longer exists. Since the fishing tackle collecting boom of the past decade, Winchester tackle probably brings higher prices at fishing tackle shows than it does from the Winchester collector.

Fishing tackle collecting is one of the most active facets of the collector marketplace today. Whether it is the economy or the desire to invest in high return collectibles, there are a lot of people in the market for *quality* fishing tackle. When you add to that interest the name "Winchester," you've got more searchers than the market has quality products. This creates an ideal situation for the seller, but a very tough marketplace for the collector.

However, there is still a lot of Winchester fishing tackle to be found in yard or garage sales, estate sales, and from personal contacts. This tackle is usually available at less-than-market price. Most non-collectors just see a spinner or reel, not the name Winchester. Even if they do see the famous Winchester lightning letters, they have no idea of the value that this name adds to the item. This is where the student of Winchester fishing tackle will have the advantage. Knowledge is the key to collecting.

Finding Winchester Fishing Tackle

Twenty years ago the problem facing most Winchester fishing tackle collectors was finding the tackle. Fishing tackle collectors were not really impressed by the quality of the reels, and the painting of the lures, so Winchester tackle was not displayed prominently at auctions and flea markets. However, judicious searching of tackle boxes and looking for insignificant stampings on reels and reel seats could turn up some real bargains. Today, Winchester tackle is the featured item in locked showcases at tackle shows, gun shows and antique malls.

Much of the fun of collecting is the search, and there is still Winchester tackle in those farm sale tackle boxes and among those old rods and reels in the attic. There are just more collectors out looking for those pieces, and sellers are quite a bit more astute than they were a few years ago.

If you don't have the inclination to search out those "field finds" you can still put together a fine collection of Winchester fishing tackle. Today we have more possibilities for the purchase of Winchester tackle than ever before. The major sources are gun, fishing tackle, and sporting collectibles shows and auctions, and perhaps the most successful of them all today, the Internet auction sites.

Gun shows will probably decrease in numbers due to government rules and regulations, but at the same time fishing tackle and sporting collectibles shows are growing in number and size. Winchester tackle collectors can usually find many Winchester items of interest at most major shows of this type. However, even these shows are being affected by the newest method of collecting – the Internet auction.

The Ebay auction site, currently the most successful of the cyber auctions, has thousands of items for sale at any one time, and many of these are Winchester. If you can't find an item for your collection today, just check back tomorrow. A recent Ebay search found 1,150 postings with Winchester in the title or description, and 30 of these were fishing items. There are hundreds of new fishing tackle items being added each day.

The Internet auctions are great for sellers, in that the finder of an item does not have to know its value. All he has to do it put it on line and let the national and international market determine the value on the day the auction closes. This has brought a lot more items to the market.

The seller does not need to sell his tackle to a local collector (the only person he knows who collects Winchester tackle); he's got a whole world out there looking at his Winchester rod, reel or lure. This does not work well for the local collector, and usually raises prices (good for the seller). However, the serious collector is seeing many more items in a month than he would usually see in a year. All you have to do is step up and pay the price.

Whether or not the interest in buying and selling on the Internet will remain at its current level, or increase or decrease is not yet known. Some of the bloom has already worn off, due to quite a few fake Winchester "sample items" (more on this later), and buyers not being able to examine and handle the merchandise in person. Most collectors would like to be able to grade a rod, reel or lure themselves, rather than trusting a seller they don't know personally.

Develop Your Own Collecting Plan

Most people do not start to collect Winchester fishing tackle with a plan in mind. They just acquire a few things and the next thing you know - it's a collection (or more likely, an "accumulation"). Most collectors are not satisfied to find one or two items for their collection per year, so Winchester collectors seldom specialize – they collect all Winchester tackle.

As a general rule, it is always wise not to purchase items in poor or damaged condition. It is very difficult to find parts for Winchester rods, reels and lures. If these collectibles are in poor condition they seldom increase in value. However, since there is a great deal of competition for the best Winchester tackle, most collectors seem to use the "first-let's-get-an-example" approach. You can then upgrade when (or if) the chance arises. Most people soon learn to purchase any tackle that is in excellent condition – if they can afford it.

Items in prime, mint or excellent condition are very hard to find. This is fishing tackle, and it was made to be used. Remember that prime pieces are great trade items even if they don't fit your collection.

Most Winchester non-gun products manufactured during the expansion times of the 1920s were of very high quality. These items were either contracted from established firms, or made by Winchester after they purchased an established company. Winchester fishing tackle seems to be an exception. Perhaps their lack of experience in this field caused them to make mistakes, or to cut corners.

Winchester fishing tackle can be divided into four main categories: Rods, Reels, Lures and Miscellaneous Tackle. Each of these categories contains some exceptional items. These particular products surpassed the mediocre quality of the majority of the fishing tackle produced by this otherwise fine old company, and it is important to the collector to recognize these gems.

We will discuss each of these areas with some general comments before giving product descriptions used by Winchester. Then we'll follow with value guides for each area. But first we want to add a few notes of caution about fakes and forgeries. We'll comment on "generic" brands of tackle. Then we'll define the grading standards we used for the value guides.

The Problem of Fakes and Forgeries

Unfortunately, some mention must be made of the recent influx of counterfeit and so-called "fantasy" Winchester fishing items. This seems to be a greater problem in the fishing tackle line than any other facet of Winchester collecting.

The biggest problem at this time seems to be with fantasy items. These are things that never were produced by Winchester. We have some very imaginative people with computer software capable of reproducing Winchester logos and drawings, then pasting them on all kinds of supposed "give-away" merchandise. Most of this fantasy stuff is labeled "Courtesy of Winchester." Among the items of this type are hook tins and packets, leader containers, oil bottles, and the wildest of them all - a supposed worm container made from a waxed cardboard container like a cottage cheese box.

There are also reproduction "Winchester" decals that have been applied to bait buckets, landing nets, and several other fishing items. The best advice seems to be that if there is no product number stamped into the metal of the item, or if the number stamping is large and not well lined up, beware!

Metal stamps with the "Winchester Repeating Arms Co./Trade Mark" are being used to counterfeit unmarked items. Many of these fakes are relatively easy to spot due to the "dishing" of the metal around the stamp. If a product number is stamped in a very irregular manner, you had better think twice before making the purchase.

The Winchester "Generic" Brands

Winchester Repeating Arms Co. also produced a great deal of unmarked, or "generic" brand fishing tackle. Among the names they used on this tackle were Armax, Barney & Berry, Crusader, and even Hendryx. This tackle was produced, starting in 1923, to quiet the rumblings of disgruntled Winchester firearms and ammunition jobbers who were not allowed to sell "Winchester" branded sporting goods.

In 1923 Winchester mailed out catalogs to their firearms jobbers that listed almost all of their line of fishing tackle, but these items did not bear the Winchester label. Jobbers could purchase this tackle for resale, and at very attractive prices. Reels, lures, terminal tackle, and even the Edwards rods were available in these "generic" brands.

Although this is the same Winchester fishing tackle with a different stamping, these items are valued much lower by collectors today. The disparity might change in the future as collectors get better educated, but the fishing tackle will probably never be worth more than 50 percent of the value of similar "Winchester" stamped items.

Several Winchester wooden lures, with Armax stampings on the metal, and in mint condition in boxes surfaced a few years ago. Little interest was shown by Winchester lure collectors, and they were finally sold for giveaway prices – at least when compared to their value if they had been marked "Winchester."

The Winchester Repeating Arms Company also manufactured fishing tackle and parts for many other tackle companies. Mostly these were metal parts such as reel seats, butt caps, and net ferrules. However, some reels were made for other major fishing tackle retailers under their own brand names. Having the yardage mark on the reel foot underlined can usually identify these reels. These reels cannot be called Winchester reels, however, and their value is not increased because Winchester might have been the contractor.

Grading Fishing Rods, Reels and Tackle

Grading of any used item seems to depend upon whether you are the buyer or the seller: the buyer always looks at items with a critical eye. What is wrong with it? Buyer's look for the defects.

Sellers look at items with a positive eye - they see the good points of the item. Thus the buyer usually sees things at a lower grade than the seller does. When attempting to grade your own tackle, try to look at the item as if you were the buyer.

One of our goals in this unique book is to provide grading standards for several levels of quality to help both buyers and sellers see their collectibles more realistically.

Excellent (Exc.)

This is an item that looks unused, and is a prime collectible. A reel or lure does not have its box, but a rod has its bag and/or tube, if provided originally.

Very Good (V.G.)

Shows very little use, but might have some minor defects. A lure might have minor age cracks and wear. Spinner blades might have a scratch with some minor paint loss, and feathers might be dirty. A reel could have minor scratches, brass wear, and minor "click" wear. A bamboo rod could show minor varnish dings and grip use, but all pieces should be full length, and rod should still have bag and tube. Steel rods must still have the bag, but there could be slight paint missing, and the cork could show use.

Good

Shows fishing use. A lure would show age cracks and minor paint chips. Hooks and hardware show rust or corrosion. Spinners and spoonbaits show plating and feather wear, with paint partially missing. Reels show scratches, light corrosion and/or pitting, and the foot and some screws might be damaged. Bamboo rods might have some thread fraying or missing, also some varnish wear and dings. Pieces might be an inch or less short. Bag or tube might be rotted or missing. Steel rods might have some paint missing, chipped cork, and the bag might be rotted or missing.

Fair

A questionable collectible that shows considerable fishing use. A lure would show major defects, such as major paint loss, cracked eyes, and/or broken hook points and hardware corrosion. Spinners would have hooks or feathers missing, no paint on back, with much plating missing. A reel would have significant problems; corrosion, damaged or missing screws, end caps, or other minor parts. A bamboo rod would have short sections, missing guides, windings, bag, and/or tube, and also chipped cork. Steel rods would have little paint, some rust present, missing guides, chipped cork, and the original bag would be missing.

In our value charts that follow each product, we will only give Excellent (Exc.), Very Good (V.G.)

and Good prices. The value for Fair items drops off considerably. There are some rare items only available in Fair condition and you would be wise to acquire them if the price is reasonable.

Lures and Reels in Boxes or on Cards

It should be recognized that reel and lure boxes and cards were packages. They were meant to hold the lure or reel until sold, and the fisherman often threw them away when using the item. However, since tackle boxes in the 1920s were metal, many fishermen often kept their reels and lures in their original boxes to protect them from wear and corrosion. Unfortunately, many of these boxes then became worn or water damaged.

The original box that a lure (either wooden or spinner) or reel came in adds a tremendous value to the collectible. New-in-box items can triple the value of a lure or reel. However, as a general rule, you can double the values listed for a reel or lure if it is in the box.

Rods are a different story. Rod tubes, bags and tip tubes were a part of the rod unit. They should be present with the rod; not having them lowers the value of the item.

Winchester Fishing Rods

The major exceptions to the average quality of Winchester's fishing tackle were their bamboo rods. When E. W. "Bill" Edwards signed a five-year contract to supervise bamboo rod production, Winchester acquired a gem. Bill Edwards had been trained by famed rod maker Hiram Leonard, and had worked with F. E. Thomas and Loman Hawes. These were the elite American craftsmen of their day in the rod-building field. Bill Edwards left Winchester when his contract expired in 1924. However, Winchester had learned their lessons from a master, and continued to produce quality rods for the next seven years.

Many of these split cane rods are bargains today. Most fishing rod collectors are looking for short rods that are eight feet or less. An example of what this does to the market is the Winchester Edwards 7' "Wandrod." It seems that each time an excellent example of this rod appears for sale, it sets a new record price for a Winchester rod. A rod of similar quality and condition in 9- or 10-foot length would bring about half as much money as this more-sought-after short rod.

If possible, a Winchester tackle collector should only be looking for rods in Excellent or Very Good condition. There are still some bargains to be found if you purchase longer fly rods of nine to ten feet in length, or short casting rods of 3 to four feet. Many collectors are unaware of the fact that rods of these lengths were quite popular in past generations.

There is also the whole class of rods called "Bait Rods" that are not eagerly collected today, and they are usually priced far below fly rods of equal quality. Bait rods were going out of style by the 1920s (in favor of the short bait casting rod), and most collectors don't even know what a "bait rod" is.

Bait rods are the 8- to 10-foot rods that were used by 19th century anglers for casting frogs, minnows, and other bait. The reel was mounted "before the hand" and was cranked with the right hand on top of the rod. Bait rods are a bit stiffer than a comparable length fly rod. Winchester's examples have 6600 and 6700 series numbers. These are the rods the famous "Kentucky" reels were paired with from the 1880s until the advent of the short bait casting rod. Most collectors today seem to think that they are light salt-water rods, and have little interest in them. Bait rods are a most-important item from our early angling heritage.

Winchester steel rods were of high quality, but they are identical to the Bristol steel rods manufactured by Horton Manufacturing Company of Bristol, Connecticut. The only difference being the "Winchester" logo and model number on the reel seat instead of the Bristol trademark. Horton was the premier manufacturer of steel rods, and the originator of most concepts in steel rod manufacture. The assumption is that either Horton totally manufactured the rods, or supplied parts to Winchester for assembly. Steel rods should not be overlooked, or denigrated, by collectors. Except for fly fishing, there were probably more fishermen using steel rods than those using split bamboo rods, until shortly after World War II and the invention of the fiberglass rod. Winchester had some very nice steel rods in their lineup, and the dark agate guides and tip, brass ferrules, and black shafts make a handsome collectible, especially in the original bag with the Winchester label.

Split Bamboo Fly Rods

Beauty, lightness, flexibility and resiliency are the features which the angler looks for most when selecting a high grade Bamboo Rod.

Winchester Bamboo Rods are designed and constructed with extreme care. They are manufactured from imported Tonkin cane which is the best obtainable for Fishing Rods. Only expert workmanship enters into the building of these Rods.

Weights given on Winchester Rods are weights of rods unpacked.

Nickel silver fittings. Nickel silver snake guides. Ring tip. Compressed cork grip. Attractively wound with red silk. Machine-welted ferrules.

No.	Weight	Length
6005	5 1/4 oz.	8 1/2 ft.
6010	6 oz.	9 ft.
6015	6 3/4 oz.	9 1/2 ft.

Rod Values:	Exc.	V.G.	Good
6005	350.00	275.00	175.00
6010	325.00	250.00	150.00
6015	325.00	250.00	150.00

Nickel silver fittings. Nickel silver snake guides. Solid cork grip. Nickel silver angle tip. Wound with purple silk. Machine welted serrated ferrules. Extra tip joint. Tips in bamboo tip case.

No.	Weight	Length
6030	4 1/2 oz.	8 1/2 ft.
6035	5 1/4 oz.	9 ft.
6040	5 1/2 oz.	9 1/2 ft.

Rod Values:	Exc.	V.G.	Good
6030	400.00	300.00	200.00
6035	375.00	250.00	130.00
6040	375.00	250.00	130.00

Nickel silver fittings. Solid ringed cork grip. Nickel silver snake guides. Machine welted serrated ferrules. Nickel silver angle tip. Attractively wound with red silk. Extra tip joint. Tips in bamboo tip case.

No.	Weight	Length
6043	3 3/4 oz.	7 1/2 ft.
6044	4 1/4 oz.	8 ft.
6045	4 3/4 oz.	8 1/2 ft.
6050	5 1/4 oz.	9 ft.
6055	5 3/4 oz.	9 1/2 ft.
6060	6 1/4 oz.	10 ft.

Rod Values:	Exc.	V.G.	Good
6043	1,000.00	650.00	450.00
6044	850.00	550.00	350.00
6045	500.00	350.00	250.00
6050	450.00	300.00	200.00
6055	450.00	300.00	200.00
6060	475.00	325.00	225.00

Nickel silver fittings. Solid ringed cork grip. Machine welted serrated ferrules. First guide is of one-ring type of genuine agate, the others of bronze steel, snake style. Angle tip of nickel-plated, file-proof, hardened steel. Bamboo used in this rod is scientifically treated to produce fine action, and strips are matched so knots will not come together. Pepper and salt winding. Extra tip joint. Tips in bamboo tip case. Packed in a partitioned cloth bag.

No.	Weight	Length
6065	4 1/2 oz.	8 1/2 ft.
6070	5 oz.	9 ft.
6075	5 1/2 oz.	9 1/2 ft.

Rod Values:	Exc.	V.G.	Good
6065	500.00	300.00	200.00
6070	450.00	275.00	185.00
6075	450.00	275.00	185.00

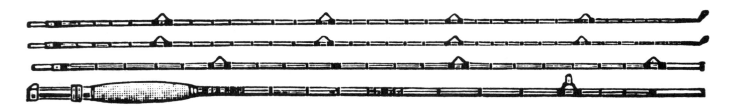

Nickel silver fittings. Solid ringed cork grip. First guide one-ring with genuine agate, others snake-style made of bronzed steel. Machine-welted, serrated ferrules. Both tip joints furnished with angle tip: one of nickel-plated steel, the other of genuine agate. Stock used in joints of these rods is scientifically treated, knots matched and sections straightened by experts. Wound with orange and black silk. Tips in bamboo tip case.

No.	Weight	Length
6080	4 1/2 oz.	8 1/2 ft.
6085	5 oz.	9 ft.
6090	5 1/2 oz.	9 1/2 ft.

Rod Values:	Exc.	V.G.	Good
6080	600.00	400.00	275.00
6085	550.00	375.00	260.00
6090	550.00	375.00	260.00

Frosted nickel silver fittings. Special ringed cork grip. First guide one-ring genuine agate. Others best quality bronzed steel. Semi-handmade, serrated, waterproofed ferrules. Tips of angle type: one nickel-plated, hardened steel; the other of genuine agate. Attractively wound with high-grade green Japan silk. Bamboo strips carefully treated to produce fine action. All six strips cut from the same piece of bamboo and matched so knots will not line up opposite each other. All strips and sections straightened by experts before assembling. Tips in bamboo tip case.

No.	Weight	Length
6115	4 1/4 oz.	8 ft.
6120	4 1/2 oz.	8 1/2 ft.
6125	5 oz.	9 ft.
6130	5 1/2 oz.	9 1/2 ft.

Rod Values:	Exc.	V.G.	Good
6115	900.00	600.00	400.00
6120	650.00	450.00	325.00
6125	600.00	400.00	300.00
6130	600.00	400.00	300.00

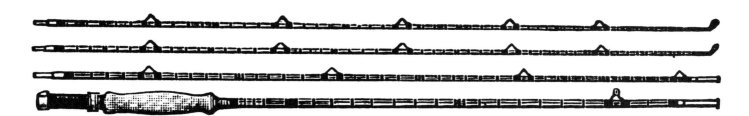

Nickel silver fittings. Solid ringed cork grip. First guide one-ring type of agate. Others, snake type of bronzed steel. Special semi-handmade, welted, serrated, waterproof ferrules. Angle tips: one of nickel-plated, hardened steel; the other genuine agate. Bamboo strips treated to insure fine action. All six strips cut from same piece of bamboo. Knots carefully matched so as not to line up opposite each other. Wound with tan color silk. All strips and sections straightened by experts before assembling. Packed in a high-grade aluminum case.

No.	Weight	Length
6135	4 1/4 oz.	8 1/2 ft.
6140	4 3/4 oz.	9 ft.
6145	5 1/4 oz.	9 1/2 ft.

Same style and grade rod as above, especially designed for dry fly casting.

No.	Weight	Length
6136	5 oz.	8 1/2 ft.
6141	5 1/2 oz.	9 ft.
6146	6 oz.	9 1/2 ft.

Rod Values:	Exc.	V.G.	Good
6135	650.00	450.00	325.00
6140	600.00	400.00	300.00
6145	600.00	400.00	300.00
6136	650.00	450.00	325.00
6141	600.00	400.00	300.00
6146	600.00	400.00	300.00

Rocky Mountain Bamboo Fly Rods

These rods are made with the extra long cork grip so strongly in demand in the Rocky Mountain States. Many fishermen like this style rod because with this long grip they can shift the position of the hand thus changing the feel and balance of the rod and resting hand and wrist. The extra long grip is also preferred in use with automatic reels with an extension-controlling lever.

Nickel silver snake guides. Nickel silver agate tip. Wound with purple silk. Machine welted serrated ferrules. Extra tip joint. Tips in bamboo tip case. A rod of unusual power. Special 10-inch cork grip. Locking band on reel seat.

No.	Weight	Length
6037	5 1/2 oz.	9 ft.
6042	6 oz.	9 1/2 ft.

Rod Values:	Exc.	V.G.	Good
6037	600.00	400.00	300.00
6042	600.00	400.00	300.00

Nickel silver fittings. First guide one ring with genuine agate. Others snake style made of bronzed steel. Special 10-inch, solid cork grip. Machine-welted, serrated ferrules. Reel seat has locking band. Both tip joints have angle tips: one of nickel-plated, hardened steel; the other of genuine agate. Stock used in all joints is scientifically treated, knots matched and sections hand-straightened. Wound with orange and black silk. Tips in bamboo tip case. Packed in partitioned cloth bag.

No.	Weight	Length
6087	5 3/4 oz.	9 ft.
6092	6 1/4 oz.	9 1/2 ft.

Rod Values:	Exc.	V.G.	Good
6087	600.00	400.00	300.00
6092	600.00	400.00	300.00

Highest grade handmade bamboo fly rod. Hand-tooled, nickel silver fittings. Serrated, welted and waterproofed ferrules. First guide one ring agate. Others bronzed steel, snake style. Angle tips: one of agate; other is nickel-plated, hardened steel. Special 10-inch, solid cork grip. All six strips cut from same piece of bamboo to insure uniformity of stock. All modern methods of treating bamboo used in preparing material for this rod. Wound with red silk. All strips and sections straightened by experts before assembling. Packed in aluminum case.

No.	Weight	Length
6157	6 oz.	9 ft.
6162	6 3/4 oz.	9 1/2 ft.

Rod Values:	Exc.	V.G.	Good
6157	600.00	400.00	300.00
6162	600.00	400.00	300.00

Special Bamboo Western Fly Rod for Heavy Fishing

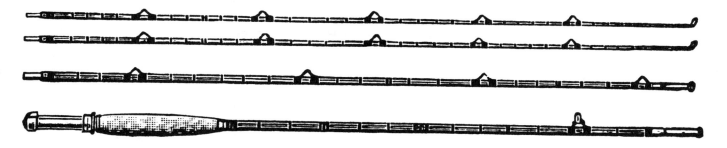

A rod that will meet the demand for the type of rod wanted in the Pacific states for steelhead fishing. Extra-heavy action. Three joints and extra tip. Steel ring tips on both tip joints. Agate first guide. Other guides large bronze steel, snake type. Has 7 1/2-inch ringed cork grip. Distinctive winding in red silk. Equipped with extra large reel seat to fit the extra-size reels used for heavy fishing. Packed in canvas bag with tips in standard bamboo tip case.

No.	Weight	Length
6220	8 1/8 oz.	9 1/2 ft.
6225	8 3/8 oz.	10 ft.

Rod Values:	Exc.	V.G.	Good
6220	600.00	400.00	300.00
6225	650.00	450.00	325.00

Bass Fly Rod

Specially designed for bass fishing. Three-piece with extra tip joint. First guide agate, all others bronzed steel, snake type. One agate angle tip and one steel angle tip. Serrated ferrules. Tips in bamboo tip case. Extra-size reel seat and good-sized solid cork grip. Orange and black silk windings.

No.	Weight	Length
6265	5 oz.	8 1/2 ft.
6270	5 1/2 oz.	9 ft.
6275	6 oz.	9 1/2 ft.

Rod Values:	Exc.	V.G.	Good
6265	600.00	400.00	300.00
6270	600.00	400.00	300.00
6275	600.00	400.00	300.00

Edwards Handmade Fly Rods

These rods are made by hand with special care to make the most perfect Bamboo Fly Rod. They are made from only the highest grades of carefully selected cane. You will find these rods will delight the most exacting lover of fine fishing tackle.

Special handmade bamboo fly rod. Nickel silver fittings. Solid ringed cork grip. Special semi-handmade, hand-welted, serrated and waterproofed ferrules. First guide one ring agate. Others, snake style in bronzed steel. Angle tips: one of agate, the other of nickel-plated, hardened steel. Hand-tooled fittings. All six strips cut from the same piece of specially selected bamboo. Carefully matched and treated to produce one of the best fly rods on the market. Carefully wound with red silk. All strips and sections straightened by experts before assembling. Packed in a high-grade aluminum case.

No.	Weight	Length
6150	4 1/2 oz.	8 1/2 ft.
6155	5 oz.	9 ft.
6160	5 3/4 oz.	9 1/2 ft.

Same style and grade as rod above, but designed for dry fly casting.

No.	Weight	Length
6151	5 oz.	8 1/2 ft.
6156	5 1/2 oz.	9 ft.
6161	6 1/4 oz.	9 1/2 ft.

Rod Values:	Exc.	V.G.	Good
6150	1,000.00	800.00	450.00
6155	900.00	700.00	400.00
6160	900.00	700.00	400.00
6151	1,100.00	900.00	500.00
6156	1,000.00	800.00	450.00
6161	1,000.00	800.00	450.00

Highest grade bamboo fly rod. Handmade throughout. Hand-tooled nickel silver fittings. Serrated, welted and waterproofed ferrules. First guide one ring agate, all others bronzed steel, snake style. Angle tips: one of agate, the other of nickel-plated, hardened steel. All six strips cut from the same piece of bamboo, insuring uniformity of stock. All modern methods of treating bamboo to insure perfect action used in the manufacture of this rod. Carefully wound with red silk, with tan trimmings. All strips and sections straightened by experts before assembling. Packed in high-grade aluminum case.

No.	Weight	Length
6165	4 oz.	8 ft.
6170	4 1/2 oz.	8 1/2 ft.
6175	5 oz.	9 ft.
6180	5 3/4 oz.	9 1/2 ft.
6185	6 1/4 oz.	10 ft.

Same style and grade as above, but designed for dry fly casting.

No.	Weight	Length
6166	4 1/4 oz.	8 ft.
6171	5 oz.	8 1/2 ft.
6176	5 1/2 oz.	9 ft.
6181	6 1/4 oz.	9 1/2 ft.
6186	6 1/2 oz.	10 ft.

Rod Values:	Exc.	V.G.	Good
6165	1,300.00	1,000.00	750.00
6170	1,100.00	750.00	600.00
6175	1,000.00	650.00	550.00
6180	900.00	600.00	500.00
6185	1,000.00	650.00	550.00
6166	1,400.00	1,150.00	850.00
6171	1,200.00	850.00	700.00
6176	1,100.00	750.00	650.00
6181	1,000.00	700.00	600.00
6186	1,100.00	750.00	650.00

Winchester Fishing Equipment • 379

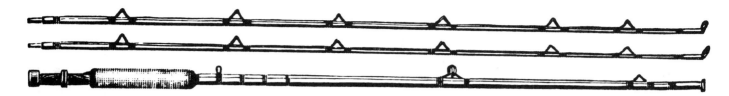

Highest grade bamboo fly rod. Handmade throughout. Hand-tooled nickel silver fittings. Serrated, welted and waterproofed ferrules. First guide one ring agate, all others bronzed steel, snake style. Angle tips: one of agate, the other of nickel-plated, hardened steel. All six strips cut from the same piece of bamboo, insuring uniformity of stock. All modern methods of treating bamboo to insure perfect action used in the manufacture of this rod. Carefully wound with tan silk, with purple trimmings. All strips and sections straightened by experts before assembling. Packed in Silkaline bag and aluminum rod case.

No.	Weight	Length
6163	2 1/2 oz.	7 ft.

Rod Values:	Exc.	V.G.	Good
6163	1,800.00	1,400.00	900.00

Comment: *This is the very desirable Edwards "Wandrod."*

Combination Fly/Bait/Bait Casting Rod

Brown bamboo. Reversible handle. Imitation agate butt guide and Roto-ring tip top on fly and butt ends with other guides snake-type hard steel. The casting tip has imitation agate tip top. Makes the following rods:

Model 6320	Weight	Length
Fly rod	8 oz.	9 1/2 ft.
Fly rod	6 oz.	7 1/4 ft.
Bait rod	8 oz.	9 1/2 ft.
Bait rod	6 oz.	7 1/4 ft.

Model 6320	Weight	Length
Bait rod	5 oz.	4 ft.
Bait casting rod	7 oz.	6 1/4 ft.
Bait casting rod	5 oz.	4 ft.

Comment: *This combination rod could be used for several purposes. It only appeared in the 1931 catalog, then was taken out of the product line.*

Rod Values:	Exc.	V.G.	Good
6320	800.00	500.00	350.00

Split Bamboo Bait Rod

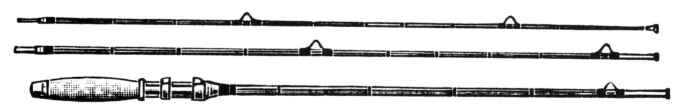

Nickel silver fittings. Has snake-type, nickel silver guides. Machine-welted ferrules. Three-ring tip. Compressed-cork grip. Attractively wound with red silk. No extra tip.

No.	Weight	Length
6780	7 oz.	8 ft.
6785	7 1/2 oz.	8 1/2 ft.
6790	8 oz.	9 ft.
6795	8 1/2 oz.	9 1/2 ft.

Rod Values:	Exc.	V.G.	Good
6780	375.00	250.00	150.00
6785	375.00	250.00	150.00
6790	375.00	250.00	150.00
6795	375.00	250.00	150.00

Solid ringed cork grip. Nickel silver fittings. Machine-welted ferrules. Nickel silver snake-style guides. Three-ring nickel silver tip. Extra tip joint. Tips in bamboo tip case. Attractively wound with purple silk.

No.	Weight	Length
6655	5 3/4 oz.	8 ft.
6660	6 1/2 oz.	8 1/2 ft.
6665	7 1/4 oz.	9 ft.
6670	8 oz.	9 1/2 ft.
6675	8 3/4 oz.	10 ft.

Rod Values:	Exc.	V.G.	Good
6655	425.00	300.00	200.00
6660	425.00	300.00	200.00
6665	425.00	300.00	200.00
6670	425.00	300.00	200.00
6675	425.00	300.00	200.00

Nickel silver fittings. Double grip of solid ringed cork. Serrated, hand-welted, waterproofed ferrules. First guide is barrel-type of a special high-grade agate. Other guides of nickel silver, bell-type. Two tip joints furnished with specially designed tips of a high-grade agate. Dark green windings. Bamboo used in this rod carefully treated to provide good action. Sections are matched to prevent knots coming together. The six strips of each section of this rod are cut from the same section of cane, making the strips absolutely uniform in action. Tips in bamboo tip case. Packed in partitioned cloth bag.

No.	Weight	Length
6735	5 3/4 oz.	8 ft.
6740	6 1/2 oz.	8 1/2 ft.
6745	7 1/4 oz.	9 ft.
6750	8 oz.	9 1/2 ft.
6755	8 3/4 oz.	10 ft.

Rod Values:	Exc.	V.G.	Good
6735	550.00	350.00	250.00
6740	550.00	350.00	250.00
6745	550.00	350.00	250.00
6750	550.00	350.00	250.00
6755	550.00	350.00	250.00

Split Bamboo Bait Casting Rod

Nickel silver fittings. Nickel silver one ring casting guides. Nickel silver coil tip. Single grip of compressed cork. Attractively wound in red silk. Machine-welted ferrules.

No.	Weight	Length
6455	4 1/2 oz.	3 1/2 ft.
6460	4 3/4 oz.	4 1/2 ft.
6465	5 1/4 oz.	5 ft.
6470	5 3/4 oz.	5 1/2 ft.

Rod Values:	Exc.	V.G.	Good
6455	275.00	175.00	125.00
6460	275.00	175.00	125.00
6465	275.00	175.00	125.00
6470	275.00	175.00	125.00

Winchester Fishing Equipment • 381

Nickel silver fittings. Machine-welted ferrules. Double grip of solid ringed cork. Equipped with strongly constructed finger hook. All guides one ring type. Crystal guides and tips. Offset tip with genuine agate. Attractively wound in purple. Packed in a cloth bag.

No.	Weight	Length
6425	4 1/2 oz.	3 1/2 ft.
6385	4 3/4 oz.	4 1/2 ft.
6390	5 1/4 oz.	5 ft.
6395	5 3/4 oz.	5 1/2 ft.

Rod Values:	Exc.	V.G.	Good
6425	325.00	200.00	150.00
6385	325.00	200.00	150.00
6390	325.00	200.00	150.00
6395	325.00	200.00	150.00

Nickel silver fittings. Machine-welted ferrules. Double grip of ringed cork. Scarlet windings of high-grade Japanese silk. Large one-ring guides fitted with genuine agate. Offset tip of genuine agate. Eccentric-locking reel band which holds the reel firmly in place so that it cannot be shaken loose. Bamboo used in this rod carefully treated to give exceptionally fine action. Sections matched to prevent knots coming together. Packed in a canvas case.

No.	Weight	Length
6415	4 1/2 oz.	3 1/2 ft.
6400	4 3/4 oz.	4 1/2 ft.
6405	5 1/4 oz.	5 ft.
6410	5 3/4 oz.	5 1/2 ft.

Rod Values:	Exc.	V.G.	Good
6415	375.00	260.00	175.00
6400	375.00	260.00	175.00
6405	375.00	260.00	175.00
6410	375.00	260.00	175.00

Nickel silver fittings. Hand-welted, serrated ferrules. Double ringed cork grip. Wound with pepper and salt silk windings. Large one-ring guides with genuine agate. Genuine agate offset tip. Winchester patented interlocking reel band. Packed in a canvas case.

No.	Weight	Length
6420	4 1/2 oz.	3 1/2 ft.
6335	4 3/4 oz.	4 1/2 ft.
6340	5 1/4 oz.	5 ft.
6345	5 1/2 oz.	5 1/2 ft.

Rod Values:	Exc.	V.G.	Good
6420	400.00	290.00	200.00
6335	400.00	290.00	200.00
6340	400.00	290.00	200.00
6345	400.00	290.00	200.00

382 • Winchester Fishing Equipment

Specially designed high grade rod fitted for the purpose of expert and tournament casting. Fittings of 18 percent nickel silver, hand-tooled. Hand-welted, serrated and waterproofed ferrules. Double solid-ringed cork grip. Screw-type reel seat. Wound with two colors of silk. One-ring guides, genuine agate. Tips of offset-type with agate. All agates of special high polish. Bamboo is brown-colored and treated to give exceptionally fine action. Sections matched to prevent knots coming together. Each section made from six strips cut from one piece of cane for uniform quality. Extra quality varnish finish. Extra tip joint. One tip made for 5/8 oz. and the other tip for 1/2 oz. lures. Packed in aluminum rod case.

No.	Weight	Length
6485	4 3/4 oz.	4 1/2 ft.
6490	5 1/4 oz.	5 ft.
6495	5 3/4 oz.	5 1/2 ft.

Rod Values:	Exc.	V.G.	Good
6485	425.00	350.00	250.00
6490	425.00	350.00	250.00
6495	425.00	350.00	250.00

Comment: Winchester introduced this high-end rod in the 1928 catalog but discontinued it by 1931.

Equipped with nickel silver fittings. Double ringed cork grip. Rich, dark green windings. Large, one-ring guides fitted with genuine agate. Genuine agate offset tip. Semi-handmade ferrules, serrated and waterproofed. The bamboo used in this rod is carefully treated to give exceptionally fine action. Sections are carefully matched. Has Winchester patented interlocking reel band. Packed in an aluminum case.

No.	Weight	Length
6365	4 3/4 oz.	4 1/2 ft.
6370	5 1/4 oz.	5 ft.
6375	5 3/4 oz.	5 1/2 ft.

Rod Values:	Exc.	V.G.	Good
6365	425.00	350.00	250.00
6370	425.00	350.00	250.00
6375	425.00	350.00	250.00

Nickel silver fittings, serrated ferrules. Eccentric reel band. Double ringed cork grip. Matched bamboo strips to eliminate parallel knots. All guides and tip genuine agate. Tan silk windings.

Rod Values:	Exc.	V.G.	Good
6310	525.00	440.00	300.00

No.	Weight	Length
6310	6 oz.	6 ft.

Edwards Handmade Casting Rod

High-grade bait casting rod designed by our bamboo expert. Specially adapted for expert bait and tournament casting. Fittings of nickel silver, hand tooled. Double solid ringed cork grip. Hand-welted, serrated and waterproofed ferrules. Guides one ring, genuine agate. Tip of offset type with agate. Rod wound with red silk with tan trimmings, the pongee being transparent after being varnished. Interlocking reel band. The bamboo used in this rod is carefully treated to give exceptionally fine action. Sections matched to prevent knots coming together. Each section made from six strips cut from one piece of cane, making the quality of the strips very uniform. Extra tip joint. Packed in an aluminum case.

No.	Weight	Length
6380	5 3/4 oz.	5 1/2 ft.

Rod Values:	Exc.	V.G.	Good
6380	950.00	700.00	500.00

Steel Fishing Rods

We are repeatedly informed that there is more life and more resiliency in Winchester steel rods than in other steel rods in the market. The reason for this is the expert heat treatment they are given and the extreme care devoted to this important operation.

The steel used is a specially tested grade containing a high percentage of carbon. It combines a desirable light weight with high tensile strength. In manufacture it is so treated that it takes on a resiliency which conveys the strike more quickly from hand to hook than is usual.

Nickel silver fittings are an exclusive feature of Winchester steel rods that add materially to the strength of this line from a selling standpoint. The rust-resisting finish on the inside also marks a distinct step forward in steel rod manufacture. Weights shown on steel rods are gross weights of rods packed.

Steel Fly Rods

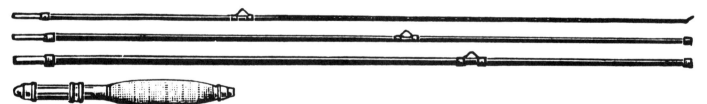

Black enamel. Nickel fittings. Cork grip. Nickel silver snake guides. One ring tip.

No.	Weight	Length
5120	7 1/2 oz.	8 ft.
5125	8 oz.	8 1/2 ft.
5130	8 1/2 oz.	9 ft.
5135	9 oz.	9 1/2 ft.

Same model with reversible handle.

5121	7 1/2 oz.	8 ft.
5126	8 oz.	8 1/2 ft.
5131	8 1/2 oz.	9 ft.
5136	9 oz.	9 1/2 ft.

Rod Values:	Exc.	V.G.	Good
5120	160.00	100.00	75.00
5125	160.00	100.00	75.00
5130	160.00	100.00	75.00
5135	160.00	100.00	75.00
5121	160.00	100.00	75.00
5126	160.00	100.00	75.00
5131	160.00	100.00	75.00
5136	160.00	100.00	75.00

Black enamel. Nickel fittings. Solid compressed cork grips. Nickel silver snake guides. Nickel silver angle tip.

No.	Weight	Length
5025	10 oz.	8 ft.
5030	10 1/2 oz.	8 1/2 ft.
5035	11 oz.	9 ft.
5040	11 1/2 oz.	9 1/2 ft.
5045	12 oz.	10 ft.

Rod Values:	Exc.	V.G.	Good
5025	160.00	100.00	75.00
5030	160.00	100.00	75.00
5035	160.00	100.00	75.00
5040	160.00	100.00	75.00
5045	160.00	100.00	75.00

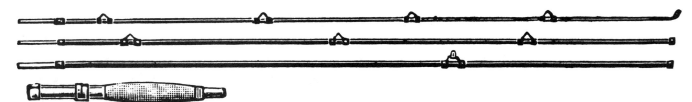

Black enamel. Nickel silver fittings. Eccentric locking reel band. Ringed cork grip. First guide is agate; others snake-style, nickel silver. Agate angle tip.

No.	Weight	Length
5005	9 oz.	8 ft.
5010	9 1/2 oz.	8 1/2 ft.
5015	10 oz.	9 ft.
5020	10 1/2 oz.	9 1/2 ft.

Same model with reversible handle.

5007	10 1/2 oz.	8 ft.
5012	11 oz.	8 1/2 ft.
5017	11 1/2 oz.	9 ft.
5020	11 oz.	9 1/2 ft.

Rod Values:	Exc.	V.G.	Good
5005	185.00	125.00	100.00
5010	185.00	125.00	100.00
5015	185.00	125.00	100.00
5020	185.00	125.00	100.00
5007	185.00	125.00	100.00
5012	185.00	125.00	100.00
5017	185.00	125.00	100.00
5020	185.00	125.00	100.00

Special Light Weight Steel Trout Rod

Black enamel. Nickel silver fittings. First guide and tip of genuine agate. This rod is considerably lighter in weight than any steel rod previously manufactured. It is especially designed for the trade that desires an extremely light rod. It has a nicety of action which will appeal to the most discriminating angler.

No. 5100   Length - 7 ft.

Rod Values:	Exc.	V.G.	Good
5100	200.00	145.00	100.00

Steel Telescopic Rods

A dependable, strong steel rod, adjustable to any length tip to nine feet, to give the fisherman a single rod adaptable to the varying conditions of fishing that often arise in a single day's sport. Equally good for fly casting when stream is open and clear and for work on streams overhung with brush or in thickets. Holds firmly in any adjustment, allowing the angler to use whatever length is most convenient.

Black enamel. Nickel silver snake guides. Three ring nickel silver tip. Reversible handle. 5-inch ringed cork grip.

No. 5090   Weight - 9 oz.

Rod Values:	Exc.	V.G.	Good
5090	145.00	100.00	75.00

Black enameled. Nickel silver snake guides. Three-ring nickel silver tip. Reversible handle. Weight is approximately 9 oz.

No. 5095   **4 1/4-inch ring cork grip**

No. 5096   **Corrugated wood grip handle not detachable from first joint**

Rod Values:	Exc.	V.G.	Good
5095	125.00	90.00	60.00
5096	115.00	85.00	55.00

Model 5450 telescopic bait casting rod. From T. Webster collection. Photo by D. Kowalski.

Bait casting telescopic rod. A dependable, strong steel rod, adjustable to any length up to 5 1/2 feet. Gives the fisherman a single rod adaptable to the varying conditions of fishing that often arise in a single day's sport. Holds firmly in any adjustment, allowing the angler to use whatever length is most convenient. Black enameled. Nickel silver one-ring guides and offset tip. Ringed cork grip with finger hook. Packed in a partitioned cloth bag.

No. 5450   Weight - 8 oz.

Rod Values:	Exc.	V.G.	Good
5450	125.00	90.00	60.00

Steel Bait Rods

Brown enamel. Nickel snake guides and three-ring tip. The guides on 5700 and 5705 are made especially large. Well-turned wooden handle. A strongly built steel rod at a minimum price.

No.	Weight	Length
5700	5 1/2 oz.	4 ft.
5705	5 3/4 oz.	5 ft.
5710	6 1/2 oz.	6 ft.
5715	7 1/2 oz.	7 ft.
5720	8 1/2 oz.	8 ft.
5725	9 1/2 oz.	9 ft.

Rod Values:	Exc.	V.G.	Good
5700	110.00	75.00	50.00
5705	110.00	75.00	50.00
5710	110.00	75.00	50.00
5715	110.00	75.00	50.00
5720	110.00	75.00	50.00
5725	110.00	75.00	50.00

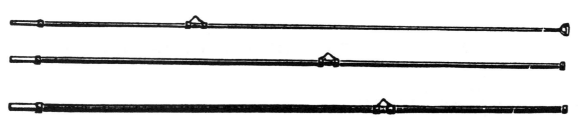

Black enamel. Nickel silver snake guides. Three ring tip. Nickel fittings. Cork grip.

No.	Weight	Length
5730	7 oz.	8 ft.
5740	8 oz.	9 ft.

Rod Values:	Exc.	V.G.	Good
5730	135.00	95.00	65.00
5740	135.00	95.00	65.00

Black enamel. Nickel fittings. Solid cork grip. Two ring nickel silver guides. Three ring nickel silver tip.

No.	Weight	Length
5635	9 1/2 oz.	7 ft.
5640	10 oz.	8 ft.
5650	11 oz.	9 ft.
5660	12 oz.	10 ft.

Rod Values:	Exc.	V.G.	Good
5635	170.00	120.00	80.00
5640	170.00	120.00	80.00
5650	170.00	120.00	80.00
5660	170.00	120.00	80.00

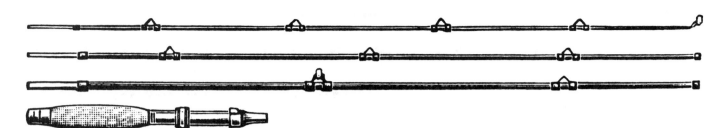

Black enamel. Nickel silver fittings. Solid ringed cork grip. Agate first guide and tip; other guides are two-ring type.

No.	Weight	Length
5665	9 1/2 oz.	7 ft.
5670	10 oz.	8 ft.
5680	11 oz.	9 ft.
5690	12 oz.	10 ft.

The same model with reversible handle.

No.	Weight	Length
5667	10 ounces	7 ft.
5672	10 1/2 oz.	8 ft.
5682	11 1/2 oz.	9 ft.
5692	12 1/2 oz.	10 ft.

Rod Values:	Exc.	V.G.	Good
5665	190.00	140.00	100.00
5670	190.00	140.00	100.00
5680	190.00	140.00	100.00
5690	190.00	140.00	100.00
5667	190.00	140.00	100.00
5672	190.00	140.00	100.00
5682	190.00	140.00	100.00
5692	190.00	140.00	100.00

Steel Bait Casting Rods

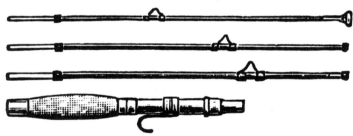

Black enamel. Nickel fittings. Cork grip. Has large, double-ring casting guides. Nickel silver stirrup tip. Equipped with finger hook.

No.	Weight	Length
5380	6 oz.	3 ft.
5385	7 oz.	4 ft.
5350	7 1/2 oz.	4 1/2 ft.
5355	8 oz.	5 ft.
5360	8 1/2 oz.	5 1/2 ft.

Rod Values:	Exc.	V.G.	Good
5380	135.00	95.00	65.00
5385	135.00	95.00	65.00
5350	135.00	95.00	65.00
5355	135.00	95.00	65.00
5360	135.00	95.00	65.00

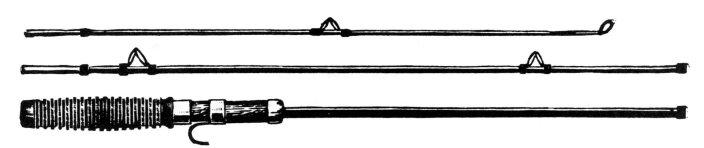

Brown enameled. Nickel fittings. Corrugated wooden handle. Nickel silver double-ringed guides and offset tip. Removable finger hook on reel band.

No.	Weight	Length
5515	7 oz.	4 1/2 ft.
5520	7 1/2 oz.	5 ft.
5525	8 oz.	5 1/2 ft.

Rod Values:	Exc.	V.G.	Good
5515	110.00	75.00	50.00
5520	110.00	75.00	50.00
5525	110.00	75.00	50.00

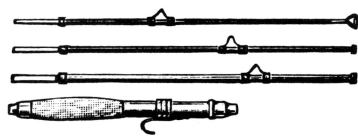

Black enamel. Cork grip. Double-ringed guides and three-ring tip. Nickel fittings. Equipped with finger hook.

No.	Weight	Length
5420	5 oz.	4 ft.
5425	5 1/2 oz.	4 1/2 ft.
5430	6 oz.	5 ft.
5435	6 1/2 oz.	5 1/2 ft.

Rod Values:	Exc.	V.G.	Good
5420	135.00	95.00	65.00
5425	135.00	95.00	65.00
5430	135.00	95.00	65.00
5435	135.00	95.00	65.00

Same as 5420 series, except with crystal first guide and tip.

5540	5 oz.	4 ft.
5545	5 1/2 oz.	4 1/2 ft.
5550	6 oz.	5 ft.
5555	6 1/2 oz.	5 1/2 ft.

Rod Values:	Exc.	V.G.	Good
5540	170.00	120.00	80.00
5545	170.00	120.00	80.00
5550	170.00	120.00	80.00
5555	170.00	120.00	80.00

Same as 5420 series, except all guides and tip are crystal.

No.	Weight	Length
5560	5 oz.	4 ft.
5565	5 1/2 oz.	4 1/2 ft.
5570	6 oz.	5 ft.
5575	6 1/2 oz.	5 1/2 ft.

Rod Values:	Exc.	V.G.	Good
5560	190.00	140.00	100.00
5565	190.00	140.00	100.00
5570	190.00	140.00	100.00
5575	190.00	140.00	100.00

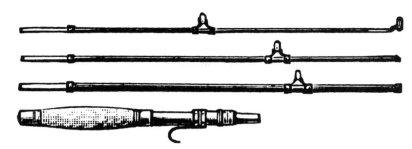

Polished nickel silver fittings. Nickel silver ends. Large one ring crystal casting guides and offset crystal agate casting tip. Single grip of ringed cork. Equipped with finger hook.

No.	Weight	Length
5475	6 oz.	3 ft.
5480	7 oz.	4 ft.
5485	7 1/2 oz.	4 1/2 ft.
5490	8 oz.	5 ft.
5495	8 1/2 oz.	5 1/2 ft.

Rod Values:	Exc.	V.G.	Good
5475	160.00	110.00	70.00
5480	160.00	110.00	70.00
5485	160.00	110.00	70.00
5490	160.00	110.00	70.00
5495	160.00	110.00	70.00

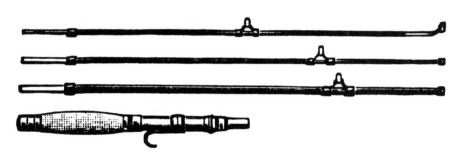

Black enamel. Nickel silver fittings. Solid ringed cork grip. Large one ring casting guides. Offset tip. Agate first guide and tip.

No.	Weight	Length
5300	7 oz.	4 ft.
5305	7 1/2 oz.	4 1/2 ft.
5310	8 oz.	5 ft.
5315	8 1/2 oz.	5 1/2 ft.

Rod Values:	Exc.	V.G.	Good
5300	170.00	120.00	80.00
5305	170.00	120.00	80.00
5310	170.00	120.00	80.00
5315	170.00	120.00	80.00

Same as 5300 series, except all guides and tip of agate.

No.	Weight	Length
5400	7 oz.	4 ft.
5405	7 1/2 oz.	4 1/2 ft.
5410	8 oz.	5 ft.
5415	8 1/2 oz.	5 1/2 ft.

Rod Values:	Exc.	V.G.	Good
5400	190.00	140.00	100.00
5405	190.00	140.00	100.00
5410	190.00	140.00	100.00
5415	190.00	140.00	100.00

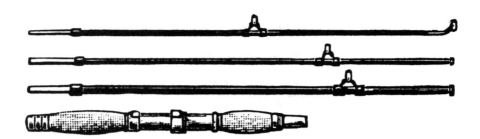

Black enamel. Nickel silver trimmings. Double solid ringed cork grips. All guides are large, one-ring genuine agate casting guides. Genuine agate offset tip. Equipped with Winchester interlocking reel band. Polished finish.

No.	Weight	Length
5320	8 oz.	4 1/2 ft.
5325	8 1/2 oz.	5 ft.
5330	9 oz.	5 1/2 ft.

Same as 5320 series, except has Satin finish.

No.	Weight	Length
5335	8 oz.	4 1/2 ft.
5340	8 1/2 oz.	5 ft.
5345	9 oz.	5 1/2 ft.

Rod Values:	Exc.	V.G.	Good
5320	190.00	140.00	100.00
5325	190.00	140.00	100.00
5330	190.00	140.00	100.00
5335	190.00	140.00	100.00
5340	190.00	140.00	100.00
5345	190.00	140.00	100.00

Lancewood/Cane Fishing Rods

Lancewood fly rod. Nickel plated brass fittings. Nickel silver snake guides. One-ring tip. Ebonized handle. Packed in partitioned cloth bag.

No.	Weight	Length
6008	5 oz.	9 ft.
6013	5 1/2 oz.	10 ft.

Rod Values:	Exc.	V.G.	Good
6008	225.00	145.00	100.00
6013	225.00	145.00	100.00

Winchester Fishing Equipment • 391

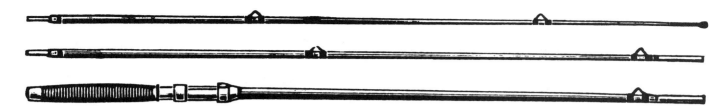

Lancewood bait rod. Nickel plated brass fittings. Spiral guides wound on with scarlet silk. Ebonized handle. Packed in partitioned cloth bag.

No.	Weight	Length
6608	8 oz.	8 ft.
6618	8 1/2 oz.	9 ft.

Rod Values:	Exc.	V.G.	Good
6608	200.00	120.00	85.00
6618	200.00	120.00	85.00

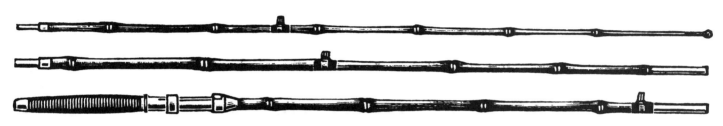

Three-piece rod of Japanese cane. Ebonized handle. Nickel-plated brass ferrules and reel seat. Spiral guides wound on with scarlet silk. Heat straightened and varnished. Extra strong tip.

No.	Weight	Length
6838	12 oz.	8 ft.
6843	12 oz.	9 ft.
6848	12 oz.	10 ft.

Rod Values:	Exc.	V.G.	Good
6838	170.00	120.00	80.00
6843	170.00	120.00	80.00
6848	170.00	120.00	80.00

Crusader Fishing Rods

Crusader three-piece rod of Japanese cane. Brass ferrules. Wound-on tips.

No.	Weight	Length
6808	8 oz.	8 ft.
6813	10 oz.	10 ft.
6818	12 oz.	12 ft.

Rod Values:	Exc.	V.G.	Good
6808	100.00	70.00	50.00
6813	100.00	70.00	50.00
6818	100.00	70.00	50.00

Comment: *Originally a very cheap three-piece cane pole for the beginner.*

Three-piece rod of Japanese cane. Brass ferrules, butt cap and reel band. Ring guides and tip wound on with scarlet silk. Heat straightened and varnished. Crusader brand.

Rod Values:	**Exc.**	**V.G.**	**Good**
6823	100.00	70.00	50.00
6828	100.00	70.00	50.00
6833	100.00	70.00	50.00

No.	*Weight*	*Length*
6823	8 oz.	8 ft.
6828	10 oz.	10 ft.
6833	12 oz.	12 ft.

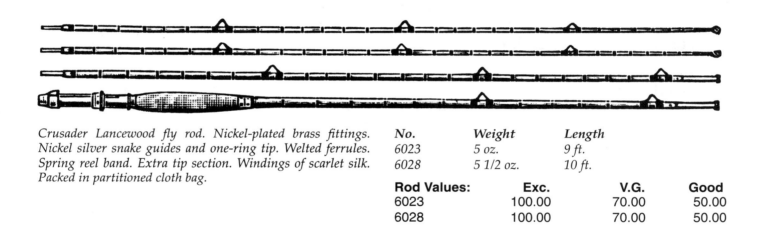

Crusader Lancewood fly rod. Nickel-plated brass fittings. Nickel silver snake guides and one-ring tip. Welted ferrules. Spring reel band. Extra tip section. Windings of scarlet silk. Packed in partitioned cloth bag.

No.	*Weight*	*Length*
6023	5 oz.	9 ft.
6028	5 1/2 oz.	10 ft.

Rod Values:	**Exc.**	**V.G.**	**Good**
6023	100.00	70.00	50.00
6028	100.00	70.00	50.00

Fishing Rod Handles

Winchester also sold fishing rod handles separately so fishermen could convert their rods to other configurations and uses. These would have been stamped "Winchester" on the reel seat.

They also made steel rod trolling tips and steel rod reducers that fit into the handle to receive the second joint of the rod. Another interesting product was an "emergency rod top" measuring 2 1/2 inches long that could be used when a tip broke off or it could be inserted directly into the second rod joint to make a shorter and stouter rod. It is unlikely these small parts were stamped.

As we get photographs of these items with their original boxes, we will present them in future editions.

Winchester Fishing Reels

Winchester fishing reels and metal baits were initially manufactured with the worn-out machinery used by the Andrew B. Hendryx Company since the 1880s. After Winchester purchased them in 1919, they retooled. But Winchester only added a few high quality casting reels that were their original designs. All other reels were the same ones that Hendryx had been selling for many years. Undoubtedly, Winchester's financial difficulties in the 1920s allowed only a minimal amount of research and development for their fishing tackle.

However, fishing reels tend to last longer than any other fishing collectible. More Winchester reels appear on the tackle market than any other fishing tackle item. Thus it is possible for a Winchester collector to put together a very nice collection of Winchester reels. There are quite a few Winchester collectors that have more than fifty reels in their collections, and some have in the hundreds.

The most common Winchester reels are "utility" models. These were inexpensive reels, usually purchased by casual fishermen, or by a father for his son. They were the 1920's equivalent of today's cheap spincast reel. They were either round plated, or had raised pillars, with a 2:1 gear ratio. These reels were the staples of the Hendryx line, and Winchester produced most of the same models under their own logo. These reels ranged in size from 40- to 100-yard capacities.

At some point in Winchester's tackle production, many of these utility reels were assigned numbers that were not catalogued. There are at least twenty, and probably more, utility reels that have numbers not used in the price section. All these reels seem to be identical to reels that Winchester catalogued, and prices should be the same.

Collectors should be cautious of reels with irregular number stampings however, for there are a great many unmarked utility reels that are waiting for the forger with the Winchester metal stamp and a set of number stamps. These counterfeit reels can usually be recognized by larger-than-normal digits, and evidence that the numbers were stamped one at a time – rather than with a continuous four-digit stamp.

Winchester saltwater reels are usually the highest priced of all Winchester reels, except for a few scarce casting reels. Fewer saltwater reels were produced, so they are scarcer today. Also the corrosion inherent in salt water makes it harder to find Excellent or Very Good examples.

The scarcest of all the reels are Winchester's top-of-the-line casting reels, the #4160 and #4161 non-level wind, and the #4345 level wind. These were original designs by Winchester and patented in 1924. All these reels were made of nickel silver and are quality products. However, they are quite scarce, so if you get a chance to grab one you'd better do so when you get the opportunity.

Winchester Fishing Reels

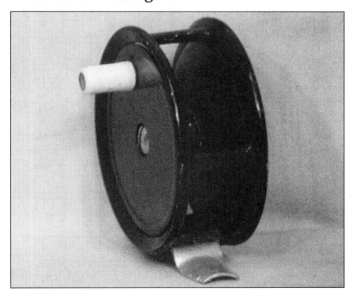

Model 1630 fly fishing reel is one of the more sought-after reels that is not nickel silver. From T. Webster collection. Photo by D. Kowalski.

Two important features of Winchester Reels are evident to the eye at first glance, their sturdy construction and beauty. Among the many styles offered in this line will be found reels that will meet the requirements of both the casual and the all-around fisherman and of all those anglers who demand a reel of the finest mechanism.

Single Action. A solidly constructed fly reel of aluminum alloy finished in dull black; beautiful in appearance and perfect in action. Its extreme lightness and strength will appeal to the most exacting anglers. Easily taken apart by removing the spool retaining screw. Adjustable click. Weight - 8 oz.

No.	Capacity	Disc Diam.	Pillar Length
1730	50 yds.	3 1/4 in.	3/4 in.
1630	35 yds.	2 7/8 in.	3/4 in.

Reel Values:	Exc.	V.G.	Good
1730	275.00	225.00	175.00
1630	275.00	225.00	175.00

Model 1236 fly fishing reel is one of a line of cheap, light reels with nickel finish. From T. Webster collection. Photo by D. Kowalski.

Single Action. A very popular reel for fly fishing. The large open drum and perforated sides of the frame permit free circulation of air which dries the line quickly. Light in weight but very strong. Removable spool, adjustable click. Nickel finish. Weight - 8 oz.

No.	Capacity	Disc Diam.	Pillar Length
1336	80 yds.	2 7/8 in.	1 in.
1236	60 yds.	2 7/8 in.	3/4 in.
1136	40 yds.	2 3/8 in.	3/4 in.

Reel Values:	Exc.	V.G.	Good
1336	200.00	150.00	100.00
1236	200.00	150.00	100.00
1136	225.00	175.00	125.00

Model 1235 fly fishing reel with black finish. From T. Webster collection. Photo by D. Kowalski.

Same reel as above in dull black finish.

No.	Capacity	Disc Diam.	Pillar Length
1335	80 yds.	2 7/8 in.	1 in.
1235	60 yds.	2 7/8 in.	3/4 in.
1135	40 yds.	2 3/8 in.	3/4 in.

Reel Values:	Exc.	V.G.	Good
1335	225.00	175.00	125.00
1235	250.00	200.00	150.00
1135	250.00	200.00	150.00

Model 1212 bait casting reel with box. Values at right are for reel only but original boxes with reel would at least double the value of the collectible. From T. Webster collection. Photo by D. Kowalski.

Single action. Strongly constructed medium-priced bait casting reel. Solidly constructed screwed frame. Adjustable click. Nickel finish. Weight - 8 oz.

No.	Capacity	Disc Diam.	Pillar Length
1412	80 yds.	2 1/2 in.	1 in.
1312	60 yds.	2 1/4 in.	1 in.
1212	40 yds.	2 in.	1 in.

Reel Values:	Exc.	V.G.	Good
1412	165.00	115.00	75.00
1312	185.00	125.00	90.00
1212	210.00	150.00	100.00

Single action. This reel is manufactured to meet the demand for an inexpensive single-action reel. Made of brass. No click. Has improved one-piece cross plate which gives added strength.

No.	Capacity	Disc Diam.	Pillar Length
1418	80 yds.	2 1/2 in.	1 in.
1318	60 yds.	2 1/4 in.	1 in.
1218	40 yds.	2 in.	1 in.
1118	25 yds.	1 3/4 in.	1 in.

Reel Values:	Exc.	V.G.	Good
1418	165.00	135.00	100.00
1318	165.00	135.00	100.00
1218	185.00	145.00	110.00
1118	200.00	150.00	115.00

Model 1118 bait casting reel (with no click). From T. Webster collection. Photo by D. Kowalski.

No.	Capacity	Disc Diam.	Pillar Length
1419	80 yds.	2 1/2 in.	1 in.
1319	60 yds.	2 1/4 in.	1 in.
1219	40 yds.	2 in.	1 in.
1119	25 yds.	1 3/4 in.	1 in.

Reel Values:	Exc.	V.G.	Good
1419	185.00	125.00	90.00
1319	185.00	125.00	90.00
1219	185.00	125.00	90.00
1119	210.00	150.00	100.00

Model 1119 bait casting reel. Has brass finish and permanent click. From T. Webster collection. Photo by D. Kowalski.

No.	Capacity	Disc Diam.	Pillar Length
1421	80 yds.	2 1/2 in.	1 in.
1321	60 yds.	2 1/4 in.	1 in.
1221	40 yds.	2 in.	1 in.
1121	25 yds.	1 3/4 in.	1 in.

Reel Values:	Exc.	V.G.	Good
1421	185.00	125.00	90.00
1321	185.00	125.00	90.00
1221	200.00	145.00	95.00
1121	200.00	145.00	95.00

Model 1121 bait casting reel is the same reel as the Model 1119 but with a nickel finish. From T. Webster collection. Photo by D. Kowalski.

Model 2647 bait casting reel is one of the rarer nickel silver models. Some collectors refer to these as "German silver" models. Note the leather thumb brake. From T. Webster collection. Photo by D. Kowalski.

Double action. A sturdily constructed reel especially adapted to heavy fishing, such as surf casting, deep lake and saltwater trolling. Made with black Bakelite side plates which are superior in strength to hard rubber. Nickel silver frame. Steel pivots. Equipped with detachable leather thumb brake. Weight each about 19 oz.

No.	Capacity	Disc Diam.	Pillar Length
2647	200 yds.	3 in.	2 1/8 in.

Reel Values:	Exc.	V.G.	Good
2647	475.00	425.00	325.00

Model 2640 bait casting reel has the same design as the Model 2647 but it has nickel-plated brass frame and no thumb brake. From T. Webster collection. Photo by D. Kowalski.

No.	Capacity	Disc Diam.	Pillar Length
2840	300 yds.	3 1/4 in.	2 3/8 in.
2740	250 yds.	3 1/4 in.	2 1/8 in.
2640	200 yds.	3 in.	2 1/8 in.
2540	150 yds.	3 in.	1 7/8 in.

Reel Values:	Exc.	V.G.	Good
2840	350.00	300.00	225.00
2740	350.00	300.00	225.00
2640	350.00	300.00	225.00
2540	350.00	300.00	225.00

Model 2644 bait casting reel. From T. Webster collection. Photo by D. Kowalski.

Double action. A reel of sturdy construction made for heavy fishing and lake trolling. Adjustable click and drag. Heavily nickel-plated. Weight each about 19 oz.

No.	Capacity	Disc Diam.	Pillar Length
2944	300 yds.	3 3/4 in.	1 7/8 in.
2844	250 yds.	3 1/2 in.	1 7/8 in.
2744	200 yds.	3 1/4 in.	1 7/8 in.
2644	150 yds.	3 in.	1 7/8 in.

Reel Values:	Exc.	V.G.	Good
2944	300.00	250.00	175.00
2844	250.00	225.00	160.00
2744	250.00	225.00	160.00
2644	250.00	225.00	160.00

Double action. A reel popular because of its quality and moderate price. Suitable for trolling and still fishing. Adjustable click and drag. Nickel finish. Weight each about 9 oz.

No.	Capacity	Disc Diam.	Pillar Length
2430	100 yds.	2 1/2 in.	1 5/8 in.
2330	80 yds.	2 1/4 in.	1 5/8 in.
2230	60 yds.	2 1/4 in.	1 3/8 in.
2130	40 yds.	2 in.	1 3/8 in.

Reel Values:	Exc.	V.G.	Good
2430	135.00	100.00	80.00
2330	135.00	100.00	80.00
2230	150.00	110.00	90.00
2130	150.00	110.00	90.00

Model 2430 bait casting reel. From T. Webster collection. Photo by D. Kowalski.

No.	Capacity	Disc Diam.	Pillar Length
2490	100 yds.	2 1/2 in.	1 5/8 in.
2390	80 yds.	2 1/4 in.	1 5/8 in.
2290	60 yds.	2 1/4 in.	1 3/8 in.
2190	40 yds.	2 in.	1 3/8 in.

Reel Values:	Exc.	V.G.	Good
2490	160.00	125.00	100.00
2390	160.00	125.00	100.00
2290	175.00	135.00	110.00
2190	175.00	135.00	110.00

Model 2490 bait casting reel is the same reel as the Model 2430 but it has red jeweled oil cap. From T. Webster collection. Photo by D. Kowalski.

Double action. A moderately priced reel, suitable for trolling and still fishing. Adjustable drag and click. Made of brass with polished nickel-plated finish. Weight each about 9 oz.

No.	Capacity	Disc Diam.	Pillar Length
2442	100 yds.	2 1/2 in.	1 5/8 in.
2342	80 yds.	2 1/4 in.	1 5/8 in.
2242	60 yds.	2 1/4 in.	1 3/8 in.
2142	40 yds.	2 in.	1 3/8 in.

Reel Values:	Exc.	V.G.	Good
2442	135.00	100.00	75.00
2342	135.00	100.00	75.00
2242	150.00	110.00	85.00
2142	150.00	110.00	85.00

Model 2342 bait casting reel. From T. Webster collection. Photo by D. Kowalski.

Double action. Nickel-plated brass. Has adjustable drag and click. Weight each about 9 1/2 oz.

No.	Capacity	Disc Diam.	Pillar Length
2336	60 yds.	2 1/4 in.	1 3/8 in.
2236	40 yds.	2 in.	1 3/8 in.

Reel Values:	**Exc.**	**V.G.**	**Good**
2336	135.00	100.00	85.00
2236	135.00	100.00	85.00

Model 2336 bait casting reel. From T. Webster collection. Photo by D. Kowalski.

Here are examples of the same model number being used on designs that changed over the years. These are front and side views of three bait casting reels, all authentic and all stamped as Model 2242. From T. Webster collection. Photos by D. Kowalski.

Similar to Model 2336 but has special 1 7/8-inch pillars, giving 40 yards larger capacity and slightly different proportions. Double action. Nickel-plated brass. Adjustable drag and click. Weight each about 9 1/2 oz.

No.	Capacity	Disc Diam.	Pillar Length
2392	100 yds.	2 1/4 in.	1 7/8 in.
2292	80 yds.	2 in.	1 7/8 in.

Reel Values:	Exc.	V.G.	Good
2392	115.00	90.00	70.00
2292	115.00	90.00	70.00

These models are the same as Model 2336 and Model 2236 but have plain oil caps. Photograph not available.

No.	Capacity	Disc Diam.	Pillar Length
2393	60 yds.	2 1/4 in.	1 3/8 in.
2293	40 yds.	2 in.	1 3/8 in.

Reel Values:	Exc.	V.G.	Good
2393	150.00	125.00	100.00
2293	150.00	125.00	100.00

Model 2392 bait casting reel. From T. Webster collection. Photo by D. Kowalski.

These models are the same as Model 2393 and Model 2293 but have red jeweled oil caps.

No.	Capacity	Disc Diam.	Pillar Length
2391	60 yds.	2 1/4 in.	1 3/8 in.
2291	40 yds.	2 in.	1 3/8 in.

Reel Values:	Exc.	V.G.	Good
2391	135.00	100.00	85.00
2291	135.00	100.00	85.00

Model 2291 bait casting reel with box. From T. Webster collection. Photo by D. Kowalski.

Model 2830 bait casting reel. From T. Webster collection. Photo by D. Kowalski.

Double action. Sturdily constructed and especially adapted to heavy fishing, such as surf casting, deep lake and saltwater trolling. Black Bakelite side plates. Nickel-plated brass frame. Steel pivots. Adjustable click. Lever at front for free spool operation. Weight about 19 oz.

No.	Capacity	Disc Diam.	Pillar Length
2830	300 yds.	3 1/2 in.	1 3/8 in.
2730	250 yds.	3 1/4 in.	2 1/8 in.

Reel Values:	Exc.	V.G.	Good
2830	350.00	290.00	250.00
2730	350.00	290.00	250.00

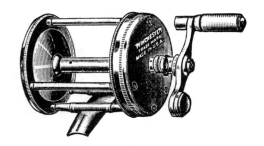

No.	Capacity	Disc Diam.	Pillar Length
4160	100 yds.	2 in.	1 3/4 in.

Reel Values:	Exc.	V.G.	Good
4160	525.00	400.00	325.00

Nickel Silver with satin finish. Quadruple action. Exceptionally high grade. For use in tournament work and for the angler who values accuracy, power and quietness in castings. The spiral-cut gears and perfectly balanced handle eliminate practically all vibration. Knurled edge, white grip. Adjustable click. Plain oil caps. Weight about 13 oz.

Model 4345 bait casting reel is nickel silver and has level-winding guide to distribute line evenly on spool. From T. Webster collection. Photo by D. Kowalski.

Quadruple action. Level winding. Nickel silver with satin finish. Exceptionally high grade. For use in tournament work and for the angler who values accuracy, power and quietness in casting. The spiral-cut gears and perfectly balanced handle eliminate practically all vibration. Knurled edge, double-handle level winding. Adjustable click. Plain Oil Caps. Weight each about 13 oz.

No.	Capacity	Disc Diam.	Pillar Length
4345	100 yds.	2 in.	1 3/4 in.

Reel Values:	Exc.	V.G.	Good
4345	525.00	400.00	325.00

Quadruple action. Nickel silver. An exceptionally high-grade reel designed for use in tournament work and for the angler who values accuracy, power and quietness in casting. The spiral-cut gears and perfectly balanced handle eliminate practically all vibration. Adjustable click. Weight about 12 oz.

No.	Capacity	Disc Diam.	Pillar Length
4161	85 yds.	2 in.	1 1/2 in.

Reel Values:	Exc.	V.G.	Good
4161	625.00	500.00	375.00

Model 4161, another nickel silver bait casting reel. From T. Webster collection. Photo by D. Kowalski.

Quadruple action. Level winding. Nickel-plated heavy brass. Knurled edge. Double handle with white grips. Spiral-cut gears. Adjustable click. Plain oil caps. Weight about 13 oz.

No.	Capacity	Disc Diam.	Pillar Length
4340	100 yds.	2 1/4 in.	1 7/8 in.

Reel Values:	Exc.	V.G.	Good
4340	350.00	250.00	175.00

Model 4340, nickel-plated brass reel with level winding bar. From T. Webster collection. Photo by D. Kowalski.

Quadruple action. Level winding. Nickel-plated heavy brass. Knurled edge. Double handle with white grips. Adjustable click. Weight about 12 oz.

No.	Capacity	Disc Diam.	Pillar Length
4339	80-100 yds.	2 in.	1 7/8 in.

Reel Values:	Exc.	V.G.	Good
4339	275.00	200.00	150.00

Comment: *This was Winchester's least-expensive level-wind reel.*

Model 4339 with box. From T. Webster collection. Photo by D. Kowalski.

Model 4350 in two versions, one arm and two. In company catalogs, this model is pictured with two arms but we know enough about Winchester manufacturing practices to not be surprised if they put a single arm on some of the models. And since this reel was so easy to take apart, some enterprising buyer might have decided he liked the reel but the extra arm got in the way so he replaced it. From T. Webster collection. Photo by D. Kowalski.

No.	Capacity	Disc Diam.	Pillar Length
4350	100 yds.	2 in.	2 5/8 in.
4250	80 yds.	2 in.	2 3/8 in.

Reel Values:	Exc.	V.G.	Good
4350	250.00	175.00	125.00
4250	250.00	175.00	125.00

Here's a drawing of the Model 4350 taken apart. Quadruple action. The simplicity of construction of this take-down reel will appeal to all bait casters. Removing the right oil cap and giving a slight turn to the right cap will make the spool and other parts accessible for cleaning and oiling. The cap is held firmly in place by a specially designed catch. The reel cannot be assembled incorrectly. Has tubular frame with nickel finish. Weight about 10 1/2 oz.

Model 4246 has double handles. From T. Webster collection. Photo by D. Kowalski.

A quadruple-action reel exceptional in appearance, balance and action. Strong brass reel with precision cut gears, and tooled parts perfectly assembled. Agate bearing caps. Double-handled balance crank. Nickel-plated emery finish with brass-finish axle and bright nickel cross plate, click button and binding screw. Weight about 10 1/2 oz.

No.	Capacity	Disc Diam.	Pillar Length
4247	100 yds.	2 1/4 in.	1 7/8 in.
4246	80 yds.	2 in.	1 7/8 in.

Reel Values:	Exc.	V.G.	Good
4247	200.00	150.00	100.00
4246	200.00	150.00	100.00

Winchester Fishing Equipment • 403

Quadruple action. A reel plain in design and of simple construction. Can easily be taken apart. Made with Winchester's patented take-down feature designed to eliminate any danger of the frame loosening while in action. Satin nickel finish. Weight about 10 1/2 oz.

No.	Capacity	Disc Diam.	Pillar Length
4356	80 yds.	2 in.	1 7/8 in.
4256	60 yds.	2 in.	1 5/8 in.

Reel Values:	Exc.	V.G.	Good
4356	225.00	160.00	110.00
4256	225.00	160.00	110.00

Model 4356, also a take-down model. From T. Webster collection. Photo by D. Kowalski.

Quadruple action. Medium-priced reel, suitable for all-around use. Has carefully cut steel gears and polished bearings which insure spool accuracy for distance in casting. Reel offered at a moderate price. Made of brass, nickel plated. Weight about 10 oz.

No.	Capacity	Disc Diam.	Pillar Length
4254	100 yds.	2 1/4 in.	1 7/8 in.
4253	80 yds.	2 in.	1 7/8 in.
4252	60 yds.	2 in.	1 5/8 in.

Reel Values:	Exc.	V.G.	Good
4254	200.00	150.00	100.00
4253	200.00	150.00	100.00
4252	200.00	150.00	100.00

Model 4252. From T. Webster collection. Photo by D. Kowalski.

Quadruple action. Brass reel, nickel-plated. Has adjustable drag and click. Weight about 9 1/2 oz.

No.	Capacity	Disc Diam.	Pillar Length
4331	80 yds.	2 1/4 in.	1 5/8 in.
4231	60 yds.	2 in.	1 5/8 in.

Reel Values:	Exc.	V.G.	Good
4331	135.00	100.00	85.00
4231	135.00	100.00	85.00

Model 4231 has adjustable drag. From T. Webster collection. Photo by D. Kowalski.

Model 4382 is a slightly larger version of the Model 4331. From T. Webster collection. Photo by D. Kowalski.

Similar to Model 4331 and Model 4231 but have a longer 1 7/8-inch pillar which increases the line capacity by 20 yards. Weight about 9 1/2 oz.

No.	Capacity	Disc Diam.	Pillar Length
4382	100 yds.	2 1/4 in.	1 7/8 in.
4282	80 yds.	2 in.	1 7/8 in.

Reel Values:	Exc.	V.G.	Good
4382	135.00	100.00	85.00
4282	135.00	100.00	85.00

Model 4328 has adjustable drag. From T. Webster collection. Photo by D. Kowalski.

Quadruple action. Brass reel, heavily nickel-plated. Adjustable drag and click. Weight about 10 oz.

No.	Capacity	Disc Diam.	Pillar Length
4328	80 yds.	2 1/4 in.	1 5/8 in.
4228	60 yds.	2 in.	1 5/8 in.

Reel Values:	Exc.	V.G.	Good
4328	165.00	125.00	100.00
4228	165.00	125.00	100.00

Model 4290 has red jewel on oil cap. From T. Webster collection. Photo by D. Kowalski.

Same models as the 4328 and 4228 but with jeweled oil caps. Weight about 10 oz.

No.	Capacity	Disc Diam.	Pillar Length
4390	80 yds.	2 1/4 in.	1 5/8 in.
4290	60 yds.	2 in.	1 5/8 in.

Reel Values:	Exc.	V.G.	Good
4390	185.00	150.00	125.00
4290	185.00	150.00	125.00

Same models as the 4328 and 4228 but with longer 1 7/8-inch pillars giving extra line capacity of 20 yards per reel. Weight about 10 oz.

No.	Capacity	Disc Diam.	Pillar Length
4391	100 yds.	2 1/4 in.	1 7/8 in.
4291	80 yds.	2 in.	1 7/8 in.

Reel Values:	Exc.	V.G.	Good
4391	185.00	150.00	125.00
4291	185.00	150.00	125.00

Model 4291 is actually a Model 4228 with a longer pillar. From T. Webster collection. Photo by D. Kowalski.

Another version of the Model 4291. From T. Webster collection. Photo by D. Kowalski.

More Models of Winchester Reels

Here are additional Winchester reels about which we have limited information. These were not described in the 1927, 1928 or 1931 Winchester catalogs, so we assume they were made for short periods of time. We will present photographs here, as well as their model numbers. The following value chart applies to all the reels in the following section, unless otherwise noted.

Reel Values:	Exc.	V.G.	Good
Models	225.00	175.00	125.00

Model 2137. From T. Webster collection. Photo by D. Kowalski.

Model 1195. From T. Webster collection. Photo by D. Kowalski.

Model 2206. From T. Webster collection. Photo by D. Kowalski.

406 • Winchester Fishing Equipment

Model 2237. From T. Webster collection. Photo by D. Kowalski.

Model 2210. From T. Webster collection. Photo by D. Kowalski.

Model 2245. From T. Webster collection. Photo by D. Kowalski.

Model 2448. From T. Webster collection. Photo by D. Kowalski.

Model 2238. From T. Webster collection. Photo by D. Kowalski.

Model 2726. From T. Webster collection. Photo by D. Kowalski.

Model 2926. From T. Webster collection. Photo by D. Kowalski.

Model 2826. From T. Webster collection. Photo by D. Kowalski.

Model 2348. From T. Webster collection. Photo by D. Kowalski.

Winchester Fishing Lures

The Winchester Repeating Arms Company listed only three wooden lures in their catalogs. These were a rather chubby three-hook minnow, a sleek five-hook minnow, and the Multi-Wobbler. The minnows were unique in that they had two different styles of propellers – a conventional one on the front, and a straight-line rear prop. The Multi-Wobbler was a reverse-running, crab-type bait, with double hooks. The diving planes were adjustable to make the lure dive deep or run on, or near, the surface. On all the wooden lures, the Winchester name and model number were stamped on the front propeller, or diving plane. Collectors should make sure that these numbers are correct for the lure and color.

Winchester used a unique photo-finish decal to apply their scale pattern to all three wooden lures. This finish was available in silver or gold. The method of finishing these lures was patented by Leavitt Lane in 1921, and assigned to the Winchester Repeating Arms Company. This finish was an attempt to provide scale-patterned bait that did not violate the very successful scale finish patent owned by the Creek Chub Bait Company. The decal finish did not hold up well and consequently it is very difficult to find examples that are in Very Good or Excellent condition. The eyes on these photo finish lures were a part of the decal pattern, not a glass eye. This lack of glass eyes makes these colors less appealing to some collectors, which lowers their value when compared to some of the other paint finishes that do have glass eyes.

Other than terminal tackle (i.e. hooks and sinkers) there were more lures manufactured and sold than any other fishing' tackle item. This makes the high prices claimed by some wooden lures a bit hard to understand. However, it is all a question of supply and demand. There are more lure collectors than rod or reel collectors, so the demand for quality baits raises the price.

Due to the limited number of catalogued wooden lures and colors produced (eight), it is still possible for the Winchester collector to put together a complete collection of Winchester wooden lures. The problem today is finding 24 lures in Very Good or better condition that the average man can afford. There are some complete color collections of Winchester wooden lures, but most were acquired before today's high prices.

In collecting wooden lures, color patterns control the price variations, with unpopular colors (fewer produced) or special-order colors usually bringing the highest prices. Winchester did not appear to manufacture any special-order colors, but there are some patterns that are more desirable than others. As mentioned above, the decal patterns did not hold up well, so representatives in Very Good or better condition command top dollar.

Collectors seem to like color #5 green crackle back, and color #0 which is commonly called "parrot" (white with green back stripes and a red head), so the demand and consequently the price is a bit higher for these colors.

Winchester also manufactured a line of generic or "Economy Minnows" which were produced by using the wooden bodies from the underwater min-

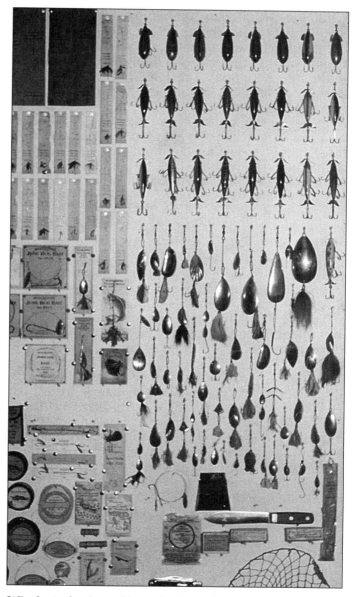

Winchester's plugs, flies and spinner baits lend themselves to wall displays. Here is part of the Tom Webster collection, including a near-complete set of the three styles of wooden plugs. Photo by D. Kowalski.

nows, fitting them with a front propeller and side and trailing treble hooks. These hooks were attached with simple screw eyes without cups. These lures had very simple paint patterns of white with either red head, or a blended green back, and no eyes.

There was also a surface minnow, which was produced by using the Multi-Wobbler body with a belly and trailing treble, and front propeller only. These lures have not been found in any catalog, and when and why Winchester manufactured them is unknown at this time. It is possible that they were produced from left-over parts after Winchester went out of the fishing tackle business.

The best opportunity to accumulate a large specialized collection of Winchester tackle would be with spoonbaits. The number of sizes and types is almost unlimited, and there are still lots of these items surfacing from America's garages and attics. Spoonbaits are generally small in size, and are easy to display. A metal bait display that was similar to the old advertising cartridge boards would be a thing of beauty.

Since there is no way to mark a fly, Winchester artificial flies must be on a card to be identified. The large gaudy bass flies common during Winchester's tackle production days are things of beauty. Since bass flies are an American innovation, perhaps they are the common man's version of the intricate and high-priced Atlantic salmon flies.

Winchester Plug Baits

Winchester plug baits are offered in three styles: the Multi-wobbler, the Minnow equipped with three treble hooks and the Minnow equipped with five treble hooks.

The Multi-Wobbler is very accurately shaped and weighted to make it active in the water and correct for casting purposes. By various simple adjustments of the blades this bait may be made to dive, dart or wobble either on or under the surface. When not in action it floats. This bait is furnished with double hooks, making it practically weedless.

The Winchester Minnow bait is also very carefully shaped and weighted to insure correct action in the water. The spinners move easily and revolve in opposite directions. All metal parts, including the detachable hooks, are nickel-plated. The Minnow bait is furnished with both three treble hooks and five treble hooks, according to the purpose for which it is desired.

Each style of bait is furnished in eight different color combinations, all carefully selected for practical use. Two of these are scale finishes, one in gold, the other in silver. The gold scale finish represents the coloring of the gold fish, while the silver scale has the effect of a minnow.

Multi-Wobbler. Made in eight finishes. Weight about 3/4 oz. each.

No. 9200. White with green back stripes, red head. From T. Webster collection. Photo by D. Kowalski.

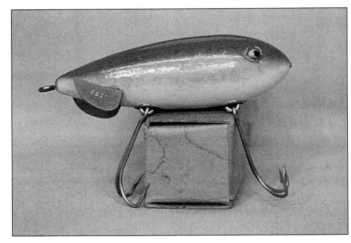

No. 9201. Green and gold back, yellow underneath. From T. Webster collection. Photo by D. Kowalski.

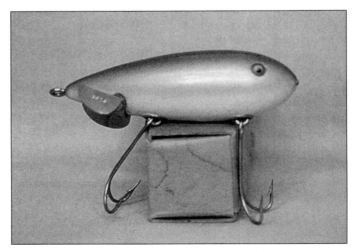

No. 9202. Green with silver sides. From T. Webster collection. Photo by D. Kowalski.

Winchester Fishing Equipment • 409

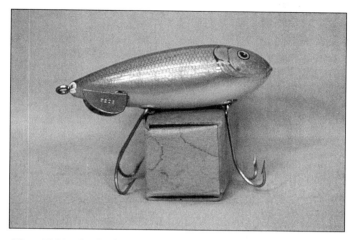

No. 9203. *Scale finish, gold. From T. Webster collection. Photo by D. Kowalski.*

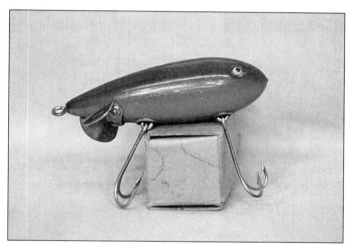

No. 9204. *Red. From T. Webster collection. Photo by D. Kowalski.*

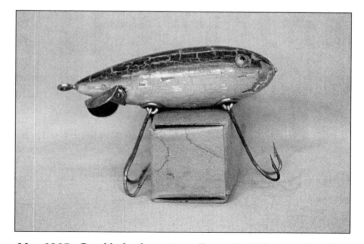

No. 9205. *Crackle-back pattern. From T. Webster collection. Photo by D. Kowalski.*

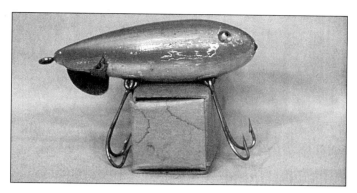

No. 9206. *Rainbow color. From T. Webster collection. Photo by D. Kowalski.*

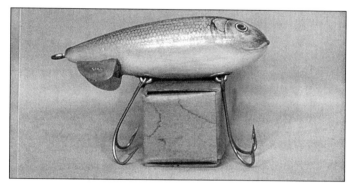

No. 9207. *Scale finish, silver. From T. Webster collection. Photo by D. Kowalski.*

Plug Values:	Exc.	V.G.	Good
9200	800.00	550.00	350.00
9201	700.00	500.00	300.00
9202	700.00	500.00	300.00
9203	800.00	550.00	350.00
9204	700.00	500.00	300.00
9205	800.00	550.00	350.00
9206	700.00	500.00	300.00
9207	800.00	550.00	350.00

Minnow with Three Treble Hooks. *Made in eight finishes. Weight about 1 oz. each.*

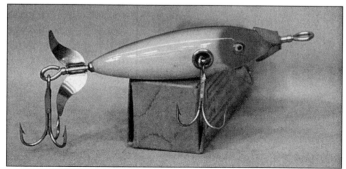

No. 9010. *White with green back stripes, red head. From T. Webster collection. Photo by D. Kowalski.*

410 • Winchester Fishing Equipment

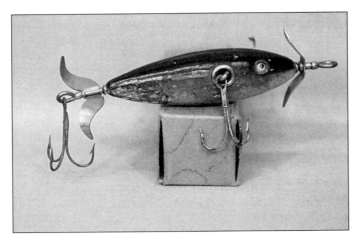

No. 9011. *Green and gold back, yellow underneath. From T. Webster collection. Photo by D. Kowalski.*

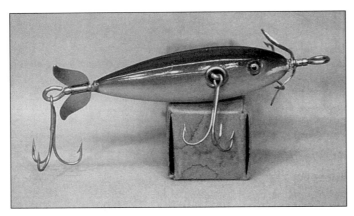

No. 9012. *Green with silver sides. From T. Webster collection. Photo by D. Kowalski.*

No. 9013. *Scale finish, gold. Photo not available.*

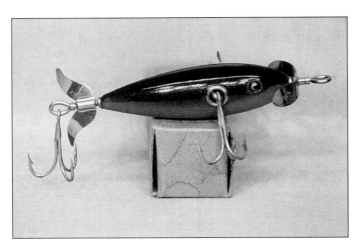

No. 9014. *Red. From T. Webster collection. Photo by D. Kowalski.*

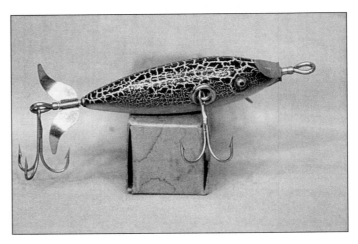

No. 9015. *Crackle-back pattern. From T. Webster collection. Photo by D. Kowalski.*

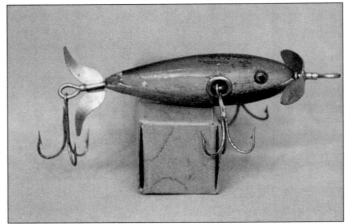

No. 9016. *Rainbow color. From T. Webster collection. Photo by D. Kowalski.*

Winchester Fishing Equipment • 411

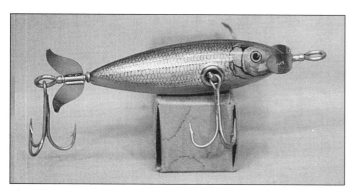

No. 9017. *Scale finish, silver. From T. Webster collection. Photo by D. Kowalski.*

Plug Values:	Exc.	V.G.	Good
9010	1,100.00	850.00	600.00
9011	900.00	700.00	500.00
9012	900.00	700.00	500.00
9013	1,100.00	850.00	600.00
9014	900.00	700.00	500.00
9015	1,100.00	850.00	600.00
9016	900.00	700.00	500.00
9017	1,100.00	850.00	600.00

Minnow with Five Treble Hooks. *Made in eight finishes. Weight about 1 1/8 oz. each.*

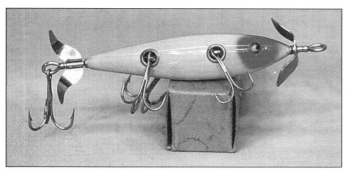

No. 9210. *White with green back stripes, red head. From T. Webster collection. Photo by D. Kowalski.*

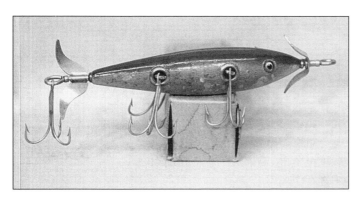

No. 9211. *Green and gold back, yellow underneath. From T. Webster collection. Photo by D. Kowalski.*

No. 9212. *Green with silver sides. Photo not available.*

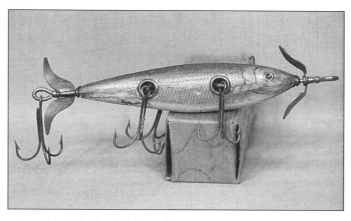

No. 9213. *Scale finish, gold. From T. Webster collection. Photo by D. Kowalski.*

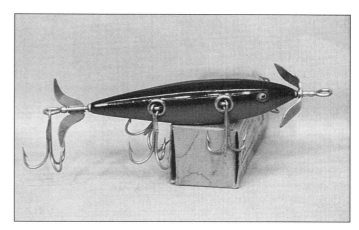

No. 9214. *Red. From T. Webster collection. Photo by D. Kowalski.*

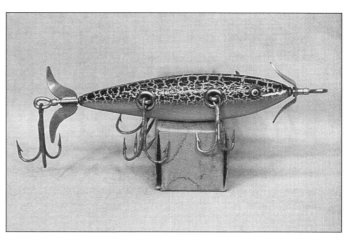

No. 9215. *Crackle-back pattern. From T. Webster collection. Photo by D. Kowalski.*

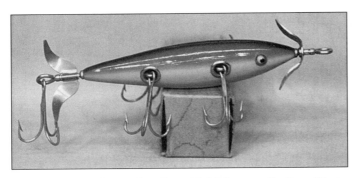

No. 9216. Rainbow color. From T. Webster collection. Photo by D. Kowalski.

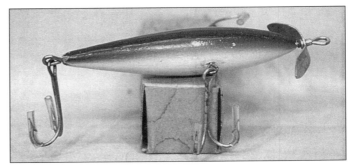

Economy Minnow with long body. Also created from spare parts. This one using long body and No. 9014 spinner. From T. Webster collection. Photo by D. Kowalski.

Plug Values:	Exc.	V.G.	Good
Long	400.00	250.00	160.00

No. 9217. Scale finish, silver. From T. Webster collection. Photo by D. Kowalski.

Plug Values:	Exc.	V.G.	Good
9210	1,500.00	1,000.00	750.00
9211	1,200.00	850.00	600.00
9212	1,200.00	850.00	600.00
9213	1,500.00	1,000.00	750.00
9214	1,200.00	850.00	600.00
9215	1,500.00	1,000.00	750.00
9216	1,200.00	850.00	600.00
9217	1,500.00	1,000.00	750.00

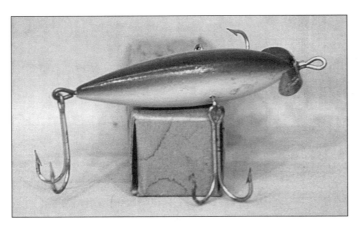

Economy Minnow with short body. Created from spare parts using short body and No. 9014 spinner. From T. Webster collection. Photo by D. Kowalski.

Plug Values:	Exc.	V.G.	Good
Short	300.00	175.00	125.00

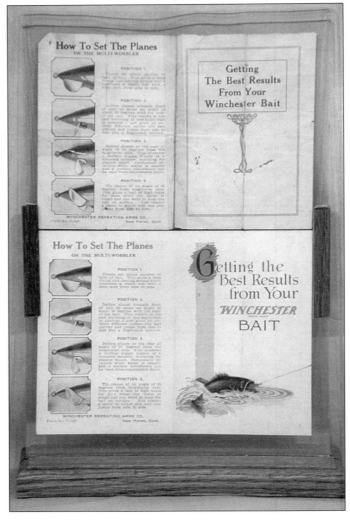

Plug Booklets, in two versions, tell anglers how to use the Winchester plug baits. A booklet was included in every Multi-wobbler, or 3-hook and 5-hook Minnow. From T. Webster collection. Photo by D. Kowalski.

Winchester Fly Patterns

All Winchester flies could be ordered in the following patterns:

Abbey	Hare's Ear
Alder	Ibis
Alexandria	Jock Scott
Beaverkill	Jungle Cock
Bee	King of the Waters
Black Ant	March Brown
Black Gnat	McGinty
Black Hackle	Mormon Girl
Blue Bottle	Dark Montreal
Blue Dun	Light Montreal
Whirling Blue Dun	Parmacheene Belle
Blue Upright	Professor
Brown Hackle (Peacock body)	Queen of Waters
	Raven
Caddis	Red Ant
Cahill	Red Hackle
Catoodle Bug	Red Palmer
Coachman	Red Spinner
Cowdung	Reuben Wood
Flight's Fancy	Royal Coachman
Ginger Quill	Seth Green
Governor	Silver Doctor
Green Drake	White Miller
Grey Hackle (Peacock body)	Wickham's Fancy
	Willow
Grizzly King	Yellow Sally

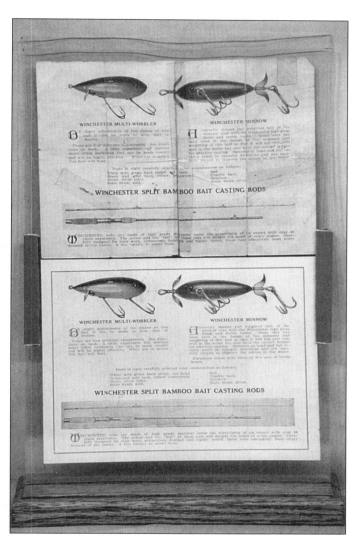

Plug booklets, inside. Booklets folded are approximately 3 1/2" wide x 6" high. From T. Webster collection. Photo by D. Kowalski.

Values:	Exc.	V.G.	Good
Short	325.00	275.00	225.00

Comment: *Values are for single plug booklet.*

Dry Flies. Highest Quality

Carefully tied on imported Pennell Eye hollow-point hooks. Wings are divided and paired and the hackle is tied over and under the wings. Selection of hackle is made for each size fly so that it will not be necessary to trim the natural ends. We cannot too strongly recommend this line of dry flies. Available in sizes 8, 10, 12 and 14. Approximate Weight per Dozen 1 1/4 Ounces.

No. 3136. Tied on Sproat Hooks. Pennell Eye Without Gut.
No. 3146. Tied on Sneck Hooks. Pennell Eye Without Gut.
No. 3131. Tied on Sproat Hooks. Pennell Eye With 4 in. Mist-Colored Gut.
No. 3141. Tied on Sneck Hooks. Pennell Eye With 4 in. Mist-Colored Gut.

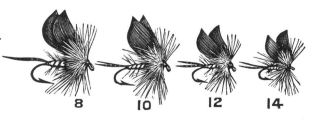

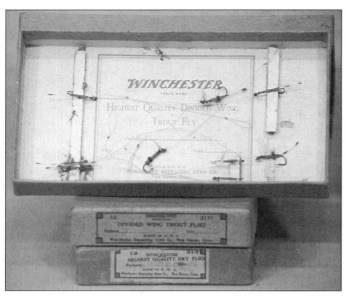

Trout flies were packed one dozen per box. From bottom - Dry Flies (No. 3131); Divided Wing Trout Flies (No. 3171); and an open box of Divided Wing Trout Flies showing the ravages of heat, humidity and insects on organic products such as feathers when they are not sealed from the outside air. From T. Webster collection. Photo by D. Kowalski.

Fly Values:	**Exc.**	**V.G.**	**Good**
Dry	175.00	125.00	90.00

Comment: *Values for dry flies on card or in box for identification purposes.*

Bass Flies

No. 3261. Superior. Tied on Sproat Hook with Gut. Tied to 4-inch mist-colored gut with large size loop. Sizes 2/0, 1/0, 1 and 2. This example is in Grizzly King pattern. From T. Webster collection. Photo by D. Kowalski.

No. 3266. Superior. Tied on Ringed Sproat Hook. Bodies of high quality silk with large wings. Sizes 2/0, 1/0, 1 and 2.

No. 3151. Highest Quality. Full natural wings and hackle, tied on imported hollow-point Pennell Sproat hooks with gut. Sizes 2/0, 1/0, 1 and 2. Three to the card, perforated in individual sections. Two dozen flies to the box.

Fly Values:	**Exc.**	**V.G.**	**Good**
Bass	200.00	150.00	100.00

Comment: *Values for bass flies (No. 3151, 3261, 3266) on card or in box for identification purposes.*

Trout Flies. Highest Quality Divided Wing

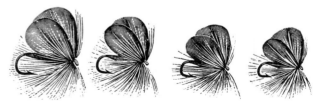

No. 3171. Tied to highest quality imported hollow point turned down eye Sneck hooks with selected gut snells with 1 inch loop. Upright divided wings, quill in center. Highest quality silk bodies. Standard patterns. Sizes 8, 10, 12 and 14. These flies are packed one dozen in a gray box. Each fly mounted on insert which keeps fly erect.

Trout Flies. Highest Quality Closed Wing

Tied on highest-quality imported Pennell Sproat hollow-point hooks with 4-inch gut. Wings paired and well proportioned. Sizes 6, 8, 10 and 12. **No. 3111** - On Sproat Hooks. **No. 3121** - On Sneck Hooks. Packed three on a card, perforated into individual sections. One-quarter gross flies to the box (12 cards).

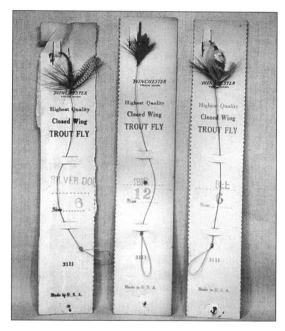

Closed Wing Trout Flies (No. 3111) came in at least 50 patterns. Here are three on cards in Silver Doctor, Ibis and Bee patterns. From T. Webster collection. Photo by D. Kowalski.

Trout Flies. Superior

No. 3201. Good quality silk bodies, dressed on imported spearpoint Sproat hooks, tied with 4-inch looped gut, mist-colored. Sizes 6, 8, 10 and 12. These flies are packed six on a card. Each card perforated for every two flies. One-half gross of flies to the box (12 cards).

Superior Trout Flies (No. 3201) in excellent condition on a display card. From T. Webster collection. Photo by D. Kowalski.

Fly Values:	Exc.	V.G.	Good
Trout	175.00	125.00	90.00

Comment: *Values for trout flies (No. 3111, 3121, 3171, 3201) on card or in box for identification purposes.*

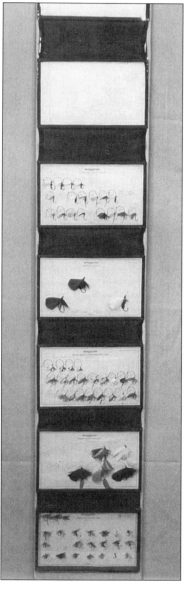

Salesman's Sample Case of flies. Has seven display areas each measuring 9" x 5 1/2"; total case unfolded is 9 5/8" wide x 57" long. Single sections of this case have come on the market and have been sold as separate units. From T. Webster collection. Photo by D. Kowalski.

Values:	Exc.	V.G.	Good
	5,000.00	4,500.00	3,800.00

Comment: *Values are for case without flies.*

416 • Winchester Fishing Equipment

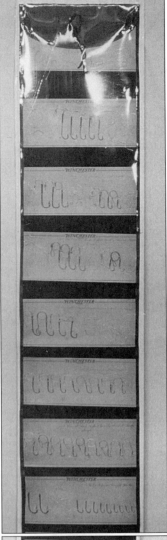

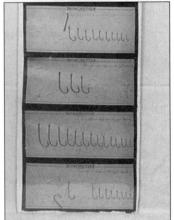

Salesman's Sample Case of hooks. Has 12 panels for display; each has a display area of 9 5/8" x 4 1/4". Total case unfolded measures 10 1/4" wide x 66" long. From T. Webster collection. Photo by D. Kowalski.

Winchester Spoon Baits

Winchester Spoon Baits will readily appeal to that class of anglers to whom quality is of first importance. The best of material combined with expert workmanship produce a quality which distinguish Winchester Spoon Baits. This workmanship is based on years of experience in this class of bait. We have endeavored to offer a wide variety with a view to meeting the demands of anglers all over the country.

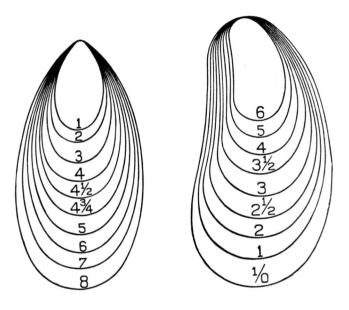

These two diagrams give the actual spoon size of each size of the Fluted Trolling and Kidney Trolling bait. The diagram on the left gives spoon sizes for Fluted Trolling bait from size 1 to 8 in which it is offered. At the right are shown the sizes of Kidney Trolling bait spoons so that the actual size of any desired spoon may be readily determined from this diagram.

Values:	Exc.	V.G.	Good
	4,500.00	3,800.00	3,000.00

Comment: *Values are for case without hooks.*

Casting and Trolling Spoons

In this classification will be found bait suitable for casting and trolling purposes which can be used effectively for large and small game fish. The larger sizes are suitable for Pickerel, Pike and Lake Trout; the medium size for Black Bass, Salmon, Trout, etc.; and the smaller size for Sunfish, Perch and Trout. Spoons are made of extra-heavy stamped brass, nickel-plated. Snaps are of extra-hard spring brass, nickel-plated treble hooks, with selected fancy feathers which are securely bound with linen threads.

Fluted Trolling Spoon (No. 9616). Nickel finish. From T. Webster collection. Photo by D. Kowalski.

Pearl Kidney Trolling Spoon. Iridescent pearl spoons.

No.	Size	Spoon Size	Oz./doz.	Hook Size
9452	2P	1 1/4	8 1/2	2
9453	3P	1 1/2	10 1/2	1
9454	4P	1 11/16	10 1/2	1/0
9455	5P	1 7/8	12	4/0
9456	6P	2 1/8	12	5/0

Bait Values: Exc. 175.00 V.G. 125.00 Good 90.00

Fluted Trolling Spoon (No. 9613) on card. From T. Webster collection. Photo by D. Kowalski.

No.	Size	Spoon Size	Oz./doz.	Hook Size
9610	1	1 x 9/16	5 1/2	6
9611	2	1 1/8 x 9/16	5 1/2	4
9612	3	1 5/16 x 23/32	9	2
9613	4	1 17/32 x 13/16	9	1
9614	4 1/2	1 11/16 x 7/8	9	1
9615	4 1/2	1 7/8 x 27/32	10 1/2	1
9616	5	2 3/32 x 11/32	12	2/0
9617	6	2 1/4 x 1 5/32	12	3/0
9618	7	2 3/8 x 1 1/8	15 1/2	4/0
9619	8	2 11/16 x 1 1/4	15 1/2	5/0

Bait Values: Exc. 75.00 V.G. 55.00 Good 35.00

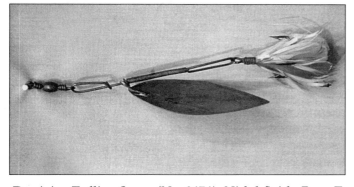

Dominion Trolling Spoon (No. 9474). Nickel finish. From T. Webster collection. Photo by D. Kowalski.

No.	Size	Spoon Size	Oz./doz.	Hook Size
9472	2	2 1/8 x 1	10 1/2	2/0
9473	3	2 3/8 x 1 1/8	12	3/0
9474	4	2 5/8 x 1 5/16	15 1/2	4/0
9475	5	2 15/16 x 1 15/32	15 1/2	5/0
9476	6	3 1/4 x 1 3/4	20	6/0

Bait Values: Exc. 90.00 V.G. 65.00 Good 45.00

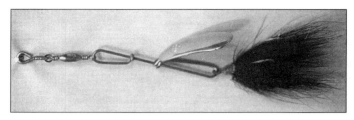

Kidney Trolling Spoon (No. 9635). Nickel finish. From T. Webster collection. Photo by D. Kowalski.

No.	Size	Spoon Size	Oz./doz.	Hook Size
9631	6	1 1/8 x 9/16	5 1/2	4
9634	5	1 1/4 x 5/8	9	2
9632	4	1 7/16 x 23/32	9	1
9635	3 1/2	1 5/8 x 7/8	10	1
9633	3	1 31/32 x 31/32	10 1/2	2/0
9636	2 1/2	2 1/8 x 1 1/8	12	3/0
9637	2	2 11/32 x 1 5/32	15 1/2	4/0
9638	1	2 17/32 x 1 8/32	17	4/0
9639	1/0	2 27/32 x 1 13/32	17	5/0

Bait Values: **Exc.** 90.00   **V.G.** 65.00   **Good** 45.00

Gold Bowl Trolling Spoon (No. 9625). Gold plated bowl. Upper half nickel-plated. From T. Webster collection. Photo by D. Kowalski.

No.	Size	Spoon Size	Oz./doz.	Hook Size
9621	5	1 1/16 x 9/16	5 1/2	4
9622	4	1 11/32 x 13/16	9	1
9623	3	1 5/8 x 7/8	9	1/0
9624	2	1 7/8 x 1 1/16	10 1/2	2/0
9625	1	2 3/16 x 1 1/4	12	4/0
9626	1/0	2 11/16 x 1 7/16	17	6/0
9627	2/0	2 7/8 x 1 1/2	18 1/2	7/0

Bait Values: **Exc.** 85.00   **V.G.** 65.00   **Good** 45.00

Original Fluted Trolling Spoon (No. 9643). Nickel finish. From T. Webster collection. Photo by D. Kowalski.

Hammered Oval Trolling Spoon. Nickel finish.

No.	Size	Spoon Size	Oz./doz.	Hook Size
9840	7	9/16 x 1 3/32	7	4
9841	6	23/32 x 1 5/16	9	4
9842	5	7/8 x 1 1/2	9	1
9843	4	15/16 x 1 23/32	9	1
9844	3	1 x 1 15/16	10 1/2	1/0
9845	2	1 1/16 x 2 1/16	12	2/0
9846	1	1 3/16 x 2 1/4	12	3/0

Bait Values: **Exc.** 90.00   **V.G.** 65.00   **Good** 45.00

No.	Size	Spoon Size	Oz./doz.	Hook Size
9641	2	1 1/8 x 9/16	5	4
9642	3	1 5/16 x 23/32	9	2
9643	4	1 17/32 x 13/16	9	1
9648	4 1/2	1 11/16 x 7/8	9	1
9647	4 3/4	1 7/8 x 27/32	10 1/2	1
9644	5	2 1/8 x 1 1/16	12	2/0
9645	6	2 1/4 x 1 5/32	12	3/0
9646	8	2 11/16 x 1 5/16	15 1/2	5/0

Bait Values: **Exc.** 90.00   **V.G.** 65.00   **Good** 45.00

Winchester Fishing Equipment • 419

No.	Size	Spoon Size	Oz./doz.	Hook Size
9780	7	1 5/8 x 9/16	9	2
9781	6	2 x 23/32	9	1
9782	5	2 5/16 x 3/4	10 1/2	1/0
9783	4	2 5/8 x 7/8	10 1/2	2/0
9784	3	2 7/8 x 15/16	12	4/0
9785	2	3 5/16 x 1 1/16	15 1/2	5/0

Bait Values: Exc.   V.G.   Good
85.00   65.00   45.00

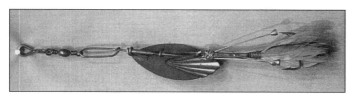

Weedless Fluted Trolling Spoon (No. 9535). Nickel finish. Long shank hooks. Weed guard cones on rustproof piano-wire springs. From T. Webster collection. Photo by D. Kowalski.

No.	Size	Spoon Size	Oz./doz.	Hook Size
9535	4 3/4	1 7/8 x 27/32	12	1/0
9536	5	2 3/32 x 1 1/32	15 1/2	3/0
9537	6	2 1/4 x 1 5/32	15 1/2	4/0
9538	7	2 3/8 x 1 1/8	17	6/0
9539	8	2 11/16 x 1 1/4	17	6/0

Bait Values: Exc.   V.G.   Good
85.00   65.00   45.00

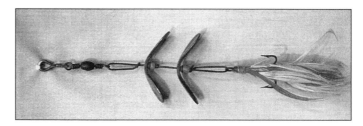

Reverse Blade Trolling Spoon (No. 9502). Nickel finish. Double spinners. From T. Webster collection. Photo by D. Kowalski.

No.	Size	Spoon Size	Oz./doz.	Hook Size
9502		1 5/8	10 1/2	1/0
9501		1 5/8	9	1/0

Bait Values: Exc.   V.G.   Good
90.00   65.00   45.00

Comment: *No. 9501 has only one blade but is valued the same as No. 9502.*

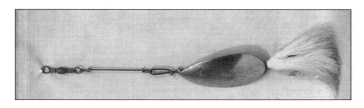

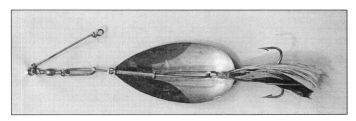

Muskallonge Spoon (No. 9491 first; No. 9492 second). Nickel finish. From T. Webster collection. Photo by D. Kowalski.

No.	Size	Spoon Size	Oz./doz.	Hook Size
9491	1/0	3 1/2 x 1 21/32	21 1/2	7/0
9492	2/0	3 11/16 x 1 7/8	26	7/0

Bait Values: Exc.   V.G.   Good
125.00   95.00   65.00

Eureka Assortment (No. 9403). One assortment on a card includes the following six items: Size 4 - Gold Bowl Bait; Size 4 - Original Fluted Trolling Bait; Size 3 1/2 - Kidney Bait; Size 4 1/2 - Fluted Bait; Size 6 - Willow Bait; Size 4 - Fluted Leaf Bait.

Bait Values: Exc.   V.G.   Good
325.00   225.00   150.00

Comment: *Values for all six baits on a card.*

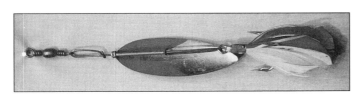

Willow Leaf Trolling Spoon (No. 9784). Nickel finish. From T. Webster collection. Photo by D. Kowalski.

Imperial Trolling Spoon (No. 9573 on card). Nickel finish. From T. Webster collection. Photo by D. Kowalski.

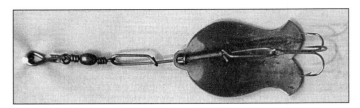

Delavan Spoon (No. 9563). Nickel finish. From T. Webster collection. Photo by D. Kowalski.

No.	Size	Spoon Size	Oz./doz.	Hook Size
9561	1	1 3/4 x 1	10 1/2	2/0
9562	2	2 x 1 7/32	12	3/0
9563	3	2 5/32 x 1 9/32	15 1/2	4/0

Bait Values: Exc.   V.G.   Good
              90.00   70.00   45.00

Sound Oval Spoon. Nickel finish. Does not come with hooks.

No.	Size	Spoon Size	Oz./doz.
9583	3	1 23/32 x 25/32	4
9584	4	2 1/16 x 1 1/32	4
9585	5	2 13/32 x 1 3/16	5 1/2
9586	6	2 5/8 x 1 7/32	5 1/2

Bait Values: Exc.   V.G.   Good
              85.00   65.00   45.00

No.	Size	Spoon Size	Oz./doz.	Hook Size
9572	2	1 1/2 x 21/32	5 1/2	6
9573	3	1 23/32 x 25/32	9	3
9574	4	2 1/16 x 1 1/32	9	1
9575	5	2 13/32 x 1 3/16	10 1/2	2/0
9576	6	2 5/8 x 1 7/32	12	3/0

Brass finish.

No.	Size	Spoon Size	Oz./doz.	Hook Size
9567	2	1 1/2 x 21/32	5 1/2	6
9568	3	1 22/32 x 25/32	9	3
9569	4	2 1/16 x 1 1/32	9	1
9570	5	2 13/32 x 1 3/16	10 1/2	2/0
9571	6	2 5/8 x 1 7/32	12	3/0

Copper finish.

No.	Size	Spoon Size	Oz./doz.	Hook Size
9577	2	1 1/2 x 21/32	5 1/2	6
9578	3	1 23/32 x 25/32	9	3
9579	4	2 1/16 x 1 1/32	9	1
9580	5	2 13/32 x 1 3/16	10 1/2	2/0
9581	6	2 5/8 x 1 7/32	12	3/0

Bait Values: Exc.   V.G.   Good
              100.00   75.00   50.00

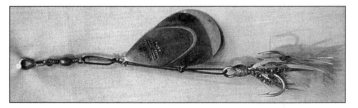

Gold Bug Trolling Spoon (No. 9674). Nickel bowl. Upper half of spoon gold-plated. From T. Webster collection. Photo by D. Kowalski.

No.	Size	Spoon Size	Oz./doz.	Hook Size
9670	1	1 1/8 x 9/16	5 1/2	4
9671	2	1 3/8 x 13/16	9	3
9672	3	1 5/8 x 7/8	9	1
9673	4	1 7/8 x 1 1/16	10 1/2	1/0
9674	5	2 1/8 x 1 1/4	12	2/0

Bait Values: Exc.   V.G.   Good
              85.00   65.00   45.00

Winchester Fishing Equipment • 421

Lake Tahoe Spoon (No. 9592) shown first without hook (the way it was sold). Photograph shows it outfitted with a hook. Nickel finish. From T. Webster collection. Photo by D. Kowalski.

No.	Size	Spoon Size	Oz./doz.
9591	1	4 3/8 x 2 5/16	17
9592	2	4 5/8 x 2 7/16	18

Bait Values:	Exc.	V.G.	Good
	125.00	95.00	65.00

Seattle Trout Spoon (No. 9408) shown first without hook (the way it was sold). Photograph shows it outfitted with a hook. Nickel finish. From T. Webster collection. Photo by D. Kowalski.

No.	Size	Spoon Size	Oz./doz.
9408	4	15/16 x 1 3/4	16 1/2

Bait Values:	Exc.	V.G.	Good
	125.00	95.00	65.00

Casting Spoon is equipped with Sproat hook. Nickel-plated blade has fluted edge.

No.	Size	Spoon Size	Hook Size
9510	1	1 x 9/16	1/0
9511	2	1 1/8 x 9/16	2/0
9512	3	1 5/16 x 23/32	3/0

Bait Values:	Exc.	V.G.	Good
	85.00	65.00	45.00

Casting Spoon has plain blade. Nickel finish. No hooks.

No.	Spoon Size	Oz./doz.
9513	1 3/32 x 5/8 - Single Spoon	5
9514	1 3/32 x 5/8 - Double Spoon	6

Pearl blade. No hooks.

9515	1 x 5/8 - Single Spoon	6
9516	1 x 5/8 - Double Spoon	6

Bait Values:	Exc.	V.G.	Good
	80.00	60.00	40.00

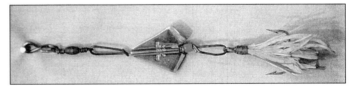

Black Bass Trolling Spoon (No. 9464). Nickel finish. From T. Webster collection. Photo by D. Kowalski.

No.	Size	Spoon Size	Oz./doz.	Hook Size
9462	5	3/4 x 11/16	8 1/2	4
9463	4	1 x 7/8	8 1/2	3
9464	3	1 1/8 x 1 1/16	9	1
9465	2	1 3/8 x 1 1/4	9	1/0
9466	1	1 5/8 x 1 3/8	10 1/2	2/0

Bait Values:	Exc.	V.G.	Good
	100.00	75.00	50.00

Trout Spinners

Winchester Trout Spinners are substantially constructed, and are handmade throughout. A special snap connection allows flies, hooks, etc. to be changed instantly. They can be obtained in several finishes, single or tandem blades, with or without flies and with different style hooks. The smaller sizes can be used satisfactorily with the fly rod, for small game fish such as Trout, Rock Bass, Sunfish, Perch, etc., while the large sizes are suitable for casting and trolling.

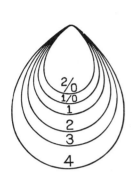 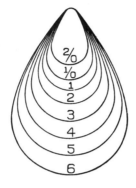

Diagram at left shows actual sizes of the spoons furnished on each size of Colorado Spinner bait listed below. Diagram at right gives same outline for sizes offered in Oregon Spinner bait.

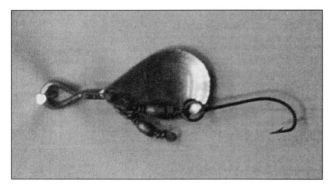

Oregon Spinner (No. 9605). Nickel finish. From T. Webster collection. Photo by D. Kowalski.

No.	Size	Spoon Size	Oz./doz.	Hook Size
9606	2/0	2 5/32 x 1 9/32	5	8
9605	1/0	1 5/16 x 11/16	5 1/2	6
9604	1	1 3/32 x 13/16	5 1/2	4
9603	2	1 1/4 x 15/16	9	2
9602	3	1 1/2 x 1 1/8	9	1
9601	4	1 3/4 x 1 1/4	10 1/2	2/0
9600	5	2 x 1 3/8	15 1/2	3/0
9599	6	2 1/4 x 1 1/2	17	4/0

Brass finish.

No.	Size	Spoon Size	Oz./doz.	Hook Size
9694	2/0	2 5/32 x 1 9/32	5	8
9695	1/0	15/16 x 11/16	5 1/2	6
9696	1	1 3/32 x 13/16	5 1/2	4
9697	2	1 1/4 x 15/16	9	2
9698	3	1 1/2 x 1 1/8	9	1
9699	4	1 3/4 x 1 1/4	10 1/2	2/0
9700	5	2 x 1 1/8	15 1/2	3/0
9701	6	2 1/4 x 1 1/2	17	4/0

Copper finish.

No.	Size	Spoon Size	Oz./doz.	Hook Size
9686	2/0	25/32 x 19/32	5	8
9687	1/0	15/16 x 11/16	5 1/2	6
9688	1	1 3/32 x 13/16	5 1/2	4
9689	2	1 1/4 x 15/16	9	2
9690	3	1 1/2 x 1 1/8	9	1
9691	4	1 3/4 x 1 1/4	10 1/2	2/0
9692	5	2 x 1 3/8	15 1/2	3/0
9693	6	2 1/4 x 1 1/2	17	4/0

Bait Values:	Exc.	V.G.	Good
	75.00	55.00	35.00

Colorado Spinner (No. 9804). Nickel finish. From T. Webster collection. Photo by D. Kowalski.

No.	Size	Spoon Size	Oz./doz.	Hook Size
9680	2/0	11/16 x 1/2	5 1/2	10
9681	1/0	15/32 x 19/32	5 1/2	8
9682	1	15/16 x 11/16	5 1/2	6
9683	2	1 3/32 x 13/16	5 1/2	4
9684	3	1 1/4 x 15/16	9	2
9685	4	1 1/2 x 1 1/8	10 1/2	1

Bait Values:	Exc.	V.G.	Good
	65.00	50.00	35.00

No.	Size	Spoon Size	Oz./doz.	Hook Size
Brass finish.				
9800	2/0	11/16 x 1/2	5 1/2	10
9801	1/0	15/32 x 19/32	5 1/2	8
9802	1	15/16 x 11/16	5 1/2	6
9803	2	1 3/32 x 13/16	5 1/2	4
9804	3	1 1/4 x 1 15/16	9	2
9805	4	1 1/2 x 1 1/8	10 1/2	1

Bait Values: Exc. 75.00   V.G. 55.00   Good 35.00

No.	Size	Spoon Size	Oz./doz.	Hook Size
Copper finish.				
9810	2/0	11/16 x 1/2	5 1/2	10
9811	1/0	25/32 x 19/32	5 1/2	8
9812	1	15/16 x 11/16	5 1/2	6
9813	2	1 3/32 x 13/16	5 1/2	4
9814	3	1 1/4 x 15/16	9	2
9815	4	1 1/2 x 1 1/8	9	1

Bait Values: Exc. 85.00   V.G. 65.00   Good 45.00

No.	Size	Spoon Size	Oz./doz.	Hook Size
Pearl.				
9820	2/0	11/16 x 1/2	5 1/2	10
9821	1/0	25/32 x 19/32	5 1/2	8
9822	1	15/16 x 11/16	5 1/2	6
9823	2	1 3/32 x 13/16	5 1/2	4

Bait Values: Exc. 150.00   V.G. 115.00   Good 75.00

Colorado Spinner with Fly. Nickel finish.

No.	Size	Spoon Size	Oz./doz.	Hook Size
9541	620	11/16 x 1/2	5 1/2	8
Pearl.				
9540	600	11/16 x 1/2	5	8

Bait Values: Exc. 85.00   V.G. 65.00   Good 45.00

Comment: *Add 100 percent for pearl blade.*

Little Wonder Spinner. Spoon has fluted edge. Lower half of spoon gold-plated. Upper half nickel-plated.

No.	Size	Spoon Size	Oz./doz.	Hook Size
9723		7/16 x 13/16	5	1
9724		9/16 x 1	5 1/2	1
9725		9/16 x 1 1/8	5 1/2	1

Bait Values: Exc. 85.00   V.G. 65.00   Good 45.00

Single Trout Spinner Without Flies. Nickel finish.

No.	Size	Spoon Size	Oz./doz.
9650	HS	1/2 x 9/32	4 1/2
9651	H1	5/8 x 3/8	4 1/2
9652	H2	27/32 x 7/16	5
9653	H3	1 3/32 x 5/8	5

Bait Values: Exc. 65.00   V.G. 50.00   Good 35.00

No.	Size	Spoon Size	Oz./doz.
Pearl.			
9655	HSP	1/2	4 1/2
9656	H1P	11/16	4 1/2
9657	H2P	7/8	4 1/2
9658	H3P	1 1/16	5

Bait Values: Exc. 150.00   V.G. 115.00   Good 75.00

Single Trout Spinner With Flies. Assorted flies using Professor, Royal Coachman, Brown Hackle, Red Ibis, Grey Hackle, Parmacheene Belle, Montreal, Cow Dung, Queen of Waters, Coachman, Seth Green and Yellow Sally. Nickel finish.

No.	Size	Spoon Size	Oz./doz.	Hook Size
9760	HS	1/2 x 9/32	4 1/2	8
9761	H1	5/8 x 3/8	4 1/2	6
9762	H2	27/32 x 7/16	5	4
9763	H3	1 3/32 x 5/8	5 1/2	2

Bait Values: Exc. 85.00   V.G. 65.00   Good 45.00

No.	Size	Spoon Size	Oz./doz.	Hook Size
Pearl.				
9765	HSP	1/2	4 1/2	8
9766	H1P	11/16	4 1/2	6
9767	H2P	7/8	4 1/2	4
976S	H3P	1 1/16	5	2

Bait Values: Exc. 160.00   V.G. 120.00   Good 80.00

Tacoma Bait Spinner (No. 9550). Nickel finish. Weight per dozen about 9 oz. From T. Webster collection. Photo by D. Kowalski.

No.	Size	Spoon Size	Hook Size
9550	1	1 3/32 x 9/32 - 1 5/16 x 23/32	1

Tacoma Bait Spinner (No. 9551). Nickel finish. Weight per dozen about 5 1/2 oz.

No.	Size	Spoon Size	Hook Size
9551	1 1/2	1 1/8 x 9/16	1

Tacoma Bait Spinner (No. 9552). Nickel finish. Weight per dozen about 9 oz. From T. Webster collection. Photo by D. Kowalski.

No.	Size	Spoon Size	Hook Size
9552	50	1 1/8 x 9/16 - 1 x 15/32	1

Tacoma Bait Spinner (No. 9553). Nickel finish. Weight per dozen about 9 oz.

No.	Size	Spoon Size	Hook Size
9553	60	7/8 x 13/32 - 1 1/8 x 9/16	1

Bait Values:	Exc.	V.G.	Good
	90.00	70.00	45.00

Comment: *Values are the same for all four Tacoma Bait Spinners (No. 9550, 9551, 9552, 9553).*

Tandem Trout Spinner Without Flies. Nickel finish.

No.	Size	Spoon Size	Oz./doz.
9660	HT	1/2 x 9/32	5 1/2
9664	HA	5/8 x 3/8	5 1/2
9661	HB	27/32 x 7/16	5 1/2
9662	HC	1 3/32 x 5/8	5 1/2

Bait Values:	Exc.	V.G.	Good
	75.00	55.00	35.00

Pearl.

No.	Size	Spoon Size	Oz./doz.
9665	HTP	1/2	5 1/2
9666	HAP	11/16	5 1/2
9667	HBP	7/8	5 1/2
9668	HCP	1 1/16	5 1/2

Bait Values:	Exc.	V.G.	Good
	160.00	120.00	80.00

Tandem Trout Spinner With Flies. Assorted flies using Professor, Royal Coachman, Brown Hackle, Red Ibis, Grey Hackle, Parmacheene Belle, Montreal, Cow Dung, Queen of Waters, Coachman, Seth Green and Yellow Sally. Nickel finish.

No.	Size	Spoon Size	Oz./doz.	Hook Size
9770	HT	1/2 x 9/32	5	8

No.	Size	Spoon Size	Oz./doz.	Hook Size
9771	HA	5/8 x 3/8	5 1/2	6
9772	HB	27/32 x 7/16	5 1/2	4
9773	HC	1 3/32 x 5/8	5 1/2	2

Bait Values:	Exc.	V.G.	Good
	90.00	70.00	45.00

Pearl.

No.	Size	Spoon Size	Oz./doz.	Hook Size
9775	HTP	1/2	5 1/2	8
9776	HAP	11/16	5 1/2	6
9777	HBP	7/8	8 1/2	4
9778	HCP	1 7/16	9	2

Bait Values:	Exc.	V.G.	Good
	175.00	130.00	90.00

Emerick Spinner. Nickel finish.

No.	Size	Spoon Size	Oz./doz.	Hook Size
9831	1	3/4 x 17/32	5	8
9832	2	1/2 x 11/32	5	10
9883	3	13/32 x 9/32	5	12

Bait Values:	Exc.	V.G.	Good
	85.00	65.00	45.00

Spinning Coachman. Coachman fly attached. With each bait are packed two other flies of assorted patterns, selected from the following: Queen-O-Waters, Governor, Silver Doctor, Lake George, Parmacheene Belle, Raven, Ibis, Onondaga, Professor and John Mann. All flies tied to No. 1 Sproat hooks. Nickel spinners. Weight per Dozen about 8 1/2 ozs.

No. 9400. Spoon Size - 1 3/16 x 15/32.

Bait Values:	Exc.	V.G.	Good
	190.00	150.00	110.00

June Bug Bait

For wall-eyed pike, pickerel and bass. Brass spoon is 1 17/32 x 13/16 in., gold-plated and red-enameled inside, nickel-plated outside, upper one-third gold-plated. Brass barrel swivel; Size 4/0 hook. Weight per Dozen about 3 1/2 oz.

June Bug (No. 9715 on card) has 36-inch wire leader. From T. Webster collection. Photo by D. Kowalski.

June Bug (No. 9717 on card) has 6-inch wire leader with copper safety snap. From T. Webster collection. Photo by D. Kowalski.

Bait Values:	Exc.	V.G.	Good
	100.00	75.00	50.00

Comment: *Same values for No. 9717 and 9715.*

June Bug without hook (No. 9716) is mounted on 3-inch wire snap. Weight per Dozen about 3 oz.

Bait Values:	Exc.	V.G.	Good
	85.00	65.00	45.00

Miscellaneous Fishing Tackle

Winchester miscellaneous fishing items include line spools and cards, landing nets, hook boxes and packets, tackle and bait boxes, and split shot containers. These items are uncommon enough that there is little chance to put together a collection of "Winchester Miscellaneous Tackle." However, a few of these tackle pieces certainly spice up a collection of Winchester fishing tackle.

Line spools are very difficult to find in Excellent condition because fishermen stuck a pencil through the hole at the center of the spool when they installed the line on a reel. By punching the hole they did some serious damage to the graphics on the label. However, some nice spools can still be found, but they are usually very high-priced.

Winchester tackle boxes were a contract item, and are not uncommon. They are tin boxes that had a Japanned finish, with gold decorating lines. The "Winchester" logo is stencil painted inside the box lid, and thus is usually in good condition. Several companies used the same boxes during this time period, with the only difference being the name stenciled on the inside of the lid.

The smaller, belt-mounted bait cans are quite scarce. They have a Winchester decal applied to the front. Since there are people out there with identical decals, it would be advisable to be very cautious in purchasing any bait box. It would also pay to be very careful when purchasing any Winchester landing nets marked with a decal. Most Winchester nets are marked with a metal stamp on the frame, but at the close of their tackle production many Winchester items had identifying decals applied. The addition of the original cloth bag for the net would alleviate fears of counterfeits.

Probably the most common Winchester miscellaneous products found in collections are the celluloid-topped split shot containers. These have colorful labels and fish graphics and were available in several sizes. However, the split shot container that looks like a common BB tube is actually quite a bit less common.

Landing Net Frames

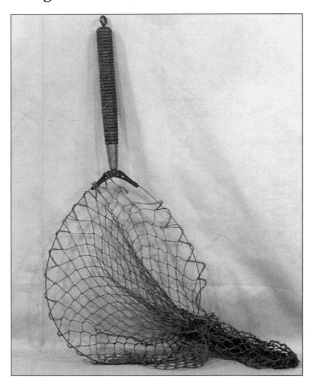

Winchester sold its landing nets both with and without nets attached. This is a No. 9470, which is actually the No. 9430 frame equipped with a 20-inch, square-bottom, waterproofed landing net. From T. Webster collection. Photo by D. Kowalski.

No. 9430. "Trout" model. Corrugated wood handle nine inches in length with black enamel finish. Collapsible frame enameled in black. Nickel plated ferrule on end of handle with 42 inches of black elastic cord attached to nickel plated screw-eye on end of handle. Approximate size of ring 11 x 10 1/2 in. Packed individually in bag. Approximate weight 1/2 lb.

No. 9431. One-piece, 12-inch bamboo handle. Black enameled collapsible frame. Nickel swivel hook at one end. Nickel-plated ferrule at the other. Approximate ring size 11 x 10 1/2 inches. Packed individually in bag. Approximate weight 1/2 lb.

No. 9432. One-piece, 30-inch bamboo handle. Black enamel collapsible frame. Nickel-plated ferrules on each end. Approximate size of ring 13 1/2 x 11 1/4 inches. Packed individually in bag. Approximate weight 1/2 lb.

Winchester Fishing Equipment • 427

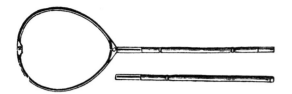

No. 9433. Jointed bamboo handle, 48 inches long overall. Collapsible steel frame of special construction to give added strength. Enameled black. Nickel-plated joining ferrules. Approximate size of ring 15 x 14 inches. (This model designed for 24-inch, square-bottom waterproofed net.) Packed individually in bag. Approximate weight 1 1/4 lbs.

Net Values:	Exc.	V.G.	Good
9430	300.00	200.00	150.00
9431	350.00	235.00	175.00
9432	350.00	235.00	175.00
9433	425.00	350.00	300.00

Comment: *Winchester also supplied cotton nets: minnow dip nets in four sizes; square-bottom landing nets in four sizes for their landing-net frames; and a pointed-bottom capelin net in four sizes. A landing net in excellent condition would also include the appropriate net, itself, also in excellent condition.*

Winchester Fish Hooks

Whenever you're dealing with collectibles that were virtually sold in bulk, rather than "eaches," such as fish hooks or individual "BBs" in a box of shot, accurate identification of original pieces is problematic. These small items were not individually stamped with the "Winchester" logo. And both fish hooks and individual BBs were "consumables" meant to be used on the fishing trip or in the field. That makes them more difficult to find today.

Fish hooks have a unique position as a collectible because of these factors. But Winchester sold them in a variety of identifiable sizes and patterns, perhaps with other unique features such as bronzed points or blued points. That makes them fair game, as it were, for the collector who is seeking all the variations of certain products.

We're presenting Winchester line art on hooks because it was well rendered. And it should help the collector make sure the hooks he or she finds in a package are the ones that belong there.

There were basically two types of fish hooks. The "ringed" hook allowed the angler to tie his own line to the hook. The "snelled" hook had a short section of leader material attached to the hook shaft. Each type of hook also came in two grades, "Superior" and "Highest Quality" and in several styles.

Values given are for full boxes or bags.

Superior Ringed Fish Hooks

Best grade of spear point hooks, imported. High grade steel with finely tempered points. Carefully tested to assure a correct temper. Packed 100 per box; ten boxes in a carton.

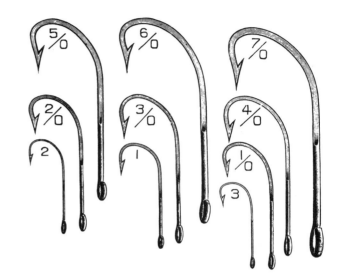

Superior O'Shaughnessy Ringed Hooks. No. 7000. Bronzed, spear point. Sizes - 10/0, 8/0, 7/0, 6/0, 5/0, 4/0, 3/0, 2/0, 1/0, 1 to 6. Box of 100.

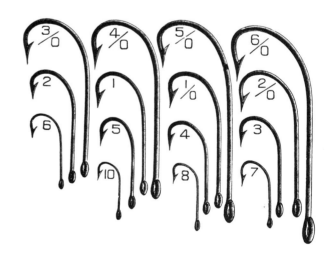

Superior Sproat Ringed Hooks. No. 7100. Bronzed, spear point. Sizes 6/0, 5/0, 4/0, 3/0, 2/0, 1/0, 1 to 10. Box of 100.

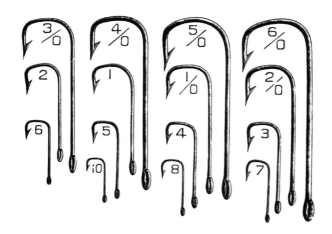

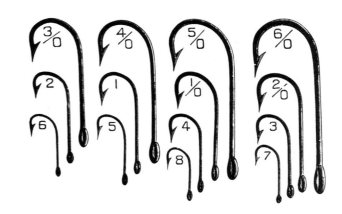

Superior Sneck Ringed Hooks. No. 7200. Bronzed, spear point. Sizes - 6/0, 5/0, 4/0, 3/0, 2/0, 1/0, 1 to 10. Box of 100.

Superior Kirby Ringed Hooks. No. 7500. Japanned, spear point. Sizes - 6/0, 5/0, 4/0, 3/0, 2/0, 1/0, 1 to 10. Box of 100.

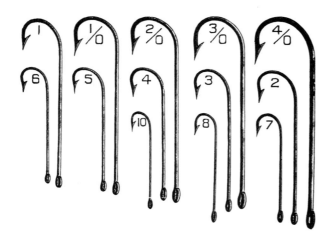

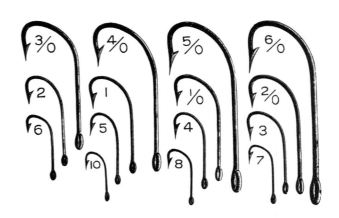

Superior Carlisle Ringed Hooks. No. 7300. Blued spear point. Sizes - 6/0, 5/0, 4/0, 3/0, 2/0, 1/0, 1 to 10. Box of 100.

Superior Limerick Ringed Hooks. No. 7600. Japanned, spear point. Sizes - 6/0, 5/0, 4/0, 3/0, 2/0, 1/0, 1 to 10. Box of 100.

Superior Aberdeen Ringed Hooks. No. 7400. Bronzed spear point. Sizes - 6/0, 5/0, 4/0, 3/0, 2/0, 1/0, 1 to 10. Box of 100. (Photo not available.)

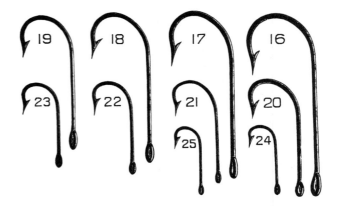

Superior Cincinnati Bass Ringed Hooks. No. 7700. Polished bright, spear point. Sizes - 16 to 25. Box of 100.

Highest Quality Ringed Fish Hooks

Pennell Limerick hooks, size 1/0. Box of 100 (No. 6600) Highest Quality. Made in Norway. From T. Webster collection. Photo by D. Kowalski.

Highest Quality Limerick Ringed Hooks. *No. 6600. Pennell ringed hooks, bronzed hollow point. Sizes - 6/0, 5/0, 4/0, 3/0, 2/0, 1/0, 1 to 10. Box of 100.*

Superior Grade Treble Hooks

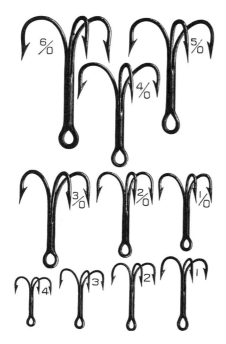

Superior Treble Hooks. *No. 7110. Nickel-plated, spear point. Sizes - 7/0, 6/0, 5/0, 4/0, 3/0, 2/0, 1/0, 1 to 10. One Gross in a Box.*

Superior Treble Hooks, Feathered. *No. 7120. Nickel-plated, spear point. Sizes - 6/0, 5/0, 4/0, 3/0, 2/0, 1/0, 1 to 4. One Dozen in a Box.*

Hook Values:	Exc.	V.G.	Good
Box	200.00	150.00	90.00

Comment: *Values are for full box, any style, size or grade.*

Superior Snelled Fish Hooks

High grade spear point hooks, tied to Superior gut with extra-high-grade red silk. Silk covered with two coats of varnish. All hooks are thoroughly tested to assure correctly tempered points. Packed one-half dozen in a glassine waterproof envelope; 24 envelopes in a carton.

Superior O'Shaughnessy Snelled Hooks. *No. 7004 - 4-ply Gut. No. 7009 - 4-ply Looped Gut. Sizes - 7/0 to 1/0. No. 7005 - 12-inch Piano Wire - Sizes 8/0-6/0 and 5/0-3/0.*

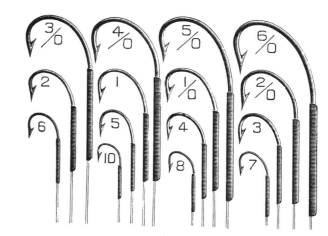

Superior Sproat Snelled Hooks. *No. 7101 - Single Gut. No. 7102 - Double Gut. No. 7103 - Treble Gut. Sizes - 6/0, 5/0, 4/0, 3/0, 2/0, 1/0, 1 to 12.*

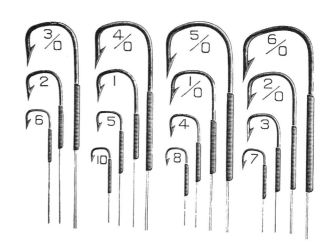

Superior Sneck Snelled Hooks. *No. 7201 - Single Gut. No. 7202 - Double Gut. No. 7203 - Treble Gut. Sizes - 6/0, 5/0, 4/0, 3/0, 2/0, 1/0, 1 to 12.*

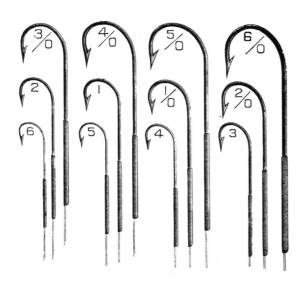

Superior Carlisle Snelled Hooks. No. 7301 - Single Gut. No. 7302 - Double Gut. No. 7303 - Treble Gut. Sizes - 6/0, 5/0, 4/0, 3/0, 2/0, 1/0, 1 to 12.

Superior Aberdeen Snelled Hooks. No. 7401 - Single Gut. No. 7402 - Double Gut. Sizes - 6/0, 5/0, 4/0, 3/0, 2/0, 1/0, 1 to 12.

Superior Kirby Snelled Hooks. No. 7501 - Single Gut. No. 7502 - Double Gut. Sizes - 6/0, 5/0, 4/0, 3/0, 2/0, 1/0, 1 to 12.

Superior Limerick Snelled Hooks. No. 7601 - Single Gut. No. 7602 - Double Gut. Sizes - 4/0, 3/0, 2/0, 1/0, 1 to 12.

Bag of Cincinnati Bass Superior Snelled Hooks. Hook size No. 23. From T. Webster collection. Photo by D. Kowalski.

Superior Cincinnati Bass Snelled Hooks. No. 7701 - Single Gut. No. 7702 - Double Gut. No. 7703 - Triple Gut. Sizes - 16 to 25.

Superior Kinsey Snelled Hooks. No. 7801 - Single Gut. No. 7802 - Double Gut. Sizes - 9 to 18.

Superior New York Trout Snelled Hooks. No. 7901 - Single Gut. No. 7902 - Double Gut. No. 7903 - Triple Gut. Sizes - 4/0, 3/0, 2/0, 1/0, 1 to 10.

Hook Values:	Exc.	V.G.	Good
Envelope	75.00	45.00	30.00

Comment: *Values are for Superior Snelled Hooks in envelopes, any style or size.*

Highest Quality Snelled Fish Hooks

Imported hollow point hooks tied to Selecto Gut with bronzed silk. Silk is thoroughly covered with two coats of varnish. All hooks are carefully tested to assure proper temper in the points. Packed one-half dozen in a gray slotted folder; one gross in a carton.

Highest Quality O'Shaughnessy Snelled Hooks. No. 6001 - Single Gut. No. 6002 - Double Gut. Sizes - 6/0, 5/0, 4/0, 3/0, 2/0, 1/0, 1 to 12.

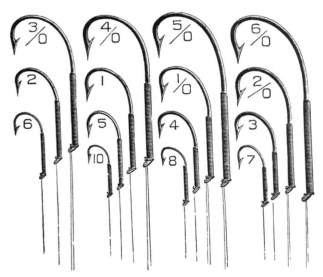

Highest Quality Sproat Snelled Hooks. No. 6101 - Single Gut. No. 6102 - Double Gut. No. 6103 - Treble Gut. No. 6106 - Pennell Single. No. 6107 - Pennell Double. Sizes - 6/0, 5/0, 4/0, 3/0, 2/0, 1/0, 1 to 12.

Winchester Fishing Equipment • 431

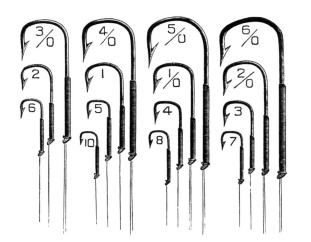

Highest Quality Sneck Snelled Hooks. No. 6201 - Single Gut. No. 6202 - Double Gut. No. 6203 - Treble Gut. No. 6206 - Pennell Single. No. 6207 - Pennell Double. Sizes - 6/0, 5/0, 4/0, 3/0, 2/0, 1/0, 1 to 12.

Highest Quality Carlisle Snelled Hooks. No. 6301 - Single Gut. No. 6302 - Double Gut. No. 6303 - Treble Gut. Sizes - 6/0, 5/0, 4/0, 3/0, 2/0, 1/0, 1 to 14.

Highest Quality Aberdeen Snelled Hooks. No. 6401 - Single Gut. No. 6402 - Double Gut. No. 6403 - Treble Gut. Sizes - 6/0, 5/0, 4/0, 3/0, 2/0, 1/0, 1 to 12.

Highest Quality Kirby Snelled Hooks. No. 6501 - Single Gut. No. 6502 - Double Gut. Sizes - 6/0, 5/0, 4/0, 3/0, 2/0, 1/0, 1 to 12.

Highest Quality Limerick Snelled Hooks. No. 6601 - Single Gut. No. 6602 - Double Gut. No. 6603 - Treble Gut. No. 6606 - Pennell Single. No. 6607 - Pennell Double. Sizes - 6/0, 5/0, 4/0, 3/0, 2/0, 1/0, 1 to 12.

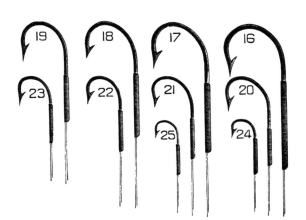

Highest Quality Cincinnati Bass Snelled Hooks. No. 6701 - Single Gut. No. 6702 - Double Gut. No. 6703 - Treble Gut. No. 6706 - Pennell Single. No. 6707 - Pennell Double. Sizes - 16 to 25.

Highest Quality Kinsey Snelled Hooks. No. 6801 - Single Gut. No. 6802 - Double Gut. Sizes - 9 to 18.

Hook Values:	Exc.	V.G.	Good
Cards	150.00	100.00	60.00

Comment: *Values are for Highest Quality Snelled Hooks in folders or on cards, any style or size.*

Winchester Leaders

All Winchester Leaders are made from selected imported silk worm gut. Silk worm gut is the raw silk as it is taken from the worm before it has matured. If the worm were allowed to live this raw silk would be woven into its cocoon.

When the raw silk is removed from the worm, it is stretched and dried, after which it is graded into three qualities: Estriada, which is the cheapest grade, Superior and Selecto. It is also divided according to sizes.

All Winchester Highest Quality leaders are tied from Selecto gut only. Winchester Superior leaders are tied from Superior gut. No Estriada gut is used for Winchester leaders.

Highest Quality Leaders

Made from selected Imported silk worm gut; tied from Selecto gut only.

Fina - *Light Trout Leaders. Approximate Size .011.*

No.	Gut	Length	Loops
5121	Single	1 yard	No dropper loop
5122	Single	1 yard	One dropper loop
5123	Single	2 yards	Two dropper loops

No. 5131. Medium Trout Leader. From T. Webster collection. Photo by D. Kowalski.

No. 5132. Medium Trout Leader. From T. Webster collection. Photo by D. Kowalski.

Regular - Medium Trout Leaders. Approximate Size .013.

No.	Gut	Length	Loops
5131	Single	1 yard	No dropper loop
5132	Single	1 yard	One dropper loop
5133	Single	2 yards	Two dropper loops

Padron 1 - Bass Leaders. Approximate Size .015.

No.	Gut	Length	Loops
5151	Single	1 yard	No dropper loop
5152	Single	1 yard	One dropper loop
5153	Single	2 yards	Two dropper loops

Marana 1 - Extra Heavy Bass Leaders. Approximate Size .018.

No.	Gut	Length	Loops
5171	Single	1 yard	No dropper loop
5172	Single	1 yard	One dropper loop
5173	Single	2 yards	Two dropper loops

Marana 2 - Special Leader for use with Light Weight Lures. Approximate Size .017. No. 5161. 4-foot leader with large loop on one end, regular loop at other end.

Tapered Leaders

No.	Weight	Length	Description
5101	Light	7 1/2 foot	Loop one end only. Padron 1 to 3X drawn.
5102	Medium	7 1/2 foot	Loop one end only. Padron 1 to 2X fine.

Superior Leaders.

Made from selected imported silk worm gut; tied from Superior gut.

Superior Medium Trout Leaders

No.	Gut	Length	Loops
5231	Single	1 yard	No dropper loop
5232	Single	1 yard	One dropper loop
5233	Single	2 yards	Two dropper loops
5237	Double	1 yard	No dropper loop
5238	Double	2 yards	No dropper loop

Superior Bass Leaders

No.	Gut	Length	Loops
5241	Single	1 yard	No dropper loop
5242	Single	1 yard	One dropper loop
5243	Single	2 yards	Two dropper loops
5247	Double	1 yard	No dropper loop

All Superior Leaders listed above attached to individual card. One dozen leaders to the box. Superior Treble Machine Twisted.

Superior Treble (3-ply) Machine Twisted Leaders. No. 5291 - 1 foot. No. 5292 - 2 feet. No. 5293 - 3 feet.

Superior 6-ply Machine Twisted Leaders. No. 5296 - 1 foot. No. 5297 - 2 feet. No. 5298 - 3 feet.

All 3-ply and 6-ply Superior Leaders packed one dozen to the box. Approximate Weight per dozen 1/4 lb.

Values:	Exc.	V.G.	Good
Cards	150.00	100.00	60.00

Comment: *Values are for Leaders on cards, any style or size.*

Joe Welsh "Telarana Nova" Leaders

Suitable for every kind of fresh and salt water fishing and unaffected by climate. Knotless leader well known for its strength and invisibility. Packed one in a glassine envelope; one dozen leaders to the carton.

Leader Size - Breaking Strain: 1 - 30 lbs., 2 - 15 lbs., 3 - 10 lbs., 4 - 7 lbs., 5 - 4 lbs., 6 - 2 1/2 lbs.

No.	Size	Length	Loops
5310	1	3 ft.	none
5320	2	3 ft.	none
5321	2	3 ft.	one
5330	3	3 ft.	none
5331	3	3 ft.	one
5332	3	6 ft.	none
5333	3	6 ft.	two
5340	4	3 ft.	none
5341	4	3 ft.	one
5342	4	6 ft.	none
5343	4	6 ft.	two
5350	5	3 ft.	none
5351	5	3 ft.	one
5352	5	6 ft.	none
5353	5	6 ft.	two
5360	6	6 ft.	none

Values:	Exc.	V.G.	Good
	150.00	100.00	60.00

Tinned Piano Wire Leaders. One Dozen in a Package.

No.	Weight	Length
5401	Light	39 in.
5403	Medium	60 in.
5407	Heavy	75 in.

Values:	Exc.	V.G.	Good
	225.00	150.00	100.00

Comment: *Values for package with at least six leaders.*

Wire Leaders with Swivel and Snap

No. 5410. Six inch. Cable Bronze; swivel on one end, snap on the other. Six to the card perforated in individual sections. Two cards to the box.

No. 5415. Three foot. Cable Bronze. Swivel on one end, snap on the other. Individual coils, one dozen to the box.

No. 5420. Six inch. Phosphor bronze wire. Swivel on one end, snap on the other. Six on individually perforated cards. Two cards to the box.

Values:	Exc.	V.G.	Good
	150.00	100.00	65.00

Comment: *Values for one leader on card or in box.*

Winchester Fishing Floats

Superior grade and finish. Adjustable. Float made in two colors. Packed one dozen in a carton.

Barrel-shaped Float.
No.	Size
	2 in.
	2 1/2 in.
	3 in.
9593	3 1/2 in.
9594	4 in.

Egg-shaped Float.
No.	Size
9580	1 1/2 in.
	1 3/4 in.
	2 in.
9583	2 1/4 in.
9584	2 1/2 in.

Values:	Exc.	V.G.	Good
Floats	250.00	200.00	175.00

No. 5420 wire leader, six inches. Card is 6 3/4" long. From T. Webster collection. Photo by D. Kowalski.

Fishing Lines Furnished with Hook, Float and Sinker

No. 8701. 15-foot green twisted cotton line. Furnished with 1 1/2 in. egg-shaped wood float in three colors. Ringed hook. Split shot sinker. Wound on stained wood winder.

No. 8703. 25-foot green twisted cotton line. Furnished with fancy natural cork float, assorted 1 1/2 in. egg and 2 1/4 in. barrel float. Snelled hook, adjustable sinker. Wound on enameled winder.

No. 8705. 30-foot green twisted cotton line. Three-color wood float - egg-shaped, 1 1/2-inch size. Snelled hook, adjustable sinker. Wound on enameled square winder.

No. 8707. 30-foot green twisted cotton line. Furnished with egg sinker, ringed hook. Wound on enameled square winder.

Values:	Exc.	V.G.	Good
	250.00	200.00	175.00

Comment: *For any size "furnished" line.*

Winchester Enameled Silk Fishing Line

Winchester Enameled Silk Lines represent the highest quality obtainable in enameled silk fishing lines. Only the finest of imported silk is used in their manufacture. This together with our special vacuum-enamel process enables us to produce a line of remarkable finish and value.

Halford Fly Line. Imported double-tapered fly line of the highest quality. Brown in color. Vacuum dressed, carefully tapered, waterproof, flexible, strong and long wearing. Dressed by hand. 30 Yards to the Coil.

No.	Size
8071	HEH
8072	HDH
8073	HCH

Optimo Fly Line. Another imported high-grade double-tapered fly line. Olive green in color. Vacuum dressed. Waterproof. A strong, durable line second only to the Halford. Dressed by hand. 30 Yards to the Coil.

No.	Size
8081	HEH
8882	HDH
8083	HCH

Values:	Exc.	V.G.	Good
Coil	160.00	125.00	90.00

Adirondack. White with black thread. Made from highest grade silk obtainable. Enameled by improved process, producing a highly glossy finish. Unexcelled in waterproof quality by any enameled line on the market. Semi-transparent, flexible, durable and strong. 25 yards on a card; 4 cards connected.

No.	Size	Test
8001	H	18 lb.
8002	G	24 lb.
8003	F	28 lb.
8004	E	32 lb.
8005	D	36 lb.

Winchester Fishing Equipment • 435

Seneca. *White with black cross stripes. One of the best enameled silk lines. Highest quality Japan silk, braided hard to insure strength. Coated with a special enamel which will not crack or peel. Core enameled, as well as outside, making a line of exceptional value. 25 Yards on a Card; 4 Cards Connected.*

No.	Size	Test
8051	H	18 lb.
8052	G	24 lb.
8053	F	28 lb.
8054	E	32 lb.
8055	D	36 lb.
8056	C	42 lb.

Salica. *One of the most popular silk enameled lines. Hard braided of extra heavy quality Japan silk, and coated with a fine transparent finish. 25 Yards on a Card; 4 Cards Connected. Green and black mottled.*

No.	Size	Test
8041	H	14 lb.
8042	G	18 lb.
8043	F	22 lb.
8044	E	26 lb.

White and black mottled.

8031	H	14 lb.
8032	G	18 lb.
8033	F	22 lb.
8034	E	26 lb.

Elite. *White with black thread. Guaranteed braided from pure silk, thoroughly waterproofed and coated with highest-grade elastic enameled finish, soft and pliable. 25 Yards on a Card; 4 Cards Connected.*

No.	Size	Test 100
8021	H	12 lb.
8022	G	15 lb.
8023	F	20 lb.

Evergreen. *Black and white. Designed especially to meet the demand for moderate-priced enameled lines. A line that will give good satisfaction and stand up under the hardest use. Enamel transparent. 25 Yards on a Card; 4 Cards Connected.*

No.	Size	Test
8012	G	12 lb.
8013	F	17 lb.

Values:	Exc.	V.G.	Good
Card	160.00	125.00	90.00

Comment: *Values for one card of Enameled Silk line.*

Oiled Silk Fishing Line

Winbos. *Green and white. Best grade oiled silk line; hard, glossy finish. 25 Yards on a Card; 4 Cards Connected.*

No.	Size	Test
8501	H	12 lb.
8502	G	15 lb.

Values:	Exc.	V.G.	Good
Card	160.00	125.00	90.00

Comment: *Values for one card of Oiled Silk line.*

Braided Silk Casting Line

Titan. *Black. Extra-high-grade casting line. Hard-braided and waterproofed. A line that cannot be too highly recommended. 50-yard spools, 2 connected.*

No.	Test
8112	15 lb.
8113	18 lb.
8116	24 lb.
8117	30 lb.

Lakeside. *Winchester gray in color. Extra-hard-braided casting line of highest-grade Japan silk. Braided over 3-ply core, making an exceptionally high-test, durable line. 50-yard spools, 2 connected.*

No.	Test
8183	15 lb.
8184	20 lb.
8186	25 lb.
8187	30 lb.

One side of Pocahontas spool (No. 8156). Wooden spool measures 2 5/8" across. From T. Webster collection. D. Kowalski photo.

Other side of same Pocahontas spool showing the striking Largemouth Bass used on several Winchester packages. From T. Webster collection. D. Kowalski photo.

Pocahontas. *Pepper and salt mottled. A standard pattern and one of the most popular casting lines. Made of high quality Japan silk. 25-yard spools, 4 connected.*

No.	Test
8152	15 lb.
8154	20 lb.
8156	25 lb.

Silkaline Casting Line

Jupiter. Mottled red and olive bronze. Hard braided over 3-ply core, making a smooth round casting line. 50-yard spools, 2 connected.

No.	Test
8132	16 1b.
8135	22 1b.

Mayflower. Black and white. Good quality braided silk lines. Specially designed to be sold at a popular price. Strong and durable. 25-yard spools, 4 connected. No. 8602. 16 lb. Test.

Pond Lily. White with black stripes. A strong line of staple pattern known to all bait casters. Braided over a 3-ply core which keeps the line from wearing flat. 50-yard spools, 2 connected.

No.	Test
8141	12 lb.
8142	15 lb.
8144	20 lb.
8146	25 lb.

Triton. A similar line to the Mayflower. Black in color. 25-yard spools, 4 connected. No. 8612. 16 lb. Test.

Sebago. Jet-black line made of highest grade No. 1 Japan silk. Waterproofed by a special process which insures a very pliable line, the silk being thoroughly treated. Medium-hard braided, making a fine, flexible line for casting. 50-yard spools, 2 connected.

No.	Test
8122	14 lb.
8123	18 lb.
8125	22 lb.
8127	28 lb.

25-yard spools, 4 connected.
| 8192 | 14 lb. |
| 8193 | 18 lb. |

Bay State. Black mottled with red. Another line of the same quality and strength as the Mayflower. 25-yard spools, 4 connected. No. 8622. 16 lb. Test.

Values:	Exc.	V.G.	Good
Spool	250.00	200.00	150.00

Comment: *Values for one spool (25-yard or 50-yard) of Braided Silk Casting line.*

Values:	Exc.	V.G.	Good
Spool	250.00	200.00	150.00

Comment: *Values for one spool (25-yard) of Silkaline line.*

Cotton Fishing Line

Ironsides. 50 Feet on a Card. Black and white mottled. A well-finished line selling at moderate price. Lines are coiled around cards in the same manner as the enameled lines. No. 8391.

Clover. 50 Feet on a Card. Brown and red mottled. No. 8392.

Seamaid. 50 Feet on a Card. Green and black. No. 8393.

Achilles. 50 Feet on a Card. Green and red. No. 8394.

Values:	Exc.	V.G.	Good
Card	150.00	125.00	90.00

Comment: *Values for 50 feet of Cotton line on a card.*

Braided Sea Island Cotton

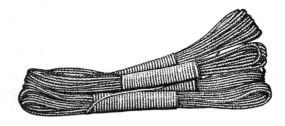

Made of combed, long-fibre Sea Island cotton. Hard braided with a glazed finish. Olive green and blue. 25-foot Hanks, 12 connected. Six Dozen Hanks in a Box.

No.	Size
8351	1
8352	2
8353	3
8354	4
8355	5
8356	6

84-foot Loops, 4 connected. One Dozen Loops in a Box.

No.	Size
8341	6
8342	5
8343	4
8344	3
8345	2
8346	1
8347	1/0
8348	2/0

Values:	Exc.	V.G.	Good
	250.00	200.00	150.00

Comment: *Values for at least one "Hank" or "Loop" in a box.*

Twisted Linen Fishing Line

Cuttyhunk. Available in either natural-linen color or green. Highest-quality twisted line. A very carefully laid line with fine, smooth finish. Wound on 25-yard spools, 4 connected. 100 Yards in a Box. Natural linen color.

No.	Size
8271	9
8272	12
8273	15
8274	18

Green color.

8251	9
8252	12

No.	Size
8253	15
8254	18

Wound on 50-yard spools, 2 connected. 100 Yards in a Box. Natural linen color.

No.	Size
8261	9
8262	12
8268	15
8264	18

Green color.

No.	Size
8241	9
8242	12
8243	15
8244	18

Wound on 100- yard spools, 2 connected. 200 Yards in a Box. Natural linen color.

No.	Size
8231	9
8282	12
8233	15
8234	18
8235	21
8236	24
8237	27

Values:	Exc.	V.G.	Good
Spool	250.00	200.00	150.00

Comment: *Values for any size spool of Cuttyhunk.*

No. 8221 Dunleer line on a "display circle" card. From T. Webster collection. Photo by D. Kowalski.

Dunleer. *This is a twisted line of grade equal to the Twistlyne. Natural linen color. 50 feet to the card. Four cards connected. One dozen cards to the carton.*

No.	Size
8221	9
8222	12

Values:	Exc.	V.G.	Good
Card	150.00	125.00	90.00

Comment: *Values for one card of either Twistlyne or Dunleer.*

Braided Linen Fishing Line

Twistlyne. *Natural linen color. A good quality twisted linen line that will meet the demand for a popular-priced linen line for stream and lake fishing. 25-yard coils on card, 4 connected. 300 Yards in a Box.*

No.	Size
8211	9
8212	12

No. 8462 Erin line on a wooden spool. "Winchester" logo is red. From T. Webster collection. D. Kowalski photo.

Erin. *Made of best imported linen stock. Hard braided, very pliable and exceptionally strong. Small sizes suitable for fresh water fishing, while the medium and larger sizes cover sufficient range to meet the demands of saltwater use. 50-yard spools, 2 connected. 100 Yards in a Box. Natural linen color.*

No.	Size
8461	9
8462	12
8463	15
8464	18

Green color.

No.	Size
8441	9
8442	12
8443	15
8444	18

Values:	Exc.	V.G.	Good
Spool	250.00	200.00	150.00

Comment: *Values for any size spool of Erin.*

Shamrock. *Natural color. Made from the best Irish linen. A strong, well-finished line for stream, pond or lake fishing. 25 Yards on card, 4 cards connected. 300 Yards in a Box.*

No.	Size
8411	9
8412	12

Glenmore. *A braided linen line of grade equal to the Shamrock line. Natural linen color. 50 feet to the card. Four cards connected. One dozen cards to the carton.*

No.	Size
8421	9
8422	12

Values:	Exc.	V.G.	Good
Card	150.00	125.00	90.00

Comment: *Values for one card of either Shamrock or Glenmore.*

Winchester Tackle Boxes

Winchester tackle boxes are made of extra-heavy tin. Strongly built with reinforced seams. The outside is japanned green with gold stripes. Inside is japanned black.

All three sizes of Winchester Tackle Boxes stacked to show comparative sizes. From T. Webster collection. Photo by D. Kowalski.

The smallest Tackle Box (No. 9531). Has one 5-compartment scoop tray. Dimensions of box are 3 3/4 inches high, 10 1/2 inches long, 5 3/4 inches wide. (Editor's note: the actual measurements of the No. 9531 tackle box in the T. Webster collection are 4 inches high x 10 3/4 inches long x 6 inches wide.)

The intermediate size Tackle Box (No. 9532). Has two trays: one scoop tray with 6 compartments and one long tray with 3 compartments. Dimensions are 5 inches high, 12 1/2 inches long, 5 3/4 inches wide. (Editor's note: the actual measurements of the No. 9532 tackle box in the T. Webster collection are 5 1/8 inches high x 12 3/4 inches long x 6 inches wide.)

Winchester Fishing Equipment • 441

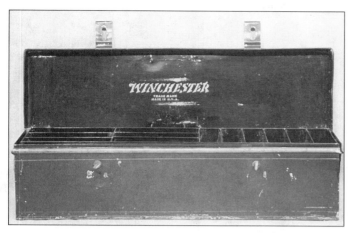

The largest of the Tackle Boxes (No. 9533). With one small tray and one large plug tray with 12 compartments. Catalog dimensions are 5 1/4 inches high, 19 1/2 inches long, 5 1/4 inches wide. . (Editor's note: the actual measurements of the No. 9533 tackle box in the T. Webster collection are 5 1/4 inches high x 19 7/8 inches long x 5 1/2 inches wide.) From T. Webster collection. Photo by D. Kowalski.

Values:	Exc.	V.G.	Good
9531	450.00	300.00	200.00
9532	650.00	425.00	300.00
9533	800.00	575.00	400.00

Winchester Bait Boxes

No. 9520. Crescent-shaped bait box is 6 inches wide with metal belt loops on back. Japanned in green.

No. 9521. Basket-shaped bait box is 3 1/2 inches by 2 3/4 inches by 2 inches. Pin soldered on back for fastening. Japanned in green.

Values:	Exc.	V.G.	Good
9520	550.00	375.00	250.00
9521	450.00	300.00	200.00

Leader Boxes. *No. 9522. Round boxes are 3 3/4 inches in diameter by 5/8 of an inch high. Satin aluminum finish. Hinged cover with two heavy felt pads inside.*

Values:	Exc.	V.G.	Good
9522	425.00	350.00	275.00

Split Buckshot and BB Sinkers

Packed in two ways for convenience. Either 25 Split BB or 10 Buckshot may be obtained packed in metal container with revolving cover. Shot may be removed by turning cover until hole comes over hole in container. They are also packed in paper tubes, 10 split buckshot to the tube, 25 BB shot to the tube. Fifty boxes or tubes to the carton. Approximate weight per carton 2 1/2 lbs.

Split BB sinkers in a metal container (No. 9114). Container is 1 1/2 inches across. From T. Webster collection. D. Kowalski photo.

Split buckshot sinkers in a metal container (No. 9115). Container is also 1 1/2 inches across. From T. Webster collection. D. Kowalski photo.

Split BB sinkers in a paper tube (No. 9134). Tube is 1 3/4 inches high. From T. Webster collection. D. Kowalski photo.

Split buckshot sinkers in a paper tube (No. 9135). Tube is 2 5/8 inches high. From T. Webster collection. D. Kowalski photo.

No.	Shot	Container		
9114	25 Split BB	Metal Container		
9115	10 Split Buck	Metal Container		
9134	25 Split BB	Paper Tube		
9135	10 Split Buck	Paper Tube		
Values:		**Exc.**	**V.G.**	**Good**
9114		300.00	225.00	150.00
9115		300.00	225.00	150.00
9134		200.00	150.00	100.00
9135		200.00	150.00	100.00

Lead BB sinkers in a small envelope. Here's another way Winchester offered these to customers. From T. Webster collection. D. Kowalski photo.

Values:	**Exc.**	**V.G.**	**Good**
	150.00	115.00	80.00

> *Phil White is the author of three books on fishing tackle including:* Winchester Fishing Tackle. *A fishing tackle collector for 30 years, he is also the editor of "Reel News" - the official publication of the Old Reel Collectors Association (ORCA).*

Baseball and Football Equipment

by David D. Kowalski

Historians still argue about whether Abner Doubleday gets credit for creating the "modern" game of baseball in 1839 at Cooperstown, New York. But by the time Winchester was ready to significantly expand its product lines in 1919, there was no doubt baseball was the "national game" of the United States. A new Winchester sporting goods line clearly needed baseball products.

Football, in the meantime, was also coming of age in America. American football was originally a combination of English rugby football and association football or soccer. By 1885 the evolution of rugby football played "the American way" had advanced to the point we could call it simply "football." The first Rose Bowl was held in 1902 and then annually starting in 1916.

Our coverage of Winchester's full line of sporting goods will start with this chapter on baseball and football products. Grouped together, baseball and football equipment included as many line items as all the other sports products combined. In these first two groups are also many very rare and one-of-a-kind items.

While baseball bats were durable products with clear stamps and model numbers burned into wood, many other products had only a small Winchester label to identify them.

Other baseball and football products, if they can be found, often suffer from clear evidence that children growing up in the 1920s and 1930s took their sports seriously. They got used. Baseballs were thrown and hit around the sandlots, ruining the logo stamps. Footballs were passed and kicked and pounded into submission, then tossed into a corner for next year's season. All that playground use was tough on original labels, logos and stamps. That's why baseball and football products in excellent condition bring a premium.

As with most other Winchester products, having a box for a football will conservatively double its value. An original baseball box, however, in mint or excellent condition will add 400 or 500 percent to the value of the baseball it holds.

Where appropriate, we'll also show you a few advertising items in this chapter that supported Winchester's baseball and football products. We will reserve the bulk of these related collectibles, particularly the colorful five-panel store displays, for the upcoming book, *Winchester Rarities*.

Winchester promoted all its major product lines with five-panel advertising sets. This one features baseball equipment on this side. The opposite side promoted trout fishing and related fishing tackle. This set would be valued at $2,800.00 in excellent condition. From T. Webster collection. Photo by D. Kowalski.

Winchester Baseballs

No. 2010. Winchester Official League. Constructed to National and American League specifications. Standard and official in every detail. Pure Para rubber center wound with 100% pure live wool yarn and strong outer cording which gives full, hard, smooth surface. Best selected horsehide cover, red and black Sea Island Cotton stitched. Every ball especially inspected for roundness, even, smooth stitching, perfect balance, weight and circumference and quality of material. Individually wrapped in tissue and silver foil and sealed in a bright red carton with the special Winchester Official League Ball seal. One dozen to the multi-carton. EVERY BALL GUARANTEED FOR 27 INNINGS.

No. 2012. Major League. Made from material almost identical with that used in the Official League ball. Pure 1-ounce Para rubber center, wool wound with strong cord outer winding for smooth hard surface. Selected horsehide cover is double stitched with red and purple waxed cord. Each ball wrapped in tissue and silver foil and sealed in an attractive carton. One dozen to the multi-carton.

No. 2013. Professional League. Rubber center wound with wool yarn and strong cording. Genuine horsehide cover, stitched with black and red waxed thread. Each ball wrapped in tissue and sealed in a carton. One dozen to the multi-car-

No. 2015. City League. Regulation specifications in size and weight. Rubber center and wool core, yarn wound. Horsehide cover, red and green waxed thread stitched. Each ball wrapped in tissue and sealed in a carton. One dozen to the multi-carton.

No. 2017. Amateur League. Standard weight and dimensions. Rubber center. Compressed-felt core wound with good quality yarn. Horsehide cover, double red and blue thread stitched. Each ball wrapped in tissue and sealed in a carton. One dozen to the multi-carton.

Baseball and Football Equipment • 445

No. 2019. Chaser Model. Compressed center, yarn wrapped. Imitation leather cover, red thread stitched. A leader in medium-sized, low-priced balls. Each ball wrapped in tissue, twelve to the carton.

A variation of the "Practice" ball was the "Special Practice" baseball shown here next to the smaller No. 3283 model. From T. Webster collection. Photo by D. Kowalski.

No. 2021. Practice. Regulation size. Compressed center, imitation leather waterproof cover. Red and green twisted thread stitched. A good practice ball and a big value at a low price. Each ball wrapped in tissue and sealed in a carton. One dozen to the multi-carton.

No. 2022. Champion Model. Compressed center, wound in yarn. Imitation leather cover, red thread stitched. The most popular ball for small boys. Each ball wrapped in tissue, twelve to the carton.

No. 2023. Boys League. Rubber center compressed felt core wound with strong cotton cording. Genuine leather cover. 8 1/2-inch circumference. Red and green twisted thread stitched. Each ball wrapped in tissue and sealed in a carton. One dozen to the multi-carton.

No. 2025. Intercollegiate League. 5 oz. 9-inch ball. Pure rubber center, wound with special yarn under tension to produce a perfectly round and balanced ball. Genuine horsehide cover with double blue and red waxed thread stitching. Each ball wrapped in tissue and sealed in a carton. One dozen to the multi-carton.

No. 2026. Junior Special. Lively rubber center in compressed core, wound with strong cotton cording, 4 1/2 oz. in weight, 8 1/2-inch circumference. Genuine horsehide cover with double red and green thread stitching. Each ball wrapped in tissue and sealed in a carton. One dozen to the multi-carton.

446 • Baseball and Football Equipment

No. 2027. Junior Official League. Junior size official ball preferred by boy's leagues. 1 oz. pure rubber center, wound with pure rubber center, wound with pure wool yarn and strong outer cording. 4 1/2 oz. in weight, with 8 1/2-inch circumference. Genuine horsehide cover, double red and blue thread stitched. Each ball wrapped in tissue and sealed in a carton. One dozen to the multi-carton.

No. 13 1/2. Leader model. Imitation leather cover, good quality felt shoddy center, red stitching. Regulation size and weight; circumference 9 in., 5 oz. Put up in separate boxes. One dozen in a cardboard box. Fifty dozen in a case.

No. 19 1/2. Rocket Boys' model. Compressed cotton center. Artificial leather covered. Circumference 8 1/4 in., 4 oz. One dozen in a cardboard box. Seventy-five dozen in a case.

Ball Values:	Exc.	V.G.	Good
2010	2,000.00	1,500.00	700.00
2012	2,000.00	1,500.00	700.00
2013	2,000.00	1,500.00	700.00
2015	2,000.00	1,500.00	700.00
2017	2,000.00	1,500.00	700.00
2019	2,000.00	1,500.00	700.00
2021	2,000.00	1,500.00	700.00
2022	2,000.00	1,500.00	700.00
2023	2,000.00	1,500.00	700.00
2025	2,000.00	1,500.00	700.00
2026	2,000.00	1,500.00	700.00
2027	2,000.00	1,500.00	700.00
13 1/2	2,000.00	1,500.00	700.00
19 1/2	2,000.00	1,500.00	700.00
3283	1,700.00	1,300.00	700.00

No. 3721. Indoor Baseball (14-inch). Lively hand-wound center and horsehide cover. Official for any game. Guaranteed to hold shape and also against any defects for one full game. Measures 14 inches in circumference. One to the Carton. Approximate weight 3/4 lb.

No. 3720. Indoor Baseball (12-inch). Hand-wound center horsehide cover. Guaranteed for one full game. Measures 12 inches in circumference. One to the Carton. Approximate weight 10 ounces.

Outing Balls. Heavy imitation leather cover stitched with strong cord. Packed one-half dozen to the carton.

No.	Circumference	Weight
3761	14 in.	5 oz.
3762	11 in.	4 oz.
3763	9 in.	3 1/2 oz.

Ball Values:	Exc.	V.G.	Good
3720	1,700.00	1,500.00	1,200.00
3721	1,700.00	1,500.00	1,200.00
3761	1,700.00	1,500.00	1,200.00
3762	1,700.00	1,500.00	1,200.00
3763	1,700.00	1,500.00	1,200.00

Baseball and Football Equipment • 447

Playground Balls. With outseam. This ball is made like the Indoor baseball except that it has its seams turned out. Hand-wound center. Horsehide cover. Specially recommended for picnic and playground use. Guaranteed for one full game.

No.	Circumference	Weight
3751	14 in.	12 oz.
3750	12 in.	10 oz.

With Outseam. Compressed felt center. Fine grade pearl grain horsehide cover. Single-stitched. Packed one to the carton.

No.	Circumference	Weight
W12	12 in.	7 1/2 oz.
W14	14 in.	10 oz.

No. 12/S. Regulation Playground. Center made of resilient material, yarn wound. Horsehide cover. Outside seams. Well made and very serviceable. Circumference is 12 inches. One-half dozen in a carton.

Ball Values:	Exc.	V.G.	Good
3750	1,200.00	1,000.00	800.00
3751	1,200.00	1,000.00	800.00
W12	1,200.00	1,000.00	800.00
W12/S	1,200.00	1,000.00	800.00
W14	1,200.00	1,000.00	800.00

Winchester Catchers' Mitts

Correct in every detail. Constructed from materials prepared expressly for us. Palms of our higher-grade mitts are molded to shape and the asbestos felt pads are hand formed and so made that padding cannot shift. These features assure the user of a well-formed pocket in the right spot, enabling him to keep up with the increased speed of the game. Particular attention is given to the forming of the pocket in this line of catchers' mitts. Long wear and protection of the user are built into Winchester mitts and backed by the Winchester Guarantee.

Mitts furnished are designed to be worn on the left hand of players who throw right handed. If right hand mitts are wanted for players who throw left handed add RH to numbers when ordering.

No. 2050. Designed and perfected to meet every requirement of the Major League catcher. Made of finest selected cowhide, especially tanned. Small size gives perfect balance enabling the user to shift quickly. Pad made of several layers of finest-quality asbestos felt, hand-formed and closely stitched to give longer service after being broken in. Full leather lined and leather roll binding. Individually packed in Winchester gray carton.

No. 2052. An extra-large mitt fully molded. Made of finest black calfskin. Fully laced with black leather lace. Leather welted seams. Four layers of asbestos pad, shaped to form deep pocket. New style fingers with outseams making surface against the back of the hand perfectly smooth. Adjustable buckle fastening at thumb. Double wrist protectors. Individually packed in Winchester gray carton.

No. 2053. A large-size molded mitt of finest calfskin. Dark tan color. Made of soft, pliable, yet tough, leather. Fully laced with rawhide lace. Four layer pad of finest quality asbestos felt, hand-formed, making a deep natural pocket. Leather welted seams, roll-style binding. Special wrist strap and buckle. Packed one in a Winchester gray carton.

No. 2055. Made of selected brown horsehide. Tan leather binding. Fully laced with tan leather lace running through brass eyelets. Leather welted seams. Padding is combination of asbestos felt and compressed hair, forming a deep natural pocket. Individually packed in Winchester gray carton.

No. 2056. Made of specially selected chocolate calfskin. Genuine asbestos felt hand-formed and making a deep pocket. Black leather roll-style binding. Leather welted seams, tan rawhide laced. Buckle fastening with non-chafing wrist protector. Individually packed in Winchester gray carton.

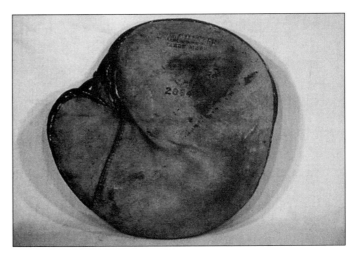

Catchers' Mitt (No. 2054) clearly shows model number stamped in the palm of a glove lightly used, if at all. From its position near the palm, you can see how easily the model number would have been obscured by heavy use of the mitt. With many used mitts, it is necessary to use a reading glass to discern the imprint of the model number. From T. Webster collection. Photo by D. Kowalski.

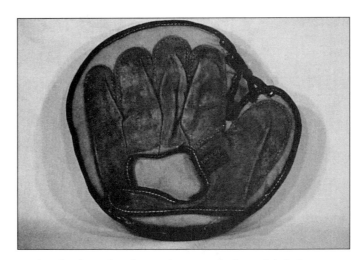

Back side of Catchers' Mitt (No. 2054) shows label placement, as well as finger and strap detail. From T. Webster collection. Photo by D. Kowalski.

No. 2054. Palm and fingers of finest black cowhide. Black mitten leather back, brown leather binding and tan leather laced. Large pocket made by hand-formed asbestos felt pad. Leather-welted seams. Individually packed in Winchester gray carton.

Baseball and Football Equipment • 449

No. 2057. Made of selected tan cowhide. Hand-made asbestos felt pad, black leather binding, fully laced with tan leather lace. Leather welted seams. Padding compressed at finger tips to facilitate "scooping up" low balls. Individually packed in Winchester gray carton.

No. 2062. Palm and fingers of finest selected mitten leather, deep wine-colored. Back and panel of oak tan grained leather, red binding, full leather laced, hand-formed padding. Packed one in a Winchester gray carton.

No. 2059. Palm and fingers chocolate-colored cowhide. Oak tan grained leather back and panel. Brown binding. Full leather lacing allows padding adjustment to suit players. Fingers and band double stitched with heavy white thread. Individually packed in Winchester gray carton.

No. 2063. Palm and fingers of tan imitation leather, khaki canvas back. Black imitation-leather band. Bound edge, waxed tan thumb lace. Packed one in a Winchester gray carton.

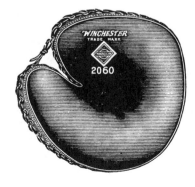

No. 2060. Full-sized mitt of highest-grade black mitten leather throughout. Double-stitched fingers and band, red binding, full leather laced. Individually packed in Winchester gray carton.

No. 2064. Good quality khaki canvas with a circular leather patch, stitched in center of palm. Leather fingers, black imitation-leather band. Black binding. Packed one in a Winchester gray carton.

No. 2066. Palm and fingers of tough brown grain leather, brown imitation leather back and band. Also has laced edge, red binding. Packed one in a Winchester gray carton.

No. W3. Big League model. Selected brown-color cowhide throughout. Molded palm. Combination felt pad. Leather lace. Special wrist strap and buckle wrist fastener. Packed one in a Winchester gray carton.

No. 2067. Back, palm and fingers of olive-colored mitten leather. Strong, black imitation-leather binding, fully laced with heavy white lace. Tan strap leather buckle fastening. Packed one in a Winchester gray carton.

No. W5. Semi-professional model. Tan-color cowhide throughout. Welded seam between band and palm. Well padded with deep natural pocket. Leather lace. Special wrist strap with buckle fastener. Packed one in a Winchester gray carton.

No. 2069. Boy's mitt, good quality leather palm and fingers; heavy canvas back, imitation-leather band. Has bound edge, strap and button fastening. Packed one in a Winchester gray carton.

No. W7. School League model. Black-colored cowhide palm and fingers. Brown leather back band. Well padded with deep ball pocket. Leather lace. Leather wrist strap with buckle fastener. Packed one in a Winchester gray carton.

No. W9. Genuine cowhide. Dark-tan cowhide palm and fingers. Brown-leather back and band. Well padded. Full laced. Strap and buckle wrist fastener. Packed one in a Winchester gray carton.

No. W13. Small Size. Dark-tan leather palm and fingers. Dark-tan imitation-leather band. Well padded. Strap and button fastener. Packed one in a Winchester gray carton.

No. W11. Medium Size. Dark-tan leather palm and fingers. Dark-tan imitation-leather back. Full laced. Well padded. Strap and button fastener. One in a carton.

No. W15. Small Size. Light-tan leather palm and fingers. Dark-tan imitation-leather back. Black imitation-leather band. Well padded. Strap and button fastener. One in a carton.

Values:	Exc.	V.G.	Good
Catcher	800.00	600.00	300.00

Comment: *Values are for all models of Catchers' Mitts. Add 25 percent for mitts worn on right hand.*

Winchester Basemen's Mitts

Winchester presents a selection of basemen's mitts in which any player will find his own particular choice in style. Skillful combination of the proper materials and careful construction make correctly fashioned mitts in which the player will have confidence. Particular attention is given to the forming of the pocket in this line of mitts.

No. 2101. Made of finest tan calfskin throughout. Oil treated with "ready broke" pad formed of best-quality felt reinforced at finger tips to protect fingers when going after low balls. Roll style leather binding, leather welted seams, fully leather laced. Extra-long panel back extending far down over back of the wrist under special strap and buckle adjustments. Strap and buckle a thumb. Packed one in a Winchester gray carton.

No. 2102. Made of finest black horsehide throughout, fully laced with black leather lace. Roll-style black leather binding. Best quality hand-formed felt pad, sewed to make a large ball pocket. Packed one in a Winchester gray carton.

No. 2105. Palm of selected brown horsehide, panel back and lining of black grain leather. Roll-style leather binding. Special-quality hand-formed felt pad. Special wrist strap and buckle fastening. Packed one in a Winchester gray carton.

No. 2103. Made of finest calfskin, especially tanned, soft yet tough, golden-tan color. Leather-welted hand-turned seams. Panel back and leather laced. Adjustable strap and buckle a thumb. Best quality hand-sewed felt pad. Packed one in a Winchester gray carton.

No. 2108. Full-sized mitt of olive-colored mitten leather. Invisible fingers. Double stitched with black thread. Black binding, fully laced with brown waxed lace. Hand-formed felt pad. Black strap and button fastening at wrist. Packed one in a Winchester gray carton.

No. 2104. Glove thumb model of soft, pliable black calfskin. Finest-quality hand-formed felt padding, so constructed and sewed that it cannot get out of position. Brown leather roll-style binding and welted seams. Laced, panel back made of tan leather. Full black leather-lined. Packed one in a Winchester gray carton.

No. 2109. Invisible-finger model, made of finest black grain mitten leather noted for long-wearing qualities. Fully laced with tan leather lace. Brown binding, strap and buckle fastening at wrist. Packed one in a Winchester gray carton.

No. 2110. Invisible-finger model, made of high-grade pearl cowhide. Brown leather binding, laced with tan leather. Felt pad. Packed one in a Winchester gray carton.

No. 2118. Full-sized mitt. Palm and fingers made of brown grain leather, brown imitation-leather back. Black lace and binding. Individual fingers. Strap and buckle fastening at wrist. Packed one in a Winchester gray carton.

No. 2115. New invisible-finger model, made of selected heavy mitten leather, light brown color, roll edge. Wine-color leather bound, tan leather lace. Special wrist strap and buckle. Packed one in a Winchester gray carton.

No. 2119. Small boy's mitt with tan leather palm, olive green canvas back and lining. Made with finger compartment and leather wrist strap with button. Packed one in a Winchester gray carton.

No. 2116. Palm and fingers made of good-quality black grain leather. Back of heavy olive green canvas. Red binding, fully laced, leather wrist fastening. A well-padded, strong, durable mitt. Packed one in a Winchester gray carton.

No. WB2 - Left Hand; WB2RH - Right Hand. Professional Model. Made of genuine horsehide, oil treated. Dark tan color. Combination felt pad. Leather bound. Leather-laced welted seams. Panel back. Adjustable-loop leather thumb lace. Strap and buckle wrist strap. Packed one in a Winchester carton.

454 • Baseball and Football Equipment

No. WB4. *Full Finger Model. Selected light-tan heavy genuine horsehide. Leather laced throughout. Special combination pad. Wrist strap and buckle. Adjustable loop thumb lace. Packed one in a Winchester carton.*

No. WB6 - *Left Hand; WB6RH - Right Hand. Palm made of light-tan genuine horsehide. Fingers and back are dark-tan leather. Fully laced with brown waxed lace. Strap and buckle wrist fastener. Packed one in a Winchester carton.*

No. WB8 - *Left Hand; WB8RH - Right Hand. Made of black grain leather throughout, well padded. Red binding with brown lace. Strap and buckle fastening at wrist. Packed one in a Winchester carton.*

No. WB10. *Good-quality dark-tan grained leather, well padded. Full laced. Button fastener at wrist. Packed one in a Winchester carton.*

No. WB12 - *Left Hand; WB12RH - Right Hand. Light tan leather. One-piece palm. Olive green canvas back and lining with finger compartments. Leather wrist strap with button. Packed one in a Winchester carton.*

Values:	Exc.	V.G.	Good
Basemen	800.00	600.00	300.00

Comment: *Values are for all models of Basemen's Mitts. Add 25 percent for mitts worn on right hand.*

Winchester Fielders' Gloves

Outstanding features of Winchester Fielders' Gloves are designs to suit individual tastes with the natural catching ability of the hand built into them. Finest materials and skillful construction give these mitts long-wearing qualities. Our special detailed attention in the selection of material and in manufacture are given to the pliability of the leather, and padding arrangement for especially formed deep pocket. Winchester gloves are made with the following special features: larger and heavily padded little finger; fully laced, permitting adjustment of padding; welted seams; edges bound with colored leather and special lacing between thumb and first finger. All "ready broke" with that soft "glovy" feel. Professional models also offered in boys' gloves.

No. 2141. Chocolate-colored grain leather glove, leather lined in palm and front of fingers. Tan binding, welted seams. Packed one in a Winchester gray carton.

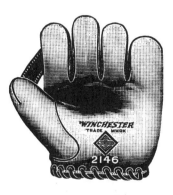

No. 2146. Extra-large glove of drab buff horsehide, pliable yet tough. Leather lined throughout, double stitched for additional strength. All seams leather welted, leather laced at heel. Packed one in a Winchester gray carton.

No. 2142. Medium-sized tan-color leather glove. Palm is leather lined. Tan binding, leather web between thumb and forefinger. Packed one in a Winchester gray carton.

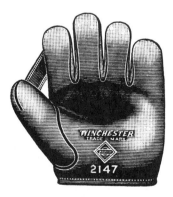

No. 2147. Large pattern, oil-treated glove of finest tan calfskin. Kid-leather lined, felt pad raised at heel, black leather roll-style binding, leather-welted seams. Packed one in a Winchester gray carton.

No. 2148. Full-sized glove of chocolate-colored horsehide. Tan leather lined throughout, leather-welted seams, roll-style binding, double horsehide web at thumb and forefinger. Packed one in a Winchester gray carton.

No. 2149. Made of genuine tan horsehide, brown leather binding, leather-welted seams, full leather lined and leather laced at heel. Double web at thumb. Packed one in a Winchester gray carton.

No. 2151. Long-fingered model, full-sized glove of chocolate-colored grain leather, full leather lined, tan binding and leather-welted seams. Leather laced at heel. Packed one in a Winchester gray carton.

No. 2152. Entire glove of finest selected black horsehide. Roll-style black leather binding and leather welted seams. Black-leather-laced heel, double-horsehide web at thumb. Hand-formed padding of best quality felt, slightly raised at heel and very thin at center of palm. Packed one in a Winchester gray carton.

No. 2153. Black horsehide, tan leather lined; Leather laced at heel. Wine-color leather binding and welted seams, double-horsehide web. Packed one in a Winchester gray carton.

No. 2154. Extra-large glove of toughest drab horsehide throughout. Laced at heel to allow adjustment. Roll-style tan leather binding. Double-stitched, leather-welted seams. Double horsehide web at thumb and forefinger. Packed one in a Winchester gray carton.

Baseball and Football Equipment • 457

No. 2155. Made of finest-grade tan horsehide leather, lining of tan mitten leather, tan leather lace at heel, roll-style binding, welted seams. Adjustable leather lace through loops between thumb and forefinger. Same model as 2158 but not "doped" with oil treatment. Packed one in a Winchester gray carton.

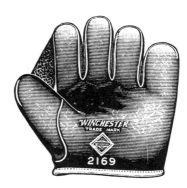

No. 2169. Black leather glove, full leather lined, bound in white with white welted seams. Handmade padding. Packed one in a Winchester gray carton.

No. 2158. Large glove of extra-quality flexible tan horsehide throughout, with extra-large thumb and little finger. Special leather loops on thumb and forefinger with adjustable leather lace to hold thumb in any position. Leather laced at heel, roll-style binding and leather-welted seams. Outside of glove oil treated which preserves and makes the leather pliable. Packed one in a Winchester gray carton.

No. 2182. Medium-sized tan-color leather glove. Perspiration-absorbing felt palm and felt lining. Packed two in a Winchester gray carton.

No. 2159. Made of cream-colored horsehide, oil treated for flexibility. Full leather lined, leather loops and adjustable lace at thumb and forefinger. Leather binding, welted seams. Built with all the features of the higher-priced gloves but within reach of the boys' pockets. Packed one in a Winchester gray carton.

No. 2183. Outseam model, made of tan leather, felt palm and finger lining, red binding. Packed two in a Winchester gray carton.

458 • *Baseball and Football Equipment*

No. 2184. *Small boy's all-leather glove, tan colored. Palm and fingers lined with felt. Brown binding, leather web between thumb and forefinger. Packed two in a Winchester gray carton.*

No. WG6 - Left Hand; WG6RH - Right Hand. *Professional Model. Genuine dark-tan, oil-treated horsehide. Cream-color leather lined. Welted seams and binding. Leather laced at wrist. Tough rawhide adjustable thumb lace. Packed one in a Winchester carton.*

No. 2185. *Medium-sized olive-green leather glove. Palm is leather lined. White welted seams, black binding, tan leather, web between thumb and forefinger. Packed one in a Winchester gray carton.*

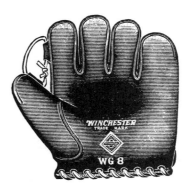

No. WG8. *Professional Model. Genuine oil-treated, dark-tan horsehide. Brown leather lined. Leather welted. Leather laced at wrist. Adjustable rawhide thumb lace. Packed one in a Winchester carton.*

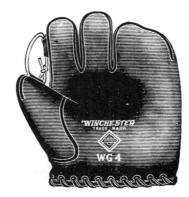

No. WG4. *Three Finger Model. Finest selected oil-treated, dark-tan horsehide. Full leather lines. Black-leather binding. Welted seams. Hand-tailored felt pad. Deep natural "ready broke" ball pocket. Adjustable rawhide thumb lace. Leather laced at wrist. Packed one in a Winchester carton.*

No. WG10 - Left Hand; WG10RH - Right Hand. *Large Youth's Model. Genuine horsehide, oil-treated, dark-tan color. Leather binding. Welted seams. Full leather lined. Laced wrist. Leather strap thumb lace. Packed one in a Winchester carton.*

Baseball and Football Equipment • 459

No. WG12. Large Youth's Model. Genuine horsehide, light tan color Palm, dark tan leather lined. Welted seams. Laced wrist. Leather web between thumb and forefinger. Packed one in a Winchester carton.

No. WG14 - Left hand; WG14RH- Right Hand. Large Youth's Model. Black grain leather. Palm is dark-tan leather lined. Bound wrist. Welted seams. Web thumb. Packed one in a Winchester carton.

No. WG16. Medium Size. Oil-treated, dark-tan leather. Palm is tan-leather lined. Web thumb. Packed one in a Winchester carton.

No. WG20 - Left Hand; WG20RH - Right Hand. Boy's Size. Genuine horsehide. Outseam model. Felt lined. Web thumb. Packed one in a Winchester carton.

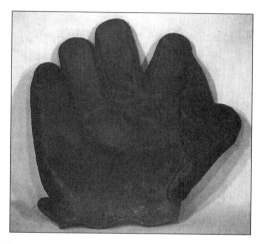

No. WG18RH. Boy's Fielder's Glove shows heavy use that has worn off the model number on heel of glove. From T. Webster collection. Photo by D. Kowalski.

No. WG18RH. Top side of the same Boy's Fielder's Glove. A rare item; gloves worn on the right hand are much rarer than those worn on the left hand. From T. Webster collection. Photo by D. Kowalski.

No. WG18 - Left Hand; WG18RH - Right Hand. Boy's Size. Tan leather. Palm is tan-leather lined. Web thumb. Packed one in a Winchester carton.

Youths' Professional Model Fielders' Gloves

Winchester offers below three Professional model gloves for the coming ball players of the nation. The younger players fitted with any of the models detailed below will get the proper start and "a proper start is a race half won." These gloves have built in them, in cadet sizes, all the features of the high-class Winchester line.

No. 2143. Cadet-size glove of black horsehide, Tan-leather binding and lining. Leather laced at heel. Leather-welted seams, double-horsehide web between thumb and forefinger. Packed one in a Winchester gray carton.

No. 2145. Cadet-size glove of oil-treated tan horsehide, full leather lined, leather loops and adjustable lace between thumb and forefingers. Laced at heel with leather lace. Roll-style leather binding. Leather-welted seams. A practical, professional model glove for boys. Packed one in a Winchester gray carton.

No. 2144. Cadet-size glove of drab-buff horsehide, full leather lined, leather laced at heel. Tan leather binding, leather-welted seams, horsehide web between thumb and forefinger. Packed one in a Winchester gray carton.

Values:	Exc.	V.G.	Good
Fielder	650.00	450.00	250.00

Comment: *Values are for all models of Fielders' Gloves, Adult and Youth. Add 25 percent for gloves worn on right hand.*

Winchester Baseball Bats

Winchester bats are manufactured by experts in wood turning. The very utmost of inspection is applied to the selection of materials and their manufacture. Only close-fibered, heavy, slow second-growth white ash, proved to be the most resilient wood giving the greatest driving power, is used. The factory selects only a certain percentage of the wood in the tree. After that is made into billets they are inspected and re-inspected during their one or two years of seasoning for a positive elimination of cross grain, knots, bark, worm holes or any other slightest imperfection. Five inspections during manufacture, each more rigid than the previous, and the final inspection of their super finish assure in Winchester bats only those fit for their use and purpose in keeping with the standards of Winchester quality. We cannot guarantee Winchester bats against breakage.

Super Quality. *Rubbed Gray Finish. Made from the very choicest selection of open-air dried ash billets. Highly polished rubbed gray finish. New Red Winchester trademark. "Super Quality" burnt on bat near end. Made in eight models, assorted lengths and weights. Furnished only one dozen assorted models packed in a fibre shipping container. No. 2300 line.*

Baseball and Football Equipment • 461

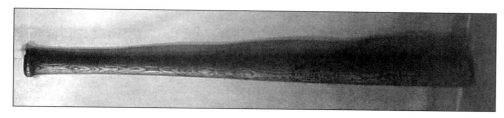

Model 2411. Professional Oil Finish bat. This 36-inch version actually measures 35 3/4 inches. From T. Webster collection. Photo by D. Kowalski.

Professional Oil Finish. *Made of best-quality straight-grain, white ash. Finished with plain-oil finish which brings out the quality of the grain to best advantage. Made in eight models as below. One dozen of only one model in various lengths and weights packed in a fibre shipping container.*

No.	Code	Lengths
2402	BR	34, 35, 36 inches
2404	FF	34, 35, 36 inches
2406	KW	34, 35, 36 inches
2407	TC	33, 34, 35 inches
2408	GK	34, 35 inches
2409	TS	33, 34, 35 inches
2410	RH	34, 35 inches
2411	ER	34, 35, 36 inches

Bat Values:	Exc.	V.G.	Good
Super Q.	550.00	400.00	225.00
Pro. Oil	550.00	400.00	225.00

Model 2707. College League bat. From T. Webster collection. Photo by D. Kowalski.

College League. *High-quality, straight-grain white ash, golden-brown finished, with natural taped handle.*

No. 2700 line. Made in eight models, assorted lengths and weights. Furnished only one dozen assorted models packed in a fibre shipping container.

No. 2702 - BR only. Assorted lengths 34, 35, and 36 in. Assorted weights 30 to 42 oz. Furnished only one dozen assorted weights and lengths in a fibre shipping carton.

Senior Professional League. *Thoroughly seasoned straight-grain white ash. Mottled-burnt, yellow-stained, and polished. Made in eight models. Assorted lengths and weights. Furnished only one dozen assorted models packed in a fibre shipping container. No. 2800 line.*

Model 2906. Sandlot League bat. From T. Webster collection. Photo by D. Kowalski.

Sandlot League. *Selected-quality, straight-grain white ash finished in a rich dark brown. Made in eight models, assorted lengths and weights. Furnished only one dozen assorted models packed in a fibre shipping container. No. 2900 line.*

Model 2240. Fungo bat is one of the rarer models. Winchester obviously made these in other lengths; this one measures 34 3/4 inches. From T. Webster collection. Photo by D. Kowalski.

Fungo. *Professional model, 33-inch Fungo bat made of selected straight-grain, air-dried white ash. Packed one dozen in a fibre shipping container.*

Bat Values:	Exc.	V.G.	Good	Bat Values:	Exc.	V.G.	Good
College	700.00	550.00	375.00	Sandlot	700.00	550.00	375.00
Senior	700.00	550.00	375.00	Fungo	800.00	600.00	425.00

Indoor Baseball Bat. Made of tough, well-seasoned ash, 33 inches long. Stained dark-walnut finish except handle which is natural. Handle wound with gray tape. Packed one dozen in a fibre shipping container. No. 2880.

Playground Bat. A 33-inch long model, made of straight-grain hardwood thoroughly seasoned. Oil finish. Packed one dozen in a fibre shipping container. No. 2890.

Bat Values:	Exc.	V.G.	Good
Indoor	850.00	650.00	425.00
Playgr.	750.00	600.00	400.00

Comment: *The Indoor model is another of the rarer Winchester bats.*

Winchester Boys' Baseball Bats

Model 2425. Public School League bat. From T. Webster collection. Photo by D. Kowalski.

Public School League. *Bat is 31 inches long, made of selected straight-grain white ash. Oil finish. Handle wound with Winchester gray tape. Packed one dozen in a fibre shipping container. No. 2425.*

Model 2825. Boys' Special bat. From T. Webster collection. Photo by D. Kowalski.

Boys' Special. *This Special boys' model is 30 inches long. A high-grade seasoned and air-dried hardwood bat. Mottled-burnt and yellow-stained finish. Packed one dozen to a fibre shipping container. No. 2825.*

Model 2725. Junior League bat. From T. Webster collection. Photo by D. Kowalski.

Junior League. High-grade seasoned and air-dried hardwood bat. Oil and mottled-burnt finish. Packed one dozen in a fibre shipping container. No. 2725.

Model 2240. Boys' League bat measures 28 1/2 inches long. From T. Webster collection. Photo by D. Kowalski.

Boys' League. Small boys' bat of straight-grain, seasoned hardwood. Oil and mottled-burnt finish. Packed one dozen in a fibre shipping container. No. 2925.

Bat Values:	Exc.	V.G.	Good	Bat Values:	Exc.	V.G.	Good
Public	700.00	550.00	375.00	Junior	700.00	550.00	375.00
B. Special	700.00	550.00	375.00	B. League	700.00	550.00	375.00

Winchester Baseball Bat Bags

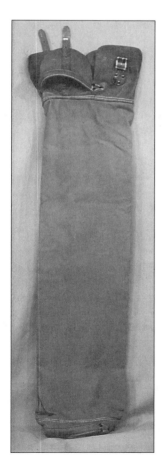

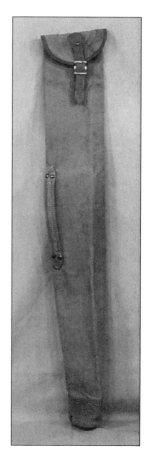

Model 1933 bat bag holds six bats. This bag was never used. Measures about 37 inches when closed. From T. Webster collection. Photo by D. Kowalski.

Bat Bags. Made of heavy khaki duck with heavy tan grain leather straps and trimming. Strong and durable. Each bag packed in a heavy manila envelope. No. 1932 - capacity 12 bats. No. 1933 - capacity 6 bats.

Model 1935 bat bag holds two bats. This bag was never used. Measures 35 1/2 inches closed. From T. Webster collection. Photo by D. Kowalski.

Bat Bag. Made of khaki canvas with football-leather end and trimming. Packed one to a heavy manila envelope. No. 1935.

Bag Values:	Exc.	V.G.	Good
1932	1,800.00	1,500.00	1,000.00
1933	1,600.00	1,250.00	900.00
1935	1,500.00	1,100.00	500.00

Winchester Baseball Catchers' Masks

No. 2201. Aluminum Mask. This is a new model mask. It is light in weight, gives the best of protection and a greater range of vision without shadow. Special pads are adjustable to give maximum comfort. Proved to be the most satisfactory type in use. This style used by practically all catchers in the big leagues and colleges. Packed one in a folding gray carton.

No. 2204. Curved vision. "Spitter" model. Electrically welded wire. Continous curled hair-filled pads. Adjustable elastic head strap. Packed one in a folding gray carton.

Heavy, electrically welded wire mask. Wide-open vision. Metal frame. Ear protectors. Continuous hair-filled pad and chin cushion. Detachable sun shade. Adjustable elastic head strap. "Spitter" model. Packed one in a folding gray carton.

No. 2205. Open-vision mask of heavy welded wire. Hair-filled pads; molded-leather head and chin pieces. Packed one in a folding gray carton.

No. 2206. Youths' Mask. Made of strong wire. Padded with continuous hair-stuffed cushions and leather chin straps. Packed in bulk.

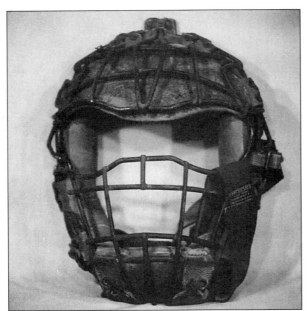

Catcher's Mask (Model 2203) with a padded inner cap. One of the "Spitter" models Winchester created because they empathized with those tobacco-chewing catchers who said, "When ya gotta spit, ya gotta spit!" From T. Webster collection. Photo by D. Kowalski.

No. 2207. Boys' Mask. Made of strong wire, well-padded with leather head and chin straps. Elastic head strap. Packed in bulk.

Values:	Exc.	V.G.	Good
Masks	600.00	450.00	300.00

Comment: *Values are for all models of Catchers' Masks.*

Catchers' Leg Guards

Leg Guards (No. 2251) show only minor wear that would put them somewhere between Excellent and Very Good condition. From T. Webster collection. Photo by D. Kowalski.

No. 2251. Leg section of strong molded fibre with shock absorbing back. Molded leather knee cap lined with heavy felt. Flexible pad joint between knee cap and leg guard allowing perfect freedom of movement. Heavy ankle pads. Packed one pair to a manila envelope.

No. 2252. Leg section of strong reeds covered with heavy white canvas. Knee cap of felt-lined, heavy molded leather. Flexible joint between kneecap and leg section. Reeds extend down and protect the ankle on both sides. Packed one pair to a manila envelope.

Values:	Exc.	V.G.	Good
Guards	700.00	550.00	400.00

Comment: *Values are for either model of Leg Guards.*

Umpires' and Catchers' Body Protectors

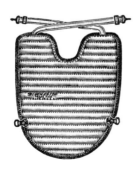

No. 2231. Umpires' Chest Protector. Heavy army duck padded with hair, a lightweight material giving maximum protection. Roll-style leather binding and adjustable shoulder straps. Packed one to a heavy manila envelope.

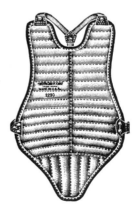

No. 2230 Heavy army duck sewed in the form of parallel reeds. Each section padded with hair, a lightweight material giving maximum protection. Roll-style leather binding. Elastic shoulder straps and adjustable web back straps. Attached by non-rusting nickel buckle. Packed one to a heavy manila envelope.

466 • Baseball and Football Equipment

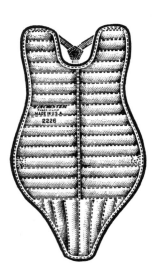

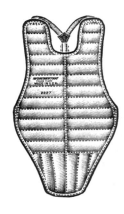

No. 2226. *Good-quality khaki cloth leather bound. Padded with curled hair. Elastic shoulder straps. Adjustable web back strap. Packed one to a manila envelope.*

No. 2227. *Youths' size of good-quality olive-colored khaki cloth. Padded with curled hair. Leather bound. Equipped with elastic shoulder strap and adjustable back strap. A good lightweight protector. Packed one to a manila envelope.*

Values:	Exc.	V.G.	Good
	700.00	550.00	400.00

Comment: *Values are for all models of Body or Chest Protectors.*

Winchester Sliding Pads

No. 2914. *Regulation model sliding pads made of special washable padding, well quilted and covered with white cotton. Packed one pair to a manila envelope.*

No. 2916. *Combination sliding pad and supporter. Made of special washable material with detachable elastic supporter. Snug fitting, giving the player every protection and comfort. Packed one pair to a manila envelope.*

Values:	Exc.	V.G.	Good
Pads	700.00	550.00	400.00

Comment: *Values are for either model of Sliding Pads.*

Winchester Baseball Shoes

No. 2507. Highest-quality Wollowby yellow-backed Kangaroo uppers and lining. Made on Goodyear last. Finest-quality oak-tanned leather sole. Professional lightweight sprint model. Genuine leather inner sole. Outside foxing. Genuine leather counter pocket. Extra-wide tongue. Hand-forged steel spikes. Fibre plate reinforcement in sole to hold spikes rigid. Half sizes 6 to 10 inclusive. One pair in a carton.

No. 2506. Low-cut, extra-quality, lined cowhide uppers. Made on Goodyear last. Best-quality oak-tanned soles. Semi-sprint model. Campbell stitched. Outside foxing. Counter pocket. Extra-long tongue. Forged steel spikes. Fibre plate reinforcement in sole to hold spikes rigid. Half sizes 5 1/2 to 10 1/2 inclusive. One pair in a carton.

No. 2505. Low-cut Wollowby yellow-backed Kangaroo uppers with Kangaroo lining. Made on Goodyear last. Best-quality oak-tanned leather soles. Sprint model. Campbell stitched. Genuine leather counter and leather sock lining. Extra-long tongue. Rawhide lacing. Forged steel toe and heel spikes. Fibre plate reinforcement in sole to hold spike rigid. Half sizes 5 1/2 to 10 1/2 inclusive. One pair in a carton.

No. 2512. Good-quality black leather shoe with a straight sole. MacKay sewed. Steel spikes. Inside reinforcement. Sizes 5 to 12 inclusive. One pair in a carton.

Values:	Exc.	V.G.	Good
Shoes	700.00	550.00	400.00

Comment: *Values are for all models of Baseball Shoes.*

No. 2501. Low-cut best-quality leather uppers. Made on Goodyear last. Plain oak-tanned leather soles. Reinforced foxing. Fibre counters. Extra-long tongues. Forged steel spikes. Fibre plate reinforcement in sole to hold spikes rigid. Half sizes 5 1/2 to 10 1/2. One pair in a carton.

Baseball Bases

No. 2810. Major League Regulation size base. White canvas double-quilted top. Extra-heavy double-web straps and wrought iron spikes.

No. 2811. High-quality heavy-canvas base, firmly stuffed and quilted. Heavy web straps and steel spikes.

No. 2812. Long-wearing white-canvas base, complete with straps and spikes.

Values:	Exc.	V.G.	Good
Bases	500.00	400.00	200.00

Comment: Values are for any of the three models of Baseball Bases.

Home Plates

No. 2901. Regulation-size heavy white-rubber home plate furnished complete with five removable spikes that screw into the bottom of the plate and fasten it firmly into the ground. Wrapped in manila brown paper.

Values:	Exc.	V.G.	Good
Home	500.00	400.00	200.00

Pitcher's Box Plate

No. 2954. Regulation-size plate for pitcher's box made of strong heavy white rubber. Furnished with three removable spikes that screw into the plate. Wrapped in brown manila paper.

Values:	Exc.	V.G.	Good
	500.00	400.00	200.00

Uniform Protector Rolls

No. 2920. Made of tan canvas, waterproof. Large and well-adapted for taking neat care of uniforms while traveling. High-quality russet-leather straps and handle. One in an individual brown manila envelope.

Values:	Exc.	V.G.	Good
	500.00	400.00	200.00

Baseball Score Book

Nos.	Description
2935	7 Game Book, Paper cover.
2938	23 Game Book, Cloth Cover
2937	47 Game Book, Cloth Cover
2939	33 Game Book, Cloth Cover

Values:	Exc.	V.G.	Good
	500.00	400.00	300.00

Attractively bound in Winchester gray, special copyrighted scoring sheet and simple instructions make scoring easy. Contains Winchester baseball advertisements at front and back. Measures 9 1/4 x 8 in. Packed one-half dozen to the carton.

Umpires' Ball-and-Strike Indicator

Values:	Exc.	V.G.	Good
	1,000.00	850.00	700.00

No. 2930. Regulation-size Umpires' indicators. Packed in individual gray cartons.

Baseball Caps

No. 7482. New York Style. Deep crown, sewed eyelets. Made of finest quality athletic flannel. Colors: gray with navy visor; gray with maroon visor; gray, with green visor; and solid colors, navy, maroon and black.

No. 7483. Brooklyn Style. Deep crown cap of high grade flannel, metal eyelets. Colors: gray with navy visor; navy with white visor; and solid colors, navy, maroon and black.

No. 7484. Philadelphia Style. Made of special cap flannel with deep crown. Colors: gray with navy visor; navy with white visor; maroon with white visor; and solid colors, navy and black.

No. 7481. Cap of finest-quality uniform flannel, deep crown, sewed eyelets. Special sun vision insert in visor protecting the players eyes while facing the sun and going after "high flies." Solid colors only, navy and black.

Values:	Exc.	V.G.	Good
Caps	700.00	500.00	300.00

Comment: *Values are for any style adult Baseball Cap.*

Baseball Uniforms

Winchester ready-to-wear baseball uniforms are made on large, roomy pattern, double stitched throughout, reinforced at all points under strain. Comfort, fit and workmanship unexcelled. Tunnel belt loops in all pants. All caps with unbreakable buckram visor. Uniforms trimmed in contrasting colors. Winchester uniforms are snappy and individual in appearance and beauty.

Carried in the Following Sizes:

SHIRTS - Sizes 36, 38, 40, 42, 44 (Chest measurement).
PANTS - Sizes 30, 32, 34, 36, 38 (Waist measurement).
CAPS - Sizes 6 7/8, 7, 7 1/8, 7 1/4, 7 3/8.

No.	Patterns	Description
7500	7501	White with wide navy stripes, trimmed with white and navy braid.
		Brownish gray with green stripe, trimmed with red and green silk braid.
		Gray with wide two tone stripe, trimmed with red and navy silk braid.
		Gray with navy stripe trimmed with royal and gold silk braid.

Made as follows:

SHIRTS - coat style, V neck, insert to match stripe in goods, 5/8 sleeves trimmed with braid. Ventilated eyelets under arms.
PANTS - plain tunnel loops, perspiration-proof ventilated crotch.
CAPS - New York Style. Deep ventilated crown, visor and button to match trimmings.
HOSE - wool, footless, color to match uniform.
BELT - black cowhide leather, nickel buckle and loop.

No.	Patterns	Description
7510	7511	White with fine navy stripe, trimmed with navy and white silk braid.
		Gray with alternating maroon and navy fine stripe, trimmed with maroon and navy silk braid.
		Gray with double green stripe, trimmed with red and green silk braid.
		Gray with two tone red and navy stripe, trimmed with red and navy silk braid.

Made as follows:

SHIRTS - coat style, V neck, two rows two tone silk braid around neck and down front, one row on 5/8 sleeve.
PANTS - plain tunnel loops.
CAPS - Cleveland Style, deep ventilated crown with silk braid around crown and visor. Button to match trimmings.
Hose - wool mixture, footless, color to match uniform.
BELT - black all leather.

No.	Patterns	Description
7520	7521	Harvard gray with alternating single navy stripe and two tone navy and crimson stripe, trimmed with crimson silk braid.
		Yale gray with wide navy stripe, trimmed with navy silk braid.
		Gray with alternating maroon and navy stripes, trimmed with navy silk braid.
		White with navy wide stripe, trimmed with navy silk braid.

Made as follows:

SHIRTS - coat style, V neck, silk braid around neck and sleeves, 5/8 sleeves.
PANTS - plain tunnel loops.
CAPS - New York Style, deep ventilated crown, visor and button to match stripe, silk braid around crown.
HOSE - cotton ribbed footless, color to match uniform.
BELT - black all leather.

No.	Patterns	Description
7530	7531	Gray with navy stripe, trimmed with two tone navy and white silk cordage.
		Gray with green stripe trimmed with red and royal two tone silk cordage.
		Gray with alternating maroon and navy stripes trimmed with red silk cordage.
		Brownish gray with alternating single black, and two tone red and black stripes, trimmed with silk cordage.

Made as follows:

SHIRTS - V neck, closed front, two rows silk cordage around neck and down front. Elbow sleeves with 1/2 in. band, one row cord through band.
PANTS - corded seams, tunnel loops.
CAPS - Brooklyn Style, visor and button to match trimmings, deep crown, two rows cord on visor.
HOSE - cotton ribbed footless, color to match uniform.
BELT - all leather.

Values:	Exc.	V.G.	Good
	1,500.00	1,300.00	1,000.00

Comment: *Values are for the adult Baseball Uniform with at least Shirt, Pants and Cap. Photograph not available.*

Boys' Baseball Uniform

Complete uniforms for boys, furnished already made up, and consisting of baseball shirt, pants, cap, belt and hose, are offered in stock as part of Winchester baseball equipment. These uniforms are made in two patterns, gray flannel with green stripe, and gray flannel with blue stripe. These uniforms are carried in stock in 6-, 8-, 10- and 12-year sizes and are ready for immediate delivery.

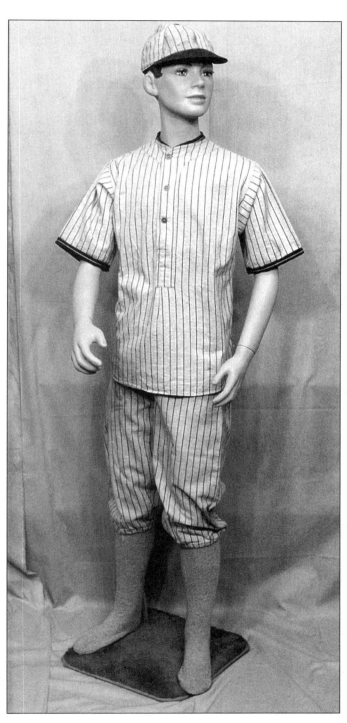

Boy's Baseball Uniform on manikin with the only known original boy's cap. Gray with blue stripes (No. 7495). From T. Webster collection. Photo by D. Kowalski.

Each complete uniform will consist of the following pieces:

SHIRTS - Made with V style neck with double row of piping around the collar and extending down the front of shirt as far as the bottom opening. Another row of double piping is placed around the ends of the half sleeves.

PANTS - Well made, strong baseball pants with piped seams.

CAPS - With piped seams and button on top. Visor to match stripe color of uniform.

HOSE - Footless cotton ribbed hose with double calf stripe to match stripe color of uniform. Strong, heavy ribbed cotton.

BELT - All black leather belt with nickel-plated buckle.

No.	Patterns	Description
7490		*Gray with Green Stripes.*
7495		*Gray with Blue Stripes.*

Values:	Exc.	V.G.	Good
	1,500.00	1,300.00	1,000.00

Comment: *Values are for the Boys' Baseball Uniform with at least Shirt, Pants and Cap.*

Winchester Footballs

Rule No. 2, Sec. I, Official Football Rules, reads: "The ball shall be made of leather, enclosing a rubber bladder. It shall be tightly inflated and shall have the shape of a prolate spheroid, circumference long axis, from 28 inches to 28 1/2 inches, short axis from 22 1/2 to 23 inches, weight from 14 ounces to 15 ounces."

High School Football (No. 3003), another football that was never used. From T. Webster collection. Photo by D. Kowalski.

No. 3003. High School Model. Regulation size and shape. Made of heavy tan cowhide. Furnished complete with pure gum-rubber bladder and lacing needle. One to the carton.

Official Intercollegiate Football (No. 3000), initially found in an old hardware store, was never used. From T. Webster collection. Photo by D. Kowalski.

No. 3000. Official Intercollegiate Football. The Winchester Official Intercollegiate football conforms strictly to the above specifications. It is made from selected parts of the best American steer hides, especially tanned and prepared. It is as perfect as expert workmanship and the best materials can make it. Our No. 3000 ball is official for any game. Furnished with heavy pure gum bladder and rawhide lacing. Our No. 3000 Winchester Official Intercollegiate Football has been inflated, inspected and thoroughly tested before leaving the factory and is official in size and weight. It is of Winchester Quality, perfect in shape, workmanship, and materials, free from defects, and will not be replaced after being put in play. Our Official Intercollegiate Ball, with proper care, will last an entire season. Individually boxed.

Baseball and Football Equipment • 473

No. 3001. College Model. Regulation size, weight and shape, made of heavy pebble-grained steer hide. Furnished with pure gum bladder and lacing needle. One to a carton.

No. 3002. Interscholastic Model. Regulation size and shape. Heavy cowhide leather, heavily sewed. Equipped with heavy, pure gum-rubber bladder, and lacing needle. One to the carton.

No. 3004. School League. Regulation size and shape. Extra-heavy pebbled-grain leather. Equipped with pure gum-rubber bladder and lacing needle. One to the carton.

No. 3005. Youth's Model. Pebbled grain leather. Equipped with pure gum-rubber bladder. Slightly smaller than regulation size. One-quarter dozen in a carton.

No. 3006. Boy's Model. Regulation size. Made of pebble-finish cowhide. Furnished with pure gum-rubber bladder and rawhide lacing. One-half dozen in a carton.

Values:	Exc.	V.G.	Good
	900.00	700.00	450.00

Comment: *Values are for any Football model.*

American Boy Rugby Football, never used and doesn't even have the bladder inside. It's stuffed with paper to give it shape. From T. Webster collection. Photo by D. Kowalski.

Values:	Exc.	V.G.	Good
Ball	900.00	700.00	450.00

Comment: *Values are for American Boy Rugby Football.*

474 • Baseball and Football Equipment

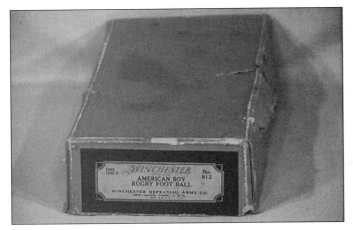

Values:	Exc.	V.G.	Good
Box	2,000.00	1,700.00	1,500.00

Comment: *Values are for this box for American Boy Rugby Footballs. An example of a box being worth at least twice the value of the product contained in it.*

Box for the American Boy Rugby Football (model 912) held one rugby ball in "flat" position. From T. Webster collection. Photo by D. Kowalski.

Football Bladders

No. 3673. *Four-piece, regulation-size stem bladder of special extra-heavy, pure gum rubber for all regulation-size Winchester footballs. This bladder is especially recommended for use with Official ball 3000. One dozen to a carton.*

No. 3675. *Four-piece, regulation-size pure gum bladder, lighter in weight than the Official, for use in footballs 3001, 3002 and 3003. One dozen to a carton.*

No. 3671. *Two-piece pure gum bladder. Regulation size. One dozen to a carton.*

No. 3672. *Pure gum bladder for all Winchester undersize balls. One dozen to a carton.*

No. 3680. *Heavy pure gum-rubber bladder with new-style valve vulcanized into the bladder instead of the usual stem. This is a big improvement over the old-type stem bladder. Each bladder is furnished with rubber tube and nipple, so that an inflator may be used to inflate the ball. The end of the valve protrudes through the bladder hole in the ball flap and a rubber button screws on to the valve end. This holds the bladder in place. It is much easier to lace the ball over this bladder than over the old-type bladders. It can be nearly laced before inflating bladder. One dozen to a carton.*

Values:	Exc.	V.G.	Good
	150.00	125.00	100.00

Comment: *Values for any model*

Ball Inflators

No. 3012. *A nine-inch brass cylinder pump 1 1/2 inches in diameter. Brass nozzle corrugated at base. Smoothed and milled to make bladder fit easily. Straight wooden handle. Nozzle soldered to cylinder. One to a carton.*

Values:	Exc.	V.G.	Good
	350.00	275.00	200.00

No. 3011. *A 9 1/2-inch brass cylinder pump, 3/4 inch in diameter. Small black wooden handle. Corrugated brass nozzle screws into cylinder. One to a carton.*

Comment: *Values are for either model of Inflator.*

Football Helmets

No. 3246. *This is a new helmet in the Winchester line. It is made of 6-ounce black strap leather. Hand-molded crown, reinforced and stiffened with three fibre cross pads. Padded with best-quality sanitary white wool felt and has a specially constructed sponge-rubber cushion ring in the crown. Deep back extension, stiffened with fibre strips, protects the base of the brain. Ear pads of molded leather with sponge-rubber cushion surrounding the ear. This construction gives additional protection and comfort and also permits the player to hear signals much more easily. The ear pads extend well forward, giving full protection to the temples. Kid-lined leather sweat band. Every possible protection has been built into this helmet to make it the best on the market. One to the carton.*

No. 3247. *Made of 6-ounce black strap leather with leather molded and stiffened crown. Molded ear pads. Deep back extension with special hinge pad, leather covered, which protects the back of the neck. Padded with best-quality white sanitary felt. Soft sponge rubber in the crown. Ear pads extend well forward to protect the temples and the forehead piece has an elastic adjustment and kid-lined sweat band. Adjustable elastic chin strap. One to the carton.*

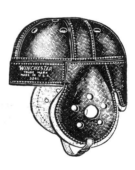

No. 3241. *This helmet is made of heavy black strap leather with best white wool felt lining. Specially treated cardboard reinforcement used to give added stiffness. Soft leather sweat band. Adjustable forehead piece. Deep back. Large molded-leather ear protectors, elastic chin strap with snap fastening. One to a carton.*

No. 3240. *Made of 6-ounce russet strap leather lined with finest-grade white wool felt. Adjustable suspension cushion of soft chrome-tan and suede leather. Adjustable forehead piece and leather sweat band. Crown inner lined with fibre. Molded leather ear protectors made extra large to protect cheeks and temples. Adjustable elastic chin strap with snap fastening. One to the carton.*

No. 3245. *Tan strap leather helmet, lined with heavy white felt. Flexible ear protectors. Adjustable forehead piece. soft leather sweat band. Elastic chin strap. One to the carton.*

Boys' Football Helmets

No. 3242. Boy's helmet made of heavy black strap leather with molded and stiffened crown. Molded ear pads and deep back extension. Padded with white wool felt and has a sponge rubber cushion in the crown. Forehead piece has an elastic adjustment. Helmet is well-ventilated and has an adjustable elastic chin strap. It is made throughout of the same high-grade material and with the same care as we make our best men's helmets. One to a carton.

No. 3237. Crown made of black artificial leather with heavy canvas sides and ears. Reinforcement of heavy artificial leather on ears, felt lined. Two to the carton.

Values:	Exc.	V.G.	Good
Helmets	1,500.00	1,200.00	800.00

Comment: *Values are for any adult or boys' Helmet.*

Boys' Football Helmet (model 3236) on a manikin only has 1/4 inch of felt lining. Another unused helmet in excellent condition. From T. Webster collection. Photo by D. Kowalski.

No. 3236. Strong black waterproof imitation leather heavily padded with gray felt, well ventilated. Made to stand the abuse of boys' play. Two to the carton.

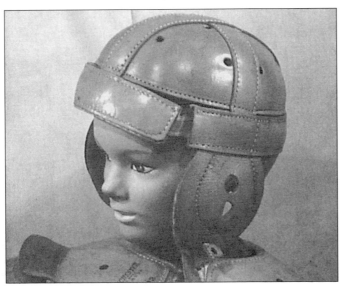

Boys' Football Helmet (model 3243) on a manikin is in unused, excellent condition. From T. Webster collection. Photo by D. Kowalski.

No. 3243. Boy's helmet of mahogany-color cowhide leather. Molded and stiffened crown with deep back extension. Padded throughout with white sanitary felt. Has an elastic forehead adjustment and elastic chin strap. A well-made, well-ventilated helmet and an excellent value at a popular price. Packed one to the carton.

Football Shoulder Pads

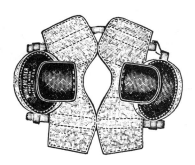

No. 3208. Made of two layers of heavy white wool felt with sections of fibre between to protect shoulder blade and collar bone. Russet leather molded shoulder cap with fibre reinforcement and felt lining. Curved sole-leather shoulder piece extends over cap. Shoulder piece and cap attached to pads by adjustable rawhide lace. Elastic webs inside rubber tubing under arm pits. Heavy elastic bands hold pads together so they conform to the body in any position. Packed in individual Manila Envelope.

No. 3209. This is a new-style pad and is made long in front and in back to give the utmost protection to the chest, shoulders and back of the player. It is made of heavy white wool felt, sole-leather top and strips in front and rear, reinforced with fibre over the collarbone. Fitted by elastic and leather straps around the body and elastic bands under the arm. Although this pad covers a greater portion of the player's body, it is so built and it fits in such a way that it is not cumbersome. Packed in individual Manila Envelope.

No. 3210. Made of two layers of heavy white felt. Molded leather shoulder caps reinforced with fibre, also equipped with fibre protection to collarbone. Heavy elastic hinge between pad and shoulder caps allows free action of the arms. Adjustable lace fastener. Packed in individual Manila Envelope.

No. 3206. Made of heavy white wool felt covered with black strap leather extending over molded-fibre shoulder cap. Wide elastic arm bands. Soft leather strips with metal eyelets over felt padding. Packed in individual Manila Envelope.

No. 3212. Made of 6-ounce russet strap leather. Double thickness of white felt padding faced with solid strap leather completely covers chest and collarbone. Strap-leather shoulder pieces give additional protection over the shoulder joints. Caps of extra heavy molded and stiffened strap leather. This pad was designed by a prominent coach and is light in weight and offers full protection. Has a lacing device by which the player can quickly adjust the pad to fit himself. Elastic arm bands. Packed in individual Manila Envelope.

No. 3207. Made of two thicknesses of white felt, reinforced over collarbone. Black leather strips over chest and back give added protection and prevent laces from ripping out. Molded-leather shoulder caps with fibre reinforcement. Broad elastic arm band. A lightweight pad built along the lines of the best pads made and an excellent value. Packed in individual Manila Envelope.

No. 3211. Boy's shoulder pad of felt reinforced with leather pieces at the collarbone. Molded leather caps. Laced front and back. Packed in individual Manila Envelope.

478 • Baseball and Football Equipment

Boy's shoulder pads (model 3203) are very similar to the No. 3211. Pads are unused and in excellent condition. From T. Webster collection. Photo by D. Kowalski.

Values:	Exc.	V.G.	Good
	1,500.00	1,200.00	800.00

Boy's shoulder pads (model 3204) are in excellent condition, another unused pair. From T. Webster collection. Photo by D. Kowalski.

No. 3204. Heavy gray felt reinforced with leather and fibre. Gives good protection to shoulder and collarbone. Packed in individual Manila Envelope.

Comment: *Values are for any adult or boys' Shoulder Pads.*

Football Knee Cap Pads

No. 3225. Made of heavy gray felt reinforced with molded fibre. Fastens by elastic straps and buckles. Each pair comes in a Manila Envelope.

Values:	Exc.	V.G.	Good
	700.00	500.00	300.00

Felt Shoulder Pads

No. 3214. Felt Shoulder Pads. To be worn under the regulation leather shoulder pads. Heavy gray felt, with brass eyelets; complete with laces. Each pair in a Manila Envelope.

Values:	Exc.	V.G.	Good
	900.00	750.00	600.00

Kidney Pads

No. 3221. Heavy white-felt pieces reinforced at top by wide strips of russet strap leather jointed in back by two elastic bands. Tie strings sewed under leather reinforcement. Has insert piece to protect end of spine. Each pair in a Manila Envelope.

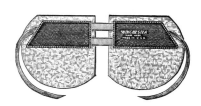

Values:	Exc.	V.G.	Good
	900.00	750.00	600.00

Elbow Pads

No. 3217. Shearling pad with wide-web elastic band at each end and narrow elastic band across center. Each pair in a Manila Envelope.

Values:	Exc.	V.G.	Good
	1,500.00	1,100.00	750.00

Thumb and Wrist Supporters

No. 3073. Made of russet strap leather. Has buckle fastening around wrist. Thumb laces. Packed six to a carton.

Values:	Exc.	V.G.	Good
	800.00	550.00	300.00

Football Gloves

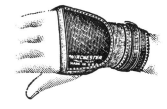

A soft leather glove that laces to the hand. Strap leather wrist supporter with buckle. Back of hand protected by piece of sole leather sewed to glove. No fingers or thumb. One to a carton. No. 3074 - Right Hand. No. 3075 - Left Hand.

Values:	Exc.	V.G.	Good
	450.00	375.00	300.00

Football Pants

No. 3280. Made of best-quality eight-ounce D. F. Army duck in olive-drab color; double stitched throughout. Bellows crotch; leather reinforced. Hips, kidneys and spine protected by fibre strips, inlaid in heavy white felt, reinforced by heavy duck. Patented five-piece, non-warpable, pipe-curved fibre covered with white felt used in leg guard. The hip pad is securely riveted to pants, and is provided with web tie strips for adjustment. Pliable knee guard constructed of felt and leather with fibre cup, laced in, which permits it being adjusted to correct position for the knee. Laced front; special adjustable lacing feature at back of leg, cowhide reinforced. Stocked in Sizes 30 to 44, inclusive. Each pair in Manila Envelope.

No. 3281. Made of khaki-colored eight-ounce duck; double stitched. Reinforced crotch; tunnel loops; flexible hip pad of heavy white felt with one-piece fibre guard, sewed-in pliable fibre kidney guard protected by felt and covered with canvas; one-piece fibre spine guard; patented curved fibre thigh guards covered with felt; inside-felt knee pad; elastic bottoms. Stocked in Sizes 28 to 42, inclusive. Each pair in a Manila Envelope.

No. 3283. Made of eight-ounce olive-colored duck. Sewed-on kidney pads of duck-covered gray felt. Hips quilted with mattress felt in drill pocket. Flat-fibre-reinforced thigh guards. Mattress-felt knee pads. Lace front. Stocked in sizes 28 to 42, inclusive. Each pair in Manila Envelope.

No. 3285. Made of olive-colored canvas. Inside hip and knee pads. Rattan-cane thigh guards. Stocked in boys' sizes 26 to 32, inclusive. Each pair in Manila Envelope.

Values:	Exc.	V.G.	Good
Pants	1,500.00	1,100.00	750.00

Comment: *Values are for any model of Football Pants.*

No. 3284. Same style and construction as 3283 pants but made in boys' sizes from 26 to 32, inclusive. Each pair in Manila Envelope.

Football Jerseys

These jerseys are offered in three grades, two in solid colors only and one in both solid colors and alternating sleeve stripe style as shown on this page. They are finely made of high-grade materials and designed for the requirements of the football player.

No. 7601. A jersey of the same quality and construction as the 7600 but with alternating sleeve stripes instead of solid colors. Stocked in these combinations: Navy and White, Maroon and White, Black and Orange, Black and Cardinal. Sizes 34 to 44, inclusive. Two to the carton.

No. 7605. Cotton and worsted mixture jersey with large shoulders and sleeves. This jersey also has regulation football collar and self seam cuffs. Solid colors, Navy, Maroon, black, and Cardinal. Sizes 34 to 44, inclusive. Two to the carton.

No. 7610. Heavy cotton jersey with large sleeves and shoulders. Solid colors only: Navy, Maroon, and Black. Regulation football collar and self-seam cuffs. Sizes 34 to 44, inclusive. Two to the carton.

No. 7600. Heavy worsted jersey with extra-large sleeves and shoulders. Regulation football collar. Self seam cuffs. Solid colors only, Navy, Maroon, Black, and Gray. Chest sizes 34 to 44, inclusive. Two to the carton.

Values:	Exc.	V.G.	Good
Jerseys	800.00	600.00	350.00

Comment: *Values are for any model of Football Jersey. No. 7605 was medium weight. No. 7610 was lightest weight.*

Football Shoes

No. 3260. Finest yellow-back kangaroo uppers, half lined. High-cut, 6-inch uppers on sprint last. Goodyear welt. Half lined. Equipped with 3/4-inch cleats firmly attached. Rawhide lacing. Carried in stock in sizes 5 to 12, inclusive. One pair to the carton.

No. 3261. Chrome-tanned veal uppers. Half lined. High-cut sprint model. Goodyear welt. Equipped with 3/4-inch cleats firmly attached. Stocked in sizes 5 to 12 inclusive. One pair to the carton.

No. 3262. Chrome-tanned cowhide. Half lined. Full sole. Reinforced with outside sole-leather counter. Wide last. Goodyear welt. Has 3/4-inch cleats firmly attached. Stocked in sizes 5 to 12 inclusive. One pair to the carton.

No. 3263. Sprint model with white-oak soles. Black shanks. Regulation 3/4-inch cleats firmly attached. Steel plate in sole to hold cleats rigid. Gun-metal calf uppers, half lined. Brass eyelets. Cotton felt sock lining. McKay sewed. Stocked in sizes 5 to 12, inclusive. One pair to the carton.

No. 3264. Gun-metal calf uppers, half lined. McKay sewed. Full white-oak soles. Regulation 3/4-inch cleats. Steel plate in soles to hold cleats rigid. Cotton felt sock lining. Brass eyelets. Stocked in sizes 5 to 12, inclusive. One pair to the carton.

Values:	Exc.	V.G.	Good
	1,500.00	1,100.00	700.00

Comment: *Values are for any model of Football Shoes.*

Football Timers

Values:	Exc.	V.G.	Good
	600.00	450.00	300.00

No. 3066. Nickel case, open faced, 60-minute dial. Stem wind and set. Attachment at side of case to start and stop. An essential to the game. Made by skilled clock and watch makers. One to the carton.

Referee's Whistles

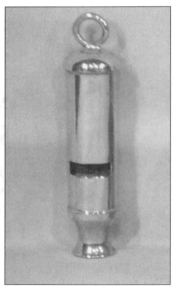

Police-type whistle, nickel-plated, with ring (No. 1805). From T. Webster collection. Photo by D. Kowalski.

Values:	Exc.	V.G.	Good
1805	700.00	500.00	300.00
1806	700.00	500.00	300.00
1807	900.00	700.00	450.00

Police-type whistle, nickel-plated, (No. 1806). From T. Webster collection. Photo by D. Kowalski.

Tubular whistle, nickel-plated, produces double tone (No. 1807). From T. Webster collection. Photo by D. Kowalski.

Umpire's Horn

Values:	Exc.	V.G.	Good
	900.00	700.00	450.00

No. 1810. Bulb horn furnished with large rubber bulb. Straight neck, oval-mouthed nickel-plated horn. Horn unscrews from bulb at neck. One to the carton.

Basketball, Volleyball, Soccer, Boxing, Handball, Tennis and Golf Equipment

by David D. Kowalski

Following the end of World War I, sports of all kinds again captured the American public's imagination. And sports participation at all levels increased. By no means was the renewed focus on sports confined to just baseball and football. In fact, many sports organizations governing many other sports, still alive today, were born in the 1920s.

For the expansion-minded Winchester company, this American love of sports inspired their decision to supply equipment for nearly every sport played in America in the 1920s. This growing line of sporting goods became very broad and ultimately included basketball, volleyball, soccer, boxing, handball, tennis and golf products. We'll feature those sports (preceded by a brief history of each) in this chapter.

In addition, Winchester sold hockey skates and related equipment, ice skates, roller skates, cross-country skis in five lengths and snowshoes. Wagons, scooters and bicycles also seemed natural line extensions. We'll cover this final group of sports and outdoor equipment in the next chapter.

The far-reaching sports environment of the day called out to Winchester when it was searching for new marketing avenues in 1919. Sports equipment was a natural for them. And they produced lines for every level of the sports ... professionals, amateurs and the kids down the city block or down the country road.

However, their general sporting goods lines basically ended with their fall into bankruptcy and their subsequent purchase by Western Cartridge Company in 1931. Pocketknives, flashlights and batteries, and roller skates were the only significant product lines to survive Western's refocusing on Winchester ammunition and firearms.

Basketball

Basketball History. Basketball was already going strong after having been invented by Dr. James Naismith in 1891. He was then a physical education instructor at the YMCA College in Springfield, Massachusetts.

Finding a Winchester basketball with a complete, readable logo is still a major goal of serious Winchester collectors. When the new ball came out of the box, it didn't take many games on gravel for it to take a "nosedive" as a collectible.

Official Basket Ball Rule No. 4, Section 1, describes the official ball required thus:

"The ball shall be round. It shall be made of a rubber bladder covered with a leather case. It shall not be less than 30 inches nor more than 32 inches in circumference and it shall weigh not less than 20 oz. nor more than 23 oz."

Basketball Supplies were the focus of this panel that was part of a five-piece advertising display set. The rest of the display featured the Model 3000 Intercollegiate Football. From T. Webster collection. Photo by D. Kowalski.

No. 3712. Regulation Model. Made of heavy pebble-grain cowhide leather, lined with the best-quality drill fabric. All seams are roll-style, welted with the best-quality leather. This ball will give continuous service under the most severe conditions and is especially suitable for outdoor play as the welted seam is well protected and does away with the objection made to the outseam ball. One in a carton.

No. 3718. Pebble-grain cowhide leather. Lined with good quality canvas. Regulation size and shape. A well-made ball slightly lighter in weight than the official. It will give good service for a long time in ordinary play. One in a carton.

No. 3711. The Winchester Official Intercollegiate Basketball conforms to these regulations in every way. It is made of a continuous four-piece or hog-yoke American pattern, of the best leather obtainable, especially treated and prepared. This ball is official for any game and will give satisfactory service. Furnished with heavy pure gum-rubber bladder and lacing needle.

Our No. 3711 Winchester Official Intercollegiate Basketball has been inflated, inspected and thoroughly tested before leaving the Factory and is Official in Size and Weight. It is of Winchester Quality, perfect in shape, workmanship and materials, free from defects, and will not be replaced after being put in play. Our Official Intercollegiate Ball, With Proper Care, will Last an Entire Season. One in a carton.

No. 3714. Interscholastic Model. Heavy American oak-tanned cowhide. Four sections and regulation size and shape. Pure gum-rubber bladder. One in a carton.

Basketball, Volleyball, Soccer, Boxing, Handball, Tennis and Golf Equipment • 485

No. 3756. *Playground Basketball. Made of best cowhide. Seams turned out to protect stitching. This ball is official for any playground league game. Furnished with pure gum-rubber bladder and lacing needle. One in a carton.*

No. 3757. *Playground Basketball. This ball is made of heavy chrome cowhide. Seams turned out to protect stitching. Regulation size and shape. Furnished with gum-rubber bladder and lacing needle. One in a carton.*

Values:	Exc.	V.G.	Good
	5,000.00	3,500.00	2,000.00

Comment: *We do not know of any Basketball found in excellent condition with clean and thoroughly legible logo.*

No. 3717. *School League Model. Pebble-grained-finish cowhide. Eight sections. Regulation size and shape. Pure gum-rubber bladder. One-half dozen in a carton.*

Basketball Carrier

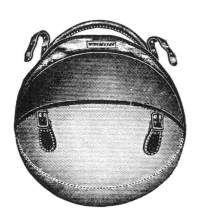

Values:	Exc.	V.G.	Good
	6,000.00	4,000.00	2,500.00

No. 3966. *Tan khaki. One leather handle with two leather straps and buckles for fastening. Made to carry inflated ball. One-half dozen in a carton.*

Basketball Bladders

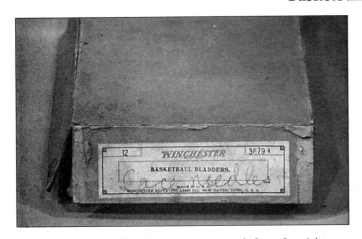

Box for Basketball Bladders is not in good shape but it's rare, like many basketball products. From T. Webster collection. Photo by D. Kowalski.

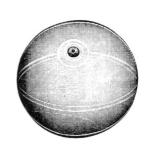

No. 3681. Heavy pure gum-rubber bladder. Official, size No. 7 for basketball equipped with the new valve instead of the old-style stem. The end of valve protrudes through bladder in the ball flap and a rubber button screws on to hold bladder in place. Each bladder furnished with rubber tube and nipple so that it may be inflated by the use of any inflator. One dozen in a carton.

Values:	Exc.	V.G.	Good
	750.00	600.00	400.00

Comment: *Values for box only.*

Values:	Exc.	V.G.	Good
	350.00	275.00	200.00

Comment: *Values for any model Basketball Bladder.*

No. 3679. No. 7 size, extra-heavy gray gum four-piece bladder. Made of the heaviest stock for Winchester official basketballs. One dozen in a carton.

No. 3661. Heavy pure gum-rubber bladder of good quality for use in any of the Winchester basketballs. One dozen in a carton.

No. 3663. Two-piece bladder. One dozen in a carton.

Basketball Goals

No. 3960. This is the most rigid basketball goal made. A 5/8-inch steel ring extends through an angle-bar frame forming a double brace. No side braces to interfere with balls played from under the goal. Equipped with six heavy bolts for securing to the back.

No. 3961. Basketball goal complete with net. Frame made of heavy wrought iron.

No. 3964. Half-inch round-steel bar frame held in position by heavy malleable casting. Bracket takes up small space and does not affect a ball thrown from an angle. This goal is rigid without the aid of side braces, fits in a bracket and is demountable.

Values:	Exc.	V.G.	Good
	1,200.00	1,000.00	700.00

Comment: *Values for any model Basketball Goal.*

Basketball, Volleyball, Soccer, Boxing, Handball, Tennis and Golf Equipment • 487

Basketball Knee Pads

No. 3190. Roll-style padding made of russet leather. Lined with white twill and stuffed with curled hair. Wide elastic bands at both ends. Narrow elastic band across center. Packed one pair to Manila Envelope.

No. 3191. Heavy imitation-leather pad. Lined with cotton. Stuffed with curled hair. Fastened at both ends with elastic bands. Packed one pair to Manila Envelope.

Values: Exc.   V.G.   Good
            500.00   350.00   200.00

Comment: *Values for either model Basketball Knee Pads.*

Eyeglass Protectors

No. 3999. Made of heavy steel wire electrically welded. Heavy padding. Leather covered. Made adjustable to head by wide elastic bands. One to the carton.

Values: Exc.   V.G.   Good
            500.00   350.00   200.00

Basketball Shirts

No. 7655. Made of heavy pure worsted. Round neck. Solid colors. Stocked in navy, maroon, cardinal and white. Sizes 32 to 44 inclusive. Three to the carton.

No. 7665. Medium-weight pure worsted shirt of same style with six-inch chest stripe. Round neck. Colors include navy and white, black and orange, Kelly green and white, purple and gold, royal and white, cardinal and white. Sizes 32 to 44 inclusive. Three to the carton.

No. 7666. Same shirt as 7665 furnished in these solid colors, navy, maroon, cardinal and white. Three to the carton.

No. 7650. Heavy pure worsted V-neck-style shirt. Has four-inch chest stripe and 1/2-inch stripe above and below. Colors are navy and white, royal and white, cardinal and white, black and orange, Kelly green and white, purple and gold. Sizes 32 to 44 inclusive. Three to the carton.

No. 7660. Medium-weight pure worsted V-neck-style with four-inch chest stripe and 1/2-inch stripes above and below. Navy and white, royal and white, cardinal and white, black and orange, Kelly green and white, purple and gold. Sizes 32 to 44 inclusive. Three to the carton.

Values: Exc.   V.G.   Good
            800.00   600.00   350.00

Comment: *Values for any Basketball Shirt.*

Basketball Pants

No. 3156. Fine-quality drill. Half belt. Button front. Short inseam. Loose-hanging hip pads. Selection of the following colors: navy, white, cardinal, purple, royal blue, burnt orange, maroon, black, old gold, Kelly green, myrtle green. Each pair in Manila Envelope.

Values:	Exc.	V.G.	Good
	2,000.00	1,600.00	1,200.00

No. 3155. Strong, durable pants. Made of heavy drill khaki canvas with hips padded with loose quilted pads which are adjustable to the body. Half belt with nickel buckle. Furnished from stock. Cannot be had trimmed. Sizes 26 to 42. Each pair in Manila Envelope.

Comment: *Values for any Basketball Pants.*

Basketball Shoes

No. 3185. Basketball Shoes. Made of white canvas with loose duck lining. Black trim and outside ankle patch. Pure gum non-slip sole. Reinforced shank. Back stay inside and out. Cork insole. Double stitched throughout. Made on foot form last insuring perfect fit. Sizes 5 to 11 inclusive. One Pair to the carton.

Values:	Exc.	V.G.	Good
	1,500.00	1,100.00	800.00

Basketball Score Book

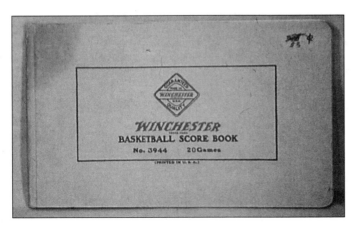

Basketball Score Book measures 9 1/4" wide. It also shows how people who conduct yard and garage sales de-value collectibles when they use pen or permanent markers to write prices on the item. From T. Webster collection. Photo by D. Kowalski.

No. 3944. Simple, efficient scoring method for 20 games. Will appeal to the average fan as well as to the professional scorer. Introduction by "Joe" Fogarty - Yale's Basketball coach, and five goal-scoring basketball team plays.

Values:	Exc.	V.G.	Good
	600.00	450.00	300.00

Volleyball

Volleyball History. Volleyball, another American creation, originated in Holyoke, Massachusetts. William G. Morgan invented it. And the Young Men's Christian Association fostered its growth in the early years. The U.S. Volleyball Association became the sport's governing body in the United States in 1928.

No. 3738. Official in size, shape and weight. Made of fine tan calf's skin lined with non-stretchable fabric. Sewed with waxed-linen cord. Furnished with pure gum bladder and lacing needle. One to the carton.

No. 3736. Made of brown-leather canvas. Regulation size and shape. Lined and strongly sewed. Furnished with pure gum-rubber bladder. One to the carton.

No. 3735. Official volley ball made of special tanned white leather. Regulation size, perfect shape and well-made. Complete with pure gum-rubber bladder and lacer. One to the carton.

No. 3737. Outseam ball made of pebble-grained-finish cowhide, with seams turned outward to prevent wear from rough surfaces. Complete with pure gum-rubber bladder and lacer. One to the carton.

Values:
Exc.	V.G.	Good
2,000.00	1,600.00	1,200.00

Comment: *Values for any model Volley Ball.*

Volleyball Bladders

No. 3682. Official, size No. 5 pure gum-rubber bladder. Equipped with the new-style valve. Adaptable to soccer or volley balls. One dozen in a carton.

No. 3683. Two-piece stem-type volley ball bladder. One dozen in a carton.

Values:
Exc.	V.G.	Good
200.00	160.00	100.00

Comment: *Values for any model of Volley Ball Bladder.*

No. 3994. **Volley Ball Net.** Made of No. 12 twine, single center. 27 feet long x 3 feet wide. Strictly Official. One to the carton. Photo not available.

Values:
Exc.	V.G.	Good
3,000.00	2,000.00	1,500.00

Comment: *Values for Volley Ball Net in carton.*

Soccer

Soccer History. The English gave us soccer, called "football" by them. Historians speculate it may date back to 200 A.D. Derby, England, hosted a Shrove Tuesday game annually for centuries to celebrate the victory of English solders over a contingent of Roman Troops in 217 A.D. The invention of rugby football in 1823 led to name confusion. When the London Football Association was formed in 1863, an evolution of the game's name began; "Soccer" appears to have been derived from the abbreviation for association.

Imported English Soccer Footballs

No. 3501. Imported English Soccer Football. Official size, weight and shape. Made of green chrome leather. 18 panels. Hand-sewed. An excellently made ball in every respect. One in a carton.

No. 3504. Regulation size, weight and shape. Made of hand-sewed cowhide. 12 panels. One in a carton.

No. 3503. Official in size, weight and shape. Made of the finest cowhide. Non-tear lacing hole. 11 panels. Hand-sewed. One in a carton.

Values:	Exc.	V.G.	Good
	2,000.00	1,600.00	1,200.00

Comment: *Values for any model of Soccer Ball.*

No. 3571. **Soccer Goal Net.** *Tarred nets complete ready for use except for posts and cross pieces. Furnished only on special order. Each pair wrapped in Manila Paper. Photo not available.*

Values:	Exc.	V.G.	Good
	3,300.00	2,500.00	1,750.00

Comment: *Values for pair of Soccer Nets in carton.*

Soccer Shoes

No. 3540. Hotspur pattern. Super-quality all-leather shoe. Double brass-riveted soles. Wood-reinforced shank. White laces. Stocked in half sizes from 5 to 1 1/2 inclusive. One Pair to the carton.

No. 3545. Fine-quality all-leather shoe. Brass-riveted soles. Rigid shank. Studs of heavy leather. White laces. Stocked in half sizes from 3 to 11 1/2 inclusive. One Pair to the carton.

Values:	Exc.	V.G.	Good
	1,500.00	1,100.00	800.00

Comment: *Values for any model of Soccer Shoe.*

Soccer Football Bladders

No. 3682. Official, Size No. 5, heavy rubber stemless bladder. Valve type. Packed 12 to the carton.

Values:	Exc.	V.G.	Good
	200.00	160.00	100.00

Soccer Football Pants

No. 3530. Half-belt, loose fitting. Heavy white drill. One-half dozen to the carton.

No. 3531. Half-belt, loose fitting. Medium-weight white drill. One-half dozen to the carton.

Values:	Exc.	V.G.	Good
	2,000.00	1,600.00	1,200.00

Comment: *Values for any style of Soccer Pants.*

Soccer Shin Guards

No. 3587. These shin guards are made with nine pieces of cane covered with leather unbound. Strap and buckle fastenings. One pair to the carton.

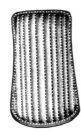

Values:	Exc.	V.G.	Good
	1,200.00	1,000.00	800.00

Boxing

Boxing History. Boxing was popular with the early Romans, even being mentioned by Homer, author of *The Iliad* and *The Odyssey*. The use of boxing gloves became part of the sport in England when the Marquees of Queensbury introduced his code of boxing rules in 1865. The World Boxing Association was founded in 1921.

Boxing was popularized in the United States in the late 1800s and early 1900s. American men, particularly, of this era followed the ring exploits of such heavyweight champions as James J. Corbett (1892-97), Robert L. Fitzsimmons (1897-99), Jack Johnson (1910-15); Jess Willard (1915-19); and William H. "Jack" Dempsey (1919-26).

Boxing Gloves

No. 3807. Instructor's Gloves. These boxing gloves are of the finest quality and design. Made of green Napa kid leather. Weigh between 12 and 13 ounces. This is a large, heavily padded glove, made with double wrist extension pads as a protection to the forearm. Long extra-large thumb. Special palm grip. Jim Corbett pattern. One set to the carton.

Model 3806. Boxing Gloves with box. A set of gloves, two pair, came with this box. The original box more than doubles the value of the gloves. From T. Webster collection. Photo by D. Kowalski.

No. 3806. Men's. Good-grade Napa kid-leather face and palm with laced wrist. Fitzsimmons' style. Weight 6 to 7 oz. One set to the carton.

No. 3801. Men's Pattern. A heavy-duty glove, 10 oz. in weight. Made of best-quality tan kid leather. Double-pad lining and padded wrist extension. Leather-roll binding and is double sewed in all places subject to strain. This is the style used by the Army and Navy in training their men and will stand all kinds of treatment being built especially for rough, continuous work. One set to the carton.

Values:

	Exc.	V.G.	Good
	4,500.00	3,750.00	3,000.00

Comment: *Values are for any model of Boxing Gloves, two pair in a box.*

No. 3802. Corbett Pattern. Made of green kid with padded wrist extension. Palm grips. Weight 10 ounces. One set to the carton.

No. 3804. Men's. Best-grade Napa kid leather, well stuffed. Padded wrists and grip. Weight 7 to 8 oz. One set to the carton.

No. 3819. Boy's Glove. Good leather. Well-padded glove with flat-palm grip. This glove is made to fit boys from 12 to 14 years. One set to the carton.

No. 3816. Men's. High-grade kid-leather fist and palm. Full size. Weight 6 to 7 oz. One set to the carton.

No. 3812. Boy's Glove. Good-grade leather. Fitzsimmons' style. One set to the carton.

No. 3811. Boy's Glove. Corbett style leather glove. One set to the carton.

No. 3818. Boy's Glove. Made of the best Napa kid leather, with padded wrist extension. Roll-palm grip. Deep laced. One set to the carton.

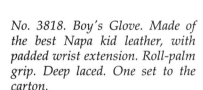

Values:

	Exc.	V.G.	Good
	1,000.00	750.00	400.00

Comment: *Values are for one pair of any standard Men's or Boy's model of Boxing Gloves, listed above.*

No. 3813. Youth's Glove. High-grade leather. Fitzsimmons' style. One set to the carton.

Fighting Gloves

No. 3820. Corbett Style. Finely made set of five-ounce gloves made of plum-color leather. White leather welted seams. One set to the carton.

No. 3825. Same glove made in six-ounce weight. One set to the carton.

No. 3821. Corbett Style. This is a five-ounce glove made on the long model and is extremely popular because of the new color which is almost a blood color and does not show stains. Made with leather-welted seams throughout and inside of thumbs reinforced with white leather. Genuine white leather roll binding. One set to the carton.

No. 3823. Same glove made in six-ounce weight. One set to the carton.

No. 3824. Fitzsimmons' style. Made of brown Napa kid leather. Thin back. Extension thumb which brings pad down over wrist bone. Weight 5 oz. One set to the carton.

No. 3826. Same glove made in six-ounce weight. One set to the carton.

Values:	Exc.	V.G.	Good
	1,700.00	1,400.00	1,000.00

Comment: *Values are for one pair of any model of the Fighting Gloves.*

Striking Bag Gloves

No. 3867. Full-size glove made of soft green Napa leather lined with felt. Roll-palm grip. Bound with roll-leather binder. Elastic wrist. One pair to the carton.

No. 3868. Open-palm style. Made of soft wine-colored leather. Lined with felt. Padded finger grip. Elastic catch. One pair to the carton.

Values:	Exc.	V.G.	Good
	700.00	500.00	300.00

Comment: *Values are for one pair of either style of Striking Bag Gloves.*

Striking Bag Platforms

No. 3885. Cyclo platform, nickel-plated finish, large heavy rim and fittings. Furnished with screws, chart and wall flange, but not with bag. One to the carton.

No. 3886. Cyclo Striking Bag Platform. Aluminum finish with rosewood disc. Furnished with screws, chart and wall flange, but no bag. One to the carton.

No. 3887. Cyclo Platform. Aluminum finish with hardwood disc. Furnished with screws, chart and wall flange, but no bag. One to the carton.

Values:	Exc.	V.G.	Good
	1,200.00	1,000.00	800.00

Comment: *Values are for one complete set of any style of Striking Bag Platform.*

Striking Bag Disk looks like a bicycle wheel with a wooden tire. To the uninitiated, this item is unique enough to keep; yet the owner or his or her heirs didn't realize there was other hardware that went with the whole kit. That would explain why these disks have sometimes gotten separated from the rest of the hardware. From T. Webster collection. Photo by D. Kowalski.

Values:	Exc.	V.G.	Good
	900.00	750.00	600.00

Comment: *Values are for one Disk from any style of Striking Bag Platform.*

Striking Bags

No. 3840. Heavy bag of pearl-colored horsehide. Reinforced at top with brown leather. Welted seams. Furnished with pure gum-rubber bladder and top cord. A large, heavy gymnasium bag. One to the carton.

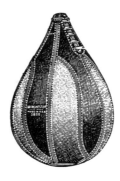

No. 3850. Made of Napa kid leather with alternating black and tan panels. Triple sewed and welted. Specially adapted to exhibition work. Furnished with pure gum-rubber bladder and top cord. One to the carton.

No. 3860. Made of genuine kangaroo leather, with special reinforcement at top to prevent tearing out. Welted and stayed seams. Sewed with heavy linen thread. Furnished with pure gum-rubber bladder and top cord. A very fast bag for expert use. One to the carton.

No. 3842. Popular pear shape of olive-green-colored leather. Triple seamed and welted. One to the carton.

No. 3854. Double-end style of black Yucatan leather. Stayed seams, reinforced with elastic cables and hooks. One to the carton.

No. 3851. Made of black Napa leather. Triple sewed and welted. Seams in white. Furnished with gum-rubber bladder and top cord. One to the carton.

No. 3852. Made of brown Napa leather. Triple-sewed seams. Regulation size. Furnished with gum-rubber bladder and top cord. One to the carton.

No. 3846. Popular pear shape of tanned Yucatan leather. One to the carton.

No. 3848. Pear shape. Vulcanized khaki, double fabric. Triple-seamed, reinforced at top with imitation leather. One to the carton.

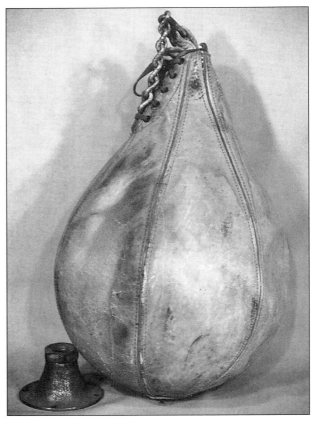

This No. 3844 Striking Bag probably saw only limited use. The "Winchester" logo and model No. are very clearly stamped in the leather just above the centerline of the bag (although they are not visible in this photograph). From T. Webster collection. Photo by D. Kowalski.

No. 3844. Pear shape of black Napa leather. Triple-stayed seams with one seam reinforced. One to the carton.

Values:	Exc.	V.G.	Good
	800.00	600.00	350.00

Comment: *Values are for any of the above models of pear-shaped Striking Bags with chain and anchor. The double-end style bag, No. 3854, would bring a 25 percent premium.*

Striking Bag Bladders. *Packed 12 to the carton. Photos not available.*

No. 3696. Size No. 6. Pear-shaped, four-piece bladder of gray pure gum rubber. Adapted to gymnasium and exhibition bags.

No. 3643. Two-piece bladder for lighter-weight bags.

No. 3695. Strong gray pure gum, four-piece bladder designed for double-end bags.

Values:	Exc.	V.G.	Good
	200.00	150.00	100.00

Hand Ball

Handball History. Four-wall handball has been played in Ireland since the Middle Ages. It was introduced to the United States in the late 1800s. One-wall handball, an American variation of the game, originated in Brooklyn, New York.

Well-made rubber hand balls. Strong and long wearing. Two sizes. No. 3773: 1 7/8-inch diameter, Official. No. 3774: 2 1/4-inch diameter, Practice. One dozen to the carton.

Values:	Exc.	V.G.	Good
	400.00	300.00	200.00

Comment: *Values are for a single Hand Ball of either style.*

Hand Ball Gloves

The only pair of Hand Ball Gloves (of either style) we're aware of that have ever been found. These were probably never used and their excellent condition is obvious. From T. Webster collection. Photo by D. Kowalski.

No. 3799. Made of fine brown Napa leather, felt padded. Circular quilting in palm to give hard striking surface. Leather lined, stitched fingers. Strap and buckle fastening. One pair to the carton.

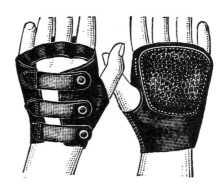

No. 3797. Fingerless Model. Made of chocolate-color elk leather. With palm patch of pebbled cowhide. Inside finger loops. Back straps with snap fasteners. One pair to the carton.

Values:	Exc.	V.G.	Good
	2,500.00	2,000.00	1,500.00

Comment: *Values are for one pair of Hand Ball Gloves of either style.*

Tennis

Tennis History. An Englishman, Major Walter C. Wingfield, invented tennis in 1873. And it was first played at a garden party in Wales that same year. It came to the United States via Bermuda when a friend of Major Wingfield introduced Mary Ewing Outerbridge, a New Yorker vacationing there, to the game in 1874. She and her brother then set up the first U.S. tennis court in Staten Island, New York.

The game grew quickly in popularity with both sexes. The first National Championship, for men only, was held in 1881 at Newport, Rhode Island. The women's championship began six years later. Finally, in 1915, the National Championship was moved to its present home at the West Side Tennis Club in Forest Hills, New York. The Davis Cup international team tournament was initiated in 1900. Courts were built on school and community playgrounds across the country. Professional tennis was launched in the United States in 1927 with formation of the United States Professional Lawn Tennis Association.

Winchester Tennis Rackets

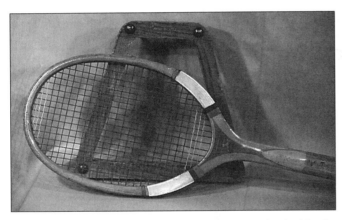

A stabilizer frame for a tennis racket will nearly double the value of the racket it holds. From T. Webster collection. Photo by D. Kowalski.

Values:	Exc.	V.G.	Good
Frame	500.00	400.00	350.00

No. W2. Repeater Model. For beauty, for quality of materials, workmanship and for its durability, this racket has no superior. Built of the finest second-growth, air-dried Vermont white ash, with full bevel bow. Reinforced with attractive cable-cord binding and fibreloid at throat, shoulders and top of handle. Four-sided cedar handle. Strung with special crest stringing. Weights: Light, Medium and Heavy. Packed in glassene envelope. One in a paper bag.

No. W1 Leader Model. A handsome racket that is built to give the maximum of service. Made of highest q-quality second growth, air-dried Vermont ash with three-piece lamination bow for greater strength. Full bevel. Bound with cable cord and reinforced with fibreloid at throat, shoulders and top of handle. Four-sided, white basswood handle. Strung with Crest Highest quality stringing. A strikingly beautiful, well-balanced racket. Weights: Light, Medium and Heavy. Packed in glassene envelope. One in a paper bag.

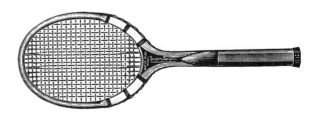

No. W3. Suzanne Lenglen Model. Match-play model. A duplicate of the racket the famous French star used in her hundreds of victories. A beautifully balanced frame of the finest ash, with a full-beveled bow. Reinforced with three rows of binding and vellum at shoulders and throat. White basswood handle. Strung with highest-quality oriental stringing. Weights: Light, Medium and Heavy. Packed in glassene envelope. One in a paper bag.

No. W4. Precision Model. This racket is one of the most attractive models on the market today. It has proven the most popular seller, too. Made of fine ash with bow having full bevel; handsomely reinforced with five rows of binding and fibreloid at throat and shoulders. Has a combination of pleasing color combinations that make for sales. White basswood handle. Highest-quality Oriental stringing. Weights: Light, Medium and Heavy. Packed one in a paper bag.

No. W5. Hi-Speed Model. A high-grade three-piece laminated frame of second-growth white ash, with a bow chamfered inside and out to give better balance. Reinforced at throat, shoulders and top of handle with heavy cable-cord binding and fibreloid in attractive color combinations. White basswood handle. Finest Oriental stringing. Weights: Light, Medium and Heavy. Packed one in a paper bag.

No. W6. Sure Shot Model. This racket will prove a "sure-shot" seller because of its appearance alone. Fine-quality white ash with inside-bevel bow. Reinforced with heavy cable-cord binding and Dutch Linen Tape at throat and shoulders in attractively harmonized color. Four-sided cedar handle. High-quality Oriental stringing. Weights: Light, Medium and Heavy. Packed one in a paper bag.

No. W7. Bull's Eye Model. For the money, the "Bull's Eye" defies competition. Of good-quality ash with a double-chamfered bow. Bound at throat and shoulders, basswood handle. Fine Oriental stringing. Weights: Light, Medium and Heavy. Packed one in a paper bag.

No. W8. Ranger Model. A durable, ash-frame racket with full bow. Bound at throat. Cedar handle. Good-quality Oriental stringing. An inexpensive racket that will stand up under lots of punishment. Weights: Light, Medium and Heavy. Packed one in a paper bag.

Values:	**Exc.**	**V.G.**	**Good**
	2,500.00	2,000.00	1,500.00

Comment: *Values are for any model of Tennis Racket.*

Winchester Tennis Balls

Richard Hecht finally opened his tennis ball can in early 2000. Here is one of three ball inside. Photo by R. Hecht.

No. W1. The best tennis ball that can be made. They serve "like a rifle shot" from Winchester Tennis Rackets. No fear of dead balls with Winchester Inventory control and the damp-proof package which preserves freshness. Balls have two-piece PLUGLESS construction with an inner-seal lining. A stitchless cover of the finest wear-resisting Australian wool felt has been vulcanized on each ball. Officially approved by United States Lawn Tennis Association. Packed three balls in a fibre tube, four tubes in a four-color Bull's Eye display box which is a "knockout."

Values:	Exc.	V.G.	Good
Ball Only	3,000.00	2,500.00	2,000.00

Comment: *Values are for a single Tennis Ball. These are rare items, in part because they were first introduced in 1928.*

This is the only tennis ball display box that has ever been found, to date. It would have held four cans of tennis balls. From T. Webster collection. Photo by D. Kowalski.

Values:	Exc.	V.G.	Good
Box Only	1,700.00	1,600.00	1,400.00

This is the only can of tennis balls that has ever been found, to date. In this photo, it is still factory sealed. Photo by R. Hecht.

Values:	Exc.	V.G.	Good
Full Can	8,500.00	8,000.00	7,500.00
Can Only	3,500.00	3,300.00	3,000.00

Golf

Golf History. Golf, that invention of the Scottish dating back to at least 1457, may have had Americans chasing a ball around the cow pastures as early as the 17th century. But the first permanent golf club wasn't organized until 1888 at the St. Andrews Golf Club in Yonkers, New York. The United States Golf Association was founded in 1894. The United States Professional Golf Association began in 1916.

Winchester paid prominent golfers of the day to endorse their equipment, a marketing tactic they also employed in other areas. Jock Hutchinson has his name on the following clubs, but other golfers were also part of this program.

Winchester "Jock Hutchison" autograph Wood and Iron Clubs. Exact duplicates of models Hutchison has used in his matches here and abroad. These graceful, superbly balanced clubs represent the height of the club-maker's art and can be recommended without reservation to your customers.

All models, wood and iron, have the finest selected hickory shafts, fitted with Special Bell-Top treated grips. Wood heads of finest persimmon with weighted backs and fibre faces. Irons, from driving iron to putter, bear the closest possible relationship in design, weight and "feel." Made with perfect graduated lofts. Blue-steel finish facings with "Aim-Rite" scoring on hitting face. Clubs illustrated are men's right hand.

Woods or Drivers

 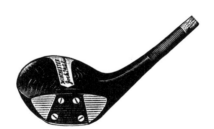 

No. W3500D. Driver.   *No. W3500B. Brassie.*   *No. W3500S. Spoon.*

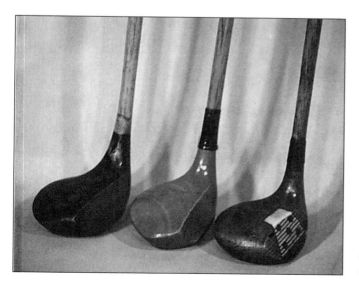

Values:	Exc.	V.G.	Good
Woods	250.00	225.00	175.00

Comment: *Values are for "Woods" with wood handles. Add 25 percent for left-hand clubs.*

These three right-hand drivers with wood handles include two older examples with plain "non-corrugated" hitting face on the club. From T. Webster collection. Photo by D. Kowalski.

Ranger Woods with Steel Shafts

*Heads of fine persimmon, plain face, conservative model. Medium lie.
Fitted with Union Hardware Seamless steel shafts. "Bell-Top" tapered calf grip.*

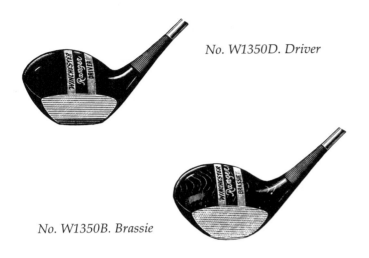

No. W1350D. Driver

No. W1350B. Brassie

Values:	Exc.	V.G.	Good
Woods	250.00	225.00	175.00

Comment: *Values are for "Woods" with steel handles. Add 25 percent for left-hand clubs.*

Irons and Putters

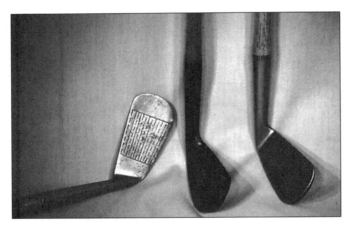

Three left-handed golf irons with wood shafts. Left-handed clubs are much rarer than those for right-handers. From T. Webster collection. Photo by D. Kowalski.

No. W3402. No. 2 Midiron

No. W3401. No. 1 Driving Iron

No. W3403. No. 3 Mid-Mashie

Basketball, Volleyball, Soccer, Boxing, Handball, Tennis and Golf Equipment • 503

No. W3404. No. 4 Mashie Iron

No. W3405. No. 5 Mashie

No. W3406. No. 5 Spade Mashie

No. W3407. No. 7 Mashie Niblic

No. W3408. No. 8 Niblic

No. W3409. No. 9 Putter

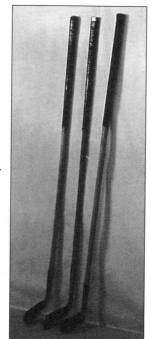

Three right-handed putters. Putters are among the rarest of golf clubs. From T. Webster collection. Photo by D. Kowalski.

Ranger Golf Outfits

No. W1M - Men; No. W1L - Ladies. An excellent-quality beginner's outfit consisting of four clubs: specially selected "Ranger" Brassie, Midiron, Mashie and Putter. Clubs of specially selected hickory shafts and heads. Bag of Oxford gray heavy waterproof whipcord, trimmed in light-tan leather. Aluminum bottom. Caddy comfort sling strap. Large ball pocket with zipper fastener. One set in a carton.

Values:	Exc.	V.G.	Good
Irons	125.00	100.00	80.00

Comment: *Values are for "Irons" with wood handles. Add 25 percent for left-hand clubs. Add another 25 percent for putters.*

Values:	Exc.	V.G.	Good
Outfit	1,200.00	1,000.00	800.00

Comment: *Values are for bag with four specified clubs. Deduct 50 percent for bag only.*

Miscellaneous Sports Equipment

Skis, Snowshoes, Hockey and Ice Skates, Roller Skates, Athletic Supplies, Scooters, Wagons and Bicycles

by David D. Kowalski

As you've seen in the prior two chapters, Winchester provided equipment for virtually all the competitive sports. We say "virtually all" because Winchester appears not to have made or supplied any cricket equipment, for example. Even though cricket came to this country in the mid-1700s shortly after it was developed in England; it was largely replaced by the growing popularity of baseball, a game that derived in part from cricket.

The only major team sport we haven't covered yet is hockey. We decided to include it here because Winchester promoted all of their skating equipment together. In fact, their advertising clearly implies they saw roller skating as an extension of ice skating, and vice versa.

Winchester also made products for other winter and outdoor sports. Both cross country skis and snowshoes were part of their line. And when winter was over, American children needed transportation. They needed bicycles, scooters and wagons. We'll cover all these remaining areas in this final chapter on sporting goods. And we've included, once again, photography of very rare and authentic collectibles from this group.

To lead off the chapter, we'll present Winchester's miscellaneous apparel and sports supplies. Some of these products are very similar to products included with specific sports. For example, Winchester's "athletic pants" are very similar to one of their styles of "basketball pants" although they have separate model numbers. They also share something else. Not too many have been found, especially in excellent condition in the box.

Miscellaneous Athletic Supplies and Apparel

No. 3975. Sweatshirt. A fine grade of sweatshirt for the use of baseball players and other athletes. Made of heavy cotton, fleece-lined. These shirts are cut full and are excellently made. Round necks. Furnished in all sizes from 32 to 44. Packed two in a Winchester gray telescope carton.

Values:	Exc.	V.G.	Good
	500.00	350.00	200.00

Comment: *Values are for one Sweatshirt.*

No. 3986. Athletic Shirt. High-grade open-knit white cotton shirt with large round neck, narrow shoulder straps and extra-large armholes. High quality and careful workmanship throughout. Sizes 26 to 44 inclusive. Six in a Winchester gray telescope carton.

No. 3080. Cotton ribbed, footless hose. Solid colors. May be had in Navy, Maroon, Myrtle Green and Black. Six pairs to the carton.

No. 3085. Cotton and worsted mixture. Ribbed. Solid colors only: Navy, Maroon, Black and Gray.

No. 3090. Heavy, pure-worsted, ribbed, footless hose. Solid colors only: Navy, Maroon and Black.

No. 3095. Special Order Only. Extra-heavy, ribbed, worsted, footless, athletic hose in solid colors only. Any colors desired.

Values: **Exc.**   **V.G.**   **Good**
500.00   350.00   200.00

Comment: *Values are for one Athletic Shirt.*

No. 3981. White Muslin Athletic Pants. Made with button front and size-adjusting lace in back. Waist sizes 26 to 42 inclusive. No. 3982 - White Jean. One-half dozen pairs to the carton.

No. 3119. Half-length, unbleached-cotton sanitary hose for use with any of the footless athletic stockings in the Winchester line. Furnished in three sizes: small, medium and large. Please specify size desired in ordering. Two dozen pairs in a carton.

Values: **Exc.**   **V.G.**   **Good**
2,000.00   1,600.00   1,200.00

Comment: *Values are for one pair of Athletic Pants.*

Values: **Exc.**   **V.G.**   **Good**
300.00   250.00   200.00

Comment: *Values are for one pair of Athletic Hose, any style.*

Athletic Hose

No. 3081. Cotton-ribbed footless hose with broad calf stripe and narrow stripe above and below. Offered in these combinations: Navy and White, Royal Blue and White, Black and Orange, Maroon and White, Myrtle Green and White, Black and Cardinal, Gray and Navy. Six pairs to the carton.

No. 3086. Cotton and worsted mixture, striped. Offered in Navy and White, Maroon and White, Black and Orange, Purple and White, Myrtle Green and White. Other color combinations on special order.

No. 3091. Heavy, pure-worsted, ribbed, striped, footless hose in Navy and White, Maroon and White, and Black and Orange. Other color combinations on special order.

No. 3096. Special Order Only. Extra-heavy, ribbed worsted, footless, athletic hose, striped. Any color combination desired.

Abdominal Supporters

No. 3958. Abdominal Supporter with Cup. Aluminum cup is well-padded. Adjustable strap fastener. May be used with any elastic supporter. One to the carton.

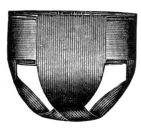

No. 3955. Abdominal Supporter. All-elastic 7-inch waist band. Made of heavy elastic webbing. Stocked in small, medium and large sizes. One in a carton.

No. 3950. Abdominal Supporter. Comfortable and strong. Made of cotton, all-elastic web. Furnished in three sizes, small, medium and large. One in an individual Winchester gray telescope carton. Six to the multi-carton.

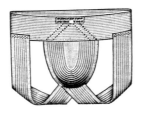

No. 3954. Wrist Bandage. Firm-fitting cotton-elastic web to support the wrist. Furnished in three sizes, small, medium and large. One in Manila Envelope.

Values:	Exc.	V.G.	Good
	1,200.00	1,000.00	900.00

Comment: *Values are for one Abdominal Supporter, any style, in the original box.*

No. 3953. Ankle Supporter. High-grade cotton-elastic web. Fits around ankle and under foot with opening at heel. Furnished in three sizes, small, medium and large. One in Manila Envelope.

Other Elastic Supporters

No. 3956. Knee Cap Supporter. Elastic knee cap of special design. The lightest and most comfortable double protection made. Padded with felt strips sewed to webbing. Stocked in small, medium and large sizes. One in Manila Envelope.

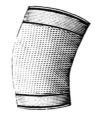

No. 3952. Elbow Cap Supporter. Made to protect this vulnerable part of the athlete. Like the kneecap supporter, this protector is made of cotton-elastic web. Furnished in three sizes, small, medium and large. One in Manila Envelope. Six supporters of one size to the carton.

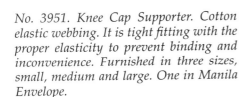

No. 3951. Knee Cap Supporter. Cotton elastic webbing. It is tight fitting with the proper elasticity to prevent binding and inconvenience. Furnished in three sizes, small, medium and large. One in Manila Envelope.

Values:	Exc.	V.G.	Good
	700.00	500.00	300.00

Comment: *Values are for one Elastic Supporter, any style, in the original box.*

Cross Country Skis

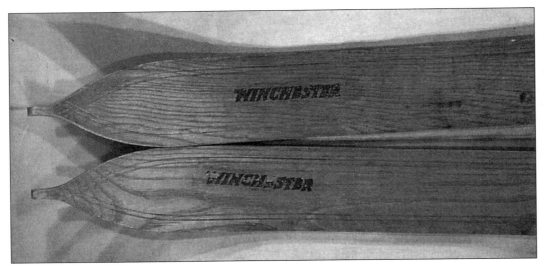

The tips of this pair of 7-foot cross country skis are typical of the design of all five lengths Winchester sold. Winchester used decals on this product line and they could be worn off by rough use or too much exposure to moisture and sunlight. From T. Webster collection. Photo by D. Kowalski.

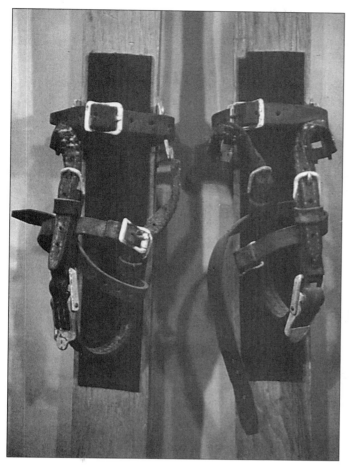

Values:	Exc.	V.G.	Good
4 Foot	700.00	600.00	500.00
5 Foot	600.00	500.00	400.00
6 Foot	600.00	500.00	400.00
7 Foot	600.00	500.00	400.00
8 Foot	700.00	600.00	500.00

Comment: *The actual measurements of authentic pairs we've examined are: 4 foot - 47 3/4"; 5 foot - 59 1/2"; 6 foot - 71 1/2"; 7 foot - 83"; 8 foot - 95". The shortest and longest skis are the rarest.*

Here are typical leather bindings on cross country skis. This pair shows these skis got used. From T. Webster collection. Photo by D. Kowalski.

Snowshoes

On snowshoes, the Winchester decal (barely visible here) is placed on the first cross bar behind the tip. This is a spot where snow accumulates during use, once again exposing the decal to the effects of moisture and sunlight. When examining a pair of snowshoes, the would-be buyer should analyze whether the wear on the decal appears to match the wear exhibited on the wooden members of the snowshoe generally. From T. Webster collection. Photo by D. Kowalski.

508 • Miscellaneous Sports Equipment

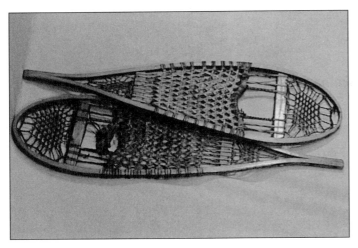

Values:	Exc.	V.G.	Good
	3,000.00	2,700.00	2,500.00

Comment: *Values are for one pair of snowshoes similar to the above pair.*

Here is a photo of the pair of snowshoes bearing the decal we showed above. These are the only authentic pair of Winchester snowshoes we're aware of. Each member of this pair measures 39 3/8" long. From T. Webster collection. Photo by D. Kowalski.

Hockey

Hockey Sticks

Winchester hockey sticks offer a compact range of styles and prices in high-grade Canadian-made sticks for this popular winter sport. These sticks are made from selected second growth rock elm, made with great care by experts who know the requirements of hockey players.

The inscription on the decal on the handle of this Winchester hockey stick reads: "Designed for players who will appreciate the highest grade of perfection in quality and design." From T. Webster collection. Photo by D. Kowalski.

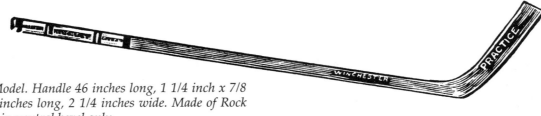

No. 4864. Practice Model. Handle 46 inches long, 1 1/4 inch x 7/8 inch thick. Blade 12 inches long, 2 1/4 inches wide. Made of Rock Elm, second-growth, in neutral bevel only.

No. 4866. Special Model. Handle 47 inches long, 1 1/4 inch x 7/8 inch thick. Blade is 11 1/2 inches long, 2 1/4 inches wide. Made of finest Canadian second-growth Rock Elm, in neutral bevel only.

Miscellaneous Sports Equipment • 509

No. 4868. Championship Model. Handle 48 inches long, 1 1/4 inch x 7/8 inch thick. Blade is 11 1/2 inches long, 2 1/2 inches wide. Made of the finest selected Canadian second-growth Rock Elm. Smooth-polished finish and blade so shaped that it will lie flat on the ice.

No. 4860. Boy's Practice Stick. Handle 39 inches long, 1 1/16 inch x 3/4 inch thick. Blade 9 inches long, 1 3/4 inches wide. Made in neutral bevel only. Not quite as good as Boy's Expert, but on the whole a good-selling stick because of very attractive price.

No. 4862. Boy's Expert Stick. Handle 38 inches long, 1 1/16 inch x 3/4 inch thick. Blade 10 inches long, 2 inches wide. Made of Rock Elm, second-growth, in neutral bevel only. This stick is of the same quality as the men's but smaller in size. Will stand plenty of hard use.

No. 4870. Goal Hockey Stick. Handle 47 inches long, 1 1/4 inch x 7/8 inch thick. Blade 12 inches long, 3 3/8 inches wide. Standard two-piece goaltender's stick. Made up to the full limit of the size allowed under the rules. Built up by adding a strip of wood attached firmly to the top of the blade, making the stick more effective for a goal tender than the ordinary size.

Values:

	Exc.	V.G.	Good	**Comment:** *Values are for all models of Hockey Stick except "Goal" Stick. Add 25 percent premium for a goalie stick.*
	1,200.00	900.00	500.00	

Hockey Puck

Hockey pucks are difficult to find in excellent condition. From T. Webster collection. Photo by D. Kowalski.

Values:	Exc.	V.G.	Good
	600.00	525.00	450.00

Hockey Shin Guards

No. 3891. *Hockey Shin Guards are made of heavy fibre with white felt padding over knee. Two leather strips riveted to fibre. Fastens with two straps. Each pair in a Manila Envelope.*

Values:	Exc.	V.G.	Good
	1,500.00	1,100.00	700.00

Hockey Gloves

No. 3898. *Hockey Gloves are made of strong tan leather. Heavy roll padding over backs of fingers and thumb. Roll pad around glove to protect wrist. Horsehide palm, ventilated. Long gauntlet reinforced with reeds. One pair to the carton.*

Values:	Exc.	V.G.	Good
	1,500.00	1,100.00	700.00

Goaltender's Leg Guards.

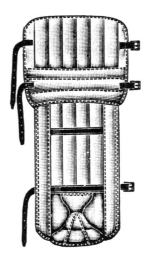

No. 4890. *Goaltender's Leg Guards are long and extra heavy. Made of heavy white canvas well padded and reinforced with heavy cane ribs. Extensions to protect ankles and instep. Fastened to leg by five straps. Each pair in a Manila Envelope.*

Values:	Exc.	V.G.	Good
	1,500.00	1,100.00	700.00

Winchester Skating Outfits and Skates

Winchester actually sold two basic kinds of skate assemblies, either with shoes or without them.. The skates with shoes already on them were called "Skating Outfits." They also sold various forms of blade assemblies that screwed on, clamped on or were strapped onto street shoes or boots. These latter versions were called "Ice Skates." Winchester basically started with their selection of blade assemblies, then added shoes to them to create the various mens' and ladies' full-shoe models.

Compared to other Winchester collectibles, ice skates are relatively common, hence the lower prices.

In the following section, we will first present skates and skating outfits that pertained to hockey. Then we'll profile and price the remainder of the ice skating, figure skating and speed skating models.

Men's Hockey Skating Outfits (Full Shoe)

No. 7861KM. Tubular Hockey Skate (No. 7761) has aluminum finish and men's shoes. Shoe sizes: 6, 7, 8, 9, 10, 11 and 12. With McKay Sewed Shoes.

No. 7861HTH With Goodyear Welt Hard Toe Shoes

No. 7861KHT With McKay Sewed Hard Toe Shoes

No. 9761KM. Tubular Hockey Skate (No. 9761) has nickel-plated and buffed finish and men's shoes. With McKay Sewed Shoes.

No. 7761KM. Tubular Hockey Skates (No. 7761) has nickel-plated and buffed finish and men's shoes. With McKay Sewed Shoes. All Hockey Skate Outfits packed one pair to the carton.

No. 6213KM. Consists of Winchester American Club Hockey skates (No. 6213) and pair of men's shoes. Shoe Sizes: Boys' - 2, 3, 4, 5. Mens' - 6, 7, 8, 9, 10, 11, 12. With McKay Sewed Shoes. One outfit to the carton.

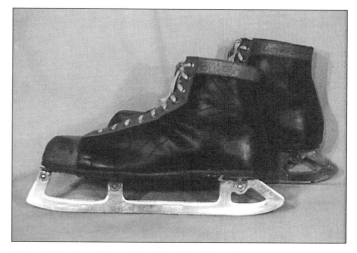

Pair of Hockey Skates has black leather shoe with brown trim. "American Club" hockey blades appear to have been screwed onto a hockey "shoe" with a hard toe. From T. Webster collection. Photo by D. Kowalski.

Values:	Exc.	V.G.	Good
	150.00	110.00	75.00

Comment: *Values are for Men's Hockey Skating Outfits (with shoes). Men's hockey skating outfits have standard high-top shoes. Women's models have taller, calf-length shoes. All Hockey Skate Outfits packed one pair to the carton.*

Ladies' Hockey Skating Outfits (Full Shoe)

No. 7861KL. Tubular Hockey Skate (No.7861) has aluminum finish, combined with ladies' shoes. Shoe Sizes: 3, 4, 5, 6, 7 and 8. With McKay Sewed Shoes.

No. 9761 KL. Tubular Hockey Skates (No. 9761) with nickel-plated and buffed finish, combined with ladies' shoes. With McKay Sewed Shoes.

No. 7761KL. Tubular Hockey Skates (No. 7161) with nickel-plated and buffed finish, combined with ladies' shoes. With McKay Sewed Shoes.

No. 6213KL. Made up of Winchester American Club Skate (No. 6213) and ladies' shoes. Shoe Sizes: 3, 4, 5, 6, 7 and 8. With McKay Sewed Shoes. One pair to the carton.

Values:	Exc.	V.G.	Good
	200.00	160.00	125.00

Comment: *Values are for Ladies' Hockey Skating Outfits (with shoes). Men's hockey skating outfits have standard high-top shoes. Women's models have taller, calf-length shoes. All Hockey Skate Outfits packed one pair to the carton.*

Tubular Skates (Blades Only)

Blades are of thin high-carbon cutlery steel, carefully hardened and tempered. Stanchions and tubes are of seamless, drawn, special spring steel. Formed foot plates are used throughout.

No. 7761. Hockey Model. Blades, foot plates and stanchions spot-welded, rivetless. Half sizes 9 to 12. Full nickel-plated and buffed. No. 7861. Satin aluminum finish. Packed one pair in a paper package.

No. 7751. Racing Model. Blades, foot plates and stanchions spot-welded, rivetless. Half sizes 9 to 12. Full nickel-plated and buffed. No. 7851. Satin aluminum finish. Packed one pair in a paper package.

Values:	Exc.	V.G.	Good
	70.00	50.00	25.00

Comment: *Values are for one pair of Tubular Ice Skates (blades), either hockey or speed style.*

Ice Skates (Blade Assemblies without Shoes).

Winchester presents a comprehensive, well-balanced line of skates from the low-priced rocker models to full hockey, figure and tubular skates that will give full measure of satisfaction to the most expert skaters in each class. Every Winchester skate represents maximum quality and satisfaction in its class for materials, design, workmanship and manufacturing skill.

Men's and Boys' Clamp Models

No. 6121. Half Hockey Model. Blades of hardened carbon steel. Cold-rolled steel foot plates. Bright polished finish. Half sizes 8 1/2 to 12. Packed one pair in a paper package.

No. 6223. American Club Half Hockey Model. Blades of carbon steel (hardened). Cold-rolled steel toe and heel plates. Embossed clamps. Full nickel-plated and bluffed. Half sizes 8 1/2 to 12. Packed one pair in a paper package.

Ladies' Clamp Models (with Strap)

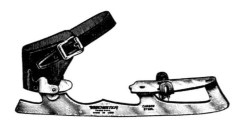

No. 5131. Saranac Rocker Model. Blades of carbon steel (hardened). Cold-rolled steel foot plates. Bright polished finish. Genuine russet-leather back and heel strap. Toe clamps. Half sizes 8 to 11. Packed one pair in a paper package.

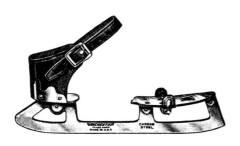

No. 6232. American Club Half Hockey Model. Blades of hardened carbon steel. Foot plates of cold-rolled steel. Full nickel-plated and buffed. Genuine russet-leather back and heel strap. Toe clamps. Half sizes 81/2 to 11. Packed one pair in a paper package.

Screw-on Models (Blade Only)

No. 6213. American Club Half Hockey Model. Blades of carbon steel (hardened). Foot plates of cold-rolled steel. Skate is full nickel-plated and buffed. Half sizes 8 1/2 to 12. Packed one pair in a paper package.

No. 9315. Figure Skates. St. Moritz Model. A high-grade figure skate made to sell at a popular price. Men's and Women's screw-on model. Blades of chrome-nickel steel. Saw-tooth toe for pivoting. Blades tapered at ends. Top edge of blades polished. Toe and heel plate of cold-rolled steel. Half sizes from 9 to 12. Packed one pair in a paper package.

Arena Model. Splayed blade of welded tool steel. Carefully hardened and tempered. Hollow ground with correct radius for best fancy skating. Special teeth for pivoting, jumping and similar feats. Forged foot and heel plates, dovetailed and brazed to the blade, making a one-piece skate. Full nickel-plated, polished and buffed to a mirror finish. One pair wrapped in cotton-lined paper, in a fancy display carton.
No. 9410. Mens' model: 10, 10 1/4, 10 1/2, 10 3/4, 11, 11 1/2 and 12.
No. 9411. Ladies' model: 9, 9 1/4, 9 1/2 and 9 3/4.

Values:	Exc.	V.G.	Good
	70.00	50.00	25.00

Comment: *Values are for a pair of Mens', Womens' or Boys' clamp-on, strap-on or screw-on models (blades only).*

Other Men's Skating Outfits (Full Shoe)

No. 9315WM. Made up of the new St. Moritz model figure skate (No. 9315) and men's shoes. Shoe Sizes: 6, 7, 8, 9, 10, 11 and 12. With Goodyear Welt Shoes. One outfit to the carton.

No. 7751KM. Made up of tubular racing skate (No. 7751), nickel-plated and buffed and men's shoes. Shoe Sizes: 6, 7, 8, 9, 10, 11 and 12. With McKay Sewed Shoes.

No. 7851KM. Made up of tubular racing skate (No. 7851) in aluminum finish and men's shoes. With McKay Sewed Shoes. One pair to the carton.

Values:	Exc.	V.G.	Good
	150.00	110.00	75.00

Comment: *Values are for one pair of Mens' Skating Outfits (full-shoe skates).*

Other Ladies' Skating Outfits (Full Shoe)

No. 9315WL. The new St. Moritz figure skate (No. 9315) combined with ladies' shoes. Shoe Sizes: 3, 4, 5, 6, 7 and 8. With Goodyear Welt Shoes. One outfit to the carton.

No. 7751KL. Tubular racing skates (No. 7751) with nickel-plated and buffed finish and ladies' shoes. Shoe Sizes: 3, 4, 5, 6, 7 and 8. With McKay Sewed Shoes.

No. 7851KL. Tubular racing skates (No. 7851) with aluminum finish and ladies' shoes. With McKay Sewed Shoes. One pair to the carton.

Values:	Exc.	V.G.	Good
	200.00	160.00	125.00

Comment: Values are for one pair of Ladies' Skating Outfits (with full shoe).

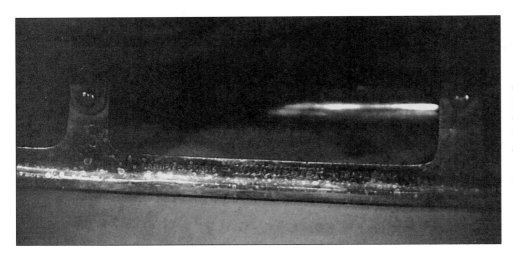

"BARNEY & BERRY - WINCHESTER - TRADE MARK" is the inscription on this ice skate blade. The Barney & Berry Co., a manufacturer of roller and ice skates, was a Winchester acquisition in 1919. From T. Webster collection. Photo by D. Kowalski.

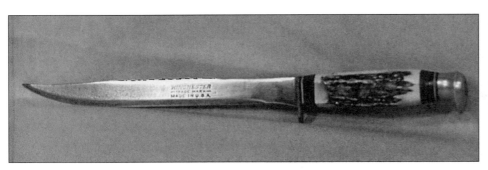

Here's a Winchester ice skate blade put to another use by a creative knifemaker. This is a harmless exercise, provided the resulting product isn't sold as an original Winchester product. Before you purchase a Winchester product, especially one that seems too good to be true, consult a Winchester expert with integrity. Buyer Beware! From T. Webster collection. Photo by D. Kowalski.

Winchester Roller Skates Survive Bankruptcy

Roller Skates are one of the items that Western decided to retain when they bought the Winchester assets in 1931. We will present and price only the early models that were advertised in the 1927 Catalog.

Box for Roller Skates from the 1960s shows plenty of red color on a buff-colored box. Type is black and red. This box also shows the Winchester penchant for piling on the advertising claims ... "The Skate with a Backbone, Most Mileage, Utmost Strength, Light Weight, Free Wheeling." From T. Webster collection. Photo by D. Kowalski.

Values: | Exc. | V.G. | Good
| 250.00 | 210.00 | 175.00

Comment: *Values are for this box only, without skates.*

Roller Skates counter sign from the 1920s promotes roller skating as "great sport" and "wonderful exercise." Colors are green and buff with red "Winchester" logo. The other side of this reversible display promotes Red W Brand House Paint. Live matter area of sign measures 12 7/8" wide x 16 1/4" high. From T. Webster collection. Photo by D. Kowalski.

Values: | Exc. | V.G. | Good
| 900.00 | 825.00 | 750.00

Comment: *Values are for this two-sided counter display.*

Roller Skate Rolls

Rolls are the heart of the skate. The new improved Winchester double ball-bearing, military-disc roll, combines unusual wear with smooth and free action. Tests have shown this disc will stand up remarkably under hard, long service.

Values: | Exc. | V.G. | Good
| 400.00 | 325.00 | 275.00

Comment: *Values are for a single "cutaway" version of a roller skate roll. Winchester provided these to salesmen and to retail stores to use for sales and display purposes. Some Winchester collectors have actually thrown these away because they originally thought they were defective parts.*

Box of Roller Skate Rolls shows the effects of holding its heavy contents. Box is buff-colored stock with bright green panels; "Winchester" logo is red and there are also a few other red highlights. The individual rolls are not marked. From T. Webster collection. Photo by D. Kowalski.

Values: | Exc. | V.G. | Good
| 400.00 | 325.00 | 275.00

Comment: *Values are for a box with at least three rolls inside.*

Roller Skates

No. 3831. Boys' Double Ball Bearing Extension Skate with steel rolls. Reinforced double-girder frame. New double-row self-contained ball-bearing rolls. Tops of cold-rolled steel, nickel-plated and buffed. Cushion action. Toe plate reinforced to prevent bending. Best-quality leather strap. Steel heel support. Extension 8 to 10 1/2 inches. No. 3731 - with fibre rolls. Packed 12 pairs to the case.

No. 3636. Girls' Double Ball Bearing Girder Frame. Double row self-contained ball-bearing steel rolls, nickel-plated. Reinforced girder frame. Tops of cold-rolled steel, nickel-plated and buffed. Cushion action. Best-quality leather strap and heel-cup support. Extension 8 to 10 1/2 inches. Packed 12 pairs to the case.

No. 3832. Girls' Double Ball Bearing Extension Skates with steel rolls. Reinforced double-girder frame. New double row self-contained ball-bearing rolls. Foot plates reinforced to prevent bending. Tops of cold-rolled steel, nickel-plated and buffed. Cushion action. Best-quality leather straps and russet-leather heel cups. Extension 8 to 10 1/2 inches. No. 3732 - with fibre rolls. Packed 12 pairs to the case.

No. 3736. Women's and Girls, Girder Frame Rink Model. Girder-frame extension skate fitted with new fibre rink rolls. Tops of cold-rolled steel. Nickel-plated and buffed on top. Cushion action. Best-quality leather back and strap. Reinforced girder frame. Extension 8 to 10 1/2 inches. Packed 12 pairs to the case.

No. 3635. Boys' Double Ball Bearing Girder Frame. Double row self-contained ball-bearing steel rolls, nickel-plated. Reinforced girder frame. Tops of cold-rolled steel, nickel-plated and buffed. Cushion action. Best-quality leather strap. Extension 8 to 10 1/2 inches. Packed 12 pairs to the case.

No. 2731. Men's and Boys' Professional Model Rink Skates. This solid-frame non-extension model is a rink skate of highest quality designed for general rink use with a view to giving maximum strength with the least weight. Foot plate construction is rigid and trucks are fastened securely in a way that assures proper alignment of rolls. The large rubber cushions give excellent action and are adjusted to individual requirements. Rolls are of red fibre. They are constructed with a double row of ball bearings. Nickel-finish steel frame. Half sizes 9 to 11 1/2. Packed 12 pairs to the case.

Miscellaneous Sports Equipment • 517

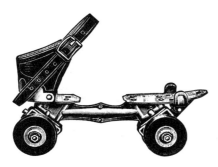

No. 2732. Women's and Girls' Professional Model Rink Skates. Solid-frame, non-extension rink skate of highest quality, designed for general rink use with a view to maximum strength with the least weight. Foot plate construction is rigid and trucks are fastened securely to assure proper alignment of rolls. Large rubber cushions. Rolls of red fibre constructed with double row of ball bearings. Nickel-finish steel frame. High-quality leather heel support. Half sizes from 8 to 10 1/2. Packed 12 pairs to the case.

No. 1331. Children's Ball Bearing Extension Skate. Tops of best cold-rolled steel. Mounted on single-row ball-bearing steel rolls. Skate nickel-plated throughout. Cushion action. Best-quality leather strap and heel support. Toe clamps. Extension 7 to 8 1/2 inches. Packed 12 pairs to the case.

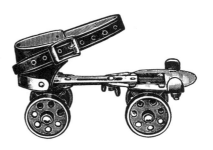

No. 1131. Children's Extension, toe-clamp model. Plain bearing. Malleable iron rolls. No cushions. Strong leather backs and straps. Well finished. Extension 6 to 7 1/2 inches. Packed 12 pairs to the case.

No. 1142. Children's Extension, all-strap model. Plain bearing. Malleable iron rolls. No cushions. Strong leather heel support and toe strap. Well finished. Extension 6 to 7 1/2 inches. Packed 12 pairs to the case.

Values:	**Exc.**	**V.G.**	**Good**
	50.00	35.00	20.00

Comment: *Values are for one pair of any model of metal-frame Roller Skates.*

Box of Roller Skate Ankle Pads is bright red with yellow banner and blue type. This box is in excellent condition and so are the bright red individual pads, shown front and back. Winchester designed them with double slots for the leather skate straps so the skater could use the outer slots first. When they broke, the straps could be inserted through the inside slots. From T. Webster collection. Photo by D. Kowalski.

Values:	**Exc.**	**V.G.**	**Good**
	400.00	325.00	275.00

Comment: *Values are for early models of boxes of pads with all pads inside.*

518 • *Miscellaneous Sports Equipment*

Values:	Exc.	V.G.	Good
	250.00	225.00	200.00

Comment: *Values are for early box of skate keys with at least three keys inside.*

Individual Skate Keys were not marked. This box is buff-colored with red "Winchester" logo and black type. From T. Webster collection. Photo by D. Kowalski.

Scooters

Scooter Skates

No. 9002. Scooter Skates are designed to be used on one foot only, the other foot being used to act as a brake and to steer. This skate is made of high-grade material. Reinforced steel frame. Adjustable toe plate to fit any size of shoe. Equipped with double-row ball-bearing military-disc rolls. Straps of high-quality russet leather. One in a carton. Weight each 2 1/2 lbs.

Values:	Exc.	V.G.	Good
	500.00	400.00	300.00

Comment: *Values are for one Scooter Skate.*

Winchester Scooters

No. 9001. Scooter frame made of high-quality steel, nickel-plated, with wooden platform and steering handle. Easy-action ball-bearing rolls. Easy to operate and control. Safe to use. Platform has corrugated rubber mat. Packed one in a carton. Approximate weight each 7 3/4 lbs.

Values:	Exc.	V.G.	Good
	2,500.00	2,000.00	1,500.00

Comment: *A rare item.*

Miscellaneous Sports Equipment • 519

Wagons

Winchester Coaster Wagons

BODY - *One-piece extra-heavy steel, strongly reinforced with steel cleats. Edge of bottom turned up. Bottom of box formed to allow it to slide over bottom, making an extra-strong and sturdy construction. The extra-large top and bottom rolls give handsome appearance.*

GEARS - *Heavy steel channel construction, extra-well braced and very strong. The hound extends sufficiently in front of wagon to permit easy steering when coasting.*

AXLES - *Heavy steel.*

TONGUE - *Tubular steel, neatly formed, with shaped grip.*

WHEELS - *Double-disc type, 10 inches in diameter. Highest-grade solid-rubber tires, self-contained roller bearings, auto-style hubcaps.*

FINISH - *Body and wheels gray enameled; bottom and tongue black enameled; running gear bright red enameled.*

No. WS2. Removable box. *1-inch solid-rubber tires. Body 15 in. x 35 in. Packed one in a fibre carton.*

Here's a refinished version of the Model WS2 Coaster Wagon showing how box could be unbolted and slid off backward. From T. Webster collection. Photo by D. Kowalski.

Model WS2. Coaster Wagon has box that can slide backward and off to create a flat-bed-type wagon. Actual measurements of the box of the pictured wagon are 34 7/8" long x 14 3/4" wide x 5" high. From T. Webster collection. Photo by D. Kowalski.

Values:	Exc.	V.G.	Good
	1,000.00	750.00	500.00

Comment: *Values are for a Model WS2 Coaster Wagon that has not been refinished.*

520 • *Miscellaneous Sports Equipment*

No. WS1. Junior Model. Stationary box. Has 3/4-inch solid-rubber tires. Body 14 3/4 in. x 30 1/4 in. Packed one in a fibre carton.

Model WS1. This is the Junior Coaster Wagon with a stationary box. Actual measurements of the box of the pictured wagon are 30 3/4" long x 14 3/4" wide x 4 1/8" high. From T. Webster collection. Photo by D. Kowalski.

Identifying decal on the bottom of the Model WS1 Junior Coaster Wagon shows typical label placement on wagons. As the metal rusts, it also unfortunately degrades the label. From T. Webster collection. Photo by D. Kowalski.

Values:	Exc.	V.G.	Good
	1,000.00	750.00	500.00

Comment: *Values are for a Model WS1 Junior Coaster Wagon that has not been refinished.*

Here's a coaster wagon with a wooden box. The red decal on the side reads "THE WINCHESTER STORE." The actual measurements of the box of the pictured wagon are 34 1/8" long x 14 3/4" wide x 4 1/8" high. From T. Webster collection. Photo by D. Kowalski.

Values:	Exc.	V.G.	Good
	2,000.00	1,850.00	1,700.00

Comment: *Values are for wooden "Winchester Store" Wagon that has not been refinished.*

Winchester Bicycles

Winchester made bicycle models for both girls and boys. They had balloon tires, probably available in standard black-wall versions. We also see models with wire front baskets, as well as battery-powered lights mounted on the front fender. Rear wheels had metal frames fastened to the rear axle that could be flipped down and the rear wheel raised off the ground so the bike could be kept erect when not in use.

Identification on Winchester bicycles appears to have been limited to metal tags mounted on the front neck post.

Models for girls are more rare than models for boys.

Boy's Bicycle is painted light brown with white trim. This one has a wire front basket. From T. Webster collection. Photo by D. Kowalski.

Girl's Bicycle is painted dark blue with white trim. This one has a battery-powered light mounted on front fender. From T. Webster collection. Photo by D. Kowalski.

Logo plate on the front of Boy's Bicycle generally reflects the very "used" condition of this bike. Screws holding in both sides of logo plate are also heavily rusted. From T. Webster collection. Photo by D. Kowalski.

Logo plate on the front neck of Girl's model is clean and clear; it has large red "W" in white circle. "WINCHESTER" is printed in gold letters on a blue banner below the white circle. This photograph also shows original paint job is in better condition than on Boy's Bicycle shown above. From T. Webster collection. Photo by D. Kowalski.

Values:	Exc.	V.G.	Good
	1,000.00	800.00	600.00

Comment: *Values are for Boy's Bicycle, any model, that has not been refinished.*

Values:	Exc.	V.G.	Good
	1,200.00	1,000.00	750.00

Comment: *Values are for Girl's Bicycle, any model, that has not been refinished.*

Farm, Yard and Garden Tools

by David D. Kowalski

Walking through Winchester's 1927 Catalog is like walking through every region of agricultural, rural and suburban America of that era. The company had developed a very broad line of outdoor hand tools and implements for farmers and gardeners. Wheelbarrows and lawn mowers were among their offerings. Winchester sold everything from cotton and beet hoes to alfalfa forks and grass hooks, from floral tools to garden cultivators.

Here is another niche where collectors are challenged to find equipment in excellent condition. Tools that were used outside were stored outside, too often with little protection from the elements.

Many of these items are also long-handled tools, typically very difficult to photograph and present with identifying detail. For that reason, we will rely heavily on line art. However, we also had access to rare and unique pieces and we present their photographs here where appropriate.

Winchester Steel Goods

A complete selection of steel farm and garden tools, including, forks, hoes, rakes, hooks, garden sets, cultivators, turf edgers and like goods has now been added to the Winchester lines. Every item in this line is a Winchester quality tool. They are made by expert workmen, from high-carbon steel. Forging is done under scientific methods that insure the correct degree of hardness to give the utmost in service and satisfaction. Every tool is inspected repeatedly at various stages of manufacture to insure the maintenance of Winchester standards of quality. This line has been standardized to include a list of staple items in general demand that will meet the great bulk of demand and keep moving.

HANDLES - *All made of extra selected second-growth northern white ash. They are carefully sanded, polished and waxed to a smooth, high white finish.*

FINISH - *All ferrules and caps enameled in rich vermilion with upper portion of tines or heads in bright gold bronze. Each tool attractively labeled in red, gold, gray and black. As an additional distinction each Winchester tool bears a neat four-color decalcomania seal bearing the guarantee of Winchester quality.*

PACKING - *Handles encased in individual Winchester gray Kraft envelopes with red Winchester. Heads in individual paper scabbards of same-grade paper. All tools tied in bundles of one dozen or half-dozen as specified by the purchaser.*

Hay Fork, Boy's Pattern

Three-tine, 10 1/2-inch Boy's Pattern Hay Fork. Tines are oval with 7-inch spread. Bent handle, strap ferrule. Models and handle lengths: WYB304 - 4 ft.

Values:	Exc.	V.G.	Good
	200.00	175.00	150.00

Comment: *Values are for Boy's Pattern.*

Farm, Yard and Garden Tools • 523

Hay Forks, Bent Handle

Three-tine, 12-inch Hay Fork. Tines are oval with 7 1/4-inch spread. Regular pattern, strap ferrule. Models and handle lengths: WB303 1/2 - 3 1/2 ft.; WB304 - 4 ft.; WB304 1/2 - 4 1/2 ft.; WB305 - 5 ft.; WB305 1/2 - 5 1/2 ft.

Three-tine, 13-inch Hay Fork. Tines are oval with 9-inch spread. Regular pattern, strap ferrule. Models and handle lengths: WB133 1/2 - 3 1/2 ft.; WB134 - 4 ft.; WB134 1/2 - 4 1/2 ft.

Three-tine, 14-inch Hay Fork. Tines are oval with 9-inch spread. Regular pattern, plain ferrule. Models and handle lengths: WB43 1/2 - 3 1/2 ft.; WB44 - 4 ft.; WB44 1/2 - 4 1/2 ft.; WB45 - 5 ft.;

Three-tine, 13-inch Hay Fork. Tines are oval with 9-inch spread. Regular pattern, plain ferrule. Models and handle lengths: WB33 1/2 - 3 1/2 ft.; WB34 - 4 ft.; WB34 1/2 - 4 1/2 ft.

Hay Fork, Straight Handle

Three-tine, 12-inch Hay Fork. Tines are oval with 7 1/4-inch spread. Regular pattern, strap ferrule. Models and handle lengths: W304 - 4 ft.; W304 1/2 - 4 1/2 ft.; W305 - 5 ft.; W305 1/2 - 5 1/2 ft.; W306 - 6 ft.

Values:	Exc.	V.G.	Good
	180.00	150.00	130.00

Comment: *Values are for any model of three-tine Hay Fork, except Boy's Pattern.*

Barley Fork

Four-tine, 18-inch Barley Fork. Tines are oval with 14-inch spread. Regular pattern, square-shoulder-dish type, spring-wire bail. Bent handle, strap ferrule. Models and handle lengths: WX404 1/2 - 4 1/2 ft.; WX405 - 5 ft.; WX505 (five tines) - 5 ft.

Values:	Exc.	V.G.	Good
	235.00	210.00	185.00

Comment: *Values are for any model.*

Silage Fork

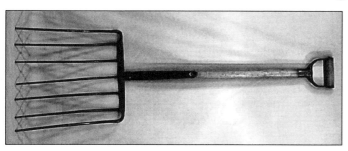

"D" handle, 16-inch Silage Fork. The seven oval tines measure 16 inches long from tip to the top of the shoulder; spread is 13 1/2 inches. Regular pattern, square shoulders, strap ferrule. Overall length is 44 inches. This Silage Fork not shown in any Winchester Catalog but it is believed to be authentic. It is also the only one known. From T. Webster collection. Photo by D. Kowalski.

Values:	Exc.	V.G.	Good
	900.00	800.00	700.00

Header Forks

Four-tine, 15-inch Header Fork. Tines are oval with 10 1/2-inch spread. Regular pattern, round shoulders, riveted shanks. Bent handle, strap ferrule. Models and handle lengths: WC404 - 4 ft.; WC404 1/2 - 4 1/2 ft.; WC405 - 5 ft.; WX405 1/2 - 5 1/2 ft.

Four-tine, 15-inch Header Fork - Kansas deep-dish pattern has deeper pattern than previous fork; and tines are oval with 11 1/4-inch extreme spread. Regular pattern, round shoulders, riveted shanks. Bent handle, strap ferrule. Models and handle lengths: WH404 - 4 ft.; WH404 1/2 - 4 1/2 ft.; WH405 - 5 ft.

Values:	Exc.	V.G.	Good
	235.00	200.00	160.00

Comment: *Values are for any model of Header Fork.*

Grain Fork

Four-tine, 16-inch Grain Fork. Tines are oval with 12 1/2-inch spread. Square-shouldered, dish Dakota pattern, riveted shanks. Bent handle, strap ferrule. Models and handle lengths: WD404 - 4 ft.; WD404 1/2 - 4 1/2 ft.; WD405 - 5 ft.

Values:	Exc.	V.G.	Good
	235.00	200.00	160.00

Comment: *Values are for any model.*

Alfalfa or Clover Fork

Four-tine, 13-inch Alfalfa or Clover Fork. Tines are oval with 9 3/8-inch spread. Round-shouldered, deep-dish regular pattern, riveted shanks. Bent handle, strap ferrule. Models and handle lengths: WA404 1/2 - 4 1/2 ft.; WA405 - 5 ft.

Values:	Exc.	V.G.	Good
	235.00	200.00	160.00

Comment: *Values are for any model of Clover Fork.*

Manure Forks

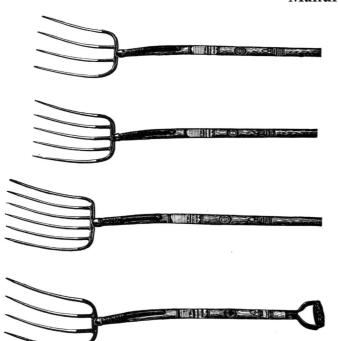

Four-tine, 13-inch Manure Fork. Tines are oval with 9-inch spread. Regular pattern, bent handle, strap ferrule. Models and handle lengths: W404 - 4 ft.; W404 1/2 - 4 1/2 ft.

Five-tine, 12-inch Manure Fork. Tines are oval with 9 5/16-inch spread. Regular pattern, bent handle, strap ferrule. Models and handle lengths: W504 - 4 ft.; W504 1/2 - 4 1/2 ft.

Six-tine, 13 1/2-inch Manure Fork. Tines are oval with 10-inch spread. Regular pattern, bent handle, strap ferrule. Models and handle lengths: W604 - 4 ft.; W604 1/2 - 4 1/2 ft.

Steel "D" handle, 13 1/2-inch Manure Fork. Handle is 32-inches long on all models; tines are oval. Regular pattern, bent handle, strap ferrule. Models, number of tines, tine spread: WD40, 4 tines, 9 inches; WD50, 5 tines, 9 5/16 inches; WD60, 6 tines, 10 inches.

Values:	Exc.	V.G.	Good
	225.00	190.00	150.00

Comment: *Values are for any model of Manure Fork.*

Spading Forks

"D" handle, 11-inch Spading Fork (No. WSD40). Four tines are flat diamond back; spread is 8 1/4 inches. Handle is 32 inches long with regular pattern, square shoulders, strap ferrule.

Values:	Exc.	V.G.	Good
	135.00	115.00	100.00

Long handle, bent pattern, 11-inch Spading Fork (No. WS40). Four tines are flat diamond back; spread is 8 1/4 inches. Handle is four feet long with regular pattern, square shoulders, strap ferrule.

Values:	Exc.	V.G.	Good
	165.00	135.00	110.00

Winchester Garden Plow

Garden Plow is in Excellent to Very Good condition with very little rust. It is the only one discovered to date. The "Winchester" logo is a red-letter decal in italicized capital letters on the metal frame placed between the hand grips and the junction of the vertical support with the main frame. From T. Webster collection. Photo by D. Kowalski.

No. W25. Garden Plow has wrought flat-steel frame, 1 inch x 1/4 inch, securely bolted. Handles adjustable to three different heights. The upright to which implements are bolted can be adjusted forward or backward. Painted gray with narrow red striping. Malleable-iron bent-pattern hand grips painted black, riveted to frame. Spread of handles is 21 inches. Steel wheel is 24 inches in diameter, painted black, with 1 1/4-inch-wide tread.

Complete with one crucible-steel polished shovel eight inches long; one calf tongue eight inches long; one five-prong cultivator; one mouldboard 12 inches long with polished landslide; one malleable-iron wrench six inches long. Length overall is 54 inches; height overall is 42 inches. Weight about 25 lbs.

The draft of these plows can easily be changed to suit the different kinds of soil, making the plow easy to operate and very efficient. One in a fibre carton.

Values:	Exc.	V.G.	Good
	2,400.00	2,100.00	1,800.00

Comment: *Values are for Garden Plow with all attachments.*

Garden Cultivators

No. WHC5. 4 1/3 ft. smooth-belted and waxed ash handle. Steel socket and head. Five adjustable one-piece forged blades. Has eight-inch spread; six inches high.

No. WHC3. 4 1/3 ft. smooth-belted and waxed ash handle. Steel socket and head. Three adjustable one-piece forged blades. Has 4 1/4-inch spread; 4 1/4 inches high.

Values:	Exc.	V.G.	Good
	225.00	200.00	175.00

Comment: *Values are for either model.*

No. WSC4. Speedy Cultivator. High-grade forged-steel head and teeth; steel shank; blued finish; rich vermilion enameled-steel ferrule riveted on. Extra-select, straight-ash handle is 4 1/3 feet long. Has five-inch spread; teeth are four inches long.

Values:	Exc.	V.G.	Good
	185.00	165.00	150.00

Garden Rakes

Solid forged bow; Ash handle is 5 1/2 feet, polished and waxed. Teeth are 3 inches, curved. Models and number of teeth: WSB12 - 12 teeth; WSB14 - 14 teeth; WSB16 - 16 teeth.

Values:	Exc.	V.G.	Good
	135.00	115.00	100.00

Level head is forged from one piece of solid steel. Ash handle is 5 1/2 feet. Straight teeth. Models and number of teeth: W90/12 - 12 teeth; W90/14 - 14 teeth; W90/16 - 16 teeth.

Comment: *Values are for either head style with 14 or 16 teeth. Add 100 percent for either style with 12 teeth.*

Wire Lawn Rake

No. W24. New pattern. Tubular-steel reversible, reinforced head is 20 5/8 inches long; 14-gauge bent-steel teeth, 5 1/2 inches overall. Other side has 24 reversible wire teeth. Ski-bar has solid protecting tooth on each end. Ash handle is 5 1/2 feet, selected and polished.

Values:	Exc.	V.G.	Good
	225.00	200.00	175.00

Farm, Yard and Garden Tools • 527

Coal or Road Rakes

No. W95/16. Straight shank. Straight ash handle is 5 1/2 feet, waxed. Head is 18 inches with 16 teeth, each 3 1/2 inches long.

Values:	Exc.	V.G.	Good
	135.00	115.00	100.00

Gravel Rakes

Gravel Rake comes in three widths. Has straight shank. Straight ash handle is 5 1/2 feet, waxed. Teeth are each 1 1/8 inches long; spaced 11/16 inches apart. No. WG14 has 14 teeth on a 14-inch head; No. WG16 has 16 teeth on a 16-inch head; No. WG18 has 18 teeth on an 18-inch head.

Values:	Exc.	V.G.	Good
	135.00	115.00	100.00

Comment: *Values are for any width.*

Manure Hook

No. WM40. Regular pattern. Has four 8 1/4-inch round tines. Extreme spread at points is 9 3/4 inches. Straight handle, five feet long, plain ferrule.

Values:	Exc.	V.G.	Good
	185.00	165.00	150.00

Potato Hooks

No. W4R. Regular Pattern. Four 7-inch round tines. Extreme spread at points is 6 inches. Straight handle, 4 1/2 feet long, plain ferrule.

No. W6R. Regular Pattern. Six 7-inch round tines. Extreme spread at points is 7 1/4 inches. Straight handle, 4 1/2 feet long, plain ferrule.

No. W5RT. Regular Pattern. Five 7-inch oval tines. Extreme spread at points is 6 3/8 inches. Straight handle, 4 1/2 feet long, plain ferrule.

No. W6RT. Regular Pattern. Six 7-inch oval tines. Extreme spread at points is 7 1/4 inches. Straight handle, 4 1/2 feet long, plain ferrule.

Values:	Exc.	V.G.	Good
	185.00	165.00	150.00

Comment: *Values are for any model of Potato Hook.*

Winchester Floral Tools

Garden or Floral Hoe

No. WY4. Polished blade is 3 1/2 inches deep x 5 inches wide. Handle is 45 inches.

Values:	Exc.	V.G.	Good
	175.00	150.00	130.00

Garden or Floral Rake

No. WR5. Head is 4 1/2 inches wide; unpolished teeth are 3 1/8 inches long. Handle is 47 inches.

Values:	Exc.	V.G.	Good
	450.00	400.00	375.00

Garden or Floral Spading Fork

No. WDF4. Four flat, diamond-back, tumbled-finish tines, each 6 1/4 inches long; spread is six inches. Malleable "D" handle with wood grip; Length overall 36 1/2 inches.

Values:	Exc.	V.G.	Good
	150.00	130.00	110.00

Garden or Floral Shovel

No. W7. Polished round-point blade is 4 3/4 inches wide x 7 1/2 inches long. Malleable "D" handle with wood grip. Overall length 38 inches.

Values:	Exc.	V.G.	Good
	165.00	145.00	125.00

Garden or Floral Sets

No. W3. Three-piece Floral Set: shovel, hoe and rake. Shovel: Malleable iron "D" handle has wood grip. Shovel is 38 inches long. Round-point blade is 7 1/2 inches x 4 3/4 inches. Hoe: 45-inch handle, shank pattern. Blade is 3 1/2 inches x 4 inches. Rake: Garden Pattern has 47-inch handle. Head is 4 1/2 inches wide with 3 1/8-inch teeth.

Values:	Exc.	V.G.	Good
	900.00	800.00	700.00

Comment: Values are for full set of three pieces.

No. W4. Four-piece Floral Set: same as set above with Spading Fork added. Fork has malleable-iron "D" handle with wood grip, 30 inches long. Four diamond-back tines, each 6 1/4 inches long. Tines have 6-inch spread. Specifications of other tools as above.

Values: **Exc.**   **V.G.**   **Good**
                1,000.00   900.00   800.00

Comment: *Values are for full set of four pieces.*

Garden Set

No. W375. Full-size three-piece set, all Winchester quality. Handles polished and finished in live blue. Very attractive.

Rake has wide-bow pattern with gold-bronzed bow. Red-lacquered ferrule and gold-bronzed cap. Has 14 teeth, each three inches long. Handle is 5 1/2 feet long.

Four-tine fork with gold-bronzed head. Red-lacquered strap ferrule with gold-bronzed cap. Flat diamond-back tines are 11 inches long with polished face and natural-finished back. Bent handle is 32 inches long with red-lacquered, pressed-steel "D" handle with wood grip.

Polished hoe is 7 inches wide x 4 3/4 inches deep with gold-bronzed shank and red-lacquered ferrule. Handle is 4 1/2 feet long.

Values: **Exc.**   **V.G.**   **Good**
                850.00   750.00   650.00

Comment: *Values are for full set.*

Garden Hoes

Shank pattern. Angle of blades is 74 1/2 degrees.

No. WG10. Regular size. Handle is 4 1/3 feet. Blade depth 4 1/4 inches. Assorted blade widths 6 1/2 to 7 1/2 inches.

No. WL105. Ladies' size. Handle is 4 feet. Blade depth 3 1/2 inches. Width of cut 5 inches.

No. WL106. Boys' size. Handle is 4 feet. Blade depth 4 inches. Width of cut 6 inches.

No. WG20. Socket pattern. Angle of blades is 74 1/2 degrees. Regular size. Handle is 4 1/3 feet. Blade depth 4 3/4 inches. Assorted blade widths 6 1/2 to 7 1/2 inches.

Values: **Exc.**   **V.G.**   **Good**
                90.00   65.00   40.00

Comment: *Values are for any model.*

Field and Garden Hoes

No. WSN7 1/2. Washington County. Shank pattern. Blade depth is 4 1/2 inches. Handle is 4 feet long. Width of cut is 7 1/2 inches.

Values:	Exc.	V.G.	Good
	90.00	65.00	40.00

No. WG207 1/2. Socket pattern. Set of blade is 70 degrees. Handle is 4 1/3 feet. Blade depth 4 3/4 inches. Width of cut is 7 1/2 inches.

Comment: *Values are for either model.*

Beet Thinning Hoes

Shank pattern. Blade depth is 3 1/2 inches. Handle is 15 inches long. No. WB615 is six inches wide. WB715 is seven inches wide.

Values:	Exc.	V.G.	Good
	135.00	115.00	90.00

Southern Meadow Hoes

No. WT207 - 7 inches; No. WT208 - 8 inches; No. WT209 - 9 inches; No. WT210 - 10 inches.

Values:	Exc.	V.G.	Good
	90.00	65.00	40.00

Comment: *Values are for any model.*

Socket pattern. Angle of blade is 74 degrees. Handle is 5 feet; neck is 7/16 inch. Blade depth 4 inches. No. and width of cut:

Meadow Hoes

WM099 - 9 inches, 4 inches; No. WM099 1/2 - 9 1/2 inches, 3 1/2 inches.

Values:	Exc.	V.G.	Good
	90.00	65.00	40.00

Comment: *Values are for either model.*

Socket pattern. Angle of blade is 74 degrees. Handle is 4 1/2 feet; neck is 7/16 inch. No., width of cut, blade depth: No.

Light Cotton or Corn Hoes

- 7 1/2 inches, 4 1/4 inches; No. WC108 - 8 inches, 4 1/4 inches.

Values:	Exc.	V.G.	Good
	90.00	65.00	40.00

Comment: *Values are for any model.*

Shank pattern. Angle of blade is 74 degrees. Handle is 5 feet; neck is 7/16 inch. Blade depth 4 inches. No., width of cut, and blade depth: No. WC107 - 7 inches, 4 inches; No. WC107 1/2

Regular Cotton Hoes

Shank pattern. Riveted shank; neck is 1/2 inch. Angle of blade is 75 degrees. Blade depth 4 inches.

No.	Cut	Handle	Blade Depth
WHC104 1/2	6 1/2 in.	4 1/2 ft.	5 in.
WHC106 1/2	6 1/2 in.	5 ft.	5 in.
WHC107	7 in.	5 ft.	5 in.
WHC107 1/2	7 1/2 in.	5 ft.	5 1/4 in.
WHC1088 in.		5 ft.	5 1/4 in.

Values:	Exc.	V.G.	Good
	90.00	65.00	40.00

Comment: *Values are for any model.*

Red River Cotton Hoes

Close-bent, 1/2-inch steel shank. Handle is 5 feet long.

No.	Cut	Blade Depth
WRC/7	7 in.	5 in.
WRC/7 1/2	7 1/2 in.	5 in.
WRC/8	8 in.	5 in.

Values:	Exc.	V.G.	Good
	90.00	65.00	40.00

Comment: *Values are for any model.*

Planters' Hoes

Shank pattern. Riveted shank; neck is 5/8 inch. Angle of blade is 74 degrees.

No.	Cut	Handle
WP107	7 in.	5 ft.
WP108	8 in.	5 ft.

Values:	Exc.	V.G.	Good
	90.00	65.00	40.00

Comment: *Values are for either model.*

Nurserymen's Hoes

Shank pattern.

No.	Cut	Handle	Blade Depth
WN6 1/2	6 1/2 in.	4 1/3 ft.	3 1/2 in.
WN7 1/2	7 1/2 in.	4 1/3 ft.	3 1/2 in.

Socket Pattern.

No.	Cut	Handle	Blade Depth
WN07 1/2	7 1/2 in.	4 1/3 ft.	3 1/2 in.

Values:	Exc.	V.G.	Good
	90.00	65.00	40.00

Comment: *Values are for any model.*

Rhode Island Hoes

 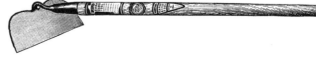

No. W19. Shank pattern; 1/2-inch shank. Set of blade is 74 degrees. Handle is 4 1/3 feet. Blade depth 4 inches. Width of cut is 9 inches.

No. W109. Socket pattern; 1/2-inch shank. Set of blade is 74 degrees. Handle is 4 1/3 feet. Blade depth 4 inches. Width of cut is 9 inches.

Values:	Exc.	V.G.	Good
	90.00	65.00	40.00

Comment: *Values are for either model of Rhode Island Hoe.*

Tobacco Hoe

No. WT9. Socket pattern. Set of blade is 70 degrees. Handle is 4 1/3 feet. Blade depth is 2 3/4 inches. Width of cut is 9 inches.

Values:	Exc.	V.G.	Good
	125.00	100.00	75.00

Mattock Hoe

No. WDE3. Solid-steel shank and blade. Riveted shank, plain ferrule. Handle length is 4 1/2 feet. Cutter width at top is 1 1/2 inches; cutter width at bottom is 3 inches. Total blade length - 12 inches; maximum blade thickness - 1/2 inch.

Values:	Exc.	V.G.	Good
	200.00	180.00	160.00

Weeding Hoes

No. W10. One prong. Points and edges tapered and edged. Handle is 4 1/3 feet. Width of cut is 3 5/8 inches. Blade length 9 inches.

No. W20. Two spear-shaped prongs. Points and edges tapered and edged. Handle is 4 1/3 feet. Width of cut is 3 3/4 inches. Blade length 9 inches.

Values:	Exc.	V.G.	Good
	200.00	180.00	160.00

Comment: *Values are for either model of Weeding Hoe.*

Mortar Hoes

No. WPM10. Shank pattern; 1/2-inch shank. Two-hole perforated blade. Handle is 5 1/2 feet. Blade depth 6 inches. Width of cut is 10 inches.

No. WM010. Socket pattern; 9/16-inch shank. Handle is 6 feet. Solid blade has depth of 6 inches. Width of cut is 10 inches.

Values:	Exc.	V.G.	Good	Values:	Exc.	V.G.	Good
	150.00	125.00	100.00		90.00	65.00	40.00

Turf Edgers

No. WTE40. Shank pattern. Blade is 9 inches x 5 inches. Handle is 4 feet.

Values:	Exc.	V.G.	Good
	200.00	180.00	160.00

Shovels, Spades and Scoops

Here is a short, highly standardized line of patterns covering the bulk of those sold through the retail trade, the big volume-selling patterns. This line, in addition to the Steel Goods line, will take care of the bulk of Winchester Dealers' requirements in farm and garden tools.

BLADES - Made from high-carbon steel.
FROGS - Special closed-type forming perfect socket.
STRAPS - Wide, well tapered, rolled flush with the handle, and securely riveted through the handle with three oversize double-countersunk, flush rivets.
HANDLES - First-grade selected northern Ash. Lightweight-type shovels are fitted with split "D" handles riveted to the pressed-steel corner caps. A rivet at bottom of split prevents "continued split." This is the coming handle.
SPECIAL CARE AND INSPECTION guarantees **BALANCE AND HANG OF WINCHESTER SHOVELS.**

Finish and Packing:
BLADES - Full bright polish, lacquered. HANDLES are fine sanded, polished and waxed, "D" type enameled Winchester Red to bottom of split. TRADE MARK rolled in straps and burned into handle. Attractive gold, red, gray and black labels. Packed and tied in bundles of six.

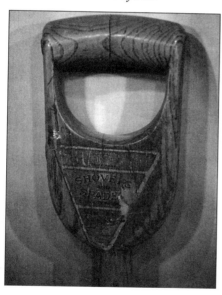

Common "D" wood handles of early spades were skillfully cut and finished. From T. Webster collection. Photo by D. Kowalski.

Dirt Shovels, Short Handle

Common "D" Handle. Socket strap pattern.

Blade Size No. 2 - 12 inches long x 9 3/4 inches wide.

No.	Handle Length	Point
WDS/2	26 1/2 in.	Square
WDR/2	26 1/2 in.	Round
WDS/2/30	30 in.	Square
WDR/2/30	30 in.	Round

Blade Size No. 3 - 12 1/2 inches long x 9 7/8 inches wide.

No.	Handle Length	Point
WDS/3	26 1/2 in.	Square

Blade Size No. 3 - 13 inches long x 9 1/4 inches wide.

No.	Handle Length	Point
WDR/3	26 1/2 in.	Round

Blade Size No. 4 - 12 3/4 inches long x 10 5/8 inches wide.

No.	Handle Length	Point
WDS/4	26 1/2 in.	Square

Values:	Exc.	V.G.	Good
	200.00	175.00	150.00

Comment: *Values are for any model.*

Split "D" Handle. Socket strap pattern.

Blade Size No. 2 - 12 inches long x 9 3/4 inches wide.

No.	Handle Length	Point
WSDS/2	26 1/2 in.	Square
WSDR/2	26 1/2 in.	Round

Values:	Exc.	V.G.	Good
	180.00	165.00	135.00

Comment: *Values are for either model.*

Lightweight Split "D" Handle. Solid shank and socket pattern. Handle assembly is full heat-treated.

Blade Size - 11 3/4 inches long x 9 3/4 inches wide.

No.	Handle Assembly	Point
WSDSST/2	25 1/2 in.	Square

Values:	Exc.	V.G.	Good
	180.00	165.00	135.00

Lightweight Split "D" Handle. Solid shank and socket pattern. Handle assembly is full heat-treated.

Blade Size - 11 1/2 inches long x 9 inches wide.

No.	Handle Assembly	Point
WSDRSST/2	25 1/2 in.	Round

Values:	Exc.	V.G.	Good
	200.00	175.00	150.00

Dirt Shovels, Long Handle

Regular weight. Socket strap pattern. Handle is bent pattern, 51 inches.

Blade Size No. 2 - 12 inches long x 9 3/4 inches wide.

No.	Point
WLS/2	Square
WLR/2	Round

Lightweight. Socket strap pattern. Handle is bent pattern, 51 inches.

Blade Size - 12 inches long x 9 3/4 inches wide.

No.	Point
No. WLSL/2	Square Point

Blade Size No. 4 - 12 3/4 inches long x 10 5/8 inches wide.

No.	Point
WLS/4	Square

Blade Size No. 4 - 13 inches long x 10 1/4 inches wide.

No.	Point
WLR/4	Round

Values:	Exc.	V.G.	Good
	200.00	175.00	150.00

Comment: *Values are for any model.*

Blade Size - 11 1/2 inches long x 9 inches wide.

No.	Point
No. WLRL/2	Round Point

Values:	Exc.	V.G.	Good
	200.00	175.00	150.00

Comment: *Values are for either model.*

Farm, Yard and Garden Tools • 535

No.	Point
No. WLRSST/2	Round Point

Values:	Exc.	V.G.	Good
	200.00	175.00	150.00

Lightweight. Solid shank and socket pattern. Handle assembly 47 inches long, full heat-treated.

Irrigation Shovels, Long Handle

Socket strap pattern. Handle is bent pattern, 51 inches. Medium Lift 5 1/2 inches. Blade Size - 11 inches long x 8 1/2 inches wide. No. WLI/S. Round Point.

Values:	Exc.	V.G.	Good
	200.00	175.00	150.00

Solid shank and socket pattern. Handle assembly 47 inches long, full heat-treated. Medium Lift 5 1/2 inches.

No. WLISST1. Blade Size - 11 inches long x 8 1/2 inches wide. Round Point.

No. WLISST1. Lift 4 1/2 inches. Blade Size - 11 3/4 inches long x 9 1/4 inches wide. Round Point.

Values:	Exc.	V.G.	Good
	200.00	175.00	150.00

Comment: *Values are for either model.*

Spades, Socket Strap Pattern

Iowa Pattern. Split "D" Handle. Blade is 12 inches long x 6 1/4 inches wide. Handle 30 inches long. No. WSR2. Round Point.

Values:	Exc.	V.G.	Good
	170.00	155.00	125.00

Iowa Pattern. Long Handle. Blade is 12 inches long x 6 1/4 inches wide. Handle 51 inches long. No. WSLR2. Round Point.

Values:	Exc.	V.G.	Good
	200.00	175.00	150.00

Luther Burbank Pattern. Split "D" Handle. Blade is 12 inches long x 6 1/2 inches wide. Handle 30 inches long. No. WBS2. Half Round Point.

Values:	Exc.	V.G.	Good
	150.00	125.00	100.00

Luther Burbank Pattern. Long Handle. *Blade is 13 inches long x 6 3/4 inches wide. Handle 51 inches long. No. WBLS2. Half Round Point.*

Values:	Exc.	V.G.	Good
	200.00	175.00	150.00

Plain Back. Common "D" Handle. *Blade Size No. 2 - 12 inches long x 7 3/4 to 7 1/2 inches wide. Handle 27 inches long. No. WSD/2. Square Point.*

Values:	Exc.	V.G.	Good
	150.00	125.00	100.00

Plain Back. Long Handle. *Blade Size No. 2 - 12 inches long x 7 3/4 to 7 1/2 inches wide. Handle 51 inches long. No. WSL/2. Square Point.*

Values:	Exc.	V.G.	Good
	200.00	175.00	150.00

Plain Back. Common "D" Handle Drain. *Blade tapered concave; taper is 5 1/2 inches to 4 5/8 inches wide; sharpened. Handle 27 1/2 inches long. Round Point. No. and blade length: No. W14, 14 inches; No. W16, 16 inches; No. W18, 18 inches.*

Values:	Exc.	V.G.	Good
	150.00	125.00	100.00

Comment: *Values are for any model.*

Plain Back. Common "D" Handle Ditching. *Blade tapered concave; taper is 6 1/4 inches to 5 3/4 inches wide; sharpened. Handle 27 1/2 inches long. Half Round Point. No. and blade length: No. WD14, 14 inches; No. WD16, 16 inches; No. WD18, 18 inches.*

Values:	Exc.	V.G.	Good
	150.00	125.00	100.00

Comment: *Values are for any model.*

Grain Scoop

Western Pattern. Split "D" Handle. *Hollow back. Socket shank. Blade corrugated, 27 1/2 inches long.*

No.	Blade Length	Width
WDW6	16 1/2 in.	13 1/4 in.
WDW8	17 1/2 in.	14 in.
WDW10	18 1/2 in.	14 3/4 in.
WDW12	19 in.	15 in.

Values:	Exc.	V.G.	Good
	260.00	225.00	190.00

Comment: *Values are for any model Grain Scoop.*

Winchester Agricultural Tool Handles

Extra-quality, selected, second-growth northern white Ash. Chucked and bored, with vermilion enameled strap ferrule and cap. Square hole. Available in the following patterns: Bent Hay Fork; Bent Manure Fork; Bent Header Fork; Bent Alfalfa Fork; Long Handle Shovel; Split "D" Shovel; and Scoop Shovel. Photos not available.

Values:

Exc.	V.G.	Good
125.00	100.00	75.00

Comment: *Values are for any model Farm or Garden Tool Handle that has not been attached to tool.*

Winchester Wheelbarrows

Metal Wheelbarrow in Very Good to Good condition showing much of the original color and striping. In Excellent condition, the tray would show red stripe around edge. This is the only metal one that has ever been found. From T. Webster collection. Photo by D. Kowalski.

All Purpose Barrow. No. W100. Capacity is three cubic feet. Hardwood frame and legs, painted Winchester gray. Legs have wrought-iron shoes. Handles are 1 1/2 in. x 2 in. x 56 in. Painted Winchester gray with narrow strips and black hand holds. Steel tray is 18 gauge with turned edge, painted Winchester gray with red band around edge, bolted and riveted to frame. Tray is 28 inches wide x 32 inches long x 7 inches deep at wheel, 5 inches deep at handles. Black wheel. Packed loose; tray packed in burlap bag.

Values:

Exc.	V.G.	Good
2,000.00	1,750.00	1,500.00

Comment: *Values are for Metal Winchester Wheelbarrow, assembled.*

538 • *Farm, Yard and Garden Tools*

Winchester-Simmons Co. Wooden Wheelbarrow. Produced after 1922 when Winchester merged with the Simmons Hardware Company. Color is wine red with yellow stripes and highlights. From Richard Hecht collection. Photo by R. Hecht.

The front of the tray of the Winchester-Simmons Co. Wooden Wheelbarrow. Inscription was overprinted in black: First line - WINCHESTER - SIMMONS CO.; Second line - OF BOSTON; Third line - NO. 6. From Richard Hecht collection. Photo by R. Hecht.

Values:	Exc.	V.G.	Good
	1,500.00	1,200.00	900.00

Comment: *Values are for Winchester-Simmons Wooden Wheelbarrow.*

Winchester Lawn Mowers

Double Gear. Ball Bearing. High-grade, cast-side frames, spoke flange raised-drive wheels, gear casings and bed plate, all thoroughly braced and reinforced. High-grade-steel, oil-tempered revolving knives and adjustable and self-sharpening bed knife, screwed to reinforced bed plate. Malleable-iron reel braces and adjustable roller brackets, with hook extension for grass catcher. Heavy cast drive-wheel-bearing rear axle. Double gearing on both sides, with steel-bushed hardened gear and double-sliding steel-pin ratchet. Double screw adjustment for cones and ball retainer. Simple and strong rocking adjustment for lower steel bed knife. Steel handle braces. White maple handle is 3 1/2 feet long, nicely varnished. Hardwood roller. Patented non-loosening clamp attachment for handle bar. All running parts carefully milled. Metal parts extra finished. Painted Winchester gray with red trim.

High Wheel Lawn Mower - Five Reel Knives. Drive wheels are 11 inches in diameter. Diameter of reel is 7 inches. Other diameters: front bar - 11/16 inches; reel axle - 5/8 inches; drive wheel hub bearing - 2 1/10 inches; roller - 2 1/2 inches. Adjustable to cut grass to a height of 3/4 inches to 1 1/2 inches. Will cut grass standing about 7 inches high.

No.	Width of Cut	Total Width
WH14	14 in.	19 3/4 in.
WH16	16 in.	21 3/4 in.
WH18	18 in.	23 3/4 in.
WH20	20 in.	25 3/4 in.

Model WL13. Low Wheel Lawn Mower. Actual outside width of this model is 18 3/8 inches; actual cutting edge of blades is 13 3/4 inches. The outside hubs of the wheels have indented inscriptions "WINCHESTER DOUBLE GEAR WL13." The inside hubs have "WINCHESTER REPEATING ARMS CO." inscription. Just a few flecks of red paint are left on the steel handle braces. From T. Webster collection. Photo by D. Kowalski.

Model WL13. The length of the handle compared to the width of the head almost makes this model look disproportionate. Weight is about 44 pounds. From T. Webster collection. Photo by D. Kowalski.

Model WL13. Close-up of top of handle shows words "WINCHESTER" and "BALL BEARING" painted in red. From T. Webster collection. Photo by D. Kowalski.

Low Wheel Lawn Mower - Four Reel Knives. *Drive wheels are 9 inches in diameter. Diameter of reel is 5 1/2 inches. Other diameters: front bar - 5/8 inches; reel axle - 5/8 inches; drive wheel hub bearing - 2 1/10 inches; roller - 2 inches. Adjustable to cut grass to a height of 1/2 inch to 1 inch. Will cut grass standing about 5 1/2 inches high.*

No.	Width of Cut	Total Width
WL12	12 in.	17 3/4 in.
WL13	13 in.	18 3/4 in.

No.	Width of Cut	Total Width
WL14	14 in.	19 3/4 in.
WL16	16 in.	21 3/4 in.
WL18	18 in.	23 3/4 in.

Values:

Exc.	V.G.	Good
500.00	400.00	300.00

Comment: *Values are for any model of Winchester Lawn Mower. Add 60 percent for Winchester Store models.*

Scythe or Grass Hook

No. W1. Scythe has 12 1/2-inch cut. High-grade forged steel. Back of blade is ribbed. Full polished, with gray upper web striped in red; screwed to gray ridged, drop-forged, bent-steel shank that is 7 1/2 inches long, striped in red. Black rubberoid-finish, ribbed handle is 5 3/4 inches long.

Values:

Exc.	V.G.	Good
250.00	225.00	200.00

Grass Shears

This Grass Shears is one of the very few that has ever been found. From T. Webster collection. Photo by D. Kowalski.

No. W97. Grass Shears has single-bow pattern. Highest-grade steel, polished blades and grips. Trowel shanks and spring-tempered bow forged from one piece of high-grade steel. Straight blades, tempered, set and sharpened. Length of blades is 6 inches; overall length is 13 inches.

Values:

Exc.	V.G.	Good
200.00	175.00	150.00

Comment: *These were packed one-half dozen in a cardboard box.*

Lawn Sprinkler

Lawn Sprinkler from the 1920s has cast-iron base with indented "WINCHESTER" logo. Arms rotate. Measures 8 1/8 inches wide at the base and is 10 inches high. A fairly rare item. From T. Webster collection. Photo by D. Kowalski.

Values:

Exc.	V.G.	Good
1,200.00	1,100.00	900.00

Comment: *Values are for rotating model.*

Axes, Hatchets and Hammers

by David D. Kowalski

Winchester purchased the Mack Axe Company of Beaver Falls, Pennsylvania in 1920, giving them a broad line of single- and double-bit axes, a variety of hatchets, and several unique hammers. We present here the Winchester models being sold as of the printing date of the 1927 catalog. And we have added a few items, such as draw knives, that we can authenticate.

One of the challenges of identifying axes, hatchets and hammers originally made by Winchester is that they did not stamp the model number on all the metal heads. Some of the hatchets do have model number stamps on their heads. Winchester typically used a decal on the axe heads. And from what we have seen, they appear to have put their decals on all handles. However, they would also typically stamp the model number on the butt end of original handles, particularly hammer handles.

A further complication in this area is that a long-ago owner (or not-so-long-ago owner) of a hammer might have snapped the handle, then re-handled it with the wrong handle. Winchester also sold axe heads, for example, separately. That gave a buyer the chance to put whatever handle on it he or she wanted to.

Furthermore, Winchester's full-size axes were sent to retailers packed in a case containing one dozen pieces. The small axes came in cartons with one-half dozen units. There are no single boxes for any axe, large or small, to help corroborate model numbers.

When assessing authenticity and value, the would-be collector should look for all the right parts in the right place on a tool. And the premium price is reserved for those tools with all the right parts and numbers, never used, perhaps even with an original case or carton.

Speaking of numbers, yet another complication in the tool arena is that Winchester published both old product numbers and new product numbers. As far as we are able, we will publish both the old and new model numbers here.

Finally, Winchester tools typically got used. That resulted in decals getting rubbed off or worn. Or axe heads were sharpened. Here again, items in Excellent condition or New In Case are particularly desirable and valuable.

We have included photographs of Winchester tools we could authenticate by the presence of original decals or stamped model numbers. And we have made every effort to correctly identify the model of the axe head. Some of them were a challenge. If we had a very worn example of a model that would have made identification difficult for you, the reader, we chose to use line art.

In the case of axes, we will also give length measurements of axe heads where possible. But keep in mind that the length of an axe head that has been sharpened does not reflect the actual length of the original head. You will have to judge the amount of wear shown. However, we believe this additional information will help you identify tools and model numbers in the field.

Winchester also made most of their axe heads in several weights; we will list these. And they put handles on them of various lengths; we will also identify these.

Winchester Axes

Great care is taken in handling Winchester axes to give them the proper "hang." The contour and shape are such as to make them cut faster and with less effort. It is this care in handling and attention to securing the right contour plus the excellent grind given the bit that makes for the superiority of Winchester axes.

Our axes are made by the overlaid method with bits of the highest-grade crucible steel carefully tempered and ground. Eyes are punched from the solid steel and tapered from the outer to inner opening, which prevents the handle loosening. Heads have smooth BLACK FINISH with cutting edges and tops bright. Handled axes are hung with selected hickory handles in white-wax finish. Wedged with hardwood wedges locked with double-locking wedge.

Winchester Axes, Single Bit

Notice the finely ground blade and the tight-holding interlocking wedge of Winchester axes.

Single Bit, Dayton Pattern, Handled

Dayton Pattern axe head measures 7 5/8" long. From T. Webster collection. Photo by D. Kowalski.

Nos.	Head Wt. Lbs.	Handle No., Size, Style
WD301A	3 to 4	WR36 - 36 in. Oval
	3 1/4 to 3 3/4	
	3 1/2 to 4 1/2	
	4 to 5	
	4 1/2 to 5 1/2	
	5 to 6	
WD301B	3 to 4	W36 - 36 in. Octagon
	3 1/4 to 3 3/4	
	3 1/2 to 4 1/2	
	4 to 5	
	4 1/2 to 5 1/2	
	5 to 6	
WD301C	3 to 4	WR34 - 34 in. Oval
	3 1/4 to 3 3/4	
	3 1/2 to 4 1/2	
	4 to 5	
	4 1/2 to 5 1/2	
WD301D	3 to 4	WR32 - 32 in. Oval
	3 1/4 to 3 3/4	
	3 1/2 to 4 1/2	
WD301H	3 to 4	WR30 - 30 in. Oval
	3 1/4 to 3 3/4	
	3 1/2 to 4 1/2	
WD301K	3 to 4	WR28 - 28 in. Oval
	3 1/4 to 3 3/4	
WD301	3 to 4	UNHANDLED
	3 1/4 to 3 3/4	
	3 1/2 to 4 1/2	
	4 to 5	
	4 1/2 to 5 1/2	
	5 to 6	

Values:	Exc.	V.G.	Good
	75.00	65.00	50.00

Comment: *Values are for any model of Single Bit Dayton Pattern.*

Single Bit, Connecticut Pattern, Handled

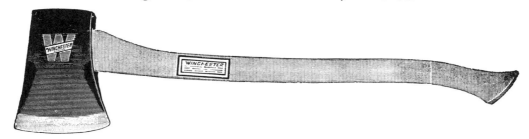

Nos.	Head Wt. Lbs.	Handle No., Size, Style
WC306A	3 to 4 3 1/4 to 3 3/4 3 1/2 to 4 1/2	WR36 - 36 in. Oval
WC306H	3 to 4 3 1/4 to 3 3/4 3 1/2 to 4 1/2	WR30 - 30 in. Oval
WC306K	3 to 4 3 1/4 to 3 3/4 3 1/2 to 4 1/2	WR28 - 28 in. Oval

Nos.	Head Wt. Lbs.	Handle No., Size, Style
WC306	3 to 4 3 1/4 to 3 3/4 3 1/2 to 4 1/2	UNHANDLED

Values:

Exc.	V.G.	Good
75.00	65.00	50.00

Comment: *Values are for any model of Single Bit Connecticut Pattern.*

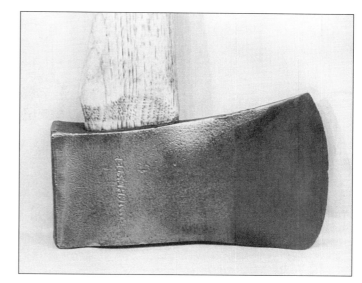

Connecticut Pattern axe head measures 7 1/8" long. From T. Webster collection. Photo by D. Kowalski.

Single Bit, Baltimore Jersey Pattern, Handled

Nos.	Head Wt. Lbs.	Handle No., Size, Style
WBJ305A	2 1/2 to 3 3 to 4 3 1/4 to 3 3/4 3 1/2 to 4 1/2 4 to 5 4 1/2 to 5 1/2 5 to 6	WR36 - 36 in. Oval
WBJ305C	2 1/2 to 3 3 to 4 3 1/4 to 3 3/4 3 1/2 to 4 1/2 4 to 5 4 1/2 to 5 1/2	WR34 - 34 in. Oval

Baltimore Jersey Pattern axe head measures 7 1/8" long. From T. Webster collection. Photo by D. Kowalski.

544 • *Axes, Hatchets and Hammers*

Nos.	Head Wt. Lbs.	Handle No., Size, Style
WBJ305D	2 1/2 to 3	WR32 - 32 in. Oval
	3 to 4	
	3 1/4 to 3 3/4	
	3 1/2 to 4 1/2	
	4 to 5	
	4 1/2 to 5 1/2	
WBJ305H	2 1/2 to 3	WR30 - 30 in. Oval
	3 to 4	
	3 1/4 to 3 3/4	
	3 1/2 to 4 1/2	
WBJ305K	2 1/2 to 3	WR28 - 28 in. Oval
	3 to 4	
	3 1/4 to 3 3/4	
	3 1/2 to 4 1/2	

Nos.	Head Wt. Lbs.	Handle No., Size, Style
WBJ305	2 1/2 to 3	UNHANDLED
	3 to 4	
	3 1/4 to 3 3/4	
	3 1/2 to 4 1/2	
	4 to 5	
	4 1/2 to 5 1/2	
	5 to 6	

Values:	Exc.	V.G.	Good
	90.00	80.00	60.00

Comment: *Values are for any model of Single Bit Baltimore Jersey Pattern.*

Single Bit, Michigan Pattern, Handled

Nos.	Head Wt. Lbs.	Handle No., Size, Style
WM302A	3 to 4	WR36 - 36 in. Oval
	3 1/4 to 3 3/4	
	3 1/2 to 4 1/2	
	4 to 5	
	4 1/2 to 5 1/2	
WM302B	3 to 4	W36 - 36 in. Octagon
	3 1/4 to 3 3/4	
	3 1/2 to 4 1/2	
	4 to 5	
	4 1/2 to 5 1/2	
WM302C	3 to 4	WR34 - 34 in. Oval
	3 1/4 to 3 3/4	
	3 1/2 to 4 1/2	
	4 to 5	
WM302D	3 to 4	WR32 - 32 in. Oval
	3 1/4 to 3 3/4	
WM302	3 to 4	UNHANDLED
	3 1/4 to 3 3/4	
	3 1/2 to 4 1/2	
	4 to 5	
	4 1/2 to 5 1/2	

Values:	Exc.	V.G.	Good
	75.00	65.00	50.00

Comment: *Values are for any model of Single Bit Michigan Pattern.*

Axes, Hatchets and Hammers • 545

Single Bit, Rockaway Pattern, Handled

Nos.	Head Wt. Lbs.	Handle No., Size, Style
WRJ320D	3 1/2 to 4 1/2	WR32 - 32 in. Oval
WRJ320	3 1/2 to 4 1/2	UNHANDLED

Values: Exc. 85.00   V.G. 75.00   Good 55.00

Comment: *Values are for any model of Single Bit Rockaway Pattern.*

Single Bit, Southern Kentucky Pattern, Handled

Nos.	Head Wt. Lbs.	Handle No., Size, Style
WSK302A	3 to 4	WR36 - 36 in. Oval
	3 1/4 to 3 3/4	
	3 1/2 to 4 1/2	
	4 to 5	
	4 1/2 to 5 1/2	
	5 to 6	
WSK303D	3 to 4	WR32-32 in. Oval
	3 1/4 to 3 3/4	
	3 1/2 to 4 1/2	
WSK303D	4 to 5	WR32 - 32 in. Oval
	4 1/2 to 5 1/2	
	5 to 6	
WSK303	3 to 4	UNHANDLED
	3 1/4 to 3 3/4	
	3 1/2 to 4 1/2	
	4 to 5	
	4 1/2 to 5 1/2	
	5 to 6	

Values: Exc. 90.00   V.G. 80.00   Good 60.00

Comment: *Values are for any model of Single Bit Southern Kentucky Pattern.*

Single Bit, Wedge Pattern, Handled

Nos.	Head Wt. Lbs.	Handle No., Size, Style
WW308D	3 to 4 3 1/4 to 3 3/4	WR32 - 32 in. Oval
WW308H	3 to 4 3 1/4 to 3 3/4	WR30 - 30 in. Oval
WW308K	3 to 4 3 1/4 to 3 3/4	WR28 - 28 in. Oval
WW308	3 to 4 3 1/4 to 3 3/4	UNHANDLED

Values:	Exc.	V.G.	Good
	75.00	65.00	50.00

Comment: *Values are for any model of Single Bit Wedge Pattern.*

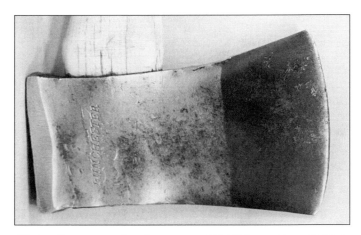

Wedge Pattern axe head measures 7 1/8" long. From T. Webster collection. Photo by D. Kowalski.

Single Bit, Wisconsin Pattern, Handled

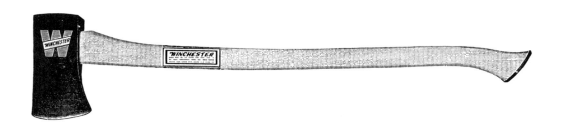

Nos.	Head Wt. Lbs.	Handle No., Size, Style
WW304X	3 to 4 3 1/4 to 3 3/4 3 1/2 to 4	WWS36 - 36 in. Slim
WW304Z	3 to 4 3 1/4 to 3 3/4 3 1/2 to 4	WWS34 - 34 in. Slim
WW304	3 to 4 3 1/4 to 3 3/4 3 1/2 to 4	UNHANDLED

Values:	Exc.	V.G.	Good
	75.00	65.00	50.00

Comment: *Values are for any model of Single Bit Wisconsin Pattern.*

Axes, Hatchets and Hammers • 547

Single Bit, Baltimore Kentucky Pattern, Handled

Nos.	Head Wt. Lbs.	Handle No., Size, Style	Values:	Exc.	V.G.	Good
WBK315A	3 to 4	WR36 - 36 in. Oval		90.00	80.00	60.00
	3 1/2- to 4 1/2					
	4 to 5		**Comment:** *Values are for any model of Single Bit Baltimore Kentucky Pattern.*			
	4 1/2 to 5 1/2					
	5 to 6					
WBK315	3 to 4	UNHANDLED				
	3 1/2 to 4 1/2					
	4 to 5					
	4 1/2 to 5 1/2					
	5 to 6					

Winchester Axes, Double Bit

Double Bit, Western Pattern, Handled

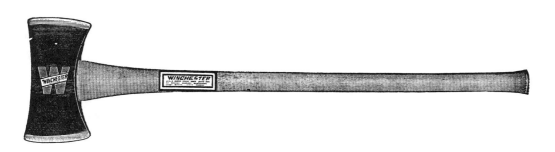

Nos.	Head Wt. Lbs.	Handle No., Size, Style	Values:	Exc.	V.G.	Good
WR350DA	3 to 4	WDR36 - 36 in. Oval		135.00	115.00	90.00
	3 1/4 to 3 3/4					
	4 to 5		**Comment:** *Values are for any model of Double Bit Western Pattern.*			
	4 1/2 to 5 1/2					
WR350	3 to 4	UNHANDLED				
	3 1/2 to 4 1/2					
	4 to 5					
	4 1/2 to 5 1/2					

Double Bit, California Reversible Pattern, Handled

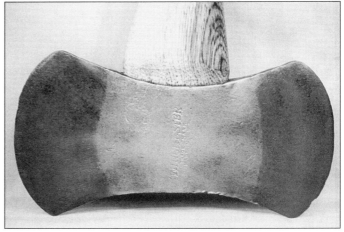

California Reversible Pattern axe head measures 8 7/8" long. From T. Webster collection. Photo by D. Kowalski.

Nos.	Head Wt. Lbs.	Handle No., Size, Style
WCR355DA	3 to 4	WDR36 - 36 in. Oval
	3 1/2 to 4 1/2	
	4 to 5	
WCR355	3 to 4	UNHANDLED
	3 1/2 to 4 1/2	
	4 to 5	

Values:	Exc.	V.G.	Good
	150.00	125.00	100.00

Comment: *Values are for any model of Double Bit California Reversible Pattern.*

Double Bit, Michigan Pattern, Handled

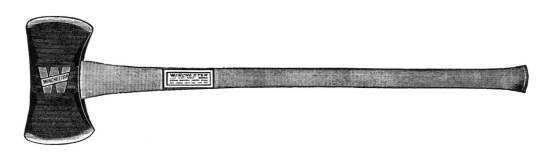 

Nos.	Head Wt. Lbs.	Handle No., Size, Style	Nos.	Head Wt. Lbs.	Handle No., Size, Style
WM352DA	3 to 4	WDR36 - 36 in. Oval	WM352	4 to 5	UNHANDLED
	3 1/2 to 4 1/2			4 1/2 to 5 1/2	
	4 to 5			5 to 6	
	4 1/2 to 5 1/2				
	5 to 6				
WM352	3 to 4	UNHANDLED			
	3 1/2 to 4 1/2				

Values:	Exc.	V.G.	Good
	135.00	115.00	90.00

Comment: *Values are for any model of Double Bit Michigan Pattern.*

Axes, Hatchets and Hammers • 549

Double Bit, Wedge Double Pattern, Handled

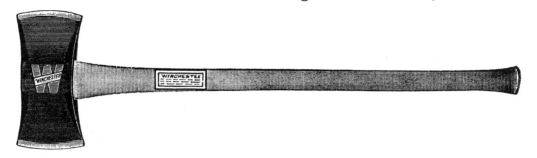

Nos.	Head Wt. Lbs.	Handle No., Size, Style	Values:	Exc.	V.G.	Good
WW356DA	3 to 4	WDR36 - 36 in. Oval		135.00	115.00	90.00
WW356	3 to 4	UNHANDLED				

Comment: *Values are for any model of Double Bit Wedge Double Pattern.*

Double Bit, Wisconsin Pattern, Handled

Wisconsin Pattern double axe head measures 8 5/8" long. From T. Webster collection. Photo by D. Kowalski.

Nos.	Head Wt. Lbs.	Handle No., Size, Style	Values:	Exc.	V.G.	Good
WW351DX	3 to 4	WWD36 - 36 in. Slim		135.00	115.00	90.00
	3 1/4 to 3 3/4					
	3 1/2 to 4					
WW351DZ	3 to 4	WWID34 - 34 in. Slim				
	3 1/4 to 3 3/4					
	3 1/2 to 4					
WW351	3 to 4	UNHANDLED				

Comment: *Values are for any model of Double Bit Wisconsin Pattern.*

Nos.	Head Wt. Lbs.	Handle No., Size, Style
	3 1/4 to 3 3/4	
	3 1/2 to 4	

Double Bit, Adirondack Pattern, Handled

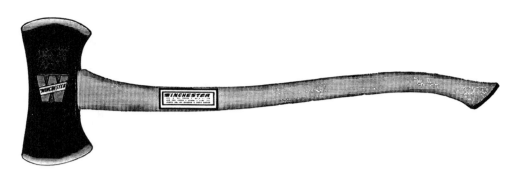

Nos.	Head Wt. Lbs.	Handle No., Size, Style	Values:	Exc.	V.G.	Good
WA357H	3 1/4 to 3 3/4 3/4	WR30 - 30 in. Oval		165.00	135.00	110.00
WA357	3 1/4 to 3 3/4 3 3/4	UNHANDLED				

Comment: *Values are for any model of Double Bit Adirondack Pattern.*

Double Bit, Puget Sound Pattern, Handled

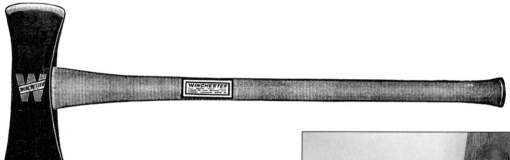

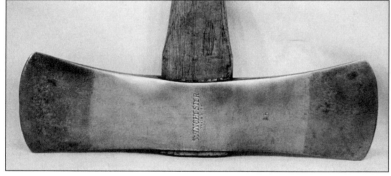

Puget Sound double axe head measures 13 1/4" long. From T. Webster collection. Photo by D. Kowalski.

Nos.	Head Wt. Lbs.	Handle No., Size, Style	Values:	Exc.	V.G.	Good
WPS358DA	3 1/2 to 4 1/2 4 to 5	WDR36 - 36 in. Oval		600.00	500.00	400.00
WPS358	3 1/2- to 4 1/2 4 to 5	UNHANDLED				

Comment: *Values are for any model of Double Bit Puget Sound Pattern.*

Double Bit, California Redwood Pattern, Handled

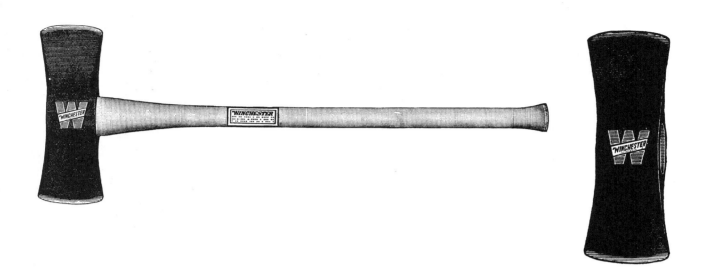

Nos.	Head Wt. Lbs.	Handle No., Size, Style	Values:	Exc.	V.G.	Good
WRW157DA	3 to 4	WDR36 - 36 in. Oval		600.00	500.00	400.00
	3 1/2 to 4 1/2					
	4 to 5		**Comment:** *Values are for any model of Double Bit California Redwood Pattern.*			
WRW157	3 to 4	UNHANDLED				
	3 1/2 to 4 1/2					
	4 to 5					

Hunter's Axe

New No. WYO; Old No. F5607T. Curved handle of selected hickory, 16 inches in length with white wax or Winchester gray finish. Head has black rustless finish. Cutting edges and top of head have bright finish. Securely locked with Winchester interlocking wedge. Weight about 1 3/4 lbs. One-half dozen in a carton.

Values:	Exc.	V.G.	Good
	75.00	55.00	40.00

Comment: *Values are for any model of Double Bit California Redwood Pattern.*

552 • *Axes, Hatchets and Hammers*

Camper's Axe with Sheath

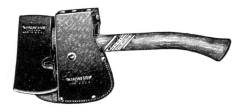

New No. W20; Old No. F5601T. A practical axe designed for use of campers and for general use. Furnished with leather sheath. Curved handle, 14 inches long, with Winchester gray finish. Head has black rustless finish. Edge and top bright. Winchester interlocking wedge. Weight each 1 1/4 lbs.

Values:	Exc.	V.G.	Good
	165.00	150.00	130.00

Comment: *Values are for the axe and sheath together. Winchester also sold the axe alone as New Model W10; Old Model F5602T. The axe alone would be valued at about 35 percent of the combination.*

Sheath for Camper's Axe.

New No. WS; Old No. F9991T. Axe sheath only. One-half dozen in a carton.

Values:	Exc.	V.G.	Good
	100.00	90.00	75.00

Boy's Axe

New No. WB95; Old No. F5609T. Curved handle of selected hickory, 28 inches long. Made in either white wax or Winchester gray finish. Head of Dayton pattern, black rustless finish. Cutting edge and top of head bright. Winchester interlocking wedge. Weight each about 2 1/4 lbs. One dozen in a case.

Values:	Exc.	V.G.	Good
	80.00	65.00	45.00

House Axe

New No. WHA; Old No. F5608T. Curved handle of selected hickory, 18 inches long, with white wax or Winchester gray finish. Head has black rustless finish; cutting edges and top bright. Securely locked with Winchester interlocking wedge. Weight about 2 1/2 lbs. One-half dozen in a carton.

Values:	Exc.	V.G.	Good
	75.00	55.00	40.00

Winchester Hatchets

Drop forged from one solid piece of high-grade tool steel. Bits carefully tempered and ground to a keen edge. Striking polls hardened to the proper degree to withstand severe service. Handled with selected hickory handles of exclusive Winchester design with fashioned handle grip and a bell end. Smooth-sanded and polished.

Handles furnished in Winchester gray as standard. Natural white finish may be had when specified. Heads securely locked to handle with Winchester patented two-piece interlocking wedge. Nail slots especially beveled to give natural firm grip in pulling nails.

Haines Hatchet Patterns

Made with several exclusive features that make Winchester Haines patterns a superior tool in this type. Blades carefully lined up so that center of cutting edge, center of eye and center of striking poll are on an even line. Sure-grip nail slot. Full true adze eye of uniform thickness, designed to prevent buckling. Deep striking poll. Superior contour and bright, full polish.

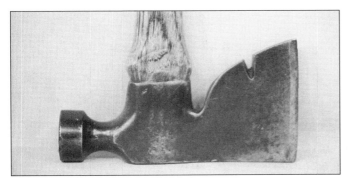

The head of this Haines Half Hatchet is 5 3/4 inches long. From T. Webster collection. Photo by D. Kowalski.

New No. WP301; Old No. F5305C. Haines Half Hatchet. Width of cut is 3 1/4 inches; handle is 13 inches. Packed one-half dozen to the carton.

Values: | Exc. | V.G. | Good
| 75.00 | 60.00 | 45.00

Comment: *Values for old or new model of Haines Half Hatchet.*

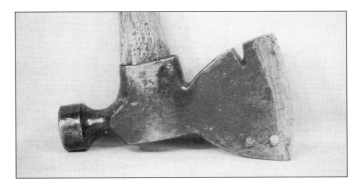

The head of this Haines Shingling Hatchet is 5 3/4 inches long. From T. Webster collection. Photo by D. Kowalski.

New No. WP201; Old No. F5300C. Haines Shingling Hatchet. Width of cut is 3 1/2 inches; handle is 13 inches. Packed one-half dozen to the carton.

Values: | Exc. | V.G. | Good
| 75.00 | 60.00 | 45.00

Comment: *Values for old or new model of Haines Shingling Hatchet.*

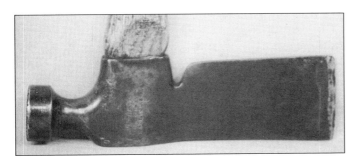

The head of this Haines Lathing Hatchet is 6 3/4 inches long. From T. Webster collection. Photo by D. Kowalski.

New No. WP401; Old No. F5352C. Haines Lathing Hatchet. Has thin blade, carefully milled cut head. Width of cut is 2 inches; handle is 13 inches. Packed one-half dozen to the carton.

Values: | Exc. | V.G. | Good
| 75.00 | 60.00 | 45.00

Comment: *Values for old or new model of Haines Lathing Hatchet.*

Underhill Hatchet Pattern

The true Underhill Pattern made with Winchester exactness, balance, heat-treating and finish. Full polished. Large square head. Milled cut face. 81 points.

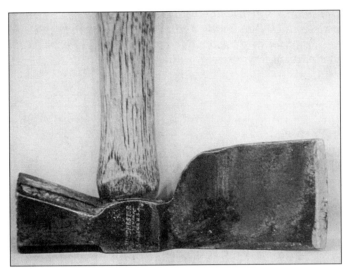

The head of this Underhill Lathing Hatchet is 6 1/8 inches long. From T. Webster collection. Photo by D. Kowalski.

New No. WP420; Old No. F5350C. Underhill Lathing Hatchet. Width of cut is 2 1/16 inches; handle is 13 inches. Packed one-half dozen to the carton.

Values:	Exc.	V.G.	Good
	75.00	60.00	45.00

Comment: *Values for old or new model of Underhill Lathing Hatchet.*

Winchester Standard Hatchet Patterns

Heads finely polished and finished in dull black rustless enamel. Top of poll, cutting and side edges polished. Packed one-half dozen to the carton.

Standard Half Pattern

The head of this Standard Half Pattern Hatchet is 7 1/8 inches long. From T. Webster collection. Photo by D. Kowalski.

New No.	Old No.	Blade Width
WBH1	F5316C	3 1/4 in.
WBH2	F5317C	3 5/8 in.
WBH3	F5322C	4 in.

Values:	Exc.	V.G.	Good
	75.00	60.00	45.00

Comment: *Values for old or new models of Standard Half Pattern Hatchet.*

Standard Shingling Pattern

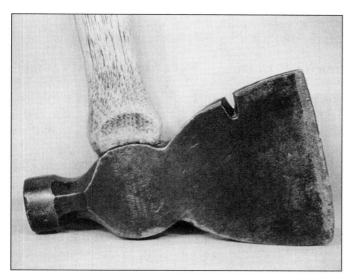

The head of this old model No. 5310 Standard Shingling Pattern Hatchet is 6 5/8 inches long. From T. Webster collection. Photo by D. Kowalski.

New No.	Old No.	Blade Width
WBS1	F5310C	3 1/2 in.
WBS2	F5311C	4 in.

The head of the new model WBS1 Standard Shingling Pattern Hatchet is 6 1/4 inches long. It also has metal cutaways not seen on the old Model 5310. From T. Webster collection. Photo by D. Kowalski.

Values:	Exc.	V.G.	Good
	75.00	60.00	45.00

Comment: *Values for old or new models of Standard Shingling Pattern Hatchet.*

Standard Broad Pattern

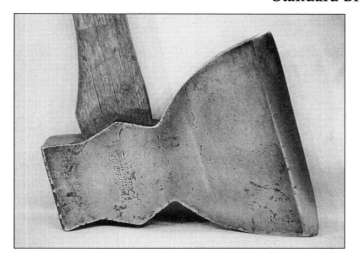

The head of the Standard Broad Pattern Hatchet is 6 1/8 inches long. From T. Webster collection. Photo by D. Kowalski.

Single Bevel.

New No.	Old No.	Blade Width	Handle Length
WBB1	F5340C	4 in.	14 in.
WBB2	F5341C	4 1/2 in.	15 in.
WBB3	F5342C	5 in.	16 in.
WBB4	F5343C	5 1/2 in.	16 in.

Double Bevel.

New No.	Old No.	Blade Width	Handle Length
WDBB1	F5380C	4 in.	14 in.
WDBB2	F5381C	4 1/2 in.	15 in.
WDBB3	F5382C	5 in.	16 in.
WDBB4	F5383C	5 1/2 in.	16 in.

Values:	Exc.	V.G.	Good
	75.00	60.00	45.00

Comment: *Values for old or new models of Standard Broad Pattern Hatchet.*

Standard Claw Pattern

Claw Patterns are exclusive Winchester design with tapered bevel, slotted fine enough to draw out small brads. Claw ends of striking poll are pitched to prevent striking when driving nails and are shaped to pull nails even when heads barely protrude from the surface.

New No.	Old No.	Blade Width	Handle Length
WBC1	F5330C	3 1/2 in.	13 in.
WBC2	F5331C	4 in.	13 1/2 in.

Values:	Exc.	V.G.	Good
	90.00	75.00	60.00

Comment: *Values for old or new models of Standard Claw Pattern Hatchet.*

The head of the Standard Claw Pattern Hatchet is 6 3/8 inches long. From T. Webster collection. Photo by D. Kowalski.

Standard Household Shingling Pattern

New No. WS10; Old No. F5360C. Plain poll. Head polished and finished in dull black Japan with striking poll and cutting edge bright polished. Plain nail slot. Blade width is 3 1/2 inches; handle is 13 1/2 inches long.

Values:	Exc.	V.G.	Good
	75.00	60.00	45.00

Comment: *Values for old or new models of Standard Household Shingling Pattern.*

The head of the Standard Household Shingling Pattern Hatchet is 6 1/8 inches long. From T. Webster collection. Photo by D. Kowalski.

Standard Rig Builders' Pattern

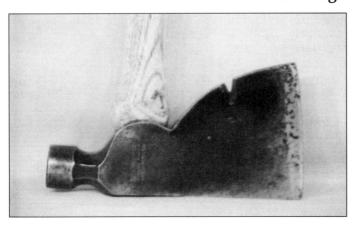

New No. WRBG; Old No. F5351C. Western type with octagon neck. Head and face accurately milled. 80 points. Undercut blade. Special flare-end handle, sure-grip nail slot. Blade width is 3 1/2 inches; handle is 17 inches long.

Values:	Exc.	V.G.	Good
	75.00	60.00	45.00

Comment: *Values for old or new model of Rig Builders' Pattern.*

The head of the Standard Rig Builders' Pattern Hatchet is 7 1/4 inches long. From T. Webster collection. Photo by D. Kowalski.

Standard Produce Pattern

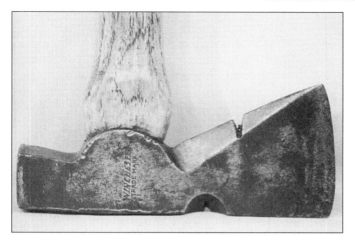

The head of the Standard Produce Pattern Hatchet is 5 3/8 inches long. From T. Webster collection. Photo by D. Kowalski.

Deep, well-balanced, square striking poll of special design. Two formed nail slots. Square checkered face. Special shaped eye.

New No.	Old No.	Blade Width	Head	Handle
WBGP10	F5355C	2 1/4 in.	17 oz.	13 in.
WBGP20	F5356C	2 1/2 in.	21 oz.	13 in.

Values:	**Exc.**	**V.G.**	**Good**
	75.00	60.00	45.00

Comment: *Values for old or new models of Standard Produce Pattern.*

Standard Box Hatchet

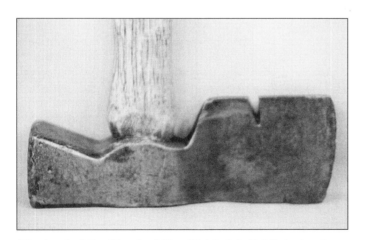

The head of the Standard Box Hatchet is 5 1/2 inches long. From T. Webster collection. Photo by D. Kowalski.

Another of the Winchester full-polished hatchets. Special shaped eye designed to prevent buckling. Has a deep, well-balanced, square striking poll. Checkered face accurately scored. Sure-grip nail slot. Blade width is 2 inches; handle is 13 inches long.

Values:	**Exc.**	**V.G.**	**Good**
	75.00	60.00	45.00

Comment: *Values for old or new models of Standard Box Hatchet.*

Winchester Hammers

All Winchester hammers have heads forged from high-grade steel scientifically heat-treated. They are tough and long wearing. Special attention is given to the distribution of weight to effect the proper "balance" and "hang." Handles are of selected hickory, expertly proportioned. Heads are securely fastened with the famous Winchester patented interlocking wedge.

Bell Face, Plain Neck, Curved Claw Pattern

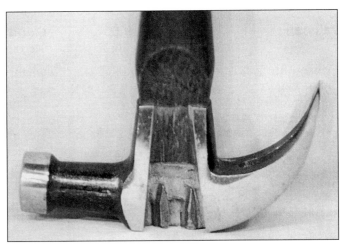

Cutaway model (No. 6008) of the Bell Face, Curved Claw Hammer is a rare example of this salesman's sample. From T. Webster collection. Photo by D. Kowalski.

Values:

Exc.	V.G.	Good
1,700.00	1,600.00	1,500.00

Comment: *Values for Cutaway models without box.*

Bell Face, Curved Claw Hammer. From T. Webster collection. Photo by D. Kowalski.

Adze eye. Bell face. Curved claw. Forged from special steel, carefully hardened and tempered. Full polished with dull black finish on poll, neck and under claws. Handles of selected hickory in either Winchester gray or white wax finish. Specially designed adze eye prevents buckling or cracking at the corners. Packed one-half dozen in a carton.

New No.	Old No.	Head Weight
W613	F6001C	7 oz.
W612	F6002C	13 oz.
W611 1/2	F6003C	16 oz.
W611	F6004C	20 oz.

Values:

Exc.	V.G.	Good
100.00	90.00	75.00

Comment: *Values for old or new models of Bell Face, Curved Claw Hammer.*

Axes, Hatchets and Hammers • 559

Octagon Head, Curved Claw Pattern

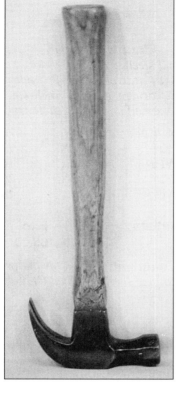

The Octagon Head, Curved Claw Hammer. From T. Webster collection. Photo by D. Kowalski.

Octagon pattern. Adze eye. Octagon striking poll and neck. Curved claw. Forged from special steel carefully hardened and tempered. Full polished head. Handles are of selected 'hickory with octagon hand-shaved neck in white wax or gray finish. Packed one in a carton.

New No.	Old No.	Head Weight
WP112	F6027C	14 oz.
WP110 1/2	F6028C	17 oz.

Same pattern with full-polished, nickel-plated head and black ebony finished handle.

W512	F6037C	14 oz.
W511 1/2	F6038C	17 oz.

Values: | Exc. | V.G. | Good
| 100.00 | 90.00 | 75.00

Comment: *Values for old or new models of Octagon Head, Curved Claw Hammer.*

Bell Face, Plain Neck, Straight Claw Pattern

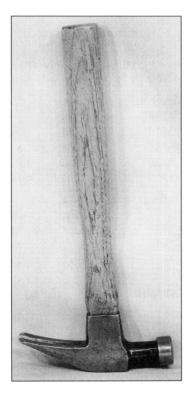

A Bell Face, Plain Neck, Straight Claw Hammer. From T. Webster collection. Photo by D. Kowalski.

Adze eye. Bell face. Straight claw. Forged from special steel, carefully hardened and tempered. Full polished. Dull black finish on poll, neck and under claws. Selected hickory handles. Finished in Winchester gray or white wax finish. One-half dozen in a carton.

New No.	Old No.	Head Weight
W411 1/2	F6013C	16 oz.
W411	F6014C	20 oz.

Values: | Exc. | V.G. | Good
| 120.00 | 110.00 | 90.00

Comment: *Values for old or new models of Bell Face, Plain Neck, Straight Claw Hammer.*

Plain Face, Angled Neck, Curved Claw

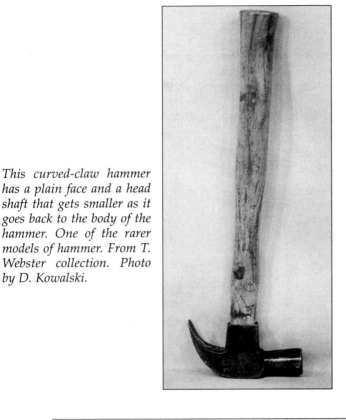

This curved-claw hammer has a plain face and a head shaft that gets smaller as it goes back to the body of the hammer. One of the rarer models of hammer. From T. Webster collection. Photo by D. Kowalski.

Adze eye. Plain face. Curved claws. Forged from special steel, carefully hardened and tempered. Full polished, with dull black finish under claws. Handles of selected hickory in either Winchester gray or white wax finish. One-half dozen in a carton.

New No.	Old No.	Head Weight
W2	F6022C	13 oz.
W1 1/2	F6023C	16 oz.
W1	F6024C	20 oz.
W0		28 oz.

Values:	Exc.	V.G.	Good
	165.00	145.00	120.00

Comment: *Values for old or new models of Plain Face, Angled Neck, Curved Claw Hammer.*

Machinists' Ball Pein Hammer

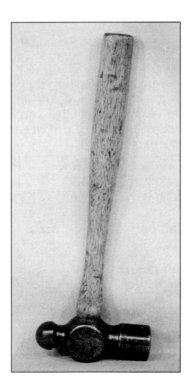

The Machinists' Ball Pein Hammer was produced in more models and weights than any other Winchester hammer. From T. Webster collection. Photo by D. Kowalski.

Forged from special steel, carefully hardened and tempered. Plain eye. Dull black finish with sides, pein and striking poll polished. Handles of selected hickory. Winchester gray or white wax finish. Packed six in a carton.

New No.	Old No.	Head Weight
WM5/0	F6200M	4 oz.
WM4/0	F6201M	6 oz.
WM3/0	F6202M	8 oz.
WM2/0	F6203M	12 oz.
WM0	F6204M	16 oz.

Packed four in a carton.

New No.	Old No.	Head Weight
WM1	F6205M	20 oz.
WM2	F6206M	24 oz.
WM3	F6207M	28 oz.
WM4	F6208M	32 oz.

Values:	Exc.	V.G.	Good
	110.00	100.00	85.00

Comment: *Values for old or new models of Machinists' Ball Pein Hammer.*

Machinists' Plain Eye Riveting Hammer

The Machinists' Plain Eye Riveting Hammer was manufactured in three sizes. The smallest one was sometimes referred to as a "tack" hammer and was used for hammering very small nails or tacks. From T. Webster collection. Photo by D. Kowalski.

Forged from special steel, carefully hardened and tempered. Plain eye. Full polished. Selected hickory handle. Winchester gray or white wax finish. Packed six per carton.

New No.	Old No.	Head Weight
WPR0	F621M	4 oz.
WPR1	F6212M	8 oz.
WPR3	F6213M	12 oz.

Values:	Exc.	V.G.	Good
	90.00	80.00	70.00

Comment: *Values for old or new models of Machinists' Plain Eye Riveting Hammer.*

Handles for Axes, Hatchets and Hammers

To meet the demand for replacement handles, we are offering high-grade handles such as are used in Winchester tools. These handles are turned from well-seasoned hickory and are correctly cut and shaped. Natural white, wax finish. Packed either two dozen to the crate, or one dozen to the carton or box.

Values:	Exc.	V.G.	Good
	175.00	150.00	125.00

Comment: *Winchester produced a variety of axe handles, small axe handles, hatchet handles, hammer handles, and machinist hammer handles. These handles have a Winchester decal on them. Values are for any types of labeled handles that have not been attached to a tool head.*

Winchester Draw Knives

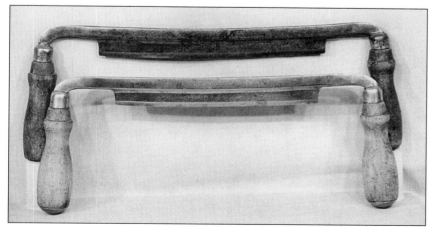

Draw Knives were used by lumberjacks to take the bark off trees. They're shown here in two sizes. The 9-inch version (top) has an actual blade length of 9 1/8 inches. The 8-inch knife has a blade length of 8 1/8 inches. From T. Webster collection. Photo by D. Kowalski.

Values:	Exc.	V.G.	Good
	175.00	150.00	125.00

Comment: *Values are for either size of Draw Knife.*

Winchester Small Pry Bar

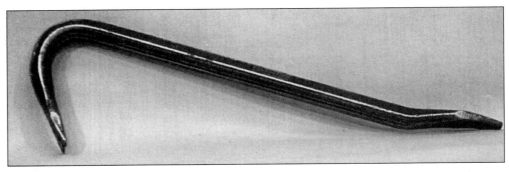

Pry Bars have never been shown in any Winchester Catalog. However, veteran collectors believe they would have been a natural additional product for a manufacturer of axes, hatchets and hammers. This version is 10 1/8 inches long from the long end to the outside edge of the curved end. It is also the only one known to have been discovered to date. From T. Webster collection. Photo by D. Kowalski.

Values:	Exc.	V.G.	Good
	400.00	350.00	300.00

Comment: *Values are only for this 10-inch version.*

Carpentry Tools
Saws, Planes, Levels, Rules, Squares, Braces and Bits

by David D. Kowalski

This chapter will be devoted to the bulk of the Winchester tools primarily involved in carpentry. However, we will start the next chapter with the wood chisels, then move into cold chisels and the other tools more generally associated with mechanics and metalworking.

Many of these carpentry tools are listed in Winchester catalogs with both old and new numbers. While we will note the style differences between old and new model designs if they seem of interest, the values for old and new number models are generally identical. If not, we will note that after the pertinent value charts.

We will maintain our general policy here, as well, of only giving model numbers in photo captions if we have actually seen the model number on a tool. However, a few exceptions come to mind. Winchester apparently never stamped the model number on the small pocket level, for example.

Dimensions for tools shown in photographs only apply to that pictured tool. There may be some differences in old and new models. There may also be some differences between actual tools produced and dimensions provided in catalogs. Winchester, after all, did not consider their tool specifications in catalogs to have the stature or sanctity of government specifications. Styles changed, improvements were made, molds were adjusted slightly.

Having said that, such facts should, once again, underscore the importance of carefully checking the authenticity of Winchester tools before purchasing them. Know your source. Get second opinions. And if the "deal" seems too good to be true, it probably is.

Carpenter's Pencil

Carpenter's Pencil made of strong, heavy lead for marking lumber plainly. Finished in Winchester gray with red bevels. Packed one-half gross in a carton. No. 1915 - 7 inches; No. 1917 - 9 inches.

Values:

	Exc.	V.G.	Good
	140.00	120.00	90.00

Comment: *Values for one Pencil, either size.*

Lumber Crayon

Lumber Crayon, black. From T. Webster collection. Photo by D. Kowalski.

Hexagon Lumber Crayon, paper covered. Measures 1/2 in. x 5 3/4 in. Made of finely ground composition; molded and pressed into hexagon form by hydraulic pressure. Colored with high-grade dyes; will not rub or wash off; will mark clearly on wet or dry lumber, also on steel or iron. Packed one-quarter gross in a cardboard box; three gross in a case. No. W61 - Black; No. W21 - Blue; No. W20 - Red.

Values:

	Exc.	V.G.	Good
	375.00	350.00	300.00

Comment: *Values for one Crayon, any color.*

Saws

Old Trusty Hand and Rip Saws

The Winchester idea of the finest development of the hand saw is expressed in this new series to which that expressive name applied by countless numbers of owners to their Winchester guns, "Old Trusty," has been most appropriately given.

The blades of "Old Trusty" saws are made of a steel of special analysis which contains certain alloys which give exceptional toughness combined with keen edge-holding qualities. All blades are hardened and tempered under electrical control insuring uniformity of temper. They are also expertly taper-ground and smithed. The teeth are accurately filed, set and sharpened by hand. The blades are polished to a full-mirror finish. Handles are selected air-dried walnut, full carved, varnished and hand polished. Fastened to blade with five special nickel-plated telescopic screws. Each blade etched with standard Winchester trade mark and special Old Trusty design.

Straight Back. No. W45/26 - Length of blade is 26 in.; Points to the inch; 7, 8, 9, or 10.
No. W45/24 - Length of blade is 24 in.; Points to the inch; 7, 8, 9, or 10. Each saw encased in paper scabbard and packed in individual carton.

Values:

	Exc.	V.G.	Good
	800.00	750.00	650.00

Comment: *Values for either 24-inch or 26-inch blade, and any number of points.*

Skew back. No. W40/26 - Length of blade is 26 in.; Points to the inch; 7, 8, 9, 10, or 11.
Skew back. No. W45/24 - Length of blade is 24 in.; Points to the inch; 7, 8, 9, 10, or 11.
Skew back, Rip Saw. No. W40R/26 - Length of blade is 26 in.; Points to the inch; 5, 5 1/2, 6. Each saw encased in paper scabbard and packed in individual carton.

Values:

	Exc.	V.G.	Good
	650.00	550.00	400.00

Comment: *Values for either 24-inch or 26-inch blade, skew back, and any number of points ("Rip" version has fewer points per inch). Double these values for a saw with original scabbard and carton as seen in the following example.*

Carpentry Tools • 565

A very rare "Old Trusty" skew back with the individual box and paper scabbard that it came in. This saw was probably never used. From T. Webster collection. Photo by D. Kowalski.

Logo on paper sheath of previous "Old Trusty" skew back. From T. Webster collection. Photo by D. Kowalski.

Logo on blade of previous "Old Trusty" skew back. From T. Webster collection. Photo by D. Kowalski.

Hand, Rip and Panel Saws

All Winchester saws are expertly made from high-grade steel by experienced saw makers. They have carefully set and filed teeth, are carefully ground and will meet the approval of particular workmen. Blades are of high-quality extra-spring steel. Taper ground and tempered. Full polished and etched. Hand filed and set. Perfection pattern handles, finely carved and varnished. Rip and hand saws fastened with five improved brass screws, panel saws with four. Packed four per carton.

Skew Back Saws

No.	Type	Blade	Points/inch
W8/24	Panel	24 in.	7, 8, 9, 10, 11
W8/22	Panel	22 in.	9, 10, 11
W8/20	Panel	20 in.	9, 10
W8/18	Panel	18 in.	9, 10, 11

Skew Back

No.	Type	Blade	Points/inch
W8R28	Rip	28 in.	5, 5 1/2, 6
W8R26	Rip	26 in.	5, 5 1/2, 6
W8/26	Hand	26 in.	7, 8, 9, 10, 11

Values:

	Exc.	V.G.	Good
	100.00	80.00	55.00

Comment: Values for any skew back; rip, hand or panel, and any number of points. Add 25 percent for 18-inch length.

Ship Saws

Skew Back

No.	Type	Blade	Points/inch
W8S	Ship	26 in.	8, 9, 10

Values:	Exc.	V.G.	Good
	125.00	100.00	75.00

Comment: *Values for either straight back or skew back ship saw; these had narrower tip than standard models.*

Straight Back

No.	Type	Blade	Points/inch
W16S	Ship	26 in.	8, 9, 10

Straight Back Saws

No.	Type	Blade	Points/inch
W16/24	Panel	24 in.	7, 8, 9, 10, 11
W16/22	Panel	22 in.	9, 10, 11
W16/20	Panel	20 in.	9, 10, 11

Values:	Exc.	V.G.	Good
	100.00	80.00	55.00

Comment: *Values for any straight back; rip, hand or panel, and any number of points.*

Straight Back

No.	Type	Blade	Points/inch
W16R28	Rip	28 in.	5, 5 1/2, 6
W16/26	Hand	26 in.	7, 8, 9, 10, 11

Some of the Model 16 straight back saws had "starter knicks" on the top edge of the blade. From T. Webster collection. Photo by D. Kowalski.

No. 13 Grade, Straight Back

Straight Back. No. 13 Grade. A good serviceable saw of high-grade steel. Plain hardwood handles, varnished edges. Four brass screws.

No.	Type	Blade	Points/inch
W13R26	Rip	26 in.	5, 5 1/2, 6
W13H26	Hand	26 in.	7, 8, 9, 10, 11

Values: Exc. 90.00   V.G. 75.00   Good 55.00

Comment: *Values for either style and any number of points. This was originally Winchester's "economy" saw. Shows "starter knick" on top edge of blade.*

Cross Cut Saws, Two Man (Shown without Handles)

Perforated Lance Tooth. Made of high-grade crucible steel. Polished blade. Four gauges thinner on back than at tooth edge.

No.	Length	Center Width
W4025 1/2	5 1/2 ft.	5 3/4 in.
W4026	6 ft.	6 in.
W4026 1/2	6 1/2 ft.	6 3/8 in.

Values: Exc. 750.00   V.G. 700.00   Good 600.00

Comment: *Values for any length.*

Narrow Perforated Lance Tooth. Made of high-grade crucible steel. Polished blade; made two gauges thinner on back than at tooth edge. Width at center - 3 3/4 inches.

No.	Length
W2055	5 ft.
W2055 1/2	5 1/2 ft.
W2056	6 ft.

Values: Exc. 900.00   V.G. 850.00   Good 750.00

Comment: *Values for any length.*

Perfection Lance Tooth. Made of high-grade crucible steel. Polished blade. Four gauges thinner on back than at tooth edge. Full patent ground.

No.	Length	Center Width
W1085	5 ft.	6 in.
W1085 1/2	5 1/2 ft.	6 1/4 in.
W1086	6 ft.	6 1/2 in.

Values: Exc. 750.00 V.G. 700.00 Good 600.00

Comment: *Values for any length.*

Western Felling Tooth. Made of high-grade tool steel, crescent ground, polished and etched. Special lance teeth carefully filed and set. Four gauges thinner on back than at tooth edge. Cut ends.

No.	Length
W4036	6 ft.
W4036 1/2	6 1/2 ft.
W4037	7 ft.

Values: Exc. 750.00 V.G. 700.00 Good 600.00

Comment: *Values for any length.*

Champion Tooth. Made of highest-grade crucible steel. Four gauges thinner on back than at tooth edge.

No.	Length	Center Width
W1065	5 ft.	6 3/4 in.
W1065 1/2	5 1/2 it-	7 in.
W1066	6 ft.	7 1/4 in.

Values: Exc. 750.00 V.G. 700.00 Good 600.00

Comment: *Values for any length.*

Narrow Champion Tooth. Highest-grade crucible steel. Blade is polished. Width at center - 3 1/4 inches.

No.	Length
W2015	5 ft.
W2015 1/2	5 1/2 ft.
W2016	6 ft.

Values:	**Exc.**	**V.G.**	**Good**
	900.00	850.00	750.00

Comment: *Values for any length.*

Cross Cut Saws, One Man

Perforated Lance Tooth. Made of high-grade crucible steel. Polished blade. Varnished handle. Four screws. Packed with supplementary handle. Taper ground.

No.	Length	Butt Width
W3044	4 ft.	7 5/8 in.
W3044 1/2	4 1/2 ft.	7 3/4 in.
W3045	5 ft.	7 7/8 in.

Values:	**Exc.**	**V.G.**	**Good**
	700.00	600.00	500.00

Comment: *Values for any length.*

Champion Tooth. One Man Cross Cut. The supplemental handles are not on this example but you can see the holes drilled for them, both front and rear. From Tom Webster collection. Photo by D. Kowalski.

Champion Tooth. Polished high-grade crucible steel blade. Varnished-edge handle. Complete with supplementary handle. Taper ground.

No.	Length	Butt Width
W3003	3 ft.	6 1/8 in.
W3003 1/2	3 1/2 ft.	6 1/4 in.
W3004	4 ft.	6 3/4 in.

Values:	**Exc.**	**V.G.**	**Good**
	600.00	500.00	400.00

Cross Cut Saw Handles

No. W11. Climax reversible. Malleable iron bolt and nut. Natural finish. Pair packed individually. Length - 13 1/2 in.; maximum diameter - 1 3/8 in.

No. W122. Loop rod through handle making positive connection with blade and overcoming any lost motion. Natural finish. Pair packed individually. Length - 8 in.; maximum diameter - 1 1/4 in.

No. W800. Loop Pattern. Malleable iron ferrule, washer and loop are painted red. Natural Finish. Pair packed individually. Length - 13 1/2 in.; maximum diameter - 1 1/4 in.

No. W1100. Heavy Climax Reversible Pattern. Malleable iron sheaths, clasp and thumbnut are painted red. Natural Finish. Pair packed individually. Length - 15 1/4 in.; maximum diameter - 1 1/4 in.

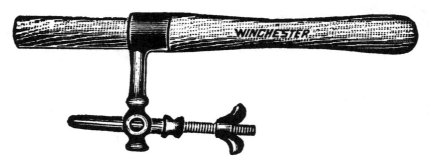

No. W900. Universal Reversible. May be used in four positions. Double grip. Heavy malleable iron casting-loop rod. Pair packed individually. Length - 14 1/2 in.; maximum diameter - 1 7/16 in.

Values:	Exc.	V.G.	Good
	125.00	110.00	85.00

Comment: *Values for any model.*

Wood Saw

A rare 32-inch blade next to a 30-inch saw frame. A 32-inch frame has never been found to date. Winchester made both gray enameled frames and stained maple frames. But purchaser had option to change blades from original set-up. From T. Webster collection. Photo by D. Kowalski.

No. W75. *Selected maple frame. Enameled gray. Extra-thin back, improved common-tooth, straight-breast blade; 30 in. x 2 3/8 in. wide. Polished. Jumbo tinned rod. No. W75/32 - 32 in. blade.*

No. W80. *Selected maple frame. Enameled gray. Thin-back, polished champion blade, 30 in. x 2 3/8 in. wide. Polished. Jumbo tinned rod.*

No. W85. *Maple frame. Stained and varnished dark mahogany. Round-breasted, extra-thin back, blued blade, 30 in. x 1 3/4 in. wide. Duplex rod.*

Values:	Exc.	V.G.	Good
	150.00	135.00	100.00

Comment: *Values for any style of 30-inch frame and blade. Add 200 percent for 32-inch frame and blade.*

Wood Saw Blades

No. W25. *Made of crucible steel, patent ground and tempered. Set and sharpened.*

No.	Dimensions
W25	30 in. x 2 3/8 in. Improved, polished
W25/32	32 in. x 2 3/8 in. Improved, polished

No. W26. *30 in. x 1 3/4 in. Narrow, round-breasted blade, blued.*

No. W27. *30 in. x 2 3/8 in. Wide, round-breasted blade, blued.*

572 • *Carpentry Tools*

No. W28.   30 in. x 2 3/8 in. Champion tooth, Polished.

Values:	Exc.	V.G.	Good
	50.00	45.00	35.00

Comment: *Values for any style of 30-inch blade. Add 100 percent for 32-inch blade.*

Saw Kit

Saw Kit. Four blades, handle and canvas case. From Tom Webster collection. Photo by D. Kowalski.

No. W201. A combination of blades that provides a handy kit for the practical mechanic, householder and farmer. Made of highest-grade crucible spring steel. Adjustable beechwood varnished handle, with patented tightening lever. Packed in a durable canvas case. Old No. F2182B. Contains the following assortment of blades:

14 inch Compass Saw
16 inch Special Blade
18 inch Plumber's Blade
20 inch Hand Saw

Values:	Exc.	V.G.	Good
	600.00	500.00	450.00

Comment: *Values for complete set with case.*

Nest of Saws

No. W96. Consists of hardwood handle fitted with nickel-plated screw, together with three interchangeable blades: one 10-inch keyhole blade; one 14-inch compass blade; and one 18-inch pruning blade. Old No. F2181B. Packed three to a carton.

Values:	Exc.	V.G.	Good
	350.00	300.00	250.00

Comment: *Values for complete set.*

Keyhole Saw

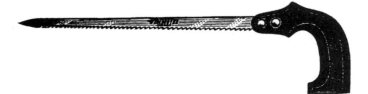

No. W95/10. Length is 10 inches. Narrow, very flexible blade made of fine steel. Old No. F1801B. Packed one-half dozen in a carton.

Values:	Exc.	V.G.	Good
	75.00	65.00	50.00

Carpentry Tools • 573

Back Saw

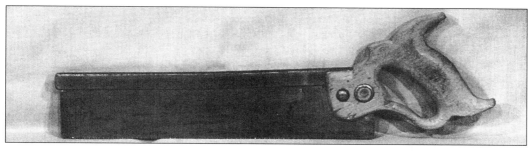

Back Saw. This 12-inch model has overall length of 16 1/2 inches. From T. Webster collection. Photo by D. Kowalski. Back Saw has beech handle. Polished, varnished edges. Blued back. Packed four in a box.

New No.	Old No.	Length
W44/10	F2301B	10 in.
W44/12	F2302B	12 in.
W44/14	F2303B	14 in.

Values: Exc. 85.00   V.G. 75.00   Good 60.00

Comment: *Values for any length.*

Compass Saw

Compass Saw. This 14-inch model (No. 1902) has actual blade length of 13 3/4 inches and overall length of 19 1/4 inches. From T. Webster collection. Photo by D. Kowalski.
Compass Saw is similar to keyhole saw, but with wider blade. Refined crucible steel. Varnished applewood handle. Packed six in a carton.

New No.	Old No.	Length
W93/12	F1901B	12 in.
W93/14	F1902B	14 in.
W93/16	F1903B	16 in.

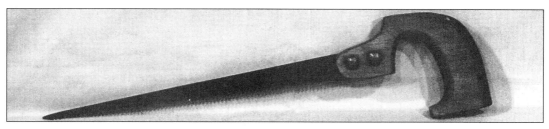

Compass Saw (No. 2001) has actual blade length of 11 5/8 inches and overall length of 17 1/4 inches. From T. Webster collection. Photo by D. Kowalski.
Compass Saw has polished crucible steel blades. Handle is beech. Varnished edges. Packed six in a carton.

New No.	Old No.	Length
W86/12	F2001B	12 in.
WS6/14	F2002B	14 in.

Values: Exc. 75.00   V.G. 65.00   Good 50.00

Comment: *Values for either style Compass Saw, any length.*

Coping Saw

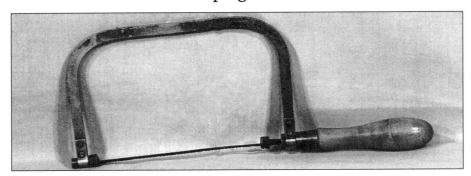

Coping Saw shows "Winchester" logo clearly visible across top of frame. From T. Webster collection. Photo by D. Kowalski.
No. W50. Coping Saw has heavy nickel-plated steel frame. Hardwood handle. Blade is tightened by turning handle, and may be adjusted for any angle. Complete with one W6 1/2 blade. Packed two in a box. Old No. F2188B.

Values:	Exc.	V.G.	Good
	75.00	70.00	60.00

Hack Saws

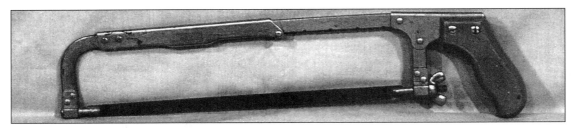

Hack Saw with pistol grip and 12 1/8" blade accommodated by adjustable frame. From T. Webster collection. Photo by D. Kowalski.

No. W48. Adjustable, pistol-grip frame that is nickel-plated and buffed. Handle is molded rubber composition. Frame adjustable to take blades from 8 to 12 inches and is strongly made with riveted sockets. Old No. F3902B.

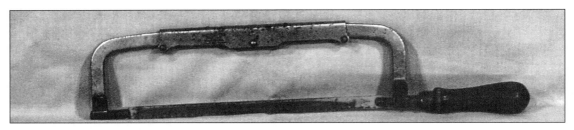

Hack Saw with straight grip (No. 3602); this one with 10 3/8" blade and adjustable frame. From T. Webster collection. Photo by D. Kowalski.

No. W188A. Adjustable, straight-grip frame made of strong steel, nickel-plated and buffed. Hardwood handle stained and varnished with mahogany finish. Regular-pattern extension frame that will take blades from 8 to 12 inches. Screw handle adjustment. Old No. F3602B.

No. W188. Hack Saw has solid frame, nickel-plated and buffed. Mahogany finished handle. Screw handle adjustment. Made for 8-inch blade only. Old No. F3801B.

Values:	Exc.	V.G.	Good
	60.00	55.00	45.00

Comment: *Values for any style Hack Saw.*

Kitchen Saw

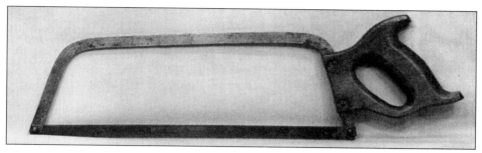

Kitchen Saw (No. 2901) is 14-inch model. From T. Webster collection. Photo by D. Kowalski.
Kitchen Saw has flat back; polished steel frame; varnished beechwood handle. Handle fastened to frame by two brass screws.

New No.	Old No.	Size
W2/14	F2901B	14 in.
W2/16	F2902B	16 in.

Values:	Exc.	V.G.	Good
	125.00	100.00	75.00

Butcher Saw

Butcher Saw with old-style frame. Some models have new-style frame similar to Kitchen Saw. From T. Webster collection. Photo by D. Kowalski.
Butcher Saw comes with beechwood handle with varnished edges. Brass screws. Frame is flat; 1 in. x 1/4 in. Depth from inside center edge of 24-inch frame to tooth edge of blade is 5 inches. Blade finished bright; 5/8 in. wide.

New No.	Old No.	Size
W15/18	F2851B	18 in.
W15/20	F2852B	20 in.
W15/22	F2853B	22 in.
W15/24	F2854B	24 in.

Values:	Exc.	V.G.	Good
	125.00	100.00	75.00

Coil Saw Blade

Coil Saw Blade comes in 25-toot length. Packed individually.

New No.	Old No.	Size
WF 3/4	F2184B	3/4 in. wide
WF 5/8	F2185B	5/8 in. wide

Values:	Exc.	V.G.	Good
	160.00	145.00	125.00

Comment: *Values for either width.*

Planes

Winchester planes embody three important essentials that mean more sales and more satisfied customers. Efficient, high-quality tempered cutters, made in accordance with the formulas developed by Winchester engineers as a result of Winchester experience in heat treatment of steel. Their outstanding features are rigidity which averts chattering, and quick, accurate, easy adjustment.

Wood Bottom Planes

Comparisons of bottoms of Wood Bottom Smooth Plane (No. 3040) and the handled version (No. 3041). Plane on bottom is model without handle; base measures 9 1/4 in. long; 2 5/8 in. at widest part, and 2 in. at narrowest part. Plane on top is handled model; base measures 8 3/4 in. long; 2 5/8 in. at widest part, and 1 3/4 in. at narrowest part. From T. Webster collection. Photo by D. Kowalski.

Wood Bottom Smooth Plane (No. 3040). From T. Webster collection. Photo by D. Kowalski.

No. W24. Wood Bottom Smooth Plane. Screw adjustment. Iron frame. Beechwood bottom. Highest-grade crucible steel cutter. Black enamel frame. Wood sides and knob handle varnished. Cutters oil-tempered and sharpened; ready for use. Old No. F3040C. Length 9 in.; Cutter 2 in. Weight 2 3/4 lbs. Packed one in a carton.

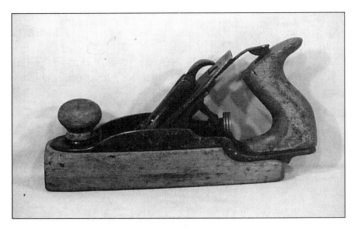

Wood Bottom Smooth Plane, handled (No. 3041). From T. Webster collection. Photo by D. Kowalski.

No. W35. Wood Bottom Smooth Plane (Handled). Screw adjustment. Iron frame. Beechwood bottom. Highest-grade crucible steel cutter. Black enamel frame. Sides and knob handle varnished. Cutters oil-tempered and sharpened; ready for use. Old No. F3041C. Length 9 in.; Cutter 2 in. Weight 3 1/4 lbs. Packed one in a carton.

Values:	**Exc.**	**V.G.**	**Good**
	100.00	85.00	65.00

Comment: *Values for either handled or unhandled, old or new model.*

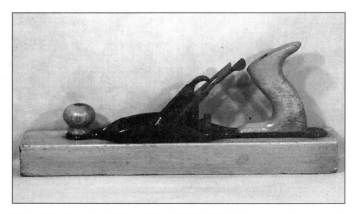

Wood Bottom Jack Plane (No. 3045). Model number is stamped into wood on top front of plane. Base is 15 in. long x 2 3/4 in. wide. From T. Webster collection. Photo by D. Kowalski.

Carpentry Tools • 577

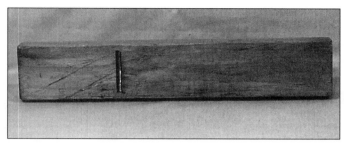

The bottom of the Wood Bottom Jack Plane (No. 3045) is perfectly rectangular (no taper front to back). From T. Webster collection. Photo by D. Kowalski.

No. W26. Wood Bottom Jack Plane. Screw adjustment, Iron frame. Beechwood bottom. Highest-grade crucible steel cutter. Black enamel frame. Sides and knob handle varnished. Cutters oil-tempered and sharpened; ready for use. Old No. F3045C. Length 15 in.; Cutter 2 in. Weight 4 1/4 lbs. Packed one in a carton.

Values:	Exc.	V.G.	Good
	100.00	85.00	65.00

Comment: *Values for either old or new model.*

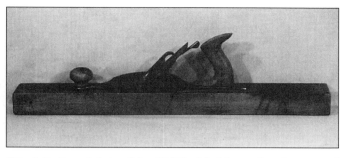

Wood Bottom Jointer (No. 3055). Model number is stamped into wood on top front of plane. Base is rectangular and measures 24 1/16 in. long x 3 3/16 in. wide. From T. Webster collection. Photo by D. Kowalski.

No. W31. Wood Bottom Jointer. Screw adjustment. Iron frame. Beechwood bottom. Highest-grade crucible steel cutter. Black enamel frame. Sides and knob handle varnished. Cutters are oil-tempered and sharpened; ready for use. Old No. F3055C. Length 21 in.; Cutter 2 3/8 in. Weight 6 5/8 lbs. Packed one in a carton.

Values:	Exc.	V.G.	Good
	100.00	85.00	65.00

Comment: *Values for either old or new model.*

Iron Planes (Large)

All large iron planes available with both corrugated and smooth bottoms.

Wood Bottom Fore Plane (No. 3050). Model number is stamped into wood on top front of plane. Base is rectangular and measures 18 1/8 in. long x 3 1/8 in. wide. From T. Webster collection. Photo by D. Kowalski.

No. W28. Wood Bottom Fore Plane. Screw adjustment. Iron frame. Beechwood bottom. Highest-grade crucible steel cutter. Black enamel frame. Sides and knob handle varnished. Cutters oil-tempered and sharpened; ready for use. Old No. F3050C. Length 18 in.; Cutter 2 3/8 in. Weight 5 3/4 lbs. Packed one in a carton.

Values:	Exc.	V.G.	Good
	100.00	85.00	65.00

Comment: *Values for either old or new model.*

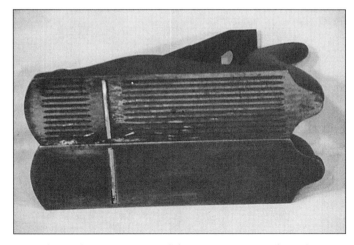

Top plane shows corrugated bottom. Bottom plane is same basic model with smooth bottom. From T. Webster collection. Photo by D. Kowalski.

Iron Bench Plane (No. 3206). The largest corrugated model in this series. Base measures 10 7/8 in. long x 2 7/8 in. wide. From T. Webster collection. Photo by D. Kowalski.

Iron Bench Plane. Screw adjustment. Iron frame. Highest-grade crucible steel cutter. Handle and knob varnished. Cutters oil-tempered and sharpened; ready for use. Packed one in a carton.

Smooth Bottom:

New No.	Old No.	Length	Cutter	Weight
W3	F3004C	8 in.	1 3/4 in.	3 1/4 lbs.
W4	F3005C	9 in.	2 in.	4 lbs.
W4 1/2	F3006C	10 in.	2 3/8 in.	5 1/8 lbs.

Corrugated Bottom:

New No.	Old No.	Length	Cutter	Weight
W3/C	F3204C	8 in.	1 3/4 in.	3 lbs.
W4/C	F3205C	9 in.	2 in.	3 3/4 lbs.
W4 1/2	F3206C	10 in.	2 3/8 in.	5 1/4 lbs.

Values: Exc.   V.G.   Good
                 85.00   75.00   50.00

Comment: *Values for either old or new models, smooth or corrugated bottoms.*

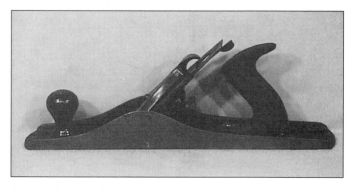

Iron Jack Plane (No. 3011). The largest smooth model in this series. Base measures 15 in. long x 2 3/4 in. wide. From T. Webster collection. Photo by D. Kowalski.

Logo and design comparisons between the same size old and new models of Iron Jack Plane. The New No. W5/C on left has corrugated bottom (and does not have the "C" after model number on plane). The Old No. 3010 on right is a smooth bottom model that shows a higher, slimmer grip knob; the "Winchester" logo is raised bronze-colored letters inside a black, recessed panel. The newer model (W5/C) on left has "Winchester" on top line and "Trade Mark" on bottom line inside panel that has been painted red. From T. Webster collection.

Iron Jack Plane. Screw adjustment. Iron frame. Highest-grade crucible steel cutter. Handle and knob varnished. Cutters are oil-tempered and sharpened; ready for use. Packed one in a carton.

Smooth Bottom:

New No.	Old No.	Length	Cutter	Weight
W5	F3010C	14 in.	2 in.	5 1/2 lbs.
W5 1/2	F3011C	15 in.	2 1/4 in.	6 lbs.

Corrugated Bottom:

New No.	Old No.	Length	Cutter	Weight
W5/C	F3025C	14 in.	2 in.	5 3/8 lbs.
W5 1/2C	F3026C	15 in.	2 1/4 in.	6 1/8 lbs.

Values: Exc.   V.G.   Good
                 85.00   75.00   50.00

Comment: *Values for either old or new models, smooth or corrugated bottoms.*

Carpentry Tools • 579

Iron Fore Plane (No. W6/C). The "C" not stamped as part of model on this plane. Base measures 18 in. long x 2 7/8 in. wide. From T. Webster collection. Photo by D. Kowalski.

Iron Fore Plane. Screw adjustment. Iron frame. Highest-grade crucible steel cutter. Handle and knob varnished. Cutters are oil-tempered and sharpened; ready for use. Packed one in a carton.

Smooth Bottom:

New No.	Old No.	Length	Cutter	Weight
W6	F3015C	18 in.	2 3/8 in.	7 3/8 lbs.

Corrugated Bottom:

| W6/C | F3030C | 18 in. | 2 3/8 in. | 7 1/8 lbs. |

Values: Exc. 85.00 V.G. 75.00 Good 50.00

Comment: *Values for either old or new models, smooth or corrugated bottoms.*

Iron Jointer Plane (No. 3035) has corrugated bottom; the "C" not stamped as part of model on this plane. Base measures 21 7/8 in. long x 2 7/8 in. wide. From T. Webster collection. Photo by D. Kowalski.

Jointer. Screw adjustment. Iron frame. Highest-grade crucible steel cutter. Handle and knob varnished. Cutters oil-tempered and sharpened; ready for use. Packed one in a carton.

Smooth Bottom:

New No.	Old No.	Length	Cutter	Weight
W7	F3020C	22 in.	2 3/8 in.	7 3/4 lbs.

Corrugated Bottom:

| W7/C | F3035C | 22 in. | 2 3/8 in. | 7 1/2 lbs. |

Values: Exc. 85.00 V.G. 75.00 Good 50.00

Comment: *Values for either old or new models, smooth or corrugated bottoms.*

Iron Planes (Small)

No. W65. Low Angle Block Plane. Screw adjustment. Cutter made of highest-grade crucible steel. Cutter oil-tempered and sharpened; ready for use. Packed one in a carton.

New No.	Old No.	Length	Cutter	Weight
W65	F3086C	7 in.	1 5/8 in.	1 5/8 lbs.

Nickel-Plated:

| W60 | F3087C | 6 in. | 1 3/8 in. | 1 1/2 lbs. |

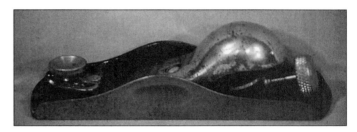

Nickel-plated Low Angle Block Plane (No. W60) shows "65" stamp on body even though it has the nickel-plated parts of the "W60." From T. Webster collection. Photo by D. Kowalski.

Values: Exc. 100.00 V.G. 85.00 Good 65.00

Comment: *Values for either old or new model, either version.*

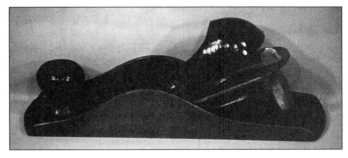

This version of the Low Angle Block Plane (No. 220) has no finger "indents" on side of body. Also has locking arm under handle. From T. Webster collection. Photo by D. Kowalski.

Low Angle Block Plane. Japanned handle. Polished trim. Screw adjustment. Cutter made of highest-grade crucible steel. Cutter oil-tempered and sharpened; ready for use. Packed one in a carton.

New No.	Old No.	Length	Cutter	Weight
W220	F3090C	7 1/2 in.	1 5/8 in.	1 1/2 lbs.

Values: Exc. 100.00 V.G. 85.00 Good 65.00

Comment: *Values for either old or new model.*

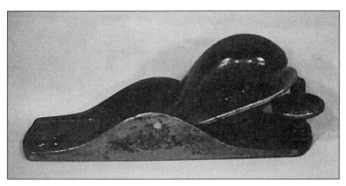

This short model of the Low Angle Block Plane (No. 103) has actual body length of 5 3/8 inches. From T. Webster collection. Photo by D. Kowalski.

Low Angle Block Plane. Japanned handle. Polished trim. Screw adjustment. Cutter made of highest-grade crucible steel. Cutter oil-tempered and sharpened; ready for use. Packed one in a carton.

New No.	Old No.	Length	Cutter	Weight
W103	F3091C	5 1/2 in.	1 3/8 in.	1 lb.

Values:	Exc.	V.G.	Good
	100.00	85.00	65.00

Comment: *Values for either old or new model.*

Low Angle Block Plane. Japanned finish. Cutter made of highest-grade crucible steel. Cutter oil-tempered and sharpened; ready for use. Packed one in a carton.

New No.	Old No.	Length	Cutter	Weight
W102	F3093C	5 1/2 in.	1 3/8 in.	1 lb.

Values:	Exc.	V.G.	Good
	100.00	85.00	65.00

Comment: *Values for either old or new model.*

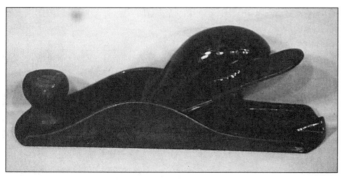

Low Angle Block Plane (No. 110) has actual body length of 7 1/4 inches. Note small raised notch at back of base. From T. Webster collection. Photo by D. Kowalski.

Low Angle Block Plane. Japanned handle. Polished sides. Cutter made of highest-grade crucible steel. Cutter has been oil-tempered and sharpened; ready for use. Packed one in a carton.

New No.	Old No.	Length	Cutter	Weight
W110	F3092C	7 1/2 in.	1 5/8 in.	1 1/2 lbs.

Values:	Exc.	V.G.	Good
	100.00	85.00	65.00

Comment: *Values for either old or new model.*

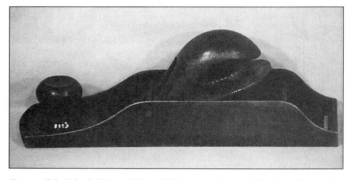

Reversible Block Plane (No. 130) has no finger "indents" on side of body and a more substantial body than the previous "small" planes. From T. Webster collection. Photo by D. Kowalski.

Reversible Block Plane. Japanned handle. Polished sides. Cutters may be reversed for planing in close corners. Cutters are made of high-grade crucible steel; oil-tempered and sharpened; ready for use. Packed one in a carton.

New No.	Old No.	Length	Cutter	Weight
W130	F3094C	7 3/4 in.	1 5/8 in.	1 1/2 lbs.

Values:	Exc.	V.G.	Good
	100.00	85.00	65.00

Comment: *Values for either old or new model.*

Knuckle Joint, Adjustable Mouth Plane. Screw adjustment, nickel-plated. Highly polished all steel. Cutters are high-grade crucible steel; oil-tempered and sharpened; ready for use. Patented side adjustment for cutter. Packed one in a carton.

New No.	Old No.	Length	Cutter	Weight
W18	F3085C	6 in.	1 5/8 in.	1 1/2 lbs.
W19	F3089C	7 in.	1 5/8 in.	1 5/8 lbs.

Values:	Exc.	V.G.	Good
	100.00	85.00	65.00

Comment: *Values for either old or new models.*

Adjustable Mouth Plane. Screw adjustment. Highly polished trimmings. Patented side adjustment for exact adjustment of the cutter with face of plane. Cutters are high-grade crucible steel; oil-tempered and sharpened; ready for use. Packed one in a carton.

New No.	Old No.	Length	Cutter	Weight
W9 1/2	F3083C	6 in.	1 5/8 in.	1 1/2 lbs.
W15	F3084C	7 in.	1 5/8 in.	1 5/8 lbs.

Values:	Exc.	V.G.	Good
	100.00	85.00	65.00

Comment: *Values for either old or new models.*

Fillister

Filister Plane (No. 3201) is the older model and measures 10 inches from front edge of base to bottom back edge of handle. From T. Webster collection. Photo by D. Kowalski.

Filister (No. W78) is the newer model showing more ornate and refined handle design and no front peg on body. It measures 10 5/8 inches from front edge of base to bottom back edge of handle flair. From T. Webster collection. Photo by D. Kowalski.

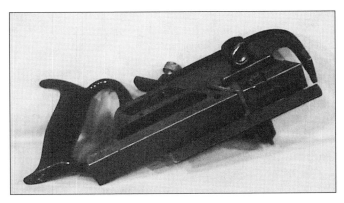

Filister (No. W78) showing the back side and bottom. From T. Webster collection. Photo by D. Kowalski.

Fillister. Japanned finish. Polished trimmings. Two seats for cutters. Depth gauge and spur, and removable arm and fence. Packed one in a carton.

New No.	Old No.	Length	Cutter	Weight
W78	F3201C	8 1/2 in.	1 1/2 in.	3 5/8 lbs.

Values:	Exc.	V.G.	Good
	350.00	300.00	225.00

Comment: *Values for either old or new models.*

Dado

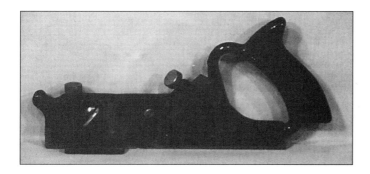

Dado (No. 3063) is the widest of four models. It measures 1 inch wide and 9 7/8 inches from front edge of base to bottom back edge of handle. From T. Webster collection. Photo by D. Kowalski.

Back side of Dado (No. 3063) showing the oak leaf pattern common to all four sizes. From T. Webster collection. Photo by D. Kowalski.

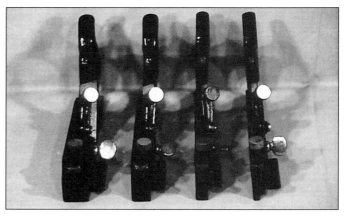

Dados, all four widths, from left: 1 inch, 3/4 inch, 1/2 inch, 1/4 inch. From T. Webster collection. Photo by D. Kowalski.

Dado. Cutter of highest-grade crucible steel. Depth gauge and two spurs. Cutter plane is 1/4 inch wide. Japanned finish. Polished trimmings. Packed one in a carton.

New No.	Old No.	Length	Cutter	Weight
W39 1/4	F3060C	8 in.	1/4 in.	2 lbs.
W39 1/2	F3061C	8 in.	1/2 in.	1 7/8 lbs.
W39 3/4	F3062C	8 in.	3/4 in.	2 1/4 lbs.
W39/1	F3063C	8 in.	1 in.	2 1/2 lbs.

Values:	Exc.	V.G.	Good
	350.00	300.00	225.00

Comment: *Values for either old or new models, any width.*

Bull Nose Rabbet Plane

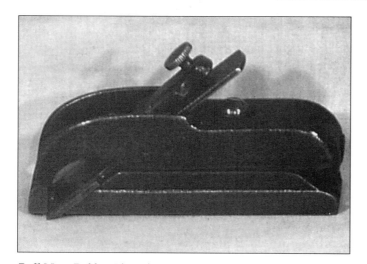

Bull Nose Rabbet Plane (No. 3098) is very rare and in excellent condition. From T. Webster collection. Photo by D. Kowalski.

Bull Nose Rabbet Plane. Cutter of highest-grade crucible steel, oil-tempered and sharpened; ready for use. Japanned frame. Packed one in a carton.

New No.	Old No.	Length	Cutter	Weight
W75	F3098C	4 in.	1 in.	3/4 lb.

Values:	Exc.	V.G.	Good
	600.00	550.00	500.00

Comment: *Values for either old or new models.*

Router Plane

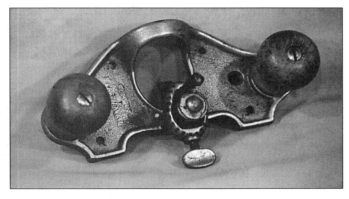

Router Plane (No. 3070) clearly shows model number in raised letters on frame. Measures 7 1/2 inches end to end. From T. Webster collection. Photo by D. Kowalski.

Router Plane. Screw adjustment, open throat, nickel-plated. Handles varnished. Cutters made of highest-grade crucible steel, oil-tempered and sharpened for use. Has quarter and half-inch cutters. Packed one in a carton.

New No.	Old No.	Weight
W171	F3070C	2 1/2 lb.

Values:	Exc.	V.G.	Good
	450.00	400.00	300.00

Comment: *Values for either old or new models.*

Cabinet Scrapers

Cabinet Scrapers. Made of highest-grade steel. Plain cutting edges. Packed one dozen in a carton.

New No.	Old No.	Size	Weight/Dozen
W36	F2220B	3 in. x 6 in.	3 1/4 lbs.
W35	F2221B	3 in. x 5 in.	2 3/4 lbs.
W34	F2222B	3 in. x 4 in.	2 1/4 lbs.
W24	F2223B	2 in. x 4 in.	1 1/2 lbs.

Values:	Exc.	V.G.	Good
	30.00	25.00	20.00

Comment: *Values for either old or new models, any size.*

Scraper Planes

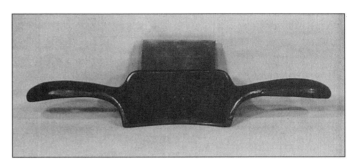

Scraper Plane (No. 3075) is the older version of the W79 and shows straight horizontal frame line. From T. Webster collection. Photo by D. Kowalski.

Scraper Plane (No. W79) measures 11 inches across handles. From T. Webster collection. Photo by D. Kowalski.

Scraper Plane; not adjustable. Cutter of highest-grade crucible steel, oil-tempered and sharpened; ready for use. Japanned frame. Packed one in a carton.

New No.	Old No.	Length	Cutter	Weight
W79	F3075C	11 in.	2 3/4 in.	1 3/4 lbs.

Values:	Exc.	V.G.	Good
	120.00	100.00	80.00

Comment: *Values for either old or new models.*

Scraper Plane (No. 3076) is adjustable and has iron handles. Measures 11 inches across handles. Base is 3 5/8 in. x 3 1/8 in. From T. Webster collection. Photo by D. Kowalski.

Scraper Plane; adjustable. Single cutter made of highest-grade crucible steel, oil-tempered and sharpened; ready for use. Japanned metal frame. Packed one in a carton.

New No.	Old No.	Face	Cutter	Weight
W81	F3076C	3 1/2 in.	2 3/4 in.	3 1/4 lbs.

Values:

Exc.	V.G.	Good
150.00	135.00	110.00

Comment: *Values for either old or new models.*

Scraper Plane (No. 3080) is adjustable and has wood handles. Measures 10 7/8 inches across handles. Base is 6 3/8 in. x 3 1/2 in. From T. Webster collection. Photo by D. Kowalski.

Scraper Plane; adjustable. Double mahogany handles. Polished trim. Single cutter made of highest-grade crucible steel, oil-tempered and sharpened; ready for use. Packed one in a carton.

New No.	Old No.	Length	Cutter	Weight
W12	F3080C	6 in.	3 in.	4 1/2 lbs.

Values:

Exc.	V.G.	Good
160.00	145.00	120.00

Comment: *Values for either old or new models.*

Spoke Shave

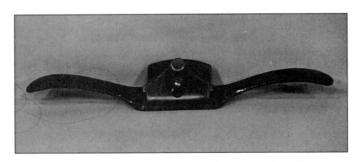

Spoke Shave (No. W91) is 10 1/4 inches across handles. From T. Webster collection. Photo by D. Kowalski.

No. W91. Spoke Shave. Cast iron frame. Double-iron type. Raised handles in black japanned finish. Has 10-inch spread cutter, 2 1/8 inches wide. Cutter and cap polished. Packed one-half dozen in a carton.

Values:

Exc.	V.G.	Good
120.00	100.00	80.00

Plane Replacement Irons

Forged from highest-grade tool steel, oil-tempered and full-polished; sharpened and whetted on an oil stone by hand, ready for use. Available in a variety of models for various planes.

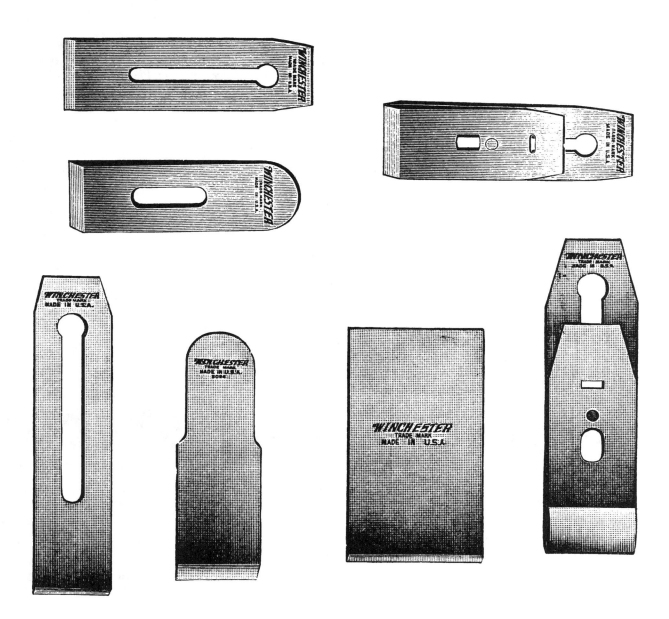

Values:	Exc.	V.G.	Good
	25.00	20.00	15.00

Comment: *Values for any style or model, one item without box.*

Wood Levels

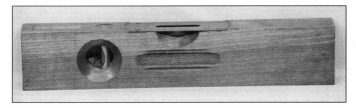

Wood Level (No. 9802) is smallest wood level with single level and plumb. From T. Webster collection. Photo by D. Kowalski.

Wood Level. Non-adjustable. Single level and single plumb. Made of seasoned hardwood. Small-size stock in one piece, measuring 2 3/8 in. x 1 1/4 in. Proved glasses. Mahogany stain finish, polished. Brass top plate. Vials filled with special opalescent fluid giving high visibility. Packed one in Winchester gray Kraft paper.

New No.	Old No.	Length	Weight
W104/12	F9802A	12 in.	7/8 lb.
W104/14	F9804A	14 in.	1 lbs.
W104/16	F9806A	16 in.	1 1/8 lbs.
W104/1S	F9808A	18 in.	1 1/4 lbs.

Values:	Exc.	V.G.	Good
	75.00	60.00	40.00

Comment: *Values for either old or new models, any length.*

Wood Level (No. 9823) is adjustable and has added brass end plates. From T. Webster collection. Photo by D. Kowalski.

Wood Level. Adjustable. Single level and single plumb. Made of seasoned hardwood. Standard-size stock in one piece, measuring 3 1/8 in. x 1 3/8 in. Proved glasses. Mahogany stain finish, polished. Brass top plate and ends. Vials filled with special opalescent fluid giving high visibility. Packed one in Winchester gray Kraft paper.

New No.	Old No.	Length	Weight
W3/24	F9821A	24 in.	2 1/2 lbs.
W3/26	F9823A	26 in.	2 3/4 lbs.
W3/28	F9825A	28 in.	3 lbs.
W3/30	F9827A	30 in.	3 1/4 lbs.

Values:	Exc.	V.G.	Good
	90.00	75.00	65.00

Comment: *Values for either old or new models, any length.*

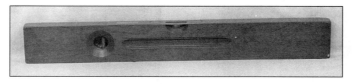

Wood Level (No. 9811) is shortest wood level in this series. From T. Webster collection. Photo by D. Kowalski.

Wood Level. Non-adjustable. Single level and single plumb. Made of seasoned hardwood. Standard-size stock in one piece, measuring 3 1/8 in. x 1 3/8 in. Proved glasses. Mahogany stain finish, polished. Brass top plate. Vials filled with special opalescent fluid giving high visibility. Packed one in Winchester gray Kraft paper.

New No.	Old No.	Length	Weight
W0/24	F9811A	24 in.	2 1/4 lbs.
W0/26	F9813A	26 in.	2 1/2 lbs.
WO/28	F9815A	28 in.	2 3/4 lbs.
WO/30	F9817A	30 in.	3 lbs.

Values:	Exc.	V.G.	Good
	75.00	60.00	40.00

Comment: *Values for either old or new models, any length.*

Wood Level (No. 9831) is adjustable and has duplex plumbs with brass cover plates. From T. Webster collection. Photo by D. Kowalski.

Wood Level. Adjustable. Single level and duplex plumbs. Made of seasoned hardwood. Standard-size stock in one piece, measuring 3 1/8 in. x 1 3/8 in. Proved glasses. Mahogany stain finish, polished. Brass top plate, duplex side plates and ends. Vials filled with special opalescent fluid giving high visibility. Packed one in Winchester gray Kraft paper.

New No.	Old No.	Length	Weight
W30/24	F9831A	24 in.	2 3/4 lbs.
W30/26	F9833A	26 in.	3 lbs.
W30/28	F9835A	28 in.	3 1/4 lbs.
W30/30	F9837A	30 in.	3 1/2 lbs.

Values:	Exc.	V.G.	Good
	200.00	175.00	125.00

Comment: *Values for either old or new models, any length.*

Carpentry Tools • 587

Mason's Level. Made of light, one-piece, air-dried, seasoned hardwood measuring 3 1/4 in. x 1 1/4 in. Proved glasses filled with special opalescent fluid giving high visibility. Two hand holes. Six glasses. Body enameled in Winchester red. Packed one in Winchester gray Kraft paper.

New No.	Old No.	Length	Weight
W48	F9875A	48 in.	3 3/4 lbs.

Values:	Exc.	V.G.	Good
	425.00	410.00	375.00

Comment: *Values for either old or new models.*

Iron Level

Iron Level (No. W36/9) is actually stamped "369." From T. Webster collection. Photo by D. Kowalski.

Iron Level. Adjustable. Single level and duplex plumbs. Frames made of gray iron of special design to ensure lightness and strength. Tops and bottoms milled and ground parallel. Black Japan finish with polished edges. Adjustable proved glasses encased in nickel-plated steel casings and filled with special opalescent fluid. Packed one in a carton.

New No.	Old No.	Length	Weight
W36/9	F9860A	9 in.	1 1/4 lbs.
W36/12	F9862A	12 in.	1 7/8 lbs.
W36/18	F9864A	18 in.	3 lbs.
W36/24	F9866A	24 in.	4 1/4 lbs.

Values:	Exc.	V.G.	Good
9 inch	500.00	450.00	400.00
12 inch	500.00	450.00	400.00
18 inch	325.00	300.00	250.00
24 inch	325.00	300.00	250.00

Comment: *Values for either old or new models.*

Pocket Level

Pocket Level never stamped with the model number. From T. Webster collection. Photo by D. Kowalski.

Pocket Level. Non-adjustable. Made of hexagon brass tubing, polished and nickel-plated. Equipped with proved glasses filled with special opalescent fluid. Three inches long. Individually wrapped in white wax paper. Packed six in a carton. New No. W31/3; Old No. F9850A. Weight 1/2 lb. per carton.

Values:	Exc.	V.G.	Good
	750.00	600.00	450.00

Comment: *Values for either old or new models.*

Butt Gauge

Butt Gauge (No. 9779) is in excellent condition. From T. Webster collection. Photo by D. Kowalski.

Close-up of calibrations on top of the Butt Gauge (No. 9779). From T. Webster collection. Photo by D. Kowalski.

Butt Gauge. Nickel-plated. Frame of cast iron. Steel bars and set screws. Tempered cutters. Length is three inches. Bars graduated in 16ths for two inches. Packed one in a carton. New No. W95; Old No. F9779A. Weight 5/8 lb.

Values:	Exc.	V.G.	Good
	100.00	80.00	50.00

Comment: *Values for either old or new models.*

Wood Gauges (Scribes)

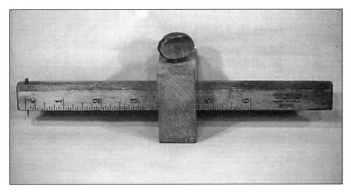

Wood Gauge (Scribe), single arm (No. 9775) is 8 1/4 inches long. From T. Webster collection. Photo by D. Kowalski.

Wood Gauge. Has eight-inch, single oval beechwood bar that is graduated in inches. Adjustable point. Adjustable head of beechwood. Boxwood screw. Entire gauge varnished. Packed one dozen in a carton. New No. W26; Old No. F9775A. Weight 2 7/8 lbs. per carton.

Values:	**Exc.**	**V.G.**	**Good**
	100.00	80.00	50.00

Comment: *Values for either old or new models.*

Wood Gauge (Scribe), double arm (No. 9776) is 8 1/2 inches long. From T. Webster collection. Photo by D. Kowalski.

Wood Gauge. Has two eight-inch, oval beechwood bars graduated in inches. Each bar works independently in the same head. Adjustable beechwood head. Boxwood screw. Entire gauge varnished. Packed one-half dozen in a carton. New No. W72; Old No. F9776A. Weight 1 7/8 lbs. per carton.

Values:	**Exc.**	**V.G.**	**Good**
	200.00	175.00	145.00

Comment: *Values for either old or new models. Double arm more rare than single arm.*

Metal Gauges (Scribes)

Metal Gauge (Scribe), single arm (No. 9777) is 6 5/8 inches long. From T. Webster collection. Photo by D. Kowalski.

Metal Gauge. Has single, nickel-plated bar that is graduated in 16ths. Cast iron double-faced adjusting head. Two markers, one pin-point and one roller. Bar graduated in 16ths. Steel bar is 6 1/2 inches long and 5/16 inch in diameter. Packed one in a carton. New No. W97; Old No. F9777A. Weight 1/2 lb.

Values:	**Exc.**	**V.G.**	**Good**
	125.00	110.00	90.00

Comment: *Values for either old or new models.*

Metal Gauge (Scribe), double arm (No. 9778) is 6 5/8 inches long. From T. Webster collection. Photo by D. Kowalski.

Metal Gauge. Has double, nickel-plated bar that is graduated in 16ths. Cast iron double-faced adjusting head. Tempered pin-points and rollers. Bar graduated in 16ths. Steel bar is 6 1/2 inches long and 5/16 inch in diameter. Packed one in a carton. New No. W98; Old No. F9778A. Weight 5/8 lb.

Values:	**Exc.**	**V.G.**	**Good**
	160.00	150.00	135.00

Comment: *Values for either old or new models. Double arm more rare than single arm.*

Rules

Folding Spring Joint Rules

Folding Rules came in both yellow and white in four sizes each. From T. Webster collection. Photo by D. Kowalski.

Yellow Folding Rule (No. 9404) in near mint condition. From T. Webster collection. Photo by D. Kowalski.

Folding Spring Joint Rules. Made of selected flexible hardwood. Concealed steel rivets. Stiff joint springs that hold rule rigid when extended. Steel joints and brass tips. Graduated in feet, inches, 8ths and 16ths. Fitted with patented strike plates. Conveniently marked with direction arrow. Each joint 6 in. x 5/8 in. Packed one-half dozen in a carton.

New No.	Old No.	Length	Folds	Weight
Enameled yellow.				
W203	F9403A	3 ft.	Six	3/4 lb.
W204	F9404A	4 ft.	Eight	1 lb.
W205	F9405A	5 ft.	Ten	1 1/2 lbs.
W206	F9406A	6 ft.	Twelve	1 3/4 lbs.
Enameled white.				
W103	F9453A	3 ft.	Six	3/4 lb.
W104	F9454A	4 ft.	Eight	1 lb.
W105	F9455A	5 ft.	Ten	1 1/2 lbs.
W106	F9456A	6 ft.	Twelve	1 3/4 lbs.

Values:	Exc.	V.G.	Good
	750.00	650.00	500.00

Comment: *Values for either old or new models, either color, any length.*

Folding Boxwood Rules

This series of rules is made of selected, thoroughly seasoned boxwood. All metal trimmings are of brass. These rules are accurately machine graduated with graduations printed in black. Natural varnished finish.

Two Foot - Four Fold. Full brass bound. Square joint. Width is one inch. Graduated with drafting scales in 8ths, 10ths, 12ths and 16ths. New No. W62; Old No. F9562A. Packed one-half dozen to the carton.

Values:	Exc.	V.G.	Good
	260.00	235.00	200.00

Comment: *Values for either old or new models.*

Two Foot - Four Fold. Half brass bound. Square joints. Width is one inch. Graduated with drafting scales in 8ths, 10ths, 12ths and 16ths. New No. W84; Old No. F9584A. Packed one-half dozen to the carton.

Values:	Exc.	V.G.	Good
	175.00	160.00	125.00

Comment: *Values for either old or new models.*

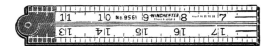

Two Foot - Four Fold. Square joints. Middle plates. Width is one inch. Graduated in 8ths and 16ths. New No. W61; Old No. F9561A. Packed one-half dozen to the carton.

Values: | **Exc.** | **V.G.** | **Good**
| 175.00 | 160.00 | 125.00

Comment: *Values for either old or new models.*

Two Foot - Four Fold. Square joints. Middle plates. Width is one inch. Graduated in 8ths and 16ths. New No. W68; Old No. F9568A. Packed one dozen to the carton.

Values: | **Exc.** | **V.G.** | **Good**
| 175.00 | 160.00 | 125.00

Comment: *Values for either old or new models.*

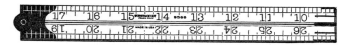

Three Foot - Four Fold. Made with arch joint and middle plates. Width is one inch. Graduated in 8ths and 16ths. New No. W66; Old No. F9566A. Packed one-half dozen to the carton.

Values: | **Exc.** | **V.G.** | **Good**
| 225.00 | 200.00 | 160.00

Comment: *Values for either old or new models.*

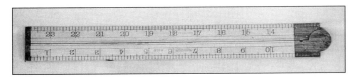

Folding Boxwood Rule (No. 9518) is the largest model. From T. Webster collection. Photo by D. Kowalski.

Two Foot - Two Fold. Square joint. Width is 1 1/2 inch. Graduated in 8ths and 16ths. New No. W18; Old No. F9518A. Packed one-half dozen to the carton.

Values: | **Exc.** | **V.G.** | **Good**
| 260.00 | 235.00 | 200.00

Comment: *Values for either old or new models.*

Boxwood Caliper Rules

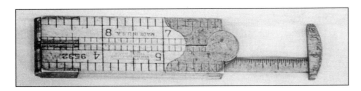

Boxwood Caliper Rule (No. 9532) with caliper extended. From T. Webster collection. Photo by D. Kowalski.

The three hinges of the Boxwood Caliper Rule (No. 9532). From T. Webster collection. Photo by D. Kowalski.

One Foot - Four Fold. Made with arch joint and middle plates. Width is one inch. Caliper slide made of brass and accurately machined to fit slot in rule. Slide graduated on top in 16ths and underside in 32nds. Rule graduated in 8ths, 10ths, 12ths and 16ths. New No. W32; Old No. F9532A. Packed one-half dozen to the carton.

Values: | **Exc.** | **V.G.** | **Good**
| 360.00 | 335.00 | 300.00

Comment: *Values for either old or new models.*

One Foot - Two Fold. Boxwood Caliper Rule. Made with square joint. Width is 1 3/8 inch. Fitted with accurately machined caliper slide of brass graduated at the top in 16ths and underside in 32nds. Rule graduated in 8ths, 10ths, 12ths and 16ths. New No. W37; Old No. F9537A. Packed one-half dozen to the carton.

Values:	Exc.	V.G.	Good
	360.00	335.00	300.00

Comment: *Values for either old or new models.*

One Foot - Two Fold. Boxwood Caliper Rule. Made with square joint. Width is 1 3/8 inch. Fitted with accurately machined caliper slide of brass graduated at the top in 16ths and underside in 32nds. Rule graduated in 8ths, 10ths, 12ths and 16ths. New No. W36; Old No. F9536A. Packed one-half dozen to the carton.

Values:	Exc.	V.G.	Good
	360.00	335.00	300.00

Comment: *Values for either old or new models.*

Squares

Try Squares

Try Square (No. 9709) has length graduations faintly visible on upper edge. From T. Webster collection. Photo by D. Kowalski.

Try Square. Steel blade with rosewood handle. Blade machined and squared inside and out. Attractive, rust-resisting electrozinc finish. Graduated in 8ths. Inner edge of handle is brass faced. Packed one-half dozen to the carton.

New No.	Old No.	Blade	Handle	Weight
W122/6	F9706A	6 in.	4 5/8 in.	2 lbs.
W122/7 1/2	F9708A	7 1/2 in.	5 3/8 in.	2 7/8 lbs.
W122/9	F9709A	9 in.	6 in.	3 5/8 lbs.

Try Square (No. 9726) has steel handle. Length graduations virtually gone from wear and corrosion. From T. Webster collection. Photo by D. Kowalski.

Try Square. Steel blade and handle. Blade machined and squared inside and out. Accurately graduated in 8ths. Handle and blade finished in electrozinc finish. Packed one-half dozen to the carton.

New No.	Old No.	Blade	Handle	Weight
W22/6	F9726A	6 in.	4 in.	2 1/4 lbs.
W22/8	F9728A	8 in.	5 in.	4 1/8 lbs.

Values:	Exc.	V.G.	Good
	75.00	65.00	50.00

Comment: *Values for either old or new models, steel or rosewood handles.*

Try and Mitre Square

Try and Mitre Square (No. W102/7 1/2) has rosewood handle. Length graduations moderately visible. From T. Webster collection. Photo by D. Kowalski.

Try and Mitre Square. Steel blades, machined and squared inside and out. Accurately graduated in 8ths. Handle of polished rosewood. Inner edge of handle and shoulder are brass-faced. Finished in attractive, rust resisting electrozinc finish. Packed one-half dozen to the carton.

New No.	Old No.	Blade	Handle	Weight
W102/6	F9716A	6 in.	4 in.	2 1/4 lbs.
W102/7 1/2	F9718A	7 1/2 in.	5 in.	2 7/8 lbs.

Values:	Exc.	V.G.	Good
	75.00	65.00	50.00

Comment: *Values for either old or new models.*

Sliding T Bevel

Sliding T Bevel (No. W125/6) has rosewood handle. From T. Webster collection. Photo by D. Kowalski.

Sliding T Bevel. Steel blades, machined and ground on edges and sides. electrozinc finish. Polished rosewood finish. Brass flush wing nut. Brass end and top plates. Packed one-half dozen to the carton.

New No.	Old No.	Blade	Handle	Weight
W125/6	F9756A	6 in.	4 7/8 in.	1 1/4 lbs.
W125/8	F9758A	8 in.	5 7/8 in.	1 3/4 lbs.
W125/10	F9760A	10 in.	7 3/8 in.	2 1/4 lbs.

Values:	Exc.	V.G.	Good
	75.00	65.00	50.00

Comment: *Values for either old or new models.*

Steel Squares

Six styles of steel squares have now been added to the Winchester line of tools. These cover a wide range of squares for every purpose of the carpenter and mechanic. They're made in varying sizes and finishes to meet every demand. Two of these squares are a take-down model that comes down in two straight sections and can be carried in a canvas case as shown below. When put together these two parts dovetail perfectly, making a rigid square. The take-down device is simple and positive. Four of the styles are made with the new Winchester electrozinc finish. This is zinc electrolytically plated, giving a bright, attractive surface that is virtually rustproof.

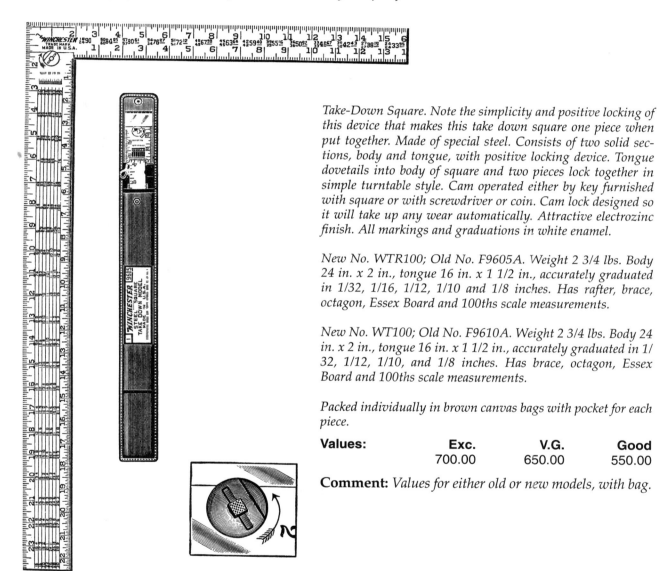

Take-Down Square. Note the simplicity and positive locking of this device that makes this take down square one piece when put together. Made of special steel. Consists of two solid sections, body and tongue, with positive locking device. Tongue dovetails into body of square and two pieces lock together in simple turntable style. Cam operated either by key furnished with square or with screwdriver or coin. Cam lock designed so it will take up any wear automatically. Attractive electrozinc finish. All markings and graduations in white enamel.

New No. WTR100; Old No. F9605A. Weight 2 3/4 lbs. Body 24 in. x 2 in., tongue 16 in. x 1 1/2 in., accurately graduated in 1/32, 1/16, 1/12, 1/10 and 1/8 inches. Has rafter, brace, octagon, Essex Board and 100ths scale measurements.

New No. WT100; Old No. F9610A. Weight 2 3/4 lbs. Body 24 in. x 2 in., tongue 16 in. x 1 1/2 in., accurately graduated in 1/32, 1/12, 1/10, and 1/8 inches. Has brace, octagon, Essex Board and 100ths scale measurements.

Packed individually in brown canvas bags with pocket for each piece.

Values:	Exc.	V.G.	Good
	700.00	650.00	550.00

Comment: *Values for either old or new models, with bag.*

One-Piece Weldless Steel Square. Tapered in thickness from the angle outward. Hardened corners. Accurately graduated. Electrozinc finish. All markings and graduations in white enamel. Accurately graduated in 1/32, 1/16, 1/12, 1/10 and 1/8 inches. Body 24 in. x 2 in., tongue 16 in. x 1 1/2 in. Has rafter or framing brace, octagon, Essex Board and 100ths scale measurements. Packed in paper scabbards, three to the carton. New No. WF100; Old No. F9606A.

Values: **Exc.**   **V.G.**   **Good**
                  150.00   125.00   90.00

Comment: *Values for either old or new models.*

Steel Square. Regular. Body 24 in. x 2 in., tongue 16 in. x 1 1/2 in. Three accurate graduations, 1/1, 1/12 and 1/8. Has Brace and Essex Board measurements. Electrozinc finish. Graduations and markings in white enamel. Packed in paper scabbards, three to the carton. New No. W3; Old No. F9616A.

Values: **Exc.**   **V.G.**   **Good**
                  150.00   125.00   90.00

Comment: *Values for either old or new models.*

Steel Square. Regular. Body 24 in. x 2 in., tongue 16 in. x 1 1/2 in. Accurately graduated 1/32, 1/16, 1/12, 1/10 and 1/8 inch. Has Brace, Octagon, Essex Board and 100ths scale measurements. Electrozinc finish. Graduations and markings in white enamel. Packed in paper scabbards, three to the carton. New No. W100; Old No. F9611A.

Values: **Exc.**   **V.G.**   **Good**
                  150.00   125.00   90.00

Comment: *Values for either old or new models.*

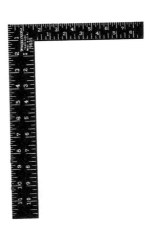

Steel Square. Small Size. A smaller-sized square than the others in the Winchester line having body 12 in. x 1 in., and tongue 8 in. x 1 in. Three accurate graduations 1/12, 1/8 and 1/4 inches. Gun-metal blued finish. Deep-cut graduations filled with white enamel. Packed in paper scabbards, three to the carton. New No. W10; Old No. F9655A.

Values: **Exc.**   **V.G.**   **Good**
                  300.00   275.00   225.00

Comment: *Values for either old or new models.*

Carpentry Tools • 595

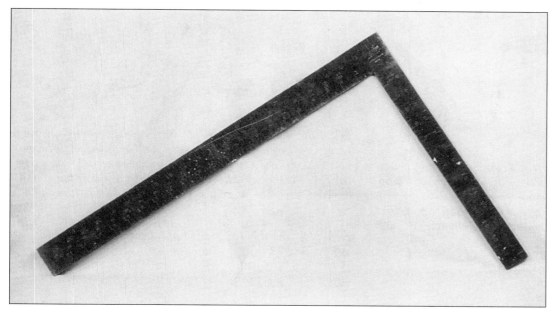

Steel Square. Both this model W14 and the small W10 have the dark blued finish. From T. Webster collection. Photo by D. Kowalski.

Steel Square. Regular. Body 24 in. x 2 in., tongue 16 in. x 1 1/2 in. Two accurate graduations, 1/8 and 1/4 inches. Has Essex Board measurements. Gun-metal blued finish. Deep-cut graduations filled with white enamel. Packed in paper scabbards, three to the carton. New No. W14; Old No. F9650A.

Values:	Exc.	V.G.	Good
	150.00	125.00	90.00

Comment: *Values for either old or new models.*

Braces

Bit Brace Display

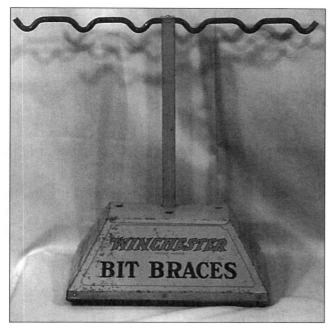

Brace Display is 17 inches high. A rare piece. From T. Webster collection. Photo by D. Kowalski.

Bit Brace Display. Here's something unusual in a display fixture. This new Winchester fixture is so designed that it shows every detail of the bit brace at a glance. The full beauty of construction of the brace can be seen right on the fixture. These fixtures are substantial looking, simple and attractive. Stands are made of wood covered with sheet metal, lithographed in three colors, Winchester red, Winchester gray and black. Cross bars are 3/8-inch iron stock. Top platform is furnished with three holes which enables the dealer to display one of each of the three styles of Winchester auger bits, making a perfect sales tie-up with the dealer's stock of Winchester auger bits. New No. WBA18; Old No. F5985C (originally shipped with 18 braces).

Values:	Exc.	V.G.	Good
	2,800.00	2,600.00	2,300.00

Comment: *Values for Brace Display without any braces or bits.*

Bit Braces

Box Ring Ratchet Jaw Type. Brace. Giant ball-bearing chuck. Universal-type jaws of forged steel. Full metal-clad ball bearing. Cocobolo head. Cocobolo sweep handle with friction sleeve. Wood parts varnished and polished. Metal parts full nickel-plated and buffed. Each brace individually wrapped and packed two to the carton.

New No.	Old No.	Size of Sweep
WBB10	F3503C	10 in.
WBB12	F3504C	12 in.
WBB14	F3505C	14 in.

Open Ring Ratchet Type. Brace. Standard hexagon-type chuck shell. Semi-steel spring-type alligator jaws. Full metal-clad hardwood handle. Hardwood sweep handle. Wood parts are stained walnut, varnished and polished. Metal parts are full nickel-plated and buffed. Each brace individually wrapped and packed two to the carton.

New No.	Old No.	Size of Sweep
W28	F3522C	8 in.
W210	F3523C	10 in.
W212	F3524C	12 in.

Open Ring Ratchet Type. Brace. Standard chuck shell. Malleable iron two-piece alligator-type jaws. Hardwood head and sweep handle. Stained and varnished dark mahogany. Metal parts bright polished with chuck shell blued. Each brace individually wrapped and packed six to the carton.

New No.	Old No.	Size of Sweep
W410	F3543C	10 in.

Box Ring Ratchet "Grip-All" Type. Brace. Straight shell. Forged spring-type alligator jaws. Full metal-clad Cocobolo head. Cocobolo sweep handle with friction sleeve. Wood parts varnished and polished. Metal parts are full nickel-plated and buffed. Each brace individually wrapped and packed two to the carton.

New No.	Old No.	Size of Sweep
W18	F3512C	8 in.
W110	F3513C	10 in.
W112	F3514C	12 in.

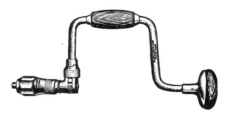

Open Ring Ratchet. Brace. Standard chuck shell. Malleable iron two-piece alligator-type jaws. Hardwood head and sweep handle, black ebonized finish. Metal parts nickel-plated and buffed. Each brace individually wrapped and packed six to the carton.

New No.	Old No.	Size of Sweep
W310	F3533C	10 in.

Plain Brace Without Ratchet. Standard chuck shell. Malleable iron two-piece alligator-type jaws. Hardwood head and sweep handle. Stained and varnished dark mahogany. Metal parts polished except blued chuck shell. Each brace individually wrapped and packed six to the carton.

New No.	Old No.	Size of Sweep
WP8	F3602C	8 in.

Values:	Exc.	V.G.	Good
	100.00	85.00	60.00

Comment: *Values for any model of Brace, old or new number.*

Carpentry Tools • 597

Breast Drills

Made with strong malleable iron frames, and are manufactured with special attention to insuring correct meshing of the gears. They are all designed to give satisfactory, long service.

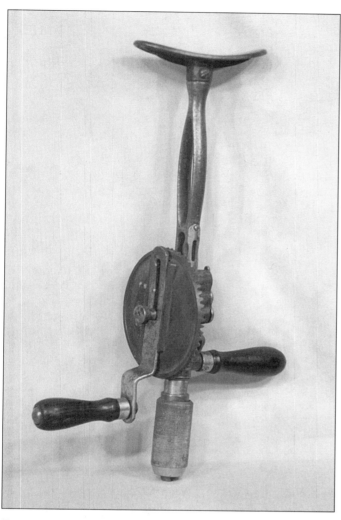

Breast Drill (No. 8744). From T. Webster collection. Photo by D. Kowalski.

Breast Drill. Malleable iron frame with polished steel shank extending to the breast plate. Cast gears with cut teeth. Pinion of steel. Made for two speeds. Adjustable breast plate. Sweep handle adjustable for three lengths. Malleable chuck shell. Forged alligator jaws carefully tempered and hardened. Adapted to small and medium round shank drills as well as taper shank bits. Frame enameled in Winchester gray. Gear enameled in and out in Winchester red. Cocobolo handles with nickel-plated ferrules. Top of breast plate is polished. Each drill individually wrapped and packed in individual carton. New No. W44; Old No. F8744M. Weight 6 lbs.

Breast Drill (No. 8733) has level in handle. From T. Webster collection. Photo by D. Kowalski.

Breast Drill With Level. This drill is furnished with level set in the frame. One-piece malleable iron frame. Gears cast with cut teeth. Pinion of steel. Made in two speeds. Adjustable breast plate. Sweep handle adjustable for three lengths. Steel chuck shell. Forged universal jaws. Hardened and adapted for round shanks from 1/8 inch to 1/2 inch in diameter as well as for tapered shank bits. Frame enameled in Winchester gray. Gears enameled in and out in Winchester red. Top of breast plate is polished. Cocobolo handles with nickel-plated ferrules. Each drill individually wrapped and packed in individual carton. New No. W33; Old No. F8733M. Weight 5 5/8 lbs.

Breast Drill. Similar to No. 8744 except that it is fitted with three-jaw chuck which is adapted to round shank drills from No. 0 to 1/2 inch. In finish and construction it is the same as the drill described above. Each drill individually wrapped and packed in individual carton. New No. W41; Old No. F8741M. Weight 5 7/8 lbs.

Values:

	Exc.	V.G.	Good
	135.00	120.00	100.00

Comment: *Values for any model, old or new number.*

Values:

	Exc.	V.G.	Good
	100.00	90.00	75.00

Comment: *Values for either model without level in handle, old or new number.*

Bits

Auger Bits

Winchester auger bits are made in three carefully designed patterns to meet the requirements of various types of work. The solid center pattern is the type especially adapted to all kinds of general work.

The electrician's or open center type, is designed for fast boring. To prevent binding and insure easy boring it is made with an open center in which the outer edges of the bit are thicker than the center.

The double twist is made with two extension lips and two spurs. The screw point has double thread. This bit is designed especially for such fine work as cabinet work and pattern making.

New No.	Old No.	Weight/Dozen	Diameter
WS14	F1214C	3 1/2 lbs.	14/16 in.
WS15	F1215C	4 lbs.	15/16 in.
WS16	F1216C	4 1/2 lbs.	16/16 in.
WS18	F1218C	5 3/4 lbs.	18/16 in.
WS20	F1220C	6 1/4 lbs.	20/16 in.
WS22	F1222C	6 1/2 lbs.	22/16 in.
WS24	F1224C	6 1/ lbs.	24/16 in.

Double Twist Drill Bit (No. 1409). From T. Webster collection. Photo by D. Kowalski.

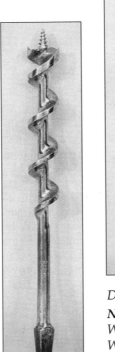

Solid Center Drill Bit (No. 1212). From T. Webster collection. Photo by D. Kowalski.

Solid Center Pattern. Packed one-half dozen in a carton.

New No.	Old No.	Weight/Dozen	Diameter
WS3	F1203C	1 1/4 lbs.	3/16 in.
WS4	F1204C	1 1/4 lbs.	4/16 in.
WS5	F1205C	1 1/4 lbs.	5/16 in.
WS6	F1206C	1 3/4 lbs.	6/16 in.
WS7	F1207C	2 lbs.	7/16 in.
WS8	F1208C	2 1/4 lbs.	8/16 in.
WS9	F1209C	2 1/2 lbs.	9/16 in.
WS10	F1210C	2 1/2 lbs.	10/16 in.
WS11	F1211C	3 lbs.	11/16 in.
WS12	F1212C	3 lbs.	12/16 in.
WS13	F1213C	3 1/2 lbs.	13/16 in.

Double Twist Pattern. Packed one-half dozen in a carton.

New No.	Old No.	Weight/Dozen	Diameter
W3	F1403C	1 1/4 lbs.	3/16 in.
W4	F1404C	1 1/4 lbs.	4/16 in.
W5	F1405C	1 1/4 lbs.	5/16 in.
W6	F1406C	1 1/2 lbs.	6/16 in.
W7	F1407C	2 lbs.	7/16 in.
W8	F1408C	2 1/4 lbs.	8/16 in.
W9	F1409C	2 1/2 lbs.	9/16 in.
W10	F1410C	2 3/4 lbs.	10/16 in.
W11	F1411C	3 1/4 lbs.	11/16 in.
W12	F1412C	3 1/4 lbs.	12/16 in.
W13	F1413C	3 1/2 lbs.	13/16 in.
W14	F1414C	4 lbs.	14/16 in.
W15	F1415C	6 1/4 lbs.	15/16 in.
W16	F1416C	4 1/4 lbs.	16/16 in.

Values:	Exc.	V.G.	Good
	20.00	15.00	10.00

Comment: *Values for single bits, either old or new number.*

Auger Bit Sets

All Winchester bits are made of carefully selected steel, treated by the most modern methods of hardening and tempering. They represent highest quality of materials, workmanship and design. All three patterns may be had in sets of 13 bits each packed in gray flannel roll or handy wooden box as shown below.

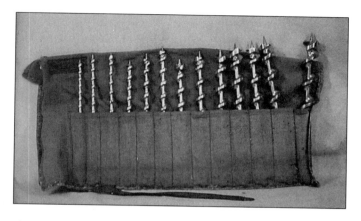

Auger Bit Set in canvas case contains solid center bits. From T. Webster collection. Photo by D. Kowalski.

Practical combinations of Open Center, Solid Center, and Double Twist bits including the 13 sizes from 4/16 inch to 1 inch diameter. Each bit made of high-grade steel. Strong and keen cutting. Packed in handy gray canvas case with compartment for each kit. Weight per Set about 3 lbs.

New No.	Old No.	
WSR13	F1231C	Solid Center
WR13	F1431C	Double Twist

Values:	Exc.	V.G.	Good
	800.00	700.00	600.00

Comment: *Values for full set with bits, either old or new number.*

Strongly made, metal bound, stained wood boxes with separate compartment for each of the 13 different size bits in the set, ranging in diameter from 4/16 inch to 1 inch. Each bit made of high grade steel. Strong and keen cutting. Weight per Set about 3 1/2 lbs.

New No.	Old No.	
WSB13	F1230C	Solid Center
WB13	F1430C	Double Twist

Auger Bit Box. Wooden box with front hinged cover folded down shows individual slots inside for holding bits. From T. Webster collection. Photo by D. Kowalski.

Auger Bit Box, closed. Measures 6 3/8 inches wide x 10 7/8 inches high x 2 1/8 inches deep when closed. From T. Webster collection. Photo by D. Kowalski.

Values:	Exc.	V.G.	Good
	800.00	700.00	600.00

Comment: *Values for full box with bits, either old or new numbers. For empty box only, deduct 20 percent from above values.*

Bit Brace Tools

Forged from high-grade octagonal steel, all carefully heat-treated and tempered. Square grips are black forged finish, blades polished.

Screw Driver Bit

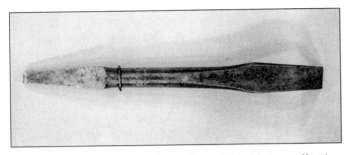

Screw Driver Bit (No. 2835). From T. Webster collection. Photo by D. Kowalski.

Screw Driver Bits packed one dozen in a carton. Weight about 1 lb.

New No.	Old No.	Width	Length
W102 1/4	F2834C	1/4 in.	4 3/4 in.
W102 5/16	F2835C	5/16 in.	4 3/4 in.
W102 3/8	F2836C	3/8 in.	4 3/4 in.

Values:	Exc.	V.G.	Good
	65.00	55.00	40.00

Comment: *Values for any size, either old or new number.*

Countersink Bit

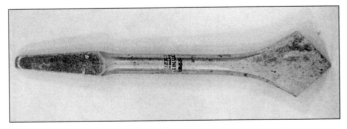

Countersink Bit (No. 2855). From T. Webster collection. Photo by D. Kowalski.

Countersink Bits packed one dozen in a carton. Weight about 1 1/4 lbs.

New No.	Old No.	Length
W120	F2855C	4 3/4 in.

Values:	Exc.	V.G.	Good
	65.00	55.00	40.00

Comment: *Values for either old or new number.*

Square Reamer Bit

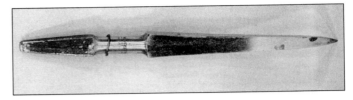

Square Reamer Bit (No. 2855). Wire around shaft used for hanging on a wall display. From T. Webster collection. Photo by D. Kowalski.

Square Reamer Bits packed one dozen in a carton. Weight about 2 1/4 lbs.

New No.	Old No.	Length
W115	F2876C	6 in.

Values:	Exc.	V.G.	Good
	65.00	55.00	40.00

Comment: *Values for either old or new number.*

Expansive Bit

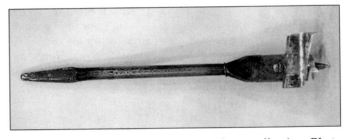

Expansive Bit (No. 1201). From T. Webster collection. Photo by D. Kowalski.

Expansive Bits have shanks and heads forged from special steel, accurately tempered, full polished except square of shank which is forged black. Spurs and cutters are hand sharpened. Adjustment of cutter is simple and positive. When adjusting screw is tightened, serrated milled edges interlock absolutely preventing moving out of position and insuring absolute uniformity of hole in boring. Each bit furnished with two cutters, graduated in sixteenth inches. Each bit wrapped in white wax rust-resisting paper and packed with extra cutter in carton. One-half dozen to the multi carton.

New No.	Old No.	Length	Boring Capacity
WS	F1200C	8 1/4 in.	5/8 to 2 in.
WL	F1201C	9 in.	7/8 to 3 in.

Values:	Exc.	V.G.	Good
	75.00	65.00	50.00

Comment: *Values for either old or new number, either length.*

Expansive Bit Cutters

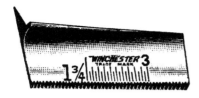

Expansive Bit Cutters are graduated by Sixteenths Inches. Packed one-half dozen to the carton. Weight 1/2 lb. per dozen.

New No.	Old No.	Boring Capacity
W1	F1241C	5/8 to 1 1/8 in.
W2	F1242C	1 1/8 to 2 in.
W3	F1243C	7/8 to 1 3/4 in.
W4	F1244C	1 3/4 to 3 in.

Values:	Exc.	V.G.	Good
	8.00	7.00	5.00

Comment: *Values for single cutter, either old or new number, any length.*

Bit Brace Extension

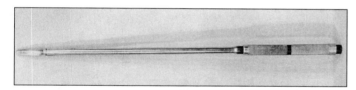

Bit Brace Extension (No. 3578) is 17 3/4 inches long. From T. Webster collection. Photo by D. Kowalski.

Steel extension rods, 3/8-inch diameter. Has 5/8-inch heavy knurled chuck. Hardened jaws, blued. Bit held in place by forged jaws of special design and reinforced by a sliding chuck shell. These extensions are so constructed that it is possible to make replacement of any of the parts, a distinctive feature of Winchester extensions. Each bit extension wrapped in white wax rust-resisting paper and packed in individual carton. One-half dozen to the multi carton.

New No.	Old No.	Length
W318	F3578C	18 in.
W324	F3579C	24 in.

Values:	Exc.	V.G.	Good
	75.00	65.00	50.00

Comment: *Values for either old or new number, either length.*

Twist Drills

Twist Drill Bit has "Winchester" stamped on it, as well as "14" for 14/32 inches. From T. Webster collection. Photo by D. Kowalski.

Twist Drills forged from highest grade tool steel, oil-tempered and full polished. Sizes 2/32 to 16/32 in. are packed one dozen in a cardboard box; larger sizes one-half dozen in a cardboard box. No. W109 - For metal or wood.

Diameter	Length (in.)	Diameter	Length (in.)
2/32	3 1/4	12/32	6
3/32	3 1/2	13/32	6 1/2
4/32	4	14/32	6 1/2
5/32	4 1/4	15/32	7
6/32	4 3/4	16/32	7
7/32	5	17/32	7 1/2
8/32	5 1/4	18/32	7 1/2
9/32	5 1/2	20/32	7 1/2
10/32	5 1/2	22/32	7 1/2
11/32	6	24/32	7 1/2

Values:	Exc.	V.G.	Good
	18.00	15.00	12.00

Comment: *Values for either old or new number, any width.*

Twist Drill Sets

No. W109M. Twist Drill Sets come in varnished hardwood cylinder boxes. Sets of nine drills - one each 2, 3, 4, 5, 6, 7, 8, 10, and 12/32 inch. Weight per set 1 1/4 lbs.

Values:	Exc.	V.G.	Good
	800.00	750.00	650.00

Comment: *Values for box with drills. For box only deduct 20 percent from above values.*

Mechanic Tools
Tool Cabinets, Tool Kits, Chisels, Nail Sets, Punches, Screwdrivers, Files, Pliers and Wrenches

by David D. Kowalski

This chapter completes our rundown of the carpentry tools with our coverage of wood chisels and nail sets. Then we'll present tool cabinets, originally filled with various carpentry tools.

Winchester also focused on the needs of mechanics and car owners generally. Their tool kits were marketed as handy selections for the garage workshop or as emergency kits carried in the family car. Finally, we'll cover the hand tools more often associated with mechanics rather than carpenters. These are the cold chisels, punches, screwdrivers, files, pliers and wrenches.

Small hand tools present another display challenge. Tom Webster used a horizontal format here with two wooden pegs under each tool for support. Photo by D. Kowalski.

Chisels

Wood Chisels

Blades and sockets are made from one solid piece of steel to give the maximum amount of strength. Edges are wide beveled so as to cut with a minimum of interference from the sides.

Winchester chisels are full mirror polished, with the blades sharpened; ready for use. Ends of handles are leather-tipped, reinforced with steel, which prevents mushrooming yet gives full resiliency.

Firmer Chisels

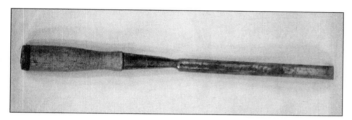

Firmer Chisel, bevel edge (No. 4983). Blade nicks and worn handle show this tool got used. From T. Webster collection. Photo by D. Kowalski.

Firmer Chisel, bevel edge, socket. One-piece full-polished blade. Special tool steel. Leather-tipped handle. Blade sharpened for use. Blade is 6 inches long. Packed one-half dozen in a carton.

New No.	Old No.	Blade Width (in.)
WB 1/8	F4980C	1/8
WB 1/4	F4981C	1/4
WB 3/8	F4982C	3/8
WB 1/2	F4983C	1/2
WB 5/8	F4984C	5/8
WB 3/4	F4985C	3/4
WB 7/8	F4986C	7/8
WB1	F4987C	1
WB1 1/4	F4989C	1 1/4
WB1 1/2	F4991C	1 1/2
WB1 3/4	F4993C	1 3/4
WB2	F4995C	2

Values: | Exc. | V.G. | Good
 | 65.00 | 50.00 | 25.00

Comment: *Values for single chisel, old or new number.*

Pocket Chisels

Pocket Chisel, bevel edge (No. 4855). Shows light pitting. From T. Webster collection. Photo by D. Kowalski.

Pocket Chisel, bevel edge, socket. One-piece mirror-finished blade of special tool steel. Leather-tipped handle. Sharpened for use. Blade is 4 1/2 inches long. Packed one-half dozen in a carton.

New No.	Old No.	Blade Width (in.)
WSB 1/4	F4841C	1/4
WSB 3/8	F4842C	3/8
WSB 1/2	F4843C	1/2
WSB 5/8	F4844C	5/8
WSB 3/4	F4845C	3/4
WSB1	F4847C	1
WSB1 1/4	F4849C	1 1/4
WSB1 1/2	F4851C	1 1/2
WSB1 3/4	F4853C	1 3/4
WSB2	F4855C	2

Values: | Exc. | V.G. | Good
 | 65.00 | 50.00 | 25.00

Comment: *Values for single chisel, old or new number.*

Butt Chisels

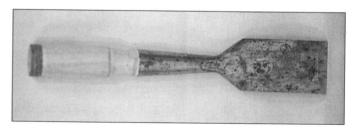

Butt Chisel, bevel edge (No. 4713). Shows significant rust. From T. Webster collection. Photo by D. Kowalski.

Butt Chisel, bevel edge, socket. One-piece mirror-finished blade of special tool steel. Leather-tipped handle. Blade sharpened for use. Blade is 3 inches long. Packed one-half dozen in a carton.

New No.	Old No.	Blade Width (in.)
W 1/4	---	1/4
W 3/8	---	3/8
W 1/2	F4703C	1/2

New No.	Old No.	Blade Width (in.)
W 5/8	F4704C	5/8
W 3/4	F4705C	3/4
W1	F4707C	1
W 1/4	F4709C	1 1/4
W1 1/2	F4711C	1 1/2
W1 3/4	F4713C	1 3/4
W2	F4715C	2

Values:	Exc.	V.G.	Good
	65.00	50.00	25.00

Comment: *Values for single chisel, old or new number.*

Cutaway Wood Chisel

Cutaway Wood Chisel. Available to stores for display purposes.

Values:	Exc.	V.G.	Good
	250.00	225.00	175.00

Comment: *Values for factory-cut model.*

Nail Sets

Nail Sets. Forged from high-grade octagonal steel, carefully heat-treated and tempered, grips finished in black enamel. Blades and ends polished. Packed one dozen in a carton.

New No.	Old No.	Pt. Diam.	Stock	Length
W100/1	F2771C	1/32 in.	3/8 in.	4 in.
W100/2	F2772C	2/32 in.	3/8 in.	4 in.
W100/3	F2773C	3/32 in.	3/8 in.	4 in.
W100/4	F2774C	4/32 in.	3/8 in.	4 in.
W100/5	F2775C	5/32 in.	3/8 in.	4 in.

Values:	Exc.	V.G.	Good
	65.00	50.00	25.00

Comment: *Values for single Nail Set, any size, old or new number.*

Nail Set Assortment

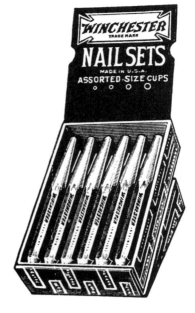

Nail Set Assortment consists of three each of the above nail sets, making one dozen packed in a "Rose" display carton. New No. W100; Old No. F2780C.

Values:	Exc.	V.G.	Good
	500.00	450.00	375.00

Comment: *Values for Nail Sets, old or new number, with display box.*

Tool Cabinets

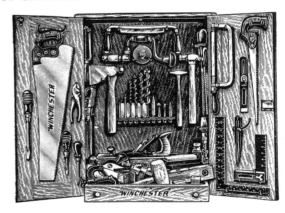

No. W9. Hardwood Wall Cabinet, with two paneled doors; has inside drawer, three inches deep. Natural finish, finely varnished and hand rubbed; brass-plated ball-tip steel hinges; two brass hangers on back; brass cylinder lock with two steel keys. Dimensions of cabinet: Outside - 31 inches high, 22 1/2 inches wide, 8 inches deep; Inside - 29 1/2 inches high, 21 inches wide, 6 1/2 inches deep. (Cabinet originally came with 48 tools and 14 other miscellaneous articles.)

Values:	Exc.	V.G.	Good
	2,800.00	2,600.00	2,200.00

Comment: *Values for Wall Cabinet without any tools.*

Tool Outfits

Tools are a necessity for every owner of an automobile and many others who need a convenient selection of most commonly used tools in handy form. The right combination of the most essential ones is a convenience every user will appreciate. Here are three handy outfits of tools required for emergency and repair work neatly encased in waterproof rolls that take the least amount of room and keep the tools where they can always be found on need. Every tool is a Winchester.

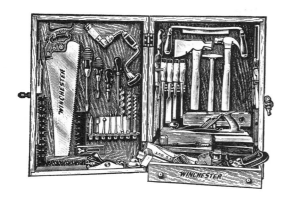

No. W7. Hardwood Wall Cabinet, with one paneled box door; has inside drawer, three inches deep. Natural finish, finely varnished and hand rubbed; brass-plated ball-tip steel hinges and hasp; two brass hangers on back; polished brass padlock with two steel keys. Dimensions of cabinet: Outside - 27 inches high, 18 1/2 inches wide, 9 inches deep; Inside - 25 1/2 inches high, 17 inches wide, 7 1/2 inches deep. (Cabinet originally came with 42 tools and 14 other miscellaneous articles.)

Values:	Exc.	V.G.	Good
	2,500.00	2,300.00	2,000.00

Comment: *Values for Wall Cabinet without any tools.*

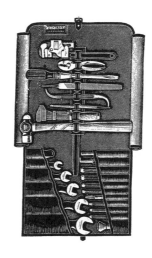

No. 1985. 25 Tool Outfit. Contains a complete selection of high-grade tools for automobile and general work. This outfit contains all the items that will generally be found needed at almost any kind of work around the car and garage and for many other purposes. It is put up in a handy roll, which makes it very convenient to carry, and to use. (Originally contained such tools as a ball pein hammer, cotter pin puller and even a pocketknife.) Roll packed in individual carton. Approximate weight 15 lbs.

Values:	Exc.	V.G.	Good
	3,500.00	3,200.00	2,800.00

Comment: *Values for Tool Outfit with all tools. Add 50 percent for original box.*

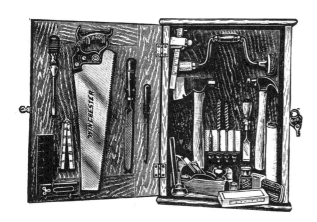

No. W3. Hardwood Wall Cabinet, with one paneled box door. Natural finish, finely varnished and hand rubbed; brass-plated steel hinges and hasp; two brass hangers on back; polished brass padlock with two steel keys. Dimensions of cabinet: Outside - 24 inches high, 16 inches wide, 6 inches deep; Inside - 22 1/2 inches high, 14 1/2 inches wide, 4 1/2 inches deep. (Cabinet originally came with 19 tools and 10 other miscellaneous articles.)

Values:	Exc.	V.G.	Good
	2,000.00	1,900.00	1,750.00

Comment: *Values for Wall Cabinet without any tools.*

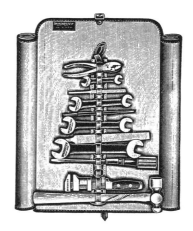

No. 1981. 11 Tool Outfit. Handy cloth roll contains a complete selection of high-grade tools especially adaptable to private garage and touring work. Roll packed in individual carton. Approximate weight 7 lbs.

Values:	Exc.	V.G.	Good
	2,800.00	2,500.00	2,200.00

Comment: *Values for Tool Outfit with all tools. Add 50 percent for original box.*

606 • *Mechanic Tools*

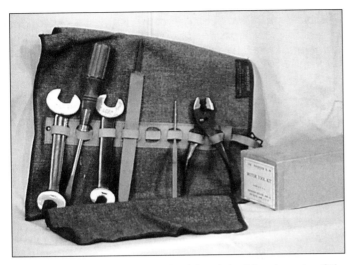

This 7 Tool Outfit (No. 1982) with original box has six of the original tools that were never used. It's only missing the 4 7/8-inch open end wrench. Some collectors would consider this outfit more valuable with the six original tools than if the missing wrench was replaced with a substitute in poor condition. From the Tom Webster collection. Photo by D. Kowalski.

No. 1982. 7 Tool Outfit. Contains the following Winchester tools that answer many requirements for repairs and emergency work. Roll packed in individual carton. Approximate weight 7 lbs.

Tool	Number	Description
Regular Champion Screw Driver	W40/5	5-inch length
Combination Slip Joint Plier	W260	6-inch length. Black finish, large and small jaw grip, wire cutter and screw driver.
Open End Wrench	W725	4 7/8-inch length
	W727	6 7/8-inch length
	W731	7 3/4-inch length
Mill Bastard File	WM8	8-inch length
Ignition File	W6	

Values:	Exc.	V.G.	Good
	2,500.00	2,300.00	2,000.00

Comment: *Values for Tool Outfit with all tools. Add 50 percent for original box.*

Cold Chisels and Punches

Winchester cold chisels and punches are forged from special high grade octagonal steel properly heat-treated and tempered to make the strong satisfactory tool that is required for the work to be done by such a tool. Edges and points are tough and strong, carefully shaped for their purpose. Grips finished in black enamel. Blades and ends full polished.

Regular Flat Cold Chisel. Sizes 3/4, 5/16, and 3/8 - one dozen; 1/2 to 1 - one-half dozen in a carton.

New No.	Old No.	Cut	Stock	Length
W14	F4512C	1/4 in.	1/4 in.	5 in.
W516	F4513C	5/16 in.	5/16 in.	5 in.
W38	F4514C	3/8 in.	3/8 in.	5 in.
W12	F4515C	1/2 in.	7/16 in.	6 in.
W58	F4516C	5/8 in.	1/2 in.	6 1/2 in.
W34	F4517C	3/4 in.	5/8 in.	7 in.
W78	F4518C	7/8 in.	3/4 in.	8 in.
W10	F4519C	1 in.	7/8 in.	8 1/2 in.

Values:	Exc.	V.G.	Good
	75.00	60.00	35.00

Comment: *Values for single chisel, any width, old or new number.*

Round Nose Cold Chisel. Sizes 3/16 and 1/4 - one dozen; 5/16 to 1/2 - one-half dozen in a carton.

New No.	Old No.	Cut	Stock	Length
W53 3/16	F4531C	3/16 in.	5/16 in.	5 in.
W53 1/4	F4532C	1/4 in.	3/8 in.	5 in.
W53 5/16	F4533C	5/16 in.	1/2 in.	5 1/2 in.
W53 3/8	F4534C	3/8 in.	5/8 in.	6 in.
W53 1/2	F4535C	1/2 in.	3/4 in.	7 in.

Values:	Exc.	V.G.	Good
	65.00	50.00	25.00

Comment: *Values for single chisel, any width, old or new number.*

Mechanic Tools • 607

Diamond Point Nose Cold Chisel. Sizes 3/16 and 1/4 - one dozen; 5/16 and 3/8 - one-half dozen in a carton.

New No.	Old No.	Cut	Stock	Length
W55 3/16	F4551C	3/16 in.	5/16 in.	5 in.
W55 1/4	F4552C	1/4 in.	3/8 in.	5 in.
W55 5/16	F4553C	5/16 in.	1/2 in.	5 1/2 in.
W55 3/8	F4554C	3/8 in.	5/8 in.	6 in.

Values: Exc. 65.00   V.G. 50.00   Good 25.00

Comment: *Values for single chisel, any width, old or new number.*

Cape Chisel

Cape Chisel. Sizes 3/16 and 1/4 - one dozen; 3/8 to 5/8 - one-half dozen in a carton.

New No.	Old No.	Cut	Stock	Length
W57 3/16	F4571C	3/16 in.	5/16 in.	5 1/2 in.
W57 1/4	F4572C	1/4 in.	3/8 in.	5 1/2 in.
W57 3/8	F4574C	3/8 in.	1/2 in.	6 in.
W57 1/2	F4575C	1/2 in.	5/8 in.	6 1/2 in.
W57 5/8	F4576C	5/8 in.	3/4 in.	7 in.

Values: Exc. 65.00   V.G. 50.00   Good 25.00

Comment: *Values for single chisel, any width, old or new number.*

Ripping Chisel

Ripping Chisel. Made to exclusive Winchester pattern. Beveled side edges. Cutting edge has special bevel designed to cut wood or metal. Perfectly tempered and may be sharpened with a file. Face, bevels and taper bit polished. Blades have just enough offset so hand will clear work. Designed especially for work of electricians and plumbers. Each chisel paper wrapped and packed one-half dozen in a carton.

New No.	Old No.	Cut	Length
WRC5/8	F4596C	5/8 in.	11 in.
WRC1	F4599C	1 in.	11 in.

Values: Exc. 75.00   V.G. 60.00   Good 35.00

Comment: *Values for single chisel, any width, old or new number.*

Solid Punch

Solid Punches. Packed one dozen in a carton.

New No.	Old No.	Stock	Length
W384	F2745C	3/8 in.	4 in.

Values: Exc. 65.00   V.G. 50.00   Good 25.00

Comment: *Values for single punch, old or new number.*

Pin Punch

Pin Punches. Packed one dozen in a carton.

New No.	Old No.	Pt. Diam.	Stock	Length
W15	F2711C	1/8 in.	3/8 in.	5 in.
W13	F2712C	3/16 in.	3/8 in.	5 in.
W11	F2713C	1/4 in.	3/8 in.	5 in.
W9	F2714C	5/16 in.	3/8 in.	5 in.
W7	F2715C	3/8 in.	3/8 in.	5 in.

Values: Exc. 65.00   V.G. 50.00   Good 25.00

Comment: *Values for single punch, any size, old or new number.*

Prick Punch

Prick Punch. Round knurled barrel. Packed one dozen in a carton.

New No.	Old No.	Stock	Length
W217	---	3/8 in.	4 in.

Prick Punch. Octagon barrel. Packed one dozen in a carton.

New No.	Old No.	Stock	Length
W117	F2725C	3/8 in.	4 in.

Values: Exc. 65.00   V.G. 50.00   Good 25.00

Comment: *Values for single Prick Punch, either style, old or new number.*

608 • *Mechanic Tools*

Center Punch

Center Punch. Round knurled barrel. Packed one dozen in a carton.

New No.	Old No.	Stock	Length
W215	---	3/8 in.	4 in.

Center Punch. Octagon barrel. Packed one dozen in a carton.

New No.	Old No.	Stock	Length
W115	F2735C	3/8 in.	4 in.

Values: | Exc. | V.G. | Good |
| 65.00 | 50.00 | 25.00 |

Comment: *Values for single Center Punch, either style, old or new number.*

Cotter Pin Puller

Cotter Pin Puller. Forged from high-grade octagonal steel, carefully heat-treated and tempered. Grips finished in black enamel. Blades and ends polished. Packed one dozen in a carton.

New No.	Old No.	Stock	Length
W8	F2795C	3/8 in.	8 in.

Values: | Exc. | V.G. | Good |
| 175.00 | 150.00 | 125.00 |

Comment: *Values for single Puller, old or new number.*

Screw Drivers

Blades of all Winchester screwdrivers are made of special alloy steel, tempered full length. This gives great strength, toughness and hardness. The distinctive lug-and-notch construction, used on all the screw drivers of the Cabinet, Regular and Mechanics' Special patterns, locks the blade and handle securely so that it is practically impossible for the blade to turn or loosen in the handle even under the severest strain.

Offset Screw Driver

Forged from high-grade octagonal steel, carefully heat-treated and tempered. Grips finished in black enamel. Blades and ends polished. Packed one dozen in a carton.

New No.	Old No.	Stock	Length
W0S6	F2815C	3/8 in.	6 in.

Values: | Exc. | V.G. | Good |
| 175.00 | 150.00 | 125.00 |

Comment: *Values for single Offset Screw Driver, old or new number.*

Cutaway Screw Driver

Cutaway Screw Driver. Available to stores for display purposes.

Values: | Exc. | V.G. | Good |
| 1,000.00 | 900.00 | 700.00 |

Comment: *Values for factory-cut model.*

Mechanics' Special Screw Driver

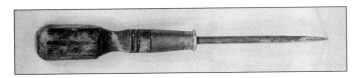

Mechanics' Special Screw Driver (No. 7123). Shows lug-and-notch handle construction. From T. Webster collection. Photo by D. Kowalski.

Mechanics' Special Screw Driver. Blade made of special alloy steel. Full tempered. Lug-and-notch construction, blade running through entire length of handle and forming the head. Steel bolster. Brass ferrule. Winchester gray handle. Wrapped in individual scabbards; one-half dozen in a carton.

New No.	Old No.	Blade Length
W20/2	F7121C	2 in.
W20/3	F7122C	3 in.
W20/4	F7123C	4 in.
W20/5	F7124C	5 in.
W20/6	F7125C	6 in.
W20/8	F7126C	8 in.
W20/10	F7127C	10 in.

Regular Pattern Screw Driver

Regular Pattern Screw Driver. Blade made of special alloy steel. Full tempered. Lug-and-notch construction. Strong steel bolster. Brass ferrule. Winchester gray handle. Wrapped in individual scabbards; one-half dozen in a carton.

New No.	Old No.	Blade Length
W40/2	F7101C	2 in.
W40/3	P7102C	3 in.
W40/4	F7103C	4 in.
W40/5	F7104C	5 in.
W40/6	F7105C	6 in.
W40/8	F7106C	8 in.
W40/10	F7107C	10 in.

Cabinet Pattern Screw Driver

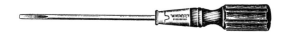

Cabinet Pattern Screw Driver. Blade made of special alloy steel. Full tempered. Lug-and-notch construction. Strong steel bolster. Brass ferrule. Winchester gray handle. Blade of small diameter, particularly designed for close and delicate work in tight places. Blade diameter on three smaller sizes is 5/32 of an inch; on three larger sizes it is 3/16 of an inch. Wrapped in individual scabbards; one-half dozen in a carton.

New No.	Old No.	Blade Length
W45/3	F7112C	3 in.
W45/4	F7113C	4 in.
W45/5	F7114C	5 in.
W45/6	F7115C	6 in.
W45/8	F7116C	8 in.
W45/10	F7117C	10 in.

Values: Exc. 75.00   V.G. 60.00   Good 35.00

Comment: *Values for single screwdriver with lug-and-notch construction (Mechanics' Special, Regular pattern, Cabinet pattern), any length, old or new number.*

Household Screw Driver

Household Screw Driver. Round polished blade of high-grade steel. Heavy steel ferrule. Mahogany stained and varnished handle. Blade securely fastened to handle so it will not turn. Packed one-half dozen in a carton.

New No.	Old No.	Blade Length
WH2	F7171C	2 in.
WH3	F7172C	3 in.
WH4	F7173C	4 in.
WH5	F7174C	5 in.
WH6	F7175C	6 in.
WH8	F7176C	8 in.

Values: Exc. 65.00   V.G. 50.00   Good 25.00

Comment: *This was Winchester's economy screwdriver without lug-and-notch handle. Values for single screwdriver, any length, old or new number.*

Pocket Screw Driver

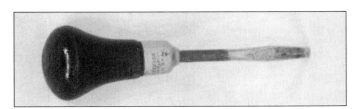

Pocket Screw Driver (No. 7160). From T. Webster collection. Photo by D. Kowalski.

Pocket Screw Driver. Blade made of special alloy steel carefully hardened and tempered. Knurled for convenience in rapid rotation. Hard maple handle shaped especially to fit the palm of the hand. Stained Winchester gray. Packed one-half dozen in a carton.

New No.	Old No.	Blade Length
WP	F7160C	1 5/8 in.

Values: Exc. 80.00   V.G. 65.00   Good 50.00

Comment: *Values for single screwdriver, old or new number.*

Screw Driver Roll

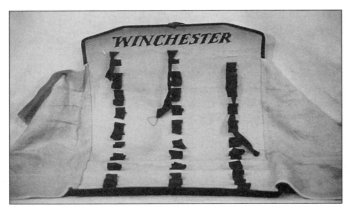

Cloth Screwdriver Roll is bright orange with black trim. From T. Webster collection. Photo by D. Kowalski.

Values:	Exc.	V.G.	Good
	425.00	375.00	300.00

Comment: *Designed for long screwdrivers.*

Screwdriver Counter Display

Screwdriver or wood chisel display for retail counters has six holes for tools. From T. Webster collection. Photo by D. Kowalski.

Values:	Exc.	V.G.	Good
	300.00	275.00	250.00

Comment: *Values for this display. There is also a version with square holes for tennis rackets that would be valued at 25 percent more than above values.*

Files

Forged from single bars of high-quality steel, tempered by a process that gives great toughness and hardness. Cut by skilled workmen.

Mill Bastard File. Packing: 4 to 10 inch - one dozen; 12 and 14 inch - one-half dozen in a carton.

New No.	Old No.	Size
WM4	F8030M	4 in.
WM5	F8031M	5 in.
WM6	F8032M	6 in.
WM7	F8042M	7 in.
WM8	F8033M	8 in.
WM10	F8034M	10 in.
WM12	F8035M	12 in.
WM14	F8036M	14 in.

Values:	Exc.	V.G.	Good
	45.00	40.00	30.00

Comment: *Values for any length, old or new number.*

Flat Bastard File. Packing: 6 to 10 inch - one dozen; 12 to 16 inch - one-half dozen in a carton.

New No.	Old No.	Size
WFB6	F8045M	6 in.
WFB8	F8046M	8 in.
WFB10	F8047M	10 in.
WFB12	F8048M	12 in.
WFB14	F8049M	14 in.
WFB16	F8050M	16 in.

Values:	Exc.	V.G.	Good
	45.00	40.00	30.00

Comment: *Values for any length, old or new number.*

Square Bastard File. Packing: 3 to 10 inch - one dozen; 12 and 14 inch - one-half dozen in a carton.

New No.	Old No.	Size
WSB3	F8075M	3 in.
WSB4	F8076M	4 in.
WSB5	F8077M	5 in.
WSB6	F8078M	6 in.
WSB8	F8079M	8 in.
WSB10	F8080M	10 in.
WSB12	F8081M	12 in.
WSB14	F8082M	14 in.

Values:	Exc.	V.G.	Good
	90.00	80.00	60.00

Comment: *Values for any length, old or new number.*

Half-Round Bastard File. Packing: 6 to 10 inch - one dozen; 12 and 14 inch - one-half dozen in a carton.

New No.	Old No.	Size
WHR6	F8090M	6 in.
WHR8	F8091M	8 in.
WHR10	F8092M	10 in.
WHR12	F8093M	12 in.
WHR14	F8094M	14 in.

Values: Exc. 55.00   V.G. 50.00   Good 40.00

Comment: *Values for any length, old or new number.*

Round Bastard File. Packing: 3 to 10 inch - one dozen; 12 and 14 inch - one-half dozen in a carton.

New No.	Old No.	Size
WRB3	F8060M	3 in.
WRB4	F8061M	4 in.
WRB5	F8062M	5 in.
WRB6	F8063M	6 in.
WRB8	F8064M	8 in.
WRB10	F8065M	10 in.
WRB12	F8066M	12 in.
WRB14	F8067M	14 in.

Values: Exc. 80.00   V.G. 70.00   Good 50.00

Comment: *Values for any length, old or new number.*

Warding Bastard File. Packed one dozen in a carton.

New No.	Old No.	Size
WWB3	F8105M	3 in.
WWB4	F8106M	4 in.
WWB5	F8107M	5 in.
WWB6	F8108M	6 in.
WWB8	P8110M	8 in.

Values: Exc. 45.00   V.G. 40.00   Good 30.00

Comment: *Values for any length, old or new number.*

Great American Cross Cut File. Packed one dozen in a carton.

New No.	Old No.	Size
WGA8	F8308M	8 in.
WGA10	F8310M	10 in.

Values: Exc. 65.00   V.G. 60.00   Good 50.00

Comment: *Values for any length, old or new number.*

Extra Slim Taper File. Packed one dozen in a carton.

New No.	Old. No.	Size
WEST3	F8001M	3 in.
WEST3 1/2	F8002M	3 1/2 in.
WEST4	F8003M	4 in.
WEST4 1/2	F8004M	4 1/2 in.
WEST5	F8005M	5 in.
WEST5 1/2	F8007M	5 1/2 in.
WEST6	F8006M	6 in.
WEST7	F8008M	7 in.

Values: Exc. 65.00   V.G. 55.00   Good 40.00

Comment: *Values for any length, old or new number.*

Slim Taper File. Packed one dozen in a carton.

New No.	Old. No.	Size
WST3	F8009M	3 in.
WST3 1/2	F8010M	3 1/2 in.
WST4	F8011M	4 in.
WST4 1/2	F8012M	4 1/2 in.
WST5	F8013M	5 in.
WST5 1/2	F8014M	5 1/2 in.
WST6	F8015M	6 in.
WST7	F8016M	7 in.
WST8	F8017M	8 in.
WST10	F8018M	10 in.

Values: Exc. 60.00   V.G. 50.00   Good 35.00

Comment: *Values for any length, old or new number.*

Double End Taper File. Packed one dozen in a carton.

New No.	Old. No.	Size
WDE7	F8207M	7 in.
WDE8	F8208M	8 in.
WDE9	F8209M	9 in.
WDE10	F8210M	10 in.

Values: Exc. 90.00 V.G. 80.00 Good 65.00

Comment: *Values for any length, old or new number.*

Ignition File. Packed one dozen in a carton.

New No.	Old. No.	Size
W6	F8145M	6 1/2 in.

Values: Exc. 225.00 V.G. 200.00 Good 175.00

Comment: *Values for old or new number.*

Half-Round Wood Rasp

Half-Round Wood Rasp. Forged from single bars of high-quality steel, tempered by a process that gives great toughness and hardness; Cut by skilled workmen. Packed one-half dozen in a carton.

New No.	Old. No.	Size
WHRWR10	F8120M	10 in.
WHRWR12	F8121M	12 in.
WHRWR14	F8122M	14 in.

Values: Exc. 50.00 V.G. 45.00 Good 35.00

Comment: *Values for any length, old or new number.*

Shoe Rasp

Shoe Rasp. Forged from single bars of high-quality steel, tempered by a process that gives great toughness and hardness; Cut by skilled workmen. Packed one-half dozen in a carton.

New No.	Old. No.	Size
WRS8	F8135M	8 in.

Values: Exc. 90.00 V.G. 80.00 Good 65.00

Comment: *Values for any length, old or new number.*

Winchester Pliers

These pliers are forged from special steel, selected and heat-treated by skilled workmen in accordance with the precise formulas developed by Winchester engineers. Jaws of Winchester pliers are tough and hard, sharply milled and designed to prevent crushing or chipping. Handles of all pliers are knurled to give good grip and specially shaped to fit the hand comfortably.

Slip Joint Pliers

Slip joint pliers are designed to give the greatest possible leverage and to give freedom of action without becoming loose. The shouldered rivets used on these pliers prevent any possibility of binding and at the same time hold pliers tight.

Combination Slip Joint Plier. Vest pocket type. A neat small plier milled with large and small jaw grip. Wire cutter attachment. Winchester knurled handles. Packed one-half dozen in a carton.

New No.	Old No.	Finish	Length
W150	F2495M	Nickel-plated	5 1/2 in.
W250	F2105M	Black	5 1/2 in.

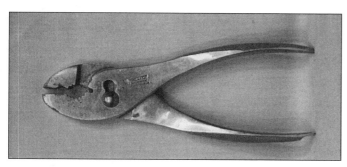

Combination Slip Joint Plier (No. 2496). From T. Webster collection. Photo by D. Kowalski.

Combination Slip Joint Plier. Large and small jaw grip. Wire cutter attachment. Has screwdriver on one handle; knurled handles. Packed one-half dozen in a carton.

New No.	Old No.	Finish	Length
W160	F2496M	Nickel-plated	6 in.
W260	F2106M	Black	6 in.

Combination Slip Joint Plier. Heavy type for severe duty. Design of jaws made to give good grip on large or small objects. Square hole for holding nuts and other square objects. Wire cutter and screwdriver attached. Packed one-half dozen in a carton.

New No.	Old No.	Finish	Length
W180	F2498M	Nickel-plated	8 in.
W28O	F2108M	Black	8 in.

Combination Slip Joint Plier. Heaviest Winchester plier of this type. Has great strength and leverage. Built for heavy service. Two sizes of gripping forms and flat end grip. Wire cutter. Packed one-half dozen in a carton.

New No.	Old No.	Finish	Length
W1100	F2499M	Nickel-plated	10 in.
W2100	F2109M	Black	10 in.

Universal Slip Joint Plier. Forged from special steel, accurately machined and finely finished. Winchester knurled hand grips. Shape of jaws enables gripping objects of any irregular shape. Teeth in jaws sharp and hard. Wire cutter in handle. This plier will do all the work of a parallel jaw plier. Packed one-half dozen in a carton.

New No.	Old No.	Length
W170	F2467M	7 in.

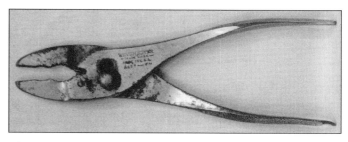

Thin Nose Slip Joint Plier (No. 2457). From T. Webster collection. Photo by D. Kowalski.

Thin Nose Slip Joint Plier. Winchester knurled handle. Furnished with wire cutter and screwdriver. The thin nose and tapered jaws valuable for use on objects difficult to reach. Packed one-half dozen in a carton.

New No.	Old No.	Finish	Length
W175	F2457M	Nickel-plated	7 in.

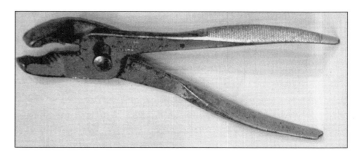

Bent Nose Combination Slip Joint Plier (No. 2488). From T. Webster collection. Photo by D. Kowalski.

Bent Nose Combination Slip Joint Plier. Shaped to permit work at odd angles and in holes without bruising the hand. Flat nose and square hole for nuts. Screw driver on one handle. Packed one-half dozen in a carton.

New No.	Old No.	Finish	Length
WB18	F2488M	Nickel-plated	8 in.
WB110	F2489M	Nickel-plated	10 in.

Values:	Exc.	V.G.	Good
	60.00	50.00	35.00

Comment: *Values for any Slip Joint Plier, any model or length, old or new number.*

Lap Joint Pliers

Lap joint pliers have sturdy, long joints designed with special attention to making jaws and handles rigid. Each style carefully tempered to right degree to fit its particular purpose.

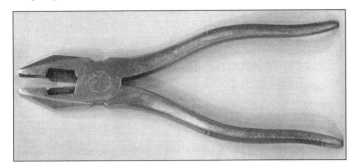

Lineman's Side Cutting Lap Joint Plier (No. 2116). From T. Webster collection. Photo by D. Kowalski.

Lineman's Side Cutting Lap Joint Plier. Heavy heads. Jaws and cutting edges accurately machined. Handles shaped to the hand. Knurled hand grip. Powerful leverage. Sharp, everlasting cutters. Winchester finish. Packed one-half dozen in a carton.

New No.	Old No.	Length
W966	F2116M	6 in.
W967	F2117M	7 in.
W968	F2118M	8 1/2 in.

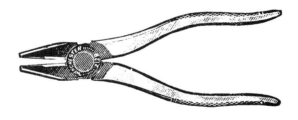

Electrician's Side Cutting Lap Joint Plier. Light-nose type. Built on graceful lines with beveled nose. Designed for work of electricians and mechanics who need a strong side cutting plier but do not require so heavy a tool as the lineman's pattern. Adaptable to interior electrical wiring. The small size is much used in the millinery trade. Packed one-half dozen in a carton.

New No.	Old No.	Length
W14	F22122M	4 in.
W15	F2124M	5 in.
W16	F2126M	6 in.

Values:	Exc.	V.G.	Good
	70.00	60.00	45.00

Comment: Values for any model or length of Lineman's Side Cutting or Electrician's Side Cutting Lap Joint Plier, old or new number. Add 25 percent premium for 4-inch Electrician's Side Cutting Lap Joint Plier

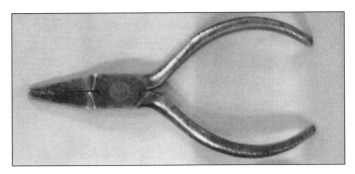

Flat Nose Lap Joint Plier (No. 2190). This 3-inch version is one of only two 3-inch tools made by Winchester. From T. Webster collection. Photo by D. Kowalski.

Flat Nose Lap Joint Plier. Forged from high-grade steel. Highly polished with knurled handles made especially to fit the hand comfortably. Hand file cut on inside of jaws. An ideal tool where a simple, plain plier is required. Packed one-half dozen in a carton.

New No.	Old No.	Length
W89F3	F2190M	3 in.
W89F4	F2192M	4 in.
W89F5	F2194M	5 in.
W89F6	F2196M	6 in.

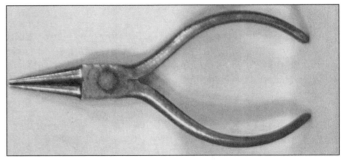

Round Nose Lap Joint Plier (No. 2180). This 3-inch version is one of only two 3-inch tools made by Winchester. From T. Webster collection. Photo by D. Kowalski.

Round Nose Lap Joint Plier. The most graceful and lightest-weight round nose plier made in this country. Nose design based on a famous French pattern with Winchester improvements in style and fitting of joints. Packed one-half dozen in a carton.

New No.	Old No.	Length
W890R3	F2180M	3 in.
W890R4	F2182M	4 in.
W890R5	F2184M	5 in.
W890R6	F2186M	6 in.

Values:	Exc.	V.G.	Good
	110.00	100.00	90.00

Comment: Values for any model or length of Flat Nose and Round Nose Lap Joint Plier, except the 3-inch versions. Add 500 percent premium for the very rare 3-inch model in either design.

Mechanic Tools • 615

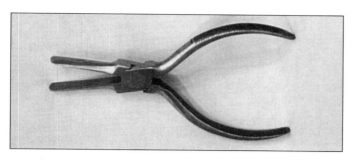

Duck's Bill Lap Joint Plier (No. 2214). From T. Webster collection. Photo by D. Kowalski.

Duck's Bill Pattern Lap Joint Plier. Made with long, slender spring-tempered jaws. Close-fitting lap joint. Packed one-half dozen in a carton.

New No.	Old No.	Length
W84	F2212M	4 in.
W85	F2214M	5 in.

Values:	Exc.	V.G.	Good
	110.00	100.00	90.00

Comment: *Values for either length, old or new model.*

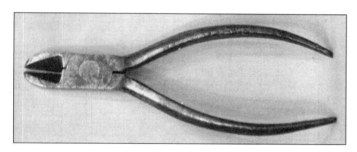

Diagonal Cutting Lap Joint Plier (No. 2234). From T. Webster collection. Photo by D. Kowalski.

Diagonal Cutting Pattern Lap Joint Plier. Made with oblique cutters that cut closely. Narrow head permits use in confined places. Knives perfectly fitted and meet accurately at all points. These pliers will cut silk-covered wire cleanly and without mashing. Packed one-half dozen in a carton.

New No.	Old No.	Length
W44	F2232M	4 in.
W45	F2234M	5 in.
W46	F2236M	6 in.

Values:	Exc.	V.G.	Good
	90.00	75.00	60.00

Comment: *Values for any length, old or new model.*

Cutting Nippers

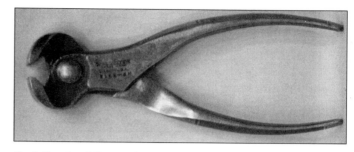

End Cutting Nippers (No. 2166). From T. Webster collection. Photo by D. Kowalski.

End Cutting Nippers. Has great strength and is easy to operate. Jaw of special design. Joint is set well toward jaws to give maximum leverage. Special beveled cutting edges, heat-treated under Winchester formula, insure easy cutting with least effort. Packed one-half dozen in a carton.

New No.	Old No.	Length
W5	F2164M	5 in.
W6	F2166M	6 in.
W8	F2168M	8 in.

Values:	Exc.	V.G.	Good
	65.00	55.00	40.00

Comment: *Values for any length, old or new model.*

Short Nose Side Cutting Chain Plier

Short Nose Side Cutting Chain Plier. Drop forged, full polished plier with knurled handles. Inside of jaws have hand-filed cut. Shackle hole in end of handle. Constructed with long joints for strength. Special cutter will cut silk-covered wire without drawing silk or bruising wire. Packed one-half dozen in a carton.

New No.	Old No.	Length
W65	F2254M	5 in.

Values:	Exc.	V.G.	Good
	110.00	100.00	90.00

Comment: *Values for old or new model.*

Universal Side Cutting Plier

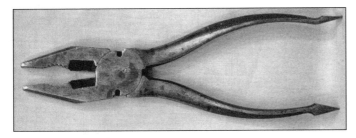

Universal Side Cutting Plier (No. 2148). From T. Webster collection. Photo by D. Kowalski.

Universal Side Cutting Plier. Drop-forged side cutting plier for universal use. Exceptionally well-designed plier with side cutters, two joint wire cutters, reamer, screwdriver and slotted jaw for brad awl use. Full polished. Knurled handle grips. Packed one-half dozen in a carton.

New No.	Old No.	Length
W96	F2146M	6 1/2 in.
W98	F2148M	8 in.

Universal Side Cutting Plier, Button's Pattern

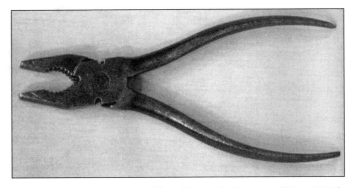

Universal Side Cutting Plier, Button's Pattern (No. 2136). From T. Webster collection. Photo by D. Kowalski.

Button's Pattern. Universal Side Cutting Plier. Perfectly designed drop-forged pliers. Jaws carefully cut and fitted to insure easy action. Designed with firm gripping milled feature and three wire cutters. Full polished. Knurled hand grips. A perfect household and general utility tool. Packed one-half dozen in a carton.

New No.	Old No.	Length
W206	F2136M	6 in.
W208	F2138M	8 in.
W210	F2139M	10 in.

Values:	Exc.	V.G.	Good
	90.00	75.00	60.00

Comment: *Values for either pattern of Universal Side Cutting Plier, any length, old or new model.*

Pipe Wrenches

The strongest wrench of this type on the market. Frames are of pressed steel. Adjustable jaw, reinforced at shoulder, is forged from nickel steel. Lower jaw is removable and inserted in a positive manner. It is made from special-grade steel. Teeth in both jaws accurately milled to a pitch which insures quick grip and easy release. This is the only pipe wrench on the market with jaws of such superior steel. Thread on movable jaw and adjusting nut is a special Winchester development, smooth and quick in action and will not jam.

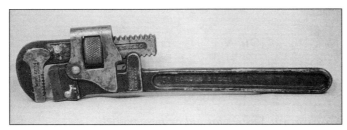

Pipe Wrench with steel handle (No. WSP10). From T. Webster collection. Photo by D. Kowalski.

Pipe Wrench, steel handle. Packed six to the carton.

New No.	Old No.	Size	Weight Each
WSP6	F1030M	6 in.	1/2 lb.
WSP8	F1031M	8 in.	3/4 lb.
WSP10	F1032M	10 in.	2 lbs.
WSP14	F1033M	14 in.	3 lbs.
WSP18	F1034M	18 in.	5 lbs.

Monkey Wrench, Coe's Pattern

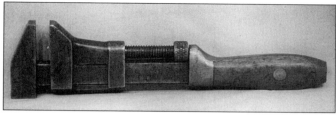

Monkey Wrench, Coe's Pattern (No. 1004). From T. Webster collection. Photo by D. Kowalski.

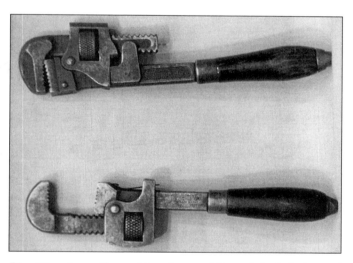

Pipe Wrench with wood handle (No. WWP10). From T. Webster collection. Photo by D. Kowalski.

Pipe Wrenches with wood handles went through both design and measurement changes. Old model 1021 (on left) is plainer and simpler in design and is 8 inches long with jaws fully extended. New model WWP8 is measured as 8 inches when jaws are closed. From T. Webster collection. Photo by D. Kowalski.

Pipe Wrench, wood handle. Packed six to the carton.

New No.	Old No.	Size	Weight Each
WWP6	P1020M	6 in.	1/2 lb.
WWP8	F1021M	8 in.	3/4 lb.
WWP10	F1022M	10 in.	2 lbs.
WWP14	F1023M	14 in.	3 1/4 lbs.

Values:
Exc.	V.G.	Good
90.00	70.00	45.00

Comment: *Values for either steel or wood handle, any length, old or new model.*

Coe's Pattern - Monkey Wrench. Knife handle. Bar and jaws forged out of special-grade steel, which produces a wrench capable of withstanding a very high degree of strain. The head and jaws are scientifically hardened. Material, construction and workmanship fit the wrench to withstand severe service. The sliding jaw is set in accurately, allowing little play. Adjusting screw is extra heavy. Sides of handles made of selected hardwood. Handles riveted through frame and bar. Black finish. Packed: 6 to 12 inch, six; 15 to 21 inch, four in a carton.

New No.	Old No.	Size	Weight Each
WB6	F1001M	6 in.	3/4 lb.
WB8	F1002M	8 in.	1 lb.
WB16	F1003M	10 in.	1 3/4 lbs.
WB12	F1004M	12 in.	2 3/4 lbs.
WB15	F1005M	15 in.	3 1/2 lbs.
WB18	F1006M	18 in.	5 1/4 lbs.
WB21	F1007M	21 in.	7 lbs.

Values:
Exc.	V.G.	Good
90.00	70.00	45.00

Comment: *Values for any length, old or new model.*

Open End Wrenches

Forged flat from bar steel. Milled carefully and case hardened. Head of each wrench marked with nut size for which it is designed. Full finished. Polished all over, handles black rustproof finish. Polished heads.

Check Nut Open End Wrench. Milled to fit U.S. bolt sizes. Packed five in a carton.

New No.	Old No.	Nut Size	Milled Size	Length
W623	F1607M	3/16-1/4	12/32-16/32	4 3/8
W627	F1619M	5/16-3/8	18/32-22/32	5 1/2
W631	F1631M	7/16-1/2	24/32-28/32	7
W635	F1643M	9/16-5/8	30/32-32/32	10 3/8

Double Head Engineers' Open End Wrench. Has 15-degree angle. Milled to fit U.S. Standard bolts and nuts. Packed: 4 to 7 3/4 inch, six; 9 3/4 to 13 1/2 inch, three in a carton.

New No.	Old No.	U.S. Size	Milled Size	Length
W23	F1197M	3/16-1/4	13/32-1/2	4
W25		1/4-5/16	1/2-19/32	4 7/8
W27	F1119M	5/16-3/8	19/32-11/16	5 7/8
W29		3/8-7/16	11/16-25/32	6 7/8
W31	F1131M	7/16-1/2	25/32-28/32	7 3/4
W33		1/2-9/16	7/8-31/32	8 3/4
W35	F1143M	1/2-5/8	7/8-1 1/16	9 3/4
W37		5/8-3/4	1 1/16-1 1/4	11 1/2
W39	F1152M	3/4-7/8	1 1/4-1 7/16	13 1/2

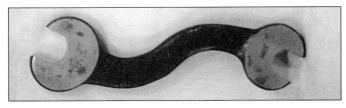

Heavy Duty Double Head "S" Open End Wrench (No. 1837). From T. Webster collection. Photo by D. Kowalski.

Heavy Duty Double Head "S" Open End Wrench. Has 22 1/2-degree angle. A type designed especially for heavy duty. Milled to fit U.S. Standard hexagon head cap screws. Packed: 4 to 9 inch, five; 10 1/2 inch, three in a carton.

New No.	Old No.	Cap Screw	Milled Size	Length
W660	F1801M	1/8-3/16	10/32-12/32	4
W661	F1810M	1/4-5/16	14/32-16/32	5
W662	F1813M	5/16-3/8	16/32-18/32	5
W663	F1814M	5/16-7/16	16/32-20/32	5
W664	F1817M	3/8-1/2	18/32-24/32	6 1/4
W665	F1823M	7/16-9/16	20/32-26/32	6 1/4
W666	F1837M	5/8-3/4	28/32-32/32	9
W667	F1849M	7/8-1	36/32-40/32	10 1/2

General Purpose "S" Open End Wrench. Milled to fit Standard bolts and nuts. Packed: 6 1/4 to 9 1/4 inch, five; 10 3/8 inch, three in a carton.

New No.	Old No.	Stan. Size	Milled Size	Length
W380	F1505M	3/16-1/4	12/32-16/32	6 1/4
W500	F1514M	1/4-5/16	10/32-20/32	7 1/8
W580	F1522M	5/16-3/8	20/32-24/32	8 1/4
W750	F1528M	3/8-7/16	24/32-28/32	9 1/4
W1000	F1537M	7/16-1/2	28/32-32/32	10 3/8

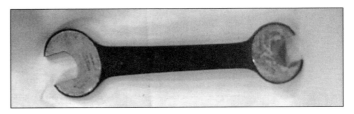

SAE Standard Open End Wrench (No. W136). From T. Webster collection. Photo by D. Kowalski.

SAE Standard Open End Wrench. Light model; forged bar steel, carefully milled and case hardened. Milled to fit S.A.E. bolts and nuts. Handles have black rustproof finish. Polished heads. Packed six in a carton.

New No.	Old No.	SAE Size	Milled Size	Length
W125	F1705M	1/4-5/16	14/32-16/32	4 7/8
W127	F1716M	3/8-7/16	18/32-20/32	6 1/8
W131	F1728M	1/2-9/16	24/32-28/32	7 1/4
W136	F1740M	5/8-11/16	30/32-32/32	8 1/2
W137	F1749M	3/4-7/8	34/32-40/32	9

Double Head Cap Screw Open End Wrench. Has 15-degree angle. Milled to fit U.S. Standard hexagon head cap screws. Packed six in a carton.

New No.	Old No.	Cap Screw	Milled Size	Length
W723	F1204M	3/16-1/4	12/32-14/32	4
W725	F1213M	5/16-3/8	16/32-18/32	4 7/8
W727	F1222M	7/16-1/2	20/32-24/32	6 7/8
W731	F1234M	9/16-5/8	26/32-28/32	7 3/4
F735	F1246M	3/4-7/8	32/32-36/32	9 3/4

Textile Open End Wrench has very slight "S" curve to handle. This is 9-inch version. From T. Webster collection. Photo by D. Kowalski.

Values:	Exc.	V.G.	Good
	45.00	35.00	20.00

Comment: *Values for any style of Open End Wrench, any length, old or new model.*

Mechanic Tools • 619

Wrench Assortments.

These display boards have been made with easel backs so that they support themselves and can be placed anywhere in your store. The easel support is firmly attached to the board by a brass chain. These boards have been designed to be effective "silent salesmen." They are attractively enameled in Winchester gray with neat stripe border in red.

These boards are offered in two sizes, one carrying a complete assortment of the 32 Winchester drop-forged open end wrenches, the other a careful selection of 26 of the 32 varieties in the complete line.

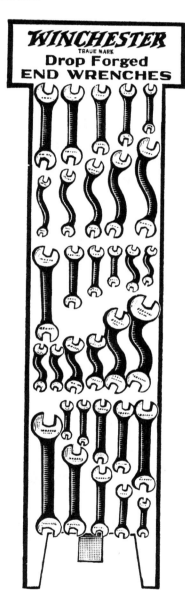

No. W179. Old No. F1091M. Complete Assortment originally had 179 wrenches. Size of Board - 5 feet 5 1/4 inches high and 14 inches wide for main body of board.

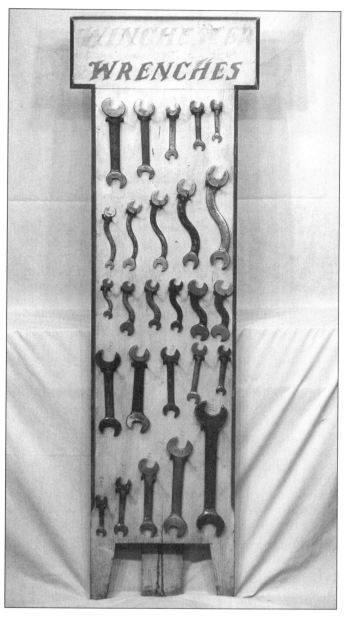

Open End Wrench Assortment Display Board (No. W146) is 58 1/4 inches high and has 14-inch wide body; header is 18 inches wide. From T. Webster collection. Photo by D. Kowalski.

No. W146. Old No. F1092M. Assortment originally had 146 wrenches. (Contains all the wrenches offered with the other board except the Double Head "S" Wrenches W666 and W667 and the check nut series.) Size of Board - 4 feet 10 1/2 inches high and 14 inches wide for main body of board.

Values:	Exc.	V.G.	Good
	1,200.00	1,000.00	800.00

Comment: *Values for either size Display Board without wrenches.*

Kitchen and Household Appliances

by David D. Kowalski

Winchester's push to expand its product line included virtually every type of major kitchen appliance. Refrigerators were one of their targets and resulted in the purchase of the National Refrigerator Company of Boston in 1925. But it only took them two years to realize gas-operated refrigerators weren't profitable. They were gone by 1928.

Winchester also got into the washing machine business in 1926. The Whirldry Corporation was a Winchester acquisition that year. Production was moved to New Haven, Connecticut. But by 1931, this part of the business produced nearly $2 million of red ink, a huge loss in that era when, as they say, "a dollar was still worth a dollar." In fact, many Winchester historians believe the Whirldry fiasco was the final nail in the Winchester coffin.

So we'll begin this chapter on household products with the end, so to speak. We'll start with the Winchester washing machine, then take you through a very broad, diverse and highly collectible array of kitchen and household appliances and equipment.

The portable washing machine fit easily on a table or counter top. This one measures 16 1/2 inches high and 14 inches across the top. It also came with a tin lid. From T. Webster collection. Photo by D. Kowalski.

Whirldry Portable Electric Washing Machine

Winchester kept the Whirldry name on their electric portable washing machine. Here's the label from a machine in Excellent condition. From Richard Hecht collection. Photo by R. Hecht.

Looking down into the Whirldry machine showing the perforated inner basket and the four-armed agitator. From T. Webster collection. Photo by D. Kowalski.

Values:	Exc.	V.G.	Good
	1,800.00	1,650.00	1,500.00

Comment: *Values are for any model of Whirldry Portable Electric Washing Machine.*

Winchester Ironing Board

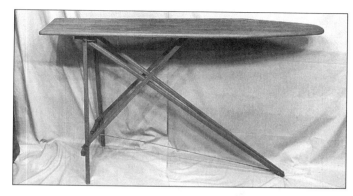

Ironing Board measures 53 3/4 inches from end to end of the wooden top and stands 31 1/2 inches high. One of only two ironing boards known. From T. Webster collection. Photo by D. Kowalski.

Label of Ironing Board glued to the underside of top identifies this model as a Winchester Store version. From T. Webster collection. Photo by D. Kowalski.

Values: **Exc.**   **V.G.**   **Good**
                      1,900.00   1,700.00   1,500.00

Comment: *Values are for any model of Winchester or Winchester Store Ironing Board.*

Electric Irons

No. W100. Iron with Patented Toggle Switch. Has cast-iron sole plate; heavy stamped-steel hood and handle bracket, full nickel-plated. Wood grip is Winchester gray, bolted; best-quality Nichrome wire heating element. Complete with 6-foot Mercerized cord, with standard screw-and-pull plug and special pull plug with spiral-spring wire guard. Has reversible heat-proof steel stand with aluminum finish. Operates on alternating or direct current. Heating element guaranteed one year. Weight 6 lbs. Packed one in a cardboard box.

Values: **Exc.**   **V.G.**   **Good**
                      300.00   250.00   200.00

Comment: *Values are for model W100 Iron.*

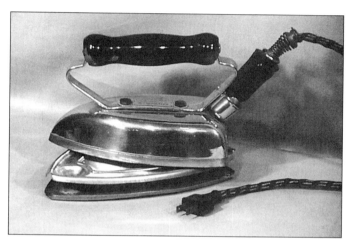

Model W110 Iron is the same as the Model W100 but has a standard plug-in cord. Photo shows detail of the steel safety stand. From T. Webster collection. Photo by D. Kowalski.

Values: **Exc.**   **V.G.**   **Good**
                      250.00   225.00   175.00

Comment: *Values are for model W110 Iron.*

Model W50 Iron is smaller and rarer than models W100 and W110. From T. Webster collection. Photo by D. Kowalski.

Values: **Exc.**   **V.G.**   **Good**
                      400.00   325.00   275.00

Comment: *Values are for model W110 Iron.*

Electric Sewing Machine

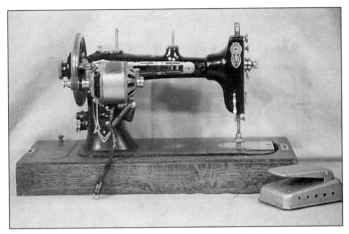

Electric Sewing Machine came with a full wooden cabinet cover (not pictured). The wooden base is 20 1/4 inches long. From T. Webster collection. Photo by D. Kowalski.

Values:	Exc.	V.G.	Good
	800.00	700.00	600.00

Comment: *Values are for any model of Electric Sewing Machine.*

Carpet Sweepers

Wooden Carpet Sweeper measures 14 1/2 inches wide at the base and the case is 4 1/2 inches high. This rare wood-case early version is the only one known. Has wooden handle. "WINCHESTER" logo is in large red letters on top of case. From T. Webster collection. Photo by D. Kowalski.

Values:	Exc.	V.G.	Good
	1,000.00	900.00	750.00

Comment: *Values are for model with wooden case.*

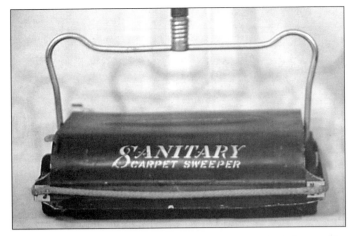

This Carpet Sweeper has a metal case. It is slightly smaller than the wooden one, measuring 14 inches wide at the base and 4 inches high. This model is also a "Winchester Store" version. Wooden handle. From T. Webster collection. Photo by D. Kowalski.

Values:	Exc.	V.G.	Good
	900.00	750.00	600.00

Comment: *Values are for Winchester or Winchester Store models with metal base.*

Electric Vacuum Cleaner

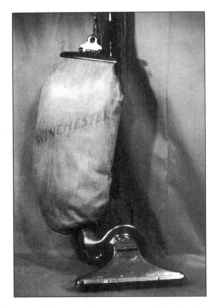

Electric Vacuum Cleaner is very rare. The bottom of the intake is 13 1/2 inches wide; top of the handle is 46 1/2 inches from the floor. From T. Webster collection. Photo by D. Kowalski.

Values:	Exc.	V.G.	Good
	1,800.00	1,700.00	1,600.00

Comment: *Values are for any model of Electric Vacuum Cleaner.*

Electric Fans

Electric Fans were sold in three sizes. The largest one (on left) is 17 1/2 inches high. The smallest one (right) measures 10 3/4 from the base to the top of the wire blade cage. From T. Webster collection. Photo by D. Kowalski.

Values: Exc.   V.G.   Good
              600.00   500.00   400.00

Comment: *Values are for the largest model. The medium size would be 30 percent less; the smallest one 50 percent less.*

Electric Radio

This table model Electric Radio has a wood cabinet that measures 25 1/2 inches long and 10 1/2 inches high. The total height of the black metal speaker (on its own stand) is 25 1/2 inches. From T. Webster collection. Photo by D. Kowalski.

Values: Exc.   V.G.   Good
              1,200.00   1,000.00   800.00

Comment: *Values are for the table model. Winchester also produced a console model valued at 200 percent of the table model (only three have been found to date).*

Electric Space Heater

The Electric Space Heater (model 600) is old but not that rare. Total height is 16 inches. The reflective dish is a bright copper color. From T. Webster collection. Photo by D. Kowalski.

Values: Exc.   V.G.   Good
              300.00   250.00   200.00

Comment: *Values are for any model of Electric Space Heater.*

Electric Toaster

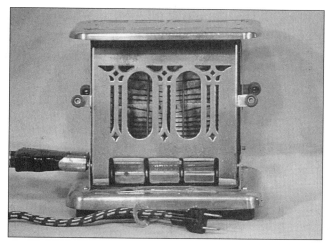

Electric Toaster is 7 1/4 inches long at the base and 7 1/8 inches high. Only five or six have been found. This one is in Excellent condition. From T. Webster collection. Photo by D. Kowalski.

Values: Exc.   V.G.   Good
              1,100.00   1,000.00   900.00

Comment: *Values are for any model of Electric Toaster.*

Electric Waffle Iron

Electric Waffle Iron is 6 1/4 inches high. This one is in Excellent condition. From T. Webster collection. Photo by D. Kowalski.

Values:
Exc.	V.G.	Good
800.00	700.00	600.00

Comment: *Values are for any model of Electric Waffle Iron.*

Electric Coffee Pots

Electric Coffee Pot has Winchester identification stamped on bottom. Total height of this six-cup model is 9 5/8 inches. Only three or four six-cup pots have been found. This one is clearly in Excellent condition. From T. Webster collection. Photo by D. Kowalski.

Nine-cup Electric Coffee Pot has bubble top of green glass. This is the only nine-cup model ever found and it's in Excellent condition. From T. Webster collection. Photo by T. Webster.

Values:
Exc.	V.G.	Good
2,500.00	2,300.00	2,100.00

Comment: *Values are for six-cup model. Add 25 percent for nine-cup model.*

Food Choppers and Food Grinders

One-piece cast-iron cylinder, hopper and stand, smoothly finished and heavily re-tinned. Cast-iron detachable crank, with red-enameled wood grip. Equipped with finest-quality worm, accurately milled and sharpened; feeds rapidly and uniformly; shoulder at rear prevents juices from leaking out. Comes complete with four cutting plates (one reversible) made of extra-quality hardened steel, accurately cut and carefully milled. Cleaned by unscrewing thumbnut holding cutting plates, then removing entire worm (one operation).

No.	Size	Plates	Height*	Cylinder	Hopper (in.)
W11	Small	2 1/4"	5"	3"	2 1/2x3 1/8
W12	Medium	2 1/2"	5 3/4"	3 1/4"	3 1/8x4
W13	Ex.Large	2 3/4"	8"	4 1/4"	4x4 3/4

* Height from base to hopper.

Kitchen and Household Appliances • 625

Food Chopper (model W12) is middle size of three models. From T. Webster collection. Photo by D. Kowalski.

Winchester also produced "Food Grinders" such as this model W105 that measures 6 1/4 inches from base to the top of the hopper. From T. Webster collection. Photo by D. Kowalski.

Values:

Exc.	V.G.	Good
75.00	60.00	40.00

Comment: *Values are for any model of Food Chopper or Food Grinder.*

Food Chopper Display Stand

Food Chopper Display Stand held six choppers or grinders for store display. From T. Webster collection. Photo by D. Kowalski.

No. W. Display Stand made from heavy sheet steel, gray enameled. Base is 11 1/2 inches and disc 7 inches in diameter with red-enameled edges. Steel center post. The "W" on each foot and the word "Winchester" on top panel are red enameled. For displaying six food choppers. Height overall is 22 1/2 inches. Approximate weight 9 lbs. NOTE - One of these display stands will be given free with each purchase of two (2) dozen Winchester Food Choppers (Assorted).

Values:

Exc.	V.G.	Good
2,200.00	2,000.00	1,750.00

Comment: *Values are for Display Stand only.*

Family Scales

Two Family Scales showing slightly different faces. From T. Webster collection. Photo by D. Kowalski.

No. W15. Heavy sheet-steel case; single steel upright with sheet-steel top 5 1/2 inches square; 7-inch white-enameled slanting dial with black figures and lines; red-enameled hand and ring; plain glass face; Base is sheet steel - 6x9 inches; Winchester gray-enameled finish. Adjusting screw on top of case. Capacity 20 pounds by ounces. Height - 8 1/2 inches. Weight each about 4 lbs. Packed one in a cardboard box.

No. W15/S. Family Scale with heavy tin scoop with foot. Scoop is 12 inches long, 6 3/4 inches wide. Height overall with scoop is 11 1/2 inches. Packed one in a cardboard box.

Values:	Exc.	V.G.	Good
	175.00	150.00	125.00

Comment: *Values are for Family Scale only. Add 15 percent with scoop.*

Vacuum Bottles

No. W1. One Pint. Cold-rolled metal case, Winchester gray finish. Seamless aluminum shoulder and cap. Highest-grade vacuum bottle or filler. Has non-rusting spring-steel shock absorber inside. Will keep liquids cold for 72 hours and hot for 24 hours. Height overall 9 3/4 inches; diameter 3 inches; weight each about 1 1/2 lbs. Packed one in a cardboard box.

No. W2. One Quart. Height overall 13 1/2 inches. diameter 3 3/4 inches; weight each about 2 lbs. Packed one in a cardboard box.

One Gallon Vacuum Bottle is 11 3/4 inches high. A rare item. From T. Webster collection. Photo by D. Kowalski.

Values:	Exc.	V.G.	Good
	175.00	150.00	125.00

Comment: *Values are for quart or gallon size. Add 75 percent for pint size.*

Vacuum Bottles. Corrugated Brass

Brass Vacuum Bottle, quart size, is 13 1/ inches high. A very rare piece in Excellent condition with a bright brass finish. From T. Webster collection. Photo by D. Kowalski.

Brass Vacuum Bottle, bottom details and cap. From T. Webster collection. Photo by D. Kowalski.

No. W1C. One Pint. Heavy seamless brass corrugated case; brass shoulder and cap; nickel-plated finish; highest-grade vacuum bottle or filler; non-rusting spring-steel shock absorber. Height overall 9 3/4 inches; diameter 3 inches; weight each about 1 1/2 lbs. Packed one in a cardboard box.

No. W2C. One Quart. Height overall 13 1/2 inches; diameter 3 3/4 inches; weight each about 2 lbs. Packed one in a cardboard box.

Values:	Exc.	V.G.	Good
	175.00	150.00	125.00

Comment: *Values are for vacuum bottles or food jars, quart size. Add 75 percent for pint size.*

Food Jars (Vacuum)

Food Jars. One quart model W7 on left; one pint model W6 on right. From T. Webster collection. Photo by D. Kowalski.

No. W6. One Pint. Cold-rolled metal case, Winchester gray finish; brass shoulder and cap, with carrying handle, nickel-plated. Highest-grade vacuum bottle or filler; non-rusting spring-steel shock absorber. Height overall 8 3/4 inches; diameter 3 inches; weight each about 1 1/2 lbs. Packed one in a cardboard box.

No. W7. One Quart. Height overall 12 1/2 inches; diameter 3 3/4 inches; weight each about 2 lbs. Packed one in a cardboard box.

Lunch Box Kit

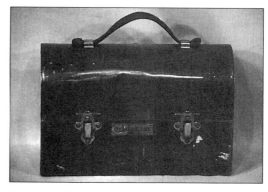

Lunch Boxes are fairly rare. This one shows the effects of having been "on the job." From T. Webster collection. Photo by D. Kowalski.

No. W10. Lunch Box with Pint Vacuum Bottle. Heavy tin double-seamed case, 10 1/4 inches long, 4 1/2 inches wide, 6 3/4 inches high. Winchester gray finish; tinned inside; hinged cover, with black enameled bottle holder; leather handle; nickel-plated catches. Weight each about 2 3/4 lbs. Packed one in a cardboard box.

Values:	Exc.	V.G.	Good
	400.00	350.00	300.00

Comment: *Values are for Lunch Box only without the Vacuum Bottle.*

Ice Cream Freezers

One Quart Ice Cream Freezer showing drain hole on side. From T. Webster collection. Photo by D. Kowalski.

One Quart and Eight Quart Ice Cream Freezers, side by side. These are the largest and smallest of six sizes and are also the rarest. From T. Webster collection. Photo by D. Kowalski.

Improved Double Motion. Second-growth white pine tubs are thoroughly saturated with paraffin and other chemicals that render them proof against the action of ice, salt and water. The staves are held perfectly tight by electric-welded galvanized-iron wire hoops, set in grooves - CANNOT COME OFF. Bottom of tub is flush with bottom of staves; 3/16-inch iron wire bail, with black-enameled bail wood; galvanized-steel wire bars; best charcoal tin-plate can, with tinned cast-iron cover; cast-iron tinned sanitary dasher; cast-iron frames, gear frames and gears; and malleable-iron improved frame catch, galvanized; cast-iron crank with wood handle. Screws on shaft. Wrapped in heavy paper.

Nos.	W21	W22	W23	W24	W26	W28
Quarts	1	2	3	4	6	8
Height of Tub (inches)	7 3/8	10 1/2	12 1/4	13 1/2	14 1/2	16 1/2
Weight each (lbs.)	6	11	13	15	19	23

Values:	Exc.	V.G.	Good
	1,200.00	1,000.00	750.00

Comment: *Values are for middle four sizes. Add 20 percent premium for the rarer One Quart and Eight Quart models.*

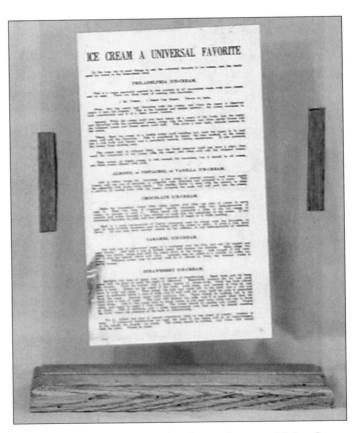

A two-sided instruction and recipe card came with Ice Cream Freezers. From T. Webster collection. Photo by D. Kowalski.

Values:	Exc.	V.G.	Good
	125.00	110.00	90.00

Winchester Refrigerators

Refrigerators, Porcelain Case

One-piece seamless porcelain lined. Porcelain outside case. The large outside sheets are porcelain on both sides and are held in place with heavy aluminum corner pieces, properly fastened to case with nickel-plated brass screws; 11 walls; one-inch cork insulation in walls and bottom lined with Cabot quilt. Cleated and air-sealed ice chamber, equipped with four studs, for electric installation. Provision chambers lined with one-piece seamless porcelain on heavy sheet steel, with rounded corners; heavy brass trimmings, nickel-plated. Removable nickel-plated brass waste pipe and trap; swinging baseboards; ball-bearing self-retaining casters; galvanized-iron ice racks; woven-wire re-tinned shelves.

Dimensions:	Size Outside	Ice Cham.	Large Prov. Cham.	Small Prov. Cham.
W18959				
Length, in.	36 1/2	14	11 3/4	15 1/4
Depth, in.	20 3/4	14 3/4	15	15
Height, in.	47 1/2	20	32 3/4	10
W18979				
Length, in.	37 3/4	14	12 3/4	15 1/4
Depth, in.	21 3/4	15 3/4	16	16
Height, in.	52 1/4	24 1/2	37 1/4	10

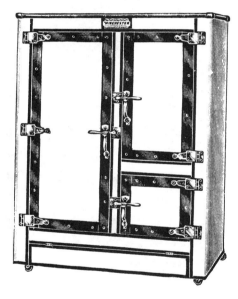

Side Icing. Two single doors on provision chamber; one door on ice chamber. Ice Capacity is the weight of a solid block of ice that can be passed through ice chamber door. Wrapped in Paper Securely Crated.

No.	W18939	W18959	W18979
Ice Capacity	75 lbs.	85 lbs.	100 lbs.
Ice Door, in.	11x16 3/4	11 1/2x18 1/2	11 1/2x23
No. of Shelves	3	3	4
Weight crated	413 lbs.	459 lbs.	515 lbs.

Dimensions:	Size Outside	Ice Cham.	Large Prov. Cham.	Small Prov. Cham.
W18939				
Length, in.	35 1/2	13 3/4	11	15
Depth, in.	19 3/4	14	14	14
Height, in.	45	18 1/4	30 1/4	9 1/2

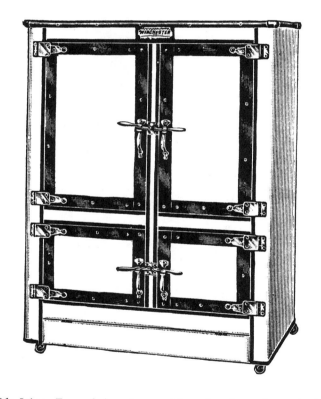

Side Icing. Four shelves in provision chambers; three single doors on provision chamber; one door on ice chamber. Ice Capacity is the weight of a solid block of ice that can be passed through ice chamber door. Wrapped in Paper Securely Crated.

No. W18999. Ice Capacity 160 lbs. Weight crated 575 lbs.

Dimensions:	Size Outside	Ice Cham.	Large Prov. Cham.	Small Prov. Cham.
W18999				
Length, in.	39 1/2	14 1/2	14 1/4	15 3/4
Depth, in.	22 3/4	16 3/4	17	17
Height, in.	56	27	41 1/2	11 1/2

Refrigerators, Ash Case

One-piece seamless porcelain lined. Made of Ash, Filled, Shellacked and Varnished, Golden Oak Finish: Extended Top, with Edges formed into Mouldings; 11 Walls and Air Spaces; one-inch Cork Insulation, Lined with Cabot Quilt; Provision Chambers Lined with one-piece Seamless Porcelain on Heavy Sheet Steel, with Rounded Corners. Cleated and air-sealed Ice Chambers, Equipped with Four Studs, for Electric Installation; Heavy Brass Trimmings, nickel-plated. Removable nickel-plated Brass Waste Pipe and Trap; Swinging Base Boards; ball-bearing self-retaining casters; galvanized-iron Ice Rack; Woven Wire Re-tinned Shelves. Apartment-style and side-icing Refrigerators have Heavy White Porcelain Lining on Ice Chamber Doors.

Dimensions:	Size Outside	Ice Cham.	Large Prov. Cham.	Small Prov. Cham.
W215				
Length, in.	33 3/4	14 1/2	11 1/2	14 1/2
Depth, in.	18	12	12	12
Height, in.	43	16 1/2	28 1/4	9 1/4
W217 and W217W				
Length, in.	33 3/4	14 1/2	11 1/2	14 1/2
Depth, in.	19	13	13	13
Height, in.	45	18 1/2	30 1/4	9
W219 and W219W				
Length, in.	35 1/2	15 1/4	12 3/4	15 1/4
Depth, in.	22	16	16	16
Height, in.	51 1/2	24 3/4	37 1/4	10

Three Door. Side Icing. Two doors on provision chambers; one door on ice chamber. Ice Capacity is the weight of a solid block of ice that can be passed through ice chamber door. Wrapped in Paper Securely Crated.

No.	W215	W217	W219
Ice Capacity	50 lbs.	75 lbs.	100 lbs.
Ice Door, in.	11 1/4x14 1/4	11 1/4x16 1/4	12x22 1/2
No. of Shelves	3	3	4
Weight crated	258 lbs.	271 lbs.	349 lbs.

With Water Cooler. Porcelain Lined; Hardwood Cover and Knob; nickel-plated Brass Faucet; nickel-plated Brass Tumbler Holder fastened to Outside of Case.

No.	W217W	W219W
Ice Capacity	75 lbs.	100 lbs.
Ice Door, in.	11 1/4x16 1/4	12x22 1/2
No. of Shelves	3	4
Weight crated	279 lbs.	357 lbs.

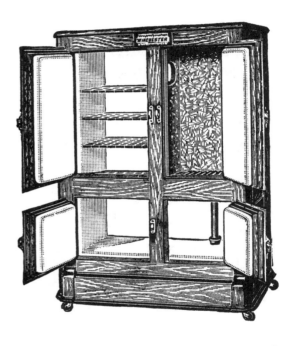

Four Door. Side Icing. Four shelves in provision chambers; three doors on provision chambers; one door on ice chamber. Ice Capacity is the weight of a solid block of ice that can be passed through ice chamber door. Wrapped in Paper Securely Crated.

No.	W221	W223
Ice Capacity	125 lbs.	150 lbs.
Ice Door, in.	11 1/2x23 3/4	12 1/2x25 1/4
Weight crated	363 lbs.	395 lbs.

With Water Cooler. Porcelain Lined; Hardwood Cover and Knob; nickel-plated Brass Faucet; nickel-plated Brass Tumbler Holder fastened to Outside of Case.

No.	W221W
Ice Capacity	125 lbs.
Ice Door, in.	11 1/2x23 3/4
Weight crated	363 lbs.

Dimensions:	Size Outside	Ice Cham.	Large Prov. Cham.	Small Prov. Cham.
W221 and W221W				
Length, in.	35 1/2	14 3/4	13	14 3/4
Depth, in.	22	16	16	16
Height, in.	54 1/4	26	39 3/4	11 1/4
W223				
Length, in.	37 1/2	15 3/4	14 1/4	15 3/4
Depth, in.	23	17	17	17
Height, in.	56 1/4	27 1/2	41 1/2	11 1/2

Refrigerators, Ash Case, Apartment Style

One-piece seamless porcelain lined. Made of Ash, Filled, Shellacked and Varnished, Golden Oak Finish; Extended Top, with Edges formed into Mouldings; 11 Walls and Air Spaces. Insulated with layers of wool felt and Cabot Quilt; Provision Chambers Lined with one-piece Seamless Porcelain on Heavy Sheet Steel, with Rounded Corners. Galvanized-iron Ice Chamber; Heavy Brass Trimmings, nickel-plated. Removable nickel-plated Brass Waste Pipe and Trap; Swinging Base Boards; ball-bearing self-retaining casters; galvanized-iron Ice Rack; Woven Wire Re-tinned Shelves. Apartment-style and side-icing Refrigerators have Heavy White Porcelain Lining on Ice Chamber Doors.

Two Door. Three shelves in provision chamber. One door on provision chamber; one door on ice chamber. Ice Capacity is the weight of a solid block of ice that can be passed through ice chamber door. Wrapped in Paper Securely Crated.

No. W210. Ice Capacity 75 lbs.; 3 Shelves. Outside Dimensions: 29 in. Long, 21 in. Deep, 54 1/4 in. High. Ice Chamber: 19 1/4 in. Long, 15 in. Deep, 13 in. High. Ice Door Opening: 19 1/4x11 in. Provision Chamber: 21 1/2 in. Long, 15 in. Deep, 24 in. High. Weight crated, 270 lbs.

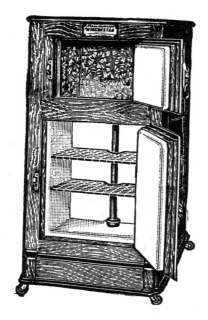

Two Door. Two shelves in provision chamber. One door on provision chamber; one door on ice chamber. Ice Capacity is the weight of a solid block of ice that can be passed through ice chamber door. Wrapped in Paper Securely Crated.

No. W209. Ice Capacity 75 lbs.; 2 Shelves. Outside dimensions: 24 in. Long, 19 in. Deep, 50 in. High. Ice Chamber: 15 in. Long, 13 1/4 in. Deep, 11 in. High. Provision Chamber: 17 in. Long, 14 in. Deep, 21 1/4 in. High. Weight crated, 220 lbs.

Refrigerators, Ash Case

One-piece porcelain lined. Three Door. Side Icing. Ash case, Varnished in Golden Oak Finish. Insulated with 3-ply Cabot Quilt and Corkboard; Interior Lined with one-piece Porcelain. Galvanized-iron Ice Chamber; corrugated galvanized-iron Ice Rack. Removable nickel-plated Brass Waste Pipe and Trap; Swinging Base Board; self-retaining casters. Nickel-plated hinges and latches. Re-tinned removable Shelves. Built in accordance with the most Advanced Principles of Refrigerator Construction and Design; Patented Construction assures Rapid Circulation of Cold Dry Air and Low Ice Consumption. Wrapped in Paper Securely Crated.

Refrigerators, White Enameled Lining

White Enameled, galvanized-iron lining, baked on. Side ice chamber. Single circulation. Made of Clear, Hard, Northern Ash; Filled, Shellacked and Varnished, Golden Oak Finish. Heavy rounding Corners; Raised Panels. Galvanized-iron Ice Chamber; Inside Lining of Provision Chamber is White Enameled Galvanized Iron on Heavy Wall of Matched Northern Pine. Walls insulated with 1/4-inch odorless, germ-proof felt, and in addition has a dead-air Chamber lined with a Second Wall of Charcoal Sheathing Inside of Casing. All Doors are insulated in same manner. Solid cast-brass trimmings, nickel-plated; air-tight Automatic Drip Cups; Detachable Zinc Drip Pipes. Swinging baseboards; ball-bearing self-retaining Casters; Tinned woven-wire Sliding Shelves. Ice Capacity is the weight of a solid block of ice that can be passed through ice chamber door. Wrapped in Paper Securely Crated.

No.	W1012	W1013	W1014	W1015
Ice Cap.	35 lbs.	50 lbs.	75 lbs.	100 lbs.
Ice Door	9 1/4x 13 1/4	11 1/4x 14 1/2	11 1/4x 16 3/4	11 5/8x 22 1/2
Shelves	2	3	3	4
Weight, lbs.	176	212	218	260

Dimensions:	Size Outside	Ice Cham.	Large Prov. Cham.	Small Prov. Cham.
W1012				
Length, in.	28	11 1/4	9 3/4	11 1/4
Depth, in.	17	12 1/8	12	12
Height, in.	40 3/4	15 5/8	28	10 1/4
W1013				
Length, in.	31 3/4	14	10 5/8	13 7/8
Depth, in.	18	13 1/4	13	13
Height, in.	42	16 3/4	30	11 1/8
W1014				
Length, in.	33 1/2	14	12 5/8	13 7/8
Depth, in.	18	13 3/8	13 1/8	13 1/8
Height, in.	44 1/4	19	31 5/8	10 3/8
W1015				
Length, in.	33 1/2	14 1/4	12 1/4	14 1/4
Depth, in.	19	14	14	14
Height, in.	50	24 1/2	7 1/4	10

Three Door. Side Icing. Three shelves in provision chamber. Two single doors on provision chambers; one door on ice chamber.

No.	W891	W893	W895	W897
Ice Cap.	50 lbs.	75 lbs.	100 lbs.	150 lbs.
Ice Door	11 1/2x 14 3/4	11 3/4x 16 3/4	11 3/4x 22 1/2	13 1/2x 22 1/2
Weight, lbs.	156	175	202	247

With Water Cooler. Porcelain Lined; Hardwood Cover and Knob; nickel-plated Brass Faucet.

Kitchen and Household Appliances • 633

No.	W893W	W895W		
Ice Cap.	75 lbs.	100 lbs.		
Ice Door	11 3/4x 16 3/4	11 3/4x 22 1/2		
Weight, lbs.	183	210		
W891				
Length, in.	32	13 1/4	13 1/4	13 3/4
Depth, in.	17	12 1/4	12 1/4	12 1/4
Height, in.	43 1/4	16 1/2	29 3/4	9 3/4
W893 and W893W				
Length, in.	33 1/2	14	14	14 1/2
Depth, in.	18	13 1/4	13 1/4	13 1/4
Height, in.	45 1/4	18 1/2	31 3/4	9 3/4
W895 and W895W				
Length, in.	33 1/2	14	14	14 1/2
Depth, in.	19	14 1/4	14 1/4	14 1/4
Height, in.	51	24 1/4	34 1/4	9 3/4
W897				
Length, in.	37	15 3/4	15 3/4	16 1/4
Depth, in.	21	16 1/2	16 1/2	16 1/2
Height, in.	51	24	37	9 1/2

Refrigerators, Hardwood Case, Polished Brass Trim

The Walls are Hollow, lined with Heavy Paper Sheathing, which makes a Perfect Tight Chamber in which the Dead Air is confined. Hollow Walls made in this manner are very effective as Non-conductors of Heat and Cold. The Entire Interior of the Provision Compartment is lined with Heavy Galvanized Iron, White Japanned, enameled, baked on, securely nailed. The Back Wall and Bottom is made of One Continuous Sheet of Metal with Turned Edges, over which is placed the sidewall Linings. The Top is Galvanized Iron over Wood, which is the Bottom of the Ice Chamber. This Point is Securely Braced by the Wood between the Galvanized Iron, coming in Direct Contact with the Front and Rear Walls of the Box. Ice Capacity is the weight of a solid block of ice that can be passed through ice chamber door. Wrapped in Paper Securely Crated.

Four Door. Side Icing. Four shelves in provision chamber. Three single doors on provision chambers; one door on ice chamber.

Three Door. Side Icing. Three shelves in provision chamber. Two single doors on provision chambers; one door on ice chamber. The Ice Chamber is fitted with a corrugated, galvanized-iron Ice Rack, Mounted on Pickled Hardwood, which Elevates it sufficiently so it does not interfere with the Free Circulation of Cold Air. Cold air enters the Provision Chamber through an Open Space in the Center of the Bottom of the Ice Chamber; After Circulating through the Entire Provision Chamber it again enters the Ice Compartment through a Top Flue above the Dividing Wall.

No.	W899
Ice Cap.	175 lbs.
Ice Door	13 1/2x 23 3/4
Weight, lbs.	266

Dimensions: W899	Size Outside	Ice Cham.	Large Prov. Cham.	Small Prov. Cham.
Length, in.	37	15 3/4	15 3/4	16 1/4
Depth, in.	22 1/4	17 1/2	17 1/2	17 1/2
Height, in.	54 1/2	25 1/2	41	12

No.	W1690	W1691	W1693	W1695
Ice Cap.	40 lbs.	50 lbs.	75 lbs.	100 lbs.
Ice Door	9x15	11 1/2x 14 3/4	11 3/4x 16 3/4	11 1/2x 22 1/2
Weight, lbs.	144	156	175	202

Dimensions:	Size Outside	Ice Cham.	Large Prov. Cham.	Small Prov. Cham.
W1690				
Length, in.	28	11 1/4	11 1/4	11 3/4
Depth, in.	16 3/4	12	12	12
Height, in.	40	16 3/4	26 1/2	6 1/2
W1691				
Length, in.	32	13 1/4	13 1/4	13 3/4
Depth, in.	17	12 1/4	12 1/4	12 1/4
Height, in.	43 1/4	16 1/2	29 3/4	9 3/4
W1693				
Length, in.	33 1/2	14	14	14 1/2
Depth, in.	18	13 1/4	13 1/4	13 1/4
Height, in.	45 1/4	18 1/2	31 3/4	9 3/4
W1695				
Length, in.	33 1/2	14	14	14 1/2
Depth, in.	19	14 1/4	14 1/4	14 1/4
Height, in.	51	24 1/4	37 1/2	9 3/4

Refrigerators, Hardwood Case, Polished Brass, Lift Lid

On account of this style of Refrigerator being Single Circulation, it is not necessary that Ice Rack be Elevated as in the Double Circulation Style, so a corrugated, galvanized-iron Ice Rack is used and is only used to allow the Waste Water to drain off and to absorb the Shock when Ice is dropped into place, and the Corrugations give sufficiently to accomplish this. The Ice Chamber is Lined Throughout with Galvanized Iron; the Lower Left Side of the Ice Chamber is fitted with a Deflector to prevent anything but the Cold Air from entering the Provision Chamber; The Right Side is fitted with a Removable galvanized-iron Flue; the sides, bottom and top fit in a Groove and are held Securely.

The Top Door is fitted with a Steel Slide that works in a Slot, and prevents the Cover from falling back and causing damage. Ice Capacity is the weight of a solid block of ice that can be passed through ice chamber door. Wrapped in Paper Securely Crated.

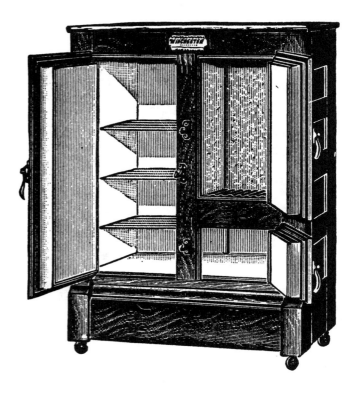

No.	W1600	W1601	W1602	W1603	W1604
Ice Cap.	20 lbs.	40 lbs.	65 lbs.	75 lbs.	100 lbs.
Ice Door	13 1/4 x9	15 1/4 x10	17 1/4 x11	19 1/4 x13	23 1/4 x14

No.	W1600	W1601	W1602	W1603	W1604
Shelves	1	2	2	2	2
Wgt. lbs.	90	109	135	150	173

Dimensions:	Size Outside	Ice Cham.	Prov. Cham.
W1600			
Length, in.	20 1/2	13	15
Depth, in.	13 5/8	10	10
Height, in.	37 1/2	8 1/4	13
W1601			
Length, in.	22 1/4	15 1/4	17 1/2
Depth, in.	15 1/4	10	10 3/4
Height, in.	40	9 1/4	14 1/2
W1602			
Length, in.	24 1/4	17 1/4	9 1/2
Depth, in.	16 1/4	11	11 3/4
Height, in.	42	11 1/4	14 1/2
W1603			
Length, in.	26 1/4	19	21 1/2
Depth, in.	18 1/4	13	13 3/4
Height, in.	44	11 1/4	16 1/2
W1604			
Length, in.	30 1/4	23 1/4	25 1/2
Depth, in.	19 1/4	14	14 3/4
Height, in.	46	11 1/4	18 1/2

Refrigerators, Hardwood Case, Polished Brass Trim

The Walls are hollow, lined with Heavy Paper Sheathing, which makes a Perfect Tight Chamber in which the Dead Air is confined; Hollow Walls made in this manner are Very Effective as Non-conductors of Heat and Cold. The Ice and Provision Compartments are lined with Heavy galvanized iron and Securely Nailed. The Back Wall and Bottom is made of one continuous Sheet of Metal with Turned Edges, over which is placed the sidewall Linings. The Top is Galvanized Iron over Wood, which is the Bottom of the Ice Chamber. This Point is Securely Braced by the Wood between the Galvanized Iron, coming in Direct Contact with the Front and Rear Walls of the Box.

On account of this style of Refrigerator being Single Circulation, it is not necessary that Ice Rack be Elevated as in the double-circulation style, so a corrugated, galvanized-iron Ice Rack is used and is only used to allow the Waste Water to drain off and to absorb the Shock when Ice is dropped into place, and the Corrugations give sufficiently to accomplish this. The Ice Chamber, like the balance of the Box, is Lined Throughout with Galvanized Iron; The Lower Left Side of the Ice Chamber is fitted with a Deflector to prevent anything but the Cold Air from entering the Provision Chamber; The Right Side is fitted with a removable galvanized-iron Flue. The Sides, Bottom and Top Fit in a Groove and are held securely. Ice Capacity is the weight of a solid block of ice that can be passed through ice chamber door. Wrapped in Paper Securely Crated.

Two Single Doors on provision chamber; one door on ice chamber. The Ice Chamber is fitted with a corrugated, galvanized-iron Ice Rack, Mounted on Pickled Hardwood, which Elevates it sufficiently so it does not interfere with the Free Circulation of Cold Air which enters the Provision Chamber Through an Open Space in the Center of the Bottom of the Ice Chamber; After Circulating through the entire Provision Chamber it again enters the Ice Compartment through a Top Flue above the Dividing Wall.

No.	W691	W693	W695
Ice Cap.	50 lbs.	75 lbs.	100 lbs.
Weight, lbs.	156	175	202

Dimensions:	Size Outside	Ice Cham.	Large Prov. Cham.	Small Prov. Cham.
W691				
Length, in.	32	13 1/4	13 1/4	13 3/4
Depth, in.	17	12 1/4	12 1/4	12 1/4
Height, in.	43 1/4	16 1/2	29 3/4	9 3/4
W693				
Length, in.	33 1/2	14	14	14 1/2
Depth, in.	18	13 1/4	13 1/4	13 1/4
Height, in.	45 1/4	18 1/2	31 3/4	9 3/4
W695				
Length, in.	33 1/2	14	14	14 1/2
Depth, in.	19	14 1/4	14 1/4	14 1/4
Height, in.	51	24 1/4	37 1/2	9 3/4

Refrigerators, Hardwood Case, Polished Brass, Lift Lid

Single Door. Lift Lid. The Top Door is fitted with a Steel Slide that works in a Slot, and prevents the Cover from falling back and causing damage.

No.	W600	W601	W602	W603	W604
Ice Cap.	20 lbs.	40 lbs.	65 lbs.	75 lbs.	100 lbs.
Ice Door	(Same as W1600 series.)				
Shelves	1	2	2	2	2
Wgt. lbs.	90	110	119	143	173

Dimensions:	Size Outside	Ice Cham.	Prov. Cham.
W600			
Length, in.	20 1/2	13 1/2	15
Depth, in.	13 5/8	10	10
Height, in.	37 1/2	8 1/4	13
W601			
Length, in.	22 1/4	15 1/4	17 1/2
Depth, in.	15 1/4	10	10 3/4
Height, in.	40	9 1/4	14 1/2
W602			
Length, in.	24 1/4	17 1/4	19 1/2
Depth, in.	16 1/4	11	11 3/4
Height, in.	42	11 1/4	14 1/2

Household Thermometers

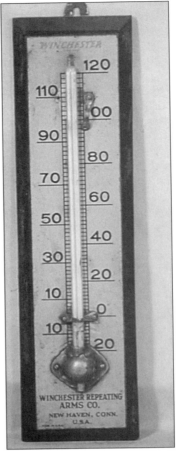

Household Thermometers continued to be made well into the 1960s. This one from the 1920s still bears the "Winchester Repeating Arms Co." logo. From T. Webster collection. Photo by D. Kowalski.

Dimensions:	Size Outside	Ice Cham.	Prov. Cham.
W603			
Length, in.	26 1/4	19 1/4	21 1/2
Depth, in.	18 1/4	13	13 3/4
Height, in.	44	11 1/4	16 1/2
W604			
Length, in.	30 1/4	23 1/4	25 1/2
Depth, in.	19 1/4	14	14 3/4
Height, in.	46	11 1/4	18 1/2

Values:	Exc.	V.G.	Good
	2,000.00	1,600.00	1,200.00

Comment: Values are for any models of Refrigerators.

Values:	Exc.	V.G.	Good
	1,000.00	800.00	600.00

Comment: Values are for models from the 1920s and early 1930s. There is actually a great deal of variability of pricing on household thermometers. Some models from the 1960s have been selling for as much as $500.

Letter Opener

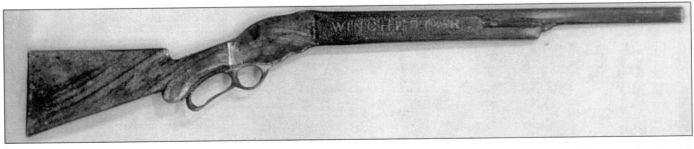

Winchester produced a letter opener to commemorate its Model 1887, the first lever-action shotgun made in the United States. It measures 8 1/4 inches long but a piece of the end has been broken off. This is one of only two that have ever been found. From T. Webster collection. Photo by D. Kowalski.

Values:	Exc.	V.G.	Good
	800.00	700.00	600.00

Cigar Boxes

Did Winchester license their name to Austin, Nichols & Co, Inc. of New Haven, Connecticut, for the distribution of cigars? It would seem so since it is unlikely another business in their hometown using their name would have gone unnoticed. This cigar box is the only one ever found and measures 9 1/4 inches wide. From T. Webster collection. Photo by D. Kowalski.

Values:	Exc.	V.G.	Good
	1,000.00	900.00	750.00

Comment: *Values are for any size or brand of Winchester cigar box, empty.*

Paints, Brushes and Padlocks

by David D. Kowalski

When Winchester merged with the Associated Simmons Hardware Company of Saint Louis, Missouri in 1922, Simmons had a controlling interest in the Mound City Paint and Color Company. Winchester upgraded this operation and increased product quality, then marketed paints, stains, varnishes and brushes. They continued to use the Simmons' brand names. On the Winchester side, the brand names were "Winchester" and "Red W Brand," as well as the Winchester Store label.

Paints and brushes were obviously consumable products, often relegated to storage in basements and garages. When old paint cans were found with layers of dust on them and their labels stained from water and dampness, they were generally perceived as unusable and thrown in the garbage. Brushes, historically, suffered an even worse fate. They were used for a few applications, probably not cleaned properly, then typically thrown out very early in their lives. We see very few of them.

Padlocks were an addition to the Winchester line in the 1927 catalog. They were produced in a variety of keyed styles. We'll also show you evidence Winchester made some padlocks for other companies.

"Paddle Board" Holder for Paint Samples

Colored wooden paint sample "paddles" hung from the hooks on this display. "Ready Mixed" and "House Paint" are colored red; so are the "W" and the four small highlight squares in each corner. Rest of copy is black; wood frame is black.

Dimensions are approximately 30 inches long x 10 inches high. From Curt Bowman collection. Photo by C. Bowman.

Values:	**Exc.**	**V.G.**	**Good**
	2,000.00	1,500.00	1,200.00

Comment: *Values for display only.*

Paint Counter Sign

Red W Brand House Paint Counter Sign (bright red and green on gray background) measures 12 7/8" wide x 16 1/4" high. Reversible counter sign promotes Roller Skates on other side. From T. Webster collection. Photo by D. Kowalski.

Values:	**Exc.**	**V.G.**	**Good**
	900.00	825.00	750.00

Comment: *Values are for this counter sign.*

Red W Brand House Paint

Prepared for Inside and Outside use under scientifically prepared formula. Red W Brand house paint brushes out well under the brush, has great covering qualities and wears exceptionally well under unusual conditions.

Ready For Use. This paint is put up in gallon and half-gallon pails with handles, quart, pint, and half pint cans, all with double friction tops.

Red W Brand House Paint Outside White No. 1033, is made in accordance with the following formula:

Pigment:
Lead Carbonate 40%
Lead Sulphate 20%
Zinc Oxide 40%
100%

Liquid:
Linseed Oil 87%
Japan 9%
Turpentine 4%
100%

Weight:
About 18 pounds per gallon.

Pint of House Paint - Light Tan (No. 1005P). Label is buff color with a red "W" and small red squares in each corner of the two major label rectangles. From T. Webster collection. Photo by D. Kowalski.

House Paint Color Chart

COLORS	One Gallon	Half Gallon	One Quart	One Pint	Half Pint No.
Cherry Red	1008G	1008HG	1008Q	1008P	1008HP
Green	1031G	1031HG	1031Q	1031P	1031HP
Dark Blue	1024G	1024HG	1024Q	1024P	1024HP
Outside White	1033G	1033HG	1033Q	1033P	1033HP
Inside Gl. White	1035G	1035HG	1035Q	1035P	1035HP
Inside Fl. White	1036G	1036HG	1036Q	1036P	1036HP
Ivory	1001G	1001HG	1001Q	1001P	1001HP
Yellow Buff	1004G	1004HG	1004Q	1004P	1004HP
Light Tan	1005G	1005HG	1005Q	1005P	1005HP
Lt. Terra Cotta	1006G	1006HG	1006Q	1006P	1006HP
Terra Cotta	1011G	1011HG	1011Q	1011P	1011HP
Warm Buff	1009G	1009HG	1009Q	1009P	1009HP
Rose Gray	1015G	1015HG	1015Q	1015P	1015HP
Tan	1010G	1010HG	1010Q	1010P	1010HP
Chestnut Brown	1012G	1012HG	1012Q	1012P	1012HP
Rich Brown	1013G	1013HG	1013Q	1013P	1013HP
Maroon	1014G	1014HG	1014Q	1014P	1014HP
Neutral Gray	1017G	1017HG	1017Q	1017P	1017HP
Puritan Gray	1019G	1019HG	1019Q	1019P	1019HP
Winchester Gray	1020G	1020HG	1020Q	1020P	1029HP
Lead Gray	1021G	1021HG	1021Q	1021P	1021HP
Italian Blue	1023G	1023HG	1023Q	1023P	1023HP
Yellow Gray	1025G	1025HG	1025Q	1025P	1025HP
Niagara Green	1026G	1026HG	1026Q	1026P	1026HP
Pea Green	1028G	1028HG	1028Q	1028P	1028HP
Olive Green	1029G	1029HG	1029Q	1029P	1029HP
Bronze Green	1032G	1032HG	1032Q	1032P	1032HP
Black	1037G	1037HG	1037Q	1037P	1037HP
Inside White	1034G	1034HG	1034Q	1034P	1034HP

1 Five-Gallon Can in a Case, Average Weight per case about 90 lbs.; 6 One-Gallon Cans in a Case; 12 Half-Gallon Cans in a Case; 24 One-Quart Cans in a Case; 48 One-Pint Cans in a Case; Average Weight per Case about 110 lbs. 48 Half-Pint Cans in a Case; Average Weight per Case about 58 lbs. Any of the above mentioned colors can be furnished on request in Five-Gallon Cans or Barrels (About 50 Gallons).

Values:	Exc.	V.G.	Good
Gallon	600.00	500.00	350.00
1/2 Gallon	500.00	400.00	300.00
Quart	400.00	300.00	200.00

Values:	Exc.	V.G.	Good
Pint	250.00	225.00	175.00
1/2 Pint	200.00	175.00	150.00

Comment: *Values are for any color of House Paint.*

Paint Color Samples

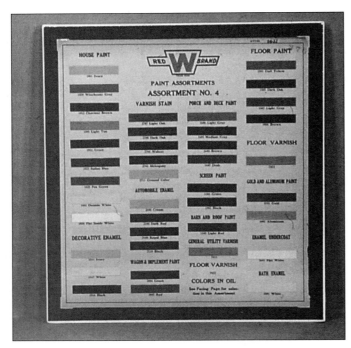

Paint Assortment was actually a page from an old catalog that was framed for display purposes. Live matter of page measures 9 1/2 inches wide x 10 1/2 inches high. From T. Webster collection. Photo by D. Kowalski.

Values:	Exc.	V.G.	Good
	300.00	275.00	250.00

Barn and Roof Paint

Prepared ready for use on wood or iron. Adapted for such uses a painting barns, fences, roofs, bridges, outhouses and structural steel. 6 One-Gallon Cans to the Case; Average Weight per Case 110 lbs. Furnished on request in barrels at $.10 net less per gallon than gallon price.

COLORS	One Gallon	Five Gallon Can
Tan	1101G	1101/5G
Light Brown	1102G	1102/5G
Light Red	1103G	1103/5G
Venetian Red	1104G	1104/5G
Light Gray	1105G	1105/5G
Lead Gray	1106G	1106/5G
Moss Green	1107G	1107/5G
Dark Brown	1108G	1108/5G

Values:	Exc.	V.G.	Good
5 Gallon	750.00	675.00	600.00
Gallon	600.00	500.00	350.00

Comment: *Values are for any color.*

Gallon can of red Oxide Paint for Barns and Roofs. Made by Winchester for Towncraft Paint & Varnish Co., Pottstown, Pennsylvania. From T. Webster collection. Photo by D. Kowalski.

Values:	Exc.	V.G.	Good
Gallon	750.00	675.00	600.00

Comment: *Values are for this private label can. For any other private label paint can, add 25 percent to the values given for comparable standard cans.*

Lawn and Porch Furniture Paint

For lawn benches, tables, swings, porch furniture and similar articles exposed to the weather. Dries with a glossy, durable finish that does not become soft or sticky when subjected to heat. Packed 24 Quarts, 48 Pints or 48 Half Pints to the Case. Average Weight per Case, Quarts or Pints, 80 lbs.; Half Pints 45 lbs.

COLORS	One Quart	One Pint	Half Pint
Red	1201Q	1201P	1201HP
Green	1202Q	1202P	1202HP
Values:	**Exc.**	**V.G.**	**Good**
Quart	600.00	500.00	350.00
Pint	500.00	400.00	300.00
1/2 Pint	400.00	300.00	200.00

Comment: *Values are for any color.*

Wire Screen Paint

Made for covering screens and all kinds of fine wire work and wire cloth and to prevent rust. Also good for frames. Made with care to assure a consistency that will not clog or fill up the mesh. Dries quickly. Gives high and durable gloss finish. Packed 6 One-Gallon Cans, 24 Quarts, 48 Pints or 48 Half Pints to the Case. Average Weight per Case, Gallons, Quarts and Pints about 70 lbs. Half Pints about 40 lbs.

Half Pint of Wire Screen Paint - Black (No. 1302HP). Label is buff color with a red "W" and small red squares in each corner of the two major label rectangles. Metal of can has rusted and blackened the label in several spots. From T. Webster collection. Photo by D. Kowalski.

COLORS	Gallon	Quart	Pint	1/2 Pint
Green	1301G	1301Q	1301P	1301HP
Black	1302G	1302Q	1302P	1302HP
Values:		**Exc.**	**V.G.**	**Good**
Gallon		600.00	500.00	350.00
Quart		400.00	300.00	200.00
Pint		250.00	225.00	175.00
1/2 Pint		200.00	175.00	150.00

Comment: *Values are for either color of Screen Paint.*

Soft Tone Flat Wall Paint

A soft-finish, sanitary and durable flat-color wall paint with the velvety appearance of a water paint plus the advantages of an oil paint. Readily washable. Suited to all interior purposes like walls, ceilings and wood work. Recommended as a sanitary finish for homes and public buildings. Also makes an excellent priming coat for enamel paints, whether on wood or metal. Any of the listed colors can be furnished in 5-gallon cans at $.05 net off gallon price per gallon. Packed 6 One-Gallon Cans, 12 Half-Gallon Cans or 24 Quart Cans to the Case; Average Weight about 100 lbs. per Case.

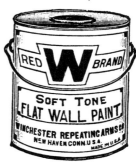

COLORS	One Quart	One Pint	Half Pint
Damask Pink	1401G	1401HG	1401Q
Ivory	1402G	1402HG	1402Q
Light Buff	1403G	1403HG	1403Q
Warm Yellow	1404G	1404HG	1404Q
Brown	1405G	1405HG	1405Q
Pompeian Red	1406G	1406HG	1406Q
Silver Gray	1407G	1406HG	1406Q
Dove Gray	1408G	1408HG	1408Q
Lilac	1409G	1409HG	1409Q
Old Rose	1410G	1410HG	1410Q
Persian Blue	1411G	1411HG	1411Q
Puritan Gray	1412G	1412HG	1412Q
Veronese Green	1413G	1413HG	1413Q
Light Sage	1414G	1414HG	1414Q
Fern Green	1415G	1415HG	1415Q
Dark Green	1416G	1416HG	1416Q
White	1417G	1417HG	1417Q
Black	1418G	1418HG	1418Q

Values:	Exc.	V.G.	Good
Quart	500.00	400.00	300.00
Pint	400.00	300.00	200.00
1/2 Pint	250.00	225.00	175.00

Comment: *Values are for any color.*

Wall Size

For use as a first coat on newly finished plastered walls that are to be finished with any oil paint. The use of size is necessary to protect the paint from free lime in green plaster. Packed 6 One-Gallon or 24 One-Quart Cans to the Case; Weight about 65 lbs. per Case.

No. 4901G - One Gallon Can; No. 4901Q - One Quart Can.

Values:	Exc.	V.G.	Good
Gallon	600.00	500.00	350.00
Quart	450.00	375.00	300.00

Comment: *Values are for either size.*

Decorative Enamel

Made for enameling walls, chairs, tables, iron beds, and other furniture; picture frames, bric-a-brac and practically all interior surfaces requiring a high-gloss finish. Can be wiped with damp cloth without affecting its luster. Packed 6 One-Gallon Cans, 24 Quarts, 48 Pints, to the Case; Average Weight about 95 lbs. per Case. 48 Half Pints per Case; Weight per Case about 50 lbs. 48 Quarter Pints per Case; Weight per Case about 30 lbs.

COLORS	Gallon	Quart	Pint	1/2 Pt.	1/4 Pt.
Cream	1501G	1501Q	1501P	1501HP	1501QP
Canary	1502G	1502Q	1502P	1502HP	1502QP
Olive Buff	1503G	1503Q	1503P	1503HP	1503QP
Turquoise Blue	1504G	1504Q	1504P	1504HP	1504QP
Dark Blue	1505G	1505Q	1505P	1505HP	1505QP
Pale Green	1506G	1506Q	1506P	1506HP	1506QP
Lt. Olive Green	1507G	1507Q	1507P	1507HP	1507QP
Sea Green	1508G	1508Q	1508P	1508HP	1508QP
Willow Green	1509G	1509Q	1509P	1509HP	1509QP
Bottle Green	1510G	1510Q	1510P	1510HP	1510QP
Light Ivory	1511G	1511Q	1511P	1511HP	1511QP
Shell Pink	1512G	1512Q	1512P	1512HP	1512QP
Rose	1513G	1513Q	1513P	1513HP	1513QP
Vermilion	1514G	1514Q	1514P	1514HP	1514QP
Maroon	1515G	1515Q	1515P	1515HP	1515QP
Black	1516G	1516Q	1516P	1516HP	1516QP
White	1517G	1517Q	1517P	1517HP	1517QP
Light Gray	1518G	1518Q	1518P	1518HP	1518QP

One-Quarter Pint of Quick Drying Enamel - Orchid (No. 3316). Label is buff color with a red "W" and small red squares in each corner of the two major label rectangles. An early label from "Red W Paint Division - Simmons Hardware Co." From T. Webster collection. Photo by D. Kowalski.

Values:	Exc.	V.G.	Good
Gallon	600.00	500.00	350.00
Quart	400.00	300.00	200.00
Pint	250.00	225.00	175.00
1/2 Pint	200.00	175.00	150.00
1/4 Pint	200.00	175.00	150.00

Comment: *Values are for any color or type of Decorative Enamel or Quick Drying Enamel.*

Bath Enamel

Available in white only. For enameling walls and ceilings of bathrooms and for bath tubs, sinks, interiors of refrigerators and other enamel-coated surfaces. Will stand action of hot and cold water and retain attractive appearance. Has long-wearing qualities. 6 One-Gallon Cans to the Case; Average Weight per case about 88 lbs.; 24 Quart Cans or 48 Pint Cans to the Case; Weight about 98 lbs.

Paints, Brushes and Padlocks • 643

No. 3501G - One Gallon Can; No. 3501Q - One Quart Can; No. 3501P - One Pint Can; No. 3501HP - Half Pint Can.

Enamel Undercoat

Designed to be used as a priming coat before enameling. Made in white only. Packed 6 One-Gallon Cans or 48 Pints to the Case, Average Weight about 90 lbs. per Case; 48 Half-Pint Cans to the Case, Weight about 50 lbs.

No. 3601G - One Gallon Can; No. 3601Q - One Quart Can; No. 3601P - One Pint Can; No. 3601HP - Half Pint Can.

White Enamel

A high-gloss, pure-white coating enamel for woodwork, inside trim and furniture. 6 One-Gallon Cans to the Case, Average Weight about 88 lbs.; 24 Quart Cans or 48 Pint Cans, Average Weight per Case about 98 lbs.; 48 Half Pints, Average Weight per Case about 50 lbs.

No. 3701G - One Gallon Can; No. 3701Q - One Quart Can; No. 3701P - One Pint Can; No. 3701HP - Half Pint Can.

Values:	Exc.	V.G.	Good
Gallon	600.00	500.00	350.00
Quart	400.00	300.00	200.00
Pint	250.00	225.00	175.00
1/2 Pint	200.00	175.00	150.00

Comment: *Values are for Bath Enamel, Enamel Undercoat or White Enamel.*

Stove Enamel

Dries completely in 14 hours. Does not chip, flake or peel. Makes very little smoke or smell. Packed 48 pints to the case, Average weight per case 68 lbs.; 48 half pints, Average weight per case about 40 lbs.; 48 quarter pints to the case, Average weight per case about 25 lbs.

No. 3401P - One Pint Can; No. 3401HP - Half Pint Can; No. 3401QP - Quarter Pint Can.

Values:	Exc.	V.G.	Good
Pint	250.00	225.00	175.00
1/2 Pint	200.00	175.00	150.00
1/4 Pint	200.00	175.00	150.00

Porch and Deck Paint

A paint that will give a lasting finish with good wearing qualities. Will not mark up easily. Not affected by water. Packed 6 One-Gallon Cans, 12 Half Gallon, 24 Quarts, 48 Pints to the Case. Average Weight per Case about 100 lbs.

COLORS	Gallon	1/2 Gal.	Quart	Pint
Light Tan	1601G	1601HG	1601Q	1601P
Dull Yellow	1602G	1602HG	1602Q	1602P
Terra Cotta	1603G	1603HG	1603Q	1603P
Venetian Red	1604G	1604HG	1604Q	1604P
Brown	1605G	1605HG	1605Q	1605P
Light Gray	1606G	1606HG	1606Q	1606P
Drab	1607G	1607HG	1607Q	1607P
Medium Gray	1608G	1608HG	1608Q	1608P
Olive Green	1609G	1609HG	1609Q	1609P
Blue	1610G	1610HG	1610Q	1610P
Values:	**Exc.**	**V.G.**	**Good**	
Gallon	600.00	500.00	350.00	
1/2 Gallon	500.00	400.00	300.00	
Quart	400.00	300.00	200.00	
Pint	250.00	225.00	175.00	

Comment: *Values are for any color.*

Floor Paint

For inside floor use only. Dries to a hard, durable surface that will not mar easily. Packed 6 One-Gallon Cans, 12 Half Gallon, 24 Quarts or 48 Pints to the Case. Average Weight per Case about 100 lbs.

COLORS	Gallon	1/2 Gal.	Quart	Pint
Dull Yellow	1801G	1801HG	1801Q	1801P
Terra Cotta	1802G	1802HG	1802Q	1801P
Venetian Red	1803G	1803HG	1803Q	1803P
Drab	1804G	1804HG	1804Q	1804P
Dark Oak	1805G	1805HG	1805Q	1805P
Brown	1806G	1806HG	1806Q	1806P
Light Gray	1807G	1807HG	1807Q	1807P
Medium Gray	1808G	1808HG	1808Q	1808P
Olive Green	1809G	1809HG	1809Q	1809P
Values:	Exc.	V.G.	Good	
Gallon	600.00	500.00	350.00	
1/2 Gallon	500.00	400.00	300.00	
Quart	400.00	300.00	200.00	
Pint	250.00	225.00	175.00	

Comment: *Values are for any color.*

Buggy Paint

For painting buggies, carriages, wagons, sleighs and other vehicles. Dries to a hard, glossy finish. Retains its new appearance over a long period and withstands washing well. Packed 24 Quart Cans to the Case, Average Weight per Case about 70 lbs.; 48 Pints to Case, Average Weight 76 lbs.; 48 Half Pints to the Case, Average Weight per Case about 40 lbs.

COLORS	One Quart	One Pint	Half Pint
Yellow	1901Q	1901P	1901HP
Vermilion	1902Q	1902P	1902HP
Carmine	1903Q	1903P	1903HP
Maroon	1904Q	1904P	1904HP
Deep Wine	1905Q	1905P	1905HP
Light Green	1907Q	1907P	1905HP
Brewster Green	1908Q	1908P	1908HP
Dark Blue	1909Q	1909P	1909HP
Black	1906Q	1906P	1906HP
Values:	Exc.	V.G.	Good
Quart	450.00	350.00	250.00
Pint	300.00	250.00	225.00
1/2 Pint	200.00	175.00	150.00

Comment: *Values are for any color.*

Wagon and Implement Paint

For painting farm implements, wagons and tools. Prevents rust and decay. Dries with a fine gloss finish. Packed 24 Quarts or 48 Pints to the Case; Average Weight per Case about 80 lbs. 48 Half Pints, Average Weight per Case about 45 lbs. One-Gallon cans furnished on request.

COLORS	1/2 Gal.	Quart	Pint	1/2 Pint
Yellow	2001HG	2001Q	2001P	2001HP
Black	2002HG	2002Q	2002P	2002HP
Red	2003HG	2003Q	2003P	2003HP
Green	2004HG	2004Q	2004P	2004HP
Blue	2005HG	2005Q	2005P	2005HP
Values:	Exc.	V.G.	Good	
Gallon	600.00	500.00	350.00	
1/2 Gallon	500.00	400.00	300.00	
Quart	400.00	300.00	200.00	
Pint	250.00	225.00	175.00	
1/2 Pint	200.00	175.00	150.00	

Comment: *Values are for any color.*

Automobile Enamel

A high-luster, long-wearing enamel that will dry hard in 24 hours and can be applied with ease by anyone. Combines highest-grade automobile varnish with non-fading colors that give a finish of excellent appearance and service. Packed 24 Quarts or 48 Pints, Average Weight per Case about 80 lbs.; 48 Half Pints, Average Weight per Case about 45 lbs. Gallon cans furnished on request.

COLORS	One Quart	One Pint	Half Pint
Cream	2101Q	2101P	2101HP
Carmine	2103Q	2103P	2101HP
Dark Red	2104Q	2104P	2104HP
Deep Maroon	2105Q	2105P	2105HP
Battleship Gray	2106Q	2106P	2105HP
Aluminum	2113Q	2113P	2113HP
Brown	2102Q	2102P	2102HP
Bright Green	2107Q	2107P	2107HP
Brewster Green	2108Q	2108P	2108HP
Royal Blue	2109Q	2109P	2109HP
White	2112Q	2112P	2112HP
Black	2110Q	2110P	2110HP
Flat Black	2111Q	2111P	2111HP
Light Undercoat	2114Q	2114P	2114HP
Dark Undercoat	2115Q	2115P	2115HP
Auto Varnish	2116Q	2116P	2116HP
Values:	**Exc.**	**V.G.**	**Good**
Gallon	600.00	500.00	350.00
Quart	400.00	300.00	200.00
Pint	250.00	225.00	175.00
1/2 Pint	200.00	175.00	150.00

Comment: *Values are for any color.*

Graphite Paint

Available in black only. Used on inside and outside iron work, structural steel and metal roofs. A good preservative for iron work. Packed 6 One-Gallon Cans to the Case, Average weight about 85 lbs.; 1-Five-Gallon Can to the Case, Weight about 75 lbs.; Barrels, Weight about 600 lbs.

No. 3801G - One Gallon Cans; No. 3801/5G - Five Gallon Cans; No. 3801B - Barrels.

Values:	**Exc.**	**V.G.**	**Good**
5 Gallon	750.00	675.00	600.00
Gallon	600.00	500.00	350.00

Shingle Stain

Especially adapted to staining shingles on homes, whether on roof or side walls. May be used either with brush or for dipping shingles. The vehicle contains creosote oil, which acts as a wood preservative and linseed oil to seal the grain.

Covering capacity-one brush coat, 150 square feet to the gallon. Two brush coats, 100 square feet to the gallon. For dipping between 2 1/2 and 3 gallons will be required per 1000 shingles. Packed One Five-Gallon Can to a Case, Average Weight of Case about 75 lbs.; 6 One-Gallon Cans per Case, Average Weight about 85 lbs.; Barrels about 600 lbs.

COLORS	1 Gallon	5 Gallon	Barrel
Gray	2204G	2204/5G	2204B
Slate	2205G	2205/5G	2205B
Light Green	2207G	2207/5G	2207B
Moss Green	2208G	2208/5G	2208B
Dark Green	2209G	2209/5G	2209B
Old Brown	2201G	2201/5G	2201B
Indian Red	2202G	2202/5G	2202B
Russet Red	2203G	2203/5G	2203B
Weather Brown	2206G	2206/5G	2206B
Values:	**Exc.**	**V.G.**	**Good**
5 Gallon	750.00	675.00	600.00
Gallon	600.00	500.00	350.00

Comment: *Values are for any color. Values for barrels not given because we consider the prospect of finding one intact to be very remote.*

Oil Wood Stain

Shades made to imitate the finest woods. Will not raise the grain in wood. Made of best grade of materials to produce a long-lasting, color-holding stain. Packed 6 One-Gallon Cans, 24 Quarts or 48 Pints to the case, Average Weight per case about 70 lbs.; 48 Half Pints to the case, Average Weight about 40 lbs. per case.

COLORS	Gallon	Quart	Pint	1/2 Pint
Light Oak	2601G	2601Q	2601P	2601HP
Dark Oak	2602G	2602Q	2602P	2602HP
Cherry	2603G	2603Q	2603P	2603HP
Walnut	2604G	2604Q	2604P	2604HP
Golden Oak	2605G	2605Q	2605P	2605HP
Antique Oak	2606G	2606Q	2606P	2606HP
Mahogany	2607G	2607Q	2607P	2607HP
Old Mahogany	2608G	2608Q	2608P	2608HP

Values:	Exc.	V.G.	Good
Gallon	600.00	500.00	350.00
Quart	400.00	300.00	200.00
Pint	250.00	225.00	175.00
1/2 Pint	200.00	175.00	150.00

Comment: *Values are for any color.*

Varnish Stain

For finishing floors, borders and old furniture. Also for decorating interior wood and ironwork of all kinds. Presents a handsome finish that is hard and long-wearing. Packed 6 One-Gallon Cans, 12 Half-Gallon, 24 Quarts or 48 Pints to the Case; Average Weight per Case about 65 lbs. 48 Half Pints to the Case; Average Weight about 35 lbs. 48 Quarter-Pints to the Case; Average Weight about 25 lbs.

One-Quarter Pint Varnish Stain - Mahogany (No. 2703QP). Label is eggshell white with red "W" and red squares in the corners of both rectangles. Fairly rare. From T. Webster collection. Photo by D. Kowalski.

"Winchester Store" version of the same can of Varnish Stain - Mahogany. This label is darker buff color with red "W" and red squares in the corners of both rectangles. "Winchester Store" printed in red below the red "W." The only "Winchester Store" can of paint or varnish ever discovered that we're aware of. From T. Webster collection. Photo by D. Kowalski.

COLORS	Gallon	1/2 Gallon	Quart
Cardinal Red	2702G	2702HG	2702Q
Mahogany	2703G	2703HG	2703Q
Walnut	2704G	2704HG	2704Q
Natural	2706G	2706HG	2706Q
Light Oak	2707G	2707HG	2707Q
Dark Oak	2708G	2708HG	2708Q
Golden Oak	2709G	2709HG	2709Q
Ground Color	2711G	2711HG	2711Q
Cherry	2701G	2701HG	2701Q
Green	2710G	2710HG	2710Q

COLORS	Pint	1/2 Pint	1/4 Pint
Cardinal Red	2702P	2702HP	2702QP
Mahogany	2703P	2703HP	2703QP
Walnut	2704P	2704HP	2704QP
Natural	2706P	2706HP	2706QP
Light Oak	2707P	2707HP	2707QP
Dark Oak	2708P	2708HP	2708QP
Golden Oak	2709P	2709HP	2709QP
Ground Color	2711P	2711HP	2711QP
Cherry	2701P	2701HP	2701QP
Green	2710P	2710HP	2710QP

Values:	Exc.	V.G.	Good
Gallon	600.00	500.00	350.00
1/2 Gallon	500.00	400.00	300.00
Quart	400.00	350.00	275.00
Pint	350.00	300.00	250.00
1/2 Pint	300.00	280.00	225.00
1/4 Pint	300.00	275.00	225.00

Comment: *Values are for any color of Varnish Stain. Double these values for any can of "Winchester Store" Varnish Stain.*

Wood Filler, Paste

Used for filling up the grain in open-grained woods. Makes a hard, smooth surface over which to lay finishing coats. Cannot be excelled for bringing out the beauty of the natural wood grain. Works well. Packed 100 lbs. to the Case.

COLORS	1 lb.	5 lb.	12 1/2 lb.	25 lb.
Natural	4801/1	4801/5	4801/12 1/2	4801/25
Oak	4802/1	4802/5	4802/12 1/2	4802/25
Golden Oak	4803/1	4803/5	4802/12 1/2	4803/25
Walnut	4804/1	4804/5	4804/12 1/2	4804/25
Mahogany	4805/1	4805/5	4805/12 1/2	4805/25

Values:	Exc.	V.G.	Good
25 lb.	500.00	400.00	300.00
12 1/2 lb.	450.00	375.00	275.00
5 lb.	400.00	350.00	250.00
1 lb.	400.00	350.00	250.00

Comment: *Values are for any color of Paste Wood Filler.*

Wood Filler, Liquid

Packed 6 One-Gallon Cans to the Case, Weight about 90 lbs.; 24 Quart Cans in a Case, Weight about 60 lbs.

SIZE	Gallon	1/2 Gal.	Quart	Pint
	5001G	5001HG	5001Q	5001P

Wood Filler, Clear Liquid

Packed 6 One-Gallon Cans to the Case, Weight about 90 lbs.; 24 Quart Cans in a Case, Weight about 60 lbs.

SIZE	Gallon	1/2 Gal.	Quart	Pint
	5002G	5002HG	5002Q	5002P

Values:	Exc.	V.G.	Good
Gallon	450.00	400.00	350.00
1/2 Gallon	400.00	350.00	300.00
Quart	350.00	300.00	250.00
Pint	300.00	250.00	200.00

Comment: *Values are for either Liquid or Clear Liquid Wood Filler.*

Crack and Crevice Filler

Made for filling cracks and crevices in old or new, hard or soft wood floors and decks of vessels before painting or enameling. Packed 100 lbs. to the Case.

No. 4601/1 - One Pound Can; No. 4601/5 - Five Pound Can.

Values:	Exc.	V.G.	Good
	450.00	375.00	300.00

Comment: *Values are for either size.*

Liquid Blackboard Slating

Gives a perfect dead-black surface. Packed 6 One-Gallon Cans, 24 Quarts or 48 Pints to a Case; Weight per Case about 70 lbs.

No. 4201G - One Gallon Can; No. 4201Q - One Quart Can; No. 4201P - One Pint Can.

Values:	Exc.	V.G.	Good
	250.00	200.00	150.00

Comment: *Values are for any size.*

Mill White Gloss

An excellent glossy white finish for walls of offices, mills and other buildings. Gives better light and working conditions as it reflects and diffuses light and is thoroughly clean and sanitary. Can be washed with water at any time without losing its brilliant finish. Will not crack, chalk, scale or flake and retains its whiteness. One Five-Gallon Can to a Case, Weight about 90 lbs.; Six One-Gallon Cans per Case, Weight about 100 lbs. Furnished on request in barrels at $.10 net less than gallon price per gallon.

No. 3901G - One Gallon Can; No. 3901/5G - Five Gallon Can.

Mill White Flat

This should always be used as a first coat before applying mill white gloss. One Five-Gallon Can to a Case, Weight about 90 lbs.; Six One-Gallon Cans per Case, Weight about 100 lbs. Furnished on request in barrels at $.10 net less than gallon price per gallon.

No. 3903G - One Gallon Can; No. 3903/5G - Five Gallon Can.

Values:	Exc.	V.G.	Good
5 Gallon	500.00	425.00	350.00
1 Gallon	450.00	375.00	300.00

Comment: *Values are for either Gloss or Flat Mill White.*

Concrete Coating Exterior

For concrete, brick or stucco work. Damp proof and weatherproof. All colors listed may be secured in 5 gallon pails at $.05 less than gallon price per gallon. Also obtainable in barrels at $.10 less than gallon price per gallon. Packed 6 One-Gallon Cans to the Case, Average Weight per Case about 110 lbs.; 1 Five-Gallon Can per Case, Average Weight about 90 lbs.; Barrels about 50 Gallons.

COLORS	Gallon
White	2301G
Milwaukee Brick	2302G
Italian Red	2303G
Ivory	2304G
Cement Gray	2305G
Stone Gray	2306G
Blue Gray	2307G
Slate Gray	2308G
Green	2309G

Values:	Exc.	V.G.	Good
5 Gallon	500.00	425.00	350.00
1 Gallon	450.00	375.00	300.00

Comment: *Values are for any color.*

Aluminum Paint

Makes a lasting silver-color finish for stoves, radiators, pipes, ranges, metal beds and like metal surfaces. Adds to their attractiveness and is a rust preventive. Not affected by extreme heat or cold. Packed 24 Quarts or 48 Pints to the Case, Weight about 70 lbs.; 48 Half Pints, Weight about 40 lbs.; 48 Quarter Pints, Weight about 25 lbs.

No. 4001Q - One Quart Can; No. 4001P - One Pint Can; No. 4001HP - Half Pint Can; No. 4001QP - Quarter Pint Can.

Gold Paint

Used similarly and for the same purposes as aluminum paint. Also acts as a good rust preventive. Packed 24 Quarts or 48 Pints to the Case, Weight about 70 lbs.; 48 Half Pints, Weight about 40 lbs.; 48 Quarter Pints, Weight about 25 lbs.

No. 4101Q - One Quart Can; No. 4101P - One Pint Can; No. 4101HP - Half Pint Can; No. 4101QP - Quarter Pint Can.

Values:	Exc.	V.G.	Good
Quart	500.00	400.00	300.00
Pint	400.00	325.00	250.00
1/2 Pint	350.00	300.00	225.00
1/4 Pint	350.00	300.00	225.00

Comment: *Values are for either Aluminum Paint or Gold Paint.*

Superior Bronzing Liquid

A special grade of bronzing liquid that has good body, floats the bronze perfectly and holds its brilliancy. Very light in color. Packed 6 One-Gallon Cans, 24 Quarts or 48 Pints to the Case; weight per Case about 35 lbs.

No. 4301G - One Gallon Can; No. 4301Q - One Quart Can; No. 4301P - One Pint Can; No. 4301HP - Half Pint Can.

Banana Bronzing Liquid

Extra-high grade that when mixed with bronze or aluminum powder gives a mixture that can be applied to metal or other surfaces with excellent results. Will stand outside as well as inside use. Must be kept tightly corked to prevent curdling. Packed 6 One-Gallon Cans, 24 Quarts or 48 Pints to the Case; weight per Case about 35 lbs.

No. 4401G - One Gallon Can; No. 4401Q - One Quart Can; No. 4401P - One Pint Can; No. 4401HP - Half Pint Can.

Values:	Exc.	V.G.	Good
	400.00	350.00	300.00

Comment: *Values are for any size Superior Bronzing Liquid or Banana Bronzing Liquid.*

American White Paste

A medium grade of white paste designed particularly for plumber's use and for priming.

No. 5601/1 - One Pound Can; No. 5601/5 - Five Pound Can.

Zinc Paste.

Ground in Bleached Linseed Oil.

Type/No.	1 lb.	5 lb.	12 1/2 lb.	25 lb.
Green Seal Zinc	5401/1	5401/5	5401/12 1/2	5401/25
Red Seal Zinc	5402/1	5402/5	5402/12 1/2	5402/25
Ground in Damar Varnish				
Zinc in Damar	5410/1	5401/5	5401/12 1/2	5401/25

Values:	Exc.	V.G.	Good
25 lb.	500.00	400.00	300.00
12 1/2 lb.	450.00	375.00	275.00
5 lb.	400.00	350.00	250.00
1 lb.	400.00	350.00	250.00

Comment: *Values are for any type of Zinc Paste or American White Paste.*

Pure Colors in Oil

Absolutely true, brilliant colors, ground in pure linseed oil. Of uniform consistency. Wide range of shades. Put up in 1 lb. cans only, except as otherwise marked.

Pure Color in Oil - Raw Umber (No. 5201), one-pound can. From T. Webster collection. Photo by D. Kowalski.

No.	Shade
Shades of Brown.	
5201/1	*Raw Umber*
5202/1	*Burnt Umber*
5203/1	*Vandyke Brown*
5204/1	*Raw Sienna*
5205/1	*Burnt Sienna*
Shades of Black.	
5210/1	*Refined Lamp Black*
5210/5	*Refined Lamp Black - 5 lb. Cans*
5211/1	*Coach Black*
5212/1	*Ivory Black*
5213/1	*Drop Black*
5214/1	*Lettering Black*
Shades of Blue.	
5220/1	*Ultramarine Blue*
5220/1/4	*Ultramarine Blue - 1/4 lb. Cans*
5221/1	*No. 1 Prussian Blue*
5221/1/4	*No. 1 Prussian Blue - 1/4 lb. Cans*
Shades of Green.	
5230/1	*Chrome Green, Light*
5231/1	*Chrome Green, Medium*
5232/1	*Chrome Green, Dark*
5233/1	*Blind and Shutter Green, Light*
5324/1	*Blind and Shutter Green, Medium*
5235/1	*Blind and Shutter Green, Dark*
5236/1	*Deep Front Door Green*
Shades of Red.	
5240/1	*Indian Red*
5241/1	*Venetian Red*
5242/1	*Tuscan Red*
5243/1	*American Vermilion*
5233/1	*Rose Pink*
5245/1	*Rose Lake*
5246/1	*Permanent Red*
Shades of Yellow.	
5250/1	*French Yellow Ochre*
5251/1	*Golden Ochre*
5252/1	*No. 1 Chrome Yellow, Light*
5253/1	*No. 1 Chrome Yellow, Medium*
5254/1	*No. 1 Chrome Yellow, Dark*
Graining Colors (in one-pound cans only).	
5260/1	*Light Oak*
5261/1	*Dark Oak*
5262/1	*Walnut*
5263/1	*Chestnut*
5264/1	*Ash*
5265/1	*Cherry*
5266/1	*Mahogany*

Values:	Exc.	V.G.	Good
1 lb.	400.00	350.00	250.00

Comment: *Values are for any color. Add 20 percent for 5-pound cans or 1/4-pound cans.*

Brushing Lacquer

A 100% Lacquer, made from the highest-grade nitrated cotton, gums, oils, pigments and solvents. Can be used on all Interior Finishes and on Metal Outside. Makes a clean, bright, long-wearing, dull satin finish, that can be polished to a high luster, and will not crack, chip or peel. Not stained by fruits or vegetables; hot dishes will leave no marks. Comes ready for use; no thinning necessary. Will surface dry in 20 minutes and can be used 2 hours after applying. All colors can be furnished in gallon and half-gallon cans.

Colors	*Quart*	*Pint*	*1/2 Pint*	*1/4 Pint*
White	1700Q	1700P	1700HP	1700QP
Black	1701Q	1701P	1701HP	1701QP
Blue	1702Q	1702P	1702HP	1702QP
Light Blue	1703Q	1703P	1703HP	1703QP
Green	1704Q	1704P	1704HP	1704QP
Jade Green	1705Q	1705P	1705HP	1705QP
Yellow	1706Q	1706P	1706HP	1706QP
Orange	1707Q	1707P	1707HP	1707QP
Oriental Red	1708Q	1708P	1708HP	1708QP
Tan	1709Q	1709P	1709HP	1709QP
Ivory	1710Q	1710P	1710HP	1710QP
Gray	1711Q	1711P	1711HP	1711QP
Clear	1712Q	1712P	1712HP	1712QP
Light Oak	1740Q	1740P	1740HP	1740QP
Dark Oak	1741Q	1741P	1741HP	1741QP
Mahogany	1742Q	1742P	1742HP	1742QP
Walnut	1743Q	1743P	1743HP	1743QP

Lacquer Thinner

Made specially for thinning Brushing Lacquer to the proper consistency while applying. 24 Quart Cans in a Case; 48 Pint Cans in a Case; Weight per Case about 65 lbs. 48 Half-Pint Cans in a Case; Weight per Case about 35 lbs. 96 Quarter-Pint Cans in a Case; Wgt. per Case about 50 lbs.

No. 1739Q - Quart Can; No. 1739P - Pint Can; No. 1739HP - Half-Pint Can; No. 1739QP - Quarter-Pint Can.

Values:	Exc.	V.G.	Good
Gallon	500.00	400.00	300.00
1/2 Gallon	500.00	400.00	300.00

Values:	Exc.	V.G.	Good
Quart	400.00	300.00	200.00
Pint	300.00	250.00	175.00
1/2 Pint	250.00	200.00	150.00
1/4 Pint	250.00	200.00	150.00

Comment: *Values are for Lacquer Thinner or any color of Brushing Lacquer.*

Red W Brand Varnishes

Any Red W Brand Varnish may be obtained in 5-gallon cans at $0.05 net less per gallon than the one-gallon price; half barrel at $0.07 1/2 net less per gallon; and barrel at $0.10 net less. Packed 12 One-Gallon Cans or 24 Half Gallon Cans to the Case, Average Weight about 108 lbs; 24 Quarts or 48 Pints to the case, Average Weight about 64 lbs.; 48 Half Pints, Average Weight about 36 lbs. (One-gallon can illustrated below.)

Floor Varnish

This varnish is especially prepared to meet the severe service required of a floor varnish. Dries to a hard glossy coat, which resists wear and water.

No. 7022G - One Gallon Can; No. 7022HG - Half Gallon Can; No. 7022Q - One Quart Can; No. 7022P - One Pint Can; No. 7022HP - Half Pint Can.

Outside Spar Varnish

A pale, full-bodied varnish that sets in five hours and dries hard and tough in twenty-four hours. Produces a tough coating that withstands all conditions of the weather in any climate. An excellent finish for outdoor woodwork, yachts, canoes, and any purpose where a weather-resisting varnish is required.

No. 7012G - One Gallon Can; No. 7012HG - Half Gallon Can; No. 7012Q - One Quart Can; No. 7012P - One Pint Can; No. 7012HP - Half Pint Can.

Interior Varnish

This varnish is designed for use on interior woodwork in homes, offices, etc. It is light in color, has good body and dries with a fine luster.

No. 7018G - One Gallon Can; No. 7018HG - Half Gallon Can; No. 7018Q - One Quart Can; No. 7018P - One Pint Can; No. 7018HP - Half Pint Can.

Rubbing Varnish

A medium-quick rubbing varnish possessing good body and working qualities. Under favorable conditions it can be rubbed in forty-eight hours without danger of "sweating out."

No. 7031G - One Gallon Can; No. 7031HG - Half Gallon Can; No. 7031Q - One Quart Can; No. 7031P - One Pint Can.

Flat Finish Varnish

For producing, without the labor of rubbing, the oil-rubbed appearance now so popular on furniture and other woodwork.

No. 7019G - One Gallon Can; No. 7019HG - Half Gallon Can; No. 7019Q - One Quart Can; No. 7019P - One Pint Can.

Automobile and Carriage Varnish

A pale, free-working varnish of heavy body, dries with the greatest luster and has excellent wearing qualities.

No. 7001G - One Gallon Can; No. 7001HG - Half Gallon Can; No. 7001Q - One Quart Can; No. 7001P - One Pint Can.

Painters' Japan

A high-quality drying Japan, free from sediment and suspended matter. A safe and satisfactory means for hastening the drying of oil paints.

No. 7030G - One Gallon Can; No. 7030HG - Half Gallon Can; No. 7030Q - One Quart Can; No. 7030P - One Pint Can; No. 7030HP - Half Pint Can.

White Drying Japan

Paler in color than the regular painters' Japan and especially prepared for use with delicate tints.

No. 7028G - One Gallon Can; No. 7028HG - Half Gallon Can; No. 7028Q - One Quart Can; No. 7028P - One Pint Can.

Black Asphaltum

A high-grade black varnish made from asphaltum. Dries quickly with a high luster and is a splendid protection for iron work and sheet metal.

No. 7032G - One Gallon Can; No. 7032HG - Half Gallon Can; No. 7032Q - One Quart Can; No. 7032P - One Pint Can.

General Utility Varnish

This varnish will give excellent satisfaction for any purpose for which varnish is intended. Sets dust-free in a few hours and dries hard over night, giving a tough, hard coating that is waterproof and retains its luster under severe usage. Equally well adapted for inside and outside use.

No. 7015G - One Gallon Can; No. 7015HG - Half Gallon Can; No. 7015Q - One Quart Can; No. 7015P - One Pint Can; No. 7015HP - Half Pint Can.

Linoleum Varnish

For re-coating and bringing out the original design in linoleum and oil-cloths; has a medium body, works easy under the brush, is flexible and dries overnight.

No. 7023G - One Gallon Can; No. 7023HG - Half Gallon Can; No. 7023Q - One Quart Can; No. 7023P - One Pint Can; No. 7023HP - Half Pint Can.

Light Hard Oil Finish

A pale varnish of good body for natural wood finishing and interior work; dries with a beautiful gloss and is dust-proof in 6 or 7 hours; hardens in 24 hours.

No. 7016G - One Gallon Can; No. 7016HG - Half Gallon Can; No. 7016Q - One Quart Can; No. 7016P - One Pint Can; No. 7016HP - Half Pint Can.

Values:	Exc.	V.G.	Good
Gallon	500.00	450.00	400.00
1/2 Gallon	450.00	400.00	350.00
Quart	400.00	375.00	350.00
Pint	350.00	325.00	300.00
1/2 Pint	350.00	325.00	300.00

Comment: *Values are for any of the above types of Varnish.*

Shellac

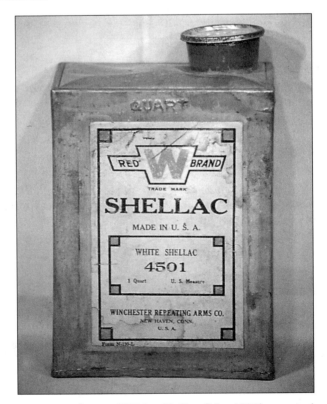

Very rare metal can of White Shellac (No. 4501), quart size. From T. Webster collection. Photo by D. Kowalski.

Shellacs are for Inside or Outside Use. Cut in denatured alcohol; gives good body.

White Shellac.

No. 4501G - One Gallon Bottle; No. 4501HG - Half Gallon Bottle; No. 4501Q - One Quart Bottle; No. 4501P - One Pint Bottle; No. 4501/2 - 2 Oz. Bottle; No. 4501/4 - 4 Oz. Bottle; No. 4501/8 - 8 Oz. Bottle.

Orange Shellac.

No. 4502G - One Gallon Bottle; No. 4502HG - Half Gallon Bottle; No. 4502Q - One Quart Bottle; No. 4502P - One Pint Bottle; No. 4502/2 - 2 Oz. Bottle; No. 4502/4 - 4 Oz. Bottle; No. 4502/8 - 8 Oz. Bottle.

Values:	Exc.	V.G.	Good
Gallon	450.00	400.00	350.00
1/2 Gallon	450.00	400.00	350.00
Quart	400.00	375.00	350.00
Pint	400.00	375.00	350.00
8 Oz.	350.00	325.00	300.00
4 Oz.	300.00	275.00	250.00
2 Oz.	300.00	275.00	250.00

Comment: *Values are for either type of Shellac in bottles. Double the values for metal cans.*

Paint and Varnish Remover

For removing varnish or paint from wood or metal surfaces; if applied freely with a soft brush and allowed to stand until the paint or varnish is thoroughly softened (one coat is usually sufficient) it can be removed with a putty knife, cloth or stiff brush. Will not discolor the wood or raise the grain. 12 One-Gallon Cans in a Case; Weight per Case about 115 lbs. 12 Half-Gallon Cans in a Case; 24 Quart Cans in a Case; 48 Pint Cans in a Case; 96 Half-Pint Cans in a Case; Weight per Case about 60 lbs.

No. 6005G - One Gallon Can; No. 6005HG - Half Gallon Can; No. 6005Q - One Quart Can; No. 6005P - One Pint Can; No. 6005HP - Half Pint Can.

Values:	Exc.	V.G.	Good
Gallon	500.00	450.00	400.00
1/2 Gallon	450.00	400.00	350.00
Quart	400.00	375.00	350.00
Values:	**Exc.**	**V.G.**	**Good**
Pint	400.00	375.00	350.00
1/2 Pint	350.00	325.00	300.00

Red W Paint Display, Willett Merchandiser

Shelves	Size of Shelves	Distance To Floor	Distance Between
Bottom	22 1/2 x 23 1/2 in.	9 in.	15 3/4 in.
Third	19 1/2 x 19 1/2 in.	25 in.	13 3/4 in.
Second	16 x 16 in.	41 in.	11 3/4 in.
Top	12 x 12 in.	52 in.	

Values:	Exc.	V.G.	Good
	2,000.00	1,800.00	1,500.00

Comment: *Values for the merchandiser only (without stock).*

No. 124. Portable display stand made of steel with four shelves; two lengths of 1/2-inch iron pipe; three supporting studs; nickel plated cap screw; four Bassick casters; lacquer finish, in a Winchester gray. Can be used for other items; easily assembled; will support a load of 755 lbs. One in a Crate; Weight each about 52 lbs.

Winchester Paint and Varnish Brushes

Warranty stamped on handles of all brushes made of Chinese or Russian bristles: WARRANTED PURE RUSSIAN HOG BRISTLES or WARRANTED PURE CHINESE HOG BRISTLES.

These brushes are made by a patented process by which the bristles are set in a rubber compound which is absolutely not affected by oil, turpentine, alcohol, water, gasoline or any substance that will not destroy the bristles and held by a seamless nickel-plated, heavy steel ferrule compressed over the bristles. Can be used in anything, will not swell and are guaranteed to hold their bristles.

Varnish Brush, Fitch Flowing - Double Thick, Chisel End

Soft hair flowing, solidly embedded in vulcanized rubber. Nailed and clinched. Polished metal ferrule. Hardwood handle, dead-black finish. Lettered in silver. Not affected by water or oil. Used for flowing varnish or enamel on fine finished woodwork or enamel work on automobiles or similar jobs. Leaves no brush marks. Packed one dozen in a cardboard box.

Fitch Flowing - Double Thick, Chisel End Varnish Brush (No. W847/1). This is the only known paint or varnish brush ever found; another example of small consumable products that were rarely saved. "VULCANIZED IN RUBBER" is imprinted on metal body facing painter as he or she used the brush. From T. Webster collection. Photo by D. Kowalski.

No.	W847/1	W847/1 1/2	W847/2
Width, in.	1	1 1/2	2
Length bristles, in.	1 3/8	1 1/2	1 5/8
Length overall, in.	6 1/2	6 3/4	7

Values:	Exc.	V.G.	Good
	1,200.00	1,100.00	950.00

Comment: *Values for any width.*

Varnish Brush, Wide End

Highest-grade Chinese black bristles. Chisel point. Solid center. Heavy nickel-plated steel ferrule. New-style dead-black hardwood handle, lettered in silver. One dozen in a cardboard box.

No.	W6	W7	W8
Width, inches	1 5/8	2 1/8	2 5/8
Length, bristles, inches	2 1/8	2 7/8	3 1/8
Length overall, inches	7 3/4	8 1/2	9

Varnish Brush, High-Class, Triple Thick

Very high-class triple-thick varnish or shellac brush for professional painters. Set in rubber. Chinese black bristles. Extra-thick, solidly embedded in vulcanized rubber. Chisel point. Nickel-plated ferrule. Hardwood handle. Dead-black finish. Lettered in Silver. Not affected by water or oil.

No.	W050	W051	W052	W053	W054
Width, inches		1 1/2	2	2 1/2	3
Lgth, bristles, in.	2 1/8	2 1/4	2 1/2	2 3/4	3
Lgth overall, in.	8	8 3/4	9 1/4	9 3/4	10 1/4

Varnish Brush, Best Grade

Best-grade Chinese black bristles. Set in rubber. Chisel point. Solidly embedded in vulcanized rubber. Nickel-plated metal ferrule. Hardwood handle, dead-black finish. Lettered in Silver. Not affected by water or oil. One dozen in a cardboard box.

No.	W091	W092	W093	W094
Width, in.	1 1/2	2	2 1/2	3
Length bristles out, in.	2 1/4	2 1/2	2 5/8	2 3/4
Length overall, in.	9	9 1/2	9 3/4	10 1/2

Varnish Brush, Oval, High-Grade Painters' Brush

Oval shape. High-grade painters' brush. Set in rubber. Chinese black bristles, solidly embedded in vulcanized rubber. Chisel point. Nickel-plated seamless steel band. Dead-black finish hardwood handle, lettered in Silver. Red stripe. Not affected by water or oil.

No.	W 4/0	W 6/0	W/80	W 10/0
Size, No.	4/0	6/0	8/0	10/0
Length bristles out, in.	3 1/8	3 3/8	3 5/8	3 7/8
Length overall, in.	10	10 1/2	10 5/8	10 7/8

Varnish Brush, Lightweight Household

A lightweight brush for household use. Set in rubber. Chinese black bristles, extra-thick, solidly embedded in vulcanized rubber. Chisel point. Nickel-plated ferrule. Hardwood handle, dead-black finish. Lettered in Silver.

No.	W110	W111	W112	W113
Width, in.	1	1 1/2	2	2 1/2
Length bristles out, in.	1 3/4	1 7/8	2	2
Length overall, in.	7 3/4	8 1/4	8 9/16	8 3/4

Varnish Brush, Oval, Medium Grade

Cement set. Oval shape. Chinese black bristles, full center. Chisel end. Seamless polished metal ferrule. Bristles held by compressed ferrule end. Dead-black finish hardwood handle, lettered in Silver. Red stripe. A medium-grade brush. Will do good work.

No.	W43	W45	W47
Size No.	2/0	4/0	6/0
Width at Ferrule, in.	1 3/4	2	2 1/4
Length, Bristles out, in.	2 1/2	2 7/8	3 1/4
Length overall, in.	9 1/4	10	10 1/2

Varnish Brush, Oval, Household Grade

Oval shape. Chinese black bristles, cement set. Full center. Chisel point. Seamless nickel-plated metal ferrule. Bristles held by compressed ferrule end. Dead-black finish hardwood handle, lettered in Silver. Red stripe. A medium-length oval brush for household use. For varnish or paint.

No. W476. Length at ferrule 2 inches. Width at ferrule 1 1/8 inches. Length of bristles out, 2 3/4 inches. Length overall 9 inches.

Values:	Exc.	V.G.	Good
	1,000.00	900.00	750.00

Comment: *Values for any width and type of Varnish Brush (except Fitch Flowing).*

Varnish Brush Assortment Box - Flat Brushes

No. W10. Assortment Box. Originally contained an assortment of four dozen flat brushes. Cardboard box with hinged top measures 17 1/2 inches long. From T. Webster collection. Photo by D. Kowalski.

Values:	Exc.	V.G.	Good
	2,000.00	1,800.00	1,500.00

Comment: *Values for box only.*

Household Brush Set

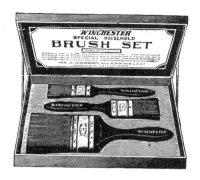

No. W333. Household Brush Assortment. An exceedingly high-quality set of brushes for use around the home or garage. Will save many hours of labor. Pure Tientsin Chinese black bristles, solidly embedded in rubber and vulcanized; nickel-plated steel ferrule; hardwood handles, dead-black finish, lettered in Silver. Assortment consists of three brushes in hinged cardboard box.

Values:	Exc.	V.G.	Good
	1,200.00	1,000.00	800.00

Comment: *Values for box only.*

Paint Brush Display

Wooden wall-mounted paint brush display. "Ready Mixed" and "House Paint" are colored red; so are the "W" and the four small highlight squares in each corner. Rest of copy is black; wood frame is black. Measures 30 1/2 inches long x 15 3/4 inches high. This is the only one known. From T. Webster collection. Photo by D. Kowalski.

Values:	Exc.	V.G.	Good
	1,800.00	1,700.00	1,500.00

Comment: *Values for display only.*

Wall Paint Brush. High-Grade, Professional

A very high-grade, extra-heavy professional painter's brush. Chinese black bristles, solidly embedded in vulcanized rubber. Heavy nickel-plated steel ferrule, with rivets extending through the brush and clinched. Beaver tail hardwood handle, dead black finish. Lettered in Silver. Not affected by water or oil.

No.	W630	W635	W640
Width, inches	3	3 1/2	4
Length, bristles out, in.	3 3/4	4	4 1/4
Length overall, inches	11	11 1/2	11 3/4

Wall Paint Brush. Mechanic's Brush

A good mechanic's brush. Best-quality Russian yellow-bristle center; Russian white-bristle casing, solidly embedded in vulcanized rubber; nickel plated steel ferrule. Beaver-tail hardwood handle, dead-black finish. Lettered in Silver.

No.	W210	W211	W212
Width, in.	3	3 2/3	4
Length, bristles out, in.	3 3/8	3 5/8	3 7/8
Length overall, inches	10 7/8	11 1/4	11 1/2

Wall Paint Brush. High-Grade Mechanic's Brush

A high-grade paint brush, recommended for mechanic's use. Black Chinese bristles, solidly embedded in vulcanized rubber. Nickel-plated steel ferrule with rivets extending through the brush and clinched. Beaver-tail hardwood handle, dead-black finish. Lettered in Silver. Not affected by water or oil.

No.	W735	W740
Width, inches	3 1/2	4
Length, bristles out, in.	3 5/8	3 7/8
Length overall, in.	11 1/4	11 3/8

Wall Paint Brush. Tientsin Bristles

Pure Tientsin Chinese black bristles, solidly embedded in rubber and vulcanized. Nickel-plated steel ferrule. Hardwood handle, dead-black finish, lettered in Silver.

No. W300. Width 3 inches; Length of bristles, out, 3 inches; Length overall 10 inches.

Wall Paint Brush, High-Grade Mechanic's, Short Bristle

A high-grade paint brush, highly recommended for mechanics' use. Best-quality Russian yellow bristle, solidly embedded in vulcanized rubber. Nickel-plated steel ferrule with rivets extending through the brush and clinched. Beaver-tail, hardwood handle, dead-black finish. Lettered in Silver. Not affected by water or oil.

No.	W330	W335	W340
Width, inches	3	3 1/2	4
Length, Bristles out, in.	3 1/8	3 1/8	3 1/8
Length overall, in.	10 1/2	10 5/8	10 3/4
Values:	Exc.	V.G.	Good
	800.00	700.00	550.00

Comment: *Values for any type or size of Wall Paint Brush.*

Stucco Brush, Best Quality

Set in rubber. Best-quality yellow Russian bristle center with white Russian bristle casing, solidly embedded in vulcanized rubber. Heavy seamless steel ferrule. Hardwood handle, dead-black finish. Lettered in Silver.

No.	W201	W202
Width, inches	3 1/2	4
Length, Bristles out, in.	4 1/8	4 3/8
Length overall, inches	10 3/4	10 7/8

Stucco Brush, General Outside

For general outside painting. Set in cement. Strictly pure Chinese selected black bristle, black leather bound. Hardwood handle, dead-black finish. Lettered in Silver.

No.	W201	W202
Width, inches	3 1/2	4
Length, Bristles out, in.	3 7/8	4 1/8
Length overall, in.	10 1/2	11

Sash Brushes or Cutters

These brushes can be used in anything. They are made by a patented process by which the bristles are set in a rubber compound which is absolutely not affected by oil, turpentine, alcohol, water, gasoline or any substance that will not destroy the bristles. Held by a seamless nickel-plated heavy steel ferrule compressed over the bristles. Can be used in anything, will not swell and are guaranteed to hold their bristles.

Sash Brush, Oval, Highest Grade

Highest-grade Chinese black bristles; chisel point; solid center. Heavy nickel-plated steel ferrule. Long, dead-black hardwood handle, lettered in Silver.

No.	W66	W77	W88
Width, inches	1 1/8	1 5/8	2 1/8

No.	W66	W77	W88
Length, Bristles out, in.	2 3/8	2 5/8	2 7/8
Length overall, in.	10 3/4	11	11 1/4

Sash Brush, General Painting

A Good Painter's Tool. Chinese fine black bristles, solidly embedded in vulcanized rubber. Metal ferrule. Hardwood handle, dead-black finish. Lettered in Silver. Not affected by water or oil.

No.	W081	W082
Width, inches	1 1/2	2
Length, Bristles out, in.	1 7/8	2
Length overall, in.	11 1/2	12

Sash Brush, Flat

Chinese fine black bristles, solidly embedded in vulcanized rubber. Chisel point. Hardwood handle, dead-black finish. Lettered in Silver. Not affected by Water or Oil.

No.	W032/1	W032/1 1/2	W032/2	W032/2 1/2
Width, in.	1	1 1/2	2	2 1/2
Length, Bristles	2	2 1/4	2 1/2	2 3/4
Length overall	10 1/2	10 3/4	11	11 1/2

Sash Brush, Trimming

For Painters' Use for Trimming Sashes and Corners. Chinese fine black bristles, solidly embedded in vulcanized rubber. Chisel point. Nickel-plated metal ferrule. Hardwood handle, dead-black finish. Lettered in Silver. Not affected by water or oil.

No.	W21	W22	W23	W24
Diameter at ferrule, in.	1/2	5/8	3/4	1
Length, Bristles out, in.	1 7/16	1 9/16	1 11/16	1 3/4
Length overall, in.	8 1/4	8 3/4	8 13/16	9

No.	W26	W28	W30
Diameter at ferrule, in.	1	1 1/8	1 1/4
Length, Bristles out, in.	2	2 3/16	2 7/16
Length overall, in.	9 15/16	10 1/8	10 1/4

Values:	Exc.	V.G.	Good
	800.00	700.00	550.00

Comment: *Values for any type or size of Stucco Brush or Sash Brush.*

Lacquer Brush

Pure Chinese black bristles, embedded in a rubber compound that will not dissolve in Lacquer or Lacquer Thinner. Square top. Tinned steel ferrule. Hardwood handle, dead-black finish, lettered in Silver. Not soluble in Lacquer or Lacquer Thinner.

No.	WL1	WL1 1/2	
Width, inches	1	1 1/2	
Length, Bristles out, in.	2 1/8	2 3/8	
Length overall, in.	8	8 3/4	
Values:	**Exc.**	**V.G.**	**Good**
	800.00	700.00	550.00

Comment: *Values for either size of Lacquer Brush.*

Radiator Bronzing Brush

Pure black goat hair, solidly embedded in vulcanized rubber. Nickel-plated steel ferrule. Long, dead-black hardwood handle, lettered in Silver. The long handle makes these brushes especially desirable for radiator bronzing.

No.	W128 3/4	W128/1	W128/1 1/2
Width, in.	3/4	1	1 1/2
Length, Bristles out	1 1/8	1 1/4	1 3/8
Length overall, in.	12 1/4	9	10
Values:	**Exc.**	**V.G.**	**Good**
	800.00	700.00	550.00

Comment: *Values for any size of Radiator Bronzing Brush.*

Camel Hair Brush, Color

Used for applying color on fine woodwork or fine varnish work. Camel hair, double thick, solidly embedded in vulcanized rubber. Nickel-plated metal ferrule. Hardwood handle, dead-black finish. Lettered in Silver. Not affected by water or oil.

No.	W500/1 1/2	W500/2	W500/2 1/2
Width, in.	1 1/2	2	2 1/2
Length, Bristles out	1 1/8	1 1/4	1 3/8
Length overall, in.	6 1/2	6 3/4	6 7/8

Camel Hair, Flat Lacquering

Used for transparent varnish, gold paint or bronzing. Set in cement set. Metal ferrule. Orange-enameled wood handle.

No.	W647 3/8	W647 1/2	W647 5/8	W647 3/4
Width at ferrule	3/8	1/2	5/8	3/4
Length, Bristles	13/16	7/8	15/16	1 1/16
Length overall	6 3/4	7 3/8	8	8 1/4

Camel Hair, Round Lacquering

Used for transparent varnish, gold paint or bronzing. Set in cement set. Metal ferrule. Orange-enameled wood handle.

No.	W646/1	W646/2	W646/3
Size, No.	1	2	3
Diameter at ferrule, in.	1/8	3/16	1/4
Length, Bristles out, in.	13/16	7/8	15/16
Length overall, in.	7	7 1/4	7 5/8

No.	W646/4	W646/5	W646/6
Size, No.	4	5	6
Diameter at ferrule, in.	1/4	5/16	5/16
Length, Bristles out, in.	1 1/16	1 1/8	1 1/4
Length overall, in.	8	8 1/8	8 3/4

Marking Brush

Pure camel hair. Cement set. Metal ferrule. Cedar handle, yellow finish.

No.	W1M	W2M	W3M	W4M
Size, No.	1	2	3	4
Diameter at ferrule, in.	1/8	3/16	1/4	1/4
Length, Bristles out, in.	1/2	5/8	11/16	1 3/16
Length over all, in.	7	7 1/4	7 5/8	8
Values:	**Exc.**	**V.G.**	**Good**	
	800.00	700.00	550.00	

Comment: *Values for any size of Marking Brush or Camel Hair Brush.*

Winchester Padlocks

Nine padlocks of various styles in an attractive display in the Curt Bowman collection. Winchester produced padlocks with solid bodies, hollow bodies, flat shackles, round shackles, in several sizes, body outlines, logo placements and type styles. Photo by C. Bowman.

The padlock and key on left would be similar to a model W16 and the one on the right is a variation of the model W23. From the Tom Webster collection. Photo by D. Kowalski

Padlock, Cast Bronze Case

Highly polished heavy cast bronze case. Bronze metal self-locking spring shackle swings both ways and has positive lock both at Nose and Heel. Full-pin tumbler construction. All interior parts of brass and bronze; cannot be jarred open. Two paracentric nickel-silver keys to each lock.

No. W16. 1 1/2 In.; Spacing of Shackle, Closed, 5/8 in. x 3/4 in.; Changes Unlimited.

No. W18. 1 3/4 In.; Spacing of Shackle, Closed, 7/8 in. x 1 in.; Changes Unlimited.

Padlock, Cast Iron Case, Black Finish.

Heavy cast iron case, black rustless iron finish; self-locking cast bronze spring shackle, swings both ways. Bronze inside works. Has 4-pin tumbler; 144 changes; two flat steel keys to each lock.

No. W15. 2 In.; Spacing of Shackle, Closed, 3/4 in. x 3/4 in.

Padlock, Cast Brass Case, Polished Finish

Cast brass case has polished finish; self-locking spring shackle; 2 brass levers; 3 brass wards, locking both heel and nose. Two nickel-plated extra heavy flat steel keys to each lock; 12 changes.

No. W12. 2 1/8 In.; Spacing of Shackle, Closed, 7/8 in. x 1 in.

Padlock, Cast Iron Case, Black Finish

Heavy cast iron case, black rustless iron finish, with wrought steel brass-plated panel; steel self-locking spring shackle, brass-plated, swings either right or left. Two nickel-plated flat steel keys to each lock; 4 changes.

No. W23. 1 1/2 In.; Spacing of Shackle, Closed, 3/4 in. x 3/4 in.

No. W25. 2 In.; Spacing of Shackle, Closed, 1 in. x 1 in.

Padlock, Cast Brass Case, Polished

Cast brass case, polished, with steel rod nickel-plated shackle that springs open to quarter turn position when unlocked. Warded construction. Two nickel-plated flat steel keys to each lock; 6 changes.

No. W33. 1 5/8 In.; Spacing of Shackle, Closed, 1 in. x 3/4 in.

No. W39. 2 In.; Spacing of Shackle, Closed, 11/8 in. x 7/8 in.

Padlock, Cast Brass Case, Round Body

Heavy cast brass case; copper-plated steel self-locking spring shackle; spring levers. Two flat steel keys with each lock.

No. W9. 2 1/8 In.; Spacing of Shackle, Closed, 1 3/16 in. x 7/8 in.

Values:	Exc.	V.G.	Good
	300.00	275.00	250.00

Comment: *Values for any size or model of Winchester Padlock, except private label.*

Railroad Padlock, Missouri Pacific Lines

Railroad Padlock produced for the Missouri Pacific Line. A rare private label model that is the only one marked for another business known to exist. Key fits in slot hidden under spring-loaded front panel. From the Tom Webster collection. Photo by D. Kowalski

Values:

Exc.	V.G.	Good
1,000.00	900.00	800.00

Comment: *Values for any size or model of Winchester Padlock produced for another company (private label).*

Door Knob and Plate Demo

A Winchester Simmons Co. Door Knob and Plate Demo on a wooden stand. There are only two such pieces known. From T. Webster collection. Photo by D. Kowalski

Values:

Exc.	V.G.	Good
600.00	550.00	450.00

Comment: *Values for this style of door lock demo.*

Flashlights, Batteries, Household Cutlery, Scissors and Barber Supplies

by David D. Kowalski

Metal Floor Display for Flashlights stands 40 inches high. Body is painted green with red pinstripes. Header is cream-colored with red "Winchester Trade Mark and B&B." From T. Webster collection. Photo by D. Kowalski.

Pocketknives, roller skates and flashlights all survived the Winchester bankruptcy and sale in 1931. So did firearms and ammunition, of course.

In this chapter, we present flashlights and batteries, some of which are bringing high prices in today's market. We follow them with Winchester's huge line of household cutlery. Finally, we wrap up the chapter with several models of scissors and shears for seamstresses and barbers, as well as related razors and razor strops.

Most of the household cutlery products were low-dollar items that probably had very low margins. Combine that with the small size of the individual pieces and the inventory necessary for maintaining such a broad line and you've got a formula for plenty of red ink on the bottom line. For these reasons, we can speculate that the Olins, father and son, didn't think twice about dropping this line when they took over Winchester. Scissors and shears suffered the same fate, even though they tended to be higher priced than cutlery.

Flashlights survived the Western takeover, in large part, because they were probably distributed through the same channels as firearms and appealed to the same buyers. We'll start with them.

Metal Flashlight Floor Display

Values:	Exc.	V.G.	Good
	800.00	700.00	600.00

Comment: *Values for display without flashlights or batteries.*

Flashlight Show Case Display

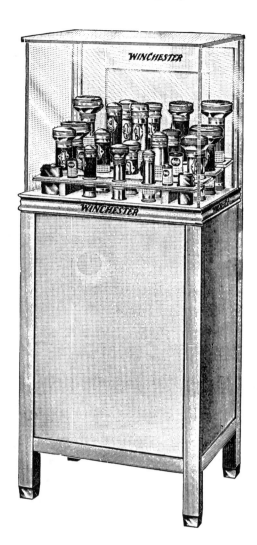

No. FS. Flashlight Show Case Display. Weight each 75 lbs. Well-made, durable and serviceable. Intended as permanent store fixture for displaying Winchester Flashlights. The entire case stands 48 inches high, 18 inches wide and 16 inches deep. Woodwork is beautifully finished in Winchester gray with the name "Winchester" in gilt on three sides The base is intended for the storage of your stock of flashlights and batteries, stands just the height of the average store counter and has hinged panel door opening from the rear. The glass display case is permanently attached to the base, and is fitted with a rack for displaying the entire line of Winchester Flashlights, this also has a panel door opening from the rear. Opening from the rear and between display case and base, there is a drawer about 1 1/2 in. deep making a convenient place for your stock of flashlights, bulbs, repairs, etc.

Values:
Exc.	V.G.	Good
2,500.00	2,200.00	1,800.00

Comment: *Values for display without flashlights. A fairly rare display.*

Flashlight Wood Counter Display

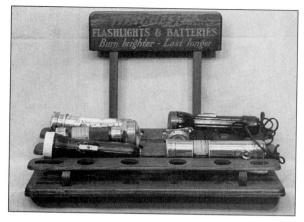

Flashlight Counter Display is made of wood, stained dark. Designed to hold flashlights in standing position. A very rare piece. From T. Webster collection. Photo by D. Kowalski.

Values:
Exc.	V.G.	Good
2,100.00	2,000.00	1,800.00

Comment: *Values for display without flashlights. Only two known to exist.*

Flashlight Wire Counter Display

Wire Flashlight Counter Display holds 12 flashlights and has two-row battery dispenser in middle. From T. Webster collection. Photo by D. Kowalski.

Values:
Exc.	V.G.	Good
325.00	300.00	275.00

Comment: *Values for display without flashlights or batteries.*

Flashlights

Winchester Flashlights have outstanding features. One-piece lens cap used on all tubular lights, which is a genuine convenience to the user as well as a protection to the lens. The coarse-pitched thread of lens cap and base cap prevents stripping the thread and makes flashlights easier to handle. Have Winchester patented switch. All nickel-plated cases are made of heavy sheet brass designed to stand hard use, with nickel plating that will resist atmospheric conditions and give long wear. Fibre cases are made from genuine vulcanized fibre free from seams or other defects. Flashlights as listed include case and Mazda bulb but do not include batteries.

Flashlight Assortment Display Panel

Flashlight Assortment Display Panel was supplied with Assortment W100. Originally contained 12 2-cell flashlights, two each in six colors. Display panel is lithographed in three colors; cut out to accommodate six flashlights.

Values:	Exc.	V.G.	Good	Comment:
	750.00	700.00	600.00	Values for display panel with six flashlights.

Three Cell Searchlight, Focusing Flashlight

No. 6921. Searchlight lens. Polished silver-plated reflector. Nickel-plated case. Focusing adjustment made with the knurled adjusting sleeve located below lens cap. Will throw a bright beam of light 500 ft. Takes battery 3511; takes 3.8 volt lamp of special brilliancy, Mazda No. 13. Packed one in a carton.

No. 6926. Similar to the nickel-plated light listed above but made with durable corrugated fibre case. Packed one in a carton.

Values:
Exc.	V.G.	Good
60.00	50.00	35.00

Comment: *Values for either model.*

Three Cell Focusing Flashlight

No. 6821. Three Cell Focusing. Fitted with special lens for this type of light. Polished silver-plated reflector. Nickel-plated case. Focusing adjustment made by means of knurled adjusting sleeve located below lens cap. Will throw a bright beam of light 300 feet. Takes battery 3511; takes 3.8 volt lamp of special brilliancy, Mazda No. 13. Packed one in a carton.

No. 6826. Similar to the nickel-plated light listed above but made with durable corrugated fibre case. Packed one in a carton.

Values:
Exc.	V.G.	Good
50.00	40.00	25.00

Comment: *Values for either model.*

Three Cell Searchlight

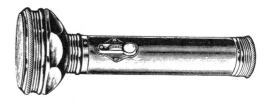

No. 6321. Three Cell Searchlight. Silver-plated reflector. Searchlight lens. Handsome nickel-plated case. Takes battery 3511; takes 3.8 volt lamp No. 17. Packed one in a carton.

No. 6326. Similar to the nickel-plated light listed above but made with durable corrugated fibre case. Packed one in a carton.

Values:
Exc.	V.G.	Good
60.00	50.00	35.00

Comment: *Values for either model.*

Three Cell Miner's Flashlight

No. 6621. Three Cell Miner's Octagon Head. Silver-plated reflector. Miner's type lens. Octagon-shaped cap. Nickel-plated case. Takes battery 3511; takes 3.8 volt lamp No. 17. Packed one in a carton.

No. 6221. Similar to the nickel-plated light listed above but made with round cap. Packed one in a carton.

No. 6226. Similar to the nickel-plated light listed above but made with round cap and durable corrugated fibre case. Packed one in a carton.

Values: Exc. V.G. Good
 50.00 40.00 25.00

Comment: *Values for any of the three models of Miner's Flashlights.*

Standard Three Cell Flashlight

No. 6121. Standard Three Cell. White enameled reflector. Bull's eye lens. Nickel-plated case. Takes battery 3511; takes 3.8 volt lamp No. 17. Packed one in a carton.

No. 6126. Similar to the nickel-plated light listed above but made with durable corrugated fibre case. Packed one in a carton.
No. 6127. Same flashlight with nickel-plated carrying chain.

Values: Exc. V.G. Good
 50.00 40.00 25.00

Comment: *Values for any model. Add 10 percent for Model 6127 with carrying chain.*

Two Cell Focusing Flashlight

No. 6811. Two Cell Focusing. Fitted with special lens for this type of light. Polished silver-plated reflector. Nickel-plated case. Focusing adjustment made by means of knurled adjusting sleeve located below lens cap. Takes battery 2511; takes 2.5 volt lamp of special brilliancy, Mazda No. 14. Packed one in a carton.

No. 6816. Similar to the nickel-plated light listed above but made with durable corrugated fibre case. Packed one in a carton.

Values: Exc. V.G. Good
 50.00 40.00 25.00

Comment: *Values for either model.*

Two Cell Searchlight

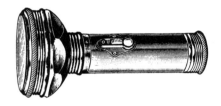

No. 6311. Two Cell Searchlight. Silver-plated reflector. Searchlight lens. Handsome nickel-plated case. Takes battery 2511; takes 2.5 volt lamp No. 16. Packed one in a carton.

No. 6316. Similar to the nickel-plated light listed above but made with durable corrugated fibre case. Packed one in a carton.

Values: Exc. V.G. Good
 55.00 45.00 30.00

Comment: *Values for either model.*

Two Cell Miner's Flashlight

No. 6611. Two Cell Miner's Octagon Head. Silver-plated reflector. Miner's type lens. Octagon-shaped cap. Nickel-plated case. Takes battery 2511; takes 2.5 volt lamp No. 16. Packed one in a carton.

No. 6211. Similar to the nickel-plated light listed above but made with round cap. Packed one in a carton.

No. 6216. Similar to the nickel-plated light listed above but made with round cap and durable corrugated fibre case. Packed one in a carton.

Values: | Exc. | V.G. | Good |
|---|---|---|
| 55.00 | 45.00 | 30.00 |

Comment: *Values for any of the three models of Miner's Flashlights..*

Standard Two Cell Flashlight

No. 6111. Standard Two Cell. White enameled reflector. Bull's eye lens. Nickel-plated case. Takes battery 2511; takes 2.5 volt lamp No. 16. Packed one in a carton.

No. 6116. Similar to the nickel-plated light listed above but made with durable corrugated fibre case. Packed one in a carton.
No. 6117. Same flashlight with nickel-plated carrying chain.

Values: | Exc. | V.G. | Good |
|---|---|---|
| 50.00 | 40.00 | 25.00 |

Comment: *Values for any model. Add 10 percent for Model 6117 with carrying chain.*

Flashlights in Metal Cases

Two Cell Focusing Flashlight. In Hammered Case. Special lens. Polished silver-plated reflector. Focusing adjustment obtained by means of knurled adjusting sleeve below lens cap. Takes No. 2511 battery and 2.5 volt lamp, No. 14 Mazda, of concentrated filament, giving extra brilliancy. One in a plush-lined gift box, in a carton.
No. 6812 - 24 carat pure gold-plated.
No. 6819 - 99.9% pure silver-plated.

Two Cell Focusing Flashlight. In Corrugated Case. Regular lens. Silver-plated reflector. Takes No. 2511 battery and 2.5 volt lamp, No. 16. One in a plush-lined gift box, in a carton.
No. 6112 - 24 carat pure gold-plated.
No. 6119 - 99.9% pure silver-plated.

Values: | Exc. | V.G. | Good |
|---|---|---|
| 250.00 | 225.00 | 175.00 |

Comment: *Values for either type in case.*

Industrial Two Cell Flashlight

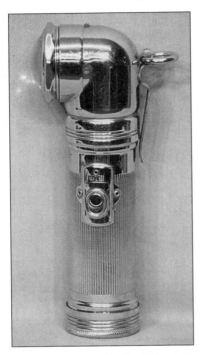

This Industrial Two Cell Flashlight (No. 6711) is a rare item in excellent condition. On thumbswitch it reads, "Patented Aug. 17, 1920 - Oct. 18, 1922." From Tom Webster collection. Photo by D. Kowalski.

Heavy brass case. Silver-plated reflector and bull's eye lens set on the side at top of case. Nickel-plated brass clip and ring riveted to back of case for hanging or attaching to belt or pocket. Takes No. 2511 battery and 2.5 volt lamp, No. 16. One in a carton.
No. 6711 - Nickel-plated case
No. 6714 - Black enameled case

Values:	Exc.	V.G.	Good
	250.00	225.00	175.00

Comment: *Values for either model.*

Railroad Lineman's Flashlight

Railroad Lineman's Two Cell Flashlight. Rare model with three bulbs - red, clear and blue - each with their own switch. From Tom Webster collection. Photo by D. Kowalski.

Head close-up of Railroad Lineman's Flashlight. From Tom Webster collection. Photo by D. Kowalski.

Values:	Exc.	V.G.	Good
	450.00	425.00	375.00

Comment: *Values for this model.*

Pointer Flashlight

The long extender-tube head of this Pointer Flashlight focuses and magnifies the light. From Tom Webster collection. Photo by D. Kowalski.

Values:	Exc.	V.G.	Good
	300.00	275.00	250.00

Comment: *Values for this model, which is fairly rare.*

Junior Flashlights

No. 6411. Junior Standard Two Cell. White enameled reflector. Small bull's eye lens. Nickel-plated case. Takes Junior battery 2311; takes 2.3 volt lamp No. 11. Packed one in a carton.

No. 6416. Similar to the nickel-plated light listed above but made with durable corrugated fibre case. Packed one in a carton.

Values:	Exc.	V.G.	Good
	50.00	40.00	25.00

Comment: *Values for either model of Junior Standard.*

Flashlights, Batteries, Household Cutlery, Scissors and Barber Supplies • 669

No. 6511. Junior Miner's Two Cell. White enameled reflector. Miner's junior lens. Nickel-plated case. Takes Junior battery 2311; takes 2.3 volt lamp No. 11. Packed one in a carton.

No. 6516. Similar to the nickel-plated light listed above but made with durable corrugated fibre case. Packed one in a carton.

Values:	Exc.	V.G.	Good
	55.00	45.00	30.00

Comment: *Values for either model of Junior Miner's Flashlight.*

Vest Pocket Flashlights

No. 7031. Vest Pocket Three Cell Flashlight. Nickel-plated case. Has Winchester patented three-position switch. Takes battery 3112; takes 3.3 volt lamp No. 2. Packed one in a carton; ten in a case.

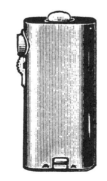

No. 7021. Vest Pocket Two Cell Flashlight. Nickel-plated case. Has Winchester patented three-position switch. Takes battery 2112; takes 2.2 volt lamp No. 1. Packed one in a carton; ten in a case.

Values:	Exc.	V.G.	Good
	225.00	200.00	175.00

Comment: *Values for either model.*

Flashlight Batteries

Winchester long-life, high-power batteries fit any standard make of flashlight. Features:

Seamless zinc cans - made of heavy zinc drawn from one piece of metal. Prevents damage to case through leakage of chemicals.

Electrolytic paste - scientifically compounded from highest-grade materials to give high electrical output and long life in use and storage.

Carbon pencil - carefully parafinned to prevent leakage or corrosion of brass contact cap.

Sealing wax - insures against leakage or evaporation of contents.

Exacting tests - each battery thoroughly tested to make sure it will live up to our established reputation.

No. 3511. Three Cell Tubular Battery. Measures 7 1/8 inches x 1 5/16 inches in diameter. Packed one dozen in a carton.

Values:	Exc.	V.G.	Good
	175.00	150.00	125.00

Comment: *Values for battery only (without box).*

No. 2511. Two Cell Tubular Battery. Measures 4 3/4 inches x 1 5/16 inches in diameter. Packed one dozen in a carton.

Values:	Exc.	V.G.	Good
	150.00	125.00	100.00

Comment: *Values for battery only (without box).*

No. 2311. Junior Tubular Battery. Measures 3 7/8 inches x 15/16 inches in diameter. Packed one dozen in a carton.

Values: **Exc.**   **V.G.**   **Good**
                 150.00   125.00   100.00

Comment: *Values for battery only (without box).*

No. 1511. Standard Single Cell Battery. Measures 2 3/8 inches x 1 5/16 inches in diameter. Packed in a carton; one dozen in a multi-carton.
No. 1311. Junior Single Cell Battery. Measures 1 5/16 inches x 15/16 inches in diameter. Packed one dozen in a carton.

Values: **Exc.**   **V.G.**   **Good**
                 35.00   30.00   20.00

Comment: *Values for Standard battery only (without box). Add 25 percent premium for Junior version.*

No. 2112. Vest Pocket Battery, Two Cell. Measures 2 1/4 inches x 1 11/32 inches x 11/16 inches. Packed one in a carton; one dozen in a case.
No. 3112. Vest Pocket Battery, Three Cell. Measures 2 1/4 inches x 1 31/32 inches x 11/16 inches. Packed one in a carton; one dozen in a case.
No. 3212. Vest Pocket Battery, Three No. 2 Cell. Measures 2 5/8 inches x 1 13/32 inches x 13/16 inches. Packed one in a carton; ten in a case.

Values: **Exc.**   **V.G.**   **Good**
                 60.00   55.00   45.00

Comment: *Values for any Vest Pocket battery only (without box).*

Battery Tester

No. 3056. Battery Tester and Lamp Tester. Developed to give you a practical, ready-to-hand device to enable you to try out each battery and lamp you sell in the customer's presence. These testers are designed for your convenience to test one, two or three-cell batteries, vest-pocket style and lamps of different voltage without trouble. Approximate weight 1 1/4 lbs. Packed one in a carton.

Values: **Exc.**   **V.G.**   **Good**
                 325.00   300.00   275.00

Comment: *A rare item.*

Radio "B" Battery

Made to provide a battery of long life and service for radio receiving sets. In designing these batteries careful study has been given to the causes of buzzing and rasping. These problems have now been largely eliminated so that smooth, quiet operation is assured insofar as the battery influences such operation. These batteries may be used for the "B" or plate circuit of any standard radio outfit. Under each positive terminal is stamped the voltage produced when that terminal is connected with the negative terminal. All Winchester Batteries have unusually long shelf life.

Flashlights, Batteries, Household Cutlery, Scissors and Barber Supplies • 671

No. 6516. Size 3 in. x 6 5/8 in. x 7 7/8 in. 45 volt "B" Battery with taps at 16 1/2, 18, 19 1/2, 21, 22 1/2 and 45 volts. Especially adapted for detector and amplifier circuits and for radio reception where a high plate voltage is desired. A silent, long-life battery constructed with 30 individual seamless No. 5 cells, carefully connected in series, and scientifically constructed to give constant steady voltage. Approximate weight 10 lbs. One in a carton; twelve in a shipping crate.

No. 5516. Size 3 in. x 4 in. x 6 5/8 in. 22 1/2 volt "B" Battery has five brass taps, making possible the following variable voltages - 16 1/2, 18, 19 1/2, 21 and 22 1/2. Especially adapted for detector and amplifier circuits on stationary wireless sets. This size battery is particularly recommended for long and efficient service. Made by the same process that gives long life to all Winchester batteries. Approximate weight 5 1/4 lbs. One in a carton; twelve in a shipping crate.

No. 5517. Size 3 1/8 in. x 4 1/8 in. x 7 in. 22 1/2 volt "B" Battery made of 15 No. 5 cells connected in series. Upright position serves the same purpose as the 5516 when full voltage (22 1/2) is desired for the plate circuit. Size adapts itself better to the available space and wiring conditions in some sets. Approximate weight 5 1/4 lbs. One in a carton; ten in a shipping crate.

No. 6518. Size 8 1/4 in. x 3 in. x 7 1/8 in. Vertical 45 volt "B" Battery with 22 1/2 volt tap. Adapted to same purposes as the 6516, but arranged in vertical position for sets in which this is more desirable. Battery comprises 30 cells each 1 1/4 in. x 2 1/4 in. Spring Grip terminals. Approximate weight 10 lbs. One in a carton; twelve in a shipping crate.

No. 6818. Size 8 in. x 3 1/8 in. x 7 in. Vertical heavy duty 45 volt "B" Battery with 22 1/2 volt tap. Adapted to same purposes as the 6516, but arranged in vertical position for sets in which this is more desirable. Battery has 30 cells, each 1 1/4 in. x 3 7/16 in. Spring Grip terminals. Approximate weight 15 lbs. One in a carton; twelve in a shipping crate.

No. 5217. Size 2 5/8 in. x 2 5/8 in. x 6 in. 22 1/2 volt "B" Battery composed of 15 No. 2 cells. An excellent plate circuit Battery made in a size that takes up the same space as the No. 6A Battery. Very popular for use with portable sets and with other sets using dry cells for the A Battery where space is considered. Approximate weight 2 1/2 lbs. Packed individually.

No. 5116. Size 2 1/2 in. 2 in. x 3 3/8 in. 22 1/2 volt "B" Battery especially adapted for detector and amplifier circuits on portable wireless sets where a lightweight battery is desirable. Although smaller and lighter than the No. 5219, it will give general satisfaction for radio work. Made by same process that gives long life to all Winchester batteries. Approximate weight 1 1/4 lbs. Packed Individually.

Values:	Exc.	V.G.	Good
	225.00	200.00	150.00

Comment: *Values for any model of Winchester "B" Battery.*

Radio "C" Battery

No. 3516. Size 1 3/8 in. x 3 in. x 4 in. 4 1/2 volt "C" Battery with taps at 3 and 4 1/2 volts. Composed of three of the famous Winchester seamless can No. 5 cells. Unequalled in filling the demands of radio fans for a stabilizing "C" Battery. Packed five in a carton; approximate weight 5 lbs.

No. 3217. Size 13/16 in. x 2 7/16 in. x 2 5/8 in. 4 1/2 Volt "C" Battery composed of three No. 2 cells in series. One in carton; approximate weight 1/2 lb.

Values:	Exc.	V.G.	Good
	225.00	200.00	150.00

Comment: *Values for any model of Winchester "C" Battery.*

Armax Batteries were one of the other Winchester brand names for batteries. From T. Webster collection. Photo by D. Kowalski.

Values:	Exc.	V.G.	Good
	800.00	700.00	600.00

Comment: *Values for any model of Armax Battery. These are considerably rarer than "Winchester" standard models.*

Flashlights, Batteries, Household Cutlery, Scissors and Barber Supplies • 673

Cutlery-related Tools and Special Knives

Ice Picks, Scraping Knives, Putty Knives and Paper Hangers' Knives are not technically "cutlery" but more accurately grouped with tools. However, this group also contains some "transitional" types of tools that have cutting edges. Examples would include Shoe Knives and even Fish Scaling Knives. So we include them all here, then move into the more typical household cutlery items.

Ice Pick

No. WR15. Ice Pick. High-grade steel, long-needle taper point, ground to shape and tempered. Hard rubber handle has six flat sides; it's sanitary, odorless and will not warp, crack, shrink or come loose. Length of point 2 1/2 in.; length overall 9 in.

Values:	Exc.	V.G.	Good
	60.00	50.00	35.00

Scraping Knife

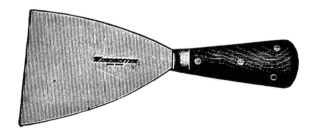

Scraping Knife. Cocobolo scale tang handle. Tempered blades. Britannia metal bolster. Four brass pins in handle. Packed one dozen in a carton.

No.	Blade
2353	4 1/4 in. x 3 in. Stiff
2356	4 1/4 in. x 3 in. Flex
2357	4 1/4 in. x 3 1/2 in. Stiff
2354	4 1/4 in. x 3 1/2 in. Flex
2355	4 7/8 in. x 4 in. Stiff

Values:	Exc.	V.G.	Good
	70.00	60.00	45.00

Comment: *Values for any model.*

Putty Knife

Putty Knife. Cocobolo scale tang handle. Tempered blades. Britannia metal bolster. Two brass pins in handle. Packed one dozen in a carton.

No.	Blade
2362	3 5/8 in. x 2 in. Stiff
2368	3 5/8 in. x 2 in. Flex
2364	3 1/2 in. x 1 5/16 in. Flex
2365	3 1/2 in. x 1 5/16 in. Stiff

Putty Knife. High-carbon steel blade is 3 1/2 in. long x 1 5/16 in. wide. Glazed finish. Scale tang Cocobolo handle is 3 3/4 in. long with 3 brass rivets. Packed one dozen in a carton. No. W115 - Stiff Blade; No. W116 - Elastic Blade.

Putty Knife. Economy model. Tempered blade. Beechwood handle is fitted with three brass pins. Packed one dozen in a carton.

No.	Blade
2369	3 1/2 in. x 1 5/16 in. Stiff
2370	3 1/2 in. x 1 5/16 in. Flex

Putty Chisel

Putty Chisel has Cocobolo scale tang handle. Tempered blades. Britannia metal bolster. Two brass pins in handle. Packed one dozen in a carton.

No.	Blade
2363	3 1/2 in. x 1 5/16 in.

Values:	Exc.	V.G.	Good
	70.00	60.00	45.00

Comment: *Values for any model of Putty Knife or Putty Chisel.*

Paper Hangers' Knives

Paper Hangers' Knife, Round Point (No. 2341). Overall length is 7 inches. From T. Webster collection. Photo by D. Kowalski.

Paper Hangers' Knife, Square Point (No. 2342). Overall length is 7 1/8 inches. From T. Webster collection. Photo by D. Kowalski.

Paper Hangers' Knives. Black solid oval handle. Nickel silver ferrule and one steel pin. Packed one-half dozen in a carton.

No.	Point	Blade Length
2341	Round	3 3/8 in.
2342	Square	3 3/8 in.

Values:	Exc.	V.G.	Good
	125.00	115.00	100.00

Comment: *Values for either model.*

Oilcloth Knife

Oilcloth Knife has high-carbon steel blade. Shaped maple handle. Zapon finished. Steel ferrule and pin. Packed one-half dozen in a carton. No. 2311. Blade length 3 in.

Values:	Exc.	V.G.	Good
	70.00	60.00	45.00

Shoe Knife

Shoe Knife has square-pointed high-carbon steel blade. Maple handle. Zapon finished. Brass ferrule and one steel pin. Packed one dozen in a carton.

No.	Blade Length
2371	3 in.
2372	4 in.

Values:	Exc.	V.G.	Good
	70.00	60.00	45.00

Comment: *Values for either model.*

Broom Corn Knife

Broom Corn Knife. High-carbon steel blade is 3 1/2 in. long. Shaped burnt-wood handle. Brass ferrule. One steel pin. Packed one dozen to the carton.

No. 2330 - with heavy leather finger guard.
No. 2331 - without finger guard.

Values:	Exc.	V.G.	Good
	125.00	115.00	100.00

Comment: *Add 20 percent with finger guard.*

Hunting Knife

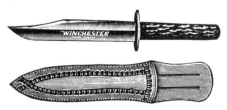

Hunting Knife. High-carbon steel, saber-clip swaged blade, highly tempered and polished, glazed finish. Scale tang. Stag handle. Three nickeled pins and nickel-silver guard. Complete with tan russet embossed leather sheath. Packed one-half dozen in a cardboard box.

No.	Blade Length
W1050-5	5 in.
W1050-6	6 in.

Values:	Exc.	V.G.	Good
	900.00	800.00	700.00

Comment: *Values for either model with sheath.*

Fish Scaling Knife

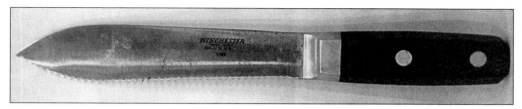

No. 1083. Fish Scaling Knife. Has double-edge carbon steel blade with both saw-cut edge for scaling and sharp edge for cutting. Highly polished scale tang black handle. Three nickel-silver telescopic rivets. Blade length is 6 inches. Packed one-half dozen in a carton.

This version of the Fish Scaling Knife (No. 1083) has the Britannia bolster and only two rivets through the handle. Total length is 10 1/2 inches. From T. Webster collection. Photo by D. Kowalski.

Values:	Exc.	V.G.	Good
	400.00	375.00	325.00

Comment: *Values for model with either two or three rivets through handle.*

Winchester Household Cutlery

Cotton Sampling or Vegetable Chopping Knife

Cotton Sampling or Vegetable Chopping Knife (No. 2321). Winchester used two different names for this product. Overall length is 9 5/8 in. From T. Webster collection. Photo by D. Kowalski.

Cotton Sampling or Vegetable Chopping Knife. Scale tang beechwood handle. Blade of high-carbon steel. Three brass telescopic rivets. Packed one-half dozen in a carton. No. 2311. Blade length 3 in.

Values:	Exc.	V.G.	Good
	125.00	115.00	100.00

Sloyd Knife

Sloyd Knife. Saber clip blade of high-carbon steel. Maple handles, Zapon finish, nickel ferrule. One steel pin. Individually wrapped in waterproof paper; one-half dozen in a carton. No. 2302; blade length 2 5/8 in.

Values:	Exc.	V.G.	Good
	70.00	60.00	45.00

Chicken Sticking Knife

Chicken Sticking Knife. Blade of high-carbon steel. Scale tang beechwood handles. Three brass telescopic rivets. Packed one-half dozen in a carton. No. 1050; blade length 3 in.

Values:	Exc.	V.G.	Good
	100.00	90.00	70.00

Oyster Knives

Oyster Knife with bulb handle (No. 2012). From T. Webster collection. Photo by D. Kowalski.

No. 2012. Oyster Knife. Oval ground blade. Bulb-shaped maple handle with Zapon finish. Brass ferrule. Packed one-half dozen in a carton. Blade length 2 3/4 in.

No. 2020. Oyster Knife with straight maple handle with Zapon finish. Semi-oval ground blade. Brass ferrule. Packed one-half dozen in a carton. Blade length 2 3/8 in.

Oyster Knife, all steel (No. 2047). From T. Webster collection. Photo by D. Kowalski.

No. 2047. All Steel Oyster Knife. Made of solid steel, forged. Tempered blade with rounded edge. Tapered sharp point. Packed one-half dozen in a carton. Overall length 5 in.

Values:	Exc.	V.G.	Good
	170.00	150.00	125.00

Comment: Values for any model of Oyster Knife.

Clam Knife

No. 2034. Clam Knife. Flat ground blade with rounded end. Highly polished Cocobolo handle. Three brass pins. Packed one-half dozen in a carton. Blade length 3 in.

Values:	Exc.	V.G.	Good
	170.00	150.00	125.00

Halibut Knife or Cleaver

No. 1078. Halibut Knife or Cleaver. Extra-heavy carbon steel, plain blade, well ground and balanced. Scale tang beechwood handle. Three brass telescopic rivets. Packed one-half dozen in a carton. Blade length 12 in.

Values:	Exc.	V.G.	Good
	110.00	95.00	75.00

Household Cleaver

Household Cleaver (No. 7814). From T. Webster collection. Photo by D. Kowalski. length 12 in.

No. 7814. Household Cleaver. A light, strong cleaver designed for use in the home. Heavy-gauge blade, made of high-carbon steel; polished walnut handle. Brass telescopic rivets. Packed one-half dozen in a carton. Blade length 7 in.

Values:	Exc.	V.G.	Good
	95.00	80.00	60.00

Butcher Steels

Butcher Steel (No. 1771). Measures 12 1/2 in. from tip to end of handle (13 in. with eye). From T. Webster collection. Photo by D. Kowalski.

No. 1771. Butcher Steel. Knurled steel with plain black handle. Metal ferrule, No guard. Wire screw eye in end of handle. Packed one-half dozen in a carton. Blade length 8 in.

Butcher Steel (No. 1762). Measures 19 3/8 in. from tip to end of handle (21 1/2 in. with eye and swivel). From T. Webster collection. Photo by D. Kowalski.

Butcher Steel. A high-grade knurled steel. Has ribbed black handle with swivel. Diamond-shaped Britannia metal guard. Packed one-half dozen in a carton.

No.	Blade Length
1760	10 in.
1761	12 in.
1762	14 in.

Butcher Steel. Knurled steel with Britannia metal ferrule. No guard. Ribbed red handle equipped with swivel. Packed one-half dozen in a carton.

No.	Blade Length
1767	10 in.
1768	12 in.
1769	14 in.

Values:	Exc.	V.G.	Good
	50.00	40.00	25.00

Comment: Values for any model. Deduct 10 percent for model 1771.

Butcher Knife Assortment Stand

Red Steer Butcher Knife Display Stand is 21 1/4 in. long, with Easel Back. Printed in five colors. Made to display six butcher knives.

Values: Exc.   V.G.   Good
                  50.00   40.00   25.00

Comment: *Values for display only (without knives).*

Butcher Knives

Butcher Knife. Swaged blade of high-carbon steel. Perfectly ground, finished and balanced. Black scale tang handle. Britannia metal bolster. Two nickel-silver telescopic rivets. Packed one-half dozen in a carton.

No.	Blade Length
1033	6 in.
1034	7 in.
1035	8 in.

Butcher Knife. Cut swaged blade of high-carbon steel. Perfectly ground, finished and balanced. Highly polished black wood scale tang handle. Three nickel-silver telescopic rivets. Packed one-half dozen in a carton.

No.	Blade Length
1006	6 in.
1007	7 in.
1008	8 in.
1010	10 in.
1012	12 in.

Butcher Knife. Cut swaged blade of high-carbon steel. Perfectly ground, finished and balanced. Zapon finished scale tang boxwood handle. Fitted with five brass pins. Packed one-half dozen in a carton.

No.	Blade Length
1136	6 in.
1137	7 in.
1138	8 in.

Household or packing house knife. High-carbon steel blade. Scale tang black wood handle. Fitted with five brass pins. Packed one-half dozen in a carton.

No.	Blade Length
1147	7 in.
1148	8 in.

Butcher Knife. Swaged blade of high-carbon steel. Perfectly ground, finished and balanced. Polished Cocobolo handle. Three brass telescopic rivets. Packed one-half dozen in a carton.

No.	Blade Length
1123	6 in.
1124	7 in.
1125	8 in.

Butcher Knife. High-carbon steel. Cut swage. Scale tang beechwood handle. Three brass telescopic rivets. Packed one-half dozen in a carton.

No.	Blade Length
1013	6 in.
1014	7 in.
1015	8 in.
1016	9 in.
1017	10 in.
1018	12 in.

Butcher Knife (No. 1013) shows excessive sharpening that has radically altered blade profile (compare to above knife). From T. Webster collection. Photo by D. Kowalski.

Household butcher knife of high-carbon steel. Cut swage. Scale tang boxwood handle, Zapon finish, fitted with five brass pins. Packed one-half dozen in a carton. No. 7163. Blade length 6 in.

Household butcher knife of high-carbon steel. Cut swage. Scale tang black wood handle, fitted with five brass pins. Packed one-half dozen in a carton. No. 7173. Blade length 6 in.

Household butcher knife. High-carbon cutlery steel blade, cut swage. Scale tang black wood handle with Britannia metal bolster. Two nickel-silver telescopic rivets. Packed one-half dozen in a carton. No. 7183. Blade length 6 in.

Values:	Exc.	V.G.	Good
	65.00	50.00	30.00

Comment: *Values for any model of Butcher Knife.*

Steak Knives

Steak Knife. Cimeter blade of high-carbon cutlery steel. Carefully ground, finished and balanced. Beechwood handle fitted with three brass telescopic rivets. Packed one-half dozen in a carton.

No.	Blade Length
1067	10 in.
1068	12 in.

Steak Knife. Cimeter blade of high-carbon steel. Carefully ground, finished and balanced. Scale tang boxwood handle, Zapon finish, fitted with five brass pins. Packed one-half dozen in a carton.

No.	Blade Length
1061	10 in.
1062	12 in.
1063	14 in.

Values:	Exc.	V.G.	Good
	75.00	60.00	40.00

Comment: *Values for any model of Steak Knife.*

Boning Knives

Boning Knife. High-carbon steel blade. Scale tang beechwood handle. Three brass telescopic rivets. Packed one-half dozen in a carton. No. 1043. Blade length 6 in.

Boning Knife. High-carbon steel blade. Scale tang black wood handle. Three nickel-silver telescopic rivets. Packed one-half dozen in a carton. No. 1044. Blade length 6 in.

Values:	Exc.	V.G.	Good
	65.00	50.00	30.00

Comment: *Values for any model of Boning Knife.*

Ribbing Knife

Ribbing Knife. Plain ribbing blade of high-carbon steel. Scale tang beechwood handle. Three brass telescopic rivets. Packed one-half dozen in a carton. No. 1055. Blade length 9 in.

Values:	Exc.	V.G.	Good
	75.00	60.00	40.00

Sticking Knives

Sticking Knife. Plain swaged blade of high-carbon steel. Scale tang beechwood handle. Three brass telescopic rivets. Packed one-half dozen in a carton. No. 1093. Blade length 6 in.

Sticking Knife. Plain swaged blade of high-carbon steel. Scale tang boxwood handle, Zapon finish, fitted with five brass pins. Packed one-half dozen in a carton. No. 1095. Blade length 6 in.

Values:	Exc.	V.G.	Good
	100.00	90.00	70.00

Comment: *Values for any model of Sticking Knife.*

Skinning Knives

Skinning Knife. Plain swaged blade of high-carbon steel. Scale tang beechwood handle. Three brass telescopic rivets. Packed one-half dozen in a carton. No. 1004. Blade length 5 in.

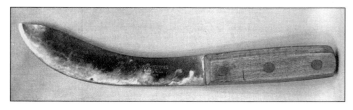

Skinning Knife (No. 1003) has overall length of 10 1/2 in. From T. Webster collection. Photo by D. Kowalski.

Skinning Knife. Extra-heavy high-carbon steel. Plain swaged blade. Scale tang beechwood handle. Three brass telescopic rivets. Packed one-half dozen in a carton. No. 1003. Blade length 6 in.

Skinning Knife (No. 1001) has overall length of 10 1/4 in. From T. Webster collection. Photo by D. Kowalski.

Skinning Knife. Extra-heavy high-carbon steel. Plain swaged blade. Scale tang boxwood handle, Zapon finish, fitted with five brass pins. Packed one-half dozen in a carton. No. 1001. Blade length 6 in.

Skinning Knife. Plain swaged blade of high-carbon steel. Scale tang black wood handle, fitted with three nickel-silver telescopic rivets. Packed one-half dozen in a carton. No. 1002. Blade length 6 in.

Values:	Exc.	V.G.	Good
	90.00	80.00	60.00

Comment: *Values for any model of Skinning Knife.*

Beef Slicers

Beef Slicer. Made of high-carbon steel. Scale tang black wood handle highly polished. Two nickel-silver telescopic rivets. Britannia metal bolster. Packed one-half dozen in a carton.

No.	Blade Length
7326	10 in.
7327	12 in.
7328	14 in.

Beef Slicer (No. 7318). From T. Webster collection. Photo by D. Kowalski.

Beef Slicer. Made of high-carbon steel. Scale tang black wood handle. Three nickel-silver telescopic rivets. Packed one-half dozen in a carton.

No.	Blade Length
7316	10 in.
7317	12 in.
7318	14 in.

Values:	Exc.	V.G.	Good
	100.00	85.00	65.00

Comment: *Values for any model of Beef Slicer.*

Ham Slicers

Ham Slicer. Flexible blade made of high-carbon steel. Highly polished Cocobolo handle. Three brass telescopic rivets. Packed one-half dozen in a carton. No. 7227. Blade length 12 in.

Ham Slicer. Blade made of high-carbon steel. Cocobolo handle, fitted with one brass telescopic rivet and two brass pins. Packed one-half dozen in a carton. No. 7228. Blade length 10 in.

Values:	Exc.	V.G.	Good
	100.00	85.00	65.00

Comment: *Values for any model of Ham Slicer.*

Bread Knives

Bread Knife (No. 7435). Overall length is 12 3/8 in. From T. Webster collection. Photo by D. Kowalski.

Bread Knife. High-carbon steel blade. Scale tang Cocobolo handle is highly polished. Three brass telescopic rivets. Packed one-half dozen in a carton. No. 7435. Blade length 8 in.

Bread Knife. High-carbon steel blade. Scale tang beech wood handle, fitted with three brass telescopic rivets. Packed one-half dozen in a carton. No. 7445. Blade length 8 in.

Values:	Exc.	V.G.	Good
	80.00	65.00	45.00

Comment: *Values for any model of Bread Knife.*

Cooks' Knives

Cooks' Knife. High-carbon forged steel blade. Solid black wood handle. Nickel-silver ferrule. Packed one-half dozen in a carton.

No.	Blade Length	No.	Blade Length
7021	4 in.	7025	8 in.
7022	5 in.	7026	10 in.
7023	6 in.	7027	12 in.

Cooks' Knife. High-carbon forged steel blade. Scale tang black wood handle. Three nickel-silver telescopic rivets. Packed one-half dozen in a carton.

No.	Blade Length	No.	Blade Length
7010	3 in.	7015	8 in.
7011	4 in.	7016	10 in.
7012	5 in.	7017	12 in.
7013	6 in.		

Values:	Exc.	V.G.	Good
	80.00	65.00	45.00

Comment: *Values for any model of Cooks' Knife with nickel-silver ferrule. Deduct 10 percent for models with three rivets.*

Kitchen Knives

Kitchen Knife. Cut swaged blade, made of high-carbon steel. Highly polished scale tang Cocobolo handle. Three brass telescopic rivets. Packed one-half dozen in a carton.

No.	Blade Length
7133	6 in.
7134	8 in.

Kitchen Knife. Flexible cut swaged blade, made of high-carbon steel. Highly polished scale tang Cocobolo handle. Three brass telescopic rivets. Packed one-half dozen in a carton.

No.	Blade Length
7107	7 1/2 in.

Kitchen Slicer. Popular model with plain high-carbon steel blade. Scale tang black wood handle, fitted with one brass telescopic rivet and two brass pins. Packed one-half dozen in a carton.

No.	Blade Length
7105	10 in.

Kitchen Knife. Cut swage blade of high-carbon steel. Scale tang Cocobolo handle, fitted with three brass telescopic rivets. Packed one-half dozen in a carton.

No.	Blade Length
7109	9 in.

Kitchen Knife. Cut swaged blade, made of high-carbon steel. Britannia metal bolster. Highly polished scale tang black wood handle. Two nickel-silver telescopic rivets. Packed one-half dozen in a carton.

No.	Blade Length
7116	10 in.

Values: Exc. 50.00   V.G. 40.00   Good 25.00

Comment: *Values for any model of Kitchen Knife or Slicer.*

Meat Forks

Meat Fork. High-carbon steel tang is inserted in Zapon finish maple handle. Steel ferrule and steel pin. Packed one-half dozen in a carton. No. 7718. Blade length 15 in.

Meat Fork (No. 7728) has overall length of 12 5/8 in. From T. Webster collection. Photo by D. Kowalski.

Meat Fork. High-carbon steel prongs. Highly polished Cocobolo scale tang handle. Three telescopic brass rivets. Packed one-half dozen in a carton. No. 7728. Blade length 13 in.

Values: Exc. 40.00   V.G. 35.00   Good 25.00

Comment: *Values for any model of Meat Fork.*

Spatulas

Spatula (No. 7633). Overall length is 9 1/4 in. From T. Webster collection. Photo by D. Kowalski.

Spatula. High-carbon steel blade. Cocobolo handle; tapered blade designed to give proper flexibility. Britannia metal bolster. Nickel-silver telescopic rivets. Packed one-half dozen in a carton.

No.	Blade Length
7631	4 in.
7633	6 in.
7635	8 in.
7636	10 in.
7637	12 in.

Spatula made without bolster sells at a price that makes it extremely popular. High-carbon steel blade. Cocobolo handle. Three brass telescopic rivets. Packed one-half dozen in a carton. No. 7654; blade length 8 in.

Values: Exc. 80.00   V.G. 65.00   Good 45.00

Comment: *Values for any model of Spatula with bolster. Deduct 10 percent for model 7654 with three rivets.*

Kitchen Set

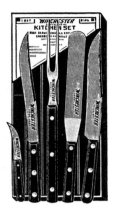

No. 6140. Kitchen Set. *A special five-piece kitchen set composed entirely of Winchester high-carbon steel cutlery with scale tang Cocobolo handles as follows: H4279K Paring Knife; H7728K Pot Fork; H7107K Slicer; H7654K Spatula; and H7125K Slicer. Each item wrapped in anti-rust paper and packed in display carton.*

Values:	Exc.	V.G.	Good
	400.00	375.00	325.00

Comment: *Values for complete set with box.*

Canning Knife

Canning Knife. *Made of high-carbon steel. Tang extends half way into special finger-shaped beechwood handle, fitted with two brass pins. Packed one-half dozen in a carton. No. 2335; blade length 3 1/2 in.*

Values:	Exc.	V.G.	Good
	55.00	45.00	30.00

Grape Knife

Grape Knife. *Made of high-carbon steel. Tang extends half way into beechwood handle, fitted with three brass pins. Packed one-half dozen in a carton. No. 2338; blade length 3 1/8 in.*

Values:	Exc.	V.G.	Good
	50.00	40.00	35.00

Paring Knife Assortment

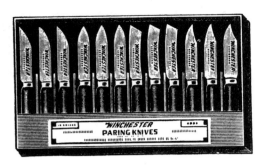

Clip

Spear

Wharncliffe

Cut Off

No. 4376. Paring Knife Assortment. *Selection of high-carbon steel standard-priced paring knives in Clip, Spear, Wharncliffe and Cut Off blade patterns. Oval black handles with nickel-silver ferrule. Three of each style as shown above. Packed one dozen assorted in a counter display carton.*

Values:	Exc.	V.G.	Good
	400.00	375.00	325.00

Comment: *Values for assortment of 12 paring knives in display carton. Winchester produced several similar sets of 12 paring knives in various blade and handle styles. All would be priced as above.*

Carving Sets

All blades used in Winchester carving knives, except the stainless steel items, are made of chrome vanadium steel. Our long steel experience and engineering research have demonstrated it to be the strongest and most satisfactory steel for cutlery blades.

Chrome vanadium steel was used by Winchester in making thousands of bayonets for the Allied armies during World War I. It was the only steel that combined the necessary tensile strength with the proper elasticity. After the war our engineers found that chrome vanadium also had wonderful cutting qualities. They experimented with it until they developed the special Winchester process of heat treating that makes it the best cutlery steel available today. Chrome vanadium steel will not chip nor break easily and holds it's cutting edge longer than any other type of cutlery steel.

All the stag handles used for Winchester carving sets are genuine stag. Two grades are used, with corresponding difference in price; one the middle and the other the curly.

There are also a number of sets in the Winchester line handled with handsome imitation grain ivory handles.

All Winchester carving sets are packed in soft gray flannel rolls and individual boxes except 5146 and 5217, which are wrapped in paper and packed in gray carton. Sets contain two or three pieces.

Stag Handle Carving Knife and/or Fork. Produced in several styles with natural ends (above) and with silver mountings on end of handle. Each set packed in soft gray flannel roll.

Values:	Exc.	V.G.	Good
	65.00	55.00	40.00

Comment: *Values are for individual pieces of carving sets, either knives or forks, either chrome steel or stainless steel, with stag handles of any style.*

Imitation Grain Ivory Handle Carving Knife and/or Fork. Produced in several blade and handle styles. Each set packed in soft gray flannel roll.

Values:	Exc.	V.G.	Good
	55.00	45.00	30.00

Comment: *Values are for individual pieces of carving sets, either knives or forks, either chrome steel or stainless steel, with imitation grain ivory handles of any style.*

Carving Set Display Boxes

Available in three grades: A, B, C. Each of these boxes is well lined and is made in three different sizes.

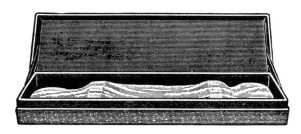

Grade A: carving set display box (above). Square end display box with hinged cover. Gray seal covering. Royal purple velvet lining.
Grade B. Cloud gray high-grade covering paper. Wood green silk and cotton poplin lining.
Grade C. Standard Winchester gray covering paper. Gray cotton crepe lining.

For Set	Box Size
Standard 3 piece	16 3/8x5 5/8x1 3/4 in.
Standard 2 piece	16 3/4X5 5/8X1 3/4 in.
Bird 2 piece	11 7/8x3 5/8x1 5/8 in.

Values:	Exc.	V.G.	Good
	135.00	120.00	100.00

Comment: *Values are for display box only, any grade or size.*

Carving Set Display Rolls

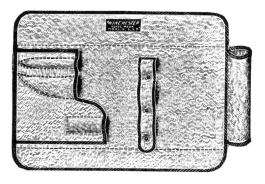

Flannel Carving Set Rolls. Made of soft gray flannel material. Same as those in which Winchester carving sets are packed as standard packing. They are furnished in three sizes as follows: No. 7060 - Standard 3 piece (above); No. 7061 - Standard 2 piece; No. 7062 - Small size (Bird) 2 piece.

Values:	Exc.	V.G.	Good
	100.00	90.00	75.00

Comment: *Values are for display roll only, any size.*

Stainless Steel Cutlery

Winchester stainless steel cutlery is made with all the qualities and care of regular Winchester cutlery plus the attractiveness of blades of stainless steel which will not stain or tarnish under fruit acids or when cutting meats, vegetables, eggs and other food articles. Combines the cutting qualities of regular high-carbon cutlery steel with the full beauty of stainless steel.

Editor's note on values: Stainless steel same as high-carbon items of similar design. We will only list those stainless steel items individually that appear to be unique to the stainless steel line.

Butcher Knife Assortment

No. 6145. An attractive assortment of the popular Winchester stainless steel butcher knives. Scale tang black wood handles with three nickel-silver telescopic rivets; two of each, 1103, 1104 and 1105.

Values:	Exc.	V.G.	Good
	400.00	375.00	325.00

Comment: *Values are for box with 12 knives as described.*

Wood Cutlery Display

Wood Display Stand. Measures 18 in. long x 12 in. high, with mahogany finish. Slotted top to insert butcher knives and slicers. Cork-filled bottom to display paring knives. Originally sold with assortment of 63 butcher knives, slicers and paring knives.

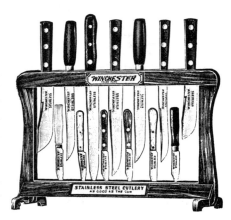

Values:	Exc.	V.G.	Good
	500.00	475.00	425.00

Comment: *Values are for display only without knives.*

Table Cutlery Assortments

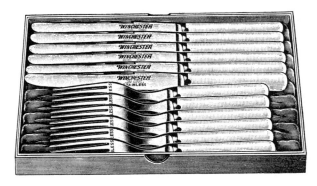

Table Cutlery Assortments. Contained six forks (four tines) and six knives with steak blades in various styles, all stainless steel. Knives had white grained celluloid handles. Box was cardboard lined with gray ribbed cloth.

Values:	Exc.	V.G.	Good
	800.00	750.00	650.00

Comment: *Values are for any assortment with all 12 pieces. Individual steak knives or forks would be valued at $90 in excellent condition; $75 in good condition.*

Kitchen Carving Set

Kitchen Carving Set with cardboard box. Also described in catalogs as "Household Carving Set." From T. Webster collection. Photo by D. Kowalski.

Values:	Exc.	V.G.	Good
	375.00	350.00	275.00

Comment: *Values are for either Kitchen Carving Set or Household Carving Set in box.*

Cheese Knife

Cheese Knife. The grocers in your town will be glad to throw away the old tinned-blade cheese knife for this Winchester stainless steel knife that will not discolor or stain cheese in its lifetime of use. Scale tang black wood handle. Three nickel-silver telescopic rivets. Packed one dozen in a carton. No. 2255; blade 10 in.

Values:	Exc.	V.G.	Good
	75.00	65.00	50.00

Butter Knife

Butter Knife. Of course, the grocer will want a butter knife that always looks bright and clean to the housewife. Stainless steel blades, cut swage. Scale tang black wood handle. Three nickel-silver telescopic rivets. Packed one dozen in a carton. No. 1030; blade 6 in.

Values:	Exc.	V.G.	Good
	45.00	35.00	25.00

Cake Turner

Cake Turner. Stainless steel flexible blade, polished. Large oval ebonized wood handle. Nickel-plated steel ferrule. Shanks extend into handle and pinned. No. 7620; blade 5 3/4 in. x 2 1/2 in. Packed one-half dozen in a carton.

Values:	Exc.	V.G.	Good
	135.00	120.00	100.00

Lemon Slicer

Lemon Slicer. Stainless steel flexible blade. Highly polished black wood handle. Three nickel-silver telescopic rivets. No. 4111; blade 4 in. Packed one dozen in a carton.

Values:	Exc.	V.G.	Good
	35.00	30.00	20.00

Citrus Fruit Knife or Soda Fountain Knife

Citrus Fruit Knife. Stainless steel plain blade. Solid black wood handle. Nickel-silver ferrule. No. 4121; blade 4 in. Packed one dozen in a carton.

Values:	Exc.	V.G.	Good
	35.00	30.00	20.00

Grape Fruit Knife Assortment

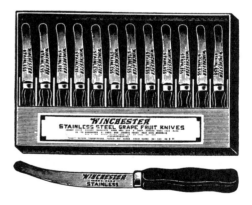

Grape Fruit Knife Assortments. Counter display boxes in various styles contained one dozen knives in various blade and handle styles.

Values:	Exc.	V.G.	Good
	400.00	375.00	325.00

Comment: *Values for various assortments of 12 grapefruit or paring knives in display box.*

Scissors, Clippers, Barber Equipment

Hair Clipper

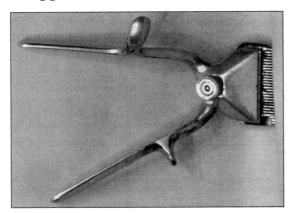

Hair Clipper (No. W784/00). From T. Webster collection. Photo by D. Kowalski.

Hair Clipper. Nickel-plated malleable iron frame and handles. Ball Bearing. Forged steel top and bottom plates. Corrugated bottom plate 1 7/8 in. wide. Length overall 5 5/8 in. Packed one in a carton. 26 fine teeth.

No. W784/00 - To cut hair to 1/32 in.
No. W785/000 - To cut hair very short.

Toilet Clipper

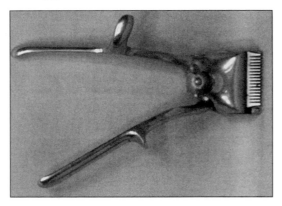

Toilet Clipper (No. W787/00). From T. Webster collection. Photo by D. Kowalski.

Toilet Clipper. Nickel-plated malleable iron frame and handles. Ball Bearing. Forged steel top and bottom plates. Corrugated bottom plate 1 5/16 in. wide. Wing nut at top; set screw on side to regulate tension of spring. Packed one in a carton. 17 fine teeth.

No. W786/00 - To cut hair to 1/32 in.
No. W787/000 - To cut hair very short.

Values:	Exc.	V.G.	Good
	175.00	150.00	125.00

Comment: *Values for either size of Hair Clipper or Toilet Clipper.*

Scissors or Shears Wood Wall Display Case

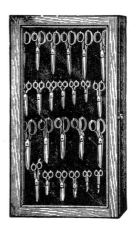

Hardwood Showcase. Measures 32 in. long, 17 in. wide, 3 in. deep. Has golden oak finish, green felt lined; complete with hooks; hinged front door (without glass) so constructed that glass can be inserted by purchaser if desired. Originally contained two dozen scissors and two dozen shears.

Values:	Exc.	V.G.	Good
	1,400.00	1,250.00	1,000.00

Comment: *Values for case without scissors or shears.*

Scissors or Shears Roll Assortments

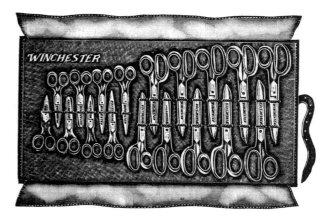

Black Leatherette Roll. Has green plush lining and green satin flaps on both sides, fitted with leatherette strap and nickel-plated buckle. Measures 23 in. long, 12 in. wide. Originally contained 18 scissors and shears.

Values:	Exc.	V.G.	Good
	550.00	450.00	350.00

Comment: *Values for roll without scissors or shears. Add 100 percent for original 18 shears and scissors. Add another 100 percent for original box.*

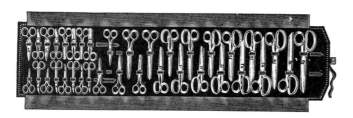

Black Leather Roll. Has green plush lining and green satin flaps on both sides, fitted with leather straps, inside and outside, and nickel-plated buckle. Measures 40 in. long, 9 in. wide. Originally contained 36 scissors and shears.

Values: **Exc.**   **V.G.**   **Good**
                    650.00   550.00   450.00

Comment: *Values for roll without scissors or shears. Add 100 percent for original 36 shears and scissors. Add another 100 percent for original box.*

Scissors, Lace Pattern

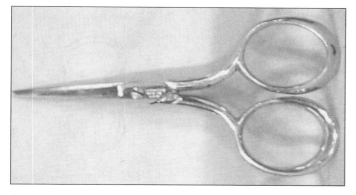

Lace Pattern Scissors (No. 9100). Rare 3-inch model. Models 9100, 9106 and 9142 were the only 3-inch scissors that Winchester made. From T. Webster collection. Photo by D. Kowalski.

Lace Pattern. Blades are full nickel-plated. High-grade forged steel. Nickel-plated, screw-fitted bows.

New No.	Old No.	Length Overall
W7/3	H9199S	3 in.
W7/3 1/2	H9101S	3 1/2 in.
W7/4	H9103S	4 in.
W7/4 1/2	H9204S	4 1/2 in.
W7/5	H9205S	5 in.
W7/5 1/2	H9206S	5 1/2 in.
W7/6	H9207S	6 in.
W7/6 1/2	H9208S	6 1/2 in.

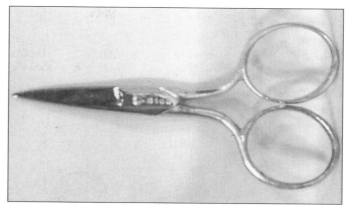

Lace Pattern Scissors (No. 9106). Rare 3-inch model. Has wider blades and smaller finger holes than model 9100. From T. Webster collection. Photo by D. Kowalski.

Lace Pattern. Blades are full nickel-plated and glazed on inside. High-grade forged steel. Nickel-plated, screw-fitted bows.

New No.	Old No.	Length Overall
W370/3	H9106S	3 in.
W370/4	H9108S	4 in.
W370/5	H9110S	5 in.
W370/6	H9112S	6 in.

Values: **Exc.**   **V.G.**   **Good**
                    60.00   40.00   20.00

Comment: *Values for old or new number, any size. Add 300 percent for 3-inch version.*

Scissors, Pocket Flat Pattern

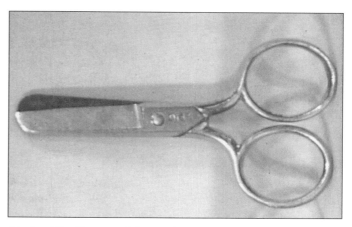

Pocket Flat Pattern Scissors (No. 9142). Rare 3-inch model. From T. Webster collection. Photo by D. Kowalski.

Pocket Flat Pattern. Plain blade, full nickel-plated. High-grade forged steel. Nickel-plated, screw-fitted bows.

New No.	Old No.	Length Overall
W6P3	H9142S	3 in.
W6P3 1/2	H9143S	3 1/2 in.
W6P4	H9144S	4 in.

New No.	Old No.	Length Overall
W6P4 1/2	H9145S	4 1/2 in.
W6P5	H9146S	5 in.

Values:	Exc.	V.G.	Good
	60.00	40.00	20.00

Comment: *Values for old or new number, any size. Add 300 percent for 3-inch version.*

Scissors, Ladies' Pattern

Ladies' Pattern. Full nickel-plated. High-grade forged steel. Blades full nickel-plated. Carefully ground and set. Nickel-plated plain, screw-fitted bows.

New No.	Old No.	Length Overall
W8/3 1/2	H9113S	3 1/2 in.
W8/4	H9114S	4 in.
W8/4 1/2	H9115S	4 1/2 in.
W8/5	H9116S	5 in.
W8/5 1/2	H9117S	5 1/2 in.
W8/6	H9118S	6 in.
W8/6 1/2	H9119S	6 1/2 in.
W8/7	H9120S	7 in.

Scissors, Ladies' Pattern, Gold Plated Shanks and Bows

Ladies' Pattern, Gold Plated Shanks and Bows. Full nickel-plated. High-grade forged steel. Blades full nickel-plated. Carefully ground and set. Nickel-plated plain, screw-fitted bows.

New No.	Old No.	Length Overall
W32/3 1/2	H9213S	3 1/2 in.
W32/4	H9214S	4 in.
W32/4 1/2	H9215S	4 1/2 in.
W32/5	H9216S	5 in.
W32/5 1/2	H9217S	5 1/2 in.
W32/6	H9218S	6 in.

Scissors, Lace Pattern, Gold Plated Shanks and Bows

Lace Pattern, Gold Plated Shanks and Bows. Full nickel-plated. High-grade forged steel. Blades full nickel-plated. Carefully ground and set. Nickel-plated plain, screw-fitted bows.

New No.	Old No.	Length Overall
W31/3 1/2	H9201S	3 1/2 in.

Scissors, Pocket Bevel Pattern

Pocket Bevel Pattern. Full nickel-plated. High-grade forged steel. Blades full nickel-plated. Carefully ground and set. Nickel-plated plain, screw-fitted bows.

New No.	Old No.	Length Overall
W389P4	H9137S	4 in.
W389P4 1/2	H9138S	4 1/2 in.
W389P5	H9139S	5 in.

Values:	Exc.	V.G.	Good
	60.00	40.00	20.00

Comment: *Values for Ladies' Pattern, Ladies' Pattern Gold Plated, Lace Pattern Gold Plated, Bevel Pattern; old or new numbers, any size.*

Button Hole Scissors

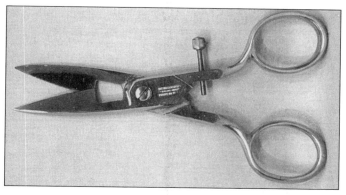

Button Hole Scissors (No. 9123). Very rare and in excellent condition. From T. Webster collection. Photo by D. Kowalski.

Button Hole Scissors. Full nickel-plated. High-grade forged steel. Blades full nickel-plated. Carefully ground and set. Inside brass set screw. Fitted bows.

New No.	Old No.	Length Overall
W1BH	H9123S	4 in.
W9BH	H9128S	4 1/2 in.

Values:

	Exc.	V.G.	Good
	75.00	60.00	35.00

Comment: *Values for either size of Button Hole Pattern, old or new numbers.*

Shears, Straight Trimmers

Straight Trimmers. Blades glazed inside. Each blade forged from one piece of highest-grade carbon steel. Carefully ground and set. Nickel-plated fitted bows. Nickel-plated screw. Winchester trademark etched on blade.

Full Nickel-Plated Blades, Shanks and Bows (Shown above)

New No.	Old No.	Length Overall
W1/5 1/2	H9009S	5 1/2 in.
W1/6	H9010S	6 in.
W1/6 1/2	H9011S	6 1/2 in.
W1/7	H9012S	7 in.
W1/7 1/2	H9013S	7 1/2 in.
W1/8	H9014S	8 in.
W1/8 1/2	H9015S	8 1/2 in.
W1/9	H9016S	9 in.
W1/10	H9017	10 in.

Japanned Finish (Shanks and Bows)

New No.	Old No.	Length Overall
W3/5 1/2	H9021S	5 1/2 in.
W3/6	H9022S	6 in.
W3/6 1/2	H9023S	6 1/2 in.
W3/7	H9024S	7 in.
W3/7 1/2	H9025S	7 1/2 in.
W3/8	H9026S	8 in.
W3/8 1/2	H9027S	8 1/2 in.
W3/9	H9028S	9 in.
W3/10	H9029S	10 in.

Shears, Bent Trimmers

Bent Trimmers. Blades glazed inside. Each blade forged from one piece of highest-grade carbon steel. Carefully ground and set. Nickel-plated fitted bows. Nickel-plated screw. Winchester trademark etched on blade.

Full Nickel-Plated Blades, Shanks and Bows

New No.	Old No.	Length Overall
W2/6	H9041S	6 in.
W2/6 1/2	H9042S	6 1/2 in.
W2/7	H9043S	7 in.
W2/7 1/2	H9044S	7 1/2 in.
W2/8	H9045S	8 in.
W2/8 1/2	H9046S	8 1/2 in.
W2/9	H9047S	9 in.
W2/10	H9049S	10 in.

Japanned Finish (Shanks and Bows - Shown above)

New No.	Old No.	Length Overall
W4/6	H9053S	6 in.
W4/6 1/2	H9054S	6 1/2 in.
W4/7	H9055S	7 in.
W4/7 1/2	H9056S	7 1/2 in.
W4/8	H9057S	8 in.
W4/8 1/2	H9058S	8 1/2 in.
W4/9	H9059S	9 in.
W4/10	H9061S	10 in.

Values:

	Exc.	V.G.	Good
	75.00	55.00	30.00

Comment: *Values for any pattern or size of Shears, old or new numbers.*

Nail Scissors

Nail Scissors. Full nickel-plated. High-grade forged steel. Blades full nickel-plated. Nickel-plated plain, screw-fitted bows.

New No.	Old No.	Length Overall
W2N3 1/2	H9155S	3 1/2 in.
W3N4	H9157S	4 in.

Values:	Exc.	V.G.	Good
	60.00	40.00	20.00

Comment: *Values for either size of Nail Scissors, old or new numbers.*

Manicure Scissors

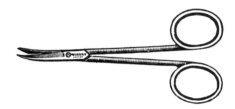

Manicure Scissors. Full nickel-plated. High-grade forged steel. Blades full nickel-plated. Nickel-plated plain, screw-fitted bows.

New No.	Old No.	Length Overall
W1M3 1/2	H9152S	3 1/2 in.
W1M4 1/4	H9153S	4 1/4 in.

Values:	Exc.	V.G.	Good
	75.00	65.00	45.00

Comment: *Values for either size of Manicure Scissors, old or new numbers.*

Manicure Sets

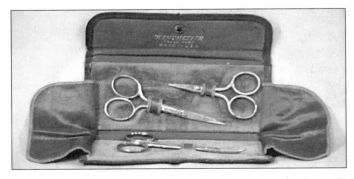

Manicure Set with three small scissors in pouch. From T. Webster collection. Photo by D. Kowalski.

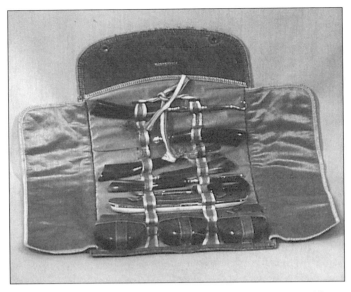

Manicure Set with multiple tools in pouch. From T. Webster collection. Photo by D. Kowalski.

Values:	Exc.	V.G.	Good
	600.00	550.00	475.00

Comment: *Values for either Manicure Set.*

Barbers' Shears German Pattern

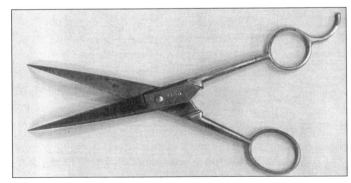

German Pattern Barber Shears (No. 9170). From T. Webster collection. Photo by D. Kowalski.

Barber Shears', German Pattern. High-grade forged steel blades. Both blades highly colored outside, glazed inside. Nickel-plated fitted bows.

New No.	Old No.	Length Overall
W35/7	H9170S	7 in.
W35/7 1/2	H9172S	7 1/2 in.

Barbers' Shears, American Pattern

Barber Shears', American Pattern. High-grade forged steel blades, nickel-plated and glazed inside. Nickel-plated plain, screw-fitted bows.

New No.	Old No.	Length Overall
W17/7 1/2	H9174S	7 1/2 in.

Shanks and bows with black japanned finish.

| W18/7 1/2 | H9175S | 7 1/2 in. |

Values:	Exc.	V.G.	Good
	125.00	100.00	75.00

Comment: *Values for any pattern or size of Barber Shears, old or new numbers.*

Safety Razor

Safety Razor. Nickel-silver head not plated. Steel handle is full nickel-plated. Handle has knurled center.

Values:	Exc.	V.G.	Good
Razor	75.00	65.00	50.00

Comment: *Values for Razor. Add 150 percent for box.*

Safety Razor Blades

Safety Razor Blades came in various style packages. From T. Webster collection. Photo by D. Kowalski.

Values:	Exc.	V.G.	Good
	165.00	150.00	125.00

Comment: *Values for single package, any style.*

Safety Razor Counter Display

Die Cut Cardboard Counter Display. Holds three razors and three packages of blades.

Values:	Exc.	V.G.	Good
	375.00	350.00	300.00

Comment: *Values for display only without blades or razors.*

Wood Safety Razor Display

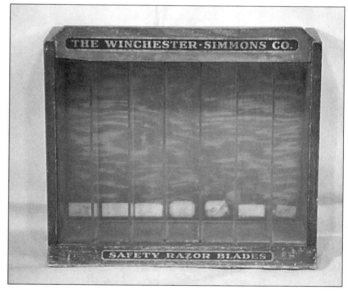

Razor Case has mahogany finish; seven partitions for various kinds of Blades. Glass front is 6 3/4 in. high, 8 3/4 in. wide. Has drop door at rear with catch. Case is 9 1/2 in. long, 8 1/4 in. high, 3 1/4 in. wide at base. From T. Webster collection. Photo by D. Kowalski.

Values:	Exc.	V.G.	Good
	550.00	500.00	425.00

Comment: *Values for display only without blades.*

Shaving Soap Brush

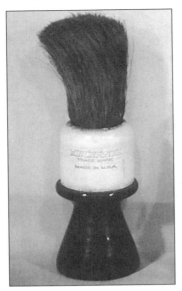

Shaving Soap Brush in excellent condition. From T. Webster collection. Photo by D. Kowalski.

Values:	Exc.	V.G.	Good
	850.00	800.00	700.00

Comment: *Rare items.*

Toilet Set

Toilet Set. Heavy blue mottled cardboard box, with partitions for each item. Contains one Winchester Safety Razor with Blade, one 3 oz. Jar Men's Powder, one 4 oz. tube Shaving Cream, and one 3 oz. bottle of Shaving Lotion with shaker top.

Values:	Exc.	V.G.	Good
	350.00	300.00	225.00

Comment: *Values for complete set.*

Barber Tools Counter Display

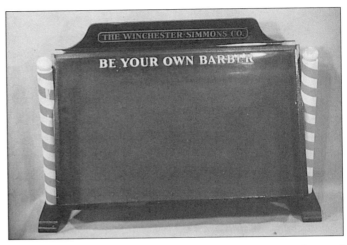

Barber Counter Display. Red mahogany-finish case fastened to two miniature ball-top barber poles. Striped in red and white, with 6 in. walnut-finish base; glass sliding front. Measures 15 3/4 in. wide, 10 1/2 in. long, 10 1/2 in. high. Green cloth back. Height overall 13 1/2 in., 18 in. long. From T. Webster collection. Photo by D. Kowalski.

Values:	Exc.	V.G.	Good
	1,400.00	1,300.00	1,200.00

Comment: *Values for display only.*

Razor Strops

Razor Strop (No. 8367). Excellent condition. From T. Webster collection. Photo by D. Kowalski.

Razor Strop (No. 8381). The biggest and best model Winchester made. From T. Webster collection. Photo by D. Kowalski.

Values:	Exc.	V.G.	Good
	175.00	150.00	125.00

Comment: *Values are for any Razor Strop. Winchester made at least 15 models of Razor Strops with various combinations of leather and canvas.*

Winchester Store Products

by David D. Kowalski

One of the hottest areas in Winchester collectibles today is the Winchester Store arena. This area includes both products made for Winchester's own company stores, as well as products supplied to other independent stores in their dealer network.

Winchester's expansion into a wide range of products had attracted retailer interest across the country. And by the end of 1920, they had 3,400 retailers signed up as part of their dealer network.

At the same time the company had launched their own chain of Winchester Stores beginning with the first one in Providence, Rhode Island, in the spring of 1920. Nine more were added before the end of the year in cities such as Boston and Springfield, Massachusetts; Troy and New York City, New York; and New Haven, Connecticut.

The search for even more revenues led to the merger with the Associated Simmons Hardware Co. in August, 1922. That move gave the newly formed Winchester Simmons Co. an established retail network with warehouses in Simmons' home base in St. Louis, Missouri, plus in other markets such as Chicago, Illinois, Sioux City, Iowa, and San Francisco, California.

This was a case of too much, too fast. By 1924 it was clear these operations were losing large amounts of money. The stores in Boston, Springfield, Providence, New Haven, Troy and New York City were closed with total loses pegged in excess of $2.35 million. While Winchester would continue to supply its dealer network through the 1920s, Winchester Store and Winchester-branded products for other retail outlets would last only 10 years.

We'll present a broad range of products here to give the reader a flavor for this era in company history. However, space does not permit an exhaustive presentation in this first volume. We'll begin with various advertising novelties Winchester offered to help its retailers sell more product.

Advertising Novelties

Specialty advertising, or the proper distribution of well-chosen advertising novelties takes advantage of the personal appeal. Such advertisements produce a friendly reaction in the mind of the customer and are generally welcomed and preserved. They serve as a constant reminder of the dealer whom they represent.

The novelties illustrated here have been chosen because they have all proved effective. Thousands of these items have been distributed to the customers of Winchester dealers throughout the country and their value thoroughly demonstrated.

Here's half of a large poster that was provided to Winchester's retail outlets, apparently touting the fact the store was a member of a large, nationwide distribution system. This rare piece is the only one known and was found being used as a backer board behind another large poster. From T. Webster collection. Photo by D. Kowalski

Yard Sticks

No. 250 - With Customer's Imprint. No. 350. Without Customer's Imprint. An economical souvenir that is practical and useful and has daily use in almost any home. Good quality white basswood 1 1/8-inches thick, with figures and graduations printed in black on one-half of both sides. One side printed in red -"QUALITY - THE WINCHESTER STORE - SERVICE." The other side can be imprinted with your name and other advertising at prices varying according to quantities ordered.

Values: | Exc. | V.G. | Good
| 350.00 | 300.00 | 250.00

Comment: *Values for either imprinted or non-imprinted yard stick.*

Rulers

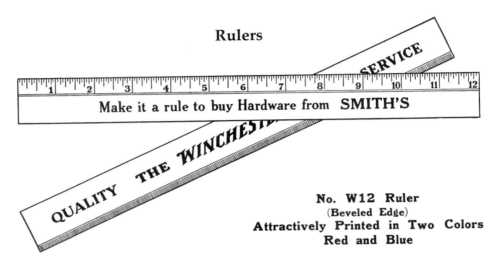

No. W12 Ruler
(Beveled Edge)
**Attractively Printed in Two Colors
Red and Blue**

No. W12. Ruler (Beveled Edge). Attractively Printed in Two Colors: Red and Blue. Here is a souvenir that will build good will for your store among the buying public of tomorrow. The boys and girls of today will soon be somebody's customers. Are you inviting their future patronage by getting and holding their good will? This inexpensive souvenir will attract the younger generation to your store. They will appreciate a ruler, especially at this season of the year. Every ruler bears your advertisement and will be carried into the homes of your community. This is very economical family advertising.

Made of good quality white basswood, beveled edge, 12 inches long, 1 inch wide, 1/8 inch thick. The back or beveled side is printed in red reading "Quality - The Winchester Store - Service" as shown in above cut. The face of the ruler will be imprinted in bright blue with your store name and address (see above cut for suggestion).

Values: | Exc. | V.G. | Good
| 300.00 | 275.00 | 225.00

Comment: *Values for either imprinted or non-imprinted ruler.*

Balloons

No. 60. Round Balloons, Air, Without Strings. One color or assorted: Green, Orange, Purple, Red, Silver, White and Yellow. Finest Quality Stock; Equipped with Valve; Can be Inflated to 10 inches in diameter. High-class, inexpensive advertising that carries your name and address. Your store name printed on one side and the Winchester Store on the other.

No. 60A. Illustrations of items you sell and your store name printed on one side and "Buy all your Hardware at the Winchester Store" on the other.

Values: | Exc. | V.G. | Good
| 300.00 | 275.00 | 225.00

Comment: *Values for a single balloon.*

Sun Hats

Sun hats came in assorted styles for men, women and children. From T. Webster collection. Photo by D. Kowalski.

No. 195. Sun Hat Assortments. These hats are imprinted "THE WINCHESTER STORE" and are excellent for advertising your business. Made of hand-woven Peanit, very strong, light, soft and pliable. Good quality cambric band and edging. For the farmer, fisherman and boatman, and styles for man, woman and child. Serviceable for outdoors, work and play.

Trimming:
Men's and Boys' - Black band, tan edging.
Ladies' - Fancy flowered band and edging.
Children's - Assorted red and navy blue band and edging.

Sold only in lots of six dozen assorted styles and sized (Specify styles and sizes when ordering). Unless otherwise specified we will ship on the basis of Two Dozen Men's; Two Dozen Boys'; One Dozen Ladies'; and One Dozen Children's to the six-dozen lot. One dozen of a style in assorted sizes in a package.

Values:	Exc.	V.G.	Good
	700.00	600.00	400.00

Comment: *Values for any style or size.*

Carpenter's Apron

This carpenter's apron from a store in northeast Wisconsin was never worn and is in excellent condition. Actual size of apron body is 18 inches wide x 21 1/2 inches long. From T. Webster collection. Photo by D. Kowalski.

No. W1. Carpenter's Apron. Made of seven-ounce white duck with extra strong, soft strings and neck band of same material. Large, deep pockets for nails. Apron is 19 inches wide and 21 inches long. Imprinted with "The Winchester Store" in red and black across bib. Your name, address and telephone number across pockets in black. An advertisement that will be on the job for you with a selected circulation every day for a long time.

Values:	Exc.	V.G.	Good
	1,500.00	1,300.00	1,000.00

Comment: *Very few have been found; another consumable item that got worn out and thrown out.*

Wagon Umbrella

No. W10. Wagon Umbrella. Made of strong union drill with alternating white and orange sections. Has spread of 64 inches. Inch and a half hardwood handle. Six japanned steel ribs. Furnished complete with wagon seat fixtures and floor plate. Imprinted in the three white sections with "The Winchester Store" in black. Three orange sections will be imprinted with your name, address and telephone number. An effective bit of advertising that drivers will appreciate the chance to display for you.

Values:	Exc.	V.G.	Good
	1,500.00	1,300.00	1,000.00

Comment: *Very few have been found.*

Cartridge Pencils

No. 3130. Souvenir Cartridge Pencil. An exact reproduction of a regular WINCHESTER high power cartridge. Stamped on side with "The Winchester Store". Bullet pulls out to bring pencil into use. A splendid souvenir for distribution at fairs, store openings, anniversaries and at Christmas.

Values:	Exc.	V.G.	Good
	200.00	175.00	125.00

Trophy Cup

No. 3133. Winchester Trophies. These beautiful Trophies are wonderful prizes for agents to award in any Contest or Athletic League in their locality; such as baseball and basketball leagues, Fishing, Skating and other contests. Furnished at a nominal cost to agents and free to Baseball Leagues adopting Winchester Official League baseballs. Trophy Cup is nickel silver, heavily silver-plated, French gray oxidized butler finish; gold lined; ebonized wood base. Will be engraved only with "WINCHESTER TROPHY, TRADE MARK".

Values:	Exc.	V.G.	Good
	600.00	500.00	400.00

Individual Trophy

No. 3056. Individual Trophy. Heavily gold-plated with "WINCHESTER TROPHY" engraved in Red, fitted with Red Silk Ribbon and Pin for attaching; can be worn as Watch Charm by substituting a regular Fob Ribbon instead of the Ribbon as furnished. These are very attractive and are of excellent quality.

Values:	Exc.	V.G.	Good
	600.00	500.00	400.00

Souvenir Paring Knife

No. 3131. Souvenir Paring Knife. Made of stainless steel of finest quality. The reverse side of the blade is etched with your name and address as shown in the illustration. Furnished in sets of a dozen with an assortment of three styles of stainless steel blades and three styles of handles: black cocobolo and boxwood.

Values:	Exc.	V.G.	Good
	200.00	175.00	125.00

Comment: *Values for a single etched knife.*

Book Matches

No W1. Book Matches. Beautifully printed in four colors: red, blue, gray and gold. Back cover carries advertising copy "tying in" your store as a member of the national chain of 6300 individually owned Winchester stores. Top shows a reproduction of your Winchester store sign. Front cover or flap carries your imprint.

Values:	Exc.	V.G.	Good
	175.00	150.00	125.00

Comment: *Values are for a single book of matches.*

Deck of Cards

Deck of Cards promotes the Winchester Stores. Card on right has dots on map pinpointing store locations. From T. Webster collection. Photo by D. Kowalski.

Values:	Exc.	V.G.	Good
	400.00	350.00	300.00

Comment: *Values are for a complete deck with store location card.*

Alarm Clocks

Alarm Clocks. Available in both Winchester and Winchester Store versions in various styles. Measure approximately four inches across face. From T. Webster collection. Photo by D. Kowalski.

Values:	Exc.	V.G.	Good
Winchester	225.00	200.00	150.00
Win. Store	700.00	600.00	500.00

Comment: *Values for alarm clocks without boxes.*

Pocket Watches

Pocket Watches. Also available in both Winchester and Winchester Store versions in various styles. From T. Webster collection. Photo by D. Kowalski.

Values:	Exc.	V.G.	Good
Winchester	200.00	175.00	150.00
Win. Store	650.00	600.00	500.00

Comment: *Values for pocket watches without boxes. Add 300 percent premium with box.*

Knife Sharpener Buttons

The back of these knife sharpener buttons had a fine whet stone. As the button on the left says, "This side will sharpen your memory. The other side will sharpen your knife." Came in oval pattern 2 3/4 inches long and round versions approximately two inches in diameter. From T. Webster collection. Photo by D. Kowalski.

Values:	Exc.	V.G.	Good
	700.00	650.00	600.00

Comment: *Values for either round or oval versions.*

License Case

The only Winchester Store License Case that has ever been found. Measures 4 3/8 inches wide x 5 1/2 inches long when open. This one was probably never used. From T. Webster collection. Photo by D. Kowalski.

Values:	Exc.	V.G.	Good
	3,000.00	2,500.00	2,000.00

Comment: *Values for any license case.*

Fishing License

This fishing license was issued to a Frank M. Buckland of West Hartford, Connecticut in the New Haven, Connecticut Winchester Store for 1925. From T. Webster collection. Photo by D. Kowalski.

Values:	Exc.	V.G.	Good
	2,000.00	1,800.00	1,500.00

Comment: *Values for any fishing or hunting license issued at a Winchester Store in the 1920s.*

Chick or Chicken Waterer

One Quart Chick Waterer was from Winchester retailer Seaboch Hardware in Marshalltown, Iowa. This is the only One Quart waterer known. Also made in one gallon and half gallon sizes. From T. Webster collection. Photo by D. Kowalski.

The vacuum created in the upper reservoir kept water at proper level in lower feeder portion. Material was glazed stoneware crock. From T. Webster collection. Photo by D. Kowalski.

Values:	Exc.	V.G.	Good
One Quart	3,000.00	2,800.00	2,500.00
Half Gallon	3,000.00	2,800.00	2,500.00
One Gallon	2,400.00	2,100.00	1,750.00

Comment: *The one gallon versions were probably the most common. Only two or three waterers of any size have ever been found.*

Oil Can

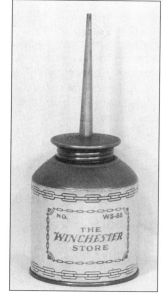

Oil Can with squirt tip measures 7 1/4 inches high. From T. Webster collection. Photo by D. Kowalski.

Values:	Exc.	V.G.	Good
	400.00	350.00	300.00

Comment: *Values for any similar oil can.*

Wrapping and Marking Supplies

Every progressive retailer knows the advertising value of distinctively wrapped packages. Such packages reach the homes of your customers and serve as an effective reminder of "The Winchester Store." The materials shown below are all of high quality and are designed to furnish Winchester dealers with wrapping and shipping material that has a splendid advertising value. By means of quantity buying, the cost of this material is kept at a very nominal figure.

Stencils

Stencils available in lengths of 9, 15 and 20 inches. A time saver in marking show cards, road signs, fair exhibit booths, parade floats, delivery trucks, packages, etc. Made of heavy oiled paper with "THE WINCHESTER STORE" carefully cut in the stencil.

Values:	Exc.	V.G.	Good
	200.00	175.00	125.00

Comment: *Values for any size.*

Gummed Stickers

Gummed Stickers are printed in red. For marking merchandise with a permanent advertisement of your store. Can be applied to vacuum sweepers, fireless cookers, lawn mowers and many similar items. Furnished four on a strip six inches long x 1 1/2 inches wide.

Values: Exc.   V.G.   Good
               50.00   40.00   25.00

Comment: *Values for one sticker on backer sheet.*

Gummed Labels

No. 1091. Labels are printed in red and black. Have gummed back.

Values: Exc.   V.G.   Good
               30.00   25.00   15.00

Comment: *Values for one sticker on backer sheet.*

Gummed Shipping Labels

No. 1094. For marking packages for shipment. Has space for writing name and address of consignee and how package is shipped. Imprinted with your name and address. Printed in red and black. Have gummed back.

Values: Exc.   V.G.   Good
               30.00   25.00   15.00

Comment: *Values for one sticker on backer sheet.*

Gummed Shipping and Package Tape

Package tape roll from O.F. Berg (city and state not identified). Measures one inch wide. From T. Webster collection. Photo by D. Kowalski.

No. 1206 - 1 1/4 inches wide, gummed inside. In 800 ft. rolls. No. 1207-1 1/4 inches wide, gummed outside. In 500 ft. rolls. For wrapping all kinds of packages. A great saving over string. Gray Kraft stock, 1 1/4 inches wide. Printed with "The Winchester Store" in red. Furnished in rolls gummed inside or outside to fit either type of standard machine.

Values: Exc.   V.G.   Good
               225.00   200.00   175.00

Comment: *Values for any similar partial roll. Add 25 percent premium for full roll.*

Shipping Tags

Durable Winchester gray stock. Order with or without string. Furnished plain or printed with your name and address. Measures 4 3/4 inches x 2 3/8 inches.

No. 1101 Plain, string attached
No. 1102 Plain, without string
No. 1103 Printed in two colors, string attached
No. 1104 Printed in two colors, without string
No. 1105 Printed in one color, string attached
No. 1106 Printed in one color, without string

Values: Exc.   V.G.   Good
               35.00   30.00   20.00

Comment: *Values for one tag of any type.*

Nail and Shot Bags

 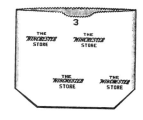

Made of tough, durable gray Kraft stock. Imprinted with the words "The Winchester Store" in red. Packed in standard bundles following the usual trade customs. Nail and Shot Bags can not be imprinted with dealer's name and address.

No. W3	3 lb. Nail Bag
No. W5	5 lb. Nail Bag
No. W10	10 lb. Nail Bag
No. W16	16 lb. Nail Bag
No. W20	20 lb. Nail Bag
No. WS1	1 lb. Shot Bag
No. WS3	3 lb. Shot Bag

Values: Exc. 110.00   V.G. 90.00   Good 60.00

Comment: *Values for one bag of any size.*

Wrapping Paper in Rolls, Printed

Excellent quality gray Kraft paper. Printed at regular intervals with "The Winchester Store" in red. Furnished in the following sizes and weights:

No. WP30/12	12 in. Rolls; 30 lb. stock
No. WP30/15	15 in. Rolls; 30 lb. stock
No. WP30/18	18 in. Rolls; 30 lb. stock
No. WP30/20	20 in. Rolls; 30 lb. stock
No. WP30/24	24 in. Rolls; 30 lb. stock
No. WP30/30	30 in. Rolls; 30 lb. stock
No. WP40/12	12 in. Rolls; 40 lb. stock
No. WP40/15	15 in. Rolls; 40 lb. stock
No. WP40/18	18 in. Rolls; 40 lb. stock
No. WP40/20	20 in. Rolls; 40 lb. stock
No. WP40/24	24 in. Rolls; 40 lb. stock
No. WP40/30	30 in. Rolls; 40 lb. stock

Values: Exc. 500.00   V.G. 400.00   Good 300.00

Comment: *Values for roll with original core, any size.*

Wrapping Paper in Rolls. Custom Printed

With Special Imprint. Excellent quality gray Kraft paper, printed at regular intervals with your name, address and telephone number and the words, "The Winchester Store" in red. Furnished in the same weights and sizes as above.

Values: Exc. 500.00   V.G. 400.00   Good 300.00

Comment: *Values for roll with original core, any size, any imprint.*

Roll Paper Designs

Here are examples of roll paper designs offered to retailers. Design would also include the store's business card.

702 • Winchester Store Products

Small Merchandise Envelopes

Small Merchandise Envelopes came in various designs printed with store name. Actual size of envelope was 3 1/8 in. x 4 3/4 in.

Values:	Exc.	V.G.	Good
	40.00	35.00	25.00

Comment: *Values for any style small envelope.*

Stationery

A very complete line of inprinted stationery is now offered Winchester Agents. Letterheads, envelopes, statements, billheads, check books, etc., all printed on Winchester gray bond paper in two colors, red and black, will serve to identify the stationery of your store. In order to permit the Sales Service Department to render the most efficient service and to offer this stationery at the lowest possible price, a standard form for each type of stationery has been developed. By standardizing these forms, they can be produced in large quantities and a big saving effected for our agents.

Receipt Pad

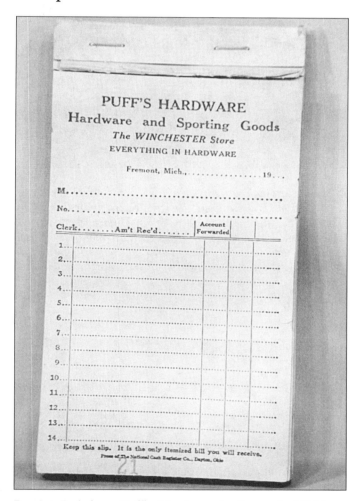

Receipt Pad from Puff's Hardware in Fremont, Michigan measures 3 5/8 inches wide x 6 7/8 inches high. From T. Webster collection. Photo by D. Kowalski.

Values:	Exc.	V.G.	Good
	300.00	275.00	250.00

Comment: *Values for any receipt pad. As examples of other stationery become available, they will be included in future editions.*

Three Ring Binders

No. 1654. Three Ring Binder. Made of heavy serviceable gray canvas. Three 1-inch rings. Patented spring opening and closing device. Holds letter size sheets 8 1/2 in. x 11 in. A great convenience for filing price lists, bulletins, letters, advertisements and other material.

Values:	Exc.	V.G.	Good
	75.00	60.00	40.00

Comment: *Values for any style small envelope.*

Lead Pencils

No. 1919. Extra grade office pencil. Round rubber-tip red eraser; nickel-plated ferrule; finest cedar, nicely finished in maroon and Winchester gray, Lettered in Silver. Extra grade compressed lead, free from grit, writes with an even smoothness. Adaptable to any business; will give satisfaction. Sharpened ready for use. Soft Lead, No. 2 grade. One-Half Gross in a Cardboard Box.

No. 1923. Hexagon lead pencil. Hexagon rubber-tip red eraser; nickel-plated ferrule; finest cedar, nicely finished in maroon and Winchester gray, Lettered in Silver. Sharpened ready for use. Medium Soft Lead. One-Half Gross in a Cardboard Box.

Values:	Exc.	V.G.	Good
	125.00	100.00	75.00

Comment: *Values for one pencil, either round or hexagon.*

Store Coats

Modern Attire - Store Coats for Winchester Agents and their Salesmen. Correct attire when worn by retail salesmen tends to create an atmosphere of refinement throughout the entire store which is very acceptable to customers and prospects. These two styles of store coats have been adopted for Winchester store employees. They present a neat trim appearance. They are economical and easily laundered, yet their outstanding quality makes them suitable for any store. You will be pleased with the fit, the set of the collar, the slope of the shoulders, the fit around the armholes and the smooth faultless hang of the garment. They are carefully designed. The stitching, felling of hems and seams is all correctly done by expert workmen.

No. 24L26. This coat is made of high-grade duck. The attractive black and white check design printed with fast colors. Four-button style with military collar. Three pockets. Removable buttons. Winchester Store Sign label mounted on each coat above pencil pocket. Our quantity purchases through one of the largest factories of its kind in the country enable us to offer these coats to you at very attractive prices. Sizes 34 to 48.

No. 24MIN24. This is a lightweight coat, made of high-grade Indianhead cloth, light tan color, three-button style, deep lapels, three pockets, detachable buttons; launders well. State size wanted. Winchester Store sign label mounted on each coat above pencil pocket. Tan color. Sizes 34 to 48.

Here is the Label. Actual Size is 1 1/8 in. x 2 1/2 in. Woven in Two Colors - Red and Blue on White. This attractive label stitched on each coat just above pencil pocket. Background is white, word "Winchester," the four "W" and "border" woven in red. The words "The," "Store," "Trade Mark" and "four corners of border" are all woven in blue. This label is a reproduction of the Winchester Store Sign.

Values:	Exc.	V.G.	Good
	500.00	400.00	300.00

Comment: *Values for coat of any size or design. Must have label attached.*

Display Materials

Good displays are the most important part of a store's advertising and the materials illustrated below will ot only enable you to make better displays but to make them more quickly. Every item has been thoroughly tested in the Sales Service Display Laboratory and found to be the best of its kind.

Show Case Displays

No. W171. Show case Display. High grade oak show case is 6 feet long, 42 inches high, and 23 inches deep. Has bevel plate-glass top, in two sections, and double-strength glass front and sides. Clear glass sliding doors at rear. Two wood shelves; one each 9 3/4 in. and 13 3/4 in. wide, on nickel-plated adjustable brackets. Originally sold with 171 items of Winchester tools. Show case knocked down and boxed; tools packed in separate cases.

Values:	Exc.	V.G.	Good
	2,000.00	1,900.00	1,750.00

Comment: *Values for show case only.*

Open Display Table

No. W86. Open Display Table. Wood table and base 68 in. long, 31 in. wide, 32 1/2 in. high; Legs 2 1/2 in. square; 55 compartments are 2 in. deep: 22 about 3 in. x 6 in.; 22 about 6 in. x 6 in.; and 11 about 6 in. x 12 in. Wood partitions are removable and can be arranged as desired. Finished in Winchester Gray. Base same size as top of table and is elevated 4 inches from floor; table legs pass through holes in base and rest on floor. Knocked down, one in crate; weight each about 175 lbs.

Values:	Exc.	V.G.	Good
	2,600.00	2,200.00	1,800.00

Comment: *Values for display table only.*

Open Top Display Table, No Dividers

Warren's Display Table made of thoroughly seasoned material; Open top and shelf; Band around top 3 1/4 in. high, 2 in. deep, inside. Overall size is 6 ft. long, 30 in. wide, 33 1/2 in. high. Packed one in a crate knocked down.

No. 377/OSG - Oak; silver gray finish; weight about 165 lbs.
No. 377PG - Poplar; Winchester gray finish; weight about 145 lbs.

Values:	Exc.	V.G.	Good
	2,500.00	2,200.00	1,700.00

Comment: *Values for display table only.*

Open Top Display Table, 27 Glass Compartments

No. G376/OSG. Thoroughly seasoned white oak; Band around top is 3 1/4 in. high, 2 in. deep, inside. Top consists of 27 bulb-edge glass compartments: 18 are 5 13/16 in. x 9 3/8 in.; and nine 11 1/4 in. x 9 3/8 in.; 2 in. deep; Outside rub rail is 4 in. high. Metal corner brackets, splicers and glass supports; poplar shelf. Overall size is 6 ft. long, 30 in. wide, 33 1/2 in. high. Silver gray finish. Weight about 215 lbs. Packed one in a crate knocked down.

Values:	Exc.	V.G.	Good
	2,500.00	2,200.00	1,700.00

Comment: *Values for display table only.*

Open Top Display Table, 27 Wood Compartments

No. W376PG. Thoroughly seasoned southern poplar throughout; Winchester gray finish. Top consists of 27 wood compartments: 18 are 5 5/8 in. x 9 3/8 in.; and nine 11 1/2 in. x 9 3/8 in.; 2 in. deep. Long and short partitions halved together. Overall size is 6 ft. long, 30 in. wide, 33 1/2 in high; weight each about 150 lbs. Packed one in a crate knocked down.

Values:	Exc.	V.G.	Good
	2,500.00	2,200.00	1,700.00

Comment: *Values for display table only.*

Open Top Display Table, 56 Compartments, Two Shelves

No. 2G374/OSG. Well-seasoned white oak; band around top is 3 1/4 in. high, 2 in. deep, inside. Top consists of 56 bulb-edge glass compartments: eight are 5 in. x 7 in.; four 5 in. x 14 1/8 in.; 24 are 4 1/2 in. x 9 3/8 in; and 20 are 4 1/2 in. x 7 in.; 2 in. deep. Outside rub rail 4 in. high. Steel corner and center splicers and partition holders, monumental bronze finish. Three-ply paneled ends are 1 3/4 inches thick. Has removable shelf. Overall size is 7 ft. long, 30 in. wide, 34 1/2 in. high. Silver gray finish. Weight about 300 lbs. Packed one in a crate knocked down.

Values:	Exc.	V.G.	Good
	2,500.00	2,200.00	1,700.00

Comment: *Values for display table only.*

Open Top Display Table, 56 Compartments, Solid Center

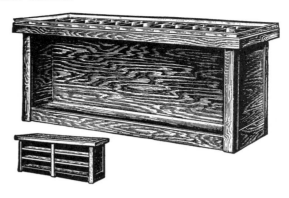

No. 2G374/OASG. Same table as above with 1/4-inch, three-ply, oak-paneled ends; three-ply fir upright center partition, dividing the lower portion into an open compartment in front and the rear with two shelves; matched fir bottom. Overall size is 7 ft. long, 30 in. wide, 34 in high. Silver gray finish. Weight about 310 lbs. Packed one in a crate knocked down.

Values:	Exc.	V.G.	Good
	2,500.00	2,200.00	1,700.00

Comment: *Values for display table only.*

Display Table Top, 27 Glass Compartments

No. G376/OTRSG. Table top. Bottom made of 3/8 in., three-ply fir built-up stock. Has oak band 2 3/8 in. high, 2 in. deep. Outside rub rail 4 in. high. Steel corner and center splicers and partition holders, monumental bronze finish. Overall size is 72 1/2 in. long, 30 1/2 in. wide. Top consists of 27 bulb-edge glass compartments: 18 are 5 13/16 in. x 9 3/8 in.; and nine are 11 1/4 in. x 9 3/8 in., 2 in. deep. Silver gray finish. Weight about 85 lbs.

Values:	Exc.	V.G.	Good
	500.00	400.00	300.00

Comment: *Values for display table top only.*

Display Table Top, 56 Glass Compartments

No. 2G373/ORSG. Same as above but top consists of 56 bulb-edge glass compartments: eight are 5 in. x 7 in.; four are 5 in. x 14 1/8 in.; 24 are 4 1/2 in. x 9 3/8 in.; and 20 are 4 1/2 in. x 7 in., 2 in. deep. Silver gray finish. Weight about 100 lbs.

Values:	Exc.	V.G.	Good
	500.00	400.00	300.00

Comment: *Values for display table top only.*

Show Case Inserts

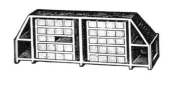

For displaying pocket knives, scissors, shears, kitchen knives, slicers, etc. Designed and specially constructed to fit inside of regular cutlery show cases. All cutlery can be sampled on removable covered panels and each item priced on special tag, which also designates the drawer inside of case where duplicate stock is kept.

The merchandise which is sampled on the insert should include not less than 50 patterns of Winchester pocket knives together with a complete line of Winchester scissors and shears, in addition to such items as safety razors, shaving brushes and other shaving accessories.

Has paneled oak case, natural finish, not varnished; can be stained and varnished by purchaser to match other store fixtures. Removable panels; height overall 24 in.; depth 19 in. Shelves inside of case, entered from rear, with 40 wood boxes 11 in. x 3 1/4 in. x 4 in. for duplicate stock. Packed one in a crate.

With green felt-covered panels.
No. 6CI - For 6 ft. show cases; length 5 1/2 ft.; Weight about 98 lbs.
No. 8CI - For 8 ft. show cases; length 6 1/2 ft.; Weight about 116 lbs.

With green plush-covered panels.
No. 6CIP - For 6 ft. show cases; length 5 1/2 ft.; Weight about 98 lbs.
No. 8CIP - For 8 ft. show cases; length 6 1/2 ft.; Weight about 116 lbs.

Values:

Exc.	V.G.	Good
3,000.00	2,800.00	2,500.00

Comment: *Values for either style or length without merchandise.*

Display Panel Boards

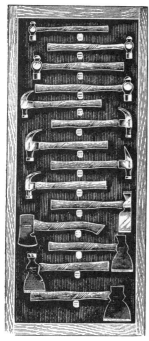

No. V24. Panel Boards. For displaying cutlery and tools. Made of kiln-dried lumber, with insert panel covered with green felt. All cutlery and tools can be sampled on boards, each item priced on special tags. Panel boards are natural finish, not varnished; can be stained and varnished by purchaser to match other store fixtures. Size each is 2 ft. x 4 ft. with 2 3/8-inch stiles. Weight of board only about 12 lbs.

Values:

Exc.	V.G.	Good
800.00	700.00	500.00

Comment: *Values for any style without merchandise.*

Portable Merchandiser, Double Post

No. W160. Portable Merchandiser (Willett) with four shelves. Steel construction; two lengths of 1/2-inch iron pipe; six supporting studs; two nickel-plated cap screws; four Bassick casters. Lacquer finish, in a Willow Green. Suitable for Special Items. Easily Assembled. Packed one in a crate. Weight about 130 lbs.

Dimensions:

Shelves	Size, in.	From Floor, in.
Bottom	23 1/2 x 59 1/2	9
Third	19 1/2 x 55 1/2	25
Second	15 1/2 x 51 1/2	39 1/2
Top	11 1/2 x 47 1/2	52

Values:	Exc.	V.G.	Good
	3,000.00	2,900.00	2,800.00

Comment: *Values without merchandise.*

Portable Merchandiser. Single Post

No. W124. Portable Merchandiser (with single post) with four shelves. Steel construction; two lengths of 1/2-inch iron pipe; three supporting studs; one nickel-plated cap screw; four Bassick casters. Lacquer finish, in a Winchester gray. Suitable for special items; easily assembled. Will support a load of 755 lbs. Packed one in a crate. Weight about 52 lbs.

Dimensions:

Shelves	Size, in.	From Floor, in.
Bottom	23 1/2 x 23 1/2	9
Third	19 1/2 x 19 1/2	25
Second	15 x 16	41
Top	12 x 12	52

Values:	Exc.	V.G.	Good
	2,500.00	2,200.00	1,800.00

Comment: *Values without merchandise.*

Window Display Pedestal

This 18-inch high Display Pedestal (No. 3139) is one of only two found to date. From T. Webster collection. Photo by D. Kowalski.

Logo close-up of 18-inch Display Pedestal. From T. Webster collection. Photo by D. Kowalski.

Improve your window displays with Winchester Standard Display Pedestals. Made of solid oak and finished a dark golden oak. Furnished in three sizes: 12, 18, and 24 inches high. Shipped in individual corrugated cartons. No. 3138 - 12 in.; No. 3139 - 18 in.; No. 3140 - 24 in.

Values:	Exc.	V.G.	Good
	800.00	700.00	500.00

Comment: *Values for 18-inch model. Add 25 percent premium for 12-inch or 24-inch models.*

Show Card Frames

No. 3111. Set of five Show Card Frames. Add to the attractiveness of your show cards with this set of show card frames. Five frames with detachable bases for show cards, plus twenty holders for small show cards or price tickets, all made of oak and finished a dark golden oak. Shipped complete in a corrugated carton.

Values:	Exc.	V.G.	Good
	800.00	700.00	500.00

Comment: *Values for complete set of five frames.*

Window Display Screen

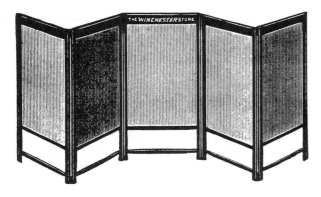

No. 1927. Window Display Screen has steel rod construction 5/16 inches in diameter, electrically welded at all corners. Steel channels with 5/8-inch facing and a 5/16-inch depth, electrically welded to the inner walls. Top of channels are open for insertion of corrugated board fillers and poster changes. Size of panels: 18 in. wide, 38 1/2 in. high, elevated 12 in. from floor. Panels permanently hinged with double action hinges and can be folded very compactly. Finished in Ebony Enamel, baked on. Has five panels with corrugated board fillers. Height overall 51 in. Weight each about 40 lbs.

Values:	Exc.	V.G.	Good
	700.00	600.00	400.00

Comment: *Values for full five-panel frames. These were the frames that held the five-panel advertising displays that Winchester created in large quantities for all their products.*

Wooden Gun Rack

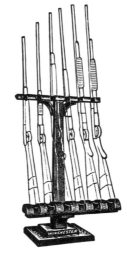

No. 3105. Gun Rack made of solid oak; finished a dark golden oak. Notches in a top bar are covered with emerald green felt to avoid scratching the gun barrels. Rack is perfectly designed and will not tip over or wobble. Shipped in individual corrugated carton, partly disassembled to save carrying charges. Holds six guns of any size.

Values:	Exc.	V.G.	Good
	2,500.00	2,200.00	1,700.00

Comment: *Values for rack only.*

Wooden Fishing Rod Rack

No. 3115. Fishing Rod Rack is a solid oak rack with ball-bearing casters. Height, 4 ft.; Base, 18 in. x 18 in. Top is 12 in. x 12 in. Holds 28 rods. Finished in dark golden oak. Shipped knocked down in individual corrugated cartons.

Values:	Exc.	V.G.	Good
	2,500.00	2,200.00	1,700.00

Comment: *Values for rack only.*

Show Window Valance (Cloth)

In daytime this Show Window Valance is very effective. The red lettering stands out against cream-colored background. At night the light shows through the cream-colored background, which brings out the lettering and makes a very attractive sign. Use this style layout for windows up to 6 ft. wide.

A cream-colored, patented, processed, transparent cloth. It is frostproof, steamproof and waterproof. The lettering is done with unfading red and shaded with an air brush. "The Winchester Store" is to appear in at least one place on each Window. Dealer's name or name of some line of merchandise can also be inserted at no extra charge; dealer to furnish his own copy. Standard width 18 inches including fringe. Can be had narrower or wider if necessary at no change in price. Use this style layout for windows 8 ft., 10 ft. or wider.

Values:	Exc.	V.G.	Good
6 foot or less	1,500.00	1,400.00	1,200.00
8 ft. plus	2,000.00	1,800.00	1,500.00

Comment: *Can have various product callouts but must have "The Winchester Store" logo.*

Road Signs (Steel)

No. 3060. Road Sign. It works every day in the year, continually flashing to the Prospective Customer as he is driving into town to buy goods; The Hardware Man's Invitation "Buy all Your Hardware at my Store, The Winchester Store." Made of 28 Gauge Steel, painted in three colors of lead and oil paints and then varnished. The words "Hardware" and "Winchester" are painted in red, all other lettering in black on a gray background. Frame made of wood molding, reinforced with steel band at corners. Size is 30 inches high, 60 inches long. Weight about 19 lbs.

Values:	Exc.	V.G.	Good
	800.00	700.00	500.00

Comment: *Values for this sign only.*

Flexlume Electric Signs (Steel)

The dazzling brilliancy of a Flexlume Electric Sign with its bold, snow-white, raised letters of glass will make your store front "reach out" and pull more business. Snow-white raised glass letters against the dark blue background gives you a sign that is clearly legible by day and brilliantly lighted by night; can be read blocks away. Constructed of 26 gauge copper-bearing steel, galvanized, then electro copper-plated and primed, then finished in "Duco". Electric Wiring bears the label of the National Board of Fire Underwriters. Complete rig furnished for hanging. Price does not include flasher, hanging or lamps; we recommend 50-watt blue or frosted-mill type lamps for best results. 20 lamps needed.

No. 1913. Flexlume Electric Sign. Size is 5 ft. long and 35 in. high; double-faced; both sides identical. Shipping weight about 250 lbs.

No. 1914. Flexlume Electric Sign. Size is 12 ft. 8 in. high; 32 inches wide; double-faced; both sides identical. Shipping weight about 300 lbs.

Values:	Exc.	V.G.	Good
Horizontal	2,000.00	1,900.00	1,700.00
Vertical	3,000.00	2,800.00	2,500.00

Comment: *Values for this sign only.*

Enameled Steel Sign

No. 1441. Enameled Steel Sign has actual measurement of 18 inches wide x 10 1/8 inches high. From T. Webster collection. Photo by D. Kowalski.

Values:	Exc.	V.G.	Good
	1,700.00	1,500.00	1,200.00

Comment: *Values for this sign only.*

Bronze Window Sign

No. 1446. Bronze Window Sign is 19 1/8 inches long x 2 7/8 inches high. From T. Webster collection. Photo by D. Kowalski.

No. 1446. *By using this handsome sign in your show windows you can be sure that every window display you make is so definitely tied up with your store name that it can never be confused with displays made by your competitor. Made of solid monumental bronze with high-polished border and letters. Your store name is made in large letters across the top of the sign in dignified runic type. "The Winchester Store" is in smaller type beneath. Sign is equipped with rubber feet and substantial folding easel. This bronze sign can also be used on show case and any other interior displays. Size is 2 3/4 in. high x 19 3/4 in long*

Values:	Exc.	V.G.	Good
	1,700.00	1,500.00	1,200.00

Comment: *Values for this sign only.*

Electric Sign for Storefront

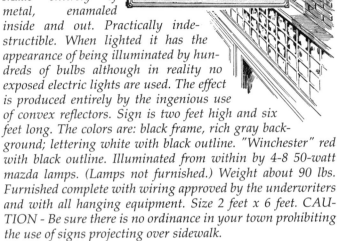

No. 1450. This illuminated sign in front of your store will be seen for blocks in either direction. It is a double-faced sign illuminated on both sides. Made entirely of metal, enameled inside and out. Practically indestructible. When lighted it has the appearance of being illuminated by hundreds of bulbs although in reality no exposed electric lights are used. The effect is produced entirely by the ingenious use of convex reflectors. Sign is two feet high and six feet long. The colors are: black frame, rich gray background; lettering white with black outline. "Winchester" red with black outline. Illuminated from within by 4-8 50-watt mazda lamps. (Lamps not furnished.) Weight about 90 lbs. Furnished complete with wiring approved by the underwriters and with all hanging equipment. Size 2 feet x 6 feet. CAUTION - Be sure there is no ordinance in your town prohibiting the use of signs projecting over sidewalk.

Values: Exc. 3,000.00   V.G. 2,800.00   Good 2,500.00

Comment: *Values for this sign only.*

Indoor Cartridges/Guns Sign (Painted on Tin)

Large green inset-door-panel sign in excellent condition is a panting on tin by Alexander Pope. It illustrates mounted moose antlers holding two guns, two powder horns and three ducks that have been shot. Bottom panel announces that "We Recommend and Sell Winchester Cartridges and Guns." From Curt Bowman collection. Photo by C. Bowman.

Values: Exc. 3,200.00   V.G. 2,200.00   Good 1,500.00

Comment: *Values for this sign only.*

Indoor Multi-Product Sign

Large horizontal indoor advertising sign pictures two men working in the woods. Entire bottom foreground of picture has a wooden tray holding Winchester guns, ammunition, knives, skate blades and tools. This was produced on canvas in 1930. From Curt Bowman collection. Photo by C. Bowman.

Values: Exc. 4,500.00   V.G. 3,000.00   Good 2,000.00

Comment: *Values for this sign only. Only three currently known to exist.*

Calendars, Posters and Advertising

by Tom Webster

Winchester believed in advertising. Lots of it! And unless you've been collecting it as long as I have, you almost cannot comprehend the volume and variety. Calendars, posters, floor displays (we'd now call them point-of-purchase displays), five-panel advertising displays on scores of products, case inserts, counter pads, counter displays, two-sided counter displays, hanging cardboard store signs (many of them die-cut), metal signs, as well as thousands of newspaper and magazine ads.

Then there are also vast quantities of other advertising-related collectibles that have captured the attention of Winchester lovers. Things like letterhead and envelopes, buttons and product booklets come to mind. Winchester also produced several catalogs for retailers and sales bulletins for the field sales staff. All of these pieces have some value to collectors.

Winchester advertising has become a specialty for many collectors. There are also specialties within the specialty, such as big game animals, birds, dogs or cowboy-related pieces. The quality of the artwork is quite good. Some of it is truly world-class. I am thinking particularly of the calendar and poster paintings done by Philip R. Goodwin. Even if the Winchester name means nothing to you, you can't help but admire the realism and drama of Goodwin's poster of the Grizzly Bear coming out of the cabin. The brilliant color and detail of the "Cock of the Woods" poster by an unknown artist also puts it in the top levels of animal art.

Our challenge is to give some focus to this area. We will start with calendars, then move to the major posters, finishing with a sample of five-panel displays, die-cuts and other memorable pieces. Most of these are very striking in color. And you will see them all in color in the upcoming *Winchester Rarities*, plus many more examples we did not have the room to include here.

Winchester Factory Poster

Values:	Exc.	V.G.	Good
	2,200.00	2,000.00	1,750.00

Comment: *Values are only for this early version. It is also one of the rarest of the Factory paintings.*

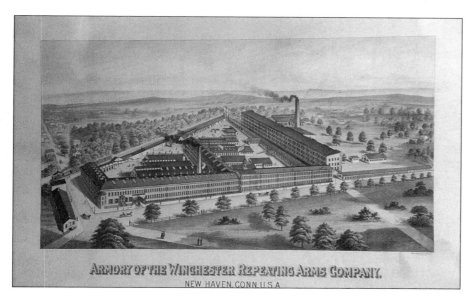

Picture of the Winchester Factory, one of the earliest versions. Live matter area is 34 inches wide x 22 1/4 inches high. Done in black and sepia-tone brown. From T. Webster collection. Photo by D. Kowalski.

Winchester Calendars

From 1887 to 1934, that span of 53 years that interests the collector of "old" Winchester products, Winchester produced 36 different poster-size wall calendars. We present all of them.

Winchester did not offer any wall calendars from 1902 through 1911. During this time they did, however, produce several full-size posters that have become very collectible. There were no Winchester calendars offered in 1931 or 1932, years when the new owners, Western Cartridge Co., were getting the company reorganized and streamlined. Then Winchester/Western produced calendars in 1933 and 1934. We've included them, as well.

We will give values for each calendar, using the same three-tier grading scale we employed for most of the other non-firearms products. Each value chart will be followed by comments about rarity and also identify the painter if that has added to a calendar's collectibility.

1887 Calendar

1887 Calendar. The first and one of the rarest of the calendars. Promotes the Model 1886 rifle. "Winchester" is in red. Painter is unknown. From Curt Bowman collection. Photo by C. Bowman.

Values:	Exc.	V.G.	Good
	15,000.00	13,000.00	10,000.00

Comment: *About 8-10 of them have been discovered.*

1888 Calendar

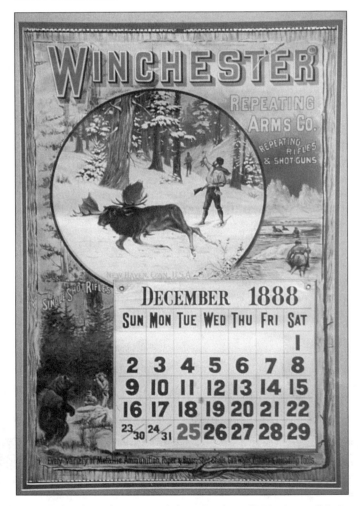

1888 Calendar. The rarest of the calendars. "Winchester" is in red; "Repeating Arms Co." is in yellow. Winchester used 1887 illustrations they purchased from Harper's Weekly. From T. Webster collection. Photo by D. Kowalski.

Values:	Exc.	V.G.	Good
	15,000.00	13,000.00	10,000.00

Comment: *Only 3 or 4 have been discovered.*

Calendars, Posters and Advertising • 715

1889 Calendar

1890 Calendar

1889 Calendar. This calendar starts a tradition used by several painters of putting a title on various scenes. This one includes "In Luck," "Just in the Nick of Time," and "Keep Low." "Winchester" is in red; "Repeating Arms Co." is in orange. Painted by A.B. Frost. From T. Webster collection. Photo by D. Kowalski.

Values:	Exc.	V.G.	Good
	12,000.00	10,000.00	8,500.00

Comment: *Not quite as rare as 1887 or 1888. The first of eight calendars painted by A.B. Frost. He also painted 1895-1901. Arthur Burdett Frost, 1851-1928, was one of the most popular illustrators of his day. He often depicted American rural life, but he is best known for his illustrations in the "Uncle Remus" stories by Joel Chandler Harris.*

1890 Calendar. Multiple hunting scenes were also typical of the earliest calendars. This specimen also shows it got hung up and used; the December page is wrinkled and torn on the bottom left corner. "Winchester Repeating Arms Co." is in red; rest of painting is heavily brown and buff. From T. Webster collection. Photo by D. Kowalski.

Values:	Exc.	V.G.	Good
	12,000.00	10,000.00	8,500.00

Comment: *Also not quite as rare as 1887 or 1888. Winchester used 1883 and 1885 illustrations they purchased from Harper's Weekly.*

1891 Calendar

1891 Calendar. Another example of multiple hunting scenes. The circular scene has the caption, "Shoot or you'll lose him." "Winchester Repeating Arms Co." is in red; rest of painting is heavily brown and buff. Painted by Frederic Remington. From T. Webster collection. Photo by D. Kowalski.

Values:	Exc.	V.G.	Good
	10,000.00	9,000.00	7,500.00

Comment: *The first of the Frederic Remington calendars. Remington lived from 1861-1909. His more than 2700 paintings and drawings typically depict accurate and action-filled scenes from his life on the Western Plains. These calendars are sought by Frederic Remington collectors, collectors of cowboy art and, of course, Winchester collectors.*

1892 Calendar

1892 Calendar. Another Western scene painted by Frederic Remington. "Winchester" is in buff; "Repeating Arms Co." is in gold; rest of painting is heavily gray and brown with green trees in canoe scene. From T. Webster collection. Photo by D. Kowalski.

Values:	Exc.	V.G.	Good
	10,000.00	9,000.00	7,500.00

Comment: *Remington includes another of his favorite images, the mounted horseman.*

1893 Calendar

1893 Calendar. The Indian guide is advised, "Hang on to them," as he carries off the bear cubs. "Winchester" is in buff; "Repeating Arms Co." is in gold; rest of painting is heavily brown with just a few red highlights such as the Indian's hat. Painted by Frederic Remington. From T. Webster collection. Photo by D. Kowalski.

Values:	Exc.	V.G.	Good
	10,000.00	9,000.00	7,500.00

Comment: *Remington shows a mule train "Protected by the Winchester."*

1894 Calendar

1894 Calendar. "Ranchmen protecting Stock from Wolves" is the major scene at top. "Winchester" is in red on a buff banner; "Repeating Arms Co." is in black; rest of painting is brown, buff and gray with a few red highlights. Painted by Frederic Remington. From T. Webster collection. Photo by D. Kowalski.

Values:	Exc.	V.G.	Good
	10,000.00	9,000.00	7,500.00

Comment: *The last of the Remington calendars.*

1895 Calendar

1895 Calendar. "Success" is the top scene; "An Unexpected Chance," is the bottom scene. "Winchester" is in red on a buff banner; "Repeating Arms Co." is in brown; "Cartridges" is in red; rest of painting is green, brown, buff and gray with a few red highlights. Painted by A.B. Frost. From T. Webster collection. Photo by D. Kowalski.

Values:	Exc.	V.G.	Good
	1,750.00	1,600.00	1,400.00

Comment: *The second A.B. Frost Winchester calendar and the first in a series of seven straight years that he painted their calendar scene.*

1896 Calendar

1896 Calendar. "The Finishing Shot" is the caption for the top scene. The other two scenes are not captioned. "Winchester" is in red on a buff banner; "Repeating Arms Co." is in brown; "Cartridges" is in red; rest of painting is green, brown, buff and gray with a few red highlights. Painted by A.B. Frost. From T. Webster collection. Photo by D. Kowalski.

Values:	Exc.	V.G.	Good
	1,500.00	1,400.00	1,200.00

Comment: *The third A.B. Frost calendar.*

1897 Calendar

1898 Calendar

1897 Calendar. "A Chance Shot" is the caption for the top scene; "An Interrupted Dinner" is the bottom scene. "Winchester" is in red on a buff banner; "Repeating Arms Co." is in black; "Cartridges" is in red; rest of painting is green, brown, buff and gray with a few red highlights. Painted by A.B. Frost. From T. Webster collection. Photo by D. Kowalski.

Values: **Exc.**   **V.G.**   **Good**
            1,500.00   1,400.00   1,200.00

Comment: *The fourth Frost calendar.*

1898 Calendar. "The 30 Did It" is the caption for the top scene; the duck-hunting scene at bottom is not captioned. "Winchester" is in red on a buff banner; "Repeating Arms Co." is in brown; "Ammunition" is in red; rest of painting is green, brown, buff and gray with a few red highlights. This calendar also has overprinted identification of the Stark & Weckesser retail store in Dayton, Ohio. Painted by A.B. Frost. From T. Webster collection. Photo by D. Kowalski.

Values: **Exc.**   **V.G.**   **Good**
            1,200.00   1,000.00   900.00

Comment: *The fifth Frost calendar shows another drop in values.*

1899 Calendar

1899 Calendar. "We've Got Him Sure" is the caption for the top scene; "Snipe Shooting" is the bottom scene. "Winchester" is in red on a light cream banner; "Repeating Arms Co." is in brown; "Ammunition" is in red; rest of painting is green, brown, buff and gray with a few red highlights. Painted by A.B. Frost. From T. Webster collection. Photo by D. Kowalski.

Values:	Exc.	V.G.	Good
	1,200.00	1,000.00	900.00

Comment: *The sixth Frost calendar.*

1900 Calendar

1900 Calendar. "Waiting for a Shot at the Old Ram" is the caption for the top scene; "Quail Shooting" is the bottom scene. "Winchester Repeating Arms Co." is in red on a buff banner; "Ammunition" is in red; rest of painting is brown, buff, light blue and gray with a few red highlights. Painted by A.B. Frost. From T. Webster collection. Photo by D. Kowalski.

Values:	Exc.	V.G.	Good
	1,200.00	1,000.00	900.00

Comment: *The seventh Frost calendar.*

1901 Calendar

1901 Calendar. "Fresh Meat for the Outfit" is the caption for the top scene; "Winter Fun on the Farm" is the bottom scene. "Winchester Repeating Arms Co." is in red on a light blue banner; "Ammunition" is in red; rest of painting is brown, buff and light blue with a few red highlights. Painted by A.B. Frost. From T. Webster collection. Photo by D. Kowalski.

Values:	Exc.	V.G.	Good
	1,500.00	1,400.00	1,200.00

Comment: *The eighth and last A.B. Frost calendar is the last Winchester calendar with multiple scenes. It is fairly rare and is valued higher than the previous three. This is also the last calendar Winchester offered until the 1912 edition.*

1912 Calendar

1912 Calendar. Winchester calendars come back with a roar in 1912. Roaring Grizzly Bear is dark brown; hunter in foreground has red highlights on coat. "Winchester" is in red; so are "Guns and Cartridges." Winchester calendars, from now on, will have one dominant scene. Painted by N.C. Wyeth. From T. Webster collection. Photo by D. Kowalski.

Values:	Exc.	V.G.	Good
	3,000.00	2,800.00	2,700.00

Comment: *This image was also a poster Winchester produced during the "poster period" from 1902-1911.*

1913 Calendar

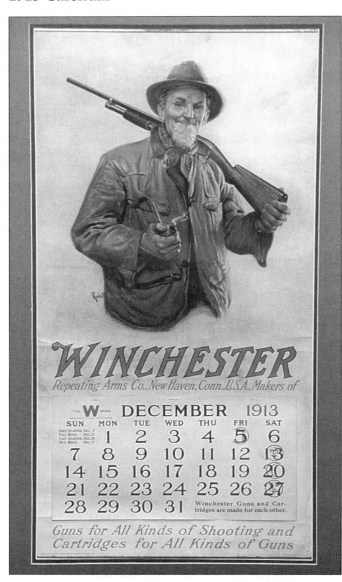

1913 Calendar. Bearded hunter is wearing a brown coat and carrying the first Model 12. "Winchester" is in red. Painted by Robert Robinson. From T. Webster collection. Photo by D. Kowalski.

Values: **Exc.**   **V.G.**   **Good**
3,000.00   2,800.00   2,700.00

Comment: *This calendar also sought after by Model 12 aficionados.*

1914 Calendar

1914 Calendar. Hunter is wearing a brown coat and darker brown pants. Pumpkins in foreground are orange; sky is yellow. "Winchester" is in red. Painted by Philip R. Goodwin. From T. Webster collection. Photo by D. Kowalski.

Values: **Exc.**   **V.G.**   **Good**
1,700.00   1,600.00   1,400.00

Comment: *The first of four calendars Philip R. Goodwin painted for Winchester.*

1915 Calendar

1915 Calendar. Female mountain goat protecting her kid from a golden eagle. "Winchester" is in red. Painted by Lynn Bogue Hunt. From T. Webster collection. Photo by D. Kowalski.

Values: | Exc. | V.G. | Good
| 1,700.00 | 1,600.00 | 1,500.00

Comment: *The first calendar Lynn Bogue Hunt painted for Winchester. He didn't do the second one until 1929.*

1916 Calendar

1916 Calendar. Two hunters with their Airedale terrier. Winchester came back to Philip R. Goodwin for this painting. Sky is yellow and buff. "Winchester" is in red. From T. Webster collection. Photo by D. Kowalski.

Values: | Exc. | V.G. | Good
| 2,000.00 | 1,900.00 | 1,700.00

Comment: *Values are 10-15 percent higher than Goodwin's 1914 calendar.*

1917 Calendar

1917 Calendar. This action-packed calendar is highly sought after by both Winchester and Western cowboy art collectors. Rearing horse is black; cowboy in blue shirt is holding him. Hunter holding elk head is wearing copper-colored shirt. "Winchester" is in red. From T. Webster collection. Photo by D. Kowalski.

Values: | Exc. | V.G. | Good
| 4,000.00 | 3,900.00 | 3,700.00

Comment: *Cowboy collectors have driven up the price of this calendar. Painted by W.K. Leigh, who was a well-regarded Western artist.*

1918 Calendar

1918 Calendar. Dad offers pointers to his son on how to stop the running rabbit. Maple tree in upper right is turning red; others are turning yellow. "Winchester" is in red with white outline on a dark blue-green background. Painted by George Brehm. From T. Webster collection. Photo by D. Kowalski.

Values: | Exc. | V.G. | Good
| 1,700.00 | 1,600.00 | 1,400.00

Comment: *Winchester tied this calendar theme into their new emphasis on the Junior Rifle Corps.*

1919 Calendar

1920 Calendar

1919 Calendar. Farmer stops his plow horses long enough to gaze at cloud pattern that appears to create the American flag. Sky is yellow with red, white and blue streaks running through it. "Winchester" is in red on a buff background. Painted by Robert Amick. From T. Webster collection. Photo by D. Kowalski.

Values:

Exc.	V.G.	Good
1,700.00	1,600.00	1,400.00

Comment: *The patriotic theme hasn't particularly excited Winchester collectors about this calendar.*

1920 Calendar. Another father and son hunting theme. "Winchester" is in red on a blue, white and yellow sky. The duck hunters are wearing dark brown clothing. Painter is unknown. From T. Webster collection. Photo by D. Kowalski.

Values:

Exc.	V.G.	Good
1,700.00	1,600.00	1,400.00

Comment: *This calendar shows some horizontal wrinkles from having been stored rolled but still getting creased.*

1921 Calendar

1921 Calendar. This father and son are hunting in an upland setting. "Winchester" is in red on a blue and white sky. The boy is wearing a red vest and standing in front of a red bush; dad is wearing a green vest. Painted by Arthur Fuller. From T. Webster collection. Photo by D. Kowalski.

Values: | Exc. | V.G. | Good
| 1,700.00 | 1,600.00 | 1,400.00

Comment: *The last calendar Winchester produced with the father-and-son theme.*

1922 Calendar

1922 Calendar. Another cowboy action shot. The hunter on horseback is wearing a red-patterned shirt. Cliff wall and trail are buff. "Winchester" is in red on a blue sky. Painted by H.C. Edwards. From T. Webster collection. Photo by D. Kowalski.

Values: | Exc. | V.G. | Good
| 3,000.00 | 2,850.00 | 2,700.00

Comment: *The cowboy collectors also like this one.*

1923 Calendar

1924 Calendar

1923 Calendar. Hunter on rock outcrop stalking big horn sheep. His clothing, except for red neck bandana, and most of scenery are tan. "Winchester" is in red on gray sky. Painted by Philip R. Goodwin. From T. Webster collection. Photo by D. Kowalski.

Values:	Exc.	V.G.	Good
	2,000.00	1,900.00	1,700.00

Comment: *Goodwin's third Winchester calendar.*

1924 Calendar. Duck hunter is holding a Model 12. A fairly nondescript calendar with blue-green water and a faint dawning sun casting a yellow glow on hunter and reeds. "Winchester" is in red on a cream-colored background. Painted by G. Ryder. From T. Webster collection. Photo by D. Kowalski.

Values:	Exc.	V.G.	Good
	1,500.00	1,400.00	1,200.00

Comment: *Unexciting values generally reflect an "unexciting" painting.*

1925 Calendar

1925 Calendar. These were reportedly Winchester's bear dogs in foreground. They're white with brown ears. Two redbone hounds are in background. "Winchester" is in red on a wood-grained background. Painted by H.R. Poore. From T. Webster collection. Photo by D. Kowalski.

Values: **Exc.**   **V.G.**   **Good**
                     3,000.00   2,850.00   2,700.00

Comment: *Values jump back up for this popular calendar. The same painting was also offered to stores in various wood frames for display purposes.*

1926 Calendar

1926 Calendar. Goodwin's hunter is again wearing his red bandana (as he was in the 1923 calendar). And the Grizzly Bear means business in this dramatic scene. "Winchester" is in red. Calendar portion is sepia-tone brown with cream-colored lettering. Painted by Philip R. Goodwin. From T. Webster collection. Photo by D. Kowalski.

Values: **Exc.**   **V.G.**   **Good**
                     3,000.00   2,850.00   2,700.00

Comment: *The last and most valuable of the four Goodwin Winchester calendars.*

1927 Calendar

1928 Calendar

1927 Calendar. The hunter on snowshoes is ready to pull off his glove with his teeth when he sees the big buck and the doe. He's wearing a red-checked coat. "Winchester" is in red on a yellow sky; sun is casting a yellow tint across snow ridges. Painted by Frank Stick. From T. Webster collection. Photo by D. Kowalski.

Values:	Exc.	V.G.	Good
	1,700.00	1,600.00	1,400.00

Comment: *This man on snowshoes should not be mistaken for Philip R. Goodwin's early 1900's poster of a hunter on snowshoes.*

1928 Calendar. Moose hunter standing in canoe is wearing dark green shirt and pants with red bandana around his neck. Water in foreground is dark green with yellow and light blue highlights. "Winchester" is in red on a yellow and gray sky; water around moose is bright yellow. Calendar page is dark green with white type. Painted by R. Farrington Elwell. From T. Webster collection. Photo by D. Kowalski.

Values:	Exc.	V.G.	Good
	2,500.00	2,350.00	2,200.00

Comment: *This calendar is more rare than the 1927 issue and considered much more desirable.*

1929 Calendar

1929 Calendar. Trio of pheasants flushed by dog and hunter. "Winchester" is in red on a light blue and gray sky; meadow grass is tan and brown. Painted by Lynn Bogue Hunt. From T. Webster collection. Photo by D. Kowalski.

Values:	Exc.	V.G.	Good
	1,800.00	1,700.00	1,500.00

Comment: *Lynn Bogue Hunt also painted the 1915 calendar.*

1930 Calendar

1930 Calendar. Winchester "Mountain Man" calendar. The "Mountain Man" is wearing a brown leather jacket and a red bandana. "Winchester" is in red on a bright blue sky. The most unique feature of this calendar is that six different outdoors and product scenes were used on the monthly pages. This photograph of the full calendar has the March/April months turned out that feature two fishermen playing a bass. Painter is unknown. From T. Webster collection. Photo by D. Kowalski.

1930 Calendar. January/February page has a household appliance scene next to a workshop and tool scene. From Curt Bowman collection. Photo by C. Bowman.

1930 Calendar. July/August page shines the spotlight on flashlights and batteries. From Curt Bowman collection. Photo by C. Bowman.

1930 Calendar. May/June page promotes roller skating. From Curt Bowman collection. Photo by C. Bowman.

1930 Calendar. September/October page pictures a flight of ducks and promotes Winchester's Model 12 and Model 97 shotguns, as well as shotshells. From Curt Bowman collection. Photo by C. Bowman.

Values:	Exc.	V.G.	Good
	1,000.00	850.00	700.00

Comment: The "Mountain Man" was heavily used by Winchester and his collectibility has suffered a bit as a result. The painter of the "Mountain Man" is unknown, perhaps an indication that this was a calendar being produced as economically as possible by a company on the verge of bankruptcy. This was also the last Winchester calendar for two years, none being produced in 1931 or 1932 while Western Cartridge Co. was reorganizing Winchester.

1930 Calendar. November/December "big buck" scene promotes Winchester rifles and cartridges. From Curt Bowman collection. Photo by C. Bowman.

1933 Calendar

1933 Winchester/Western Calendar. Hunting shack scene uses a great deal of browns and dark browns. Hunter on right is wearing a light green shirt. Light coming through window is turquoise blue. "Winchester" and "Western" both in red inside black panels. Painted by William Eaton. From T. Webster collection. Photo by D. Kowalski.

Values:	Exc.	V.G.	Good
	900.00	800.00	700.00

Comment: *Among the lowest values for a Winchester calendar.*

1934 Calendar

1934 Winchester/Western Calendar. This young hunter is thinking, "I wish I had Dad's Winchester." He's wearing a dark green coat, red tie and brown pants. The sky in background is light green. "Winchester" and "Western" both in red inside white panels. Painted by Eugene Iverd. From T. Webster collection. Photo by D. Kowalski.

Values:	Exc.	V.G.	Good
	1,400.00	1,300.00	1,200.00

Comment: *This appealing young boy was a powerful image for Winchester/Western and this calendar is a popular one.*

Posters and Other Advertising Specialties

Winchester did not produce an annual poster-sized wall calendar from 1902 through 1911. Some collectors speculate that they abandoned the calendar concept because the recent seven-year series of A.B. Frost calendars from 1895-1901 simply weren't dramatic and dynamic enough to really grab consumer attention.

But Winchester wasn't ready to stop advertising. On the contrary, they soon developed product posters featuring dramatic wildlife art or outdoor scenes. These have become highly collectible and, as a group, are bringing higher prices than calendars.

Winchester also produced many other case inserts, die-cut store signs, floor-model displays, counter pads and a host of booklets, as well as letterhead and other advertising items. We present a representative cross-section of them here. We will devote the bulk of the upcoming *Winchester Rarities* to presenting as complete a selection as has ever been done, all in four color.

Three Mallard Ducks Flying

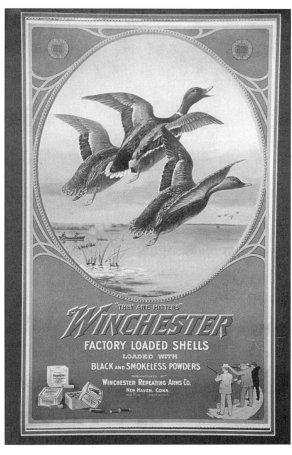

Three Mallard Ducks Flying. The earliest poster promoting factory loaded shotgun shells. Mallards are standard color against a light blue sky. Poster background is light green with yellow border around ducks. "Winchester" is red with white shadow behind it. Size slightly smaller than typical later poster. From T. Webster collection. Photo by D. Kowalski.

Values:	Exc.	V.G.	Good
	3,700.00	3,600.00	3,400.00

Comment: *Released in 1904, the first poster promoting shotguns and shotshells.*

Hunter Standing Over Big Horn Sheep

Hunter Standing over Big Horn Sheep. Earliest poster promoting rifles and ammunition. Hunter is wearing brown shirt, green pants and red bandana. Sky is light blue. Frame around photo area is gold; rest of poster background is dark green. "Winchester" is red with white shadow behind it. Larger copy is buff color; small copy is white. Size slightly smaller than typical later poster. From Curt Bowman collection. Photo by C. Bowman.

Values:	Exc.	V.G.	Good
	3,700.00	3,600.00	3,400.00

Comment: *Also released in 1904, the companion rifle poster to the previous "Mallards Flying" poster.*

Cock of the Woods

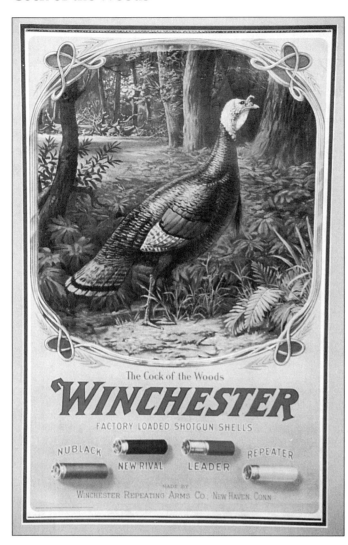

"The Cock of the Woods." A stunning and colorful wild turkey poster produced in 1905 promotes four brands of loaded Winchester shotshells. Painter is unknown. "Winchester" is in red on a turquoise blue background. Woven frame around turkey is yellow. From T. Webster collection. Photo by D. Kowalski.

Values:	Exc.	V.G.	Good
	9,000.00	8,000.00	6,500.00

Comment: *This poster is not uncommon but it is one of the most sought after of Winchester posters from the early-1900's poster era.*

Woman by Canoe

Woman by the Canoe. There are only two copies known of this poster promoting .22 Caliber Repeaters. Woman is wearing a dark blue dress; has red bandana tucked in her belt. Canoe is dark turquoise blue. "Winchester" is in red; dark copy lines are green. From T. Webster collection. Photo by D. Kowalski.

Values:	Exc.	V.G.	Good
	12,000.00	11,000.00	9,000.00

Comment: *This rare poster is also in excellent condition to very good condition with a slight water mark in upper right corner and a horizontal crease along bottom.*

Two Grouse Flying

Two Grouse Flying. Promotes the Model 97 shotgun. Forest scene with typical fall colors. "Winchester" and bottom line of copy are in red; "Repeating Shotguns" is dark gray. From T. Webster collection. Photo by D. Kowalski.

Values:	Exc.	V.G.	Good
	2,500.00	2,200.00	1,800.00

Chesapeake Retrieving Canvasback Duck

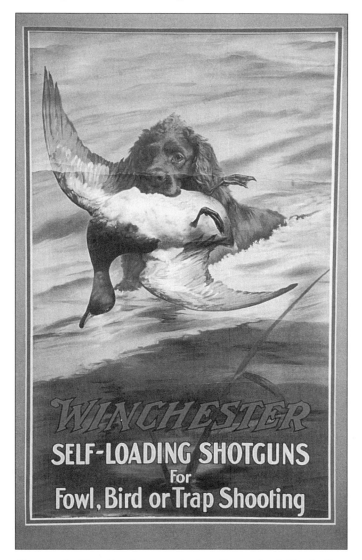

Chesapeake Bay Retriever retrieving Canvasback Duck. Promotes self-loading shotguns. Water is dark green in foreground and mixed green and white around the dog. "Winchester" is red; other copy is yellow. From T. Webster collection. Photo by D. Kowalski.

Values:	Exc.	V.G.	Good
	3,000.00	2,900.00	2,700.00

Hunter on White Horse with Bear

Hunter in Mountains on White Horse with Grizzly Bear behind Him. Promotes Winchester rifles and ammunition. Bottom lines of poster read: "The Winchester Model 54, a World's Standard High Power Bolt Action Sporting Rifle Calibers 270 W.C.F. and .30 Govt. '06." Mountains are almost rainbow-colored; hunter has green pants and red bandana. "Winchester" is red; so is outlined "W" behind it; next line is black. From T. Webster collection. Photo by D. Kowalski.

Values:	Exc.	V.G.	Good
	4,200.00	4,000.00	3,800.00

Man on Snowshoes with Wolf Pack

Man on Snowshoes with Wolf Pack. Tells a story in the snow (contrary to what we now know about there being no historical record of a wolf pack attacking a human). Hunter is wearing a tan coat with red stripes; his pants are green. "Winchester" and the line "Shoot Straight and Strong" are in red; bottom line is black; rest of copy is green. From T. Webster collection. Photo by D. Kowalski.

Values:	Exc.	V.G.	Good
	4,500.00	4,300.00	4,000.00

Comment: *One of at least five posters painted by Philip R. Goodwin, this one from 1906.*

Man on Piebald Horse on Mountain

Man on Piebald Horse on Mountain. Piebald horse is brown and white; pack horse being led is brown. Sky is egg white. "Winchester" and the line "Accuracy Reliability and Results" are in red; rest of copy is green. From T. Webster collection. Photo by D. Kowalski.

Values:	Exc.	V.G.	Good
	2,200.00	2,000.00	1,700.00

Comment: *Another poster painted by Philip R. Goodwin, from 1907.*

Grizzly Bear Coming Out of Cabin

Grizzly Bear Coming Out of Cabin. The surprised cabin owner is carrying his .401 caliber rifle; his shirt is blue and bandana is red. Sky and lake are light blue. "Winchester" and the line "Most Powerful Recoil-Operated Rifle" are in red; ".401 Caliber Self-Loading Rifle" is green; second to last line is black. From T. Webster collection. Photo by D. Kowalski.

Values:	Exc.	V.G.	Good
	4,500.00	4,300.00	4,000.00

Comment: *Another famous and desirable Philip R. Goodwin poster, from 1909.*

Two Hunters Laying on Rock

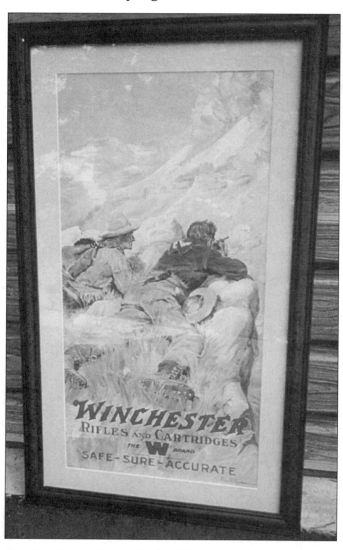

Two Hunters Laying on Rock, taking aim at Mountain Goats. Hunter on right with gun has bright blue shirt, tan pants and red bandana. His guide is wearing darker tan shirt. Sky is light blue, white and gold. "Winchester" and "W" are in red. Other larger copy is blue. From Curt Bowman collection. Photo by C. Bowman.

Values:	Exc.	V.G.	Good
	4,500.00	4,300.00	4,000.00

Comment: *Also painted by Philip R. Goodwin and one of his most sought-after Winchester posters.*

Four Deer Going Up Snowy Mountainside

Four Deer Going Up Snowy Mountainside, another painting by Philip R. Goodwin. Sky is a threatening gray and white. Far mountainside is green and gold. "Winchester" and "W" are in red. Other larger copy is dark green. From Curt Bowman collection. Photo by C. Bowman.

Values:	Exc.	V.G.	Good
	1,500.00	1,300.00	1,000.00

Comment: *The least sought-after poster by Philip R. Goodwin.*

Eight Canada Geese Flying

Eight Canada Geese Flying. Promotes factory loaded shells and repeating shotguns. Sky is bright blue with gray and white clouds. "Winchester" and "The Winning Combination" are in red. Other copy is gray. From Curt Bowman collection. Photo by C. Bowman.

Values:	Exc.	V.G.	Good
	2,500.00	2,100.00	1,700.00

Setter and Pointer - 20 Gauge

Setter and Pointer - promoting 20 gauge Shotguns. Dogs are black and white; setter is in foreground. Sky and background landscape are dark gray and blue. Meadow grass is tan. "Winchester" is red; other copy is gold. From Curt Bowman collection. Photo by C. Bowman.

Values:	Exc.	V.G.	Good
	1,200.00	1,000.00	800.00

Pointer and Setter - Repeating Shotguns

Pointer and Setter - promoting Repeating Shotguns. Dogs are black and white; pointer is in foreground. Sky and background landscape are dark gray and dark blue; tree is dark green. Meadow grass is tan. "Winchester" is red; other copy is gold. From Curt Bowman collection. Photo by C. Bowman.

Values:	Exc.	V.G.	Good
	1,100.00	900.00	700.00

Grizzly Bear on Rock above Two Hunters

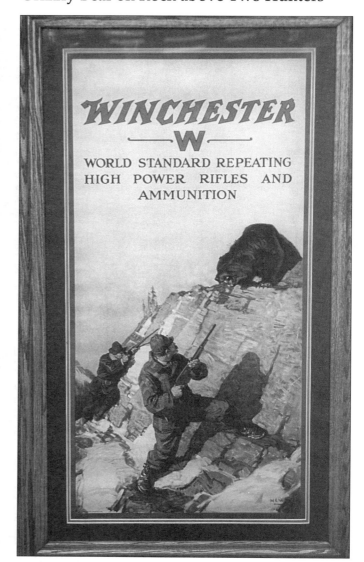

Grizzly Bear on Rock above Two Hunters. This painting by N.C. Wyeth became the dominant visual when Winchester resurrected the wall calendar concept in 1912. Roaring Grizzly Bear is dark brown; hunter in foreground has red highlights on coat. "Winchester" and "W" are in red; other copy is dark brown. Sky is yellow and gray. From T. Webster collection. Photo by D. Kowalski.

Values:	Exc.	V.G.	Good
	4,200.00	4,000.00	3,800.00

Comment: *Only two of these posters are known.*

Other Advertising Specialties.

Bear Dogs - Framed Picture

Bear Dogs Picture. H.R. Poore painted this picture of bear dogs reportedly belonging to Oliver Winchester. The painting was used for the 1925 calendar, as well as three versions of a framed picture made available to retail stores. The most desirable of these three versions is the one shown with decals around the dark wood frame. From T. Webster collection. Photo by D. Kowalski.

Comment: *Values are only for this wood-framed version with decals.*

Values:	Exc.	V.G.	Good
	5,000.00	4,700.00	4,200.00

Shoot Them and Avoid Trouble - Framed Picture

Shoot Them And Avoid Trouble. Store sign promotes Winchester loaded shotgun shells. Background colors are light green and gold. The "W" on each side in border is bright red. Live matter area (including green border) measures 32 5/8 inches wide x 24 5/8 inches high. From T. Webster collection. Photo by D. Kowalski.

Comment: *This highly controversial piece is also quite collectible. Values are only for examples with the full border.*

Values:	Exc.	V.G.	Good
	5,000.00	4,500.00	3,500.00

"Mountain Man" Floor Display

Mountain Man Floor Display produced with visuals from the 1930 wall calendar. Background behind Mountain Man is bright yellow. "Winchester" is in red on main display as well as on book pages. The display has an eight-page product promotion "book" attached to it in the left corner using the six product scenes from the same 1930 calendar. Base measures 30 1/2 inches wide x 40 inches high. From T. Webster collection. Photo by D. Kowalski.

Comment: *Values are for this floor display only. Winchester produced more than 30 such floor displays, several that were much larger than this one. Many of them will be presented in color in Winchester Rarities.*

Values:	Exc.	V.G.	Good
	1,000.00	800.00	600.00

Case Inserts (in Shotshell Cases for Store Display)

Woodcock Case Insert. Trees and brush in background are several shades of green. Dog is brown and white. "Winchester" in red; other copy is white. Measures 8 1/8 inches wide x 12 1/8 inches high. From T. Webster collection. Photo by D. Kowalski.

Quail Case Insert. Five California Quail feeding in light brown meadow grass. Sky is light blue; trees in background are green. "Winchester" is red; "The Hunters' Choice" is black with red outline; other copy is black. Measures 8 1/8 inches wide x 12 1/8 inches high. From T. Webster collection. Photo by D. Kowalski.

Calendars, Posters and Advertising • 743

Grouse Drumming Case Insert. Grouse on brown log with green, blue and brown forest scene in background. "Winchester" is red on a yellow background; "We Have a Full Stock" is black with red outline; other copy is black with green outline. Measures 8 1/8 inches wide x 12 1/8 inches high. From T. Webster collection. Photo by D. Kowalski.

Six Puppies and Gun Case Insert. The only horizontal format in this set of four. Dogs are brown and white on upper green background. "Winchester" is red on lower blue background. Other copy is white with black outline. Measures 12 inches wide x 8 inches high. From T. Webster collection. Photo by D. Kowalski.

Values:	Exc.	V.G.	Good
	1,800.00	1,500.00	1,200.00

Comment: *Values are for any one of the set of four case inserts. Add 10 percent for the California Quail version, which is the rarest of the four. Note that each of the inserts has a hole or holes punched in top so they could be hung in store.*

Die-Cut Retail Sign, From Turkey to Jacksnipe

Die-Cut. From Turkey to Jacksnipe. Promotes loaded Leader and Repeater shotshells. Upper 12 gauge Repeater shell is bright yellow; lower Leader shell is bright red with yellow head. Turkey has greenish tint to some feathers; chest is orange/bronze. "Winchester" and "W" are orange/red; other copy is black. From T. Webster collection. Photo by D. Kowalski.

Values:

	Exc.	V.G.	Good
	3,400.00	3,200.00	2,800.00

Comment: *One of the rarest of the die-cuts.*

Die-Cut Retail Sign, Dog and Two Quail

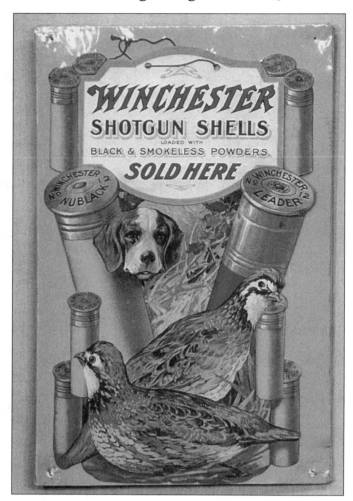

Die-Cut. Dog and Two Quail. Promotes loaded Nublack, Leader and Repeater shotshells. Dog behind Nublack shell is brown and white. All shells are yellow with gold heads except large middle shell on right which is a Leader shell with bright red body and gold head. All shells are 12 gauge. "Winchester" and "Sold Here" are red; other copy is black. Note two holes punched in top for hanging string. From T. Webster collection. Photo by D. Kowalski.

Values:

	Exc.	V.G.	Good
	2,600.00	2,400.00	2,200.00

Comment: *Another of the rarer die-cuts.*

Triangle Retail Sign, Squirrel, Bear and Canvasback

Hanging Triangle Sign. Squirrel, Bear and Canvasback. Promotes shotguns and rifles for large and small game. Each panel is light green with white highlights. Alternating dark green and black rings surround the animals. "Winchester" and "W" on each panel are red; "For Sale Here" on each panel is dark green; other copy is black. Note hole punched in top for hanging string. Each triangle is 8 inches wide at the base and 15 inches tall. From T. Webster collection. Photo by D. Kowalski.

Values:	Exc.	V.G.	Good
	8,500.00	7,500.00	6,000.00

Comment: *There are only two triangular hanging signs known; each a different version.*

Retail Store Counter Pads

Counter pad - rare version with all red type. Background is cream colored. From T. Webster collection. Photo by D. Kowalski.

Values:	Exc.	V.G.	Good
	500.00	450.00	300.00

Comment: *Values are for this pad only. Winchester produced about 20 versions. Many of them will be presented in color in Winchester Rarities.*

Winchester Letterhead and Correspondence

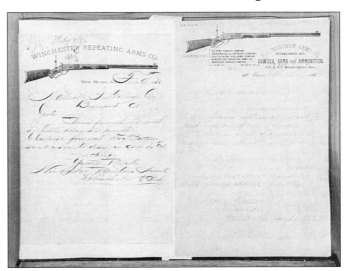

Winchester correspondence and letterhead is a category with many examples. Letter on left is from Winchester and is dated February 9, 1880. Letter on right is from E.C. Meacham Arms Co. of St. Louis, Missouri, a Winchester agent, and dated January 19, 1888. From T. Webster collection. Photo by D. Kowalski.

Values:	Exc.	V.G.	Good
	800.00		75.00

Comment: *Values are highly variable. A letter signed by Oliver Winchester would bring the high price or more.*

Winchester Envelopes

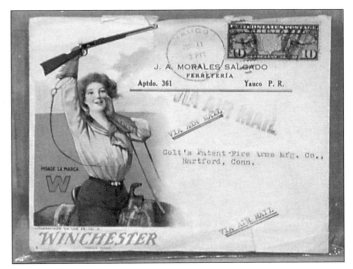

Winchester envelope in rare Spanish version shows woman on horse. From T. Webster collection. Photo by D. Kowalski.

Values:	Exc.	V.G.	Good
	1,000.00	900.00	800.00

Comment: *Values are for this version only. Envelopes are another category with many examples. Most would be priced at 50 percent of this example or less.*

Five-Panel Display Shipper

Shipper for Five-Panel Store displays. We have shown a few examples of five-piece floor display panels in this edition. They were shipped to retailers in these flat cardboard cases. Measures 40 1/2 inches long x 19 1/4 inches wide. From T. Webster collection. Photo by D. Kowalski.

Values:	Exc.	V.G.	Good
	300.00	250.00	200.00

Comment: *Values are for the shipper only. Winchester produced in excess of 100 different five-panel displays. Many of them will be presented in color in Winchester Rarities.*

Winchester Product Booklets

Values:	Exc.	V.G.	Good
	2,500.00		75.00

Comment: *Values here are also highly variable, depending on subject matter and rarity of the booklet.*

Product and educational booklets ranged from rifles to cooking, the full gamut of Winchester's product line. The booklet on Winchester .22s measures 3 inches wide x 6 1/4 inches high. The cook book is slightly larger. From T. Webster collection. Photo by D. Kowalski.

Winchester Trench Art

by David D. Kowalski

In the early chapters on cartridges and shotshells, we've presented collectible items that Winchester originally produced in production runs of hundreds of thousands of pieces, perhaps even millions of pieces. Their value is now based on several, perhaps hundreds of similar pieces that have changed hands; they generated a certain price based on a combination of rarity and condition. And we have attempted to not only set the standards for evaluating grades of condition, but we have provided a range of prices that reflect that condition.

Furthermore, this pricing structure underscores the fact most collectors take a dim view of an original Winchester item that has not been properly preserved. If we can find a piece in mint condition stored in its original box that is also in perfect condition, we've found the collector's dream. Of course, we would expect to pay far more for it than if it were scratched or dented or soiled and its box were torn or long since thrown in some garbage can.

With trench art, all these typical rules for valuing collectibles change.

First of all, "trench art" is that name given to large caliber spent shells, typically, that have been embellished in some way. Most of these pieces date from World War I. There is only a small fraction of the trench art from that period done on Winchester shells. That's because Winchester didn't produce vast quantities of large caliber military ammunition.

Historians agree that very few of these pieces were actually made in the trenches. Banging a hammer on a shell would have been an invitation to the enemy if done out in the field.

Wounded soldiers in hospitals were the ones with time on their hands and the freedom to engage in the noisy process of reshaping a cannon shell or mortar round. These spent shells were heated, filled with sand, then pounded into the desired shape. For the recuperating soldier in the hospital, creating trench art was a way to fight boredom and to earn some extra money for beer and cigarettes.

Therefore, unlike typical Winchester collectibles, we know we're starting with a product that's been fired from a cannon or some smaller weapon. The inside of the casing has usually been blackened by a powder charge. Then maybe it was carried back to base camp on a rough journey in a box or bag. In short, it started on its journey into someone's collection as a damaged item.

Then some "artist" would "damage" it some more. He heat it, beat it, smashed it, twisted it, took metal away from it. He may have added metal to it in the form of metal weld to create eagles, falcons, flowers, vines or handles.

We're not just looking at an old damaged cartridge. We've gone beyond that. We're now dealing with a new class of collectibles that deserves to be called "art."

Even though you may have purchased it simply as an investment, others may look at it differently. It moves them emotionally in some way. They think of the soldier fighting for his country who might have created it. They wonder who he was. Did he survive the war? Did he create anything else? We decided that even if we didn't know the answer to any of these questions for the pieces presented, Winchester trench art still deserved to be in this volume.

Although most trench art dates from WWI, dating can become problematic. Very little of it is dated. And if it has a date etched on it, the casual observer doesn't know if it was "back-dated." Cartridge historians can tell you when certain calibers were made, but we don't know if the artist worked on the shell right after it was fired or if he brought it home in his duffel bag, then waited thirty years to turn it into his or her artistic vision.

As with most collectibles, if you're buying a piece of trench art because it was linked to some historic event, the more documentation you can see that comes from reliable sources, the more certain you can be about dating and origin. Most trench art isn't signed.

The only thing certain we can say about Winchester trench art is that it must be made from a bona fide Winchester shell. Look to the headstamp. That will tell you if it's a Winchester shell. And you can estimate its age.

Beyond that, art is in the eye of the beholder. If it moves you emotionally, it's art, even if it doesn't affect anyone else.

Pricing trench art is a little different than pricing collectibles once made on the assembly line. It's typically a one-of-a-kind piece. It can be good art or bad art, depending on your perspective. And condition, as we already explained, is tainted by the fact the shell was fired. Then altered in other ways.

Therefore, with this group of items, we'll give you only a single price (not weighted by condition). We have asked experienced Winchester collectors to tell us what they would pay for the item, given its original link to Winchester.

Is it Winchester trench art? That's question one. Look at the headstamp first. This shell head shows a fair amount of oxidation and scratching. However, a close examination revealed "Winchester Repeating Arms Co." and other copy stamped around the primer hole. Furthermore, that stamping appears original, showing wear and damage in the same areas where the shell casing has been damaged. From T. Webster collection. Photo by D. Kowalski.

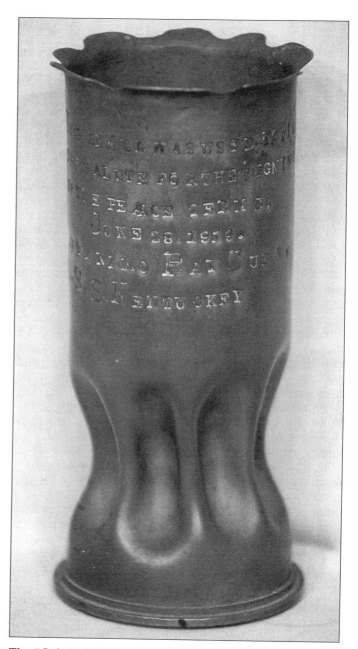

The "Cuba" shell. Here's the finished trench art attached to the previous headstamp. The inscription on this shell is presented without quote marks to more clearly convey the exact spelling and punctuation stamped there (as follows): This shell was used to fire the salute for the signing of the peace terms. June 28, 1919. Guantanimo Bay Cuba. U.S.S. Kentuckey (no period). From T. Webster collection. Photo by D. Kowalski. Value: $250.00.

The shell on the left has been decorated with a stem-and-leaf design and shaped like a flower vase. (It also appears to have been made by the same artist who created the "butterfly" vase that's the far left piece among the four pieces presented together in an adjacent photograph; the wave designs around the base and top of each look too similar to be random creations of different artists.) The ash tray design of the center shell has a carry stem that was welded into the primer hole. On the right is the "Cuba" shell described earlier. From T. Webster collection. Photo by D. Kowalski. Values (from left): $150.00; $100.00; $250.00.

These four pieces were grouped together to show various kinds of texture created on the shells. The "butterfly" shell on left has a closed top; very small texture marks were made in the darker background behind the butterfly. The second shell from the left with the bullet-shaped top has a reptile design on its side with very clearly defined scales along its body; and the entire shell has been highly polished to a light gold finish. The third shell, designed to be a flower vase, is a very dark copper color; thousands of small hammer blows were used to texture the outside of the shell casing. The dark brass shell on the far right had the main body of the casing compressed into a series of "accordion" folds. From T. Webster collection. Photo by D. Kowalski.
Values (from left): $150.00; $225.00; $225.00; $100.00.

Two pieces of trench art with squat shapes showing rounded and expanded shell walls. The piece on the left has an "urn" shape with a turned-over, "flower petal" top edge. Piece on the right has two handles and cover added for a "teapot" effect. From T. Webster collection. Photo by D. Kowalski. Values (from left): $125.00; $150.00.

Total height of this piece is 19 7/8". Lead bullet was added by its creator to simulate original loaded shell. From T. Webster collection. Photo by D. Kowalski. Value: $225.00.

Close-up of previous shell to show the detail on flower blossoms and veining on the leaves, as well as the copper strip used to "marry" bullet and shell. (Note damage to shell edge under this copper collar.) From T. Webster collection. Photo by D. Kowalski.

SET YOUR SIGHTS ON THESE EXCEPTIONAL GUN REFERENCES

2000 Standard Catalog of Firearms
by Ned Schwing
Over 80,000 prices and 5,000 photos in this must-have resource for gun collectors. Includes a full-color gallery of some of the world's most rare and beautiful firearms; and an insightful look at the firearms industry over the last 10 years. Updated and expanded to offer coverage on 12,000 firearm models.
Softcover • 8-1/2 x 11
1,312 pages
5,000+ b&w photos
40 color photos
GG10 • $32.95

Law Enforcement Memorabilia
by Monty McCord
A wide-range of items are covered from miniature vehicles to clothes, patches, and restraints. You will learn how to evaluate and expand your collection with confidence. This book contains the most comprehensive collection of badges available, and is sure to set the standard for this collectible field.
Softcover • 8-1/2 x 11
192 pages
550 b&w photos
16-page color section
SCLE • $19.95

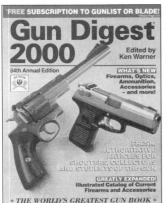

Gun Digest 2000
Edited by Ken Warner
This new edition is filled with fresh articles from firearms experts and scholars. Plus the latest prices and specifications on more than 3,000 currently available firearms from the US and around the world, as well as handloading presses, optics and ammunition. Finally, a freshly updated Directory of the Arms Trade is included.
Softcover • 8-1/2 x 11
544 pages
2,300+ b&w photos
GD2000 • $24.95

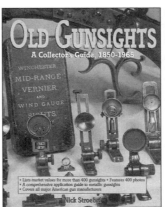

Old Gunsights: A Collectors Guide, 1850 to 1965
by Nicholas Stroebel
This unique book offers an in-depth and comprehensive examination of old gunsights and the rifles they were used on from 1850 to 1965, and features 400 photos and hundreds of market prices, covering all major American manufacturers and some foreign.
Softcover • 8-1/2 x 11
320 pages
400 b&w photos
OLGU • $29.95

Colt Memorabilia Price Guide
by John Ogle
Colt collectors will love this first-time ever compilation of non-gun Colt merchandise produced by Sam Colt's companies, and other companies using the Colt name. More than 1,500 color photos and prices help collectors identify a wide range of objects from knives to glassware.
Softcover • 8-1/2 x 11
256 pages
1,500 color photos
CCOL • $29.95

Old Rifle Scopes
by Nick Stroebel
Coverage on over 120 scope makers and 60 mount makers. Photos and market values for 300 scopes and mounts manufactured from 1950-1985. A brief company history of each maker, along with a discussion of the scopes and/or mounts manufactured by that maker. An overview of telescopic sights as well as a discussion of scope optics and mechanics.
Softcover • 8-1/2 x 11
400 pages
300 b&w photos
ORS • $31.95
(Available 5/00)

For a FREE catalog or to place a credit card order, call

800-258-0929 Dept. GNBR

M-F, 7 am - 8 pm • Sat, 8 am - 2 pm, CST
Krause Publications, Dept. GNBR, 700 E State St, Iola, WI 54990
Visit and order from our secure web site: www.krausebooks.com
Dealers call toll-free 888-457-2873 ext 880, M-F, 8 am - 5 pm

Shipping and Handling: $3.25 1st book; $2 ea. add'l. Call for UPS rates. Foreign orders $15 per shipment plus $5.95 per book.
Sales tax: CA 7.25%, IA 6%, IL 6.25%, PA 6%, TN 8.25%, VA 4.5%, WA 8.2%, WI 5.5%
Satisfaction Guarantee: If for any reason you are not completely satisfied with your purchase, simply return it within 14 days and receive a full refund, less shipping.

MUST-HAVE RESOURCES FOR
WINCHESTER COLLECTORS

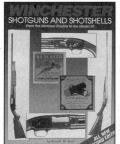

Winchester Shotguns & Shotshells
by Ronald W. Stadt
This "must have" for Winchester collectors gives you exceptional photos and text on collectible Winchester shotguns and shotshells manufactured through 1961. Author Ron Stadt also offers extensive coverage on shotshells and their boxes.
Hardcover • 8-1/2 x 11 • 288 pages
600 b&w photos
WSS01 • $34.95

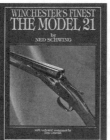

Winchester's Finest — The Model 21
by Ned Schwing
Get the most complete guide to the finest double-barrel side-by-side shotgun made in America. The Olin Corporation designated this book by Ned Schwing "the official history of the Model 21 Shotgun."
Hardcover • 8-1/2 x 11 • 360 pages
375 b&w photos • 16-page color section
WT01 • $49.95

Winchester Slide-Action Rifles, Volume I
Model 1890 and Model 1906
by Ned Schwing
Every young boy from the 1800s to the 1950s dreamed of owning his own Winchester rifle. Ned Schwing traces their history through word and picture in this chronology of the Model 1890 and 1906.
Hardcover • 8-1/2 x 11 • 352 pages
500 b&w photos
WS01 • $39.95

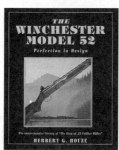

The Winchester Model 52
Perfection In Design
by Herbert G. Houze
Historical arms enthusiast Herbert Houze unravels the mysteries surrounding the development of what many consider the most perfect rifle ever made. The book covers the rifle's improvements through five modifications. Users, collectors and marksmen will appreciate each variation's history, serial number sequences and authentic photos.
Hardcover • 8-1/2 x 11 • 192 pages
190 b&w photos
WIN • $34.95

Winchester Repeating Arms Company
by Herbert G. Houze
Run, don't walk, to get your hands on this one-of-a-kind history. This book uncovers the story and development behind Winchester from 1865-1981. You'll get new truths, models and unpublished records and photos.
Hardcover • 8-1/2 x 11 • 512 pages
574 photos
WR01 • $50.00

Winchester Model 42
by Ned Schwing
This book ranks near the top as one of the all-time favorite collector firearms. Author Ned Schwing gives you the most accurate and complete book on the Model 42 ever written.
Hardcover • 8-1/2 x 11 • 160 pages
200 b&w photos
WG01 • $34.95

Winchester Slide-Action Rifles, Volume II
Model 61 & Model 62
by Ned Schwing
Take a complete historical look at the favorite slide-action guns of America through Ned Schwing's eyes. Explore receivers, barrels, markings, stocks, stampings and engraving in complete detail.
Hardcover • 8-1/2 x 11 • 256 pages
300 b&w photos
WM01 • $34.95

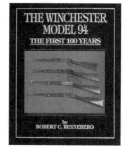

The Winchester Model 94
by Robert C. Renneberg
You'll enjoy Robert C. Renneberg's tribute to "The Gun That Won The West" as you follow the evolution of the Model 94 and the major changes that led to its perfection.
Hardcover • 8-1/2 x 11 • 208 pages
184 b&w photos
WN01 • $34.95

For a FREE catalog or to place a credit card order, call

800-258-0929 Dept. GNBR

M-F, 7 am - 8 pm • Sat, 8 am - 2 pm, CST
Krause Publications, Dept. GNBR, 700 E State St, Iola, WI 54990
Visit and order from our secure web site: www.krausebooks.com
Dealers call toll-free 888-457-2873 ext 880, M-F, 8 am - 5 pm

GUN LIST

Shipping and Handling: $3.25 1st book; $2 ea. add'l. Call for UPS rates. Foreign orders $15 per shipment plus $5.95 per book.
Sales tax: CA 7.25%, IA 6%, IL 6.25%, PA 6%, TN 8.25%, VA 4.5%, WA 8.2%, WI 5.5%
Satisfaction Guarantee: If for any reason you are not completely satisfied with your purchase, simply return it within 14 days and receive a full refund, less shipping.